‖‖‖‖‖‖‖‖‖‖‖‖‖‖‖‖‖‖‖‖‖
W9-BSQ-210   S

The Editor

ROBERT S. MIOLA, the Gerard Manley Hopkins Professor of
English and Lecturer in Classics at Loyola University Maryland, has written and lectured widely on classical back-
grounds to Shakespeare and on early modern literature. He
has edited Ben Jonson's *Every Man in His Humour* (2000)
and *The Case Is Altered* (forthcoming); several Shakespeare
plays, including the Norton Critical Edition of *Macbeth*
(2004); and *Early Modern Catholicism: An Anthology of Primary Sources* (2007).

Denmark — Elsinore Castle

King Hamlet — Gertrude → Claudius
                              doesn't like

Prince Hamlet

Tragedy/Ghost story → brings in doubt, justice

Ghost of Sr. Hamlet tells Prince
Hamlet that Claudius killed
him + now Hamlet needs to
kill Claudius

A NORTON CRITICAL EDITION

William Shakespeare
HAMLET

TEXT OF THE PLAY

THE ACTORS' GALLERY

CONTEXTS

CRITICISM

AFTERLIVES

RESOURCES

Edited by

ROBERT S. MIOLA
LOYOLA UNIVERSITY MARYLAND

W · W · NORTON & COMPANY · *New York* · *London*

This title is printed on permanent paper containing 30 percent post-consumer waste recycled fiber.

The text of this book is composed in Fairfield Medium
with the display set in Bernhard Modern.
Book design by Antonina Krass.
Composition by Westchester Book Group
Manufacturing by the Maple-Vail Book Manufacturing Group
Production manager: Eric Pier-Hocking.

ISBN: 978-0-393-92958-4

W. W. Norton & Company, Inc., 500 Fifth Avenue, New York, NY 10110-0017
wwnorton.com

W. W. Norton & Company Ltd., Castle House, 75/76 Wells Street
London W1T 3QT

2 3 4 5 6 7 8 9 0

Contents

Acknowledgments

I record permissions to reprint texts and illustrations in the notes throughout.

I am grateful to many friends and colleagues who listened, shared ideas, and answered queries, especially David Bevington, Lois Potter, Zachary Zeller, Russell Jackson, and Peter Holland. For their efficiency, I am also grateful to Norton Critical Edition editor Carol Bemis, her indefatigable associate Rivka Genesen, and the copyeditor, Benjamin Reynolds. I also owe thanks to the authors who have been generous with their works, notably Kenneth Branagh, Jawad al-Assadi, and Margaret Litvin.

This project could not have come to fruition without institutional support, especially from Loyola University Maryland—its library staff (especially the Interlibrary Loans Department), its Office of Research and Sponsored Programs (for summer grants), its Humanities Center (for a permissions subvention), and its Gerard Manley Hopkins Chair in English. The University also enabled me to hire a superb research assistant, Paul Zajac, who cast a professional eye on the text and commentary before embarking on editorial projects of his own. I am also indebted to great institutions of research for their resources and hospitality—the Folger Shakespeare Library, the British Library, and the Shakespeare Institute, Stratford-upon-Avon. The Shakespeare Association of America meetings and those at the International Shakespeare Conference provided lively forums for discussion.

This edition follows the exemplary Norton Critical Edition of *Hamlet* (1963, 1992), edited by Cyrus Hoy, who was coincidentally my doctoral supervisor many years ago. I hope it is a worthy successor.

Illustrations

Introduction

Imagining *Hamlet*[†]

Theatrical Imaginings

Imagine all the Hamlets in one place, perhaps the chandeliered ballroom of the Waldorf Astoria in New York City. At the entrance Shakespeare's Hamlet, Richard Burbage (1601), thirty-three, bearded, portly, leaps into Ophelia's grave. The stout, vigorous, bewigged Thomas Betterton, who played the role for more than forty years (1661–1709, even at age seventy-four!), knocks over a chair and struts about energetically. David Garrick's man of feeling (1742–1776), hands outstretched, starts in terror at the ghost (p. 364). In flowing black cape, the tall, mournful John Philip Kemble (1783–1817) casually holds Yorick's skull by his knee, awaiting his brother Charles as Laertes and his niece Fanny as Ophelia. Kemble's sister, Sarah Siddons, dressed in epicene costume, Hamlet herself (1776, 1778, 1781, 1802), fences brilliantly.

Edmund Kean's impassioned, unpredictable Hamlet (1814–32) kisses Ophelia's hand and then crawls menacingly on his belly to the king. Near him is his tormented Russian counterpart, Pavel Mochalov (1837); William Charles Macready, a generous but perturbed prince (1823–51); the perfect Victorian gentleman Hamlet of Charles Fechter (1861, 1864, 1870); the American Edwin Booth's gentle, thoughtful, and sensitive son (1853–91, p. 155); the dark-browed Henry Irving's "lean image of hungry speculation" (1874–85) in Yeats's phrase, the poetical, lunatic lover of Ellen Terry's mad Ophelia. Johnston Forbes-Robertson's gallant, cheerful prince (1897–1913), greatly skeletal in frame, waves his arms in Gothic gesture.

The powerful voice of Tommaso Salvini (1875) thrills American onlookers, even as they glance at their libretti to decipher his Italian;

† Quotations without page reference are from selections reprinted below (cited fully in "Resources"). I am grateful to Oxford University Press for permission to reprint and adapt here some paragraphs from my *Shakespeare's Reading* (2000), 120–24. For references to the folio I cite *Hamlet: The Texts of 1603 and 1623*, ed. Ann Thompson and Neil Taylor (London: Arden Shakespeare, 2006); for references to other Shakespeare plays, *The Complete Works of Shakespeare*, ed. David Bevington, 5th ed. (New York: Longman, 2003).

near him, Salvini's countryman, the youthful Vittorio Gassman (1952–53), sits quietly with Rosencrantz and Guildenstern, crestfallen at their betrayal, well along the road of disillusion he must travel.

On French stage and screen, the "divine" Sarah Bernhardt (1899–1901, p. 329) capers with zest and comic energy. The pale, slight, Danish Asta Nielsen (1921), silent film star, deploys her large, haunting eyes and melodramatic movements to play the Princess of Denmark—Hamlet as a woman pretending to be a man—and dies in the arms of her true love Horatio. Another movie star, John Barrymore, commands attention as a lithe, powerful, mother-loving son (1922, 1925; p. 153), intelligent but explosive, sometimes demonic, the only American to enjoy success in the role in London, despite G. B. Shaw's disapproval. Barrymore's successor, the blonde Laurence Olivier (1937, film 1948), kisses Gertrude with Oedipal ardor (p. 265), soliloquizes cerebrally, and finally leaps athletically from a fifteen-foot platform, sword in hand, to stab the king. Olivier's rival in the 1930s, John Gielgud, sweet, bitter, angry, and princely, speaks the verse with rare intelligence and musicality.

In black modern dress, Richard Burton (1964; p. 174) stabs Hume Cronyn's bantam Polonius and stalks the floor with raw power and masculine energy, improvising freely, his magnificent, mesmerizing Welsh voice ringing out. Bored, disaffected, angry, the '60s student, David Warner (1965), adjusts his scarf and rimless gold glasses and flips a middle finger at passersby, including Nicol Williamson (1969), who burns with anguish and rage, and Derek Jacobi (1980), who wields his intelligent, high-pitched tenor before the BBC television crew. The avenging Lethal Weapon Hamlet, Mel Gibson (1990), glowers and studies his lines, preparing to meet Paul Scofield's weary and infinitely sad ghost.

Contemporary international Hamlets gather together against oppressive despotisms: the black Joko Scott (1981) struggles against white enemies in front of South African high-school students. Bound in a chair under harsh light, the Romanian Ion Caramitru (1985–89) battles the espionage and interrogation of the dying Ceauşescu regime. The Polish Teresa Budzisz-Krzyżanowska (1989), in front of a mirror, portends the fall of Communism and exposes the falsity of dictatorship. After the fall of socialism and the crackdown in Tiananmen Square, the Chinese Pu Cunxin (1989) unpredictably changes roles with Polonius and Claudius; there are no heroes or villains anymore.

Or are there? The white-haired Kenneth Branagh (1996; p. 177) slashes curtains in the duel with Laertes, skewers Claudius with a hurled sword, and gives his dying voice to Fortinbras, who has already invaded the room and had Osric (Robin Williams) stabbed from behind. In skullcap and amid video rentals, Ethan Hawke (2000; p. 358) struggles against a corporate Claudius from Wall Street (see also p. 297). The German Angela Winkler (2000) alternates between quiet utterance and tempestuous outburst, between experienced woman and lost child. Famous from *Doctor Who*, David Tennant (2008; p. 240) threatens Claudius, then acts with zany wit and mad-cap humor. Amidst the din of English and non-English Hamlets— African, Asian, European, Japanese, Arab, and others—Jude Law (2009) recites "To be or not to be" in blue light under the gently fall-ing snow (see cover).

Contextual Imaginings

So many Hamlets—each enacting differently Shakespeare's infinite tragedy of fate and free will, sin and suffering, justice and revenge. Performed for the first time in 1600 or 1601, this play originated in the grim Icelandic sagas influentially compiled by Saxo Grammati-cus in *Historica Danica* (1180–1208). Saxo's work appeared, with additions and moralizations, in the French translation of François de Belleforest, *Histoires tragiques* (1576), which in turn appeared in anonymous English translation, *The Hystorie of Hamblet* (1608). Hamlet's story has analogues, as Josef Schick demonstrated (*Corpus Hamleticum*, 1938), in tales from Persia, Africa, India, Romania, Ukraine, China, and other places. Shakespeare probably knew some mediated version of Belleforest and a lost play, perhaps by Thomas Kyd, known as *Ur-Hamlet* (the Germanic prefix denoting "primitive, original, earliest"). Existing like an invisible archaic ruin beneath a classical temple, the *Ur-Hamlet* (late 1580s) lives largely in the teas-ing notice of contemporaries like Thomas Nashe and Thomas Lodge, and perhaps in *Der Bestrafte Brudermord* (Fratricide Punished), a Hamlet play performed by early seventeenth-century English players traveling in Germany, surviving now only in a transcription (1710) of the lost manuscript.

The contextual origins of the play, however, lie far beneath Ham-let stories, deep within the mythic archetypes of Greek tragedy (fifth century BCE), particularly the drama of Orestes' revenge. Shakespeare probably never read Greek tragedy directly, but he may have come across Erasmus's Latin translations and he certainly knew Latin adaptations by Seneca (c. 4 BCE–65 CE), the popular play-wright Polonius invokes as a model for tragedy ("Seneca cannot be too heavy," 2.2.327–28). The great Greek playwrights Aeschylus, Sophocles, and Euripides variously depict Orestes finally avenging the murder of his father Agamemnon by slaying his mother Clytem-nestra and her lover Aegisthus. As Gilbert Murray has shown (see pp. 255–64), Orestes prefigures Hamlet in this general action and in many significant particulars. Beset with the moral paradoxes of revenge, Orestes acts to fulfill the will of the gods and Apollo's oracle, but in so doing invites divine retribution: pursuit by the Erinyes, those relentless winged goddesses.

Hamlet similarly struggles, revenges, and suffers, but he lives and dies in a Judeo-Christian universe that is continually evoked by Biblical allusion and echo. Claudius's murder of King Hamlet reenacts Cain's murder of Abel in Genesis: "It hath the primal eldest curse upon't, / A brother's murder" (3.3.37–38; see also 1.2.105; 5.1.68–69). Hamlet compares Polonius and Ophelia to Jephthah and his ill-fated daughter from Judges 11:30–40. He likens man to a "quintessence of dust" (2.2.269), and this dust blows throughout the play (see 1.2.71; 4.2.5; 5.1.183 and 229), recalling the story of creation and Genesis 3:19: "Thou art dust, and to dust shalt thou return,"[1] a phrase repeated in the Church of England burial service. The span of human life here, as in the medieval cycle plays, stretches from these creation stories of Genesis through death to the "last trumpet" (5.1.208) of doomsday, that is, to the Last Judgment of Revelation. Doomsday appeared imminent in the apocalyptic portents attending Caesar's death (1.1.122), Horatio says, and if the world's grown honest, Hamlet cynically retorts, "then is doomsday near" (2.2.232). The Gravedigger invokes doomsday as the punch line for his end-time jest: "Who builds stronger than a mason, a shipwright, or a carpenter?" . . . "'a grave-maker.' The houses he makes lasts till doomsday" (5.1.43–44, 51–52).

As these intimations of the Last Judgment suggest, neither Apollo, the Olympians, nor Chance (*Tyche*) rules Hamlet's world, but the Judeo-Christian God, the Lord of hosts who will reward the good and punish the wicked. This God appears in gentler aspect in Hamlet's ruminations after the sea voyage. Relating his narrow escape from Claudius's plot, Hamlet assures Horatio, "There's a divinity that shapes our ends, / Rough-hew them how we will" (5.2.10–11). Cumulatively the Biblical echoes and expressions of Christian faith thus contest the classical revenge ethos and counsel instead trust and patience: As Saint Paul says, "Recompense to no man evil for evil. . . . 'Vengeance is mine, I will repay,' saith the Lord" (Romans 12:17, 19).

Such Christian imperatives everywhere complicate and contest the demands of classical revenge tragedy in *Hamlet*, generating its conflicted style, enduring ironies, and critical imaginings.

---

1. Here and throughout I cite the Geneva Bible (1560).

Critical Imaginings

ATROCITY

From the beginning Shakespeare exploits and subverts the classical traditions that bequeathed to later generations a three-part revenge action consisting of (1) Atrocity, (2) the Creation of the Revenger, and (3) Atrocity. He does not depict the initial atrocity, the killing of king and father, in the disturbingly vivid imagery of Aeschylus's *Agamemnon*, for example, or in Seneca's bright purples; he shrouds the murder in the mists of the Elsinore night. Like classical spirits, the ghost of King Hamlet begins the revenge action by revealing his foul, unnatural murder and demanding vengeance. But unlike those phantasms, King Hamlet says nothing in his first appearances, then refuses to reveal the secrets of the next life, and finally sounds strangely moral, lamenting his own spiritual unreadiness for death:

> Cut off even in the blossoms of my sin,
> Unhouseled, disappointed, unaneled,
> No reck'ning made, but sent to my account
> With all my imperfections on my head.
> O horrible, O horrible, most horrible! (1.5.76–80)

The ghost bitterly regrets missing three Catholic sacraments—the Eucharist ("unhouseled"), Penance ("disappointed"), and Extreme Unction ("unaneled"). He exhorts Hamlet to leave the punishment of the Queen "to heaven."

Voltaire preferred this unusual specter to the apparition of Darius in Aeschylus's *The Persians* because King Hamlet's revelations suggest the awful power of the Supreme Being to punish crimes outside "the reach of human laws" (Introduction, *Sémiramis*, 1748). Most have not been so reassured. Roy Battenhouse ("The Ghost in *Hamlet*," 1951) and Eleanor Prosser (*Hamlet and Revenge*, 1967) variously argue that the ghost is a malignant spirit who acts like the devil to entrap Hamlet; penitential spirits, they observe, do not return to earth to demand vengeance by murder. Noting such anomalies, Stephen Greenblatt (*Hamlet in Purgatory*, 2001) nevertheless identifies King Hamlet as a Catholic ghost from a Catholic (and officially proscribed) Purgatory. Part classical shade, part demonic spirit, part Purgatorial ghost, he sensibly concludes, King Hamlet appears to be a mix of disparate elements and incompatible theologies, classical and Christian.

The critical perplexity mirrors Hamlet's own. Moved to revenge, Hamlet nevertheless ponders the "questionable shape" (1.4.43) of the ghost, "spirit of health or goblin damned" (40). Unlike classical avengers, Hamlet wonders if the initial atrocity ever really occurred, fearing that the story might be a trap, the ghost really a devil who abuses him only to damn him (2.2.519ff.) Relocated in a Christian context, the classical imperatives of revenge imperil the soul as well as the body. Hamlet warily contrives the mousetrap play, *The Murder of Gonzago*, to discover the truth.

Discomfiting the King, the mousetrap play confirms the ghost's story but plunges Hamlet into deeper perplexities. For *The Murder of Gonzago* represents not only the actual murder of King Hamlet but also Hamlet's intended murder of King Claudius. Hamlet pointedly characterizes the assassin not as the victim's brother but as "one Lucianus, nephew to the king" (3.2.229). Urging the players, he identifies the action not as usurpation but as revenge, "Come, 'the croaking raven doth bellow for revenge'" (237–38)—echoing, in fact, two lines from an old revenge play, *The True Tragedy of Richard III* (c. 1594). The initial atrocity thus merges disturbingly with the projected one, and the killing of King Hamlet looks much like the anticipated killing of King Claudius. To revenge his father, Hamlet must reenact the initial atrocity: he must kill the king. This paradox puzzles his will and turns awry his enterprise of great pitch and moment.

THE CREATION OF THE REVENGER

Motivated by such an atrocity and beset by such doubts, Hamlet struggles to fulfill the second phase of classical revenge action, the creation of himself as revenger. Like Orestes, he disguises his true intentions and bides his time. He puts on an antic disposition, a feigned madness to deceive those around him. In his grief he turns to a friend or confidant, the ancient Pylades or *Satelles* (servant) here appearing as the faithful Horatio. Hamlet pointedly evokes classical revengers as models for imitation—Lucianus (of the Latin name) and the ruthless Greek Pyrrhus, son of Achilles. When the players arrive, Hamlet begins to recite a speech he "chiefly loved" (2.2.370), Aeneas's tale to Dido and the slaughter of King Priam by the avenging Pyrrhus, "he whose sable arms, / Black as his purpose, did the night resemble." Smeared with blood, "roasted in wrath and fire," "with eyes like carbuncles," the "hellish" Pyrrhus is the spirit of classical revenge incarnate (376–87). His sword over King Priam's head, Pyrrhus hesitates; then "A rousèd vengeance sets him new a-work." The sword falls like "Cyclops' hammers" and minces the limbs of his victim (412ff.).

In true humanist style, Hamlet conjures a classical model, Pyrrhus, revenger and king-killer, as an exercise in self-fashioning. Trying to imitate the prototype, Hamlet later speaks the violent, sanguinary language of revenge, threatening in Senecan fashion to disrupt the daily processes of nature: "Now could I drink hot blood, / And do such business as the bitter day / Would quake to look on"

(3.2.362–64). Like the Pyrrhus he admires, Hamlet soon stands over the helpless King, sword in hand, and hesitates. He refuses to slay Claudius at prayer in 3.3, however, so that he may damn him later, so "that his soul may be as damned and black / As hell, whereto it goes" (94–95). Hamlet here puts into chilling practice Atreus's famous dictum concerning revenge: *scelera non ulcisceris, / nisi vincis* ("Crimes you don't avenge, unless you outdo them," Seneca, *Thyestes*, 195–96). (Hamlet even sounds like Atreus in his bitter self-reproaches.) Hamlet's display of classical ferocity in the Prayer Scene appalled Samuel Johnson in 1765: "This speech, in which Hamlet, represented as a virtuous character, is not content with taking blood for blood, but contrives damnation for the man that he would punish, is too horrible to be read or to be uttered."

But Hamlet is not Orestes, Pyrrhus, or Atreus, nor was meant to be. The very mention of damnation and hell undermines his attempt to play the classical revenger, to outdo the crimes of his victim. These terms evoke the Judeo-Christian moral universe that is wholly alien and inimicable to such vindictive action. In this world murder and revenge are sins, God judges and punishes sinners, and hellfire awaits the damned. The Folio version of *Hamlet* (1623) presents another moment wherein Hamlet wrestles with the morality of classical revenge and the prospect of damnation. After discovering the plot against his life, he asks Horatio:

> Is't not perfect conscience
> To quit him with this arm? And is't not to be damned
> To let this canker of our nature come
> In further evil? (5.2.67–70; p. 149)

Hamlet attempts to justify revenge in Christian terms, to argue that it is "perfect conscience" to kill Claudius and that he will be damned if he doesn't rather than if he does. Horatio provides no reassuring answer. Two incompatible ethical systems, classical and Christian, here clash impossibly.

Hamlet's self-creation as a classical revenger proceeds inconsistently, by fits and starts. He stabs Polonius brutally and grapples with Laertes at Ophelia's grave, ranting in high style. This rhetoric of outrage, however, alternates with very different speech rhythms and registers—witty banter, philosophical inquiry, odd snatches of verse and song, and anguished soliloquy:

> To be or not to be—that is the question.
> Whether 'tis nobler in the mind to suffer
> The slings and arrows of outrageous fortune,
> Or to take arms against a sea of troubles
> And by opposing end them. To die, to sleep—

No more—and by a sleep to say we end
The heartache and the thousand natural shocks
That flesh is heir to. 'Tis a consummation
Devoutly to be wished. (3.1.57–65)

The famous lines reveal an acute intelligence confronting the fallen world, the "thousand natural shocks / That flesh is heir to." The melancholy mood leads to a death wish, to a desire for the sleep that ends all troubles. World-weary, aching for respite, Hamlet searches for an honorable course of action, wondering whether patient endurance or active confrontation is the better course. Soliloquies such as this further distinguish Hamlet from his classical models, full of passionate intensity. Pyrrhus's hesitation is momentary; Hamlet's hesitation is the play itself.

So conflicted and variable a revenger has evoked widely different critical responses. Some have seen and played Hamlet as a man of action, but many have taken a different view. In an extremely influential passage, Goethe characterized Hamlet as an oak tree planted in a costly jar that it shatters. In other words, "A lovely, pure, noble and most moral nature, without the strength of nerve which forms a hero, sinks beneath a burden which it cannot bear and must not cast away" (*Wilhelm Meister's Apprenticeship*, 1795, tr. 1824). The sixth American President, John Quincy Adams, praised Hamlet similarly as "Man in the ideal perfection of his intellectual and moral nature, struggling with calamity beyond his power to bear" (Letter to James H. Hackett, February 7, 1839). Whether or not one agrees with the specifically Romantic terms of praise here (Hamlet is a good and moral man trapped in a predicament he cannot handle), most actors and audiences have been sympathetic to Hamlet and his plight.

Dissenting, however, some have judged the prince to be immoral, insane, or incoherent. An early editor, George Steevens (1785), summarized him as a man who ruthlessly kills Polonius, Rosencrantz, and Guildenstern, mistreats and finally causes the death of Ophelia, and finally assassinates the king to revenge his own, not his father's, death. George Bernard Shaw, Victorian playwright and critic, thought Hamlet mad for pretending that reason could rule behavior while all the time acting on his irrational impulses:

And, indeed, there is a sense in which Hamlet is insane; for he trips over the mistake which lies on the threshold of intellectual self-consciousness: that of bringing life to utilitarian or Hedonistic tests, thus treating it as a means instead of an end. Because Polonius is "a foolish prating knave," because Rosencrantz and Guildenstern are snobs, he kills them as remorselessly as he might kill a flea, showing that he has no real belief in the superstitious reason which he gives for not killing himself, and in fact anticipating exactly the whole course of the intellectual history of Western Europe until Schopenhauer found the clue [the irrational nature of man] that Shakespeare missed.[2]

The Russian novelist Leo Tolstoy, who read Shakespeare in German, Russian, and English and found it all disappointing, thought Hamlet's many contradictions rendered him simply a jumble or a cipher: "One moment he is awestruck at his father's ghost, another moment he begins to chaff it, calling it 'old mole'; one moment he loves Ophelia, another moment he teases her, and so forth. There is no possibility of finding any explanation whatever of Hamlet's actions or words, and therefore no possibility of attributing any character to him." In 1995 the New York Bar Association assumed that Hamlet was serving a life sentence for five murders (Polonius, Rosencrantz, Guildenstern, Laertes, and Claudius) and one manslaughter (Ophelia) and staged an appeal (*The Elsinore Appeal*, 1996). (The results were inconclusive.) Objecting to the critical fascination with Hamlet's character altogether, Margreta de Grazia (*Hamlet without Hamlet*, 2007) iconoclastically recentered the play off the prince and on dispossession and imperial history.

ATROCITY

Whatever one thinks of Hamlet as character, the action of the play ends classically in final atrocity. Laertes and Hamlet stab each other with the poisoned sword; Gertrude drinks from the poisoned cup; Hamlet, dying, stabs Claudius and pours the poisoned drink down his throat:

> Here, thou incestuous, damnèd Dane,
> Drink off this potion! Is thy union here?
> Follow my mother. (5.2.299–301)

The first editor, Nicholas Rowe (1709), thought Shakespeare improved on classical prototypes such as Sophocles' *Electra* because Hamlet, unlike Orestes, does not kill his mother onstage. On his uncle, however, Hamlet wreaks the bloody and furious revenge prescribed by the ghost and demanded by the classical tradition. Or so it seems. But unlike Orestes, his descendants, and his counterparts in Saxo and Belleforest, Hamlet does not plan the culminating atrocity; instead, Claudius and Laertes conceive the treachery, set up the poisoned sword and cup, and disguise their intentions. Hamlet thus assumes the role of victim as well as that of revenger.

Moreover, in the concluding movement of the play Hamlet exhibits a new calm and a new trust in Providence.

2. *The Saturday Review*, October 2, 1897, 364.

> There is special providence in the fall of a sparrow. If it be
> now, 'tis not to come; if it be not to come, it will be now; if it be
> not now, yet it will come. The readiness is all. (5.2.189–92)

Alluding to Matthew 10:29 ("Are not two sparrows sold for a far-
thing? And one of them shall not fall on the ground without your
Father"), Hamlet depicts God as the kindly father whose loving care
extends to all creation, even to death. The three balanced conditional
clauses ("If it be . . . if it be . . . if it be"), so hypnotically similar in
sound and cadence, express Hamlet's recognition of his mortality
and his trust that all will pass as God and God alone wills. All he
need do is have faith and wait. Unlike Senecan revengers, Hamlet
does not rouse himself to *nefas*, "crime," but instead aspires to "readiness," the practice of patience and Christian submission to divine
plan. No classical avenger ever spoke like this. And none ever died as
Hamlet does, exchanging forgiveness with Laertes, begging a survivor to tell his story, receiving a final benediction that anticipates heavenly reward: "Now cracks a noble heart. Good night, sweet prince, /
And flights of angels sing thee to thy rest" (333–34).

At the end of the play Shakespeare intensifies, not resolves, the
conflict between classical and Christian ethics. Instead of concluding harmony, he creates a strangely dissonant and compelling
music of the close, one that has thrilled and captivated audiences
for over four centuries. But not everyone has applauded. Eighteenth-
century critics complained in chorus about perceived violations of
poetic justice: John Dennis (1711): "the guilty and innocent perish
promiscuously";[3] Lewis Theobald (1715): "virtue ought to be rewarded
as well as vice punished" (Vickers 2:306); Charlotte Lennox 1753):
"one fate overwhelms alike the innocent and the guilty" (Vickers
4:128). Judging the ending to be "exceedingly ill-managed," Peter
Whalley (1748) observed that Hamlet in the source survives the
usurper and dies a natural death (Vickers 3:272). Declaring that
Shakespeare neglects poetical probability as well as poetical justice, Samuel Johnson (1765) lamented "the untimely death of Ophelia, the young, the beautiful, the harmless, and the pious."

To answer such critics, the actor David Garrick radically altered
the ending. In his long-running adaptation Gertrude lies in a trance
offstage, struck with the horror of the murder; Hamlet prays that she
might experience penitence before dying; Rosencrantz and Guildenstern remain alive; Horatio and Laertes inherit the kingdom; Hamlet
moralizes his own death from Laertes: "'Tis the hand of heav'n, /
Administers by him this precious balm / For all my wounds." We are
here not a long way from the Dumas-Meurice *Hamlet* in France

---

3. *Shakespeare: The Critical Heritage*, ed. Brian Vickers, 1974–81, 2:285.

(1847), wherein the ghost reappears at the end to apportion punishments and allow Hamlet, vindicated as God's instrument, to live on. Censuring such alterations, Harry Levin (1959) affirmed Shakespeare's ending as a realistic portrayal of our inscrutable world and a grand expression of cosmic irony:

> Since we cannot altogether arrange our lives, we are constantly seeking some principle of arrangement in the universe, whether it be the finger of deity or the determination of chance. Thwarted, we may blame fickle fortune with Seneca, or malicious fate with Thomas Hardy, or original sin with Kierkegaard. Otherwise, our quest for retribution, with Dante, must be continued in another world. Lesser dramatists are easily tempted to intervene in the little worlds they have created, making sure that the good have their rewards when the evil have their punishments; but insofar as they improve upon life, they weaken their dramaturgy. With Shakespeare the dramatic resolution conveys us, beyond the man-made sphere of poetic justice, toward the ever-receding horizons of cosmic irony.

Editorial Imaginings

Shakespeare himself left behind no manuscripts of his *Hamlet* but three different printed texts—three versions of one play or three related plays, depending on your point of view: the relatively short Quarto 1 (2221 lines, printed 1603), the more familiar Quarto 2 (4056 lines, printed 1604 and 1605), and the Folio (3907 lines, printed 1623).[4] There are many other differences among these three texts (see Appendixes 1 and 2), some apparently introduced by printers and actors. Despite scholarly uncertainty about their origins, nature, and relations, every modern edition of *Hamlet* represents an editor's imagining of the play, based on the evidence, howsoever interpreted, of these three early texts.

From early times theatrical practice has adopted Q2 or F in radically abridged versions, since either uncut, even if performed speedily, runs over four hours. But if the theater has created ever shorter *Hamlet*s, editors have created ever longer ones. Not really sure about what to leave out or on what principle, editors since Alexander Pope (1723) have usually conflated Q2 and F, hoping to use all the evidence to produce some single authoritative Shakespearean text and deciding, in effect, the more *Hamlet*, the better. Some recent editors have been reluctant to choose among the alternatives

4. A quarto is a playbook about the size of a modern paperback made from sheets of paper folded in half twice; a folio, about the size of a modern coffee-table book, is made from sheets folded in half once.

and have produced instead pluralistic *Hamlet* simulcasts: Jesús
Tronch-Pérez (2002) presents a synoptic *Hamlet*, Q2 and F simultaneously with the differences signaled by typography and line
placement. Bernice W. Kliman and Benjamin Bertram (2004) have
presented all three texts in parallel columns. Charles Adams Kelly
et al. have published the second edition of *The Hamlet* 3×2 *Text
Research Toolset* (2009), which features in parallel all three texts in
facsimile and in modern typeface, with color-coded variants and
concordance arrows. The Arden 3 editors, Ann Thompson and Neil
Taylor, have published all three texts simultaneously, each separately and meticulously edited (just under 1,000 pages, 2006).
There are also some interesting digital versions available, including
The Enfolded Hamlet (Q2 and F together). One can easily access
online images of specific quarto and folio copies and view them in
separate windows on one computer screen.

   Since each early textual witness represents a more or less legitimate version of the play, this Norton Critical Edition takes one,
Quarto 2, as its copy text and tries to stay with it unless forced off
by a reading that doesn't make sense or that makes much less sense
than another reading. Of course, the criteria of "sense" and "much
less sense" is to some degree inevitably subjective, in other words, a

Hamlet 1.2.129–32

Quarto 2 (1604/5)

Ham. O that this too too sallied flesh would melt,
Thaw and resolue it selfe into a dewe,
Or that the euerlasting had not fixt
His cannon gainst seale slaughter, ô God, God,

Folio (1623)

Ham. Oh that this too too solid Flesh, would melt,
Thaw, and resolue it selfe into a Dew:
Or that the Euerlasting had not fixt
His Cannon 'gainst Selfe-slaughter. O God, O God!

Quarto 1 (1603)

Ham. O that this too much grieu'd and sallied
Would melt to nothing, or that the vniuersall
Globe of heauen would turne al to a Chaos!

matter of what an editor imagines to be a sensible, correct reading. Analysis of just four lines from a Hamlet soliloquy (1.2.129–32) gives some idea of the many textual problems *Hamlet* presents and this complicated process of editorial imagining. These lines present something easy, something moderately difficult, and something impossible.

We begin with the simplest textual problem, "seale slaughter." According to the *Oxford English Dictionary*, "seal" can mean "a willow," "stamp," or "member of the family *Phocidae*, sub-order *Pinnipedia*, of aquatic carnivorous animals, with limbs developed into flippers and adapted for swimming." Is Hamlet saying that God wants us to save the seals? Even in the wonderful world of Shakespeare scholarship, no editor has yet advanced that argument and given us Hamlet as Danish proto–Greenpeace activist. (It is only a matter of time.) Editors agree that Hamlet is talking about suicide, and the phrase should read "self-slaughter," as it does in F, which seems obviously a correction rather than a sophistication.

So far, so good. But what sort of "cannon" has the Everlasting fixed against self-slaughter? The spellings "cannon" and "canon" are interchangeable in this age (there are no fixed spellings until the eighteenth century), so the prime candidates are "cannon," a piece of ordnance, a big gun, or "canon," an ordinance, rule, law, or decree. One image is that of God aiming a gun at would-be suicides; the other is of God setting up a law prohibiting self-slaughter. First stop after the OED might be a concordance (the Open Source Shakespeare website, for example) where one can find in Shakespeare's works twenty-five instances of "cannon" and five of "canon," after eliminating the example in question which the editor has placed in the latter category. (That might well make you nervous about all the evidence available, since most concordances are based on modernized spellings—in other words, on someone else's answer to the very question you are asking.) An advanced search to see if any of these cannons/canons have been "fixed" yields nothing. What about Shakespeare's contemporaries? Did Marlowe, Jonson, Dekker, Greene, or Chapman ever fix any cannons or canons? Another database, Literature Online, can survey thousands of works of poetry and prose and drama, say from 1550 to 1650, with variant spellings in a matter of seconds. The search term "fix NEAR cannon" produces one hit: William D'Avenant (who claimed to be a bastard son of Shakespeare) in *The Platonick Lovers* (1636) wrote, "And 'gainst thy palace, fix my cannon till / I batter it to dust." The fixed cannon is a gun here. One can also check Early English Books Online, the Text Creation Partnership of over 25 thousand fully searchable early modern works, or LEME, Lexicons of Early Modern English, another online resource—to no avail, however.

Editors have to print something, though they can record alternate readings in a note, and they have differed widely on cannon /
canon. In 1726, without the benefit of the databases, Lewis Theobald, unfairly the main dunce of Pope's *Dunciad*, surveyed Shakespeare's other plays and argued for "canon": "I much doubt the
propriety of the phrase *fixing cannon* to carry the meaning here supposed. The military expression . . . is *mounting* or *planting cannon*."
Theobald noted that the usual phrase in English was "to fix a canon
or law," perhaps deriving from Virgil (*Leges fixit pretio, atque refixit*,
Aeneid 6.622) and the Latin phrase *figere legem*, "to fix a law," and
its Greek equivalents. Theobald finally invoked "the poet's own turn
and cast of thought," adducing a parallel passage from *Cymbeline*:
"'Gainst self-slaughter / There is a prohibition so divine / That cra-
vens my weak hand" (3.4.76–78) (*Shakespeare Restored*, 17).

Many editors, myself included, have followed Theobald, though
Joseph Hunter (1845) disagreed, thinking "canon" "an unhappy word
to use here," and opining that the mention of the "cannon" in the
King's speech immediately preceding (line 126) "was still ringing in
the poet's ears" (*New Illustrations*, 2:218). Still, it doesn't make much
sense for God to aim a large metaphorical gun at someone, to
threaten to kill him, in other words, to keep him from killing himself. And, of course, the specific "canon," most commentators have
argued, could well be the commandment in the Decalogue, "Thou
shalt not kill," which includes a well-recognized prohibition against
suicide. Whatever one decides, one should proceed with a proper
sense of humility. In the theater no distinction can be made; auditors heard and still hear simply "cannon" and "canon" and compre-
hend one or both meanings.

This brings us to the third and the impossible problem, Q2's "too
too sallied flesh." Let's leave aside the double "too," which has occasioned much suspicion and comment. Some few have retained the
reading "sallied," meaning "assailed," and cited Shakespearean and
contemporary parallels; that is defensible, but the phrase is unusual.
(Still, if Shakespeare always wrote what was usual, we wouldn't be
speaking of *Hamlet* today.) Some have preferred F's "solid" as a correction that either restores the original reading or as Shakespeare's
revision. "Solid" fits in with the images of melting and dissolving.
But others have argued that Q2's "sallied" is actually a misreading
or mishearing of "sullied." This appears to be the case at 2.1.40,
where Polonius says "laying these slight sallies [meaning "sullies,"
i.e. stains, imputations of dishonor] on my son," and also at 5.2.353
of *Love's Labour's Lost*, "pure as the unsallied [for "unsullied"] lily."
(A Dekker example has also led some, but not the OED, to consider
"sally" an alternate form for "sully," not even a misreading.) The idea
of misreading, however, receives some support from what we know

about Elizabethan paleography in general, and what we conjecture about Shakespeare's handwriting, based on his signatures and on some fragments of the *Sir Thomas More* manuscript, tentatively identified as his. Lowercase *a* and *u* are frequently confused, especially if the *a* is left open at the top, as many, including Shakespeare, were wont to do. ("Gertrud" is spelled "Gertrad" in many places in the early printed texts, including Q2.)

So into the lists comes "sullied," i.e., "stained, polluted, defiled" flesh, which has gained many supporters. John Dover Wilson (1934, 2:307–15) argued that Burbage, the original Hamlet, was a hefty man so that a reference to his "too too solid" flesh would convulse the house with laughter and ruin the play, and that "sullied" is the clue to Hamlet's disgust at his mother's impurity and worldly corruption. Harold Jenkins (1982, 437) says similarly that "'sullied' enlarges the meaning as 'solid' does not." Here the argument moves from textual to aesthetic grounds—to which reading the editor imagines to be preferable for literary or other nontextual reasons. Of course, whatever one decides in print, no one can finally control which of the three an actor says and which of the three an audience hears. So *Hamlet* as text and as playscript is as elusive, problematic, refractory, multidimensional, polysemous, and uncontrollable as is its main character. Shakespeare could have written "sallied," "sullied," "solid," all, or none. The editor wrestles with the alternatives, imagines a correct or defensible answer, and prints his or her choice. (This edition, hesitantly, goes with "solid.")

Global Imaginings

Despite the instability of its text, Shakespeare's *Hamlet* has come to unparalleled dramatic life in global translation, production, and adaptation.

Off the coast of what is now Sierra Leone in West Africa, September 5, 1607, sailors on an English merchant ship, the *Red Dragon*, staged the first production of *Hamlet* outside Europe. Four native Africans heard the play in English, in a running Portuguese translation, and perhaps in Temne, the local African language. Since then, the play has been translated into Afrikaans (1945) and Zulu (1954), and has enjoyed a rich theatrical history, beginning with the full production in Port Elizabeth in 1799. In South Africa, Rohan Quince explains, the play has served many different social purposes, often conferring on a racial group cultural prestige and performing one or another political function. During the resurgence of Afrikaaner nationalism, for example, the 1947 Afrikaans production in Johannesburg featured a dispossessed Hamlet who sought to get his land back. In 1969, a time of student protest against apartheid, a

University of Cape Town student Hamlet struggled against entrenched corruption in government. In 1981 in Cape Peninsula, a black actor, Joko Scott, suffered denial of his basic rights by a white Claudius and betrayal by a white Ophelia and his white friends.

Soon after *Hamlet*'s first publication in Quarto 1 (1603), a contemporary writer declared the fall of the Godunov regime in Russia (1605) "the poetical fury in a stage-action, complete yet with horrid and woeful tragedies, a first but no second to any *Hamlet*. . . . Revenge, just revenge, was coming."[5] From earliest times, *Hamlet* has reflected the various political and spiritual crises of Russia. In the 1790s the play uncomfortably echoed the situation of the murdered Peter III and his wife Catherine, who ascended to the throne with Grigori Orlov, her companion and a participant in the coup. In 1837 Pavel Mochalov portrayed a deeply sorrowful Hamlet who challenged authority; he represented those who stood against the Tsarist repression of intellectuals and artists. Ivan Turgenev's famous essay "Hamlet and Don Quixote" (1860) characterized Hamlet as a sympathetic figure who was nevertheless paralyzed into inaction by egotism and lack of faith.

Nikolay Akimov produced in Moscow (1932) a satirical version that featured an obese Hamlet who contrived the ghost scene and a drunken Ophelia who died after an orgy. This production mounted a challenge to the negative characteristics traditionally associated with Hamlet—melancholy, brooding, inaction. More positively, Boris Pasternak translated *Hamlet* as a play of duty and self-denial (1940) and wrote a poem in which Hamlet echoes Christ (see "Afterlives," p. 375). Reacting against the subversive potential of such an individualistic and rebellious hero, Stalin banned *Hamlet* (and many of Shakespeare's other works). After the dictator's death in 1953, many cities in Russia produced *Hamlet* as a play that championed human dignity against governmental oppression. Nikolay Okhlopkov's 1954 Moscow production staged Denmark as a prison whose central metaphor was a massive pair of metal doors. Grigori Kosintsev directed a film (1964), wherein the swirling sea of freedom opposed dark images of politico-spiritual oppression—jagged boulders, large Stalinist statues, the iron grills and heavy portcullis of the castle, the prison-like bars of the balustrade, the metal farthingale that literally cages Anastasiya Vertinskaya's doomed and porcelain Ophelia (p. xxix).

Germany has also had a complicated history of encounter with *Hamlet*, so much so that Gerhard Hauptmann claimed Shakespeare as a native son: he may have been born and buried in England, but "Germany is the country where he truly lives."[6] By 1626, a company

---

5. *Sir Thomas Smithes Voiage and Entertainment in Rushia*, 1605, sig. K.
6. *Shakespeare Jahrbuch*, 51, 1915, xii.

Anastasiya Vertinskaya as Ophelia in the metal farthingale, Kosintsev's film, 1964

of English actors performed something entitled *Tragoedia von Hamlet einen Printzen in Dennemarck* in Dresden. Another acting version circulated in the seventeenth century, now represented by *Der Bestrafte Brudermord* (see "Afterlives," p. 357). The trickster Hamlet of *Der Bestrafte Brudermord* and the surviving prince of some stage versions both contrast with the tragic figure who dominated later romantic readings—the Hamlet nobly inadequate to his task (Goethe, 1795), the distracted melancholic (Ludwig Tieck, 1796), the man of overactive intellect and irresolution (A. W. Schlegel, 1809). In the nineteenth century political interpretations culminated in Ferdinand Freiligrath's denunciation, "Germany Is Hamlet" (1844); here the Danish prince becomes a symbol for a nation beset by tyranny, helpless and disunited, awaiting deliverance by a Fortinbras.

In the early twentieth century Sigmund Freud analyzed Hamlet as an illustration of the Oedipus Complex. Between 1920 and 1940 Bertolt Brecht repoliticized the play by proposing a new reading: his Hamlet represents the promise of a new order founded on reason but ultimately fails because he, like the feudal Fortinbras, resorts to force. There is little promise of any kind in Heiner Müller's *Die Hamletmaschine* (*Hamletmachine*, 1977), an absurdist collage under the shadow of the East German dictatorship. Bitterly denying the possibilities of revolution and human aspiration, the play concludes with Ophelia at the end of history:

> *The deep sea.* OPHELIA *in wheelchair. Fish, debris, dead bodies and limps drift by.*

OPHELIA [*While two men in white smocks wrap gauze around her and the wheelchair, from bottom to top.*]   This is Electra speaking.

In the heart of darkness. Under the sun of torture. To the capitals of the world. In the name of the victims. I eject all the sperm I have received. I turn the milk of my breasts into lethal poison. I take back the world I gave birth to. I choke between my thighs the world I gave birth to. I bury it in my womb. Down with the happiness of submission. Long live hate and contempt, rebellion and death. When she walks through your bedrooms carrying butcher knives you'll know the truth.

> The men exit. OPHELIA *remains on stage, motionless in her white wrappings.*[7]

After the Wall came down, Peter Zadek directed a Berlin production (2000) with Angela Winkler as the lead. The embodiment of "bruised hope" after a violent century, Winkler's Hamlet showed vulnerability and a capacity for love all the more precious for existing in a world of social and political corruption (see Howard, "Women as Hamlet," p. 328).

In the east Japan has repeatedly reimagined Hamlet. In the 1870s two writers, Nozaki Bunzo and Kawatake Mokuami, adapted Hamlet for kabuki theater, a traditional song-and-dance drama with heavily made-up actors. Then there appeared translations of Charles and Mary Lamb's prose redaction, and partial versions of the play. In 1886 Kanagaki serialized his new adaptation, *Hamuretto Yamato Nishikie* ("Hamlet with Japanese Woodblock Prints"), complete with Japanese names and setting and a plot adapted to Confucian morality (p. xxix). This Laertes, for example, resolves conflicting loyalties to his father and prince by committing suicide, in the manner of a samurai warrior. In 1903 Otojiro Kawakami's production began to break free of kabuki conventions and, along with Shōyō Tsubouchi's translation and productions (1907–11), shifted the focus from staging adaptation to staging translation. By 1938 there were at least twenty Japanese translations of *Hamlet*. Japanese academics, founding the Shakespeare Association of Japan (1929) and starting academic journals, turned serious attention to understanding, appreciating, and staging Shakespeare. Their efforts laid the groundwork for the opening of the Tokyo Globe in 1988.

Norio Deguchi and Yushi Odashima staged a colloquial *Hamlet* (1975) that featured blue-jeaned actors on a bare stage and rock music. The acclaimed director Yukio Ninagawa mounted four separate productions of the play, beginning with an eclectic version in 1978 that featured Bach, Elton John, and Japanese folksongs and drew upon *Hinamatsuri* (doll festival) conventions. His fourth production (2001), set amidst barb wire and naked bulbs, reflected

---

7. Trans. Carl Weber, New York, 1984, 58. See "Afterlives," p. 379.

Hamlet in the Graveyard, a Japanese woodblock print, Tokyo, 1886. Reprinted from Kaori Ashizu, "What's *Hamlet* to Japan?" at hamlet-works.org, by permission of the publisher.

the grim realities of the post–9/11 world; Fortinbras finally has Horatio and other nobles killed with machine guns. Other versions of the play have appeared in *nōh*, a classical Japanese dance drama with stylized gesture, role, and action, and *bunraku*, Japanese puppet theater.

Japanese imaginings of *Hamlet* variously negotiate tensions between East and West, between conflicting languages, literary forms, and cultural values. One accessible and revealing example of the struggle is Akira Kurosawa's film adaptation (1960), *Warui yatshu hodo yoku nemuru* ("The Bad Sleep Well"), which transposes the story to modern corporate Japan; Hamlet becomes Nishi, a cool and calculating son who plots vengeance on his father's murderers. Nishi marries the boss's lame daughter as part of his plan but falls in love with her; he orders a wedding cake in the shape of corporate head-quarters, complete with a red rose in the seventh-floor window through which his father was pushed (the Mousetrap). He suffers some moral conflict—"It's hard to have evil. I must hate and become bad myself"—and dies betrayed.

The tensions in cross-cultural *Hamlet* adaptations are also abun-dantly evident in Arab countries, which came to *Hamlet* as early moderns came to the classics, through multilingual intermediaries. Late nineteenth-century Arab translators, for example, relied on French adaptations. After 1952 the Arab world began an extensive cultural exchange with Europe. Margaret Litvin has divided recent Arab appropriations of *Hamlet* in Egypt, Syria, Iraq, and other nations into three distinct phases. In the first, from 1952 to 1967, Arabs read *Hamlet* as simply a classic piece of world literature that con-ferred respectability on readers and actors; in the second, from 1967 to 1977, after the Arab military defeat, they interpreted Ham-let as a revolutionary hero struggling against a corrupt regime; and in the third, since 1977, Arab readers and writers have turned Hamlet into a dramatic ironist, a mocker of established institu-tions. The Egyptian Mahmoud Aboudoma's *Dance of the Scorpions* (1989–91), for example, features an ineffectual prince against a tyrant in a play about misgovernment. Iraqi playwright Jawad al-Assadi has also transformed the play into a bitter political satire, *Forget Hamlet* (1994). Everyone knows that Claudius has committed the murder but there is no possibility for justice; Claudius, a Saddam Hussein figure, controls the state and the guillotine (see "After-lives," p. 381).

The Kuwaiti Sulayman Al-Bassam has written three Arab adap-tations in English—*Hamlet in Kuwait* (2001), with a Ghost who symbolizes the 1991 Gulf War; *The Arab League Hamlet* (2001), which features an Arms Dealer; and *The Al-Hamlet Summit* (2002), in which Hamlet is a religious extremist and Ophelia a suicide bomber. In one haunting soliloquy from the last play, Hamlet echoes the prophet Muhammed in his opening line and meditates on death:

Peace be upon the grave dwellers.
I am ill, grave dwellers, I am ill,
Sick with the lies of the living,
That have spread like shredded pieces of the night,
Its end resembling its beginning.
How is the end, grave dwellers, how is it worse than the
    beginning?
I will pass these forty nights between you,
Your bones will be my books; your skulls will be my lights,

I will hold my tongue amongst you,
And eat from the dreams of the dead.[8]

Hamlet has been translated into every major language: Italians today, for example, read Agostino Lombardo's poetic renderings ("Oh, che vigliacco / E malfattore sono!" "Oh, what a rogue and peasant slave am I!"). The play has also appeared in tongues less familiar—Icelandic, Maltese, Persian, Tamil, Urdu, and Old Turkish. In what is probably the first extra-global imagining, Shakespeare's *Hamlet* has also suffered translation into Klingon (2000) as part of the grander "Shakespeare Restoration Project."

Afterlife Imaginings

Shakespeare's *Hamlet* has enjoyed a full and varied afterlife in other works, inspiring many later imaginings (see "Afterlives"). In James Joyce's *Ulysses* (1922), for example, *Hamlet* appears as a "sumptuous and stagnant exaggeration of murder," written by "a deathsman of the soul":

> Nine lives are taken off for his father's one, Our Father who art in purgatory. Khaki Hamlets don't hesitate to shoot. The blood-boltered shambles in act five is a forecast of the concentration camp sung by Mr Swinburne.

Stephen Dedalus here contrasts Hamlet with the English soldiers who do not hesitate to shoot Irish rebels. He compares the ending slaughter onstage to the cruel English policies during the Boer wars, especially the creation of retention camps. The political application of the play shifts to a topical one. Stephen then argues that Shakespeare originally played the ghost to Hamlet, an image of his own dead son Hamnet; accusing Gertrude of infidelity, then, Shakespeare brands his own Stratford wife with infamy. *Hamlet* thus becomes a many-layered meditation on female infidelity and male cuckoldry, themes central to the larger action of *Ulysses*.

Tom Stoppard has repeatedly reimagined the play (*Dogg's Hamlet*, *Fifteen Minute Hamlet*), but his most compelling reworking is *Rosencrantz and Guildenstern Are Dead* (1966). Reducing Hamlet to a minor character, the play focuses on Rosencrantz and Guildenstern, who struggle to act independently and to understand their predestined roles and fate. This play explores the nature of language, theater, free will, and determinism. Charles Marowitz continues his love-hate relationship with Shakespeare in *Hamlet* (1968), a collage of fragments from the play cut and pasted to deride the

---

8. Quoted by Graham Holderness, "Silence Bleeds: *Hamlet* across Borders: The Shakespearean adaptations of Sulayman Al-Bassam," *European Journal of English Studies* 12 (2008): 67–68.

main character as a conscience-stricken liberal. Concentrating on *Hamlet* source tales, John Updike in *Gertrude and Claudius* (2000) also reimagines the story, writing a prequel. The novel presents a beautiful and sensual Gertrude, trapped in marriage to the boorish king but beloved by the dashing brother.

From the outset many afterlives are comic. A number of dramas written early in the seventeenth century recall *Hamlet* playfully or parodically, including Chapman, Marston, and Jonson's *Eastward Ho* (1605). Here a lascivious bride named Gertrude marries hastily and echoes Ophelia's song, and a footman named Hamlet gets asked if he is mad (3.2.7). Even *Der Bestrafte Brudermord*, a serious early seventeenth-century German adaptation, contains a scene in which Hamlet ducks at the crucial moment so that would-be murderers, like cartoon characters, shoot each other. Mark Twain's con men in *Huckleberry Finn* (1885) mangle the soliloquies in high seriousness ("and just knocked the spots out of any acting ever *I* see before," Huck says). At a performance of *Hamlet*, the befuddled Partridge of Henry Fielding's *Tom Jones* (1749) thinks that the ghost is real. At another, Mr. Wopsle of Charles Dickens's *Great Expectations* (1861), playing the lead, faces a raucous and ridiculing crowd: "When he recommended the player not to saw the air thus, the sulky man said, 'And don't *you* do it, neither; you're a deal worse than *him*!'" The lecherous and grandiose ghost of John Barrymore returns to New York to tutor a reluctant actor in Paul Rudnick's *I Hate Hamlet* (1991).

Of course, so great and grand a tragedy has begotten many travesties, ludicrous and debasing imitations. The popular send-ups of the nineteenth century use light rhyme ("O Hamlet, you have done a deed felonius; / You've killed our poor lord chamberlain, Polonius!"), song, and low style for laughs: "To drink or not to drink! That is the question." Modern travesties follow suit, including Adam McNaughton's folksong, "The Three Minute Hamlet" (late 1980s): "Oh, Hamlet, Hamlet, acting balmy, / Hamlet, Hamlet, loves his mommy, / Hamlet, Hamlet, hesitating / He wonders if the ghost's a fake / And that is why he's waiting." In 1998 Shel Silverstein took a break from children's books to publish a rap version in *Playboy*: *Hamlet as Told on the Street*:

> So they run find Hamlet, they say, "Hey, sweet Prince,
> Your daddy's ghost been seen runnin' hither and hince.
> He's all full of maggots and he's grizzly and grim,
> Somethin's rotten in Denmark and—whew—we think it's him."
> Hamlet says, "Oh, are you sure it's my pop?
> Did he have matty gray hair with a bald spot on top?
> Did he have bright blue eyes that never know fear,
> And a tattoo says GERTRUDE FOREVER right here?"

In similar style Jaded Moon has been credited with *Hamlet goes Homie:* ("To O.D. or not to O.D. Know what I'm sayin, foo? My uncle killed my fatha! And my motha just married my evil Uncle. I've gotta go bust his ass.") Richard Curtis has taken the profanity to its burlesque extreme, to virtually every line, in his *The Skinhead Hamlet* ("To f*** or be f***ed"); "our hope was to achieve something like the effect of the New English Bible," Curtis solemnly says in a mock-prefatory comment.

Rock's Eye Productions staged and filmed (1995) *Green Eggs and Hamlet*, bits of the plot in Doctor Seuss–style rhymes. Parodied scenes have appeared in film and on television—for example, in *The Last Action Hero*, *Monty Python's Flying Circus*, and *Gilligan's Island*. Hamlet himself steps out of his play into Jasper Fforde's novel, *Something Rotten* (2004), where he meets the detective Thursday Next of Jurisfiction, a policing agency that works in and out of literary fictions. His many perceived inconsistencies of character, Thursday explains to him, result from the variety of different experiences each reader brings to the text: "'To each our own Hamlet.' 'Well,' snorted the Dane unhappily, 'it's a mystery to me. Do you think therapy would help?'"

As *Hamlet* continually comes to new life in the imaginations of actors, audiences, and readers, the rest (*pace* Hamlet himself), will be anything but silence.

The Text of
HAMLET

HAMLET, *Prince of Denmark, son of former King and Gertrude*
GHOST, *of King Hamlet, former King of Denmark*
CLAUDIUS, *King of Denmark, brother of the former King*
GERTRUDE, *Queen, widow of King Hamlet, now wife of Claudius*

POLONIUS, *councillor to the King*
OPHELIA, *his daughter*
LAERTES, *his son*
REYNALDO, *his servant*

HORATIO, *friend to Hamlet and fellow student*

ROSENCRANTZ
GUILDENSTERN } *courtiers and former fellow students*
CORNELIUS
VOLTEMAND } *ambassadors to Norway*
OSRIC, *a courtier*
A GENTLEMAN
A LORD
BARNARDO
FRANCISCO } *sentinels*
MARCELLUS

FORTINBRAS, *Prince of Norway*
CAPTAIN, *in his army*

PLAYERS, *three or four actors who perform as* PROLOGUE, PLAYER
    KING, PLAYER QUEEN, *and* LUCIANUS
CLOWNS, *a gravedigger and his companion*
DOCTOR, *of Divinity, a minister or priest*
MESSENGERS
SAILOR
AMBASSADOR, *from England*

Lords, Attendants, Guards, Sailors, Followers of Laertes, another
Ambassador or Ambassadors from England, Norwegian Soldiers

Scene: Denmark]

The Tragedy of Hamlet, Prince of Denmark

1.1 [THE GUARD PLATFORM OF ELSINORE CASTLE AT MIDNIGHT]

Enter [separately] BARNARDO *and* FRANCISCO, *two sentinels.*

BARNARDO   Who's there?

FRANCISCO   Nay, answer me. Stand and unfold yourself.

BARNARDO   Long live the King!

FRANCISCO   Barnardo?

BARNARDO   He.   5

FRANCISCO   You come most carefully upon your hour.

BARNARDO   'Tis now struck twelve. Get thee to bed,
     Francisco.

FRANCISCO   For this relief much thanks. 'Tis bitter cold,
   And I am sick at heart.

BARNARDO   Have you had quiet guard?   10

FRANCISCO   Not a mouse stirring.

BARNARDO   Well, good night.
   If you do meet Horatio and Marcellus,
   The rivals of my watch, bid them make haste.

Enter HORATIO *and* MARCELLUS.

FRANCISCO   I think I hear them.—Stand, ho! Who is there?   15

HORATIO   Friends to this ground.

MARCELLUS   And liegemen to the Dane.

FRANCISCO   [*Leaving*] Give you good night.

MARCELLUS   O, farewell, honest soldier. Who hath relieved
   you?

FRANCISCO   Barnardo hath my place. Give you good night.

                                                                             Exit.

MARCELLUS   Holla, Barnardo.   20

2. **unfold:** reveal
14. **rivals:** partners
15. **ho!:** stop!
16. **liegemen . . . Dane:** sworn servants of the Danish king
17. **Give:** i.e., may God give
20. **Holla:** Hello

5

BARNARDO Say, what, is Horatio there?
HORATIO   A piece of him.
BARNARDO Welcome, Horatio. Welcome, good Marcellus.
HORATIO What, has this thing appeared again tonight?
BARNARDO I have seen nothing.
MARCELLUS Horatio says 'tis but our fantasy,   25
  And will not let belief take hold of him
  Touching this dreaded sight twice seen of us.
  Therefore I have entreated him along
  With us to watch the minutes of this night,
  That if again this apparition come   30
  He may approve our eyes and speak to it.
HORATIO Tush, tush, 'twill not appear.
BARNARDO   Sit down awhile,
  And let us once again assail your ears,
  That are so fortified against our story,
  What we have two nights seen.
HORATIO   Well, sit we down,   35
  And let us hear Barnardo speak of this.
BARNARDO Last night of all,
  When yond same star that's westward from the pole
  Had made his course t'illume that part of heaven
  Where now it burns, Marcellus and myself,   40
  The bell then beating one—
              Enter GHOST [*in armor*].
MARCELLUS Peace, break thee off! Look where it comes again!
BARNARDO In the same figure like the King that's dead.
MARCELLUS Thou art a scholar; speak to it, Horatio.
BARNARDO Looks 'a not like the King? Mark it, Horatio.   45
HORATIO Most like. It harrows me with fear and wonder.
BARNARDO It would be spoke to.
MARCELLUS   Speak to it, Horatio.
HORATIO What art thou that usurp'st this time of night,
  Together with that fair and warlike form
  In which the majesty of buried Denmark   50
  Did sometimes march? By heaven, I charge thee, speak!

25. **fantasy:** imagination
31. **approve our eyes:** confirm our observation
32. **Tush:** (an expression of impatient dismissal or contempt)
35. **What:** i.e., with what
37. **Last . . . all:** this very last night
38. **yond:** yonder, that distant; **pole:** Pole Star, the North Star
39. **t'illume:** to illuminate
45. **'a:** he
46. **harrows:** lacerates, disturbs
48. **usurp'st:** wrongfully appropriates
50. **majesty . . . Denmark:** buried King of Denmark
51. **sometimes:** formerly

MARCELLUS   It is offended.
BARNARDO   See, it stalks away.
HORATIO   Stay, speak, speak! I charge thee speak!

Exit GHOST.

MARCELLUS   'Tis gone and will not answer.
BARNARDO   How now, Horatio, you tremble and look pale.   55
Is not this something more than fantasy?
What think you on't?
HORATIO   Before my God I might not this believe
Without the sensible and true avouch
Of mine own eyes.
MARCELLUS   Is it not like the King?   60
HORATIO   As thou art to thyself.
Such was the very armor he had on
When he the ambitious Norway combated;
So frowned he once when, in an angry parle,
He smote the sledded Polacks on the ice.   65
'Tis strange.
MARCELLUS   Thus twice before and jump at this dead hour,
With martial stalk hath he gone by our watch.
HORATIO   In what particular thought to work I know not,
But in the gross and scope of mine opinion,   70
This bodes some strange eruption to our state.
MARCELLUS   Good now, sit down, and tell me, he that knows,
Why this same strict and most observant watch
So nightly toils the subject of the land,
And why such daily cost of brazen cannon   75
And foreign mart for implements of war,
Why such impress of shipwrights, whose sore task
Does not divide the Sunday from the week.
What might be toward, that this sweaty haste
Doth make the night joint-laborer with the day?   80
Who is't that can inform me?

55. **How now:** How is it now (often used as an interjection)
59. **sensible:** attested by the senses; **avouch:** testimony
63. **Norway:** King of Norway
64. **parle:** parley, encounter
65. **sledded Polacks:** Polish soldiers on sleds
67. **jump:** precisely
68. **stalk:** walk
69. **In . . . work:** for which specific reason
70. **gross and scope:** general drift
72. **Good now:** (an expression of entreaty)
73. **watch:** watchfulness
74. **toils the subject:** causes the subjects to toil
76. **foreign mart:** expenditure abroad
77. **impress:** draft, conscription
79. **toward:** coming

HORATIO   That can I.
    At least the whisper goes so: our last King,
    Whose image even but now appeared to us,
    Was, as you know, by Fortinbras of Norway,
    Thereto pricked on by a most emulate pride,   85
    Dared to the combat; in which our valiant Hamlet—
    For so this side of our known world esteemed him—
    Did slay this Fortinbras; who, by a sealed compact
    Well ratified by law and heraldry,
    Did forfeit with his life all these his lands   90
    Which he stood seized of to the conqueror.
    Against the which a moiety competent
    Was gagèd by our King, which had return
    To the inheritance of Fortinbras,
    Had he been vanquisher, as by the same cov'nant   95
    And carriage of the article designed,
    His fell to Hamlet. Now, sir, young Fortinbras,
    Of unimprovèd mettle hot and full,
    Hath in the skirts of Norway here and there
    Sharked up a list of lawless resolutes   100
    For food and diet to some enterprise
    That hath a stomach in't; which is no other—
    As it doth well appear unto our state—
    But to recover of us, by strong hand
    And terms compulsory, those foresaid lands   105
    So by his father lost. And this, I take it,
    Is the main motive of our preparations,
    The source of this our watch, and the chief head
    Of this post-haste and rummage in the land.
BARNARDO   I think it be no other but e'en so.   110
    Well may it sort that this portentous figure

---

    85. **pricked on:** incited; **emulate:** competitive
    88. **sealed compact:** binding agreement
    89. **heraldry:** practices pertaining to rank, pedigree, and precedence
    91. **stood seized of:** legally possessed
    92. **moiety competent:** sufficient portion
    93. **gagèd:** pledged; **had return:** would have reverted
    95. **cov'nant:** agreement, compact
    96. **carriage:** import, meaning; **article designed:** stipulation drawn-up
    98. **unimprovèd:** (1) untested; (2) unrestrained; **mettle:** character, temperament
    99. **skirts:** boundaries
   100. **Sharked up:** gathered indiscriminately, perhaps predatorily
101–02. **For . . . in't:** (1) to supply an action that requires courage; (2) to serve as food
        for an action that will devour them
   105. **terms compulsory:** use of force
   108. **head:** source
   109. **post-haste:** hurry; **rummage:** bustle
   111. **sort:** (1) suit; (2) turn out

Comes armèd through our watch so like the King
That was and is the question of these wars.
HORATIO   A mote it is to trouble the mind's eye.
In the most high and palmy state of Rome,   115
A little ere the mightiest Julius fell,
The graves stood tenantless, and the sheeted dead
Did squeak and gibber in the Roman streets
At stars with trains of fire and dews of blood,
Disasters in the sun; and the moist star,   120
Upon whose influence Neptune's empire stands,
Was sick almost to doomsday with eclipse.
And even the like precurse of feared events,
As harbingers preceding still the Fates
And prologue to the omen coming on,   125
Have heaven and earth together demonstrated
Unto our climatures and countrymen.

    Enter GHOST.

But, soft, behold, lo, where it comes again!
I'll cross it though it blast me.—Stay, illusion! *It spreads*
If thou hast any sound or use of voice,   *his arms.* 130
Speak to me!
If there be any good thing to be done,
That may to thee do ease and grace to me,
Speak to me!
If thou art privy to thy country's fate,   135
Which, happily, foreknowing may avoid,
Oh, speak!
Or if thou hast uphoarded in thy life

---

114. **mote:** speck of dust. The phrasing echoes Matthew 7:3: "And why seest thou the
    mote that is in thy brother's eye, and perceives not the beam that is in thine own
    eye?" See also Luke 6:42.
115. **palmy:** triumphant
116. **Julius:** Julius Caesar, assassinated 44 BCE. Plutarch's *Caesar* (75 CE) describes some
    of the portents recalled here, and Shakespeare includes some of them in his *Julius
    Caesar* (1599); see Polonius's reference to playing Caesar below, 3.2.96–97.
117. **sheeted:** shrouded
120. **Disasters:** unfavorable influences; **moist star:** the moon (which controls tides)
121. **Neptune:** Roman god of the sea
122. **doomsday:** the end of the world and the dark day of the Last Judgment. See
    Matthew 24:29; Revelation 6:12.
123. **precurse:** foreshadowing
124. **As . . . Fates:** as forerunners always preceding the goddesses who control human
    destiny
125. **omen:** calamity
127. **climatures:** regions
128. **soft:** stop, be quiet; **lo:** look
129. **s.d.** *his:* its
136. **happily:** (1) by chance; (2) fortunately

Extorted treasure in the womb of earth,
For which, they say, your spirits oft walk in death,   140
Speak of it!   *The cock crows.*
              Stay, and speak!—Stop it, Marcellus!
MARCELLUS   Shall I strike it with my partisan?
HORATIO   Do, if it will not stand. [*They strike at it.*]
BARNARDO   'Tis here!
HORATIO   'Tis here!   [*Exit* GHOST.]   145
MARCELLUS   'Tis gone.
    We do it wrong, being so majestical,
    To offer it the show of violence,
    For it is as the air invulnerable,
    And our vain blows malicious mockery.   150
BARNARDO   It was about to speak when the cock crew.
HORATIO   And then it started like a guilty thing
    Upon a fearful summons. I have heard
    The cock, that is the trumpet to the morn,
    Doth with his lofty and shrill-sounding throat   155
    Awake the god of day, and at his warning,
    Whether in sea or fire, in earth or air,
    Th'extravagant and erring spirit hies
    To his confine; and of the truth herein
    This present object made probation.   160
MARCELLUS   It faded on the crowing of the cock.
    Some say that ever 'gainst that season comes
    Wherein our Savior's birth is celebrated,
    This bird of dawning singeth all night long.
    And then they say no spirit dare stir abroad,   165
    The nights are wholesome, then no planets strike,
    No fairy takes, nor witch hath power to charm—
    So hallowed and so gracious is that time.
HORATIO   So have I heard, and do in part believe it.
    But look, the morn in russet mantle clad   170
    Walks o'er the dew of yon high eastward hill.
    Break we our watch up and by my advice
    Let us impart what we have seen tonight

139. **Extorted:** wrongfully obtained
142. **partisan:** spear mounted with an axe blade
156. **god of day:** Phoebus Apollo, i.e., the sun
158. **extravagant and erring:** wandering beyond bounds; **hies:** hastens
159. **confine:** place of confinement
160. **probation:** proof
162. **'gainst:** before
166. **strike:** destroy by evil influence
167. **takes:** (1) steals (children, especially); (2) bewitches
168. **gracious:** filled with divine grace
170. **russet:** reddish brown

Unto young Hamlet, for upon my life
This spirit, dumb to us, will speak to him.   175
Do you consent we shall acquaint him with it,
As needful in our loves, fitting our duty?
MARCELLUS   Let's do't, I pray, and I this morning know
Where we shall find him most convenient.

Exeunt.

1.2 [ELSINORE CASTLE]

Flourish. Enter CLAUDIUS, *King of Denmark,* GERTRUDE
the Queen, COUNCIL, *as* POLONIUS *and his son* LAERTES,
HAMLET, *cum aliis [including* CORNELIUS, VOLTEMAND,
and ATTENDANTS].

KING   Though yet of Hamlet our dear brother's death
The memory be green, and that it us befitted
To bear our hearts in grief, and our whole kingdom
To be contracted in one brow of woe,
Yet so far hath discretion fought with nature   5
That we with wisest sorrow think on him,
Together with remembrance of ourselves.
Therefore our sometime sister, now our queen,
Th'imperial jointress to this warlike state,
Have we—as 'twere with a defeated joy,   10
With an auspicious and a dropping eye,
With mirth in funeral, and with dirge in marriage,
In equal scale weighing delight and dole—
Taken to wife. Nor have we herein barred
Your better wisdoms, which have freely gone   15
With this affair along. For all, our thanks.
Now follows that you know young Fortinbras,
Holding a weak supposal of our worth,
Or thinking by our late dear brother's death

179. **convenient:** conveniently
0.1.s.d. *Flourish:* fanfare sounded on a trumpet or cornet
0.2.s.d. *as:* including
0.3.s.d. *cum aliis:* with others. The Folio names Ophelia here.
  1. **brother:** (Succession by a brother is permissible in Denmark, which has an
     elective monarchy, as is clear from 5.2.64.)
  2. **green:** i.e., fresh; **befitted:** suited
  4. **contracted . . . woe:** contorted into one expression of grief
  5. **discretion . . . nature:** reason overmastered natural affection
  8. **sometime sister:** former sister-in-law
  9. **jointress:** widow who possesses property formerly held in common with her
     husband
  11. **auspicious . . . eye:** one eye glad and the other weeping
  13. **dole:** sorrow
  17. **follows . . . know:** it follows that you be told that
  18. **weak supposal:** low estimate

Our state to be disjoint and out of frame,　　　　　　　20
Colleagued with this dream of his advantage,
He hath not failed to pester us with message
Importing the surrender of those lands
Lost by his father, with all bands of law,
To our most valiant brother—so much for him.　　　25
Now for ourself and for this time of meeting,
Thus much the business is: we have here writ
To Norway, uncle of young Fortinbras—
Who, impotent and bedrid, scarcely hears
Of this his nephew's purpose—to suppress　　　　30
His further gait herein, in that the levies,
The lists, and full proportions are all made
Out of his subject. And we here dispatch
You, good Cornelius, and you, Voltemand,
For bearers of this greeting to old Norway,　　　　35
Giving to you no further personal power
To business with the King more than the scope
Of these dilated articles allow. [*He gives them a paper.*]
Farewell, and let your haste commend your duty.

COR. ⎫
VOL. ⎬ In that and all things will we show our duty.　　40
　　 ⎭

KING　 We doubt it nothing. Heartily farewell.
　　　　　　 [*Exeunt* CORNELIUS *and* VOLTEMAND.]
And now, Laertes, what's the news with you?
You told us of some suit; what is't, Laertes?
You cannot speak of reason to the Dane
And lose your voice. What wouldst thou beg, Laertes,　45
That shall not be my offer, not thy asking?
The head is not more native to the heart,
The hand more instrumental to the mouth,
Than is the throne of Denmark to thy father.
What wouldst thou have, Laertes?

LAERTES　　　　　　　　My dread lord,　　　　50

---

20. **disjoint:** ill connected; **out of frame:** disordered. Both are metaphors from carpentry.
21. **Colleagued:** allied
24. **bands:** binding agreements
28. **uncle:** (In Norway, as in Denmark, the brother of the dead king, rather than the son and namesake, has succeeded to the throne.)
29. **bedrid:** confined to bed
31. **gait:** proceeding
32. **proportions:** numbers, especially of soldiers
33. **Out . . . subject:** from his people
38. **dilated:** articulated
39. **commend:** advertise
47. **native:** related
48. **instrumental:** serviceable

Your leave and favor to return to France,
From whence, though willingly, I came to Denmark
To show my duty in your coronation.
Yet now I must confess, that duty done,
My thoughts and wishes bend again toward France,   55
And bow them to your gracious leave and pardon.

KING   Have you your father's leave? What says Polonius?

POLONIUS   He hath, my lord, wrung from me my slow leave
By laborsome petition, and at last
Upon his will I sealed my hard consent.   60
I do beseech you, give him leave to go.

KING   Take thy fair hour, Laertes. Time be thine,
And thy best graces spend it at thy will.
But now, my cousin Hamlet, and my son—

HAMLET   A little more than kin and less than kind.   65

KING   How is it that the clouds still hang on you?

HAMLET   Not so, my lord. I am too much in the sun.

QUEEN   Good Hamlet, cast thy nighted color off,
And let thine eye look like a friend on Denmark.
Do not forever with thy vailèd lids   70
Seek for thy noble father in the dust.
Thou know'st 'tis common—all that lives must die,
Passing through nature to eternity.

HAMLET   Ay, madam, it is common.

QUEEN   If it be,
Why seems it so particular with thee?   75

HAMLET   "Seems," madam, nay, it is. I know not "seems."
'Tis not alone my inky cloak, good mother,
Nor customary suits of solemn black,
Nor windy suspiration of forced breath,
No, nor the fruitful river in the eye,   80
Nor the dejected havior of the visage,

56. **bow them:** they bow
60. **sealed:** officially granted (as if placing a seal on a document); **hard:** reluctant
62. **Take . . . hour:** (1) go when you please; (2) enjoy your youth
63. **thy . . . will:** may your virtuous qualities guide you in spending time
64. **cousin:** kinsman
65. **more than kin:** more than a simple relative (since now you claim to be my father);
    kind: (1) natural; (2) charitable. Hamlet's opening line, sometimes read as an aside,
    seems rather the first of his edgy, punning responses here.
67. **sun:** (with a pun on "son")
68. **nighted color:** black mourning garments
69. **Denmark:** (1) king; (2) country
70. **vailèd lids:** lowered eyes
72. **common:** universal. Hamlet plays on the word as meaning "vulgar," 74.
77. **inky:** black. The color symbolized mourning and melancholy, a distemper similar to
    modern depression, thought to occur from an excess of black bile in the body.
79. **suspiration:** sighing
81. **dejected . . . visage:** downcast expression

Together with all forms, moods, shapes of grief,
That can denote me truly. These indeed "seem,"
For they are actions that a man might play;
But I have that within which passes show,   85
These but the trappings and the suits of woe.
KING   'Tis sweet and commendable in your nature, Hamlet,
To give these mourning duties to your father,
But you must know your father lost a father,
That father lost, lost his, and the survivor bound   90
In filial obligation for some term
To do obsequious sorrow. But to persever
In obstinate condolement is a course
Of impious stubbornness; 'tis unmanly grief.
It shows a will most incorrect to heaven,   95
A heart unfortified or mind impatient,
An understanding simple and unschooled.
For what we know must be and is as common
As any the most vulgar thing to sense,
Why should we in our peevish opposition   100
Take it to heart? Fie, 'tis a fault to heaven,
A fault against the dead, a fault to nature,
To reason most absurd, whose common theme
Is death of fathers, and who still hath cried
From the first corpse till he that died today,   105
"This must be so." We pray you, throw to earth
This unprevailing woe and think of us
As of a father. For, let the world take note,
You are the most immediate to our throne,
And with no less nobility of love   110
Than that which dearest father bears his son,
Do I impart toward you. For your intent
In going back to school in Wittenberg,
It is most retrograde to our desire,
And we beseech you bend you to remain   115

86. **trappings:** ornaments
90. **That father lost:** i.e., your grandfather
92. **obsequious:** appropriate to a funeral rite (obsequy)
93. **condolement:** sorrowing
96. **impatient:** incapable of suffering
99. **sense:** (1) perception; (2) understanding
103. **reason:** philosophy, as well as the rational power of the mind
104. **still:** always
105. **first corpse:** that of Abel, according to Genesis 4:8, the first fratricide. See similar allusions at 3.3.37–38, 5.1.68–69.
107. **unprevailing:** ineffectual
113. **school in Wittenberg:** famous German Lutheran university
114. **retrograde:** contrary
115. **bend you:** incline yourself

Here in the cheer and comfort of our eye,
Our chiefest courtier, cousin, and our son.
QUEEN   Let not thy mother lose her prayers, Hamlet.
I pray thee, stay with us; go not to Wittenberg.
HAMLET   I shall in all my best obey you, madam.   120
KING   Why, 'tis a loving and a fair reply.
Be as ourself in Denmark. Madam, come,
This gentle and unforced accord of Hamlet
Sits smiling to my heart; in grace whereof
No jocund health that Denmark drinks today   125
But the great cannon to the clouds shall tell,
And the King's rouse the heaven shall bruit again,
Respeaking earthly thunder. Come away.

                     Flourish. Exeunt all but HAMLET.

HAMLET   Oh, that this too, too solid flesh would melt,
Thaw, and resolve itself into a dew,   130
Or that the Everlasting had not fixed
His canon 'gainst self-slaughter. O God, God,
How weary, stale, flat, and unprofitable
Seem to me all the uses of this world!
Fie on't, ah, fie. 'Tis an unweeded garden   135
That grows to seed; things rank and gross in nature
Possess it merely. That it should come thus,
But two months dead—nay, not so much, not two!
So excellent a king that was to this,
Hyperion to a satyr, so loving to my mother,   140
That he might not beteem the winds of heaven
Visit her face too roughly. Heaven and earth,
Must I remember? Why, she would hang on him
As if increase of appetite had grown
By what it fed on, and yet within a month—   145
Let me not think on't. Frailty, thy name is woman!

[margin handwritten: wants to die]

120. **in . . . best:** to the best of my ability
124. **grace:** thanksgiving
125. **health:** toast
127. **rouse:** draft of liquor; **bruit:** report
128. **Respeaking:** echoing
129. **solid:** (A famous crux as both quartos read "sallied," which could mean "assailed" and the Folio reads "solid." Many have plausibly emended to "sullied," as lowercase "a" and "u" could frequently be confused by readers of Shakespeare's handwriting and "sallies" appears in Q2 for "sullies" at 2.1.40. See pp. xxiv–xxvii.)
132. **canon:** decree. Auditors may hear "cannon" as well.
137. **merely:** entirely
138. **two months:** (Hamlet will claim that his father died within "a month," 145, and later within "two hours," only to receive Ophelia's correction, "Nay, 'tis twice two months," 3.2.117–118.)
140. **Hyperion . . . satyr:** Titan, god of the sun, compared to satyr, a lecherous mythological creature, half-man, half-goat
141. **beteem:** allow

A little month, or ere those shoes were old
With which she followed my poor father's body,
Like Niobe, all tears, why she—
O God, a beast that wants discourse of reason
Would have mourned longer!—married with my uncle,   150
My father's brother, but no more like my father
Than I to Hercules. Within a month,
Ere yet the salt of most unrighteous tears
Had left the flushing in her gallèd eyes,
She married. Oh, most wicked speed, to post   155
With such dexterity to incestuous sheets!
It is not, nor it cannot come to good.
But break, my heart, for I must hold my tongue.

> *Enter* HORATIO, MARCELLUS, *and* BARNARDO.

HORATIO   Hail to your lordship.   160

HAMLET   I am glad to see you well. Horatio!—or I do forget
myself.

HORATIO   The same, my lord, and your poor servant ever.

HAMLET   Sir, my good friend. I'll change that name with
you.
And what make you from Wittenberg, Horatio?
—Marcellus!   165

MARCELLUS   My good lord.

HAMLET   I am very glad to see you. [*To* BARNARDO] Good
even, sir.
—But what, in faith, make you from Wittenberg?

HORATIO   A truant disposition, good my lord.

HAMLET   I would not hear your enemy say so,   170
Nor shall you do my ear that violence
To make it truster of your own report
Against yourself. I know you are no truant.
But what is your affair in Elsinore?
We'll teach you for to drink ere you depart.   175

147. **ere:** before
149. **Niobe:** a mythological figure of grief who became a perpetually weeping stone
150. **wants:** lacks
153. **Hercules:** mythological figure of strength and courage. See also 1.4.83 and Appendix 2, Folio passage 2, line 22 (p. 148)
155. **gallèd:** irritated
156. **post:** rush
157. **incestuous:** (In Shakespeare's time, some considered the marriage of a man and his brother's widow incestuous; see Leviticus 18:16; 20:21.)
163. **change that name:** exchange the name of "good friend"
164. **make:** do
167. **even:** evening
169. **truant:** idle
174. **Elsinore:** modern Helsingør, on the northeast coast of the island of Zealand, Denmark. Some of Shakespeare's fellow actors had toured there.

HORATIO   My lord, I came to see your father's funeral.

HAMLET   I prithee, do not mock me, fellow-student;
   I think it was to see my mother's wedding.

HORATIO   Indeed, my lord, it followed hard upon.

HAMLET   Thrift, thrift, Horatio. The funeral baked meats   180
   Did coldly furnish forth the marriage tables.
   Would I had met my dearest foe in heaven
   Or ever I had seen that day, Horatio.
   My father, methinks I see my father.

HORATIO   Where, my lord?

HAMLET   In my mind's eye, Horatio.   185

HORATIO   I saw him once. 'A was a goodly king.

HAMLET   'A was a man. Take him for all in all,
   I shall not look upon his like again.

HORATIO   My lord, I think I saw him yesternight.

HAMLET   Saw who?

HORATIO   My lord, the King your father.   190

HAMLET   The King my father?

HORATIO   Season your admiration for a while
   With an attent ear till I may deliver
   Upon the witness of these gentlemen
   This marvel to you.

HAMLET   For God's love, let me hear!   195

HORATIO   Two nights together had these gentlemen,
   Marcellus and Barnardo, on their watch
   In the dead waste and middle of the night,
   Been thus encountered: a figure like your father,
   Armèd at point exactly, cap-à-pie,   200
   Appears before them, and with solemn march
   Goes slow and stately by them. Thrice he walked
   By their oppressed and fear-surprisèd eyes
   Within his truncheon's length, whilst they, distilled
   Almost to jelly with the act of fear,   205
   Stand dumb and speak not to him. This to me
   In dreadful secrecy impart they did,

---

176. **funeral:** (The funeral of a king may have occurred a considerable time after his death and may have been an elaborate public spectacle.)
177. **prithee:** beg of you
179. **hard upon:** quickly thereafter
182. **dearest:** cruelest (from Old English *déor*)
183. **Or ever:** before
186. **'A:** he
187. **all in all:** all things in all respects
192. **Season your admiration:** restrain your astonishment
193. **attent:** attentive
200. **at point:** in readiness; **cap-à-pie:** head to foot
204. **truncheon:** an officer's staff; **distilled:** dissolved
205. **act:** effect

And I with them the third night kept the watch.
Where, as they had delivered, both in time,
Form of the thing, each word made true and good,   210
The apparition comes. I knew your father;
These hands are not more like.

HAMLET   But where was this?

MARCELLUS   My lord, upon the platform where we watch.

HAMLET   Did you not speak to it?

HORATIO   My lord, I did,
But answer made it none. Yet once methought   215
It lifted up its head and did address
Itself to motion, like as it would speak;
But even then the morning cock crew loud,
And at the sound it shrunk in haste away
And vanished from our sight.

HAMLET   'Tis very strange.   220

HORATIO   As I do live, my honored lord, 'tis true.
And we did think it writ down in our duty
To let you know of it.

HAMLET   Indeed, sirs, but this troubles me.
Hold you the watch tonight?

ALL   We do, my lord.   225

HAMLET   Armed, say you?

ALL   Armed, my lord.

HAMLET   From top to toe?

ALL   My lord, from head to foot.

HAMLET   Then saw you not his face.

HORATIO   O, yes, my lord, he wore his beaver up.

HAMLET   What looked he, frowningly?   230

HORATIO   A countenance more in sorrow than in anger.

HAMLET   Pale or red?

HORATIO   Nay, very pale.

HAMLET   And fixed his eyes upon you?

HORATIO   Most constantly.

HAMLET   I would I had been there.

HORATIO   It would have much amazed you.

HAMLET   Very like.   235
Stayed it long?

HORATIO   While one with moderate haste might tell a
hundred.

209–10. in . . . Form: with respect to the time and shape
216–17. address . . . motion: begin to move
    229. beaver: faceguard of a helmet
    230. What: how

MAR. ⎱ Longer, longer.
BAR. ⎰

HORATIO   Not when I saw't.

HAMLET   His beard was grizzled—no?

HORATIO   It was as I have seen it in his life,   240
  A sable silvered.

HAMLET   I will watch tonight.
  Perchance 'twill walk again.

HORATIO   I warr'nt it will.

HAMLET   If it assume my noble father's person,
  I'll speak to it, though hell itself should gape
  And bid me hold my peace. I pray you all,   245
  If you have hitherto concealed this sight,
  Let it be tenable in your silence still;
  And whatsoever else shall hap tonight,
  Give it an understanding but no tongue.
  I will requite your loves. So, fare you well.   250
  Upon the platform twixt eleven and twelve,
  I'll visit you.

ALL   Our duty to your honor.

HAMLET   Your loves, as mine to you; farewell.

     Exeunt [HORATIO, MARCELLUS, *and* BARNARDO].

  My father's spirit in arms? All is not well;
  I doubt some foul play. Would the night were come.   255
  Till then sit still, my soul. Foul deeds will rise,
  Though all the earth o'erwhelm them, to men's eyes.   *Exit.*

     1.3 [UNLOCALIZED, PERHAPS THE HOME OF POLONIUS]

     Enter LAERTES *and* OPHELIA, *his sister.*

LAERTES   My necessaries are embarked. Farewell.
  And, sister, as the winds give benefit
  And convey is assistant, do not sleep
  But let me hear from you.

OPHELIA   Do you doubt that?

LAERTES   For Hamlet, and the trifling of his favor,   5
  Hold it a fashion and a toy in blood,

239. **grizzled:** gray
241. **sable silvered:** black mixed with gray
242. **warr'nt:** guarantee
247. **tenable:** withheld
248. **hap:** occur by chance
255. **doubt:** fear
  3. **convey is assistant:** means of conveyance are ready
  5. **trifling:** frivolous conduct
  6. **toy in blood:** flirtation

A violet in the youth of primy nature,
Forward, not permanent, sweet, not lasting,
The perfume and suppliance of a minute—
No more.
OPHELIA   No more but so.
LAERTES   Think it no more.   10
For nature crescent does not grow alone
In thews and bulks, but as this temple waxes,
The inward service of the mind and soul
Grows wide withal. Perhaps he loves you now,
And now no soil nor cautel doth besmirch   15
The virtue of his will, but you must fear,
His greatness weighed, his will is not his own.
He may not, as unvalued persons do,
Carve for himself, for on his choice depends
The safety and health of this whole state,   20
And therefore must his choice be circumscribed
Unto the voice and yielding of that body
Whereof he is the head. Then if he says he loves you,
It fits your wisdom so far to believe it
As he in his particular act and place   25
May give his saying deed, which is no further
Than the main voice of Denmark goes withal.
Then weigh what loss your honor may sustain
If with too credent ear you list his songs,
Or lose your heart, or your chaste treasure open   30
To his unmastered importunity.
Fear it, Ophelia, fear it, my dear sister,
And keep you in the rear of your affection,

7. **primy:** flourishing
8. **Forward:** early blooming
9. **suppliance:** (1) supply; (2) supplication
11. **crescent:** growing
12. **thews and bulks:** bodily proportions and mass; **temple waxes:** i.e., body grows
13. **inward service:** i.e., inner life (the activity within the temple)
14. **Grows wide withal:** enlarges with it (the body). Laertes implies that the contrary is the case with Hamlet, in other words, that he is immature.
15. **soil nor cautel:** blemish nor deceit; **besmirch:** discolor, make dirty
16. **will:** (1) intention; (2) desire
17. **weighed:** properly considered
19. **Carve:** i.e., choose (a metaphor from cutting meat at table)
21–22. **circumscribed Unto:** restricted by
26. **give . . . deed:** put his words into action
27. **main voice:** popular will; **goes withal:** consents in addition
29. **credent:** believing; **list:** listen to
31. **unmastered importunity:** uncontrolled solicitation
33. **rear . . . affection:** i.e., out of the way of your own amorous feeling (here imagined as an attacking army)

Out of the shot and danger of desire.
"The chariest maid is prodigal enough   35
If she unmask her beauty to the moon;"
"Virtue itself scapes not calumnious strokes";
"The canker galls the infants of the spring"
Too oft before their buttons be disclosed,
And in the morn and liquid dew of youth   40
Contagious blastments are most imminent.
Be wary then; best safety lies in fear.
Youth to itself rebels though none else near.

OPHELIA   I shall th'effect of this good lesson keep
As watchman to my heart. But, good my brother,   45
Do not, as some ungracious pastors do,
Show me the steep and thorny way to heaven
Whiles, a puffed and reckless libertine,
Himself the primrose path of dalliance treads,
And recks not his own rede.

LAERTES   Oh, fear me not.   50
I stay too long.

     Enter POLONIUS.

               But here my father comes.
A double blessing is a double grace;
Occasion smiles upon a second leave.

POLONIUS   Yet here, Laertes? Aboard, aboard, for shame!
The wind sits in the shoulder of your sail,   55
And you are stayed for. There—my blessing with thee.
And these few precepts in thy memory
Look thou character. Give thy thoughts no tongue,
Nor any unproportioned thought his act.
Be thou familiar, but by no means vulgar.   60

---

34. shot: (1) range; (2) gunfire
35, 37, 38: (Quotation marks indicate proverbial language or wise sayings.)
35. chariest: most cautious; **prodigal:** extravagant and reckless
36. unmask: show; **moon:** symbol of chastity
37. calumnious: slanderous
38. canker . . . spring: cankerworm destroys spring blossoms
39. buttons be disclosed: buds be opened
40. liquid dew: i.e., time when dew is fresh and bright
41. blastments: blights
43. to . . . near: loses self-control even when alone
48. puffed: swollen with pride
49. primrose . . . dalliance: flowery road of pleasure. See Matthew 7:13: "Enter in at the strait gate; for it is the wide gate, and broad way that leadeth to destruction, and many there be which go in thereat."
50. recks: heeds; **rede:** advice
52. double blessing: second leave-taking. Laertes has already said good-bye to his father.
53. Occasion: opportunity (often personified)
58. Look thou character: be sure that you inscribe
59. unproportioned: intemperate

Those friends thou hast, and their adoption tried,
Grapple them unto thy soul with hoops of steel,
But do not dull thy palm with entertainment
Of each new-hatched, unfledged courage. Beware
Of entrance to a quarrel, but, being in,   65
Bear't that th'opposèd may beware of thee.
Give every man thy ear, but few thy voice.
Take each man's censure, but reserve thy judgment.
Costly thy habit as thy purse can buy,
But not expressed in fancy; rich not gaudy,   70
For the apparel oft proclaims the man,
And they in France of the best rank and station
Are of a most select and generous chief in that.
Neither a borrower nor a lender be,
For loan oft loses both itself and friend,   75
And borrowing dulls the edge of husbandry.
This above all—to thine own self be true,
And it must follow, as the night the day,
Thou canst not then be false to any man.
Farewell. My blessing season this in thee.   80

LAERTES   Most humbly do I take my leave, my lord.

POLONIUS   The time invests you. Go, your servants tend.

LAERTES   Farewell, Ophelia, and remember well
What I have said to you.

OPHELIA   'Tis in my memory locked,
And you yourself shall keep the key of it.   85

LAERTES   Farewell.   *Exit* LAERTES.

POLONIUS   What is't, Ophelia, he hath said to you?

OPHELIA   So please you, something touching the Lord Hamlet.

POLONIUS   Marry, well bethought.
'Tis told me he hath very oft of late   90
Given private time to you, and you yourself
Have of your audience been most free and bounteous.
If it be so—as so 'tis put on me,

61. **tried:** tested
62. **Grapple . . . hoops:** (The metaphor derives from naval warfare, specifically the practice of seizing ships with grapnels, or metal hooks on ropes.)
63. **dull thy palm:** wear out your hand (by handshaking)
64. **unfledged:** immature; **courage:** high-spirited youth
68. **censure:** opinion
69. **habit:** clothing
70. **fancy:** caprice, excessive ornament
73. **select . . . chief:** excellent and noble preeminence
76. **husbandry:** household management
80. **season this:** ripen my advice
82. **invests:** presses; **tend:** wait
89. **Marry:** i.e., by the Virgin Mary (an oath); **bethought:** purposed
93. **put on:** told to

And that in way of caution—I must tell you
You do not understand yourself so clearly   95
As it behooves my daughter and your honor.
What is between you? Give me up the truth.

OPHELIA   He hath, my lord, of late made many tenders
Of his affection to me.

POLONIUS   "Affection"? Pooh, you speak like a green girl,   100
Unsifted in such perilous circumstance.
Do you believe his "tenders," as you call them?

OPHELIA   I do not know, my lord, what I should think.

POLONIUS   Marry, I will teach you. Think yourself a baby
That you have ta'en these tenders for true pay,   105
Which are not sterling. Tender yourself more dearly,
Or—not to crack the wind of the poor phrase,
Wronging it thus—you'll tender me a fool.

OPHELIA   My lord, he hath importuned me with love
In honorable fashion.   110

POLONIUS   Ay, "fashion" you may call it. Go to, go to.

OPHELIA   And hath given countenance to his speech, my lord,
With almost all the holy vows of heaven.

POLONIUS   Ay, springes to catch woodcocks. I do know,
When the blood burns, how prodigal the soul   115
Lends the tongue vows. These blazes, daughter,
Giving more light than heat, extinct in both,
Even in their promise as it is a-making,
You must not take for fire. From this time
Be something scanter of your maiden presence;   120
Set your entreatments at a higher rate
Than a command to parle. For Lord Hamlet,
Believe so much in him, that he is young,
And with a larger tether may he walk

96. **behooves:** suits
98. **tenders:** offers
101. **Unsifted:** inexperienced
106. **sterling:** legal currency; **Tender . . . dearly:** (1) regard yourself more lovingly;
     (2) offer yourself at a higher rate
107. **crack the wind:** exhaust by overuse
108. **tender . . . fool:** (1) make me into a fool; (2) make a fool of yourself to me;
     (3) present me with a grandchild
112. **countenance:** credibility
114. **springes:** snares; **woodcocks:** birds supposed to be gullible
115. **prodigal:** liberally
118. **it:** i.e., the promise
121. **entreatments:** conversations
122. **command to parle:** i.e., Hamlet's wish to speak with you. In other words: "Value
     yourself and your conversation more highly than to speak with Hamlet simply
     because he wishes to speak to you." The metaphors are primarily military.
123. **in:** of

Than may be given you. In few, Ophelia,   125
Do not believe his vows, for they are brokers,
Not of that dye which their investments show,
But mere implorators of unholy suits,
Breathing like sanctified and pious bawds,
The better to beguile. This is for all: 130
I would not, in plain terms, from this time forth
Have you so slander any moment leisure
As to give words or talk with the Lord Hamlet.
Look to't, I charge you. Come your ways.
OPHELIA   I shall obey, my lord.   135

                                        Exeunt.

1.4 [THE GUARD PLATFORM OF ELSINORE CASTLE AT MIDNIGHT]

Enter HAMLET, HORATIO, *and* MARCELLUS.

HAMLET   The air bites shrewdly; it is very cold.
HORATIO   It is a nipping and an eager air.
HAMLET   What hour now?
HORATIO   I think it lacks of twelve.
MARCELLUS   No, it is struck.
HORATIO   Indeed? I heard it not.
It then draws near the season   5
Wherein the spirit held his wont to walk.

            A flourish of trumpets, and two pieces go off.

What does this mean, my lord?
HAMLET   The King doth wake tonight and takes his rouse,
Keeps wassail, and the swagg'ring upspring reels,
And as he drains his drafts of Rhenish down,   10
The kettledrum and trumpet thus bray out
The triumph of his pledge.

125. **In few:** briefly
126. **brokers:** go-betweens, especially in love affairs
127. **investments:** clothes
128. **implorators:** solicitors
129. **Breathing:** speaking; **bawds:** pimps
130. **for all:** once for all
132. **moment:** moment's
134. **Come your ways:** come along
  1. **shrewdly:** sharply
  2. **eager:** biting
  3. **lacks of:** is just before
  5. **season:** time
  6. **held his wont:** was accustomed
6.s.d. *pieces go off:* cannons fire offstage
  8. **rouse:** carousal, drinking bout
  9. **Keeps wassail:** revels; **upspring:** wild German dance; **reels:** dances (drunkenly)
 10. **Rhenish:** Rhine wine
 11. **bray out:** sound loudly and harshly
 12. **pledge:** (1) promise to drink (1.2.125–28); (2) feat of drinking a full cup in one draft

HORATIO   Is it a custom?

HAMLET   Ay, marry, is't,
But to my mind, though I am native here
And to the manner born, it is a custom   15
More honored in the breach than the observance.
This heavy-headed revel east and west
Makes us traduced and taxed of other nations;
They clepe us drunkards and with swinish phrase
Soil our addition; and indeed it takes   20
From our achievements, though performed at height,
The pith and marrow of our attribute.
So, oft it chances in particular men
That for some vicious mole of nature in them,
As in their birth—wherein they are not guilty,   25
Since nature cannot choose his origin—
By their o'ergrowth of some complexion,
Oft breaking down the pales and forts of reason,
Or by some habit that too much o'erleavens
The form of plausive manners—that these men,   30
Carrying, I say, the stamp of one defect,
Being nature's livery or fortune's star,
His virtues else, be they as pure as grace,
As infinite as man may undergo,
Shall in the general censure take corruption   35
From that particular fault. The dram of evil
Doth all the noble substance often dout
To his own scandal.

            Enter GHOST.

HORATIO   Look, my lord, it comes!

16. **in the breach:** by neglect
17. **east and west:** i.e., everywhere
18. **traduced:** defamed; **taxed of:** reproved by
19. **clepe:** call; **swinish phrase:** calling us swine
20. **addition:** titles of honor
21. **at height:** excellently
22. **pith . . . attribute:** substance of our good reputation
24. **mole of nature:** natural defect (in morals)
26. **his:** its
27. **o'ergrowth . . . complexion:** excess in one of the four humors thought to govern the human body and temperament
28. **pales and forts:** fences and fortifications. Reason is here imagined as the commander of a fortress.
29. **o'erleavens:** radically changes (as yeast in dough)
30. **plausive manners:** pleasing conduct
32. **livery:** provision (i.e., the "vicious mole" or the "o'ergrowth of some complexion"); **fortune's star:** i.e., the result of chance
33. **His virtues else:** the other virtues of these men
34. **undergo:** sustain
35. **general censure:** common opinion
36–38. **The dram . . . scandal:** A small quantity (**dram**) of evil blots out (**Doth . . . dout**) the essential good (**noble substance**) of a person or thing and brings disrepute (**scandal**).

HAMLET Angels and ministers of grace defend us!
Be thou a spirit of health or goblin damned,   40
Bring with thee airs from heaven or blasts from hell,
Be thy intents wicked or charitable,
Thou com'st in such a questionable shape
That I will speak to thee. I'll call thee Hamlet,
King, father, royal Dane. Oh, answer me!   45
Let me not burst in ignorance, but tell
Why thy canonized bones, hearsèd in death,
Have burst their cerements, why the sepulcher,
Wherein we saw thee quietly interred,
Hath oped his ponderous and marble jaws   50
To cast thee up again. What may this mean,
That thou, dead corpse, again in complete steel
Revisits thus the glimpses of the moon,
Making night hideous, and we fools of nature
So horridly to shake our disposition   55
With thoughts beyond the reaches of our souls?
Say, why is this? Wherefore? What should we do?
          [GHOST] *beckons* [HAMLET].
HORATIO It beckons you to go away with it,
As if it some impartment did desire
To you alone.
MARCELLUS   Look with what courteous action   60
It waves you to a more removèd ground.
But do not go with it.
HORATIO   No, by no means.
HAMLET It will not speak; then I will follow it.
HORATIO Do not, my lord.
HAMLET   Why, what should be the fear?
I do not set my life at a pin's fee,   65
And for my soul, what can it do to that,
Being a thing immortal as itself?
It waves me forth again. I'll follow it.
HORATIO What if it tempt you toward the flood, my lord,
Or to the dreadful summit of the cliff   70

40. **spirit of health:** good angel; **goblin:** ugly, mischievous demon
47. **canonized:** duly buried according to church law; **hearsèd:** coffined
48. **cerements:** waxed wrappings for the dead
52. **complete steel:** full armor
53. **glimpses . . . moon:** fitful moonlight
54. **fools of nature:** men naturally afraid of the supernatural
59. **impartment:** communication
65. **fee:** value
69. **flood:** sea

That beetles o'er his base into the sea,
And there assume some other horrible form
Which might deprive your sovereignty of reason,
And draw you into madness? Think of it.
The very place puts toys of desperation,   75
Without more motive, into every brain
That looks so many fathoms to the sea
And hears it roar beneath.

HAMLET   It waves me still.—Go on. I'll follow thee.

MARCELLUS   You shall not go, my lord. [*They hold him.*]

HAMLET   Hold off your hands!   80

HORATIO   Be ruled. You shall not go.

HAMLET   My fate cries out,
And makes each petty artery in this body
As hardy as the Nemean lion's nerve.

     [GHOST *beckons.*]

Still am I called. Unhand me, gentlemen!
By heaven, I'll make a ghost of him that lets me!   85
[*Breaking free*] I say, away!—Go on. I'll follow thee.

                    Exeunt GHOST *and* HAMLET.

HORATIO   He waxes desperate with imagination.

MARCELLUS   Let's follow. 'Tis not fit thus to obey him.

HORATIO   Have after. To what issue will this come?

MARCELLUS   Something is rotten in the state of Denmark.   90

HORATIO   Heaven will direct it.

MARCELLUS   Nay, let's follow him.

                              Exeunt.

1.5 [THE BATTLEMENTS OF ELSINORE CASTLE]

     Enter GHOST *and* HAMLET.

HAMLET   Whither wilt thou lead me? Speak, I'll go no further.

GHOST   Mark me.

HAMLET   I will.

GHOST   My hour is almost come,
When I to sulf'rous and tormenting flames
Must render up myself.

---

71. **beetles:** projects
73. **sovereignty of reason:** reason of its ability to govern you
75. **toys of desperation:** fancies of desperate actions (especially suicide)
82. **petty artery:** small conduit for blood and vital spirits
83. **Nemean lion's nerve:** strong tendon of the mythical beast slain by Hercules
85. **lets:** hinders
89. **Have after:** let's go after him
91. **it:** i.e., the issue (89)
 2. **Mark:** heed

HAMLET   Alas, poor ghost!
GHOST   Pity me not, but lend thy serious hearing   5
   To what I shall unfold.
HAMLET   Speak. I am bound to hear.
GHOST   So art thou to revenge, when thou shalt hear.
HAMLET   What?
GHOST   I am thy father's spirit,
   Doomed for a certain term to walk the night,   10
   And for the day confined to fast in fires,
   Till the foul crimes done in my days of nature
   Are burnt and purged away. But that I am forbid
   To tell the secrets of my prison house,
   I could a tale unfold whose lightest word   15
   Would harrow up thy soul, freeze thy young blood,
   Make thy two eyes like stars start from their spheres,
   Thy knotted and combinèd locks to part,
   And each particular hair to stand an end
   Like quills upon the fearful porpentine.   20
   But this eternal blazon must not be
   To ears of flesh and blood. List, list, oh, list!
   If thou didst ever thy dear father love—
HAMLET   O God!
GHOST   Revenge his foul and most unnatural murder.   25
HAMLET   Murder?
GHOST   Murder most foul, as in the best it is,
   But this most foul, strange, and unnatural.
HAMLET   Haste me to know't, that I with wings as swift
   As meditation or the thoughts of love   30
   May sweep to my revenge.
GHOST   I find thee apt;
   And duller shouldst thou be than the fat weed
   That roots itself in ease on Lethe wharf,
   Wouldst thou not stir in this. Now, Hamlet, hear:
   'Tis given out that, sleeping in my orchard,   35

11. **fast in fires:** do penance in purgatory. Roman Catholics believed that souls could be
    purified of sin in purgatory, a doctrine proscribed by Protestants.
12. **days of nature:** youth
13. **But that:** were it not that
16. **harrow up:** lacerate, tear
17. **spheres:** i.e., eye sockets (here compared to the enclosed crystalline channels
    wherein celestial bodies, according to Ptolemaic astronomy, moved in orbit)
18. **knotted . . . locks:** neatly arranged hair
19. **an:** on
20. **fearful porpentine:** (1) frightening porcupine (supposed to shoot its quills);
    (2) frightened porcupine
21. **eternal blazon:** list of eternal secrets
22. **List:** listen
32. **shouldst:** would; **fat:** lazy
33. **Lethe:** mythical river of forgetfulness in Hades; **wharf:** bank
35. **given out:** reported; **orchard:** garden

A serpent stung me; so the whole ear of Denmark
Is by a forgèd process of my death
Rankly abused. But know, thou noble youth,
The serpent that did sting thy father's life
Now wears his crown.   40
HAMLET   O my prophetic soul! My uncle!
GHOST   Ay, that incestuous, that adulterate beast,
   With witchcraft of his wit, with traitorous gifts—
   O wicked wit and gifts that have the power
   So to seduce—won to his shameful lust   45
   The will of my most seeming-virtuous queen.
   O Hamlet, what falling off was there
   From me, whose love was of that dignity
   That it went hand in hand even with the vow
   I made to her in marriage, and to decline   50
   Upon a wretch whose natural gifts were poor
   To those of mine.
   But virtue, as it never will be moved,
   Though lewdness court it in a shape of heaven,
   So lust, though to a radiant angel linked,   55
   Will sate itself in a celestial bed
   And prey on garbage.
   But soft. Methinks I scent the morning air;
   Brief let me be. Sleeping within my orchard,
   My custom always of the afternoon,   60
   Upon my secure hour thy uncle stole,
   With juice of cursèd hebona in a vial,
   And in the porches of my ears did pour
   The leperous distilment, whose effect
   Holds such an enmity with blood of man   65
   That swift as quicksilver it courses through
   The natural gates and alleys of the body,
   And with a sudden vigor it doth possess
   And curd, like eager droppings into milk,
   The thin and wholesome blood. So did it mine,   70

37. **forgèd process:** falsified narrative
42. **adulterate:** defiled by adultery
52. **To:** compared to
53. **moved:** induced to fall
54. **shape of heaven:** beautiful celestial form
56. **sate . . . bed:** satiate itself with the pleasure of a lawful marriage
61. **secure:** free from care, relaxed
62. **hebona:** (a) poison
63. **porches:** entranceways (to the body)
64. **leperous distilment:** distillation causing the disfigurement of leprosy (scales and sores)
69. **eager:** sour, acid

And a most instant tetter barked about,
Most lazar-like, with vile and loathsome crust,
All my smooth body.
Thus was I, sleeping, by a brother's hand,
Of life, of crown, of queen, at once dispatched,   75
Cut off even in the blossoms of my sin,
Unhouseled, disappointed, unaneled,
No reck'ning made, but sent to my account
With all my imperfections on my head.
O horrible, O horrible, most horrible!   80
If thou hast nature in thee, bear it not;
Let not the royal bed of Denmark be
A couch for luxury and damned incest.
But, howsoever thou pursues this act,
Taint not thy mind, nor let thy soul contrive   85
Against thy mother aught. Leave her to heaven,
And to those thorns that in her bosom lodge
To prick and sting her. Fare thee well at once.
The glow-worm shows the matin to be near,
And 'gins to pale his uneffectual fire.   90
Adieu, adieu, adieu. Remember me.   [*Exit.*]

HAMLET   O all you host of heaven! O earth! What else?
And shall I couple hell? Oh, fie! Hold, hold, my heart,
And you, my sinews, grow not instant old,
But bear me swiftly up. Remember thee?   95
Ay, thou poor ghost, whiles memory holds a seat
In this distracted globe. Remember thee?
Yea, from the table of my memory
I'll wipe away all trivial, fond records,

71. **tetter:** scab; **barked:** grew like tree bark
72. **lazar-like:** leper-like. **Lazar** derives from Lazarus, the leper in Luke 16:20.
77. **Unhouseled:** without having received the Eucharist (**housel**); **disappointed:** unprepared spiritually, here, without having received the sacrament of Penance and absolution; **unaneled:** unanointed, without having received the sacrament of the dying, Extreme Unction
78. **reck'ning:** settling of spiritual accounts (by confession of sins)
81. **nature:** natural filial affection
83. **luxury:** lechery
86. **aught:** anything
89. **glow-worm:** lightning bug; **matin:** morning (echoing "matins," prayers said at daybreak)
92. **host:** army
93. **couple:** (1) add (to the invocations); (2) join with
94. **sinews:** muscles; **instant:** suddenly. Hamlet asks to be speedily carried to his revenge, 94–95.
97. **globe:** (1) head; (2) world
98. **table:** writing tablet. Some believe Hamlet produces and writes in a tablet at 107ff.
99. **fond:** foolish

All saws of books, all forms, all pressures past   100
That youth and observation copied there,
And thy commandment all alone shall live
Within the book and volume of my brain,
Unmixed with baser matter. Yes, by heaven.
O most pernicious woman!   105
O villain, villain, smiling, damnèd villain!
My tables—meet it is I set it down
That one may smile and smile and be a villain.
At least, I am sure, it may be so in Denmark.
So, uncle, there you are. Now to my word.   110
It is "Adieu, adieu. Remember me."
I have sworn't.

      Enter HORATIO *and* MARCELLUS [*calling*].

HORATIO   My lord, my lord!
MARCELLUS   Lord Hamlet!
HORATIO   Heavens secure him.   115
HAMLET   [*Aside*] So be it.
MARCELLUS   Illo, ho, ho, my lord!
HAMLET   Hillo, ho, ho, boy! Come and come.
MARCELLUS   How is't, my noble lord?
HORATIO   What news, my lord?   120
HAMLET   Oh, wonderful!
HORATIO   Good my lord, tell it.
HAMLET   No, you will reveal it.
HORATIO   Not I, my lord, by heaven.
MARCELLUS   Nor I, my lord.   125
HAMLET   How say you, then? Would heart of man once think it?
  But you'll be secret?
HOR. ⎫
MAR. ⎭   Ay, by heaven.
HAMLET   There's never a villain dwelling in all Denmark
  But he's an arrant knave.   130
HORATIO   There needs no ghost, my lord, come from the grave
  To tell us this.
HAMLET   Why, right, you are in the right.
  And so without more circumstance at all,
  I hold it fit that we shake hands and part,
  You, as your business and desire shall point you—   135

100. **saws:** wise sayings; **forms . . . pressures:** shapes or images on the tablet
107. **meet:** fitting
115. **secure:** protect
117. **Illo, ho, ho:** a falconer's cry to a bird. Hamlet mimics the summons in response.
126. **once:** ever
130. **arrant knave:** thorough good-for-nothing
133. **circumstance:** ado

For every man hath business and desire,
Such as it is—and for my own poor part,
I will go pray.

HORATIO   These are but wild and whirling words, my lord.

HAMLET   I am sorry they offend you, heartily;   140
Yes, faith, heartily.

HORATIO   There's no offense, my lord.

HAMLET   Yes, by Saint Patrick, but there is, Horatio,
And much offense too. Touching this vision here,
It is an honest ghost, that let me tell you.
For your desire to know what is between us,   145
O'ermaster't as you may. And now, good friends,
As you are friends, scholars, and soldiers,
Give me one poor request.

HORATIO   What is't, my lord? We will.

HAMLET   Never make known what you have seen tonight.

HOR. ⎤
        ⎬ My lord, we will not.   150
MAR. ⎦

HAMLET   Nay, but swear't.

HORATIO   In faith, my lord, not I.

MARCELLUS   Nor I, my lord, in faith.

HAMLET [Holding out his sword]   Upon my sword.

MARCELLUS   We have sworn, my lord, already.   155

HAMLET   Indeed, upon my sword, indeed.

GHOST (Cries under the stage)   Swear.

HAMLET   Ha, ha, boy, sayst thou so? Art thou there, truepenny?—
Come on, you hear this fellow in the cellarage;
Consent to swear.

HORATIO   Propose the oath, my lord.   160

HAMLET   Never to speak of this that you have seen,
Swear by my sword.

GHOST [Beneath]   Swear.

HAMLET   Hic et ubique? Then we'll shift our ground.

                        [He moves to another place.]

Come hither, gentlemen,   165
And lay your hands again upon my sword.
Swear by my sword
Never to speak of this that you have heard.

---

142. **Saint Patrick:** associated with Purgatory because of Saint Patrick's Purgatory, a
cave in Donegal that was a popular place of penance and pilgrimage
143. **offense:** i.e., Claudius's crimes
144. **honest:** real
152. **In faith . . . I:** by my faith, I swear I shall not reveal what the ghost said
154. **sword:** i.e., the cross made by the intersection of the hilt and blade
158. **truepenny:** honest fellow
159. **cellarage:** cellars
164. *Hic et ubique:* Latin: here and everywhere

GHOST   [*Beneath*] Swear by his sword.

HAMLET   Well said, old mole! Canst work i' th' earth so fast?   170
    A worthy pioner.—Once more remove, good friends.

               [*He moves again.*]

HORATIO   O day and night, but this is wondrous strange!

HAMLET   And therefore as a stranger give it welcome.
    There are more things in heaven and earth, Horatio,
    Than are dreamt of in your philosophy. But come.   175
    Here, as before, never, so help you mercy,
    How strange or odd soe'er I bear myself—
    As I, perchance, hereafter shall think meet
    To put an antic disposition on—
    That you, at such times seeing me, never shall,   180
    With arms encumbered thus, or this headshake,
    Or by pronouncing of some doubtful phrase
    As "Well, well, we know," or "We could an if we would,"
    Or "If we list to speak," or "There be, an if they might,"
    Or such ambiguous giving out, to note   185
    That you know aught of me—this do swear,
    So grace and mercy at your most need help you.

GHOST [*Beneath*]   Swear. [*They swear.*]

HAMLET   Rest, rest, perturbèd spirit.—So, gentlemen,
    With all my love I do commend me to you,   190
    And what so poor a man as Hamlet is
    May do t'express his love and friending to you,
    God willing, shall not lack. Let us go in together;
    And still your fingers on your lips, I pray.
    The time is out of joint. O cursèd spite,   195
    That ever I was born to set it right!
    Nay, come, let's go together.

                            Exeunt.

  171. **pioner:** soldier, especially one who digs
  173. **as . . . welcome:** (Hamlet here invokes the tradition of hospitality to strangers.)
  175. **philosophy:** traditional philosophical inquiry and natural science
  176. **so . . . mercy:** as you hope to receive God's mercy
  177. **soe'er:** so ever
  179. **antic:** grotesque, fantastic
  181. **encumbered:** folded
  182. **doubtful:** ambiguous
  183. **an if:** if
  184. **list:** wished
  186. **aught:** anything
188. s.d. ***They swear:*** (Hamlet's following injunction to rest appears to confirm this
      swearing. Many envision a triple oath, the first two instances occurring at 163
      and 169.)
  192. **friending:** friendship
  194. **still:** ever
  195. **out of joint:** dislocated (said of bones)

2.1 [POLONIUS'S CHAMBERS]

Enter old POLONIUS *with his man* [REYNALDO].

POLONIUS   Give him this money and these notes, Reynaldo.
   [*He gives money and papers.*]
REYNALDO   I will, my lord.
POLONIUS   You shall do marvelous wisely, good Reynaldo,
   Before you visit him, to make inquire
   Of his behavior.
REYNALDO   My lord, I did intend it.   5
POLONIUS   Marry, well said, very well said. Look you, sir,
   Inquire me first what Danskers are in Paris,
   And how, and who, what means, and where they keep,
   What company, at what expense; and finding
   By this encompassment and drift of question   10
   That they do know my son, come you more nearer
   Than your particular demands will touch it.
   Take you, as 'twere, some distant knowledge of him,
   As thus, "I know his father and his friends,
   And in part him"—do you mark this, Reynaldo?   15
REYNALDO   Ay, very well, my lord.
POLONIUS   "And in part him, but," you may say, "not well.
   But if't be he I mean, he's very wild,
   Addicted so and so," and there put on him
   What forgeries you please—marry, none so rank   20
   As may dishonor him, take heed of that—
   But, sir, such wanton, wild, and usual slips
   As are companions noted and most known
   To youth and liberty.
REYNALDO   As gaming, my lord.
POLONIUS   Ay, or drinking, fencing, swearing,   25
   Quarreling, drabbing—you may go so far.
REYNALDO   My lord, that would dishonor him.
POLONIUS   Faith, no, as you may season it in the charge.

---

    4. **inquire:** inquiry
    6. **Look you:** take care you do this
    7. **Danskers:** Danes
    8. **means:** wealth (they have); **keep:** lodge
  10. **encompassment . . . question:** roundabout talking
11–12. **come . . . it:** you will come closer to the truth in this way than by asking specific
       questions (**particular demands**)
  13. **Take you:** assume
  19. **put on:** tell of
  20. **rank:** offensive
  23. **companions:** accompaniments
  24. **gaming:** gambling
  26. **drabbing:** visiting prostitutes
  28. **season . . . charge:** temper the accusation in your choice of phrasing

You must not put another scandal on him,
That he is open to incontinency;   30
That's not my meaning. But breathe his faults so quaintly
That they may seem the taints of liberty,
The flash and outbreak of a fiery mind,
A savageness in unreclaimèd blood,
Of general assault.   35
REYNALDO   But, my good lord—
POLONIUS   Wherefore should you do this?
REYNALDO   Ay, my lord, I would know that.
POLONIUS   Marry, sir, here's my drift,
    And I believe it is a fetch of wit:
    You laying these slight sullies on my son   40
    As 'twere a thing a little soiled wi' the working,
    Mark you, your party in converse, him you would sound,
    Having ever seen in the prenominate crimes
    The youth you breathe of guilty, be assured
    He closes with you in this consequence: 45
    "Good sir," or so, or "friend," or "gentleman,"
    According to the phrase or the addition
    Of man and country—
REYNALDO   Very good, my lord.
POLONIUS   And then, sir, does 'a this—'a does—What was I
    about to say?
    By the mass, I was about to say something. Where did I leave?   50
REYNALDO   At "closes in the consequence."
POLONIUS   At "closes in the consequence"—ay, marry.
    He closes thus: "I know the gentleman;
    I saw him yesterday," or "th'other day"
    —Or then or then with such or such—and, "as you say,   55
    There was 'a gaming," "there o'ertook in's rouse,"
    "There falling out at tennis," or perchance,
    "I saw him enter such a house of sale,"

29. **another:** a different kind of
30. **incontinency:** vicious sexual excess (not merely youthful indiscretion)
31. **quaintly:** artfully
32. **taints of liberty:** faults resulting from freedom
34–35. **savageness . . . assault:** a wildness in youthful blood that assails all
39. **fetch of wit:** clever trick
40. **sullies:** stains
41. **soiled . . . working:** dirtied, like cloth or needlepoint, by handling as it is being made
42. **converse:** conversation; **sound:** ask
43. **Having ever:** if he has ever; **prenominate:** aforenamed
44. **breathe of:** inquire about
45. **closes . . . consequence:** agrees with you as follows
47. **addition:** title
56. **o'ertook in's rouse:** drunk from his carousal
57. **falling out:** quarreling

Videlicet, a brothel, or so forth. See you now
Your bait of falsehood takes this carp of truth,   60
And thus do we of wisdom and of reach,
With windlasses, and with assays of bias,
By indirections find directions out.
So, by my former lecture and advice
Shall you my son. You have me, have you not?   65

REYNALDO My lord, I have.

POLONIUS   God be wi'ye; fare ye well.

REYNALDO Good my lord.

POLONIUS Observe his inclination in yourself.

REYNALDO I shall, my lord.

POLONIUS And let him ply his music.   70

REYNALDO Well, my lord.

POLONIUS Farewell.

                                        Exit REYNALDO.

        Enter OPHELIA.

                            How now, Ophelia, what's the matter?

OPHELIA Oh, my lord, my lord, I have been so affrighted!

POLONIUS With what, i'the name of God?

OPHELIA My lord, as I was sewing in my closet,   75
    Lord Hamlet, with his doublet all unbraced,
    No hat upon his head, his stockings fouled,
    Ungartered, and down-gyvèd to his ankle,
    Pale as his shirt, his knees knocking each other,
    And with a look so piteous in purport   80
    As if he had been loosèd out of hell
    To speak of horrors—he comes before me.

POLONIUS Mad for thy love?

OPHELIA   My lord, I do not know,
    But truly I do fear it.

POLONIUS   What said he?

OPHELIA He took me by the wrist and held me hard,   85
    Then goes he to the length of all his arm,

59. **Videlicet:** namely
60. **carp:** fish (a freshwater species found in ponds)
61. **of . . . reach:** who are wise and capable
62. **windlasses:** circuitous routes (used to surprise game in hunting);
    assays of bias: indirect attempts (like the curved paths of weighted bowling balls)
65. **have:** understand
67. **Good my lord:** my good lord (a polite salutation, here used for leave-taking)
68. **Observe . . . yourself:** adapt yourself to his likes and dislikes
70. **ply his music:** play his tunes (metaphorically)
75. **closet:** private room, often used for study or devotion
76. **doublet:** close-fitting jacket; **unbraced:** unfastened
78. **down-gyvèd . . . ankle:** fallen to his feet like chains (gyves)
80. **purport:** expression
86. **goes . . . arm:** he stands at arm's length away

And with his other hand thus o'er his brow,
He falls to such perusal of my face
As 'a would draw it. Long stayed he so.
At last, a little shaking of mine arm,   90
And thrice his head thus waving up and down,
He raised a sigh so piteous and profound
As it did seem to shatter all his bulk
And end his being. That done, he lets me go,
And, with his head over his shoulder turned,   95
He seemed to find his way without his eyes,
For out o' doors he went without their helps,
And to the last bended their light on me.
POLONIUS   Come, go with me: I will go seek the King.
This is the very ecstasy of love,   100
Whose violent property fordoes itself
And leads the will to desperate undertakings,
As oft as any passion under heaven
That does afflict our natures. I am sorry.
What, have you given him any hard words of late?   105
OPHELIA   No, my good lord, but, as you did command,
I did repel his letters and denied
His access to me.
POLONIUS   That hath made him mad.
I am sorry that with better heed and judgment
I had not quoted him: I feared he did but trifle,   110
And meant to wrack thee. But beshrew my jealousy!
By heaven, it is as proper to our age
To cast beyond ourselves in our opinions
As it is common for the younger sort
To lack discretion. Come, go we to the King.   115
This must be known, which, being kept close, might move
More grief to hide than hate to utter love.
Come.

                                        Exeunt.

88. **perusal:** scrutiny
98. **bended their light:** i.e., looked
100. **ecstasy:** altered state caused by excessive emotion
101. **violent property:** characteristic violence; **fordoes:** destroys
110. **quoted:** observed
111. **wrack:** ruin; **beshrew my jealousy:** curse my suspicions
113. **cast:** (1) reach (a metaphor from casting or "throwing" a net); (2) design, plan
116. **close:** secret; **move:** cause
117. **More . . . love:** more grief by concealment than offense by revelation (of Hamlet's love and strange behavior)

2.2 [THE CASTLE]

Flourish. Enter KING *and* QUEEN, ROSENCRANTZ *and*
GUILDENSTERN [*and* ATTENDANTS].

KING Welcome, dear Rosencrantz and Guildenstern.
Moreover that we much did long to see you,
The need we have to use you did provoke
Our hasty sending. Something have you heard
Of Hamlet's transformation—so call it,   5
Sith nor th'exterior nor the inward man
Resembles that it was. What it should be,
More than his father's death, that thus hath put him
So much from th'understanding of himself,
I cannot dream of. I entreat you both   10
That, being of so young days brought up with him,
And sith so neighbored to his youth and havior,
That you vouchsafe your rest here in our court
Some little time, so by your companies
To draw him on to pleasures, and to gather,   15
So much as from occasion you may glean,
Whether aught to us unknown afflicts him thus
That, opened, lies within our remedy.
QUEEN Good gentlemen, he hath much talked of you,
And sure I am two men there is not living   20
To whom he more adheres. If it will please you
To show us so much gentry and good will
As to expend your time with us awhile,
For the supply and profit of our hope,
Your visitation shall receive such thanks   25
As fits a king's remembrance.
ROSENCRANTZ   Both Your Majesties
Might, by the sovereign power you have of us,
Put your dread pleasures more into command
Than to entreaty.
GUILDENSTERN   But we both obey,

2. **Moreover:** besides
4. **sending:** summoning
6. **Sith:** since
7. **that:** that which
11. **of . . . days:** from your youth
12. **neighbored:** acquainted (as equals); **havior:** behavior
13. **vouchsafe your rest:** agree to stay
17. **aught:** anything
18. **opened:** revealed
22. **gentry:** good breeding
24. **supply and profit:** aid and advancement
27. **of:** over
28. **dread:** awesome

And here give up ourselves in the full bent   30
    To lay our service freely at your feet,
    To be commanded.
KING   Thanks, Rosencrantz and gentle Guildenstern.
QUEEN   Thanks, Guildenstern and gentle Rosencrantz.
    And I beseech you instantly to visit   35
    My too much changèd son.—Go, some of you,
    And bring these gentlemen where Hamlet is.
GUILDENSTERN   Heavens make our presence and our practices
    Pleasant and helpful to him.
QUEEN   Ay, amen.
                    Exeunt ROSENCRANTZ, GUILDENSTERN
                            [*and some* ATTENDANTS].

        Enter POLONIUS.

POLONIUS   Th'ambassadors from Norway, my good lord,   40
    Are joyfully returned.
KING   Thou still hast been the father of good news.
POLONIUS   Have I, my lord? I assure my good liege
    I hold my duty as I hold my soul,
    Both to my God and to my gracious king;   45
    And I do think—or else this brain of mine
    Hunts not the trail of policy so sure
    As it hath used to do—that I have found
    The very cause of Hamlet's lunacy.
KING   Oh, speak of that; that do I long to hear.   50
POLONIUS   Give first admittance to th'ambassadors;
    My news shall be the fruit to that great feast.
KING   Thyself do grace to them and bring them in.
                                    [*Exit* POLONIUS.]
    He tells me, my dear Gertrude, he hath found
    The head and source of all your son's distemper.   55
QUEEN   I doubt it is no other but the main,
    His father's death and our o'erhasty marriage.
KING   Well, we shall sift him.

        Enter AMBASSADORS [VOLTEMAND *and* CORNELIUS, *with*
        POLONIUS].

                        —Welcome, my good friends.
    Say, Voltemand, what from our brother Norway?

30. **in . . . bent:** i.e., totally (a metaphor from bending a bow to its limit)
38. **practices:** actions (with the suggestion of plots or deceits)
42. **still:** ever
47. **policy:** (1) prudent conduct; (2) statecraft
52. **fruit:** dessert
53. **grace:** courtesy (with a play on the "grace," or prayer, before a meal)
56. **doubt:** suspect; **main:** chief issue
58. **sift:** examine closely (a metaphor from working materials through a sieve)
59. **brother:** i.e., fellow ruler

VOLTEMAND   Most fair return of greetings and desires.   60
     Upon our first, he sent out to suppress
     His nephew's levies, which to him appeared
     To be a preparation 'gainst the Polack,
     But, better looked into, he truly found
     It was against Your Highness; whereat grieved   65
     That so his sickness, age, and impotence
     Was falsely borne in hand, sends out arrests
     On Fortinbras; which he, in brief, obeys,
     Receives rebuke from Norway, and, in fine,
     Makes vow before his uncle never more   70
     To give th'assay of arms against Your Majesty.
     Whereon old Norway, overcome with joy,
     Gives him three-score thousand crowns in annual fee,
     And his commission to employ those soldiers,
     So levied as before, against the Polack,   75
     With an entreaty, herein further shown, [*He gives a paper.*]
     That it might please you to give quiet pass
     Through your dominions for this enterprise,
     On such regards of safety and allowance
     As therein are set down.
KING   It likes us well,   80
     And at our more considered time we'll read,
     Answer, and think upon this business.
     Meantime we thank you for your well-took labor.
     Go to your rest; at night we'll feast together.
     Most welcome home!
                              Exeunt AMBASSADORS.
POLONIUS   This business is well ended.   85
     My liege, and madam, to expostulate
     What majesty should be, what duty is,
     Why day is day, night, night, and time is time,
     Were nothing but to waste night, day, and time.
     Therefore, since brevity is the soul of wit,   90
     And tediousness the limbs and outward flourishes,
     I will be brief. Your noble son is mad,

61. **first:** first encounter
62. **levies:** troops
67. **borne in hand:** deluded; **arrests:** orders to desist
69. **fine:** conclusion
71. **assay:** attempt, trial
73. **three-score:** sixty; **crowns:** coins of gold or silver
79. **regards:** conditions
80. **likes:** pleases
81. **more considered time:** time more suitable for consideration
86. **expostulate:** discourse on
90. **wit:** intelligence

"Mad" call I it, for to define true madness,
What is't but to be nothing else but mad?
But let that go.
QUEEN   More matter with less art.   95
POLONIUS   Madam, I swear I use no art at all.
   That he's mad, 'tis true; 'tis true, 'tis pity,
   And pity 'tis, 'tis true—a foolish figure,
   But farewell it, for I will use no art.
   Mad let us grant him then, and now remains   100
   That we find out the cause of this effect,
   Or rather say, the cause of this defect,
   For this effect defective comes by cause.
   Thus it remains, and the remainder thus.
   Perpend.   105
   I have a daughter—have while she is mine—
   Who, in her duty and obedience, mark,
   Hath given me this. Now gather and surmise.

          [*He reads a letter.*]

   "To the celestial, and my soul's idol, the most beautified
   Ophelia"— that's an ill phrase, a vile phrase, "beautified" is   110
   a vile phrase; but you shall hear. Thus: [*He reads.*]
   "In her excellent white bosom, these," etc.
QUEEN   Came this from Hamlet to her?
POLONIUS   Good madam, stay awhile; I will be faithful.

          [*He reads the*] letter.

          "Doubt thou the stars are fire,   115
               Doubt that the sun doth move,
          Doubt truth to be a liar,
               But never doubt I love.

   Oh, dear Ophelia, I am ill at these numbers. I have not art to
   reckon my groans. But that I love thee best, oh, most best,   120
   believe it. Adieu.

----

   98. **figure:** figure of speech
  103. **For . . . cause:** there is a reason for this madness
  105. **Perpend:** consider carefully
  108. **gather and surmise:** draw your conclusion
  112. **In . . . etc.:** (This line appears to represent part of a flowery salutation, the ending
        of which Polonius skips over with "etc." Three letters by Hamlet are read aloud dur-
        ing the play, the others at 4.6.12–28 and 4.7.43–46.)
  114. **be faithful:** read the letter accurately
  115. **Doubt:** suspect
  119. **ill . . . numbers:** (1) unskilled in writing verse; (2) sick while I write this verse.
  120. **reckon:** (1) count; (2) express in verse; **oh, most best:** (The phrase probably ampli-
        fies the preceding adverbial "best," but it could apostrophize Ophelia.)

Thine evermore, most dear lady, whilst this machine is to
him, Hamlet."
This in obedience hath my daughter shown me,
And, more above, hath his solicitings,   125
As they fell out by time, by means, and place,
All given to mine ear.

KING   But how hath she
Received his love?

POLONIUS   What do you think of me?

KING   As of a man faithful and honorable.

POLONIUS   I would fain prove so. But what might you think,   130
When I had seen this hot love on the wing—
As I perceived it, I must tell you that,
Before my daughter told me—what might you,
Or my dear Majesty your queen here, think,
If I had played the desk or table book,   135
Or given my heart a winking, mute and dumb,
Or looked upon this love with idle sight?
What might you think? No, I went round to work,
And my young mistress thus I did bespeak:
"Lord Hamlet is a prince out of thy star.   140
This must not be." And then I prescripts gave her
That she should lock herself from his resort,
Admit no messengers, receive no tokens.
Which done, she took the fruits of my advice;
And he, repellèd—a short tale to make—   145
Fell into a sadness, then into a fast,
Thence to a watch, thence into a weakness,
Thence to lightness, and by this declension
Into the madness wherein now he raves,
And all we mourn for.

KING   Do you think this?   150

QUEEN   It may be very like.

---

122. **machine:** i.e., body
125. **more above:** moreover
126. **fell out:** occurred
130. **fain:** gladly
135. **played . . . book:** i.e., been silent
136. **given . . . winking:** i.e., made my heart close its eyes to their love
138. **round:** openly
139. **bespeak:** address
140. **out . . . star:** above your sphere and position
141. **prescripts:** commands
142. **resort:** visitation
147. **watch:** insomnia
148. **lightness:** lightheadedness; **declension:** decline
151. **like:** likely

POLONIUS   Hath there been such a time—I would fain know
    that—
  That I have positively said " 'Tis so,"
  When it proved otherwise?
KING   Not that I know.
POLONIUS   Take this from this, if this be otherwise.   155
  If circumstances lead me, I will find
  Where truth is hid, though it were hid indeed
  Within the center.
KING   How may we try it further?
POLONIUS   You know sometimes he walks four hours together
  Here in the lobby.
QUEEN   So he does indeed.   160
POLONIUS   At such a time I'll loose my daughter to him.
  [*To the* KING] Be you and I behind an arras then.
  Mark the encounter. If he love her not,
  And be not from his reason fall'n thereon,
  Let me be no assistant for a state,   165
  But keep a farm and carters.
KING   We will try it.

      Enter HAMLET [*reading a book*].

QUEEN   But look where sadly the poor wretch comes reading.
POLONIUS   Away, I do beseech you, both away.
  I'll board him presently. Oh, give me leave.

        Exeunt KING *and* QUEEN [*with* ATTENDANTS].

  How does my good Lord Hamlet?   170
HAMLET   Well, God-a-mercy.
POLONIUS   Do you know me, my lord?
HAMLET   Excellent well. You are a fishmonger.
POLONIUS   Not I, my lord.
HAMLET   Then I would you were so honest a man.   175
POLONIUS   Honest, my lord?
HAMLET   Ay, sir. To be honest, as this world goes, is to be one
  man picked out of ten thousand.
POLONIUS   That's very true, my lord.

---

155. **this from this:** (Polonius probably gestures to his head and shoulders, or to his
    chain of office and neck.)
158. **center:** center of the earth; **try:** test
162. **arras:** curtain, tapestry
164. **thereon:** for that
166. **carters:** cart-drivers
169. **board:** approach; **give me leave:** farewell (as Polonius hurries the others out of
    sight). In Quarto 1, Hamlet speaks a version of the "To be or not to be" soliloquy
    here; see Appendix 1, passage 1, p. 140.
171. **God-a-mercy:** i.e., thank you
173. **fishmonger:** fish-dealer

HAMLET   For if the sun breed maggots in a dead dog, being a   180
   good kissing carrion—Have you a daughter?

POLONIUS   I have, my lord.

HAMLET   Let her not walk i'the sun. Conception is a blessing,
   but as your daughter may conceive, friend, look to't.

POLONIUS [Aside]   How say you by that? Still harping on my   185
   daughter. Yet he knew me not at first; 'a said I was a fishmonger. 'A is far gone. And truly in my youth I suffered much
   extremity for love, very near this. I'll speak to him again.—
   What do you read, my lord?

HAMLET   Words, words, words.   190

POLONIUS   What is the matter, my lord?

HAMLET   Between who?

POLONIUS   I mean the matter that you read, my lord.

HAMLET   Slanders, sir; for the satirical rogue says here that
   old men have gray beards, that their faces are wrinkled,   195
   their eyes purging thick amber and plum-tree gum, and that
   they have a plentiful lack of wit, together with most weak
   hams. All which, sir, though I most powerfully and potently
   believe, yet I hold it not honesty to have it thus set down; for
   yourself, sir, shall grow old as I am, if, like a crab, you could   200
   go backward.

POLONIUS [Aside]   Though this be madness, yet there is method
   in't.—Will you walk out of the air, my lord?

HAMLET   Into my grave.

POLONIUS   Indeed, that's out of the air. [Aside] How pregnant   205
   sometimes his replies are—a happiness that often madness
   hits on, which reason and sanity could not so prosperously
   be delivered of. I will leave him and my daughter.—My lord,
   I will take my leave of you.

HAMLET   You cannot take from me anything that I will not   210

181.   **good kissing carrion:** flesh (the "dead dog") good for the sun to kiss. The conceit
       turns on the idea that the sun creates life in carcasses. The phrase is sometimes
       emended to refer to the sun, "god kissing carrion."
183.   **i'the sun:** i.e., exposed to the sun that may make her pregnant (with perhaps a figu-
       rative warning about court life; cf. Hamlet's opening complaint about being "too
       much in the sun," 1.2.67)
185.   **How . . . by:** what do you think of (addressed to himself or the audience)
186.   **'a:** he
188.   **extremity:** extreme stress
196.   **purging:** discharging
197.   **wit:** understanding
198.   **hams:** thighs and buttocks
199.   **honesty:** courtesy
200.   **old:** as old
203.   **out . . . air:** (Open air was thought to be unhealthy for the sick. The unlocalized
       stage supports a shift in location to a courtyard or outdoor space here, though the
       rest of the scene seems to be inside.)
205.   **pregnant:** full of meaning
210.   **cannot . . . will not:** (Double negatives are commonly used for emphasis; Hamlet
       says he would be most willing to part with Polonius.)

more willingly part withal—except my life, except my life,
except my life.

POLONIUS   Fare you well, my lord.

HAMLET   These tedious old fools.

Enter GUILDENSTERN *and* ROSENCRANTZ.

POLONIUS   You go to seek the Lord Hamlet. There he is.   215

ROSENCRANTZ [*To* POLONIUS]   God save you, sir.

[*Exit* POLONIUS.]

GUILDENSTERN   My honored lord.

ROSENCRANTZ   My most dear lord.

HAMLET   My excellent good friends! How dost thou, Guildenstern? Ah, Rosencrantz. Good lads, how do you both?   220

ROSENCRANTZ   As the indifferent children of the earth.

GUILDENSTERN   Happy in that we are not overhappy. On Fortune's cap we are not the very button.

HAMLET   Nor the soles of her shoe?

ROSENCRANTZ   Neither, my lord.   225

HAMLET   Then you live about her waist, or in the middle of
her favors?

GUILDENSTERN   Faith, her privates we.

HAMLET   In the secret parts of Fortune? Oh, most true, she is
a strumpet. What news?   230

ROSENCRANTZ   None, my lord, but the world's grown honest.

HAMLET   Then is doomsday near. But your news is not true.
But in the beaten way of friendship, what make you at
Elsinore?

ROSENCRANTZ   To visit you, my lord; no other occasion.   235

HAMLET   Beggar that I am, I am ever poor in thanks; but I
thank you, and sure, dear friends, my thanks are too dear a
halfpenny. Were you not sent for? Is it your own inclining?
Is it a free visitation? Come, come, deal justly with me; come,
come. Nay, speak.   240

GUILDENSTERN   What should we say, my lord?

HAMLET   Anything but to the purpose. You were sent for, and
there is a kind of confession in your looks, which your

211. **withal:** with
221. **indifferent . . . earth:** ordinary run of mortals
227. **favors:** i.e., sexual favors
228. **privates:** ordinary citizens (with a pun on "private parts" or genitals)
230. **strumpet:** prostitute (a traditional image of Fortune because of her proverbial inconstancy)
232. **doomsday:** day of the Last Judgment. The Folio adds a passage after the next sentence on Denmark as a prison; See Appendix 2, passage 1, p. 146.
233. **beaten way:** well-worn path; **make:** do
237. **too dear:** not worth
242. **Anything . . . purpose:** anything except a straight answer (said sarcastically)

modesties have not craft enough to color. I know the good
King and Queen have sent for you.　　　　　　　　　245

ROSENCRANTZ　To what end, my lord?

HAMLET　That you must teach me. But let me conjure you, by
the rights of our fellowship, by the consonancy of our youth,
by the obligation of our ever-preserved love, and by what
more dear a better proposer can charge you withal, be even　250
and direct with me whether you were sent for or no.

ROSENCRANTZ [*To* GUILDENSTERN]　What say you?

HAMLET　Nay, then, I have an eye of you. If you love me, hold
not off.

GUILDENSTERN　My lord, we were sent for.　　　　　255

HAMLET　I will tell you why. So shall my anticipation prevent
your discovery, and your secrecy to the King and Queen molt
no feather. I have of late, but wherefore I know not, lost all
my mirth, forgone all custom of exercises, and indeed it goes
so heavily with my disposition that this goodly frame, the　260
earth, seems to me a sterile promontory, this most excellent
canopy, the air, look you, this brave o'erhanging firmament,
this majestical roof fretted with golden fire, why, it appeareth
nothing to me but a foul and pestilent congregation of vapors.
What a piece of work is a man! How noble in reason, how　265
infinite in faculties, in form and moving how express and
admirable, in action how like an angel, in apprehension how
like a god! The beauty of the world, the paragon of animals!
And yet to me, what is this quintessence of dust? Man
delights not me; nor women neither, though by your smiling　270
you seem to say so.

ROSENCRANTZ　My lord, there was no such stuff in my thoughts.

HAMLET　Why did ye laugh then, when I said "man delights
not me"?

ROSENCRANTZ　To think, my lord, if you delight not in man,　275

---

244. **color:** disguise
247. **conjure:** charge by oath
248. **consonancy . . . youth:** our childhood friendship
250. **proposer:** speaker; **even:** honest
253. **of:** on
256–57. **prevent your discovery:** come before your revelation
257–58. **molt no feather:** i.e. sustain no loss
261. **promontory:** land jutting out into the water
262. **brave:** splendid; **firmament:** sky
263. **fretted:** adorned (especially a ceiling)
265. **piece:** masterpiece
266. **faculties:** capacities; **express:** well-framed
267. **apprehension:** understanding
269. **quintessence:** perfect essence, the "fifth essence," beyond the four elements of
earth, air, fire, and water. The word is used here to deflate the preceding
description and to describe man as essentially dust. See Genesis 3:19: "Thou art
dust, and to dust thou shalt return," a phrase echoed in the Church of England
burial service.

what Lenten entertainment the players shall receive from
you. We coted them on the way, and hither are they coming
to offer you service.

HAMLET   He that plays the king shall be welcome. His Majesty shall have tribute of me, the adventurous knight shall   280
use his foil and target, the lover shall not sigh gratis, the
humorous man shall end his part in peace, and the lady
shall say her mind freely—or the blank verse shall halt for't.
What players are they?

ROSENCRANTZ   Even those you were wont to take such delight   285
in, the tragedians of the city.

HAMLET   How chances it they travel? Their residence, both
in reputation and profit, was better both ways.

ROSENCRANTZ   I think their inhibition comes by the means of
the late innovation.   290

HAMLET   Do they hold the same estimation they did when I
was in the city? Are they so followed?

ROSENCRANTZ   No, indeed, are they not.

HAMLET   It is not very strange; for my uncle is King of Denmark, and those that would make mouths at him while my   295
father lived give twenty, forty, fifty, a hundred ducats apiece
for his picture in little. 'Sblood, there is something in this
more than natural, if philosophy could find it out.

         A flourish.

GUILDENSTERN   There are the players.

HAMLET   Gentlemen, you are welcome to Elsinore. Your hands,   300
come then. Th'appurtenance of welcome is fashion and ceremony. Let me comply with you in this garb, lest my extent
to the players, which I tell you must show fairly outwards,

---

    276. **Lenten:** i.e., meager
    277. **coted:** overtook
    281. **foil and target:** sword and shield; **gratis:** for nothing
    282. **humorous man:** eccentric character
    283. **halt:** limp
    285. **wont:** accustomed
    287. **residence:** remaining at home
    289. **inhibition:** formal prohibition (perhaps against playing in the city)
    290. **late:** recent; **innovation:** (Rosencrantz could refer to the recent political changes
         in Denmark or to the contemporary London theater scene, as the Folio's
         extended passage on the rise of children's companies suggests; see Appendix 2,
         passage 2, p. 147.)
    291. **estimation:** reputation
    295. **mouths:** faces
    296. **ducats:** gold coins; **picture in little:** miniature portrait
    297. **'Sblood:** by God's blood (an oath)
    298. **more than natural:** unnatural; **philosophy:** science
    301. **appurtenance:** proper accompaniment
301–02. **fashion and ceremony:** adornment and courtesy
    302. **comply:** fulfill those duties; **garb:** manner; **my extent:** that which I extend, i.e., my
         welcome
    303. **fairly outwards:** obviously

should more appear like entertainment than yours. You are
welcome. But my uncle-father and aunt-mother are deceived.   305
GUILDENSTERN   In what, my dear lord?
HAMLET   I am but mad north-north-west; when the wind is
southerly I know a hawk from a handsaw.

    Enter POLONIUS.

POLONIUS   Well be with you, gentlemen.
HAMLET   Hark you, Guildenstern, and you too, at each ear a   310
hearer: that great baby you see there is not yet out of his
swaddling clouts.
ROSENCRANTZ   Haply he is the second time come to them, for
they say an old man is twice a child.
HAMLET   I will prophesy he comes to tell me of the players;   315
mark it. [*Loudly*] You say right, sir; o' Monday morning,
'twas then indeed.
POLONIUS   My lord, I have news to tell you.
HAMLET   My lord, I have news to tell you. When Roscius was
an actor in Rome—   320
POLONIUS   The actors are come hither, my lord.
HAMLET   Buzz, buzz.
POLONIUS   Upon my honor—
HAMLET   Then came each actor on his ass.
POLONIUS   The best actors in the world, either for tragedy, com-   325
edy, history, pastoral, pastoral-comical, historical-pastoral,
scene individable, or poem unlimited. Seneca cannot be too
heavy nor Plautus too light. For the law of writ and the lib-
erty, these are the only men.

---

304. **entertainment than yours:** a proper welcome than the welcome I give to you
307. **north-north-west:** i.e., only sometimes (when the wind blows from the north-northwest)
307–308. **when . . . southerly:** i.e., at other times (when the wind blows from the south)
308. **a hawk . . . handsaw:** i.e., one thing from another (with perhaps a play on "hernshaw" or heron)
309. **Well . . . you:** I wish you well
310. **Hark you:** listen. Hamlet and the others ignore Polonius and speak about him for a few lines.
312. **swaddling clouts:** cloths used for wrapping infants
313. **Haply:** by chance
314. **twice:** a second time. The sentiment is proverbial.
316–317. **You . . . indeed:** (Hamlet pretends to be in conversation.)
319. **Roscius:** famous Roman actor (first century BCE)
322. **Buzz, buzz:** (a rude interjection, suggesting that Polonius brings old news)
324. **Then . . . ass:** (another rude response to Polonius, perhaps mocking his "upon my honor" with a line from a ballad or play)
326. **historical-pastoral:** (In the Folio, Polonius adds a few more genres—"tragical-historical, tragical-comical-historical-pastoral.")
327. **scene . . . unlimited:** i.e., plays that observe the classical unities of time, place, and action as well as those that do not
327. **Seneca:** first-century writer of Latin tragedy
328. **Plautus:** (second–third centuries BCE) writer of Latin comedy
328–29. **law . . . liberty:** i.e., plays written in accordance with classical rules and those written free from regulation

HAMLET   O Jephthah, judge of Israel, what a treasure hadst   330
thou!

POLONIUS   What a treasure had he, my lord?

HAMLET   Why,

> "One fair daughter, and no more,
> The which he lovèd passing well."   335

POLONIUS [*Aside*]   Still on my daughter.

HAMLET   Am I not i'the right, old Jephthah?

POLONIUS   If you call me Jephthah, my lord, I have a daughter that I love passing well.

HAMLET   Nay, that follows not.   340

POLONIUS   What follows, then, my lord?

HAMLET   Why,

> "As by lot, God wot"

and then, you know,

> "It came to pass, as most like it was"—   345

the first row of the pious chanson will show you more, for
look where my abridgment comes.

> *Enter the* PLAYERS.

You are welcome, masters, welcome all.—I am glad to see
thee well. Welcome, good friends.—Oh, old friend! Why, thy
face is valanced since I saw thee last. Com'st thou to beard   350
me in Denmark?—What, my young lady and mistress! By'r
lady, your ladyship is nearer to heaven than when I saw you
last by the altitude of a chopine. Pray God, your voice, like
a piece of uncurrent gold, be not cracked within the ring.—
Masters, you are all welcome. We'll e'en to't like French fal-   355
coners, fly at anything we see. We'll have a speech straight.
Come, give us a taste of your quality. Come, a passionate
speech.

FIRST PLAYER   What speech, my good lord?

---

330. **Jephthah:** father who had to sacrifice his daughter in Judges 11. Hamlet below
quotes lines from a ballad on Jephthah's story.

335. **passing:** surpassingly

343. **lot:** chance; **wot:** knows

346. **row:** line; **chanson:** song

347. **abridgment:** that which cuts my speech short

350. **valanced:** fringed (with a beard); **beard:** provoke

351. **lady:** i.e., the boy actor who played female roles; **By'r:** by our

353. **chopine:** high-soled shoe

354. **uncurrent:** out of circulation; **cracked . . . ring:** i.e., changed to an adult male's
voice, hence making you unfit for women's roles. A coin with a crack in the ring
around the sovereign's head was useless.

355. **e'en to't:** go at it

356. **straight:** immediately

HAMLET   I heard thee speak me a speech once, but it was never   360
acted, or if it was, not above once, for the play, I remember,
pleased not the million; 'twas caviar to the general. But it
was—as I received it, and others, whose judgments in such
matters cried in the top of mine—an excellent play, well
digested in the scenes, set down with as much modesty as   365
cunning. I remember one said there were no sallets in the
lines to make the matter savory, nor no matter in the phrase
that might indict the author of affection, but called it an
honest method, as wholesome as sweet, and by very much
more handsome than fine. One speech in't I chiefly loved: 370
'twas Aeneas's talk to Dido and thereabout of it, especially
when he speaks of Priam's slaughter. If it live in your memory,
begin at this line—let me see, let me see—

"The rugged Pyrrhus, like th'Hyrcanian beast"—

'Tis not so. It begins with Pyrrhus—   375

"The rugged Pyrrhus, he whose sable arms,
Black as his purpose, did the night resemble
When he lay couchèd in th'ominous horse,
Hath now this dread and black complexion smeared
With heraldry more dismal. Head to foot   380
Now is he total gules, horridly tricked
With blood of fathers, mothers, daughters, sons,
Baked and impasted with the parching streets
That lend a tyrannous and a damnèd light
To their lord's murder. Roasted in wrath and fire,   385
And thus o'ersized with coagulate gore,
With eyes like carbuncles, the hellish Pyrrhus
Old grandsire Priam seeks."

362. caviar . . . general: i.e., too refined for the multitude
364. cried . . . of: spoke with more authority than
365. digested: ordered; modesty: restraint
366. cunning: skill; sallets: spicy flavors, i.e., indelicate language
368. indict: charge, accuse; affection: (1) affectation; (2) excess emotion
370. fine: gaudy
372. Priam: king of Troy. For his death and the fall of Troy, see Virgil's *Aeneid*, book 2.
374. rugged: (1) harsh; (2) hairy; Pyrrhus: Greek warrior in the Trojan war, a revenger
     for his father Achilles; Hyrcanian beast: i.e., tiger. Hyrcania, known for wildness
     in antiquity, is a region near the Caspian sea.
376. sable arms: black armor
378. couchèd: lying hidden; horse: the wooden Trojan horse, by which the Greeks
     entered and conquered Troy
380. heraldry: i.e., display. Heraldry is the art of displaying armorial or familial rights;
     dismal: ill-omened
381. total gules: red all over (a heraldic expression); tricked: adorned
383. impasted: encrusted; parching: burning (from the city on fire)
386. o'ersized: (1) larger than life; (2) covered over as with "size," a glaze or filler
387. carbuncles: red jewels, thought to emit light

So, proceed you.

POLONIUS   'Fore God, my lord, well spoken, with good accent   390
and good discretion.

FIRST PLAYER   "Anon he finds him,
Striking too short at Greeks. His antique sword,
Rebellious to his arm, lies where it falls,
Repugnant to command. Unequal matched,   395
Pyrrhus at Priam drives, in rage strikes wide.
But with the whiff and wind of his fell sword
Th'unnervèd father falls. Then senseless Ilium,
Seeming to feel this blow, with flaming top
Stoops to his base, and with a hideous crash   400
Takes prisoner Pyrrhus' ear. For lo, his sword,
Which was declining on the milky head
Of reverend Priam, seemed i'th'air to stick;
So as a painted tyrant Pyrrhus stood,
And, like a neutral to his will and matter,   405
Did nothing.
But as we often see against some storm
A silence in the heavens, the rack stand still,
The bold winds speechless, and the orb below
As hush as death, anon the dreadful thunder   410
Doth rend the region, so, after Pyrrhus' pause,
A rousèd vengeance sets him new a-work,
And never did the Cyclops' hammers fall
On Mars's armor, forged for proof eterne,
With less remorse than Pyrrhus' bleeding sword   415
Now falls on Priam.
Out, out, thou strumpet, Fortune! All you gods
In general synod, take away her power!
Break all the spokes and fellies from her wheel,

391. **discretion:** judgment
392. **Anon:** immediately
395. **Repugnant:** resistant
397. **fell:** cruel
398. **unnervèd:** rendered nerveless or weak; **senseless:** incapable of perceiving;
    Ilium: tower of Troy
402. **declining:** falling; **milky:** i.e., white-haired
405. **neutral . . . matter:** one suspended between his intention and its fulfillment
407. **against:** in preparation for
408. **rack:** clouds
409. **orb:** globe
411. **region:** sky
413. **Cyclops:** mythical one-eyed giants who forged weapons for the gods
414. **Mars:** god of war; **proof eterne:** eternal impenetrability
415. **remorse:** pity
418. **synod:** assembly
419. **fellies:** wood pieces that form the rim of a wheel (another conventional image
    associated with inconstant Fortune)

And bowl the round nave down the hill of heaven,   420
  As low as to the fiends!"
POLONIUS   This is too long.
HAMLET   It shall to the barber's with your beard.—Prithee,
  say on. He's for a jig or a tale of bawdry, or he sleeps. Say on;
  come to Hecuba.   425
FIRST PLAYER   "But who—ah woe!—had seen the moblèd
  queen"—
HAMLET   "The moblèd queen"?
POLONIUS   That's good.
FIRST PLAYER   "Run barefoot up and down, threat'ning the   430
  flames
    With bisson rheum, a clout upon that head
    Where late the diadem stood, and for a robe,
    About her lank and all o'erteemèd loins,
    A blanket, in the alarm of fear caught up—
    Who this had seen, with tongue in venom steeped,   435
    'Gainst Fortune's state would treason have pronounced.
    But if the gods themselves did see her then,
    When she saw Pyrrhus make malicious sport
    In mincing with his sword her husband's limbs,
    The instant burst of clamor that she made,   440
    Unless things mortal move them not at all,
    Would have made milch the burning eyes of heaven,
    And passion in the gods."
POLONIUS   Look whe'er he has not turned his color and has
  tears in's eyes.—Prithee, no more.   445
HAMLET   'Tis well. I'll have thee speak out the rest of this
  soon.—Good my lord, will you see the players well bestowed?
  Do you hear, let them be well used for they are the abstract
  and brief chronicles of the time. After your death you were
  better have a bad epitaph than their ill report while you live.   450
POLONIUS   My lord, I will use them according to their desert.

---

420. **nave:** hub; **hill of heaven:** Mount Olympus, home of the gods
424. **jig:** comic entertainment, usually musical, often performed at the end of a play
425. **Hecuba:** wife of Priam
426. **moblèd:** muffled
431. **bisson rheum:** blinding tears; **clout:** cloth
432. **diadem:** crown
433. **o'erteemèd:** worn out from bearing children (fifty, according to Euripides, but
     estimates varied)
435. **Who:** anyone who
436. **state:** rule; **pronounced:** declared
440. **instant:** immediate
442. **milch:** milk, i.e., wet with tears; **burning . . . heaven:** i.e., the stars
443. **passion:** strong emotion
444. **whe'er:** whether
447. **bestowed:** settled
448. **abstract:** summary account

HAMLET   God's bodikins, man, much better. Use every man
after his desert, and who shall scape whipping? Use them
after your own honor and dignity; the less they deserve, the
more merit is in your bounty. Take them in.   455
POLONIUS   Come, sirs.
HAMLET   Follow him, friends. We'll hear a play tomorrow.
      [*As they start to leave,* HAMLET *speaks aside to the* FIRST PLAYER.]
Dost thou hear me, old friend? Can you play *The Murder of
Gonzago?*
FIRST PLAYER   Ay, my lord.   460
HAMLET   We'll ha't tomorrow night. You could, for need,
study a speech of some dozen lines, or sixteen lines, which
I would set down and insert in't, could you not?
FIRST PLAYER   Ay, my lord.
HAMLET   Very well. Follow that lord, and look you mock him   465
not.
                        Exeunt POLONIUS *and* PLAYERS.
My good friends, I'll leave you till night. You are welcome to
Elsinore.
ROSENCRANTZ   Good my lord.
                        Exeunt [ROSENCRANTZ *and* GUILDENSTERN].
HAMLET   Ay, so, good-bye to you.—Now I am alone.   470
Oh, what a rogue and peasant slave am I!
Is it not monstrous that this player here,
But in a fiction, in a dream of passion,
Could force his soul so to his own conceit
That from her working all the visage wanned,   475
Tears in his eyes, distraction in his aspect,
A broken voice, and his whole function suiting
With forms to his conceit? And all for nothing.
For Hecuba.
What's Hecuba to him, or he to her,   480
That he should weep for her? What would he do,
Had he the motive and the cue for passion
That I have? He would drown the stage with tears
And cleave the general ear with horrid speech,

---

452. **God's bodikins:** by God's dear body (an oath)
461. **ha't:** have it
471. **rogue:** (1) vagrant or vagabond; (2) term of abuse applied to servants. Compare
   the speech in Quarto 1, Appendix 1, passage 2 (see p. 141).
474. **conceit:** conception
475. **from her working:** in response to the soul's activity; **wanned:** turned pale
476. **aspect:** expression
477–78. **his . . . conceit:** all his bodily powers matching outward appearances to his
   mental fiction of grief
484. **the general ear:** all ears

Make mad the guilty and appall the free,   485
Confound the ignorant, and amaze, indeed,
The very faculties of eyes and ears. Yet I,
A dull and muddy-mettled rascal, peak
Like John-a-dreams, unpregnant of my cause,
And can say nothing—no, not for a king   490
Upon whose property and most dear life
A damned defeat was made. Am I a coward?
Who calls me villain, breaks my pate across,
Plucks off my beard and blows it in my face,
Tweaks me by the nose, gives me the lie i'the throat   495
As deep as to the lungs? Who does me this,
Ha? 'Swounds, I should take it; for it cannot be
But I am pigeon-livered, and lack gall
To make oppression bitter, or ere this
I should ha'fatted all the region kites   500
With this slave's offal. Bloody, bawdy villain!
Remorseless, treacherous, lecherous, kindless villain!
Why, what an ass am I. This is most brave,
That I, the son of a dear father murdered,
Prompted to my revenge by heaven and hell,   505
Must like a whore unpack my heart with words
And fall a-cursing like a very drab,
A scullion. Fie upon't, foh!
About, my brains! Hum, I have heard
That guilty creatures sitting at a play   510
Have by the very cunning of the scene
Been struck so to the soul that presently
They have proclaimed their malefactions;
For murder, though it have no tongue, will speak
With most miraculous organ. I'll have these players   515

485. **amaze:** stun
488. **muddy-mettled:** low-spirited; **peak:** mope
489. **John-a-dreams:** a dreamy, idle fellow; **unpregnant of:** not filled by
492. **defeat:** destruction
493. **pate:** head
495. **gives . . . lie:** calls me a liar
497. **'Swounds:** by God's wounds (an oath)
498. **pigeon-livered:** i.e., cowardly. The pigeon was a symbol of meekness, reputed to be
     without **gall**, a substance thought to produce bitter and violent feelings in the liver.
499. **make oppression bitter:** render tyranny painful to itself
500. **region kites:** predatory birds in the air
501. **this slave's offal:** Claudius's carcass
502. **Remorseless:** pitiless; **kindless:** unnatural
503. **brave:** admirable
504. **dear:** (Auditors also hear "deer," a common image of innocent slaughter.)
507. **drab:** prostitute
508. **scullion:** menial kitchen servant
509. **About:** to work
511. **cunning:** art
513. **malefactions:** crimes
515. **organ:** i.e., voice

Play something like the murder of my father
Before mine uncle. I'll observe his looks;
I'll tent him to the quick. If 'a do blench,
I know my course. The spirit that I have seen
May be the devil, and the devil hath power   520
T'assume a pleasing shape; yea, and perhaps
Out of my weakness and my melancholy,
As he is very potent with such spirits,
Abuses me to damn me. I'll have grounds
More relative than this. The play's the thing   525
Wherein I'll catch the conscience of the King.   *Exit.*

3.1 [THE CASTLE]

Enter KING, QUEEN, POLONIUS, OPHELIA, ROSENCRANTZ,
GUILDENSTERN, LORDS.

KING   And can you, by no drift of conference,
Get from him why he puts on this confusion,
Grating so harshly all his days of quiet
With turbulent and dangerous lunacy?

ROSENCRANTZ   He does confess he feels himself distracted,   5
But from what cause 'a will by no means speak.

GUILDENSTERN   Nor do we find him forward to be sounded,
But, with a crafty madness, keeps aloof
When we would bring him on to some confession
Of his true state.

QUEEN   Did he receive you well?   10

ROSENCRANTZ   Most like a gentleman.

GUILDENSTERN   But with much forcing of his disposition.

ROSENCRANTZ   Niggard of question, but of our demands
Most free in his reply.

QUEEN   Did you assay him to any pastime?   15

ROSENCRANTZ   Madam, it so fell out that certain players
We o'erraught on the way. Of these we told him,
And there did seem in him a kind of joy
To hear of it. They are here about the court,

---

518. **tent . . . quick:** probe him to the painful part of his wound; **blench:** (1) flinch;
(2) turn pale
523. **spirits:** vapors which produce emotional states such as melancholy
524. **Abuses:** deludes
525. **relative:** pertinent
 1. **drift of conference:** direction of conversation
 7. **forward . . . sounded:** eager to be questioned
12. **disposition:** mood
13. **Niggard of question:** reluctant to initiate conversation
15. **assay:** try to entice
17. **o'erraught:** overtook

And, as I think, they have already order   20
  This night to play before him.
POLONIUS   'Tis most true.
  And he beseeched me to entreat Your Majesties
  To hear and see the matter.
KING   With all my heart, and it doth much content me
  To hear him so inclined.   25
  Good gentlemen, give him a further edge,
  And drive his purpose into these delights.
ROSENCRANTZ   We shall, my lord.

          Exeunt ROSENCRANTZ *and* GUILDENSTERN [*and* LORDS].

KING   Sweet Gertrude, leave us two,
  For we have closely sent for Hamlet hither,   30
  That he, as 'twere by accident, may here
  Affront Ophelia. Her father and myself,
  We'll so bestow ourselves that, seeing, unseen,
  We may of their encounter frankly judge,
  And gather by him, as he is behaved,   35
  If't be th'affliction of his love or no
  That thus he suffers for.
QUEEN   I shall obey you.
  And for your part, Ophelia, I do wish
  That your good beauties be the happy cause
  Of Hamlet's wildness. So shall I hope your virtues 40
  Will bring him to his wonted way again,
  To both your honors.
OPHELIA   Madam, I wish it may.

                              [*Exit* QUEEN.]

POLONIUS   Ophelia, walk you here.—Gracious, so please you,
  We will bestow ourselves.
  [*To* OPHELIA, *giving a book*] Read on this book,
  That show of such an exercise may color   45
  Your loneliness. We are oft to blame in this—
  'Tis too much proved—that with devotion's visage
  And pious action we do sugar o'er
  The devil himself.
KING [*Aside*]   Oh, 'tis too true!   50
  How smart a lash that speech doth give my conscience.

26. **edge:** incitement
27. **drive . . . into:** direct his attention to
30. **closely:** privately
32. **Affront:** meet
43. **Gracious:** Your Grace
45. **exercise:** devotion (i.e., reading a religious book); **color:** give plausible reason for
46. **loneliness:** solitude
47. **visage:** appearance

The harlot's cheek, beautied with plast'ring art,
Is not more ugly to the thing that helps it
Than is my deed to my most painted word.
Oh, heavy burden!   55
POLONIUS   I hear him coming. Withdraw, my lord.
                                          [*They withdraw.*]
          Enter HAMLET. [OPHELIA *pretends to read.*]
HAMLET   To be or not to be—that is the question.
  Whether 'tis nobler in the mind to suffer
  The slings and arrows of outrageous fortune,
  Or to take arms against a sea of troubles   60
  And by opposing end them. To die, to sleep—
  No more—and by a sleep to say we end
  The heartache and the thousand natural shocks
  That flesh is heir to. 'Tis a consummation
  Devoutly to be wished. To die, to sleep,   65
  To sleep, perchance to dream—ay, there's the rub,
  For in that sleep of death what dreams may come
  When we have shuffled off this mortal coil
  Must give us pause. There's the respect
  That makes calamity of so long life.   70
  For who would bear the whips and scorns of time,
  Th'oppressor's wrong, the proud man's contumely,
  The pangs of despised love, the law's delay,
  The insolence of office, and the spurns
  That patient merit of th'unworthy takes,   75
  When he himself might his quietus make
  With a bare bodkin? Who would fardels bear,
  To grunt and sweat under a weary life,
  But that the dread of something after death,

---

52. **plast'ring art:** i.e., cosmetics
53. **thing:** i.e., makeup
54. **deed . . . word:** murder of King Hamlet to my lies about his death
56. **s.d. *withdraw*:** (They may move to the side, conceal themselves behind a curtain, as Polonius suggested at 2.2.162, or leave the stage, as *Exeunt* in F stipulates. Ophelia remains onstage but Hamlet presumably does not notice her until line 89. She may or may not overhear the soliloquy. Compare the speech in Appendix 1, Quarto 1, passage 1, p. 140)
62. **No more:** i.e., to die is no more than to sleep
64. **consummation:** conclusion
66. **rub:** obstacle (in the game of bowls)
68. **shuffled:** cast; **coil:** turmoil
69. **respect:** consideration
70. **makes . . . life:** (1) makes long life such a misfortune; (2) makes misfortune last so long
72. **contumely:** insult
74. **office:** bureaucracy
76. **quietus:** release from debt
77. **bodkin:** dagger; **fardels:** burdens

[handwritten margin note: but the has seen a ghost — possible this was written before play]

The undiscovered country, from whose bourn   80
No traveler returns, puzzles the will,
And makes us rather bear those ills we have
Than fly to others that we know not of?
Thus conscience does make cowards of us all,
And thus the native hue of resolution   85
Is sicklied o'er with the pale cast of thought,
And enterprises of great pitch and moment,
With this regard, their currents turn awry,
And lose the name of action.—Soft you now,
The fair Ophelia.—Nymph, in thy orisons   90
Be all my sins remembered.

[handwritten margin note: Does he Know he's alone? Changes tone of speech]

OPHELIA   Good my lord,
How does your honor for this many a day?

HAMLET   I humbly thank you; well.

OPHELIA   My lord, I have remembrances of yours
That I have longèd long to redeliver.   95
I pray you, now receive them.

HAMLET   No, not I. I never gave you aught.

OPHELIA   My honored lord, you know right well you did,
And with them words of so sweet breath composed
As made these things more rich. Their perfume lost,   100
Take these again, for to the noble mind
Rich gifts wax poor when givers prove unkind.
There, my lord. [*She returns gifts.*]

HAMLET   Ha, ha, are you honest?

OPHELIA   My lord?   105

HAMLET   Are you fair?

OPHELIA   What means your lordship?

HAMLET   That if you be honest and fair, your honesty should
admit no discourse to your beauty.

OPHELIA   Could beauty, my lord, have better commerce than   110
with honesty?

HAMLET   Ay, truly, for the power of beauty will sooner transform honesty from what it is to a bawd than the force of

---

80. **bourn:** boundary
84. **conscience:** (1) faculty of moral judgment; (2) consciousness
85. **native hue:** natural color
87. **pitch:** height (the high point of a bird's flight); **moment:** importance
88. **regard:** consideration; **currents:** courses (as of rivers)
89. **Soft you:** wait a minute
90. **orisons:** prayers
97. **aught:** anything
102. **wax:** grow
104. **honest:** (1) chaste; (2) truthful
109. **admit . . . to:** allow no conversation with
110. **commerce:** dealing
113. **bawd:** pimp. Hamlet says that beauty will sooner corrupt chastity than chastity keep beauty virtuous.

honesty can translate beauty into his likeness. This was
sometime a paradox, but now the time gives it proof. I did   115
love you once.

OPHELIA   Indeed, my lord, you made me believe so.

HAMLET   You should not have believed me; for virtue cannot
so inoculate our old stock but we shall relish of it. I loved
you not.   120

OPHELIA   I was the more deceived.

HAMLET   Get thee to a nunnery. Why wouldst thou be a
breeder of sinners? I am myself indifferent honest, but yet I
could accuse me of such things that it were better my mother
had not borne me. I am very proud, revengeful, ambitious,   125
with more offenses at my beck than I have thoughts to put
them in, imagination to give them shape, or time to act
them in. What should such fellows as I do crawling between
earth and heaven? We are arrant knaves; believe none of us.
Go thy ways to a nunnery. Where's your father?   130

OPHELIA   At home, my lord.

HAMLET   Let the doors be shut upon him that he may play the
fool nowhere but in's own house. Farewell.

OPHELIA   Oh, help him, you sweet heavens!

HAMLET   If thou dost marry, I'll give thee this plague for thy   135
dowry: be thou as chaste as ice, as pure as snow, thou shalt
not escape calumny. Get thee to a nunnery, farewell. Or if
thou wilt needs marry, marry a fool, for wise men know well
enough what monsters you make of them. To a nunnery, go,
and quickly too. Farewell.   140

OPHELIA   Heavenly powers, restore him!

HAMLET   I have heard of your paintings well enough. God hath
given you one face, and you make yourselves another. You jig
and amble, and you lisp, you nickname God's creatures and
make your wantonness ignorance. Go to, I'll no more on't; it   145
hath made me mad. I say we will have no more marriage.

---

115. **sometime a paradox:** formerly a statement contrary to rational explanation or
received opinion
119. **inoculate . . . it:** graft goodness onto our fallen nature (**old stock**) that we do
not still retain some sin (**relish of it**)
122. **nunnery:** (1) convent; (2) brothel
123. **indifferent honest:** reasonably virtuous
126. **beck:** summons
129. **arrant:** downright
137. **calumny:** slander
139. **monsters:** cuckolds (i.e., spouses of unfaithful partners, often portrayed with
horns); **you:** i.e., you women
142. **paintings:** face paintings (with makeup)
143–44. **jig and amble:** move (or dance) quickly and slowly
144. **lisp:** speak affectedly and flirtatiously; **nickname:** call by new names
145. **make . . . ignorance:** excuse your affectation and lewdness by pretending
ignorance

Those that are married already—all but one—shall live. The
rest shall keep as they are. To a nunnery, go!　　　*Exit.*
OPHELIA　Oh, what a noble mind is here o'erthrown!
The courtier's, soldier's, scholar's, eye, tongue, sword,　　150
Th'expectation and rose of the fair state,
The glass of fashion and the mold of form,
Th'observed of all observers—quite, quite down!
And I, of ladies most deject and wretched,
That sucked the honey of his music vows,　　155
Now see that noble and most sovereign reason
Like sweet bells jangled out of time and harsh,
That unmatched form and stature of blown youth
Blasted with ecstasy. Oh, woe is me,
T'have seen what I have seen, see what I see!　　160

Enter KING *and* POLONIUS.

KING　Love—his affections do not that way tend;
Nor what he spake, though it lacked form a little,
Was not like madness. There's something in his soul
O'er which his melancholy sits on brood,
And I do doubt the hatch and the disclose　　165
Will be some danger; which for to prevent,
I have in quick determination
Thus set it down: he shall with speed to England
For the demand of our neglected tribute.
Haply the seas and countries different　　170
With variable objects shall expel
This something settled matter in his heart,
Whereon his brains still beating puts him thus
From fashion of himself. What think you on't?
POLONIUS　It shall do well. But yet do I believe　　175
The origin and commencement of his grief
Sprung from neglected love.—How now, Ophelia?
You need not tell us what Lord Hamlet said;

---

150. **courtier's . . . sword:** i.e., courtier's eye, soldier's sword, scholar's tongue (referring to the qualities of discrimination, eloquence, and courage attributed to Hamlet, the princely ideal)
151. **expectation and rose:** roselike hope (a rhetorical figure called hendiadys, which expresses one idea through two elements)
152. **glass . . . form:** mirror of ideal self-fashioning and model of proper behavior and beauty
157. **time:** rhythm
158. **blown:** blooming
159. **Blasted with ecstasy:** blighted by madness
164. **sits on brood:** hatches (as a hen her eggs)
165. **doubt:** fear; **disclose:** disclosure
171. **variable objects:** various sights and distractions
172. **something:** unidentified
173. **still:** always

We heard it all.—My lord, do as you please,
But if you hold it fit, after the play   180
Let his queen-mother all alone entreat him
To show his grief. Let her be round with him;
And I'll be placed, so please you, in the ear
Of all their conference. If she find him not,
To England send him, or confine him where   185
Your wisdom best shall think.
KING   It shall be so.
Madness in great ones must not unwatched go.

Exeunt.

3.2 [THE CASTLE]

Enter HAMLET *and three of the* PLAYERS.

HAMLET   Speak the speech, I pray you, as I pronounced it to
you, trippingly on the tongue. But if you mouth it as many
of our players do, I had as lief the town crier spoke my lines.
Nor do not saw the air too much with your hand, thus, but
use all gently, for in the very torrent, tempest, and, as I may   5
say, whirlwind of your passion, you must acquire and beget
a temperance that may give it smoothness. Oh, it offends
me to the soul to hear a robustious periwig-pated fellow tear
a passion to tatters, to very rags, to split the ears of the
groundlings, who for the most part are capable of nothing   10
but inexplicable dumb shows and noise. I would have such a
fellow whipped for o'erdoing Termagant. It out-Herods
Herod; pray you, avoid it.
PLAYER   I warrant your honor.
HAMLET   Be not too tame neither, but let your own discretion   15
be your tutor. Suit the action to the word, the word to the
action, with this special observance, that you o'erstep not
the modesty of nature. For anything so o'erdone is from the
purpose of playing, whose end, both at the first and now, was

182. **round:** plainspoken
183. **the ear:** earshot
184. **find him:** discover his problem
2. **trippingly:** quickly, fluently; **mouth:** speak pompously
3. **lief:** gladly
8. **robustious:** boisterous; **periwig-pated:** wig-wearing
10. **groundlings:** low-paying customers who stood in the yard of the theater
11. **inexplicable:** silent; **dumb shows:** summary representations of the action in a play,
performed without words (see below, 125ff.)
12. **Termagant:** an imaginary Muslim deity, thought to be violent and blustering;
Herod: Biblical tyrant who murdered the Holy Innocents, portrayed as violent and
ranting in medieval mystery plays
14. **I . . . honor:** yes, sir
18. **modesty:** moderation; **from:** remote from

and is to hold, as 'twere, the mirror up to nature, to show vir- 20
tue her feature, scorn her own image, and the very age and
body of the time his form and pressure. Now this overdone
or come tardy off, though it makes the unskillful laugh, cannot but make the judicious grieve—the censure of which one
must in your allowance o'erweigh a whole theater of others. 25
Oh, there be players that I have seen play and heard others
praise—and that highly—not to speak it profanely, that, neither having th'accent of Christians, nor the gait of Christian,
pagan, nor man, have so strutted and bellowed that I have
thought some of Nature's journeymen had made men, and not 30
made them well, they imitated humanity so abominably.

PLAYER   I hope we have reformed that indifferently with us.

HAMLET   Oh, reform it altogether. And let those that play
your clowns speak no more than is set down for them, for
there be of them that will themselves laugh to set on some 35
quantity of barren spectators to laugh too, though in the
meantime some necessary question of the play be then to be
considered. That's villainous, and shows a most pitiful
ambition in the fool that uses it. Go make you ready.

[*Exeunt* PLAYERS.]

Enter POLONIUS, GUILDENSTERN, *and* ROSENCRANTZ.

How now, my lord, will the King hear this piece of work? 40

POLONIUS   And the Queen too, and that presently.

HAMLET   Bid the players make haste.

[*Exit* POLONIUS.]

Will you two help to hasten them?

ROSENCRANTZ   Ay, my lord.

Exeunt they two.

HAMLET   What, ho, Horatio! 45

Enter HORATIO.

21. **scorn:** i.e., a thing worthy of scorn
21–22. **age . . . time:** i.e., the present as it is
22. **his . . . pressure:** its exact likeness and impression
23. **come tardy off:** accomplished inadequately
24. **censure . . . one:** judgment of even one of these
25. **allowance:** estimation
27. **not . . . profanely:** i.e., not to commit a blasphemy (by suggesting that God did
not create some of these characters)
28. **gait:** bearing
30. **journeymen:** workers, not yet masters of a trade
31. **abominably:** (spelled, as usual in Shakespeare, "abhominably," which suggests
the popular though false etymology, *ab homine,* "away from man," "inhuman")
32. **indifferently:** fairly well
34. **clowns:** (In Quarto 1, Hamlet expands the advice to the clowns; see Appendix 1,
passage 3, p. 142.)
35. **of them:** some of them
36. **barren:** witless
45. **What, ho:** (an exclamation used to call the attention of someone or to express
excitement)

HORATIO   Here, sweet lord, at your service.
HAMLET   Horatio, thou art e'en as just a man
  As e'er my conversation coped withal.
HORATIO   Oh, my dear lord—
HAMLET   Nay, do not think I flatter,
  For what advancement may I hope from thee,   50
  That no revenue hast but thy good spirits
  To feed and clothe thee? Why should the poor be flattered?
  No, let the candied tongue lick absurd pomp,
  And crook the pregnant hinges of the knee
  Where thrift may follow fawning. Dost thou hear?   55
  Since my dear soul was mistress of her choice
  And could of men distinguish her election,
  Sh'hath sealed thee for herself, for thou hast been
  As one, in suffering all, that suffers nothing,
  A man that Fortune's buffets and rewards   60
  Hast ta'en with equal thanks; and blest are those
  Whose blood and judgment are so well commeddled
  That they are not a pipe for Fortune's finger
  To sound what stop she please. Give me that man
  That is not passion's slave, and I will wear him   65
  In my heart's core, ay, in my heart of heart,
  As I do thee.—Something too much of this.—
  There is a play tonight before the King.
  One scene of it comes near the circumstance
  Which I have told thee of my father's death.   70
  I prithee, when thou seest that act afoot,
  Even with the very comment of thy soul
  Observe my uncle. If his occulted guilt
  Do not itself unkennel in one speech,
  It is a damnèd ghost that we have seen,   75
  And my imaginations are as foul
  As Vulcan's stithy. Give him heedful note,
  For I mine eyes will rivet to his face,

48. **conversation:** dealings with people; **coped:** encountered
53. **candied:** sugared, flattering
54. **crook:** bend; **pregnant:** ready
55. **thrift:** prosperity; **fawning:** servile behavior
57. **distinguish her election:** make discriminating choices
58. **sealed:** marked (a metaphor from the personal seal affixed to letters and legal documents)
59. **that:** who
62. **blood:** passion; **commeddled:** commingled
63. **pipe:** small wind instrument (such as a flute or recorder)
64. **stop:** hole in a wind instrument
72. **very . . . soul:** your most searching consideration
73. **occulted:** hidden
74. **unkennel:** reveal (as a fox is driven from its hole)
77. **Vulcan's stithy:** forge or anvil of Vulcan, blacksmith of the gods

And after we will both our judgments join
In censure of his seeming.   80
HORATIO   Well, my lord.
If 'a steal aught the whilst this play is playing
And scape detecting, I will pay the theft.

> [*Flourish.*] *Enter trumpets and kettledrums,* KING, QUEEN,
> POLONIUS, OPHELIA[, ROSENCRANTZ, GUILDENSTERN, *and
> others*].

HAMLET   They are coming to the play. I must be idle. Get you
a place.   85
KING   How fares our cousin Hamlet?
HAMLET   Excellent, i'faith, of the chameleon's dish: I eat the
air, promise-crammed. You cannot feed capons so.
KING   I have nothing with this answer, Hamlet. These words
are not mine.   90
HAMLET   No, nor mine now, my lord. [*To* POLONIUS] You played
once i'th'university, you say?
POLONIUS   That did I, my lord, and was accounted a good
actor.
HAMLET   What did you enact?   95
POLONIUS   I did enact Julius Caesar. I was killed i'the Capi-
tol; Brutus killed me.
HAMLET   It was a brute part of him to kill so capital a calf
there.—Be the players ready?
ROSENCRANTZ   Ay, my lord. They stay upon your patience.   100
QUEEN   Come hither, my dear Hamlet, sit by me.
HAMLET [*Approaching* OPHELIA]   No, good mother, here's metal
more attractive.
POLONIUS   [*To the* KING]   Oho, do you mark that?
HAMLET   Lady, shall I lie in your lap?   105
OPHELIA   No, my lord.
HAMLET   Do you think I meant country matters?

---

80. **censure:** judgment; **seeming:** (1) appearance; (2) pretense
82. **pay the theft:** make restitution for the stolen goods
87. **chameleon's dish:** i.e., air (which chameleons were thought to eat). Hamlet answers
     the King's question by construing **fares:** as "eats" instead of "does."
88. **promise-crammed:** fed only with the air of promises; **capons:** castrated and fatted
     roosters
90. **mine:** for me
91. **nor mine now:** (Once spoken, words proverbially became public property.)
96. **Julius Caesar:** Roman conqueror assassinated by Brutus in 44 BCE. Caesar and
     Brutus in Shakespeare's *Julius Caesar* (1599) may have been played by the same
     actors who played Polonius and Hamlet here.
98. **brute:** brutish (from the Latin *brutus*, "stupid"); **so . . . calf:** such an excellent fool
102. **metal:** (with a pun on "mettle" or "character")
103. **attractive:** (1) fair; (2) magnetic
107. **country matters:** lovemaking (as in the bawdy country), with a pun on the first
     syllable of **country**

OPHELIA   I think nothing, my lord.

HAMLET   That's a fair thought to lie between maids' legs.

OPHELIA   What is, my lord?   110

HAMLET   Nothing.

OPHELIA   You are merry, my lord.

HAMLET   Who, I?

OPHELIA   Ay, my lord.

HAMLET   O God, your only jig-maker. What should a man do   115
but be merry? For look you how cheerfully my mother looks,
and my father died within's two hours.

OPHELIA   Nay, 'tis twice two months, my lord.

HAMLET   So long? Nay then, let the devil wear black, for I'll
have a suit of sables. O heavens, die two months ago, and   120
not forgotten yet? Then there's hope a great man's memory
may outlive his life half a year. But, by'r Lady, 'a must build
churches then or else shall 'a suffer not thinking on, with
the hobby-horse, whose epitaph is "For O, for O, the hobby-
horse is forgot."   125

The trumpets sound. Dumb show follows.

Enter a KING *and a* QUEEN, *the* QUEEN *embracing him and he
her. He takes her up, and declines his head upon her neck. He
lies him down upon a bank of flowers. She, seeing him asleep,
leaves him. Anon comes in another man, takes off his crown,
kisses it, pours poison in the sleeper's ears, and leaves him. The*
QUEEN *returns, finds the* KING *dead, makes passionate action.
The* POISONER *with some three or four come in again, seem to
condole with her. The dead body is carried away. The* POI-
SONER *woos the* QUEEN *with gifts; she seems harsh awhile, but
in the end accepts love.*

[*Exeunt* PLAYERS.]

OPHELIA   What means this, my lord?

HAMLET   Marry, this is mitching malicho; it means mischief.

---

108. **nothing:** (a term for female genitals, as Hamlet immediately recognizes. "Thing"
could also refer to male genitals).
115. **only jig-maker:** best composer of comic entertainments
117. **within's:** within this
118. **twice two months:** (This clear statement from an objective observer may conflict
with Hamlet's "within a month" [1.2.153], and indicate his distracted state of
mind or a lapse of time between Acts 1 and 2, wherein Rosencrantz and Guildenstern have been sent for and appear, and the ambassadors have gone to and
returned from Norway.)
120. **suit of sables:** fancy clothing trimmed with sable fur
123. **suffer . . . on:** endure oblivion
124. **hobby-horse:** character costumed to look like a horse. The quoted song
immediately following laments the loss of such traditions.
125. **s.d.:** (Compare the dumb show in the Folio, Appendix 2, passage 3, page 148.)
125.9. **s.d.** *condole:* commiserate
127. **mitching malicho:** sneaking wickedness

OPHELIA   Belike this show imports the argument of the play.

Enter PROLOGUE.

HAMLET   We shall know by this fellow. The players cannot
keep counsel; they'll tell all.   130

OPHELIA   Will 'a tell us what this show meant?

HAMLET   Ay, or any show that you will show him. Be not you
ashamed to show, he'll not shame to tell you what it means.

OPHELIA   You are naught, you are naught. I'll mark the play.

PROLOGUE   For us and for our tragedy,   135
Here stooping to your clemency,
We beg your hearing patiently.   [*Exit.*]

HAMLET   Is this a prologue or the posy of a ring?

OPHELIA   'Tis brief, my lord.

HAMLET   As woman's love.   140

Enter [*two players as*] KING *and* QUEEN.

PLAYER KING   Full thirty times hath Phoebus' cart gone round
Neptune's salt wash and Tellus' orbèd ground,
And thirty dozen moons with borrowed sheen
About the world have times twelve thirties been,
Since love our hearts and Hymen did our hands   145
Unite commutual in most sacred bands.

PLAYER QUEEN   So many journeys may the sun and moon
Make us again count o'er ere love be done.
But, woe is me, you are so sick of late,
So far from cheer and from our former state,   150
That I distrust you. Yet, though I distrust,
Discomfort you, my lord, it nothing must,
For women fear too much, even as they love,
And women's fear and love hold quantity,
Either none, in neither aught, or in extremity.   155

128. **Belike:** probably
130. **counsel:** secrets
132. **Be not you:** if you be not
134. **naught:** naughty. Ophelia responds to the indecent suggestion of being not ashamed
to show herself.
138. **posy . . . ring:** saying or verse inscribed in a ring. The actor playing the Prologue
gives only a few lines instead of the argument of the play.
141. **Phoebus's cart:** the chariot of the sun
142. **salt wash:** ocean; **Tellus' orbèd ground:** the earth goddess's globe (i.e. the earth)
143. **thirty dozen moons:** i.e., thirty years
145. **Hymen:** the god of marriage
146. **commutual:** mutually
151. **distrust:** fear for
152. **nothing:** not at all
153. **For . . . love:** (This unrhymed line may have lost its answering line or been marked
for deletion)
154. **hold quantity:** keep proportion with each other
155. **Either none:** either there is no fear or love. The next phrase repeats the idea, in
neither emotion is there **aught**, "anything"; **or in extremity:** or there is excess of
fear and love

Now what my love is, proof hath made you know,
And as my love is sized, my fear is so.
Where love is great, the littlest doubts are fear;
Where little fears grow great, great love grows there.

PLAYER KING   Faith, I must leave thee, love, and shortly too;   160
My operant powers their functions leave to do,
And thou shalt live in this fair world behind,
Honored, beloved; and haply one as kind
For husband shalt thou—

PLAYER QUEEN   Oh, confound the rest!
Such love must needs be treason in my breast.   165
In second husband let me be accurst!
None wed the second but who killed the first.

HAMLET   That's wormwood.

PLAYER QUEEN   The instances that second marriage move
Are base respects of thrift, but none of love.   170
A second time I kill my husband dead
When second husband kisses me in bed.

PLAYER KING   I do believe you think what now you speak,
But what we do determine oft we break.
Purpose is but the slave to memory,   175
Of violent birth, but poor validity,
Which now, like fruit unripe, sticks on the tree,
But fall unshaken when they mellow be.
Most necessary 'tis that we forget
To pay ourselves what to ourselves is debt.   180
What to ourselves in passion we propose,
The passion ending, doth the purpose lose.
The violence of either grief or joy
Their own enactures with themselves destroy.
Where joy most revels, grief doth most lament,   185
Grief joys, joy grieves, on slender accident.
This world is not for aye, nor 'tis not strange

156. **proof:** experience
157. **sized:** measured in size
161. **operant:** vital; **leave:** cease
162. **behind:** after I have gone
167. **but who:** except the one who
168. **wormwood:** i.e., disturbing (literally, a plant proverbial for its bitterness)
169. **instances:** causes; **move:** motivate
170. **respects of thrift:** financial considerations
175. **Purpose . . . memory:** resolutions must be remembered to be acted upon
176. **validity:** strength, durability
179–80. **Most . . . debt:** we inevitably forget about self-imposed obligations
184. **enactures:** enactings. Grief or joy exhausts itself immediately.
186. **joys:** enjoys, i.e. turns into joys. Extreme grief or joy quickly turns into its
    opposite for slight reasons.
187. **aye:** ever

That even our loves should with our fortunes change;
For 'tis a question left us yet to prove
Whether love lead fortune or else fortune love.   190
The great man down, you mark his favorite flies;
The poor, advanced, makes friends of enemies;
And hitherto doth love on fortune tend,
For who not needs shall never lack a friend,
And who in want a hollow friend doth try,   195
Directly seasons him his enemy.
But, orderly to end where I begun,
Our wills and fates do so contrary run
That our devices still are overthrown;
Our thoughts are ours, their ends none of our own.   200
So think thou wilt no second husband wed,
But die thy thoughts when thy first lord is dead.
PLAYER QUEEN   Nor earth to me give food, nor heaven light,
Sport and repose lock from me day and night,
To desperation turn my trust and hope,   205
And anchor's cheer in prison be my scope,
Each opposite that blanks the face of joy
Meet what I would have well, and it destroy,
Both here and hence pursue me lasting strife,
If, once I be a widow, ever I be a wife.   210
HAMLET   If she should break it now—
PLAYER KING   'Tis deeply sworn. Sweet, leave me here awhile.
My spirits grow dull, and fain I would beguile
The tedious day with sleep.
PLAYER QUEEN   Sleep rock thy brain,
And never come mischance between us twain.   215

                    [*He sleeps.*] *Exit* [PLAYER QUEEN].

HAMLET   Madam, how like you this play?
QUEEN   The lady doth protest too much, methinks.
HAMLET   Oh, but she'll keep her word.
KING   Have you heard the argument? Is there no offense in't?

193. **hitherto:** up to this point
194. **who not needs:** whoever is rich
196. **seasons him:** ripens him into
199. **devices still:** plans ever
203. **Nor:** let neither
204. **lock:** keep
206. **anchor's cheer:** a hermit's sustenance; **my scope:** the extent of my fare and liberty
207–08. **Each . . . destroy:** May every adverse thing that causes joy to grow pale meet and destroy everything that I want to prosper
209. **hence:** in the afterlife
211. **it:** i.e., her oath
213. **spirits:** vital energies; **fain:** gladly
215. **mischance:** ill fortune; **twain:** two
219. **argument:** plot summary

HAMLET   No, no, they do but jest, poison in jest; no offense   220
i'the world.

KING   What do you call the play?

HAMLET   *The Mousetrap.* Marry, how? Tropically. This play is
the image of a murder done in Vienna. Gonzago is the
Duke's name, his wife, Baptista. You shall see anon. 'Tis a   225
knavish piece of work, but what of that? Your Majesty and
we that have free souls, it touches us not. Let the galled
jade winch, our withers are unwrung.

     Enter LUCIANUS.

This is one Lucianus, nephew to the King.

OPHELIA   You are as good as a chorus, my lord.   230

HAMLET   I could interpret between you and your love, if I
could see the puppets dallying.

OPHELIA   You are keen, my lord, you are keen.

HAMLET   It would cost you a groaning to take off mine edge.

OPHELIA   Still better, and worse.   235

HAMLET   So you mis-take your husbands.—Begin, murderer.
Leave thy damnable faces and begin. Come, "the croaking
raven doth bellow for revenge."

LUCIANUS   Thoughts black, hands apt, drugs fit, and time
    agreeing,
Confederate season, else no creature seeing,   240
Thou mixture rank of midnight weeds collected,
With Hecate's ban thrice blasted, thrice infected,
Thy natural magic and dire property
On wholesome life usurps immediately.

---

    223. **Tropically:** figuratively, as a trope. The Q1 spelling, "trapically," suggests a pun
        on "trap."
    225. **Duke's:** i.e., King's
    227. **free:** innocent
227–28. **galled jade:** horse irritated from painful chafing
    228. **winch:** kick; **withers:** the horse's back between the shoulders; **unwrung:**
        unchafed
    229. **nephew:** (Lucianus represents the past assassin Claudius, but also, as **nephew**
        suggests, the future assassin Hamlet.)
    230. **chorus:** i.e., an actor who explains or comments on a play
231–32. **I . . . dallying:** i.e., I could play the narrator at a puppet show that represented
        you playing with your lover. This sets up the bawdy suggestions following in
        keen, i.e., sexually aroused, **groaning,** i.e., orgasm or pregnancy, and **edge,** i.e.,
        sexual desire.
    236. **mis-take:** take falsely. The marriage service required spouses to "take" each
        other "for better, for worse."
237–38. **the croaking . . . revenge:** (Hamlet conflates two lines from a revenge play,
        The True Tragedy of Richard III [c. 1591]: "The screeking raven sits croaking for
        revenge. / Whole heads [herds] of beasts comes bellowing for revenge.")
    240. **Confederate season:** the time and occasion conspiring (with me); **else:**
        otherwise
    242. **Hecate's ban:** the curse of Hecate, goddess of witchcraft
    243. **dire property:** evil power
    244. **On . . . usurps:** steals away health and life

[*He pours the poison into the* SLEEPER's *ear.*]

HAMLET 'A poisons him i'the garden for his estate. His name's   245
Gonzago. The story is extant and written in very choice Ital-
ian; you shall see anon how the murderer gets the love of
Gonzago's wife.

[CLAUDIUS *stands.*]

OPHELIA The King rises.
QUEEN How fares my lord?   250
POLONIUS Give o'er the play.
KING Give me some light. Away!
POLONIUS Lights, lights, lights!

Exeunt all but HAMLET *and* HORATIO.

HAMLET "Why, let the strucken deer go weep,
     The hart ungallèd play;   255
For some must watch, while some must sleep,
     Thus runs the world away."
Would not this, sir, and a forest of feathers—if the rest of
my fortunes turn Turk with me—with Provincial roses on my
razed shoes, get me a fellowship in a cry of players?   260
HORATIO Half a share.
HAMLET A whole one, ay.
"For thou dost know, O Damon dear,
     This realm dismantled was
Of Jove himself, and now reigns here   265
     A very, very—pajock."
HORATIO You might have rhymed.
HAMLET O good Horatio, I'll take the ghost's word for a
thousand pound. Didst perceive?
HORATIO Very well, my lord.   270
HAMLET Upon the talk of the poisoning?

254. **strucken:** struck. These lines, reminiscent of old ballads, rehearse the popular belief that wounded deer retire to weep and die.
255. **ungallèd:** unhurt
256. **watch:** stay awake
258. **this:** i.e., the play; **forest of feathers:** i.e., many plumed hats (which actors wore)
259. **turn Turk with:** i.e., turn against; **Provincial roses:** rosettes of ribbons or cloth that look like the Province rose
260. **razed:** slashed ornamentally. Auditors might also have heard "raised," alluding to the high shoes actors sometimes wore; **fellowship:** partnership; **cry:** pack (of hounds)
263. **Damon:** (a traditional shepherd's name in pastoral poetry)
264. **dismantled:** stripped
266. **pajock:** (1) perhaps peacock, fabled to be cruel and lustful; (2) perhaps "patch-cock," a word Spenser used to describe degenerate English in Ireland. The spellings "paiock" (Q2) and "Paiocke" (F) are unique to Shakespeare.
267. **rhymed:** (used a word rhyming with "was," probably "ass" in contemporary pronunciation)
268–69. **for . . . pound:** i.e., as absolutely reliable

HORATIO   I did very well note him.

HAMLET   Aha! Come, some music, come, the recorders!
"For if the King like not the comedy,
Why then, belike, he likes it not, perdy."   275
Come, some music!

Enter ROSENCRANTZ *and* GUILDENSTERN.

GUILDENSTERN   Good my lord, vouchsafe me a word with you.

HAMLET   Sir, a whole history.

GUILDENSTERN   The King, sir—

HAMLET   Ay, sir, what of him?   280

GUILDENSTERN   Is in his retirement marvelous distempered.

HAMLET   With drink, sir?

GUILDENSTERN   No, my lord, with choler.

HAMLET   Your wisdom should show itself more richer to signify this to the doctor, for for me to put him to his purga-   285
tion would perhaps plunge him into more choler.

GUILDENSTERN   Good my lord, put your discourse into some
frame, and start not so wildly from my affair.

HAMLET   I am tame, sir. Pronounce.

GUILDENSTERN   The Queen, your mother, in most great   290
affliction of spirit, hath sent me to you.

HAMLET   You are welcome.

GUILDENSTERN   Nay, good my lord, this courtesy is not of the
right breed. If it shall please you to make me a wholesome
answer, I will do your mother's commandment; if not, your   295
pardon and my return shall be the end of business.

HAMLET   Sir, I cannot.

ROSENCRANTZ   What, my lord?

HAMLET   Make you a wholesome answer; my wit's diseased.
But, sir, such answer as I can make, you shall command, or   300
rather, as you say, my mother. Therefore no more, but to the
matter: my mother, you say—

ROSENCRANTZ   Then thus she says: your behavior hath struck
her into amazement and admiration.

273. **recorders:** flute-like instruments
275. **belike:** probably; **perdy:** by God (a corruption of the French *par Dieu*)
281. **distempered:** out of humor, vexed
283. **choler:** one of the four humors of early modern physiology, sometimes equated
with bile, thought to cause anger
285–86. **purgation:** i.e., blood-letting, a cure for excess of choler. Hamlet suggests that
his purgation of Claudius might take the form of forced confession or the
bloodletting of execution.
288. **frame:** order; **start:** jump away (like a horse)
294. **breed:** kind; **wholesome:** sane
299. **wit:** mind
304. **admiration:** wonder

HAMLET   Oh, wonderful son that can so stonish a mother!   305
But is there no sequel at the heels of this mother's admiration? Impart.

ROSENCRANTZ   She desires to speak with you in her closet ere
you go to bed.

HAMLET   We shall obey were she ten times our mother. Have   310
you any further trade with us?

ROSENCRANTZ   My lord, you once did love me.

HAMLET   And do still, by these pickers and stealers.

ROSENCRANTZ   Good my lord, what is your cause of distemper? You do surely bar the door upon your own liberty if you   315
deny your griefs to your friend.

HAMLET   Sir, I lack advancement.

ROSENCRANTZ   How can that be, when you have the voice of
the King himself for your succession in Denmark?

HAMLET   Ay, sir, but "While the grass grows"—the proverb is   320
something musty.

        Enter the PLAYERS *with recorders.*

Oh, the recorders. Let me see one. [*He takes a recorder.*] To
withdraw with you, why do you go about to recover the wind
of me, as if you would drive me into a toil?

GUILDENSTERN   O my lord, if my duty be too bold, my love is   325
too unmannerly.

HAMLET   I do not well understand that. Will you play upon
this pipe?

GUILDENSTERN   My lord, I cannot.

HAMLET   I pray you.   330

GUILDENSTERN   Believe me, I cannot.

HAMLET   I do beseech you.

GUILDENSTERN   I know no touch of it, my lord.

HAMLET   It is as easy as lying: govern these ventages with your
fingers and thumb, give it breath with your mouth, and it will   335
discourse most eloquent music. Look you, these are the stops.

---

    305. **stonish:** astonish
    308. **closet:** private room, often used for study or devotion
    311. **trade:** business. Rosencrantz catches the jab at their supposed friendship.
    313. **pickers and stealers:** i.e., hands. Hamlet recalls a catechism verse about keep-
        ing one's hands from "picking and stealing."
    319. **succession:** succession to the throne
    320. **While . . . grows:** (The rest of the proverb is "the silly horse starves"; see Dent,
        Shakespeare's Proverbial Language, G423; Hamlet suggests that he may not live
        long enough to rule the kingdom.)
    321. **something musty:** somewhat stale (so Hamlet does not finish the quotation)
    323. **withdraw:** speak privately
323–24. **recover . . . toil:** get to my windward side to drive me into a trap (**toil**). The
        metaphor is from hunting.
325–26. **love . . . unmannerly:** great affection causes me to intrude in your affairs
    334. **ventages:** holes in the instrument (**stops**, 336)

GUILDENSTERN   But these cannot I command to any utt'rance
of harmony; I have not the skill.

HAMLET   Why, look you now how unworthy a thing you make   340
of me. You would play upon me, you would seem to know
my stops, you would pluck out the heart of my mystery. You
would sound me from my lowest note to my compass, and
there is much music, excellent voice, in this little organ, yet
cannot you make it speak. 'Sblood, do you think I am easier
to be played on than a pipe? Call me what instrument you   345
will, though you fret me, you cannot play upon me.

    Enter POLONIUS.

God bless you, sir.

POLONIUS   My lord, the Queen would speak with you, and
presently.

HAMLET   Do you see yonder cloud that's almost in shape of a   350
camel?

POLONIUS   By the mass, and 'tis like a camel indeed.

HAMLET   Methinks it is like a weasel.

POLONIUS   It is backed like a weasel.

HAMLET   Or like a whale.   355

POLONIUS   Very like a whale.

HAMLET   Then I will come to my mother by and by. [*Aside*]
They fool me to the top of my bent.—I will come by and by.
Leave me, friends. I will. Say so. "By and by" is easily said.

                    [*Exeunt all but* HAMLET.]

'Tis now the very witching time of night,   360
When churchyards yawn, and hell itself breathes out
Contagion to this world. Now could I drink hot blood,
And do such business as the bitter day
Would quake to look on. Soft, now to my mother.
O heart, lose not thy nature! Let not ever   365
The soul of Nero enter this firm bosom.
Let me be cruel, not unnatural.
I will speak daggers to her but use none.

---

342. **sound me:** (1) play me like an instrument; (2) search out my depths, as with a
fathom line; **compass:** full range of tones
343. **organ:** musical instrument
346. **fret:** (1) equip with frets, the ridges for fingering on stringed instruments; (2) annoy
357. **by and by:** very soon; **fool me:** make me play the fool
358. **top . . . bent:** limit of my ability
360. **witching time:** time of witches and evil spells
361. **yawn:** i.e., open their graves
362. **Contagion:** plague, poison
365. **nature:** natural affection
366. **Nero:** Roman emperor (r. 54–68) who murdered his mother Agrippina.
368. **speak daggers:** (a proverbial phrase; see Dent, 8.1)

My tongue and soul in this be hypocrites,
How in my words soever she be shent,   370
To give them seals never my soul consent.   *Exit.*

3.3 [THE CASTLE]

Enter KING, ROSENCRANTZ, *and* GUILDENSTERN.

KING   I like him not, nor stands it safe with us
To let his madness range. Therefore prepare you.
I your commission will forthwith dispatch,
And he to England shall along with you.
The terms of our estate may not endure   5
Hazard so near's as doth hourly grow
Out of his brows.
GUILDENSTERN   We will ourselves provide.
Most holy and religious fear it is
To keep those many many bodies safe
That live and feed upon Your Majesty.   10
ROSENCRANTZ   The single and peculiar life is bound
With all the strength and armor of the mind
To keep itself from noyance, but much more
That spirit upon whose weal depends and rests
The lives of many. The cess of majesty   15
Dies not alone, but like a gulf doth draw
What's near it with it; or it is a massy wheel
Fixed on the summit of the highest mount,
To whose huge spokes ten thousand lesser things
Are mortised and adjoined, which, when it falls,   20
Each small annexment, petty consequence,
Attends the boist'rous ruin. Never alone
Did the king sigh, but with a general groan.
KING   Arm you, I pray you, to this speedy voyage,

369. **hypocrites:** deceivers (because the tongue will threaten harm that the soul will not allow)
370. **How . . . soever:** however much by my words; **shent:** berated, put to shame
371. **give them seals:** i.e., confirm them with deeds
  3. **forthwith dispatch:** immediately prepare
  5. **terms . . . estate:** my position as king
  7. **brows:** i.e., head, perhaps signaled by threatening looks; **provide:** make ready
  8. **fear:** duty
 11. **peculiar:** private
 13. **noyance:** harm
 14. **weal:** welfare
 15. **cess:** decease
 16. **gulf:** whirlpool
 17. **massy:** massive; **wheel:** (an allusion to the wheel of Fortune, often depicted with a king on top and others on the periphery; see 2.2.389–93)
 20. **mortised:** securely fastened
 22. **Attends:** participates in
 24. **Arm:** prepare

For we will fetters put about this fear   25
Which now goes too free-footed.

ROSENCRANTZ   We will haste us.

Exeunt GENTLEMEN [ROSENCRANTZ *and*
GUILDENSTERN].

Enter POLONIUS.

POLONIUS   My lord, he's going to his mother's closet.
Behind the arras I'll convey myself
To hear the process; I'll warrant she'll tax him home.
And, as you said, and wisely was it said,   30
'Tis meet that some more audience than a mother,
Since nature makes them partial, should o'erhear
The speech, of vantage. Fare you well, my liege.
I'll call upon you ere you go to bed
And tell you what I know.

KING   Thanks, dear my lord.   35

Exit [POLONIUS].

Oh, my offense is rank, it smells to heaven;
It hath the primal eldest curse upon't,
A brother's murder. Pray can I not,
Though inclination be as sharp as will;
My stronger guilt defeats my strong intent,   40
And like a man to double business bound
I stand in pause where I shall first begin,
And both neglect. What if this cursèd hand
Were thicker than itself with brother's blood?
Is there not rain enough in the sweet heavens   45
To wash it white as snow? Whereto serves mercy
But to confront the visage of offense?
And what's in prayer but this twofold force,
To be forestallèd ere we come to fall,
Or pardoned being down? Then I'll look up.   50
My fault is past. But, oh, what form of prayer

28. **arras:** curtain, tapestry
29. **process:** proceedings; **warrant:** guarantee; **tax him home:** reprimand him severely
30. **you said:** (Polonius, in fact, made this suggestion, 3.1.183–84.)
31. **meet:** fitting
33. **of vantage:** from the vantage point of concealment
36–72. (Compare the King's speech in Quarto 1, Appendix 1, passage 4, p. 142.)
37. **primal eldest curse:** i.e., the curse of the first fratricide, Cain, who was doomed to till the earth in vain and to become "a vagabond and a renegade" (Genesis 4:11–12). See also 1.2.105, 5.1.68–69.
45–46. **Is . . . snow:** (perhaps an echo of Old Testament passages: Psalms 51:7: "Wash me and I shall be whiter than snow"; Isaiah 1:18: "Though your sins were as crimson, they shall be made white as snow.")
46. **Whereto:** what purpose
49. **forestallèd:** prevented (from sinning)

Can serve my turn? "Forgive me my foul murder"?
That cannot be since I am still possessed
Of those effects for which I did the murder—
My crown, mine own ambition, and my queen.   55
May one be pardoned and retain th'offense?
In the corrupted currents of this world
Offense's gilded hand may shove by justice,
And oft 'tis seen the wicked prize itself
Buys out the law; but 'tis not so above.   60
There is no shuffling, there the action lies
In his true nature, and we ourselves compelled,
Even to the teeth and forehead of our faults,
To give in evidence. What then? What rests?
Try what repentance can. What can it not?   65
Yet what can it when one cannot repent?
Oh, wretched state, oh, bosom black as death!
Oh, limèd soul that, struggling to be free,
Art more engaged! Help, angels, make assay.
Bow, stubborn knees, and heart with strings of steel,   70
Be soft as sinews of the new-born babe.
All may be well. [He kneels.]

       Enter HAMLET.

HAMLET   Now might I do it. But now 'a is a-praying.
And now I'll do't. [He draws his sword.]
                  And so 'a goes to heaven,
And so am I revenged. That would be scanned: 75
A villain kills my father and for that,
I, his sole son, do this same villain send
To heaven.
Why, this is hire and salary, not revenge.
'A took my father grossly, full of bread,   80
With all his crimes broad blown, as flush as May,

    56. **offense:** i.e., that gained by the offense
    57. **currents:** courses
    58. **shove by:** push aside
    59. **wicked prize:** prize won by wickedness
    61. **shuffling:** evasion
61–62. **action . . . nature:** deed is clearly known for what it is. **Action** also means "legal
      proceeding," and this sense continues below in **evidence.**
    63. **to . . . of:** i.e., face to face with
    64. **rests:** remains
    68. **limèd:** caught as a bird in lime (a sticky paste)
    69. **engaged:** attached; **assay:** an attempt
    75. **scanned:** read as follows
    79. **hire and salary:** (Another textual crux, as Q2's "base and silly" is possible but
      suspiciously inferior to the Folio reading, here adopted.)
    80. **grossly . . . bread:** in the sinful enjoyment of earthly pleasures. See Ezekiel
      16:49 on the marks of Sodom's iniquity: "pride, fullness of bread, and abundance
      of idleness."
    81. **broad blown:** in full bloom; **flush:** lusty

+ would've gone to hell anyways
+ would've avoided future conflict
+ proven strength

And how his audit stands who knows save heaven?
But in our circumstance and course of thought,
'Tis heavy with him. And am I then revenged,
To take him in the purging of his soul,   85
When he is fit and seasoned for his passage?
No.
Up, sword, and know thou a more horrid hent.
        [*He sheathes his sword.*]
When he is drunk asleep, or in his rage,

Point of no return — not killing him

Or in th'incestuous pleasure of his bed,   90
At game a-swearing, or about some act
That has no relish of salvation in't—
Then trip him that his heels may kick at heaven,
And that his soul may be as damned and black
As hell, whereto it goes. My mother stays.   95
This physic but prolongs thy sickly days.   *Exit.*
KING   My words fly up, my thoughts remain below.
Words without thoughts never to heaven go.   *Exit.*

3.4 [THE QUEEN'S PRIVATE ROOM]

        Enter [QUEEN] GERTRUDE *and* POLONIUS.

POLONIUS   'A will come straight. Look you lay home to him.
Tell him his pranks have been too broad to bear with,
And that Your Grace hath screened and stood between
Much heat and him. I'll silence me even here.
Pray you, be round.
QUEEN   I'll warrant you. Fear me not.   5
Withdraw, I hear him coming.
                    [POLONIUS *hides behind the arras.*]
        Enter HAMLET.

HAMLET   Now, Mother, what's the matter?
QUEEN   Hamlet, thou hast thy father much offended.

82. **audit:** reckoning
83. **in . . . thought:** from my limited earthly perspective
84. **'Tis . . . him:** i.e., my father's spiritual unreadiness warrants severe punishment in the next life
85. **him:** i.e., Claudius
88. **hent:** (1) act of seizure; (2) intention
92. **relish:** trace
95. **stays:** waits
96. **physic:** medicine (attempt at prayer by the King)
 1. **lay home to:** reprove vigorously
 2. **pranks:** wicked deeds (not merely "jokes"); **broad:** unrestrained
 4. **silence:** (Q1, interestingly, reads "shroud.")
 5. **round:** blunt, severe; **I'll . . . not:** I assure you, don't worry about my part
 8. **father:** i.e., stepfather, Claudius

HAMLET   Mother, you have my father much offended.
QUEEN   Come, come, you answer with an idle tongue.   10
HAMLET   Go, go, you question with a wicked tongue.
QUEEN   Why, how now, Hamlet?
HAMLET   What's the matter now?
QUEEN   Have you forgot me?
HAMLET   No, by the rood, not so.
  You are the Queen, your husband's brother's wife,
  And, would it were not so, you are my mother.   15
QUEEN   Nay, then, I'll set those to you that can speak.
HAMLET   Come, come, and sit you down; you shall not budge.
  You go not till I set you up a glass
  Where you may see the inmost part of you.
QUEEN   What wilt thou do? Thou wilt not murder me?   20
  Help, ho!
POLONIUS [*Behind the arras*]   What ho! Help!
HAMLET [*Drawing*]   How now, a rat?
  [*He thrusts his rapier through the arras.*]
                              Dead for a ducat, dead!
POLONIUS   Oh, I am slain!   [*He falls and dies.*]
QUEEN   O me, what hast thou done?   25
HAMLET   Nay, I know not. Is it the King?
QUEEN   Oh, what a rash and bloody deed is this!
HAMLET   A bloody deed—almost as bad, good Mother,
  As kill a king and marry with his brother.
QUEEN   As kill a king!   30
HAMLET   Ay, lady, it was my word.
       [*He discovers* POLONIUS.]
  Thou wretched, rash, intruding fool, farewell.
  I took thee for thy better; take thy fortune.
  Thou find'st to be too busy is some danger.
  —Leave wringing of your hands. Peace, sit you down,   35
  And let me wring your heart, for so I shall,
  If it be made of penetrable stuff,
  If damnèd custom have not brazed it so
  That it be proof and bulwark against sense.

10. **idle:** foolish
13. **rood:** cross of Christ
18. **glass:** mirror
23. **Dead . . . ducat:** I bet a ducat (gold coin) he is dead.
29. **kill a king:** (The Ghost has never accused the Queen of complicity in the murder, and Gertrude's astonishment at the accusation may confirm her innocence. She explicitly denies involvement in the murder in Q1; see Appendix 1, passage 5, p. 143.)
34. **busy:** meddlesome
38. **brazed:** brazened, hardened
39. **proof and bulwark:** armored and fortified; **sense:** feeling

QUEEN   What have I done, that thou dar'st wag thy tongue   40
  In noise so rude against me?
HAMLET   Such an act
  That blurs the grace and blush of modesty,
  Calls virtue hypocrite, takes off the rose
  From the fair forehead of an innocent love
  And sets a blister there, makes marriage vows   45
  As false as dicers' oaths. Oh, such a deed
  As from the body of contraction plucks
  The very soul, and sweet religion makes
  A rhapsody of words. Heaven's face does glow
  O'er this solidity and compound mass   50
  With heated visage, as against the doom,
  Is thought-sick at the act.
QUEEN   Ay me, what act
  That roars so loud, and thunders in the index?
HAMLET   [*Showing her two likenesses*]
  Look here upon this picture, and on this,
  The counterfeit presentment of two brothers.   55
  See what a grace was seated on this brow,
  Hyperion's curls, the front of Jove himself,
  An eye like Mars to threaten and command,
  A station like the herald Mercury
  New-lighted on a heaven-kissing hill—   60
  A combination and a form indeed
  Where every god did seem to set his seal
  To give the world assurance of a man.
  This was your husband. Look you now what follows:
  Here is your husband, like a mildewed ear   65

---

41. **act:** i.e., the remarriage or perhaps adultery. Hamlet seems to drop the charge of murder.
45. **sets . . . there:** (perhaps an allusion to the contemporary practice of branding harlots on the forehead)
46. **dicer:** one who gambles with dice
47. **contraction:** the marriage contract
48. **sweet religion makes:** makes the marriage vows
49. **rhapsody:** jumble
50. **solidity . . . mass:** i.e., earth
51. **doom:** Last Judgment
52. **the act:** i.e., Gertrude's second marriage
53. **index:** table of contents
55. **counterfeit presentment:** portrayed representation (perhaps hung pictures or miniatures worn on chains)
57. **Hyperion:** the sun god (a Titan); **front:** brow
59. **station:** way of standing; **Mercury:** winged messenger of the gods
60. **New-lighted:** newly alighted
62. **set his seal:** i.e., give his approval
65. **ear:** (of grain)

Blasting his wholesome brother. Have you eyes?
Could you on this fair mountain leave to feed
And batten on this moor? Ha, have you eyes?
You cannot call it love, for at your age
The heyday in the blood is tame, it's humble,   70
And waits upon the judgment, and what judgment
Would step from this to this? Sense, sure, you have,
Else could you not have motion, but sure that sense
Is apoplexed, for madness would not err,
Nor sense to ecstasy was ne'er so thralled   75
But it reserved some quantity of choice
To serve in such a difference. What devil was't
That thus hath cozened you at hoodman-blind?
Eyes without feeling, feeling without sight,
Ears without hands or eyes, smelling sans all,   80
Or but a sickly part of one true sense
Could not so mope. Oh, shame! Where is thy blush?
Rebellious hell,
If thou canst mutine in a matron's bones,
To flaming youth let virtue be as wax,   85
And melt in her own fire. Proclaim no shame
When the compulsive ardor gives the charge,
Since frost itself as actively doth burn,
And reason pardons will.
QUEEN   O Hamlet, speak no more.
Thou turn'st my very eyes into my soul.   90
And there I see such black and grainèd spots
As will leave there their tinct.

---

66. **Blasting:** blighting. The passage echoes Genesis 41: 5–7, wherein Pharaoh dreams
    that seven thin ears of corn, "blasted with the east wind," devour seven "rank and full
    ears."
67. **leave to feed:** stop feeding
68. **batten:** glut yourself; **moor:** waste ground (with a pun on "Moor," a dark-skinned
    person from the East)
70. **heyday:** state of excitement; **blood:** passions
72. **Sense:** perception through the five senses
73. **motion:** locomotion, movement
74. **apoplexed:** paralyzed; **err:** misperceive (as badly as you)
75. **ecstasy:** frenzy; **thralled:** captive
76. **quantity of choice:** power of discrimination
78. **cozened:** tricked; **hoodman-blind:** blind-man's buff
80. **sans:** without
82. **mope:** be powerless
84. **mutine:** incite mutiny
85. **wax:** a candle
87. **compulsive ardor:** compelling desire (of youth)
88. **frost:** i.e., old age
89. **pardons will:** excuses (rather than restrains) desire
91. **grainèd:** engrained, deep-dyed
92. **tinct:** color

HAMLET   Nay, but to live
  In the rank sweat of an enseamèd bed,
  Stewed in corruption, honeying and making love
  Over the nasty sty—
QUEEN   Oh, speak to me no more.   95
  These words like daggers enter in my ears;
  No more, sweet Hamlet.
HAMLET   A murderer and a villain,
  A slave that is not twentieth part the tithe
  Of your precedent lord, a vice of kings,
  A cutpurse of the empire and the rule,   100
  That from a shelf the precious diadem stole
  And put it in his pocket—
QUEEN   No more!
HAMLET   A king of shreds and patches—
         Enter GHOST.

  Save me and hover o'er me with your wings,
  You heavenly guards!—What would your gracious figure?   105
QUEEN   Alas, he's mad!
HAMLET   Do you not come your tardy son to chide,
  That, lapsed in time and passion, lets go by
  Th'important acting of your dread command?
  Oh, say!   110
GHOST   Do not forget. This visitation
  Is but to whet thy almost blunted purpose.
  But look, amazement on thy mother sits.
  Oh, step between her and her fighting soul.
  Conceit in weakest bodies strongest works.   115
  Speak to her, Hamlet.
HAMLET   How is it with you, lady?
QUEEN   Alas, how is't with you,
  That you do bend your eye on vacancy,

---

93. **enseamèd**: loaded with grease. "Seam" is animal fat.
94. **Stewed**: cooked, bathed (with a suggestion of **stews**, "a brothel"); **honeying**: using sweet or flattering words
96. **like daggers**: (Hamlet has fulfilled his resolve to "speak daggers" [3.2.368] to his mother.)
98. **tithe**: tenth part
99. **precedent**: former; **vice**: (1) wickedness; (2) buffoon (with reference to the Vice of the medieval morality play)
100. **cutpurse**: thief
103. **shreds and patches**: i.e., motley, the traditional variegated costume of the fool
103. **s.d.**: (Q1 specifies that the Ghost enters "in his nightgown.")
105. **heavenly guards**: angels
109. **important**: urgent
112. **whet**: sharpen
113. **amazement**: confusion
115. **Conceit**: imagination

And with th'incorporal air do hold discourse?
Forth at your eyes your spirits wildly peep,   120
And, as the sleeping soldiers in th'alarm,
Your bedded hair, like life in excrements,
Start up and stand an end. O gentle son,
Upon the heat and flame of thy distemper
Sprinkle cool patience. Whereon do you look?   125
HAMLET   On him, on him! Look you how pale he glares!
His form and cause conjoined, preaching to stones
Would make them capable. [*To* GHOST] Do not look upon
    me,
Lest with this piteous action you convert
My stern effects. Then what I have to do   130
Will want true color—tears perchance for blood.
QUEEN   To whom do you speak this?
HAMLET   Do you see nothing there?
QUEEN   Nothing at all, yet all that is I see.
HAMLET   Nor did you nothing hear?   135
QUEEN   No, nothing but ourselves.
HAMLET   Why, look you there, look how it steals away,
My father in his habit as he lived.
Look where he goes even now out at the portal!

                                        Exit GHOST.

QUEEN   This is the very coinage of your brain.   140
This bodiless creation ecstasy
Is very cunning in.
HAMLET   My pulse as yours doth temperately keep time,
And makes as healthful music. It is not madness
That I have uttered. Bring me to the test,   145
And I the matter will reword, which madness
Would gambol from. Mother, for love of grace,

119. **incorporal:** immaterial
120. **spirits:** vital forces, conceived of as fluids that permeated the blood and
     controlled emotions
121. **in th'alarm:** roused by an alarm
122. **bedded:** flat-lying; **like . . . excrements:** as if hair, a lifeless outgrowth
     (**excrements**), had come to life
123. **an:** on
127. **form and cause:** appearance and motive
128. **capable:** receptive. The Ghost would make even stones listen to his words.
129–30. **convert . . . effects:** turn me from my harsh purposed actions
131. **want true color:** be a pale imitation of my real duty. (Hamlet will shed tears
     instead of someone's blood.)
138. **habit:** clothing
139. **portal:** door
140. **very coinage:** mere creation
141. **ecstasy:** madness
146. **reword:** relate precisely (a sign of sanity)
147. **gambol:** leap, skip

Lay not that flattering unction to your soul
That not your trespass but my madness speaks.
It will but skin and film the ulcerous place,   150
Whiles rank corruption, mining all within,
Infects unseen. Confess yourself to heaven,
Repent what's past, avoid what is to come,
And do not spread the compost on the weeds,
To make them ranker. Forgive me this my virtue,   155
For in the fatness of these pursy times
Virtue itself of vice must pardon beg,
Yea, curb and woo for leave to do him good.
QUEEN   O Hamlet, thou hast cleft my heart in twain.
HAMLET   Oh, throw away the worser part of it,   160
And live the purer with the other half.
Good night. But go not to my uncle's bed.
Assume a virtue, if you have it not.
That monster, Custom, who all sense doth eat,
Of habits devil, is angel yet in this,   165
That to the use of actions fair and good
He likewise gives a frock or livery
That aptly is put on. Refrain tonight,
And that shall lend a kind of easiness
To the next abstinence, the next more easy;   170
For use almost can change the stamp of nature,
And either shame the devil, or throw him out
With wondrous potency. Once more, good night.
And when you are desirous to be blessed,
I'll blessing beg of you. [*He gestures to* POLONIUS.]
For this same lord,   175
I do repent; but heaven hath pleased it so
To punish me with this, and this with me,

148. **unction:** ointment
150. **skin:** cover
151. **rank:** gross; **mining:** digging under the surface of
155. **this my virtue:** my admonitions and virtuous talk
156. **fatness:** grossness; **pursy:** flabby
158. **curb:** bow, cringe; **leave:** permission
159. **twain:** two
164. **all . . . eat:** consumes all natural feeling and common sense
165. **Of habits devil:** who is like the devil in his tendency to encourage evil
166. **use:** habit
167. **He:** i.e., Custom; **livery:** garb, outward appearance
168. **aptly:** easily. Custom makes bad or good actions easy to justify and to perform.
171. **stamp of nature:** natural inclinations
174. **desirous . . . blessed:** i.e., repentant
175. **blessing beg:** i.e., act as a dutiful son. Catholic popular traditions included the
     blessing of children by parents, which entailed the consecration of the child to God
     and the invocation of God's protection and favor.
176. **it:** itself

That I must be their scourge and minister.
I will bestow him and will answer well
The death I gave him. So again, good night.   180
I must be cruel only to be kind.
This bad begins, and worse remains behind.
One word more, good lady.
QUEEN   What shall I do?
HAMLET   Not this by no means that I bid you do:
Let the bloat king tempt you again to bed,   185
Pinch wanton on your cheek, call you his mouse,
And let him, for a pair of reechy kisses
Or paddling in your neck with his damned fingers,
Make you to ravel all this matter out
That I essentially am not in madness,   190
But mad in craft. 'Twere good you let him know,
For who that's but a queen—fair, sober, wise—
Would from a paddock, from a bat, a gib,
Such dear concernings hide? Who would do so?
No, in despite of sense and secrecy,   195
Unpeg the basket on the house's top,
Let the birds fly, and, like the famous ape,
To try conclusions, in the basket creep
And break your own neck down.
QUEEN   Be thou assured, if words be made of breath,   200
And breath of life, I have no life to breathe
What thou hast said to me.
HAMLET   I must to England. You know that?
QUEEN   Alack,
I had forgot. 'Tis so concluded on.
HAMLET   There's letters sealed, and my two schoolfellows,   205

178. **their . . . minister:** heaven's lash and agent of justice (to punish others and,
    perhaps, himself)
179. **bestow:** put away
182. **This:** i.e., the killing of Polonius; **behind:** to come
185. **bloat:** bloated, puffy with self-indulgence
186. **Pinch wanton:** i.e., leave marks of his pinching which proclaim you a wanton, or
    loose woman
187. **reechy:** filthy
188. **paddling in:** fingering playfully
189. **ravel . . . out:** reveal everything
191. **in craft:** in contrivance, by cunning; **'Twere . . . know:** (said sarcastically, as are
    the next eight lines)
192. **but:** merely
193. **paddock:** toad; **gib:** tomcat. These animals and the bat were witches' familiars.
194. **dear concernings:** important and pertinent matters
196. **Unpeg the basket:** open the cage. The story, now lost, tells of an ape who freed
    birds from a cage on a rooftop and then, in foolish imitation of their flight, crept
    into the cage and then out, only to fall to his death.
198. **try conclusions:** experiment
199. **down:** (1) falling down; (2) utterly

Whom I will trust as I will adders fanged,
They bear the mandate; they must sweep my way
And marshal me to knavery. Let it work.
For 'tis the sport to have the enginer
Hoist with his own petard, and 't shall go hard   210
But I will delve one yard below their mines
And blow them at the moon. Oh, 'tis most sweet,
When in one line two crafts directly meet.
This man shall set me packing.
I'll lug the guts into the neighbor room.   215
Mother, good night. Indeed, this counselor
Is now most still, most secret, and most grave,
Who was in life a most foolish, prating knave.
—Come, sir, to draw toward an end with you.
—Good night, Mother.   *Exit* [HAMLET *dragging* POLONIUS].   220

4.1 [THE CASTLE]

Enter KING *to* QUEEN, *with* ROSENCRANTZ *and*
GUILDENSTERN.

KING   There's matter in these sighs, these profound heaves,
You must translate. 'Tis fit we understand them.
Where is your son?
QUEEN   Bestow this place on us a little while.

[*Exeunt* ROSENCRANTZ *and* GUILDENSTERN.]

Ah, mine own lord, what have I seen tonight!   5
KING   What, Gertrude? How does Hamlet?
QUEEN   Mad as the sea and wind when both contend
Which is the mightier. In his lawless fit,
Behind the arras hearing something stir,
Whips out his rapier, cries "A rat, a rat!"   10
And in this brainish apprehension kills
The unseen good old man.

---

206. **adders:** poisonous snakes
207. **mandate:** orders for Hamlet's removal; **sweep:** i.e., prepare
209–10. **enginer . . . petard:** military engineer blown up by his own bomb
210–11. **'t shall . . . But:** (1) there will be serious consequences unless; (2) unless luck is against me
211. **delve:** dig; **mines:** tunnels used in attacking a town
213. **in one line:** i.e., on a collision course; **crafts:** (1) tricks; (2) boats
219. **draw . . . end:** finish up
4.1. **s.d.:** (Because there is no exit for the Queen in Q2, Q1, and F at the end of 3.4, and because the action appears to be continuous, the notation for the Queen's entrance in Q2 4.1 appears to be an error. Editorial tradition, problematically, has placed an act and scene division here, which is retained above simply for ease of cross reference rather than for marking any shift in dramatic action.)
1. **matter:** significance
11. **brainish apprehension:** headstrong conception

KING   Oh, heavy deed!
  It had been so with us, had we been there.
  His liberty is full of threats to all—
  To you yourself, to us, to everyone.   15
  Alas, how shall this bloody deed be answered?
  It will be laid to us, whose providence
  Should have kept short, restrained, and out of haunt
  This mad young man. But so much was our love,
  We would not understand what was most fit,   20
  But, like the owner of a foul disease,
  To keep it from divulging, let it feed
  Even on the pith of life. Where is he gone?
QUEEN   To draw apart the body he hath killed,
  O'er whom his very madness, like some ore   25
  Among a mineral of metals base,
  Shows itself pure: 'a weeps for what is done.
KING   O Gertrude, come away!
  The sun no sooner shall the mountains touch
  But we will ship him hence, and this vile deed   30
  We must with all our majesty and skill
  Both countenance and excuse.

          Enter ROSENCRANTZ *and* GUILDENSTERN.

                              —Ho, Guildenstern!
  Friends both, go join you with some further aid.
  Hamlet in madness hath Polonius slain,
  And from his mother's closet hath he dragged him.   35
  Go seek him out, speak fair, and bring the body
  Into the chapel. I pray you, haste in this.
          [*Exeunt* ROSENCRANTZ *and* GUILDENSTERN.]
  Come, Gertrude, we'll call up our wisest friends
  And let them know both what we mean to do
  And what's untimely done. So, haply, slander,   40
  Whose whisper o'er the world's diameter
  As level as the cannon to his blank
  Transports his poisoned shot, may miss our name

12. **heavy:** grievous
17. **providence:** foresight
18. **short:** i.e., on a short leash; **haunt:** company
22. **divulging:** becoming known
23. **pith:** marrow
25. **ore:** precious metal
26. **mineral:** (1) metallic vein; (2) mine
32. **countenance:** bear, face
40. **And . . . done:** (The second half of this line is missing and editors have conjectured a
    phrase like "So, haply, slander" in order to supply a subject for the following lines.)
41. **diameter:** extent
42. **As level:** with as direct aim; **his blank:** its target center at point-blank range

And hit the woundless air. Oh, come away.
My soul is full of discord and dismay.   45

Exeunt.

4.2 [THE CASTLE]

Enter HAMLET.

HAMLET   Safely stowed. But soft, what noise? Who calls on
Hamlet? Oh, here they come.

[*Enter* ROSENCRANTZ, GUILDENSTERN, *and others.*]

ROSENCRANTZ   What have you done, my lord, with the dead
body?

HAMLET   Compound it with dust, whereto 'tis kin.   5

ROSENCRANTZ   Tell us where 'tis, that we may take it thence,
and bear it to the chapel.

HAMLET   Do not believe it.

ROSENCRANTZ   Believe what?

HAMLET   That I can keep your counsel and not mine own.   10
Besides, to be demanded of a sponge! What replication
should be made by the son of a king?

ROSENCRANTZ   Take you me for a sponge, my lord?

HAMLET   Ay, sir, that soaks up the King's countenance, his
rewards, his authorities. But such officers do the King best   15
service in the end. He keeps them, like an ape, in the corner of his jaw, first mouthed to be last swallowed. When he
needs what you have gleaned, it is but squeezing you, and,
sponge, you shall be dry again.

ROSENCRANTZ   I understand you not, my lord.   20

HAMLET   I am glad of it. A knavish speech sleeps in a foolish
ear.

ROSENCRANTZ   My lord, you must tell us where the body is
and go with us to the King.

HAMLET   The body is with the King, but the King is not with   25
the body. The King is a thing.

44. **woundless:** invulnerable
 5. **Compound:** compounded. Or the verb could be a mocking imperative. On dust, see 2.2.269n.
10. **counsel:** secrets
11. **demanded of:** questioned by; **replication:** reply (a legal term)
14. **countenance:** favor
16. **ape:** (Q2 reads "apple," which appears to be an error; the correct reading is signaled by a similar passage in Q1 earlier, 9.215–16; "he doth keep you as an ape doth nuts—in the corner of his jaw.")
21. **sleeps in:** is meaningless to
25. **The body . . . body:** The corpse of Polonius is in the palace but not near the king. Saying that the King is not with the body, Hamlet might also mean that Claudius is not yet dead. He also alludes to the doctrine of the "king's two bodies," one the immaterial office of kingship, the other his mortal human self. Hamlet suggests as well that Claudius wears the crown but does not possess true kingship.

GUILDENSTERN   A thing, my lord?
HAMLET   Of nothing. Bring me to him.

Exeunt.

4.3 [THE CASTLE]

Enter KING, *and two or three.*

KING   I have sent to seek him and to find the body.
How dangerous is it that this man goes loose!
Yet must not we put the strong law on him;
He's loved of the distracted multitude,
Who like not in their judgment, but their eyes,   5
And where 'tis so, th'offender's scourge is weighed,
But never the offense. To bear all smooth and even,
This sudden sending him away must seem
Deliberate pause. Diseases desperate grown
By desperate appliance are relieved,   10
Or not at all.

Enter ROSENCRANTZ, [GUILDENSTERN,] *and all the rest.*

How now, what hath befall'n?
ROSENCRANTZ   Where the dead body is bestowed, my lord,
We cannot get from him.
KING   But where is he?
ROSENCRANTZ   Without, my lord, guarded, to know your
pleasure.
KING   Bring him before us.
ROSENCRANTZ   Ho! Bring in the lord.   15

They enter [with HAMLET].

KING   Now, Hamlet, where's Polonius?
HAMLET   At supper.
KING   At supper? Where?
HAMLET   Not where he eats, but where 'a is eaten. A certain
convocation of politic worms are e'en at him. Your worm is   20
your only emperor for diet. We fat all creatures else to fat
us, and we fat ourselves for maggots. Your fat king and your

---

  4. **of:** by; **distracted:** troubled, irrational
  5. **their eyes:** by appearances
  6. **scourge:** punishment
  7. **bear . . . even:** manage affairs without offense
  9. **Deliberate pause:** well-considered action
9–10. **Diseases . . . relieved:** Desperate diseases require desperate remedies
         (**appliance**) (a proverbial sentiment; see Dent, 357).
 14. **Without:** outside
 20. **convocation . . . worms:** (A joking allusion to the Diet of Worms [1521], an
         assembly [**convocation**] at the city of Worms, Germany, which charged Martin
         Luther with heresy.); **politic:** cunning

lean beggar is but variable service—two dishes, but to one
table.That's the end.

KING   Alas, alas!   25

HAMLET   A man may fish with the worm that hath eat of a
king, and eat of the fish that hath fed of that worm.

KING   What dost thou mean by this?

HAMLET   Nothing but to show you how a king may go a prog-
ress through the guts of a beggar.   30

KING   Where is Polonius?

HAMLET   In heaven. Send thither to see. If your messenger
find him not there, seek him i'th'other place yourself. But,
indeed, if you find him not within this month, you shall
nose him as you go up the stairs into the lobby.   35

KING   [*To some* ATTENDANTS] Go seek him there.

HAMLET   'A will stay till you come.

                                        [*Exeunt* ATTENDANTS.]

KING   Hamlet, this deed, for thine especial safety—
Which we do tender, as we dearly grieve
For that which thou hast done—must send thee hence.   40
Therefore prepare thyself.
The bark is ready, and the wind at help,
Th'associates tend, and everything is bent
For England.

HAMLET   For England?   45

KING   Ay, Hamlet.

HAMLET   Good.

KING   So is it, if thou knew'st our purposes.

HAMLET   I see a cherub that sees them. But come, for England.
Farewell, dear Mother.   50

KING   Thy loving father, Hamlet.

HAMLET   My mother. Father and mother is man and wife;
man and wife is one flesh, so, my mother. Come, for England.
                                                                 Exit.

KING   Follow him at foot; tempt him with speed aboard.
Delay it not. I'll have him hence tonight.   55
Away, for everything is sealed and done

   23. **service:** food served at table
   26. **hath eat:** hath eaten (pronounced *et*)
29–30. **progress:** official (especially royal) journey
   39. **tender:** feel compassion for
   42. **bark:** ship
   43. **tend:** wait; **bent:** prepared
   49. **cherub:** angel (from *Cherubim,* the second of the nine orders of angels, having
       the special attribute of knowledge and vision). Hamlet hints that he does see
       Claudius's darker purpose.
   53. **one flesh:** (Hamlet echoes Biblical formulations; e.g., Matthew 19:5–6, Mark
       10:8, and the marriage service, "they two shall be one flesh.")
   54. **at foot:** at his heels, closely; **tempt:** urge

That else leans on th'affair. Pray you, make haste.
                    [*Exeunt all but the* KING.]
And, England, if my love thou hold'st at aught—
As my great power thereof may give thee sense,
Since yet thy cicatrice looks raw and red   60
After the Danish sword, and thy free awe
Pays homage to us—thou mayst not coldly set
Our sovereign process, which imports at full,
By letters congruing to that effect,
The present death of Hamlet. Do it, England,   65
For like the hectic in my blood he rages,
And thou must cure me. Till I know 'tis done,
Howe'er my haps, my joys will ne'er begin.   *Exit.*

4.4 [THE COAST OF DENMARK]

Enter FORTINBRAS *with his army over the stage.*

FORTINBRAS   Go, Captain, from me greet the Danish king.
Tell him that by his license Fortinbras
Craves the conveyance of a promised march
Over his kingdom. You know the rendezvous.
If that His Majesty would aught with us,   5
We shall express our duty in his eye;
And let him know so.
CAPTAIN   I will do't, my lord.
FORTINBRAS   Go softly on.
                    [*Exeunt all but the* CAPTAIN.]

Enter HAMLET, ROSENCRANTZ, [GUILDENSTERN,] *etc.*

HAMLET   Good sir, whose powers are these?
CAPTAIN   They are of Norway, sir.
HAMLET   How purposed, sir, I pray you?   10
CAPTAIN   Against some part of Poland.

57. **leans on:** depends on, appertains to
58. **England:** i.e., King of England; **at aught:** at any value
59. **thereof . . . sense:** over you may have taught you to appreciate
60. **cicatrice:** scar
61. **free awe:** uncompelled respect
62. **set:** regard, rate
63. **process:** command
64. **congruing:** agreeing
65. **present:** immediate
66. **hectic:** continual fever
68. **haps:** fortunes
 2. **license:** permission
 3. **the conveyance of:** an escort during
 5. **aught:** anything
 6. **duty:** respect; **eye:** presence
 7. **let . . . so:** (a command)
 8. **softly:** slowly

HAMLET   Who commands them, sir?

CAPTAIN   The nephew to old Norway, Fortinbras.

HAMLET   Goes it against the main of Poland, sir,   15
Or for some frontier?

CAPTAIN   Truly to speak, and with no addition,
We go to gain a little patch of ground
That hath in it no profit but the name.
To pay five ducats, five, I would not farm it.   20
Nor will it yield to Norway or the Pole
A ranker rate, should it be sold in fee.

HAMLET   Why, then the Polack never will defend it.

CAPTAIN   Yes, it is already garrisoned.

HAMLET   Two thousand souls and twenty thousand ducats   25
Will not debate the question of this straw.
This is th'imposthume of much wealth and peace
That inward breaks and shows no cause without
Why the man dies. I humbly thank you, sir.

CAPTAIN   God be wi'you, sir.   [*Exit.*]   30

ROSENCRANTZ   Will't please you go, my lord?

HAMLET   I'll be with you straight. Go a little before.
                              [*Exeunt all but* HAMLET.]
How all occasions do inform against me
And spur my dull revenge! What is a man,
If his chief good and market of his time   no purpose   35
Be but to sleep and feed? A beast, no more.
Sure he that made us with such large discourse,
Looking before and after, gave us not
That capability and godlike reason
To fust in us unused. Now, whether it be   40
Bestial oblivion, or some craven scruple
Of thinking too precisely on th'event—
A thought which, quartered, hath but one part wisdom
And ever three parts coward—I do not know
Why yet I live to say "This thing's to do,"   45

15. **main:** main part
17. **addition:** ornament
19. **name:** i.e., the mere name of conquest
20. **To . . . it:** I would not pay even five ducats to rent it
22. **ranker:** higher; **in fee:** outright
24. **garrisoned:** furnished with defending troops
26. **debate . . . straw:** contest this trivial matter
27. **imposthume:** pus-filled swelling
28. **without:** on the outside
33. **inform:** bring a charge or complaint
35. **market:** profit
37. **discourse:** power of reasoning
40. **fust:** become moldy
41. **oblivion:** forgetfulness; **craven scruple:** cowardly uncertainty
42. **precisely:** punctiliously, with complete propriety; **event:** outcome

Sith I have cause, and will, and strength, and means
To do't. Examples gross as earth exhort me:
Witness this army of such mass and charge,
Led by a delicate and tender prince,
Whose spirit with divine ambition puffed   50
Makes mouths at the invisible event,
Exposing what is mortal and unsure
To all that fortune, death, and danger dare,
Even for an eggshell. Rightly to be great
Is not to stir without great argument,   55
But greatly to find quarrel in a straw
When honor's at the stake. How stand I then,
That have a father killed, a mother stained,
Excitements of my reason and my blood,
And let all sleep, while to my shame I see   60
Th'imminent death of twenty thousand men
That for a fantasy and trick of fame,
Go to their graves like beds, fight for a plot
Whereon the numbers cannot try the cause,
Which is not tomb enough and continent   65
To hide the slain? Oh, from this time forth,
My thoughts be bloody or be nothing worth!   *Exit.*

4.5 [THE CASTLE]

Enter HORATIO, [QUEEN] GERTRUDE, *and a* GENTLEMAN.

QUEEN   I will not speak with her.
GENTLEMAN   She is importunate,
   Indeed distract. Her mood will needs be pitied.
QUEEN   What would she have?
GENTLEMAN   She speaks much of her father, says she hears
   There's tricks i'the world, and hems, and beats her heart,   5
   Spurns enviously at straws, speaks things in doubt

---

   46. **Sith:** since
   47. **gross:** obvious
   48. **charge:** expense
   49. **delicate and tender:** fine and youthful
   51. **mouths:** faces (in a show of contempt)
54–57. **Rightly . . . stake:** greatness does not consist in fighting only on great provoca-
      tion, but on the slightest matter (**a straw**) if honor is at risk (**at the stake**)
   62. **fantasy:** illusion; **trick:** (1) trifle; (2) deceit
   63. **plot:** piece of land
   64. **Whereon . . . cause:** on which there are more people to fight than land to stage
      the battle
   65. **continent:** container
    1. **importunate:** persistently troublesome
    2. **distract:** mad
    5. **tricks:** deceits; **hems:** makes the "hem" sound, a cough or a throat clearing
    6. **Spurns . . . straws:** takes offense peevishly at trivial things; **in doubt:** with no
      clear meaning

That carry but half sense. Her speech is nothing,
Yet the unshapèd use of it doth move
The hearers to collection; they yawn at it,
And botch the words up fit to their own thoughts,   10
Which, as her winks, and nods, and gestures yield them,
Indeed would make one think there might be thought,
Though nothing sure, yet much unhappily.

HORATIO   'Twere good she were spoken with, for she may strew
Dangerous conjectures in ill-breeding minds.   15
Let her come in.

                         [*Exit* GENTLEMAN.]

QUEEN   [*Aside*] To my sick soul, as sin's true nature is,
Each toy seems prologue to some great amiss.
So full of artless jealousy is guilt,
It spills itself in fearing to be spilt.   20

     Enter OPHELIA.

OPHELIA   Where is the beauteous majesty of Denmark?
QUEEN   How now, Ophelia?
OPHELIA (*She sings.*)   "How should I your true love know
     From another one?
  By his cockle hat and staff   25
     And his sandal shoon."
QUEEN   Alas, sweet lady, what imports this song?
OPHELIA   Say you? Nay, pray you, mark.
  "He is dead and gone, lady,   *Song.*
     He is dead and gone;   30
  At his head a grass green turf,
     At his heels a stone."
  Oho!
QUEEN   Nay, but Ophelia—
OPHELIA   Pray you, mark.   35
  [*Sings*] "White his shroud as the mountain snow"—

---

    7. **nothing:** nonsense
    8. **unshapèd use:** disordered manner
    9. **collection:** inferences about meaning; **yawn:** gape
  10. **botch:** patch; **fit** fitted
  11. **Which:** i.e. the words; **yield:** represent
  12. **thought:** supposed, conjectured
  13. **unhappily:** 1) unskillfully; 2) maliciously
  18. **toy:** trifle; **amiss:** disaster
18–20. (Quotation marks in Q1 may indicate wise or proverbial sayings.)
  19. **artless jealousy:** uncontrollable suspicion
  20. **spills . . . spilt:** destroys itself in fearing to be destroyed
  20. **s.d.:** (Q1 adds "playing on a lute, and her hair down, singing"; F1 describes her as
     "distracted.")
  25. **cockle hat:** a hat with a **cockle,** or shell, worn by pilgrims who visited the shrine
     of Saint James of Compostella in Spain
  26. **shoon:** shoes
  32. **stone:** gravestone
  33. **Oho:** (a sigh or groan)

Enter KING.

QUEEN   Alas, look here, my lord.

OPHELIA   "Larded all with sweet flowers;   *Song.*
  Which bewept to the ground did not go
   With true-love showers."   40

KING   How do you, pretty lady?

OPHELIA   Well, God 'ild you. They say the owl was a baker's
daughter. Lord, we know what we are, but know not what
we may be. God be at your table.

KING   Conceit upon her father.   45

OPHELIA   Pray, let's have no words of this; but when they ask
you what it means, say you this:

  "Tomorrow is Saint Valentine's day,   *Song.*
   All in the morning betime,
  And I a maid at your window,   50
   To be your Valentine.
  Then up he rose and donned his clothes,
   And dupped the chamber door,
  Let in the maid, that out a maid
   Never departed more."   55

KING   Pretty Ophelia.

OPHELIA   Indeed, without an oath, I'll make an end on't:

[*Sings*] "By Gis and by Saint Charity,
   Alack, and fie for shame!
  Young men will do't if they come to't;   60
   By Cock, they are to blame.
  Quoth she, 'Before you tumbled me,
   You promised me to wed.'"

He answers:
  "'So would I ha' done, by yonder sun,   65
   An thou hadst not come to my bed.'"

---

38. **Larded:** i.e., decorated
39. **Which bewept:** who lamented; **not:** (This word, unexpected and unmetrical, refers to the secret [**hugger-mugger**, 82] burial of Polonius.)
40. **showers:** i.e., tears
42. **'ild:** yield (i.e., reward)
42–43. **owl . . . daughter** (an allusion to a folktale about a baker's daughter, turned into an owl for being stingy with bread for a beggar who was really Jesus)
44. **God . . . table:** (a blessing before meals)
45. **Conceit:** fanciful thinking
48. **Valentine's:** (The song alludes to the belief that the first girl seen by a man on Valentine's Day was his valentine or true love.)
49. **betime:** early
53. **dupped:** opened
54. **a maid:** as a virgin
58. **Gis:** Jesus
61. **Cock:** (a perversion of "God" in oaths, with a bawdy pun)
62. **tumbled me:** took my virginity
66. **An:** if

KING   How long hath she been thus?

OPHELIA   I hope all will be well. We must be patient, but I
cannot choose but weep to think they would lay him i'the
cold ground. My brother shall know of it. And so I thank   70
you for your good counsel.—Come, my coach! Good night,
ladies, good night. Sweet ladies, good night, good night.

                                                    [*Exit.*]

KING   Follow her close; give her good watch, I pray you.

                                          [*Exit* HORATIO.]

Oh, this is the poison of deep grief; it springs
All from her father's death—and now behold!   75
O Gertrude, Gertrude,
When sorrows come, they come not single spies,
But in battalions. First, her father slain;
Next, your son gone, and he most violent author
Of his own just remove; the people muddied,   80
Thick and unwholesome in thoughts and whispers
For good Polonius' death—and we have done but greenly
In hugger-mugger to inter him; poor Ophelia,
Divided from herself and her fair judgment,
Without the which we are pictures or mere beasts;   85
Last, and as much containing as all these,
Her brother is in secret come from France,
Feeds on this wonder, keeps himself in clouds,
And wants not buzzers to infect his ear
With pestilent speeches of his father's death,   90
Wherein necessity, of matter beggared,
Will nothing stick our person to arraign
In ear and ear. O my dear Gertrude, this,
Like to a murdering piece, in many places
Gives me superfluous death.   95
        A noise within.

KING   Attend!
Where is my Switzers? Let them guard the door.

---

77. **spies:** scouts
80. **muddied:** stirred up, confused
82. **greenly:** unwisely
83. **hugger-mugger:** secrecy
85. **pictures:** mere semblances (of human beings)
88. **in clouds:** i.e., of suspicion
89. **buzzers:** gossips
91. **of matter beggared:** lacking facts
92. **stick:** hesitate; **arraign:** accuse
93. **In . . . ear:** to everyone
94. **murdering piece:** cannon that fires many small shots
95. **Gives . . . : death:** kills me over and over
96. **Attend:** listen
97. **Switzers:** Swiss guards, mercenaries

Enter a MESSENGER.

What is the matter?

MESSENGER   Save yourself, my lord!
The ocean, overpeering of his list,
Eats not the flats with more impiteous haste   100
Than young Laertes, in a riotous head,
O'erbears your officers. The rabble call him lord,
And, as the world were now but to begin,
Antiquity forgot, custom not known,
The ratifiers and props of every word,   105
They cry, "Choose we! Laertes shall be king!"
Caps, hands, and tongues applaud it to the clouds,
"Laertes shall be king! Laertes king!" *A noise within.*

QUEEN   How cheerfully on the false trail they cry.
Oh, this is counter, you false Danish dogs!   110

Enter LAERTES *with* OTHERS.

KING   The doors are broke.
LAERTES   Where is this king?—Sirs, stand you all without.
ALL   No, let's come in.
LAERTES   I pray you, give me leave.
ALL   We will, we will.   115
LAERTES   I thank you. Keep the door. [OTHERS *retire.*]
                   O thou vile king,
Give me my father!
QUEEN [*Holding him*]   Calmly, good Laertes.
LAERTES   That drop of blood that's calm proclaims me
   bastard,
Cries cuckold to my father, brands the harlot
Even here, between the chaste unsmirchèd brows   120
Of my true mother.
KING   What is the cause, Laertes,
That thy rebellion looks so giant-like?
Let him go, Gertrude; do not fear our person.
There's such divinity doth hedge a king,

99. **overpeering . . . list:** overflowing its boundaries
100. **flats:** flatlands; **impiteous:** ruthless, unpitying
101. **head:** army
103. **as:** as if
105. **ratifiers and props:** confirmers and supporters (referring to **antiquity** and **custom**, now unused)
107. **Caps:** (i.e., caps are thrown into the air)
110. **counter:** in the opposite direction (a hunting term)
119. **cuckold:** husband of an unfaithful wife. Laertes thinks calmness an unnatural response that would show him to be no true son and his mother a harlot.
123. **fear our:** fear for my
124. **hedge:** protect as with a surrounding hedge

That treason can but peep to what it would,   125
Acts little of his will. Tell me, Laertes,
Why thou art thus incensed. Let him go, Gertrude.
Speak, man.
LAERTES   Where is my father?
KING   Dead.
QUEEN   But not by him.
KING   Let him demand his fill.
LAERTES   How came he dead? I'll not be juggled with.   130
To hell, allegiance! Vows, to the blackest devil!
Conscience and grace, to the profoundest pit!
I dare damnation. To this point I stand,
That both the worlds I give to negligence.
Let come what comes, only I'll be revenged   135
Most throughly for my father.
KING   Who shall stay you?
LAERTES   My will, not all the world's.
And for my means, I'll husband them so well,
They shall go far with little.
KING   Good Laertes,
If you desire to know the certainty   140
Of your dear father, is't writ in your revenge
That, swoopstake, you will draw both friend and foe,
Winner and loser?
LAERTES   None but his enemies.
KING   Will you know them, then?
LAERTES   To his good friends thus wide I'll ope my arms,   145
And like the kind life-rend'ring pelican
Repast them with my blood.
KING   Why, now you speak
Like a good child and a true gentleman.
That I am guiltless of your father's death,
And am most sensibly in grief for it,   150

125. **peep . . . would:** glimpse what it would like to effect
126. **his:** its
130. **juggled with:** deceived
132. **profoundest:** deepest (a reference to the "bottomless pit" of hell in Revelation 20:1–3)
134. **both . . . negligence:** I don't care what happens in this world or the next
136. **throughly:** thoroughly; **stay:** stop
138. **husband:** manage
142. **swoopstake:** indiscriminately; **draw . . . foe:** i.e., take revenge on the innocent and guilty. The metaphor is from gambling, as Laertes is imagined to sweep up all the bets, not just his winnings.
146. **pelican:** (The pelican was thought to feed her young with her own blood.)
147. **Repast:** feed
150. **sensibly:** feelingly

It shall as level to your judgment 'pear
As day does to your eye. *A noise within.*

      Enter OPHELIA [*singing, meeting* LAERTES' *followers*].

LAERTES   Let her come in.
How now, what noise is that?
O heat, dry up my brains! Tears seven times salt,
Burn out the sense and virtue of mine eye!   155
By heaven, thy madness shall be paid with weight,
Till our scale turn the beam. O rose of May,
Dear maid, kind sister, sweet Ophelia!
O heavens, is't possible a young maid's wits
Should be as mortal as a poor man's life?   160

OPHELIA   "They bore him barefaced on the bier   *Song.*
           And in his grave rained many a tear"—
      Fare you well, my dove.

LAERTES   Hadst thou thy wits, and didst persuade revenge,
It could not move thus.   165

OPHELIA   You must sing "A-down, a-down," and you "call him
a-down-a." Oh, how the wheel becomes it! It is the false
steward that stole his master's daughter.

LAERTES   This nothing's more than matter.

OPHELIA   There's rosemary, that's for remembrance; pray you,   170
love, remember. And there is pansies, that's for thoughts.

LAERTES   A document in madness, thoughts and remembrance
fitted.

OPHELIA   There's fennel for you, and columbines. There's
rue for you, and here's some for me; we may call it "herb   175
of grace" o' Sundays. You may wear your rue with a difference. There's a daisy. I would give you some violets, but they

---

     151. **level:** plain
     155. **virtue:** power
156–157. **paid . . . beam:** i.e., avenged. The image is of putting weight in a scale till the
        crossbar (**beam**) tilts to a level position or further down.
     164. **persuade:** argue for
     166. **You . . . a-down-a:** (Ophelia assigns refrains to her song to various people, real
        or imagined.)
     167. **wheel:** refrain; **false steward:** (The story is unknown.)
     169. **nothing . . . matter:** nonsense is more moving than reasonable speech
     170. **rosemary:** (Ophelia begins to distribute real or imagined flowers, each with a
        symbolic function.)
     171. **pansies:** (symbols of love and courtship, perhaps from French *pensées*,
        "thoughts")
     172. **document:** lesson
     173. **fitted:** aptly joined
     174. **fennel:** (symbol of flattery); **columbines:** (symbol of unchastity or ingratitude);
     175. **rue:** (symbol of repentance)
176–177. **difference:** mark in a coat of arms that distinguished among different family
        members (Ophelia suggests that she and the recipient, perhaps the Queen, have
        different causes for sorrow and repentance)
     177. **daisy:** (symbol of dissembling); **violets:** (symbol of faithfulness)

withered all when my father died. They say 'a made a good
end.
   [*Sings*] "For bonny sweet Robin is all my joy."   180
LAERTES   Thought and afflictions, passion, hell itself
  She turns to favor and to prettiness.
OPHELIA   "And will 'a not come again?   *Song.*
    And will 'a not come again?
      No, no, he is dead,   185
      Go to thy deathbed,
    He never will come again.
    "His beard was as white as snow,
    Flaxen was his poll.
      He is gone, he is gone,   190
      And we cast away moan.
    God ha' mercy on his soul."
  And of all Christians' souls. God be wi'you.   [*Exit.*]
LAERTES   Do you see this, O God?
KING   Laertes, I must commune with your grief,   195
  Or you deny me right. Go but apart,
  Make choice of whom your wisest friends you will,
  And they shall hear and judge twixt you and me.
  If by direct or by collateral hand
  They find us touched, we will our kingdom give,   200
  Our crown, our life, and all that we call ours
  To you in satisfaction; but if not,
  Be you content to lend your patience to us,
  And we shall jointly labor with your soul
  To give it due content.
LAERTES   Let this be so.   205
  His means of death, his obscure funeral—
  No trophy, sword, nor hatchment o'er his bones,
  No noble rite, nor formal ostentation—
  Cry to be heard, as 'twere from heaven to earth,
  That I must call't in question.
KING   So you shall.   210
  And where th'offense is, let the great axe fall.
  I pray you, go with me.
                        Exeunt.

181. **Thought:** melancholy; **passion:** suffering
189. **poll:** head
195. **commune with:** share and discuss
197. **whom:** whichever
199. **collateral:** indirect
207. **trophy:** memorial; **hatchment:** tablet showing the coat of arms of the deceased
208. **ostentation:** ceremony

4.6 [THE CASTLE]

Enter HORATIO[, a GENTLEMAN,] *and others.*

HORATIO   What are they that would speak with me?

GENTLEMAN   Seafaring men, sir. They say they have letters
for you.

HORATIO   Let them come in.

[*Exit* GENTLEMAN.]

I do not know from what part of the world I should be   5
greeted, if not from Lord Hamlet.

Enter SAILORS.

SAILOR   God bless you, sir.

HORATIO   Let him bless thee too.

SAILOR   'A shall, sir, an't please him. There's a letter for you,
sir—it came from th'ambassador that was bound for Eng-   10
land—if your name be Horatio, as I am let to know it is.

[*He gives a letter.*]

HORATIO   [*Reads*] "Horatio, when thou shalt have overlooked
this, give these fellows some means to the King; they have
letters for him. Ere we were two days old at sea, a pirate of
very warlike appointment gave us chase. Finding ourselves   15
too slow of sail, we put on a compelled valor, and in the grapple I boarded them. On the instant they got clear of our ship,
so I alone became their prisoner. They have dealt with me like
thieves of mercy, but they knew what they did; I am to do a
turn for them. Let the King have the letters I have sent and   20
repair thou to me with as much speed as thou wouldst fly
death. I have words to speak in thine ear will make thee
dumb, yet are they much too light for the bore of the matter.
These good fellows will bring thee where I am. Rosencrantz
and Guildenstern hold their course for England; of them I   25
have much to tell thee. Farewell.

He that thou knowest
thine, Hamlet."

Come, I will give you way for these your letters,

9. **an't:** if it

10. **ambassador:** i.e., Hamlet

12. **overlooked:** looked over

13. **means:** means of access

15. **appointment:** equipage, outfit

16–17. **grapple:** wrestling. Naval battles, especially pirate actions, featured the "grapple"
or iron hook on a rope, which attackers used to immobilize and board ships.

21. **repair:** come

23. **bore:** caliber (diameter of a gun tube, through which the bullet is dis-
charged). Hamlet says that the words he has, though they would strike the lis-
tener dumb, are inadequate for the matter.

29. **way:** means of access

4.6. (Quarto 1 provides an additional encounter between Horatio and the Queen; see
Appendix 1, passage 6, p. 144)

And do't the speedier that you may direct me   30
To him from whom you brought them.

                                                    Exeunt.

                    4.7 [THE CASTLE]

         Enter KING *and* LAERTES.

KING   Now must your conscience my acquittance seal,
    And you must put me in your heart for friend,
    Sith you have heard, and with a knowing ear,
    That he which hath your noble father slain
    Pursued my life.

LAERTES   It well appears. But tell me   5
    Why you proceed not against these feats,
    So criminal and so capital in nature,
    As by your safety, greatness, wisdom, all things else,
    You mainly were stirred up.

KING   Oh, for two special reasons,   10
    Which may to you, perhaps, seem much unsinewed,
    But yet to me they're strong. The Queen his mother
    Lives almost by his looks, and for myself—
    My virtue or my plague, be it either which—
    She is so conjunctive to my life and soul,   15
    That, as the star moves not but in his sphere,
    I could not but by her. The other motive
    Why to a public count I might not go
    Is the great love the general gender bear him,
    Who, dipping all his faults in their affection,   20
    Work like the spring that turneth wood to stone,
    Convert his gyves to graces, so that my arrows,
    Too slightly timbered for so loud a wind,
    Would have reverted to my bow again,
    But not where I have aimed them.   25

---

  1. **my acquittance seal:** recognize my innocence
  3. **Sith:** since
  6. **feats:** deeds
  7. **capital:** punishable by death
  9. **mainly:** greatly
 11. **unsinewed:** weak
 15. **conjunctive:** united
 16. **star . . . sphere:** (According to Ptolemaic astronomy, each star moved in orbit through a crystalline sphere.)
 18. **count:** reckoning
 19. **general gender:** common people
 21. **work . . . stone:** function like the spring of water that petrifies wood, i.e., transform his faults to virtues
 22. **gyves:** shackles
 23. **slightly timbered:** light; **loud:** strong

LAERTES   And so have I a noble father lost,
  A sister driven into desp'rate terms,
  Whose worth, if praises may go back again,
  Stood challenger on mount of all the age
  For her perfections. But my revenge will come.   30
KING   Break not your sleeps for that. You must not think
  That we are made of stuff so flat and dull
  That we can let our beard be shook with danger
  And think it pastime. You shortly shall hear more.
  I loved your father, and we love ourself,   35
  And that, I hope, will teach you to imagine—
      Enter a MESSENGER *with letters.*
MESSENGER   [*Giving letters*] These to Your Majesty, this to
  the Queen.
KING   From Hamlet! Who brought them?
MESSENGER   Sailors, my lord, they say. I saw them not:
  They were given me by Claudio. He received them   40
  Of him that brought them.
KING   Laertes, you shall hear them.
  —Leave us.   [*Exit* MESSENGER.]
[*Reads*] "High and mighty, you shall know I am set naked on
  your kingdom. Tomorrow shall I beg leave to see your kingly
  eyes, when I shall, first asking you pardon, thereunto recount   45
  the occasion of my sudden return."
  What should this mean? Are all the rest come back?
  Or is it some abuse, and no such thing?
LAERTES   Know you the hand?
KING   'Tis Hamlet's character. "Naked,"
  And in a postscript here, he says "alone."   50
  Can you devise me?
LAERTES   I am lost in it, my lord. But let him come.
  It warms the very sickness in my heart
  That I shall live and tell him to his teeth,
  "Thus didst thou."
KING   If it be so, Laertes—   55
  As how should it be so, how otherwise?—

27. **terms:** condition
28. **go back again:** i.e., recall what she was
29. **on mount:** set up on high
43. **naked:** (1) without belongings; (2) unarmed
45. **pardon:** permission
48. **abuse:** deceit
49. **character:** handwriting
51. **devise:** explain to
55. **Thus didst thou:** i.e., I kill you just as you killed my father
56. **As . . . otherwise:** how can Hamlet be in England and how not (since we have the
    letters for evidence)

Will you be ruled by me?

LAERTES   Ay, my lord,
So you will not o'errule me to a peace.

KING   To thine own peace. If he be now returned,
As checking at his voyage, and that he means   60
No more to undertake it—I will work him
To an exploit, now ripe in my device,
Under the which he shall not choose but fall,
And for his death no wind of blame shall breathe,
But even his mother shall uncharge the practice   65
And call it accident.

LAERTES   My lord, I will be ruled,
The rather if you could devise it so
That I might be the organ.

KING   It falls right.
You have been talked of since your travel much,
And that in Hamlet's hearing, for a quality   70
Wherein they say you shine. Your sum of parts
Did not together pluck such envy from him
As did that one, and that, in my regard,
Of the unworthiest siege.

LAERTES   What part is that, my lord?   75

KING   A very ribbon in the cap of youth,
Yet needful too, for youth no less becomes
The light and careless livery that it wears
Than settled age his sables and his weeds,
Importing health and graveness. Two months since   80
Here was a gentleman of Normandy—
I have seen myself, and served against, the French,
And they can well on horseback, but this gallant
Had witchcraft in't; he grew unto his seat,
And to such wondrous doing brought his horse,   85
As had he been incorpsed and demi-natured

60. **checking at:** recoiling from (a hawking term); **that:** if
62. **device:** devising
65. **uncharge the practice:** excuse the deceit (because she won't recognize it)
67. **The rather:** all the more quickly
68. **organ:** instrument
71. **Your . . . parts:** all your good qualities
74. **siege:** category
76. **very ribbon:** mere decoration
77. **no less becomes:** is no less suited by
78. **livery:** clothing
79. **sables:** black or furred robes; **weeds:** garments
80. **Importing:** (1) signifying concern for; (2) promoting
83. **well:** perform well
86. **incorpsed and demi-natured:** joined into one body to form a double-natured
    creature like the centaur (half man, half horse)

With the brave beast. So far he topped my thought
That I in forgery of shapes and tricks
Come short of what he did.

LAERTES   A Norman was't?

KING   A Norman.   90

LAERTES   Upon my life, Lamord.

KING   The very same.

LAERTES   I know him well. He is the brooch indeed
And gem of all the nation.

KING   He made confession of you,
And gave you such a masterly report   95
For art and exercise in your defense,
And for your rapier most especial,
That he cried out 'twould be a sight indeed
If one could match you. Th'escrimers of their nation
He swore, had neither motion, guard, nor eye,   100
If you opposed them. Sir, this report of his
Did Hamlet so envenom with his envy
That he could nothing do but wish and beg
Your sudden coming o'er, to play with you.
Now, out of this—

LAERTES   What out of this, my lord?   105

KING   Laertes, was your father dear to you?
Or are you like the painting of a sorrow,
A face without a heart?

LAERTES   Why ask you this?

KING   Not that I think you did not love your father,
But that I know love is begun by time,   110
And that I see in passages of proof
Time qualifies the spark and fire of it.
There lives within the very flame of love
A kind of wick or snuff that will abate it,
And nothing is at a like goodness still,   115

87. **topped:** surpassed
88. **forgery:** imagining
92. **brooch:** jeweled ornament
94. **confession:** testimonial
96. **your defense:** i.e., the art of fencing
97. **rapier:** light and fashionable Continental sword
99. **escrimers:** fencers
104. **play:** fence
110. **begun by time:** created by circumstances and hence mutable. Claudius echoes the
     Player King in this passage.
111. **passages of proof:** actual instances
112. **qualifies:** moderates
114. **snuff:** charred part of a wick. Claudius suggests that love changes also by
     self-consumption.
115. **nothing . . . still:** nothing stays at a constant level of goodness, immune to
     deterioration

For goodness, growing to a pleurisy,
Dies in his own too much. That we would do,
We should do when we would; for this "would" changes,
And hath abatements and delays as many
As there are tongues, are hands, are accidents,   120
And then this "should" is like a spendthrift sigh,
That hurts by easing. But to the quick o' th'ulcer
Hamlet comes back. What would you undertake
To show yourself in deed your father's son
More than in words?

LAERTES   To cut his throat i'the church.   125

KING   No place, indeed, should murder sanctuarize;
Revenge should have no bounds. But good Laertes,
Will you do this, keep close within your chamber.
Hamlet returned shall know you are come home.
We'll put on those shall praise your excellence   130
And set a double varnish on the fame
The Frenchman gave you, bring you in fine together,
And wager o'er your heads. He, being remiss,
Most generous, and free from all contriving,
Will not peruse the foils, so that with ease,   135
Or with a little shuffling, you may choose
A sword unbated, and in a pass of practice
Requite him for your father.

LAERTES   I will do't.
And for that purpose I'll anoint my sword.
I bought an unction of a mountebank   140
So mortal that, but dip a knife in it,
Where it draws blood no cataplasm so rare,
Collected from all simples that have virtue
Under the moon, can save the thing from death
That is but scratched withal. I'll touch my point   145

116. **pleurisy:** excess
117. **his . . . much:** its own superfluity; **would:** intend to
119. **abatements:** diminutions
121. **spendthift:** excessive, wasteful. Sighs were thought to ease distress but to draw blood from the heart.
122. **quick o' th'ulcer:** i.e., main point
126. **murder sanctuarize:** shelter murder by affording protection
128. **Will you:** if you will
130. **put . . . shall:** incite those who will
132. **in fine:** finally
133. **o'er:** on; **remiss:** inattentive
134. **generous:** noble-minded
136. **shuffling:** sleight of hand
137. **unbated:** not blunted (as rapiers should be for exhibitions); **pass of practice:** (1) thrust in exercise; (2) treacherous thrust
140. **mountebank:** phony doctor or potion seller
142. **cataplasm:** dressing for a wound
143. **simples:** medicinal herbs; **virtue:** power

With this contagion, that if I gall him slightly,
It may be death.
KING   Let's further think of this.
Weigh what convenience both of time and means
May fit us to our shape. If this should fail,
And that our drift look through our bad performance,   150
'Twere better not assayed. Therefore this project
Should have a back or second that might hold
If this did blast in proof. Soft, let me see.
We'll make a solemn wager on your cunnings—
I ha't!   155
When in your motion you are hot and dry—
As make your bouts more violent to that end—
And that he calls for drink, I'll have prepared him
A chalice for the nonce, whereon but sipping,
If he by chance escape your venomed stuck,   160
Our purpose may hold there. [*A noise within*] But stay, what
    noise?

            Enter QUEEN.

QUEEN   One woe doth tread upon another's heel,
So fast they follow. Your sister's drowned, Laertes.
LAERTES   Drowned! Oh, where?
QUEEN   There is a willow grows askant the brook,   165
That shows his hoary leaves in the glassy stream;
Therewith fantastic garlands did she make
Of crowflowers, nettles, daisies, and long purples,
That liberal shepherds give a grosser name,
But our cold maids do dead men's fingers call them.   170
There on the pendent boughs her crownet weeds
Clamb'ring to hang, an envious sliver broke,

146. **gall**: scratch
149. **fit . . . shape**: suit us for our roles
150. **drift . . . performance**: intention be exposed by our bungling
151. **assayed**: attempted
152. **back or second**: backup plan
153. **blast in proof**: blow up in the testing
154. **your cunnings**: your and Hamlet's fencing skills
156. **motion**: exercise
157. **As**: i.e., and you should
159. **nonce**: occasion
160. **stuck**: thrust
165. **willow**: (emblem of mourning and disappointed love); **askant**: on the side of
166. **hoary**: white or grey
167. **Therewith**: with that
168. **long purples**: orchids
169. **liberal**: free speaking; **grosser name**: (The tubers the orchid have been called
    dogstones, cullions [testicles] and the like.)
170. **cold**: chaste
171. **crownet weeds**: coronet of wild flowers
172. **envious sliver**: malicious branch

When down her weedy trophies and herself
Fell in the weeping brook. Her clothes spread wide,
And mermaid-like awhile they bore her up,   175
Which time she chanted snatches of old lauds,
As one incapable of her own distress,
Or like a creature native and endued
Unto that element. But long it could not be
Till that her garments, heavy with their drink,   180
Pulled the poor wretch from her melodious lay
To muddy death.

LAERTES   Alas, then she is drowned.

QUEEN   Drowned, drowned.

LAERTES   Too much of water hast thou, poor Ophelia,
And therefore I forbid my tears. But yet   185
It is our trick; nature her custom holds,
Let shame say what it will. [*He weeps.*] When these are
        gone,
The woman will be out. Adieu, my lord.
I have a speech o' fire that fain would blaze,
But that this folly drowns it.   *Exit.*

KING   Let's follow, Gertrude.   190
How much I had to do to calm his rage!
Now fear I this will give it start again.
Therefore let's follow.

                                        Exeunt.

5.1 [A CHURCHYARD]

Enter two CLOWNS [*one a* GRAVEDIGGER].

GRAVEDIGGER   Is she to be buried in Christian burial when
she willfully seeks her own salvation?

OTHER   I tell thee she is; therefore make her grave straight.
The crowner hath sat on her and finds it Christian burial.

GRAVEDIGGER   How can that be, unless she drowned herself   5
in her own defense?

---

176. **lauds:** hymns
177. **incapable:** without ability to understand
178. **endued:** naturally adapted
186. **trick:** habit
187–88. **When . . . out:** when these tears are shed I will have spent all the female
        tenderness in me
s.d. **CLOWNS:** rustics
2. **willfully . . . salvation:** i.e., commits suicide. Suicides were denied Christian
   burial in consecrated ground. Perhaps **salvation** is simply the Gravedigger's
   error for "damnation."
3. **straight:** straightaway
4. **crowner:** coroner; **sat on her:** conducted a formal session on her case; **finds it:**
   decided that Ophelia is eligible for

OTHER   Why, 'tis found so.

GRAVEDIGGER   It must be *se offendendo*; it cannot be else. For
here lies the point: if I drown myself wittingly, it argues an
act, and an act hath three branches—it is to act, to do, to   10
perform. Argal, she drowned herself wittingly.

OTHER   Nay, but hear you, goodman delver—

GRAVEDIGGER   Give me leave. Here lies the water—good. Here
stands the man—good. If the man go to this water and
drown himself, it is, will he, nill he, he goes. Mark you that.   15
But if the water come to him and drown him, he drowns not
himself. Argal, he that is not guilty of his own death short-
ens not his own life.

OTHER   But is this law?

GRAVEDIGGER   Ay, marry, is't—crowner's quest law.   20

OTHER   Will you ha' the truth on't? If this had not been a
gentlewoman, she should have been buried out o' Christian
burial.

GRAVEDIGGER   Why, there thou sayst. And the more pity that
great folk should have countenance in this world to drown or   25
hang themselves more than their even-Christian. Come, my
spade. There is no ancient gentlemen but gardeners, ditch-
ers, and grave-makers. They hold up Adam's profession.

OTHER   Was he a gentleman?

GRAVEDIGGER   'A was the first that ever bore arms. I'll put   30
another question to thee. If thou answerest me not to the
purpose, confess thyself—

OTHER   Go to.

GRAVEDIGGER   What is he that builds stronger than either the
mason, the shipwright, or the carpenter?   35

OTHER   The gallows-maker, for that outlives a thousand ten-
ants.

GRAVEDIGGER   I like thy wit well, in good faith. The gallows
does well. But how does it well? It does well to those that do
ill. Now thou dost ill to say the gallows is built stronger than   40

---

8. *se offendendo*: "in self-offense" (the Gravedigger's mistake for the Latin phrase *se defendendo*, "in self-defense," a legal reason for justifiable homicide)
9. **wittingly**: knowingly
11. **Argal**: (Gravedigger's corruption of the Latin *ergo*, "therefore")
12. **goodman delver**: neighbor digger. **Goodman** is a respectful term of address.
15. **will . . . nill he**: whether he will or not, willy nilly
20. **quest**: inquest
25. **countenance**: permission
26. **even-Christian**: fellow Christians
30. **arms**: (1) coat of arms (the badge of nobility); (2) limbs (**arms**, literally). The Grave-digger's joke turns on the double meaning, as the Folio makes clear: "The Scrip-ture says Adam digged; could he dig without arms?"
32. **confess thyself**: (The saying continues, "and be hanged.")
33. **Go to**: (an expression of impatience or dismissal)
39. **does well**: (1) is a good answer; (2) functions aptly

the church. Argal, the gallows may do well to thee. To't again,
come.

OTHER   Who builds stronger than a mason, a shipwright, or a
carpenter?

GRAVEDIGGER   Ay, tell me that, and unyoke.   45

OTHER   Marry, now I can tell.

GRAVEDIGGER   To't.

OTHER   Mass, I cannot tell.

GRAVEDIGGER   Cudgel thy brains no more about it, for your
dull ass will not mend his pace with beating. And when you   50
are asked this question next, say "a grave-maker." The houses
he makes lasts till doomsday. Go get thee in and fetch me a
stoup of liquor.

[*Exit* OTHER.]

[GRAVEDIGGER *digs.*]

"In youth when I did love, did love,   *Song.*
   Methought it was very sweet,   55
To contract—oh—the time for—a—my behove,
   Oh, methought there—a—was nothing—a—meet."

Enter HAMLET *and* HORATIO.

HAMLET   Has this fellow no feeling of his business? 'A sings
in grave-making.

HORATIO   Custom hath made it in him a property of easiness. 60

HAMLET   'Tis e'en so. The hand of little employment hath the
daintier sense.

GRAVEDIGGER   "But age, with his stealing steps,   *Song.*
   Hath clawed me in his clutch,
And hath shipped me into the land,   65
   As if I had never been such."

[*He throws up a skull.*]

HAMLET   That skull had a tongue in it and could sing once.
How the knave jowls it to the ground, as if 'twere Cain's

45. **unyoke:** cease from labor
48. **Mass:** by the mass (an oath)
49. **Cudgel:** beat with a stick
53. **stoup:** jug or cup
54ff.: (The Gravedigger's song, continued below, appeared with variations in a poetry
anthology, *Tottel's Miscellany,* 1557, under the title "The aged lover renounceth
love.")
56. **contract . . . behove:** shorten the time for my advantage. (The "oh" and "a"
interjections perhaps signify his grunts as he digs.)
57. **meet:** suitable. This stanza makes little sense.
60. **property of easiness:** thing he can do easily
62. **daintier sense:** more delicate feeling
65. **into the land:** toward my grave
68. **jowls:** dashes (with a play on **jowl,** jawbone); **Cain:** the first murderer, killer of
his brother Abel (see 1.2.105, 3.3.37). Medieval tradition, not Scripture, portrayed the weapon as the jawbone of an ass.

jawbone, that did the first murder. This might be the pate
of a politician—which this ass now o'erreaches—one that   70
would circumvent God, might it not?

HORATIO   It might, my lord.

HAMLET   Or of a courtier, which could say, "Good morrow,
sweet lord. How dost thou, sweet lord?" This might be my
Lord Such-a-one, that praised my Lord Such-a-one's horse   75
when 'a went to beg it, might it not?

HORATIO   Ay, my lord.

HAMLET   Why, e'en so, and now my Lady Worm's, chapless,
and knocked about the mazard with a sexton's spade. Here's
fine revolution, an we had the trick to see't. Did these bones   80
cost no more the breeding but to play at loggets with them?
Mine ache to think on't.

GRAVEDIGGER   "A pickaxe and a spade, a spade,   *Song.*
        For and a shrouding sheet;
    Oh, a pit of clay for to be made   85
        For such a guest is meet."

        [*He throws up another skull.*]

HAMLET   There's another. Why may not that be the skull of a
lawyer? Where be his quiddities now, his quillities, his cases,
his tenures, and his tricks? Why does he suffer this mad
knave now to knock him about the sconce with a dirty shovel,   90
and will not tell him of his action of battery? Hum, this fellow might be in's time a great buyer of land, with his statutes, his recognizances, his fines, his double vouchers, his
recoveries. To have his fine pate full of fine dirt! Will vouchers vouch him no more of his purchases and doubles than   95
the length and breadth of a pair of indentures? The very

---

69. **pate:** head
70. **politician:** schemer; **o'erreaches:** gets the better of
71. **circumvent** get around, outwit
76. **beg:** borrow
78. **chapless:** without the lower jaw
79. **mazard:** head; **sexton:** church worker who rang bells, dug graves, and performed other duties
80. **revolution:** change, a turn of Fortune's wheel; **an:** if; **trick:** ability
81. **loggets:** a game in which pieces of wood are thrown to a stake
84. **For and:** and moreover
88. **quiddities:** subtleties, quibbles; **quillities:** verbal niceties (a variation of **quiddities**)
89. **tenures:** holdings of property or office (a legal term)
90. **sconce:** head
91. **action of battery:** lawsuit for assault
92–4. **statutes, his recognizances:** his legal documents guaranteeing debt by securing lands or properties; **fines . . . recoveries:** his legal means of transferring property not available for simple sale
95. **vouch:** guarantee; **doubles:** double vouchers (guarantees signed by two parties)
96. **pair of indentures:** contract in duplicate (with a pun perhaps on the skull's two rows of teeth)

conveyances of his lands will scarcely lie in this box, and
must th'inheritor himself have no more, ha?

HORATIO   Not a jot more, my lord.

HAMLET   Is not parchment made of sheepskins?   100

HORATIO   Ay, my lord, and of calves' skins too.

HAMLET   They are sheep and calves which seek out assurance
in that. I will speak to this fellow.—Whose grave's this,
sirrah?

GRAVEDIGGER   Mine, sir.   105
    [Sings.] "Oh, a pit of clay for to be made"—

HAMLET   I think it be thine, indeed, for thou liest in't.

GRAVEDIGGER   You lie out on't, sir, and therefore 'tis not yours.
For my part, I do not lie in't, yet it is mine.

HAMLET   Thou dost lie in't, to be in't and say it is thine. 'Tis   110
for the dead not for the quick; therefore thou liest.

GRAVEDIGGER   'Tis a quick lie, sir; 'twill away again from me
to you.

HAMLET   What man dost thou dig it for?

GRAVEDIGGER   For no man, sir.   115

HAMLET   What woman then?

GRAVEDIGGER   For none neither.

HAMLET   Who is to be buried in't?

GRAVEDIGGER   One that was a woman, sir, but, rest her soul,
she's dead.   120

HAMLET   How absolute the knave is! We must speak by the
card or equivocation will undo us. By the Lord, Horatio,
this three years I have took note of it: the age is grown so
picked that the toe of the peasant comes so near the heel of
the courtier he galls his kibe.—How long hast thou been   125
grave-maker?

GRAVEDIGGER   Of the days i'the year, I came to't that day that
our last king Hamlet overcame Fortinbras.

HAMLET   How long is that since?

---

97. **conveyances:** deeds; **box:** coffin (perhaps also skull)
98. **inheritor:** owner
100. **parchment:** animal skin used for a writing surface, especially for legal documents
102–03. **assurance in that:** security in legal documents. Only fools rely on such
     documents.
104. **sirrah:** (term of address to inferiors)
108. **on't:** of it
111. **quick:** living
121. **absolute:** precise
121–22. **by the card:** i.e., exactly
122. **equivocation:** ambiguity, double meanings
124. **picked:** (1) finicky; (2) pointed (with reference to shoes)
125. **galls his kibe:** chafes the sore on the courtier's heel

GRAVEDIGGER   Cannot you tell that? Every fool can tell that.   130
It was that very day that young Hamlet was born, he that is
mad and sent into England.

HAMLET   Ay, marry, why was he sent into England?

GRAVEDIGGER   Why, because 'a was mad. 'A shall recover his
wits there, or if 'a do not, 'tis no great matter there.   135

HAMLET   Why?

GRAVEDIGGER   'Twill not be seen in him there. There the men
are as mad as he.

HAMLET   How came he mad?

GRAVEDIGGER   Very strangely, they say.   140

HAMLET   How strangely?

GRAVEDIGGER   Faith, e'en with losing his wits.

HAMLET   Upon what ground?

GRAVEDIGGER   Why, here in Denmark. I have been sexton
here, man and boy, thirty years.   145

HAMLET   How long will a man lie i'the earth ere he rot?

GRAVEDIGGER   Faith, if 'a be not rotten before 'a die—as we
have many pocky corpses that will scarce hold the laying
in—'a will last you some eight year or nine year. A tanner
will last you nine year.   150

HAMLET   Why he more than another?

GRAVEDIGGER   Why, sir, his hide is so tanned with his trade
that 'a will keep out water a great while, and your water is a
sore decayer of your whoreson dead body. Here's a skull
now hath lien you i'th'earth three-and-twenty years.   155

HAMLET   Whose was it?

GRAVEDIGGER   A whoreson mad fellow's it was. Whose do you
think it was?

HAMLET   Nay, I know not.

GRAVEDIGGER   A pestilence on him for a mad rogue! 'A poured   160
a flagon of Rhenish on my head once. [*He picks up a skull.*]
This same skull, sir, was, sir, Yorick's skull, the King's jester.

HAMLET   This?

GRAVEDIGGER   E'en that.

HAMLET [*He takes the skull.*]   Alas, poor Yorick. I knew him,   165
Horatio, a fellow of infinite jest, of most excellent fancy. He
hath bore me on his back a thousand times, and now how

143. **ground:** cause
145. **thirty years:** (Since the Gravedigger came to his profession the day that young
Hamlet was born [131], this line—along with Yorick's death twenty-three years
ago—sets Hamlet's age at thirty, somewhat older than audiences like to imagine.)
148. **pocky:** rotten (especially with syphilis)
148–49. **hold . . . in:** hold together long enough for burial
154. **sore:** grievous; **whoreson:** vile
155. **lien you:** lain.
161. **flagon of Rhenish:** bottle of Rhine wine

abhorred in my imagination it is! My gorge rises at it. Here
hung those lips that I have kissed I know not how oft. Where
be your gibes now, your gambols, your songs, your flashes of   170
merriment that were wont to set the table on a roar? Not one
now, to mock your own grinning? Quite chopfallen? Now,
get you to my lady's table and tell her, let her paint an inch
thick, to this favor she must come. Make her laugh at that.
Prithee, Horatio, tell me one thing.   175

HORATIO   What's that, my lord?

HAMLET   Dost thou think Alexander looked o' this fashion
i'th'earth?

HORATIO   E'en so.

HAMLET   And smelt so? Pah! [*He puts down the skull.*]   180

HORATIO   E'en so, my lord.

HAMLET   To what base uses we may return, Horatio! Why
may not imagination trace the noble dust of Alexander till 'a
find it stopping a bunghole?

HORATIO   'Twere to consider too curiously to consider so.   185

HAMLET   No, faith, not a jot, but to follow him thither with
modesty enough, and likelihood to lead it: Alexander died,
Alexander was buried, Alexander returneth to dust, the dust
is earth, of earth we make loam, and why of that loam
whereto he was converted might they not stop a beer barrel?   190

Imperious Caesar, dead and turned to clay,
Might stop a hole to keep the wind away.
Oh, that that earth which kept the world in awe
Should patch a wall t'expel the winter's flaw!

> *Enter* KING, QUEEN, LAERTES, *and the corpse* [*of* OPHELIA,
> *with a* DOCTOR OF DIVINITY, *and* ATTENDANTS.]

But soft, but soft awhile. Here comes the King,   195
The Queen, the courtiers. Who is this they follow?
And with such maimed rites? This doth betoken

168. **My gorge rises:** i.e., I feel like vomiting
170. **gibes:** taunts; **gambols:** tricks
172. **grinning:** (Because they showed teeth, skulls were thought to grin.); **chopfallen:**
      (1) lacking the lower jaw; (2) dejected
173. **table:** dressing table; **paint:** apply cosmetics
174. **favor:** appearance
177. **Alexander:** Alexander the Great (356–323 BC), Greek conqueror, and, with Julius
      Caesar, symbol of worldly achievement
184. **bunghole:** hole of a cask
185. **curiously:** ingeniously
187. **modesty:** moderation; **it:** i.e., imagination
189. **loam:** clay mortar
191. **Imperious:** imperial
194. **flaw:** gust of wind
195. **soft:** be silent
197. **maimed:** mutilated, diminished

The corpse they follow did with desp'rate hand
Fordo its own life. 'Twas of some estate.
Couch we awhile and mark.   200

    [*They withdraw.* OPHELIA's *body is taken to the grave.*]

LAERTES What ceremony else?
HAMLET [*To* HORATIO] That is Laertes, a very noble youth.
  Mark.
LAERTES What ceremony else?
DOCTOR Her obsequies have been as far enlarged
  As we have warranty. Her death was doubtful,   205
  And but that great command o'ersways the order
  She should in ground unsanctified been lodged
  Till the last trumpet. For charitable prayers,
  Flints and pebbles should be thrown on her.
  Yet here she is allowed her virgin crants,   210
  Her maiden strewments, and the bringing home
  Of bell and burial.
LAERTES Must there no more be done?
DOCTOR   No more be done.
  We should profane the service of the dead
  To sing a requiem and such rest to her   215
  As to peace-parted souls.
LAERTES   Lay her i'th'earth,
  And from her fair and unpolluted flesh
  May violets spring. I tell thee, churlish priest,
  A minist'ring angel shall my sister be
  When thou liest howling.
HAMLET [*To* HORATIO]   What, the fair Ophelia?   220
QUEEN [*Strewing flowers*] Sweets to the sweet. Farewell.
  I hoped thou shouldst have been my Hamlet's wife.
  I thought thy bride-bed to have decked, sweet maid,
  And not have strewed thy grave.
LAERTES   Oh, treble woe
  Fall ten times double on that cursèd head   225

    199. Fordo: destroy; **estate:** rank
    200. Couch we: let us hide
    205. warranty: ecclesiastical permission; **doubtful:** suspicious
    206. o'ersways the order: overrides prescribed practices
    207. been: have been
    208. last trumpet: i.e., Judgment Day (see 1 Corinthians 15:52; 1 Thessalonians 4:16); **For:** instead of
    210. crants: garland
    211. strewments: flowers scattered on the coffin
 211–12. bringing . . . burial: burial in consecrated ground to the ringing of bells
    215. requiem: funeral hymn or mass; **such rest:** (pray for) such rest
    216. peace-parted souls: those who died naturally
    218. violets: (symbol of faithfulness, as at 4.5.177)
    220. howling: (in hell)

Whose wicked deed thy most ingenious sense
Deprived thee of!—Hold off the earth awhile,
Till I have caught her once more in mine arms.

    [*He leaps into the grave and embraces* OPHELIA.]

Now pile your dust upon the quick and dead,
Till of this flat a mountain you have made,   230
T'o'ertop old Pelion or the skyish head
Of blue Olympus.

HAMLET [*Advancing*]   What is he whose grief
  Bears such an emphasis, whose phrase of sorrow
  Conjures the wand'ring stars, and makes them stand
  Like wonder-wounded hearers? This is I,   235
  Hamlet the Dane!

LAERTES [*Grappling with him*]   The devil take thy soul!

HAMLET   Thou pray'st not well.
  I prithee, take thy fingers from my throat,
  For though I am not splenitive and rash,
  Yet have I in me something dangerous,   240
  Which let thy wisdom fear. Hold off thy hand.

KING   Pluck them asunder.

QUEEN   Hamlet, Hamlet!

ALL   Gentlemen!

HORATIO   Good my lord, be quiet.   245

    [*The* ATTENDANTS *part them.*]

HAMLET   Why, I will fight with him upon this theme
  Until my eyelids will no longer wag.

QUEEN   O my son, what theme?

HAMLET   I loved Ophelia. Forty thousand brothers
  Could not with all their quantity of love   250
  Make up my sum.—What wilt thou do for her?

KING   Oh, he is mad, Laertes.

QUEEN   For love of God, forbear him.

HAMLET   'Swounds, show me what thou'lt do.

---

226. **ingenious sense:** lively mind
228. (The line implies that Ophelia was in an open coffin or on a bier.)
229. **quick:** living
231–32. **Pelion, Olympus:** mountains in Greece. The Titans piled Pelion on Mount
      Ossa (243) to scale Olympus, home of the gods.
233. **emphasis:** intensity
234. **wand'ring stars:** planets
235. **wonder-wounded:** struck with amazement
236. **Dane:** ruler of Denmark (see 1.1.16)
236. **s.d.:** (Hamlet may have leapt into the grave as in Q1, or Laertes may have come
      out.)
239. **splenitive:** hot-tempered
247. **wag:** move
253. **forbear:** tolerate
254. **'Swounds:** by His (Christ's) wounds (an oath)

Woo't weep? Woo't fight? Woo't fast? Woo't tear thyself?   255
Woo't drink up eisel? Eat a crocodile?
I'll do't. Dost come here to whine,
To outface me with leaping in her grave?
Be buried quick with her, and so will I.
And if thou prate of mountains, let them throw   260
Millions of acres on us till our ground,
Singeing his pate against the burning zone,
Make Ossa like a wart! Nay, an thou't mouth,
I'll rant as well as thou.
QUEEN   This is mere madness,
And this awhile the fit will work on him.   265
Anon, as patient as the female dove,
When that her golden couplets are disclosed,
His silence will sit drooping.
HAMLET   Hear you, sir.
What is the reason that you use me thus?
I loved you ever. But it is no matter.   270
Let Hercules himself do what he may,
The cat will mew, and dog will have his day.   *Exit.*
KING   I pray thee, good Horatio, wait upon him.
                                  [*Exit* HORATIO.]

[*To* LAERTES] Strengthen your patience in our last night's speech;
We'll put the matter to the present push.   275
—Good Gertrude, set some watch over your son.—
This grave shall have a living monument.
An hour of quiet thereby shall we see;
Till then in patience our proceeding be.
                                  Exeunt.

---

255. **Woo't:** wilt thou
256. **eisel:** vinegar
262. **his pate:** its head, i.e., the top; **burning zone:** solar sphere or orbit
263. **Ossa:** Greek mountain; **an . . . mouth:** if you will rant
264. **mere:** utter
267. **couplets:** twin baby birds; **disclosed:** hatched
268. **His . . . drooping:** i.e., he will be quiet
271–72. **Let . . . day:** Despite even the best efforts of Hercules, my turn will come. "Every dog has his day" was proverbial; See Dent, D464. Perhaps there is a sarcastic jab at Laertes, as Hercules was known as a blusterer.
274. **in:** by remembering
275. **present push:** immediate action
277. **living:** lasting (also referring to the plot against Hamlet's life)

5.2 [THE CASTLE]

Enter HAMLET *and* HORATIO.

HAMLET   So much for this, sir; now shall you see the other.
    You do remember all the circumstance?
HORATIO   Remember it, my lord!
HAMLET   Sir, in my heart there was a kind of fighting
    That would not let me sleep. Methought I lay   5
    Worse than the mutines in the bilboes. Rashly,
    And praised be rashness for it—let us know
    Our indiscretion sometime serves us well,
    When our deep plots do pall and that should learn us
    There's a divinity that shapes our ends,   10
    Rough-hew them how we will—
HORATIO   That is most certain.
HAMLET   Up from my cabin,
    My sea-gown scarfed about me, in the dark
    Groped I to find out them, had my desire,
    Fingered their packet, and in fine withdrew   15
    To mine own room again, making so bold,
    My fears forgetting manners, to unfold
    Their grand commission, where I found, Horatio,
    A royal knavery, an exact command,
    Larded with many several sorts of reasons,   20
    Importing Denmark's health and England's too,
    With—ho!—such bugs and goblins in my life,
    That on the supervise, no leisure bated,
    No, not to stay the grinding of the axe,
    My head should be struck off.
HORATIO   Is't possible?   25
HAMLET [*Giving a paper*]   Here's the commission. Read it at
    more leisure.
    But wilt thou hear now how I did proceed?
HORATIO   I beseech you.

---

1. **see the other:** i.e., hear the other news
6. **mutines:** mutineers; **bilboes:** shackles affixed to a long iron bar; **Rashly:** impulsively.
    The adverb modifies Hamlet's actions, 12ff.
8. **indiscretion:** impulsive action
9. **pall:** falter; **learn:** teach
11. **Rough-hew:** shape roughly. The metaphor is from work with stone or timber.
13. **scarfed:** wrapped loosely
15. **Fingered:** stole; **in fine:** finally
20. **Larded:** ornamented
22. **such . . . life:** report of fantastic disasters if I were allowed to live; **bugs:** bugbears,
    imaginary objects of terror
23. **supervise:** reading; **leisure bated:** delay allowed
24. **stay:** wait for

HAMLET   Being thus benetted round with villains—
Ere I could make a prologue to my brains,   30
They had begun the play—I sat me down,
Devised a new commission, wrote it fair.
I once did hold it, as our statists do,
A baseness to write fair, and labored much
How to forget that learning, but, sir, now   35
It did me yeoman's service. Wilt thou know
Th'effect of what I wrote?
HORATIO   Ay, good my lord.
HAMLET   An earnest conjuration from the King,
As England was his faithful tributary,
As love between them like the palm might flourish,   40
As peace should still her wheaten garland wear
And stand a comma 'tween their amities,
And many suchlike "as"es of great charge,
That on the view and knowing of these contents,
Without debatement further more or less,   45
He should those bearers put to sudden death,
Not shriving time allowed.
HORATIO   How was this sealed?
HAMLET   Why, even in that was heaven ordinant.
I had my father's signet in my purse,
Which was the model of that Danish seal,   50
Folded the writ up in the form of th'other,

---

   29. **benetted round:** hemmed in; **villains:** (Some editors emend to "villainies.")
30–31. **Ere . . . play:** before I started thinking about a course of action, my brains had
         already started to carry out a plan. A **prologue** presents the outline of a play.
   32. **fair:** in a formal handwriting
   33. **statists:** statesmen
   34. **baseness:** lower-class skill
   36. **yeoman's:** i.e., good. A **yeoman** is a servant in a royal or noble household.
   37. **effect:** substance
   38. **conjuration:** solemn request
   39. **tributary:** nation that pays tribute
40–43. (Hamlet here sarcastically recalls the formal language of his letter.)
   40. **palm might flourish:** (A curious echo of Psalm 92:12: "The righteous shall
         flourish like a palm tree.")
   41. **still:** always; **wheaten garland:** (symbol of peace and prosperity)
   42. **stand a comma:** i.e., serve as a link. (The phrase is probably corrupt, as none of
         the meanings of **comma**—"mark of punctuation," "trench," "slight musical
         interval"—makes sense in context); **amities:** friendships
   43. **"as"es:** repetitions of "as," with a pun on "asses" that is picked up in **charge,**
         meaning (1) importance; (2) burden
   46. **He:** i.e., the King of England; **those bearers:** i.e., Rosencrantz and
         Guildenstern
   47. **shriving time:** time for confession; **sealed:** marked as authentic with a seal
         impressed in wax
   48. **ordinant:** directing
   49. **signet:** small seal, usually in a finger ring
   50. **model:** replica
   51. **writ:** writing; **form:** likeness

Subscribed it, gave't th'impression, placed it safely,
The changeling never known. Now, the next day
Was our sea fight, and what to this was sequent
Thou knowest already.   55

HORATIO   So Guildenstern and Rosencrantz go to't.

HAMLET   They are not near my conscience; their defeat
Does by their own insinuation grow.
'Tis dangerous when the baser nature comes
Between the pass and fell incensèd points   60
Of mighty opposites.

HORATIO   Why, what a king is this!

HAMLET   Does it not, think thee, stand me now upon?
He that hath killed my king and whored my mother,
Popped in between th'election and my hopes,
Thrown out his angle for my proper life,   65
And with such coz'nage—is't not perfect conscience?

                  Enter [OSRIC], a courtier.

OSRIC   Your lordship is right welcome back to Denmark.

HAMLET   I humbly thank you, sir. [Aside to HORATIO] Dost
know this water-fly?

HORATIO [Aside]   No, my good lord.   70

HAMLET [Aside]   Thy state is the more gracious, for 'tis a vice
to know him. He hath much land and fertile. Let a beast be
lord of beasts, and his crib shall stand at the King's mess. 'Tis
a chough, but, as I say, spacious in the possession of dirt.

OSRIC   Sweet lord, if your lordship were at leisure, I should   75
impart a thing to you from His Majesty.

---

52. **Subscribed:** signed (with a forged signature)
53. **changeling:** substitute
54. **was sequent:** followed
57. **They . . . conscience:** (In the Folio, Hamlet picks up the bawdy innuendo in "go
    to't" with a bitter rejoinder before this line, "Why, man, they did make love to
    this employment.")
58. **insinuation:** stealthy intrusion (into my affairs)
60. **pass:** thrust; **fell incensèd points:** fierce enraged swords
61. **opposites:** opponents, i.e., Hamlet and Claudius
62. **stand . . . upon:** become my obligation now. The unspecified it refers to the
    anticipated murder of Claudius.
64. **election:** (Denmark here is an elective monarchy.)
65. **angle:** fishing hook or line; **proper** very
66. **coz'nage:** deception; **perfect conscience:** perfectly justifiable. In the Folio
    Hamlet asks if it is damnable to allow Claudius to live and repents his attack on
    Laertes in the graveyard; see Appendix 2, passage 4, p. 149.
69. **water-fly:** (The insult suggests a trifling busybody, perhaps decked out in
    gaudy apparel. The stage direction in Q1 nominates him "a braggart
    gentleman.")
72–73. **Let . . . mess:** i.e., No matter how bestial, a man who has money may eat with
    the king.
73. **crib:** foodbox for animals; **mess:** meal or meal-table
74. **chough:** crow or jackdaw (noisy birds). Editors sometimes spell "chuff," which
    means boor or churl.

HAMLET   I will receive it, sir, with all diligence of spirit. Your
bonnet to his right use; 'tis for the head.

OSRIC   I thank your lordship; it is very hot.

HAMLET   No, believe me, 'tis very cold; the wind is northerly.   80

OSRIC   It is indifferent cold, my lord, indeed.

HAMLET   But yet methinks it is very sultry and hot for my
complexion.

OSRIC   Exceedingly, my lord. It is very sultry, as 'twere—I cannot tell how. My lord, His Majesty bade me signify to you   85
that 'a has laid a great wager on your head. Sir, this is the
matter—

HAMLET   I beseech you, remember.

          [HAMLET *gestures to* OSRIC *to put on his hat.*]

OSRIC   Nay, good my lord, for my ease, in good faith. Sir, here
is newly come to court Laertes—believe me, an absolute gen-   90
tleman, full of most excellent differences, of very soft society and great showing. Indeed, to speak feelingly of him, he
is the card or calendar of gentry, for you shall find in him
the continent of what part a gentleman would see.

HAMLET   Sir, his definement suffers no perdition in you, though   95
I know to divide him inventorially would dozy th'arithmetic
of memory, and yet but yaw neither in respect of his quick
sail. But, in the verity of extolment, I take him to be a soul of
great article, and his infusion of such dearth and rareness
as, to make true diction of him, his semblable is his mirror,   100
and who else would trace him, his umbrage, nothing more.

OSRIC   Your lordship speaks most infallibly of him.

HAMLET   The concernancy, sir? Why do we wrap the gentleman in our more rawer breath?

77. **diligence:** attentiveness
78. **bonnet:** hat (which Osric has taken off); **his:** its
81. **indifferent:** somewhat
83. **complexion:** temperament
88. **remember:** i.e., remember your courtesy (put on your hat)
89. **ease:** convenience. Osric declines to put his hat back on.
91. **differences:** distinctions
91–92. **soft society:** refined manners
92. **showing:** appearance; **feelingly:** accurately
93. **card:** map, chart; **calendar:** guide; **gentry:** nobility
94. **continent:** container; **what part:** whatever quality
95. **definement:** definition (Hamlet mocks Osric by adopting his fancy style of
speech); **perdition:** loss
96. **divide him inventorially:** list his attributes; **dozy:** make dizzy
96–97. **arithmetic of memory:** ability of memory to calculate
97–98. **yaw . . . sail:** veer off course (**yaw**) only in comparison with his true excellence
98. **verity of extolment:** truth of praise (to praise him truly)
99. **article:** matter (for an inventory); **infusion:** natural character; **dearth and
rareness:** rareness
100. **diction:** speech; **semblable:** only true likeness
101. **trace:** follow; **umbrage:** shadow
103. **concernancy:** relevance, purpose
104. **more rawer breath:** i.e., speech too crude to do him justice

OSRIC   Sir? 105

HORATIO   Is't not possible to understand in another tongue? You will do't, sir, really.

HAMLET   What imports the nomination of this gentleman?

OSRIC   Of Laertes?

HORATIO   [*To* HAMLET] His purse is empty already; all's golden 110 words are spent.

HAMLET   Of him, sir.

OSRIC   I know, you are not ignorant—

HAMLET   I would you did, sir. Yet, in faith, if you did, it would not much approve me. Well, sir? 115

OSRIC   You are not ignorant of what excellence Laertes is—

HAMLET   I dare not confess that, lest I should compare with him in excellence. But to know a man well were to know himself.

OSRIC   I mean, sir, for his weapon. But in the imputation laid 120 on him by them in his meed, he's unfellowed.

HAMLET   What's his weapon?

OSRIC   Rapier and dagger.

HAMLET   That's two of his weapons—but well.

OSRIC   The King, sir, hath wagered with him six Barbary 125 horses, against the which he has impawned, as I take it, six French rapiers and poniards, with their assigns, as girdle, hanger, and so. Three of the carriages, in faith, are very dear to fancy, very responsive to the hilts, most delicate carriages, and of very liberal conceit. 130

HAMLET   What call you the "carriages"?

106. **another tongue:** someone else's mouth. Horatio may mock Osric for failing to understand his fancy style of speech when spoken by another. Alternatively, Horatio could be addressing Hamlet (**tongue** meaning "language") and calling for simpler speech.
107. **You . . . really:** you can if you try
108. **nomination:** naming
115. **approve:** commend
117–19. **I dare . . . himself:** I do not presume to say I know Laertes' excellence lest I imply that I am his equal. And only through self-knowledge can one claim to know another.
120. **for:** with
120–21. **imputation . . . meed:** reputation given him by those in his service
121. **unfellowed:** unmatched
123. **Rapier and dagger:** (The **rapier,** a Continental light, sharp-pointed sword, and **dagger** were replacing the English broadsword and shield in fencing at the time of the play.)
125. **Barbary:** Arabian
126. **he:** i.e., Laertes; **impawned:** staked
127. **poniards:** daggers; **assigns:** accessories; **girdle:** belt
128. **hanger:** sword-strap, often ornamented; **carriages:** hangers
128–29. **dear to fancy:** elaborately designed
129. **responsive:** matching; **delicate:** finely wrought
130. **liberal conceit:** lavish ingenuity

HORATIO [*To* HAMLET] I knew you must be edified by the
margent ere you had done.

OSRIC The carriages, sir, are the hangers.

HAMLET The phrase would be more germane to the matter if   135
we could carry a cannon by our sides. I would it might be
"hangers" till then. But, on: six Barbary horses against six
French swords, their assigns, and three liberal-conceited
carriages; that's the French bet against the Danish. Why is
this all "impawned," as you call it?   140

OSRIC The King, sir, hath laid, sir, that in a dozen passes
between yourself and him, he shall not exceed you three hits.
He hath laid on twelve for nine, and it would come to immediate trial if your lordship would vouchsafe the answer.

HAMLET How if I answer no?   145

OSRIC I mean, my lord, the opposition of your person in trial.

HAMLET Sir, I will walk here in the hall. If it please His Majesty, it is the breathing time of day with me; let the foils be
brought. The gentleman willing, and the King hold his purpose, I will win for him an I can; if not, I will gain nothing   150
but my shame and the odd hits.

OSRIC Shall I deliver you so?

HAMLET To this effect, sir, after what flourish your nature
will.

OSRIC I commend my duty to your lordship.   155

HAMLET Yours.

[*Exit* OSRIC.]

'A does well to commend it himself; there are no tongues else
for's turn.

HORATIO This lapwing runs away with the shell on his head.

HAMLET 'A did comply so, sir, with his dug before 'a sucked   160
it. Thus has he—and many more of the same breed that I
know the drossy age dotes on—only got the tune of the time

---

133. **margent:** margin of a book, place for explanatory notes
135. **phrase:** i.e., "carriage," a term for the wheeled support of big guns
139. **French bet:** i.e., the bet of Laertes, who studied in Paris
141. **passes:** bouts or rounds. The precise nature of the bet is unclear, particularly the **twelve for nine** phrase below, but the King wagers that Hamlet will be within three hits of Laertes.
144. **vouchsafe the answer:** i.e., accept the challenge (but Hamlet takes the phrase literally to mean "make a reply")
148. **breathing . . . day:** time for exercise; **foils:** light blunted swords with a button at the point, used for fencing
151. **odd hits:** any hits I happen to make (despite losing the match)
158. **for's turn:** for his purposes
159. **lapwing:** bird thought to run about when newly hatched with the shell on its head (an allusion to Osric's youthful pretension or hat)
160. **comply:** use compliments or ceremonies; **dug:** mother's or nurse's breast
162. **drossy:** worthless; **tune:** style (as opposed to substance)

and, out of an habit of encounter, a kind of yeasty collection,
which carries them through and through the most profane
and winnowed opinions; and do but blow them to their trial,   165
the bubbles are out.

    Enter a LORD.

LORD   My lord, His Majesty commended him to you by young
Osric, who brings back to him that you attend him in the
hall. He sends to know if your pleasure hold to play with
Laertes, or that you will take longer time.   170

HAMLET   I am constant to my purposes; they follow the King's
pleasure. If his fitness speaks, mine is ready, now or when-
soever, provided I be so able as now.

LORD   The King and Queen and all are coming down.

HAMLET   In happy time.   175

LORD   The Queen desires you to use some gentle entertainment to Laertes before you fall to play.

HAMLET   She well instructs me.

                              [Exit LORD.]

HORATIO   You will lose, my lord.

HAMLET   I do not think so. Since he went into France, I have   180
been in continual practice. I shall win at the odds. Thou
wouldst not think how ill all's here about my heart, but it is
no matter.

HORATIO   Nay, good my lord.

HAMLET   It is but foolery, but it is such a kind of gaingiving as   185
would perhaps trouble a woman.

HORATIO   If your mind dislike anything, obey it. I will forestall their repair hither and say you are not fit.

HAMLET   Not a whit, we defy augury. There is special providence in the fall of a sparrow. If it be now, 'tis not to come;   190
if it be not to come, it will be now; if it be not now, yet it will
come. The readiness is all. Since no man of aught he leaves
knows, what is't to leave betimes? Let be.

    A table prepared. [ENTER] *trumpets, drums, and officers with*
    cushions, KING, QUEEN, *and all the state, foils, daggers,*

---

    163. **out . . . encounter:** from social intercourse; **yeasty collection:** frothy assortment
          (of foolish manners and fashionable talk)
164–65. **carries . . . opinions:** enables them to converse with both the vulgar and refined
165–66. **blow . . . out:** i.e., put Osric and his kind to any test, and they collapse (like
          bubbles in froth)
176–77. **gentle entertainment:** courteous greeting
    185. **gaingiving:** misgiving, feeling of mistrust or apprehension
187–88. **forestall their repair:** intercept their coming
    189. **augury:** omens, forebodings
189–90. **There . . . sparrow:** (an echo of Matthew 10:29: "Are not two sparrows sold for
          a farthing, and one of them shall not fall on the ground without your Father?")
192–93. **Since . . . betimes:** since no man knows anything (**aught**) of what he leaves
          behind, what does it mean to die early (**betimes**)
  193.2. **s.d. state:** nobility, court

[*cups of wine,* OSRIC,] *and* LAERTES

KING   Come, Hamlet, come, and take this hand from me.

[*The* KING *puts* LAERTES'*s hand into* HAMLET'*s.*]

HAMLET   Give me your pardon, sir. I have done you wrong,   195
But pardon't, as you are a gentleman.
This presence knows,
And you must needs have heard, how I am punished
With a sore distraction. What I have done
That might your nature, honor, and exception   200
Roughly awake, I here proclaim was madness.
Was't Hamlet wronged Laertes? Never Hamlet.
If Hamlet from himself be ta'en away,
And when he's not himself does wrong Laertes,
Then Hamlet does it not. Hamlet denies it.   205
Who does it, then? His madness. If't be so,
Hamlet is of the faction that is wronged;
His madness is poor Hamlet's enemy.
Let my disclaiming from a purposed evil
Free me so far in your most generous thoughts   210
That I have shot my arrow o'er the house
And hurt my brother.

LAERTES   I am satisfied in nature,
Whose motive in this case should stir me most
To my revenge. But in my terms of honor
I stand aloof, and will no reconcilement   215
Till by some elder masters of known honor
I have a voice and precedent of peace
To keep my name ungored. But till that time
I do receive your offered love like love,
And will not wrong it.

HAMLET   I embrace it freely,   220
And will this brother's wager frankly play.
—Give us the foils.

LAERTES   Come, one for me.

HAMLET   I'll be your foil, Laertes. In mine ignorance

197. **presence:** royal assembly
200. **nature:** natural feelings; **exception:** disapproval
207. **faction:** party
209. **disclaiming from:** denial of
211. **That I have:** as if I had
212. **in nature:** as far as my feelings are concerned
214. **in . . . honor:** according to the principles of my honor
217. **voice . . . peace:** authoritative pronouncement for reconciliation
218. **name ungored:** reputation unharmed
221. **frankly:** freely, without ill will
223. **foil:** background setting against which jewels show more brightly (with a play on **foil** as fencing sword)

Your skill shall, like a star i'the darkest night,
Stick fiery off indeed.
LAERTES   You mock me, sir.   225
HAMLET   No, by this hand.
KING   Give them the foils, young Osric. Cousin Hamlet,
You know the wager?
HAMLET   Very well, my lord;
Your Grace has laid the odds o' the weaker side.
KING   I do not fear it; I have seen you both.   230
But since he is better, we have therefore odds.
LAERTES   This is too heavy. Let me see another.
HAMLET   This likes me well. These foils have all a length?

[*They prepare to play.*]

OSRIC   Ay, my good lord.
KING   Set me the stoups of wine upon that table.   235
If Hamlet give the first or second hit,
Or quit in answer of the third exchange,
Let all the battlements their ordnance fire.
The King shall drink to Hamlet's better breath,
And in the cup an union shall he throw,   240
Richer than that which four successive kings
In Denmark's crown have worn. Give me the cups,
And let the kettle to the trumpet speak,
The trumpet to the cannoneer without,
The cannons to the heavens, the heaven to earth,   245
"Now the King drinks to Hamlet." Come, begin.

            Trumpets the while.

And you, the judges, bear a wary eye.
HAMLET   Come on, sir.
LAERTES   Come, my lord.

            [*They play.* HAMLET *scores a hit.*]

HAMLET   One.   250
LAERTES   No.
HAMLET   Judgment?

225. **Stick fiery off:** show its shine to its best advantage
229. **laid . . . o':** bet on
231. **odds:** i.e., the three-hit spread
233. **likes:** pleases; **all a length:** all the same length
235. **stoups:** jugs or cups
237. **quit . . . exchange:** requite Laertes for earlier hits by scoring the third hit or by drawing even in the third bout
238. **ordnance:** cannons
240. **union:** pearl
243. **kettle:** kettledrum
244. **without:** outside
246. s.d. *the while:* for a while

OSRIC   A hit, a very palpable hit.

    Drum, trumpets, and shot. Flourish. A piece goes off.

LAERTES   Well, again.

KING   Stay, give me drink. Hamlet, this pearl is thine.   255
  Here's to thy health. [*He drinks.*] Give him the cup.

HAMLET   I'll play this bout first. Set it by awhile.
  Come. [*They play.*] Another hit; what say you?

LAERTES   I do confess't.

KING   Our son shall win.

QUEEN   He's fat and scant of breath.   260
  Here, Hamlet, take my napkin, rub thy brows.
  The Queen carouses to thy fortune, Hamlet.

HAMLET   Good madam.

KING   Gertrude, do not drink.

QUEEN   I will, my lord. I pray you pardon me. [*She drinks.*]   265

KING [*Aside*]   It is the poisoned cup; it is too late.

HAMLET   I dare not drink yet, madam; by-and-by.

QUEEN   Come, let me wipe thy face.

LAERTES [*Aside*]   My lord, I'll hit him now.

KING [*Aside*]   I do not think't.

LAERTES [*Aside*]   And yet it is almost against my conscience.   270

HAMLET   Come, for the third, Laertes; you do but dally.
  I pray you pass with your best violence;
  I am sure you make a wanton of me.

LAERTES   Say you so? Come on.

    [*They play.*]

OSRIC   Nothing neither way.   275

LAERTES   Have at you now!

    [LAERTES *wounds* HAMLET; *then, in scuffling, they*
    change rapiers, and HAMLET *wounds* LAERTES.]

KING   Part them! They are incensed.

HAMLET   Nay, come again!

    [*The* QUEEN *falls.*]

OSRIC   Look to the Queen there, ho!

HORATIO   They bleed on both sides. How is it, my lord?

OSRIC   How is't, Laertes?   280

---

253. s.d. *Flourish:* a trumpet fanfare; *piece:* cannon
260. **fat:** out of shape
261. **napkin:** handkerchief
262. **carouses:** drinks a toast
272. **pass:** thrust
273. **make . . . of:** i.e., toy with. A **wanton** is a spoiled child.
276.1–2. s.d. *they change rapiers:* (In some stagings, Hamlet, realizing that Laertes'
    sword is unbated, makes the exchange intentionally.)

LAERTES   Why, as a woodcock to my own springe, Osric;
  I am justly killed with mine own treachery.
HAMLET   How does the Queen?
KING   She swoons to see them bleed.
QUEEN   No, no, the drink, the drink—O my dear Hamlet!—
  The drink, the drink! I am poisoned. [*She dies.*]   285
HAMLET   O villainy! Ho, let the door be locked!
  Treachery! Seek it out!

                              [LAERTES *falls. Exit* OSRIC.]

LAERTES   It is here, Hamlet, thou art slain.
  No med'cine in the world can do thee good;
  In thee there is not half an hour's life;   290
  The treacherous instrument is in thy hand,
  Unbated and envenomed. The foul practice
  Hath turned itself on me. Lo, here I lie,
  Never to rise again. Thy mother's poisoned.
  I can no more. The King, the King's to blame.   295
HAMLET   The point envenomed too? Then, venom, to thy work!

      [*He stabs the* KING.]

ALL   Treason! treason!
KING   Oh, yet defend me, friends! I am but hurt.
HAMLET   [*Forcing the* KING *to drink*]
  Here, thou incestuous, damnèd Dane,
  Drink off this potion! Is thy union here?   300
  Follow my mother.

      [*The* KING *dies.*]

LAERTES   He is justly served;
  It is a poison tempered by himself.
  Exchange forgiveness with me, noble Hamlet.
  Mine and my father's death come not upon thee,
  Nor thine on me. [*He dies.*]   305
HAMLET   Heaven make thee free of it. I follow thee.
  I am dead, Horatio. Wretched Queen, adieu.
  You that look pale and tremble at this chance,
  That are but mutes or audience to this act,
  Had I but time—as this fell sergeant, Death,   310

---

  281. **woodcock:** bird supposed to be gullible; **springe:** snare
  292. **practice:** trickery
296ff.: (Compare the sequence of action with that in Quarto 1, Appendix 1, passage 7,
          p. 145.)
  300. **union:** pearl (with a pun on marriage)
  302. **tempered:** mixed
  308. **chance:** misfortune
  309. **mutes:** actors without speaking parts
  310. **fell sergeant:** cruel sergeant-at-arms (a civil officer who makes arrests). "Death is
          God's sergeant" was proverbial; see Dent 142.2.

Is strict in his arrest—oh, I could tell you—
But let it be. Horatio, I am dead;
Thou livest. Report me and my cause aright
To the unsatisfied.

HORATIO   Never believe it.
I am more an antique Roman than a Dane.   315
Here's yet some liquor left.

    [He attempts to drink from the poisoned cup but HAMLET
    restrains him.]

HAMLET   As thou'rt a man,
Give me the cup! Let go! By heaven, I'll ha't.
O God, Horatio, what a wounded name,
Things standing thus unknown, shall I leave behind me.
If thou didst ever hold me in thy heart,   320
Absent thee from felicity awhile,
And in this harsh world draw thy breath in pain,
To tell my story.   *A march afar off [and shot within].*
        What warlike noise is this?

    Enter OSRIC.

OSRIC   Young Fortinbras, with conquest come from Poland,
To th'ambassadors of England gives   325
This warlike volley.

HAMLET   Oh, I die, Horatio.
The potent poison quite o'ercrows my spirit.
I cannot live to hear the news from England,
But I do prophesy th'election lights
On Fortinbras. He has my dying voice.   330
So tell him, with th'occurrents more and less,
Which have solicited—the rest is silence. *[He dies.]*

HORATIO   Now cracks a noble heart. Good night, sweet prince,
And flights of angels sing thee to thy rest. *[March within.]*
Why does the drum come hither?   335

---

311. **strict:** (1) just; (2) inescapable
315. **Roman:** (Romans committed suicide to avoid dishonor and sometimes to follow a
    master in death.)
321. **Absent . . . felicity:** keep yourself from the happiness of death. Perhaps an echo
    of the burial service, in which the deceased are said to be "in joy and felicity."
323. **s.d. *march*:** (probably indicated by a drumbeat)
327. **o'ercrows:** triumphs over
329. **election lights:** election of a new king alights
331. **occurrents:** events
332. **solicited:** prompted. Hamlet does not finish the thought, presumably referring to
    his vengeance or his naming of Fortinbras the next king.
333. **cracks:** (The heartstrings, tendons supporting the heart, were supposed to crack
    at death.)
334. **flights of angels:** may flying companies of angels

Enter FORTINBRAS, *with the* [*English*] AMBASSADORS
[*with drums, colors, and* ATTENDANTS].

FORTINBRAS   Where is this sight?

HORATIO   What is it you would see?
  If aught of woe or wonder, cease your search.

FORTINBRAS   This quarry cries on havoc. O proud Death,
  What feast is toward in thine eternal cell,
  That thou so many princes at a shot   340
  So bloodily hast struck?

AMBASSADOR   The sight is dismal,
  And our affairs from England come too late.
  The ears are senseless that should give us hearing
  To tell him his commandment is fulfilled,
  That Rosencrantz and Guildenstern are dead.   345
  Where should we have our thanks?

HORATIO   Not from his mouth,
  Had it th'ability of life to thank you.
  He never gave commandment for their death.
  But since, so jump upon this bloody question,
  You from the Polack wars, and you from England,   350
  Are here arrived, give order that these bodies
  High on a stage be placèd to the view,
  And let me speak to th'yet unknowing world
  How these things came about. So shall you hear
  Of carnal, bloody, and unnatural acts,   355
  Of accidental judgments, casual slaughters,
  Of deaths put on by cunning, and for no cause,
  And, in this upshot, purposes mistook
  Fall'n on th'inventors' heads. All this can I
  Truly deliver.

FORTINBRAS   Let us haste to hear it,   360
  And call the noblest to the audience.
  For me, with sorrow I embrace my fortune.

335.2. s.d. *colors:* flags
   338. **quarry:** heap of dead (literally, parts of a deer carcass); **cries on havoc:** proclaims
         a general slaughter
   339. **toward:** in preparation
   341. **dismal:** disastrous. From *dies mali,* "evil days," **dismal** denoted a stronger sense
         of calamity than it does today.
   344. **him:** i.e., Claudius
   349. **jump:** precisely; **question:** dispute
   352. **stage:** platform
   355. **carnal:** fleshly, sensual (referring to the incestuous marriage); **bloody . . . acts:**
         the fratricide and murder of Hamlet
   356. **accidental judgments:** retributions in apparent accidents; **casual:** occurring by
         chance
   358. **upshot:** conclusion

I have some rights of memory in this kingdom,
Which now to claim my vantage doth invite me.

HORATIO   Of that I shall have also cause to speak,   365
And from his mouth whose voice will draw on more.
But let this same be presently performed,
Even while men's minds are wild, lest more mischance
On plots and errors happen.

FORTINBRAS   Let four captains
Bear Hamlet like a soldier to the stage,   370
For he was likely, had he been put on,
To have proved most royal; and for his passage,
The soldiers' music and the rite of war
Speak loudly for him.
Take up the bodies. Such a sight as this   375
Becomes the field, but here shows much amiss.
Go bid the soldiers shoot.

> *Exeunt [marching, with the bodies;*
> *after which a peal of ordnance is shot off].*

FINIS.

363. **of memory:** unforgotten
364. **vantage:** favorable opportunity
366. **draw on more:** induce further voices (for Fortinbras)
369. **On:** (1) in consequence of; (2) on top of
371. **put on:** put to the test
372. **passage:** death
373–74. **The . . . Speak:** let the . . . speak
377.2. s.d. **peal of ordnance:** discharge of a cannon

TEXTUAL NOTES

These notes record substantive departures from the copy text (Q2), and do not normally include changes in lineation and punctuation and what appear to be typographical errors. Rejected Q2 readings appear after the bracket in roman type. There are no designations for acts or scenes in Q2, but I have added them from the Folio and from editorial tradition. Proofreading changes made in the printing house are designated as *Q2 corrected* or *Q2 miscorrected*.

1.1.
18 soldier] souldiers
46 harrows] horrowes
65 sledded Polacks] sleaded pollax
75 why] with
95 cov'nant] comart
96 designed] desseigne
109 rummage] Romadge
110 e'en so] enso
114 mote] moth
119 At] As
123 feared] feare
141 s.d.] *opposite 140–41*

1.2.
1 *and elsewhere* s.p. KING] *Claud.*
38 dilated] delated
58 He] *not in Q2*
67 so, my] so much my
77 good] coold
82 shapes] chapes
83 denote] deuote
105 corpse] course
112 you. For] you for
118 lose] loose
129 solid] sallied
132 canon] cannon
132 self-slaughter] seale slaughter
133 weary] wary
140 satyr] satire
143 would] should
178 see] *not in Q2*
200 cap-à-pie] *Capapea*
209 Where, as] Whereas
216 its] it
238 s.p. MAR., BAR.] *Both.*
241 tonight] to nigh

248   whatsoever] what someuer
251   eleven] a leauen
253   s.d.] *after 252*
256   Foul] fonde

1.3.

3   convey is] conuay, in
28   weigh] way
30   lose] loose
47   steep] *Q2 corrected*; step *Q2 uncorrected*
51   s.d.] *after* "rede" *(50)*
73   Are] Or
74   be] boy
75   loan] loue
76   dulls the] dulleth
108   Wronging] Wrong
114   springes] springs
124   tether] tider
128   implorators] imploratotors
129   bawds] bonds
130   beguile] beguide

1.4.

2   a] *not in Q2*
6   s.d. go] *goes*
17   revel] reueale
19   clepe] clip
36   evil] eale
37   often dout] of a doubt
69   lord] *Q2 corrected; not in Q2 uncorrected*
70   summit] somnet
80   off] of
82   artery] arture
86   away!—Go] away, goe
86   s.d. *Exeunt] Exit*
87   imagination] imagion

1.5.

1   Whither] Whether
43   wit] wits
55   lust] but
56   sate] sort
58   scent] sent
67   alleys] allies
84   howsoever] howsomeuer
128,150   s.p. hor., mar.] *Booth.*

146   O'ermaster't] Oremastret
159   cellarage] Sellerige
164   *et*] &
177   soe'er] so mere

2.1.

       s.d. *man.*] *man or two.*
28   no] *not in Q2*
40   sullies] sallies
41   wi'the] with
56   there o'ertook] there, or tooke
60   takes] take
66   be wi'ye; fare] buy ye, far
72   s.d. *Exit* reynaldo.] *after 71*
72   s.d. *Enter* ophelia.] *after 71*
97   o' doors] adoores
103   passion] passions
110   quoted] coted

2.2.

58   s.d.] *after 57*
90   since] *not in Q2*
120   oh, most] O most
124   This] pol. This
125   above] about
136   winking] working
142   his] her
147   watch] wath
169   s.d. *Exeunt*] *Exit (after 168)*
207   sanity] sanctity
214   s.d.] *after 210*
219   excellent] extent
222   overhappy. On] euer happy on
223   cap] lap
265   What a] What
280   of] on
283   blank] black
302   lest my] let me
313   Haply] Happily
316   o'] a
328   light. For] light for
351   By'r] by
355   e'en to't] ento't
355–356 French falconers] friendly Fankners
359   *and elsewhere* s.p. first player] player.
380   heraldry] heraldy

380   dismal. Head] dismall head
398   Then senseless Ilium] *not in Q2*
405   And] *not in Q2*
419   fellies] follies
426   ah] a
431   bisson rheum] *Bison* rehume
439   husband's] husband
444   whe'er] where
452   bodikins] bodkin
461   ha't] hate
466   s.d.] *after 465*
470   good-bye] God buy
475   wanned] wand
482   the cue] that
500   ha'fatted] a fatted
504   father] *not in Q2*
508   scullion] stallyon
520   the devil . . . devil] a deale . . . deale

3.1.
46   loneliness] lowlines
56   s.d.] *after 55*
65   wished. To] wisht to
76   quietus] quietas
84   of us all] *not in Q2*
86   sicklied] sickled
108   your honesty] you
119   inoculate] euocutat
122   to] *not in Q2*
143   jig] gig
144   lisp] list
155   music] musickt
156   that] what
160   ] *Q2 miscorrected has an Exit for Ophelia.*
187   unwatched] vnmatcht

3.2.
3   lief] liue
9   tatters] totters
9   split] spleet
27   praise] praysd
39   s.d.] *after 40*
45   ho] howe
58   Sh'hath] S'hath
83   detecting] detected
122   by'r] ber

125.1   s.d. *sound*] *sounds*
125.5   s.d. *comes*] *come*
127   is mitching malicho] munching *Mallico*
128   s.d.] *after* "fellow" *(129)*
130   counsel] *not in Q2*
141   *and elsewhere* s.p. PLAYER KING] *King.*
142   orbèd] orb'd the
147   *and elsewhere* s.p. PLAYER QUEEN] *Quee.*
156   love] Lord
157   sized] ciz'd
168   ] *opposite 167, 169*
169   s.p. PLAYER QUEEN] *not in Q2*
177   like] the
186   joys] ioy
186   grieves] griefes
211   ] *opposite 209–210*
215   s.d. *Exit.*] *Exeunt.*
223   how? Tropically.] how tropically,
228   s.d.] *after 229*
236   mis-take] mistake
240   Confederate] Considerat
242   infected] inuected
262   ay] I
288   start] stare
321   s.d.] *after 319*
335   thumb] the vmber
346   me,] me not,
346   s.d.] *after 347*
357   s.p. HAMLET] *as catchword (sig. H4)*
361   breathes] breakes
368   daggers] dagger
370   soever] someuer

3.3.

18   summit] somnet
19   huge] hough
22   ruin] raine
23   with] *not in Q2*
24   voyage] viage
35   s.d.] *after* "know"
56   pardoned] pardon
58   Offense's] Offences
58   shove] showe
75   revenged] reuendge
79   hire and salary] base and silly

3.4.

5   *and elsewhere* s.p. QUEEN] *Ger.*
5   warrant] wait
6   s.d.] *after* "round" (5)
19   inmost] most
43   off] of
53   ] That] *Ham.* That
54   s.p. HAMLET] *at* 53
60   heaven-kissing] heaue, a kissing
77   was't] wast
91   grainèd] greeued
98   tithe] kyth
103   s.d.] *after 102*
146   I] *not in Q2*
161   live] leaue
168   on. Refrain tonight] on to refraine night
172   shame] *not in Q2*
189   ravel] rouell
201   to breathe] to breath

4.1.

   s.d. to] *and*
32   s.d.] *after 31*
40   So, haply, slander] *not in Q2*

4.2.

   s.d.] *Enter Hamlet, Rosencraus, and others.*
16   ape] apple

4.3.

11   ] s.p. *"King." before* "How"
15   Ho] How

4.4.

30   be wi'you] buy you

4.5.

20   s.d.] *after 16*
29   *Song.] after 30*
38   *Song.] after 39*
42   God 'ild] good dild
97   s.d.] *after 95*
106   They] The
108   s.d.] *after 109*
120   brows] browé
142   swoopstake] soopstake
157   Till] Tell

176	o'] a

192–93 soul." / And] soule, and
193 be wi'you] buy you
194 see] *not in Q2*
207 trophy, sword] trophe sword
208 rite] right

4.6.

9 an't] and
23 bore] bord
27 He] *So*
29 Come] *Hor.* Come
29 give] *not in Q2*

4.7.

11 unsinewed] vnsinnow'd
12 they're] tha r
15 conjunctive] concliue
22 gyves] Giues
23 loud a wind] loued Arm'd
47 What] *King.* What
54 shall] *not in Q2*
60 checking] the King
76 ribbon] ribaud
86 demi-natured] demy natur'd
87 my] me
99 Th'escrimers] the Scrimures
114 wick] weeke
121 spendthrift] spend thirfts
122 o'] of
124 in deed] indeede
137 pass] pace
139 that] *not in Q2*
149 shape. If] shape if
155 ha't] hate
158 prepared] prefard
170 cold] cull-cold
189 o'] a

5.1.

1 *and elsewhere* s.p. GRAVEDIGGER] *Clowne*
8 *se offendendo*] so offended
11 Argal,] or all;
21 on't] an't
22 o'] a
53 stoup] soope

62	daintier] dintier
78	chapless] Choples
79	mazard] maffene
106	Oh] or
155	three-and-twenty] 23.
162	sir, Yorick's] sir *Yoricks*
177	o'] a
194	winter's] waters
194	s.d.] *opposite 195–97*
199	its] it
239	and] *not in Q2*
254	thou'lt] th'owt
272	s.d.] *Exit Hamlet and Horatio. (opposite 272–73)*
279	thereby] *Q2 corrected;* thirtie *Q2 uncorrected*
279	Till] Tell

5.2.

5	Methought] my thought
6	bilboes] bilbo
9	pall] *Q2 uncorrected;* fall *Q2 miscorrected*
30	Ere] Or
43	"as"es] as sir
52	Subscribed] Subscribe
67	s.p. *and elsewhere]* Cour.
68	humbly] humble
82	sultry] sully
82	for] or
90–91	gentleman] gentlemen
92	feelingly] sellingly
96	dozy] *Q2 uncorrected* (dosie); *dazzie Q2 miscorrected*
97	yaw] *Q2 uncorrected;* raw *Q2 miscorrected*
107	do't] *Q2 corrected;* too't *Q2 uncorrected*
120	his] this
134	carriages] carriage
136	it might be] it be *Q2 uncorrected;* it be might *Q2 miscorrected*
140	"impawned," as] *not in Q2*
156–7	Yours. 'A does] Yours doo's
160	comply] *not in Q2*
160	so] *Q2 corrected; not in Q2 uncorrected*
164	yeasty] histy
165	winnowed] trennowed
185	gaingiving] gamgiuing
190	now] *not in Q2*
191	yet it will] yet it well

193	betimes? Let] betimes, let
218	keep] *not in Q2*
218	till] all
229	o'] a'
235	stoups] stoops
240	union] Vnice *Q2 uncorrected;* Onixe *Q2 corrected*
246	s.d.] *opposite 246–47*
253	s.d.] *opposite 253–54*
278	ho] howe
283	swoons] sounds
286	Ho] how
291	thy] my
300	off] of
300	thy union] the Onixe
317	ha't] hate
323	s.d.] *opposite 322–23*
338	proud] prou'd
353	th'yet] yet
366	on] no

APPENDIX 1

Passages from Quarto 1 (1603)†

I.

Hamlet's "To be or not to be" soliloquy occurs in different form at the equivalent of Quarto 2, 2.2.169 instead of at 3.1.57. In Quarto 1 the speech and subsequent nunnery scene precede instead of follow the fishmonger sequence with Polonius, Hamlet's meeting with Rosencrantz and Guildenstern, the arrival of the Players, the Pyrrhus speech, the "Rogue and peasant slave" soliloquy, and the meeting of the King, Queen, Polonius, Rosencrantz, and Guildenstern. Compare Q2, 3.1.57–91.

HAMLET To be or not to be—ay, there's the point.
To die, to sleep—is that all? Ay, all.
No, to sleep, to dream—ay, marry, there it goes,
For in that dream of death, when we're awake,
And borne before an everlasting judge   5
From whence no passenger ever returned,
The undiscovered country, at whose sight
The happy smile and the accursèd damned.
But for this, the joyful hope of this,
Who'd bear the scorns and flattery of the world—   10
Scorned by the right rich, the rich cursed of the poor,
The widow being oppressed, the orphan wronged,
The taste of hunger, or a tyrant's reign,
And thousand more calamities besides,
To grunt and sweat under this weary life—   15
When that he may his full quietus make
With a bare bodkin? Who would this endure
But for a hope of something after death,
Which puzzles the brain and doth confound the sense,
Which makes us rather bear those evils we have   20
Than fly to others that we know not of?

---

† Line references are to *Hamlet: The Texts of 1603 and 1623*, ed. Ann Thompson and Neil Taylor (London: Arden Shakespeare, 2006).
As in Q2, Corambis [Polonius] and the King withdraw, leaving Ophelia on stage.
3. **there it goes:** that (i.e., dreaming) is the problem
4. **we're:** (Q1: "wee")
5. **borne:** carried; **judge:** (This figure is not in Q2 or F.)
8. **damned:** are damned
8–9. **happy smile . . . joyful hope:** (These emphases are not in Q2 or F.)
9. **But for this:** if it were not for this hope of salvation in the next life
11. **right:** (1) very; (2) deservedly
16. **quietus:** release from debt
17. **bodkin:** dagger

Ay, that—oh, this conscience makes cowards of us all.
—Lady, in thy orisons be all my sins remembered.
(Sigs. D4v–E; 7.115–37)

2.

Compare this speech to Hamlet's "Rogue and peasant slave" soliloquy
at Q2, 2.2.471–526.

HAMLET   Why, what a dunghill idiot slave am I!
    Why, these players here draw water from eyes
    For Hecuba. Why, what is Hecuba to him,
    Or he to Hecuba?
    What would he do an if he had my loss—   5
    His father murdered and a crown bereft him?
    He would turn all his tears to drops of blood,
    Amaze the standers-by with his laments,
    Strike more than wonder in the judicial ears,
    Confound the ignorant, and make mute the wise.   10
    Indeed, his passion would be general.
    Yet I, like to an ass and John-a-dreams,
    Having my father murdered by a villain,
    Stand still and let it pass. Why, sure I am a coward.
    Who plucks me by the beard or twits my nose,   15
    Gives me the lie i'the throat down to the lungs?
    Sure, I should take it; or else I have no gall
    Or, by this, I should ha' fatted all the region kites
    With this slave's offal. This damnèd villain,
    Treacherous, bawdy, murderous villain!   20
    Why, this is brave, that I, the son of my dear father,
    Should like a scullion, like a very drab,
    Thus rail in words. About my brain!
    I have heard that guilty creatures sitting at a play
    Hath, by the very cunning of the scene,   25

22. **conscience:** (1) faculty of moral judgment; (2) consciousness
23. **Lady:** i.e., Ophelia; **orisons:** prayers
 5. **an if:** if (Q1: "and if")
 6. **bereft:** deprived. Not in Q2 or F, this grievance suggests Hamlet's ambition and a
    personal reason for animosity toward Claudius.
 8. **Amaze:** stun
11. **general:** universal
12. **John-a-dreams:** a dreamy, idle fellow
15. **twits:** (1) hits; (2) finds fault with
16. **Gives . . . lie:** calls me a liar
17. **gall:** a substance thought to produce bitter and violent feelings in the liver
18. **region kites:** predatory birds in the air
19. **this slave's offal:** i.e., Claudius's carcass
21. **brave:** admirable
22. **scullion:** menial kitchen servant (Q1: "scalion"); **drab:** prostitute
23. **About:** to work
25. **cunning:** art

Confessed a murder committed long before.
This spirit that I have seen may be the devil,
And out of my weakness and my melancholy—
As he is very potent with such men—
Doth seek to damn me.   30
I will have sounder proofs. The play's the thing
Wherein I'll catch the conscience of the King.
(Sigs. E4v–F; 7.404–35)

3.

Hamlet's advice to the players includes this additional passage, an expanded warning for the Clown; compare Q2, 3.2.33–39.

HAMLET   And—do your hear?—let not your Clown speak more
than is set down. There be of them, I can tell you, that will
laugh themselves to set on some quantity of barren spectators to laugh with them, albeit there is some necessary point
in the play then to be observed. Oh, 'tis vile and shows a piti-   5
ful ambition in the fool that useth it. And then you have
some again that keeps one suit of jests—as a man is known
by one suit of apparel—and gentlemen quotes his jests down
in their tables before they come to the play, as thus: "Cannot
you stay till I eat my porridge?" and "You owe me a quarter's   10
wages!" and "My coat wants a cullison!" and "Your beer is
sour!" and, blabbering with his lips and thus keeping in his
cinquepace of jests when, God knows, the warm Clown cannot make a jest unless by chance, as the blind man catcheth
a hare. Masters, tell him of it.   15
(Sigs. F2r–v; 9.23–38)

4.

The King's remorseful prayer, in this text the first direct confirmation of his guilt; compare Q2, 3.3.36–72.

KING   Oh, that this wet that falls upon my face
Would wash the crime clear from my conscience!
When I look up to heaven I see my trespass;

---

2. **of them:** i.e., some of them
3. **barren:** dull, stupid
7. **suit of jests:** routine of jokes
9. **tables:** notebooks. Examples of punchlines or comic catch phrases follow in quotation marks.
10. **a quarter's:** i.e., three months
11. **cullison:** badge indicating one's crest or patron
13. **cinquepace:** lively dance
13. **warm:** eager, ardent
 1. **this wet:** these tears (an indication of the stage action)

The earth doth still cry out upon my fact.
Pay me the murder of a brother and a king   5
And the adulterous fault I have committed.
Oh, these are sins that are unpardonable.
Why, say thy sins were blacker than is jet,
Yet may contrition make them as white as snow.
Ay, but still to persever in a sin,   10
It is an act 'gainst the universal power.
Most wretched man, stoop, bend thee to thy prayer,
Ask grace of heaven to keep thee from despair.

He kneels.

(Sig. G1v; 10. 1–13)

5.

The closet scene, wherein the Queen explicitly denies knowledge
of the murder and agrees to assist Hamlet, in contrast to Q2,
3.4.137–220.

HAMLET No? Why, see the King my father,
My father in the habit as he lived!
Look you how pale he looks.
See how he steals away out of the portal.
Look, there he goes.   5

Exit GHOST.

QUEEN   Alas, it is the weakness of thy brain
Which makes thy tongue to blazon thy heart's griefs.
But, as I have a soul, I swear by heaven
I never knew of this most horrid murder.
But, Hamlet, this is only fantasy,   10
And for my love forget these idle fits.
HAMLET   "Idle"? No, mother, my pulse doth beat like yours.
It is not madness that possesseth Hamlet.
O mother, if ever you did my dear father love,
Forbear the adulterous bed tonight   15
And win yourself by little, as you may.

---

4. **fact:** crime
5. **Pay me:** punish me for
6. **adulterous:** (The King does not refer to adultery in Q2 or F.)
8. **jet:** shiny coal
10. **persever:** (accented on the second syllable)
11. **universal power:** i.e., God. The phrase does not appear in Q2 or F.
4. **portal:** door (one of the usual doors backstage and not the trapdoor in the stage)
7. **blazon:** proclaim
10. **this . . . fantasy:** the ghost is simply a product of your imagination
11. **idle:** delirious
15. **Forbear:** refrain from, avoid
16. **win . . . little:** distance yourself gradually

In time it may be you will loathe him quite.
And, mother, but assist me in revenge,
And in his death your infamy shall die.

QUEEN   Hamlet, I vow by that Majesty   20
That knows our thoughts and looks into our hearts,
I will conceal, consent, and do my best,
What stratagem soe'er thou shalt devise.

HAMLET   It is enough. Mother, good night.
Come, sir, I'll provide for you a grave,   25
Who was in life a foolish, prating knave.

Exit HAMLET *with the dead body.*
(Sigs. G3r–v; 11.77–103)

6.

Scene 14, equivalent to parts of Q2, 4.6, 4.7, and 5.2, is unique in presenting a conspiratorial conversation between Horatio and the Queen.

Enter HORATIO *and the* QUEEN.

HORATIO   Madam, your son is safe arrived in Denmark.
This letter I even now received of him,
Wherein he writes how he escaped the danger
And subtle treason that the King had plotted.
Being crossed by the contention of the winds,   5
He found the packet sent to the King of England,
Wherein he saw himself betrayed to death,
As at his next conversing with Your Grace,
He will relate the circumstance at full.

QUEEN   Then I perceive there's treason in his looks   10
That seemed to sugar o'er his villainy.
But I will soothe and please him for a time,
For murderous minds are always jealous.
But know not you, Horatio, where he is?

HORATIO   Yes, madam, and he hath appointed me   15
To meet him on the east side of the city
Tomorrow morning.

QUEEN   Oh, fail not, good Horatio,
And withal commend me a mother's care to him.

---

20. **Majesty:** i.e., God
23. **What stratagem soe'er:** in whatever plot
3–7. (The Queen hears no comparable revelation of the King's treachery toward Hamlet in Q2 or F.)
  3. **Wherein:** (Q1: "Whereas")
  4. **crossed . . . winds:** delayed by contrary winds or a storm
  8. **conversing:** (Q1: "conversion")
13. **jealous:** suspicious
14. **he:** i.e., Hamlet
18. **withal:** at the same time; **commend me:** convey for me

Bid him awhile be wary of his presence,
Lest that he fail in that he goes about.   20
HORATIO   Madam, never make doubt of that. I think by this
The news be come to court he is arrived.
Observe the King and you shall quickly find,
Hamlet being here, things fell not to his mind.
QUEEN   But what became of Gilderstone and Rossencraft?   25
HORATIO   He being set ashore, they went for England.
And in the packet there writ down that doom
To be performed on them 'pointed for him.
And by great chance he had his father's seal,
So all was done without discovery.   30
QUEEN   Thanks be to heaven for blessing of the prince!
Horatio, once again I take my leave,
With thousand mother's blessings to my son.
HORATIO   Madam, adieu.

                                                            [*Exeunt.*]
(Sigs. H2v–H3; Scene 14)

7.

The deaths of the King, Laertes, and Hamlet; compare Q2, 5.2.296–336.

HAMLET   The poisoned instrument within my hand?
Then, venom to thy venom! [*He stabs the* KING.] Die damned
villain!
Come, drink. [*Forcing the* KING *to drink*] Here lies thy union,
here!
       The KING *dies.*
LAERTES   Oh, he is justly served.
Hamlet, before I die, here take my hand   5
And, withal, my love. I do forgive thee. LAERTES *dies.*
HAMLET   And I thee.
Oh, I am dead, Horatio. Fare thee well.
HORATIO   No, I am more an antique Roman than a Dane.
Here is some poison left. [*He takes the cup.*]   10

19. **wary . . . presence:** careful about where he appears
24. **to his mind:** according to his plan
25. **But . . . Rossencraft:** (In Q2 and F Horatio raises this concern directly with Hamlet
       and he responds; see 5.2.56ff.)
27. **doom:** i.e., order for execution
28. **'pointed:** appointed
29. **seal:** impress, usually on a ring, for the authentication of documents
2. **venom . . . venom:** (1) poison, do your work; (2) poison, return to your source. In Q1,
       the King suggests both the poisoned sword and poisoned drink.
3. **union:** marriage with the Queen (now dead). In Q2 and F the King produces a
       "union," i.e., pearl (perhaps the poison), and drops it in the cup.
6. **withal:** in addition
9. **Roman:** (Romans committed suicide to avoid dishonor and sometimes to follow a
       master in death.)

HAMLET   Upon my love I charge thee, let it go.
  Oh, fie, Horatio, an if thou shouldst die,
  What a scandal wouldst thou leave behind!
  What tongue should tell the story of our deaths
  If not from thee? Oh, my heart sinks, Horatio.   15
  Mine eyes have lost their sight, my tongue his use.
  Farewell, Horatio. Heaven receive my soul. HAMLET *dies.*

  Enter VOLTEMAR *and the* AMBASSADORS *from England.*

  Enter FORTENBRASSE *with his train.*

FORTENBRASSE   Where is this bloody sight?
  (Sigs. I3v–I4; 17.95–112)

APPENDIX 2

Passages from the Folio (1623)[†]

I.

Dialogue with Rosencrantz and Guildenstern on Denmark as prison,
an addition after Q2, 2.2.232, "But your news is not true."

HAMLET   Let me question more in particular. What have you,
  my good friends, deserved at the hands of Fortune that she
  sends you to prison hither?
GUILDENSTERN   Prison, my lord?
HAMLET   Denmark's a prison.   5
ROSENCRANTZ   Then is the world one.
HAMLET   A goodly one, in which there are many confines,
  wards, and dungeons, Denmark being one o'the worst.
ROSENCRANTZ   We think not so, my lord.
HAMLET   Why, then, 'tis none to you, for there is nothing either   10
  good or bad but thinking makes it so. To me it is a prison.
ROSENCRANTZ   Why, then, your ambition makes it one; 'tis too
  narrow for your mind.

---

12. **an if:** if (Q1: "and if")
17. **Heaven . . . soul:** (Perhaps an attempt to substitute for Horatio's lovely valediction in
    Q2 and F, "Good night, sweet prince, / And flights of angels sing thee to thy rest," Q2
    5.2.333–34.)
  † Line references are to *Hamlet: The Texts of 1603 and 1623*, ed. Ann Thompson and
    Neil Taylor (London: Arden Shakespeare, 2006).
 3. **prison:** (The Arden 2 editors observe that the concept of the state as prison domi-
    nated productions of *Hamlet* in the Soviet Union and eastern Europe, notably the
    "Iron Curtain *Hamlet*," directed by Nikolay Okhlopkov, Moscow, 1954, and Grigori
    Kosintsev's filmed *Hamlet*, 1964.)
 7. **confines:** places of confinement
 8. **wards:** cells

HAMLET   O God, I could be bounded in a nutshell and count
myself a king of infinite space were it not that I have bad   15
dreams.

GUILDENSTERN   Which dreams, indeed, are ambition, for the
very substance of the ambitious is merely the shadow of a
dream.

HAMLET   A dream itself is but a shadow.   20

ROSENCRANTZ   Truly, and I hold ambition of so airy and light
a quality that it is but a shadow's shadow.

HAMLET   Then are our beggars bodies and our monarchs and
outstretched heroes the beggars' shadows. Shall we to the
court? For, by my fay, I cannot reason.   25

BOTH   We'll wait upon you.

HAMLET   No such matter. I will not sort you with the rest of
my servants, for to speak to you like an honest man, I am
most dreadfully attended.
(Sig. oo3v; 2.2.238–67)

2.

Discussion of the children's companies, an addition to Q2, 2.2.290.

HAMLET   How comes it? Do they grow rusty?

ROSENCRANTZ   Nay, their endeavor keeps in the wonted pace.
But there is, sir, an aerie of children, little eyases, that cry
out on the top of question and are most tyrannically clapped
for't. These are now the fashion, and so berattle the com-   5
mon stages—so they call them—that many wearing rapiers
are afraid of goose quills and dare scarce come thither.

HAMLET   What, are they children? Who maintains 'em? How
are they escoted? Will they pursue the quality no longer than

18. **substance . . . ambitious:** object of ambition
23. **bodies:** i.e., substantial things (because not ambitious, in contrast to the **monarchs** and **outstretched heroes**)
25. **fay:** faith; **reason:** continue in disputation
26. **wait upon:** accompany (with a sense of "serve")
27. **sort:** classify
29. **dreadfully attended:** badly served
1ff. (This passage alludes to the rivalry between the children's companies and adult
actors.)
2. **keeps:** maintains; **wonted:** usual
3. **aerie:** brood (literally, nest of a bird of prey); **eyases:** young hawks (F: "Yases")
3–4. **cry . . . question:** make more noise than others in the controversy
4. **tyrannically clapped:** vehemently applauded
5. **berattle:** assail with noise (F: "be-ratled")
5–6. **common stages:** public theaters (where the adults acted)
6. **many wearing rapiers:** i.e., fashionable young men
7. **goose quills:** i.e., the pens of satirists (who work for the children and would
mock patrons of the adult players)
9. **escoted:** paid for; **quality:** profession (of acting)
9–10. **no . . . sing:** i.e., until their voice breaks (at which point they must become adult
actors or change professions)

they can sing? Will they not say afterwards if they should   10
grow themselves to common players—as it is most like if
their means are no better—their writers do them wrong to
make them exclaim against their own succession?

ROSENCRANTZ   Faith, there has been much to-do on both sides
and the nation holds it no sin to tar them to controversy.   15
There was for a while no money bid for argument unless the
poet and the player went to cuffs in the question.

HAMLET   Is't possible?

GUILDENSTERN   Oh, there has been much throwing about of
brains.   20

HAMLET   Do the boys carry it away?

ROSENCRANTZ   Ay, that they do, my lord—Hercules and his
load too.
       (Sigs. oo3v–oo4; 2.2.335–60)

                              3.

The dumb show; compare Q2, 3.2.125 s.d.

        Hautboys play. The dumb show enters.
        Enter a KING *and* QUEEN *very lovingly, the* QUEEN
        embracing him. She kneels and makes show of protesta-
        tion unto him. He takes her up and declines his head
        upon her neck, lays him down upon a bank of flowers.   5
        She, seeing him asleep, leaves him. Anon comes in a fel-
        low, takes off his crown, kisses it, and pours poison in
        the King's ears, and exits. The QUEEN *returns, finds the*
        KING *dead, and makes passionate action. The* POISONER
        with some two or three mutes comes in again, seeming to 10
        lament with her. The dead body is carried away. The

    11. **to:** into; **most like:** most likely (F: "like most")
    12. **means:** means of support; **their writers:** i.e., the poets wielding the goose quills
        above
    13. **exclaim . . . succession:** rail at their own future profession
    14. **to-do:** ado (F: "to do")
    15. **holds . . . sin:** does not think it wrong; **tar:** incite
    16. **argument:** plot of a play (to be sold to theater companies)
    17. **cuffs . . . question:** blows in the dispute
19–20. **throwing . . . brains:** (1) mental energy expended; (2) heads cracked in violence
    21. **it:** i.e., victory
22–23. **Hercules . . . load:** (a probable allusion to the sign of the public Globe Theatre,
        which featured Hercules carrying the world)
   s.d. *Hautboys:* high-pitched wind instruments, similar to modern oboes
  3–4. *kneels . . . protestation:* (This detail may clarify the stage action in Q2.)
    5. *him:* himself
    6. *Anon:* directly
    7. *his:* i.e., the King's
   10. *mutes:* actors with non-speaking parts

POISONER *woos the* QUEEN *with gifts; she seems loath and unwilling awhile, but in the end accepts his love.*

Exeunt.

(Sig. oo6; 3.2.131 s.d.)

4.

Hamlet and Horatio's conversation, an addition after "is't not perfect conscience?", Q2, 5.2.66.

HAMLET   Is't not perfect conscience
  To quit him with this arm? And is't not to be damned
  To let this canker of our nature come
  In further evil?
HORATIO   It must be shortly known to him from England   5
  What is the issue of the business there.
HAMLET   It will be short. The interim's mine,
  And a man's life's no more than to say "one."
  But I am very sorry, good Horatio,
  That to Laertes I forgot myself   10
  For by the image of my cause I see
  The portraiture of his. I'll court his favors.
  But sure the bravery of his grief did put me
  Into a tow'ring passion.
HORATIO   Peace, who comes here?

  Enter young OSRIC.

(Sig. pp6; 5.2.67–81)

---

  1. **perfect conscience:** perfectly justifiable
  2. **quit:** requite, pay back
  3. **canker:** ulcer; **our nature:** i.e., the human race
3–4. **come In:** grow into
  7. **It:** i.e., the time between the present moment and the revelation of the news from England or Hamlet's revenge (**the interim**)
  8. **a . . . "one":** a man lives no longer than the time it takes to say "one"
  10. **forgot myself:** behaved badly (at the graveyard)
11–12. **by . . . his:** i.e., by remembering my feelings toward my father and need for revenge, I understand his feelings toward his father and his need for revenge
  12. **court:** (F: "count")
  13. **bravery:** bravado

THE ACTORS' GALLERY

John Barrymore's demonic Hamlet, 1922

EDWIN BOOTH

Notes (1878)†

At 1.2.65, Hamlet's first speech: Courteous, easy, kindly with all, to the lowest in rank he is most affable. Above all things, a *gentleman*, even to those he hates. Feminine, but not effeminate, in feeling. This is the basis on which you may build whatever Hamlet pleaseth thee.

At 1.4.86, Hamlet's exit after the Ghost: The traditional action here is to trail the sword while the left hand is extended towards the ghost. By way of improvement Forrest[1] changed this and pointed the sword and shook it threateningly at the impalpable shade. (I believe Garrick[2] used a similar gesture.) By an awkward movement on the part of Horatio I once lost my grasp of the hilt and caught the sword by the blade. I avoided grief of this lucky accident and held the weapon up as a moral guard against the spirit—the hilt and handle forming the sign of the cross.

At 1.5.2, the Ghost's first words "Mark me": A shudder at this—the first sound of his father's voice. Such delicate touches may be lost upon the audience, but no matter, give them if you feel them.

At 1.5.179, Hamlet's decision to put on "antic disposition": Undoubtedly the keynote to his character; it is frequently heard throughout the play: "I essentially am not in madness but mad in craft." "'I must be idle'—meaning 'I must play the fool.'" "My wit's diseased"—(if it was he would not think so), etc., etc., etc.

At 4.3.50, Hamlet calling the King his mother: I think I was the first to kneel and address the King as *mother*. The traditional method was to speak as to his absent parent without reference to the King, to whom he explains his meaning thus: "My mother, being absent, I bid her farewell by proxy; you, being her husband and her representative (husband and wife being one flesh), I bid you as my mother but not as my father, farewell."

At 5.1.200 s.d., Ophelia's burial: I was the first in America to give the corpse (not on a bier, nor in a coffin, but swathed and strapped to a board) to women bearers.

---

† For thirty-eight years (1853–91), Edwin Booth (1833–1893) played Hamlet as a reflective and refined gentleman, unshaken by passion and possessed of tender feelings. Edwin Booth, manuscript notes, in *Shakespeare's Tragedy of Hamlet, as Presented by Edwin Booth*, ed. William Winter (New York: Francis Hart and Co., 1878).
1. Edwin Forrest (1806–1872), American Shakespearean actor.
2. David Garrick (1717–1779), English Shakespearean actor and theater manager (see "Afterlives," p. 363)

Edwin Booth's gentle Hamlet, 1870

Letter to William Winter (1882)†

* * * The *"Mystery of Hamlet"* is an argument by Mr. Vining, dedicated to H. H. Furness, attempting to prove that Hamlet is really a woman.[3] (Good for Anna!)[4] It is very ingenious and aside from the absurdity of the writer's theory I agree with much that he urges in support of it. I have always endeavored to make prominent the femininity of Hamlet's character and therein lies the secret of my success—I think. I doubt if ever a robust and masculine treatment of the character will be accepted so generally as the more womanly and refined interpretation. I know that frequently I fall into effeminacy, but we can't always hit the proper keynote. You must see the book—it will amuse and I think it will interest you too.

HENRY IRVING

Introduction to *Hamlet* (1890)‡

There is one deep note in this play of *Hamlet* which sounds through all the discords of fate, love, and ambition. This note is Hamlet's profound affection for his father. In no literature is there any filial devotion which surpasses that. It is outraged by the beloved father's murder and by the mother's frailty; it is tortured by doubt and irresolution; it is the motive and the cue for the passion which wrecks Ophelia's hopes and ruins her life.

If we do not bear this in mind, Hamlet's conduct in the last interview with the unhappy girl [3.1] becomes inexplicable, and may easily be assigned to that insanity which is the simplest but most unsatisfactory solution of the problem. In this scene, perhaps, the actor has the most difficult task in the whole range of the drama. He has to present the conflict in Hamlet's soul so clearly that it shall connect itself in the minds of the audience with the whole train of thought which precedes it, instead of seeming the brutal outbreak of a mere madman. So grave is the difficulty of interpretation that I am anxious, in the interests of any young actor who may undertake it, that playgoers should think out the story before they see the tragedy.

† Booth to William Winter, manuscript letter, Folger Shakespeare Library, Y.c.215 (412b).
3. Edward Payson Vining, *The Mystery of Hamlet: An Attempt to Solve an Old Problem* (Philadelphia: J. B. Lippincott & Co., 1881). The book inspired the 1921 silent film *Hamlet*, in which Asta Nielsen starred as the female prince of Denmark disguised as a male.
4. Anna Elizabeth Dickinson played Hamlet in 1882.
‡ *The Works of William Shakespeare*, ed. Henry Irving and Frank A. Marshall, vol. 8 (London: Blackie, 1890), 23–25. Henry Irving (1838–1905) broke with the declamatory style to focus on Hamlet's inner life. In 1878 his *Hamlet* ran for 200 consecutive nights. Portraying the prince on the border line of insanity, Irving also showed the anguish of a lover forced by duty to be cruel to Ellen Terry's Ophelia.

Let us remember that the terrible duty which has been laid upon Hamlet by the spirit of his dead father forces him to wipe away from the tablets of his brain all "trivial, fond records," for in the soul doomed to be the avenger of "a dear father murdered," there is no room for the love of woman. Was it not a woman, too, who was the cause of this appalling crime? What crime? "What evidence," reasons Hamlet with himself, "what evidence have I to sustain my story? The testimony of a visitor from another world! With a disclosure made only to me—for nobody else heard it. Who will believe it? Who will believe such witness to the justice of my vengeance?" Should Hamlet revenge himself upon his father's murderer, *he* will appear to the people of Denmark just what he charges Claudius with being—a murderer—and the people will wreak their vengeance upon him. Distracted by doubt, he is actually contemplating suicide when he is disturbed by the approach of Ophelia, and on this innocent victim of destiny, who had been the idol of this sweet prince's heart—by a process familiar in human experience—all the elements in his mental struggle are at once concentrated with overwhelming force, spurred, too, by the suspicion that she is privy to the eavesdropping of her father and Claudius.

In all Hamlet's assumptions of mental wandering he is greatly aided by the excitability of his temperament. His emotions are always ready to carry him away, and his wild imaginings easily lend themselves to the maddest disguises of speech. A flash of volition may often be the exponent of a chain of thought, and perhaps the action of Hamlet's mind was somewhat after this manner: He feels the woe of Ophelia and his own. He writhes under the stigma of heartlessness which he cannot but incur. How remove it? How wipe away the stain? It is impossible. Cursed then be the cause. His whole nature surges up against it—the incestuousness of this king; the havoc of illicit passion, which has killed his noble father, wrecked his fairest hopes, stolen from him his mother's love—nay, robbed him even of the maternal idea, which remains to many a man in unblemished purity and even sweetness, long after a breach has taken place between his mother and himself. His (Hamlet's) mother was once fair and honest, honest as Ophelia now. *Is* Ophelia honest? Impossible to think otherwise. But it were a mad quip to ask her, and let the after dialogue take its own course. Take what course it will, it must dwell on the one subject which will harden Hamlet's heart, and give rigour to his nature. Thus comes the paradox:

HAMLET   Ha, ha! are you honest?
OPHELIA   My lord!
HAMLET   Are you fair?
OPHELIA   What means your lordship?

HAMLET   That if you be honest and fair, your honesty should admit
no discourse to your beauty.
OPHELIA   Could beauty, my lord, have better commerce than with
honesty?
HAMLET   Ay, truly, for the power of beauty will sooner transform
honesty from what it is, than the force of honesty can translate
beauty into his likeness; this was some time a paradox, but now
the time gives it proof. [3.1.104–15]

Hamlet's mother's beauty had been her snare, had tempted her
adulterous lover. His mother's honesty had fallen a victim to her
beauty. Let beauty and honesty therefore—here was the stroke of
mad exaggeration—have no discourse.

HAMLET   I did love you once.
OPHELIA   Indeed, my lord, you made me believe so.
HAMLET   You should not have believed me: for virtue cannot so
inoculate our old stock, but we shall relish of it. [115–119]

The thought underlying this is one of almost peevish aggravation of
the root-grievance cankering in the speaker's mind: "I am nothing
but vicious. You should not have believed me. My old stock—that
is, the vice I had from my mother—would so contaminate all that
was honest in my nature, or all the good I might have got through
my intercourse with you, would be so polluted by the overpowering
bad impulses in me, that you had better not have known me—
infinitely better not have loved me."
    And then with a wild "bolt." as it were, he utters the words that
may most sharply end all—"I loved you not." This is the surgeon's
knife for such complaints, and many a man has used it coolly and
callously. But such men were not Hamlets. He uses it more in
frenzy than in judgment, in an agony of pain, amid a thousand fond
remembrances, but dominated by the one conviction that he must
break with Ophelia, cost what it may. His instincts were accurate,
though his temperament was not calculating, and the impetus of
necessity drove him, in that moment of miserable stress, to use
words that could not have been more ruthlessly and effectually
chosen by the most cold-blooded of deceivers.
    There is nothing more pitiable, tender, or forlorn, in the whole
range of the drama, than Ophelia's reply: "I was the more deceived."
These are her last voluntary words, except her ejaculations of prayer
that Heaven may help and restore her lover; but these do not come
till further wild and whirling words have convinced her that it is
with a madman she is talking. For the moment it is enough that she
is abandoned, and the past repudiated. Her heart is wrecked. She
incoherently answers the one question Hamlet puts to her—

"Where's your father?"—and gazes and listens in frozen horror to
the tirades which he has now worked himself up to deliver.

But his words are not devoid of sequence, nor is their harshness
untouched with sympathy. "Get thee to a nunnery." Where else, but
in such a sanctuary, should so pure a being be sheltered? Where
else could Ophelia so well escape the contamination on which her
lover's mind was still running? The next lines, violent, self-accusing,
cynical, almost gross in their libel of humanity, are probably uttered
in desperate and yet restrained anxiety to snatch at and throw to
the heart-pierced maiden some strange, morbid consolation, but
without giving her any faint shadow of the one solace which he so
well knows would be all-sufficing. It is neither necessary nor possible to suppose that all this was deliberately thought out by Hamlet.
At such moments as he was passing through, the high pressure of a
forcible mind carries it over the difficulties in its course, and as
truly so when the leaps and bounds seem without system as when
the progress seems more regular. But for any purpose of comfort, how
utterly is this without effect! Mute is Ophelia, and after his burst of
self-condemning, man-condemning fury, her lover is mute also.

Let us now pause and imagine them thus together, when suddenly Hamlet remembers—there is no need for him to have any
reminder—the hidden presence of the King. He sharply asks Ophelia "Where's your father?" How shall we interpret her reply?

Her words are, "At home, my lord." How comes she to say this? If
she had known her father and the King were behind the arras, she
might still have made the same reply, so wrapt in her thoughts that
all recollection of the King's, and Polonius's presence might have
left her: in short, the words might have been spoken in mere
vacancy. If she did not know the King and her father were watching, of course the words were simple sincerity and truth; or, taken
by surprise by the question, and feeling herself to be an unwilling
instrument in something that was going on, while, though her
own motive was pure, she was at a loss how to explain it, she may
have given a reply which she knew to be false in the desire to clear
herself of complicity in what Hamlet would certainly think mean
and despicable. This or worse is probably Hamlet's opinion for
the moment, but that he banishes the thought is curiously proved
by the tender passage which follows; for, after sternly rebuking
Polonius, Hamlet may be said to excuse himself by implication, and to
ask pardon indirectly for the seeming reproach. "Be thou as chaste,"
he says, "as ice, as pure as snow, thou shalt not escape calumny."

And now Hamlet's excitement reaches its greatest height. Goaded
within and without, nay, dragged even by his own feelings in two
opposite directions, in each of which he suspects he may have gone
too far under the eyes of malignant witnesses, he is maddened by

the thought that they are still observing him, and as usual, half in wild exultation, half by design, begins to pour forth more and more extravagant reproaches on his kind. He must not commit himself to his love, nor unbosom his hate, nor has he a moment's pause in which to set in order a contrived display of random lunacy. As usual, passion and preconceived gloomy broodings abundantly supply him with declamation which may indicate a deep meaning or be mere madness according to the ears that hear it, while through all his bitter ravings there is visible the anguish of a lover forced to be cruel, and of a destined avenger almost beside himself with the horrors of his provocation and his task. The shafts fly wildly, and are tipped with cynic poison; the bow from which they are sped is a strong and constant though anxious nature, steadily, though with infinite excitement, bent upon the one great purpose fate has imposed upon it. The fitful excesses of his closing speech are the twangings of the bow from which the arrow of avenging destiny shall one day fly straight to the mark.

SARAH BERNHARDT

Why I Have Played Male Parts (1924)[†]

I have often been asked why I am so fond of playing male parts, and in particular why I prefer the part of Hamlet to that of Ophelia. As a matter of fact, it is not male parts, but male brains that I prefer, and among all the characters, that of Hamlet has attracted me because it is the most original, the most subtle, the most tortuous, and yet the most simple for the unity of his dream.

This being who appears to be so complex has only one idea: to avenge his father. It is true that this idea is divided into two parts: first of all, is it certain that the death of his father was the result of a crime? Further, is not this drama and the circumstances that surround it the work of the Evil One?

It is around this primary uncertainty that revolve continually the suspicions, the inquietudes, the remorse, and the terrors of being the puppet of a malignant spirit. When his father appears to him, Hamlet still suspects the malign spirit that appears as a beloved relative in order to deceive the better. And we observe him discussing the most painful alternatives.

† Sarah Bernhardt, *The Art of the Theatre*, trans. H. J. Stenning (London: Geoffrey Bles, 1924), 137–39. The French actress Sarah Bernhardt (1844–1923) was the first Hamlet on film (1900) and played the prince on stage as strong, volatile, and passionate (1899–1901). She inspired many women throughout Europe to attempt the role.

By some it is affirmed that Hamlet is mad. For my part I decline to accept this view. I find him the most sensible, the most artful, but the most unhappy of men. He tortures himself; he discovers himself a coward, and yet the fear of being a plaything of the infernal powers obsesses him. He discusses with himself, elaborates a plan which will ease his conscience; he proceeds to arrange the details of a play representing the assassination of his father such as it was recounted to him by the latter's shade. All this is the conduct of a very sensible person, of a thinker, and not of a madman.

In the famous monologue, "To be or not to be," Hamlet reveals himself completely. His life is a burden, and yet he does not kill himself. His marshalling of all the doubts is heartrending. How he suffers to see the mother he loves as the loving wife of his father's assassin! He struggles with all the thoughts that crowd thick upon him. And all the psychology of Hamlet's character is revealed to us by himself.

The fact that Hamlet arranges with great skill his plan of investigation into the conscience of the king his uncle is ample evidence that he is in his right mind. And when at length he is persuaded that the latter is his father's assassin, what intense joy surges through him at the idea of being free. The uncertainty had stifled the explosion of his vengeance. Now he is free, and will be able to avenge his father.

It is unquestionably a great delight for an artist to be able to interpret such a complex character. It had been my desire for many years to play Hamlet, and I was unable to decide to do so until I read the admirable translation by Marcel Schwob. I have played Ophelia in the Hamlet of Cressonnois,[1] but Ophelia brought nothing new to me in the study of character.

A very learned Englishman, who was also a great Shakespearian enthusiast, once asked me who had initiated me into this mysterious Hamlet. "Why . . . himself!" I replied. "Every time that Hamlet finds himself alone and reveals the depths of his mysterious soul."

Generally speaking, male parts are more intellectual than female parts. This is the secret of my preference. No female character has opened up a field so large for the exploration of sensations and human sorrows as that of Hamlet. Phèdre alone has afforded me the charm of prying into a heart that is really afflicted.[2]

---

1. Marcel Schwob and Eugène Morand wrote a French prose translation of *Hamlet* in 1897; Lucien Cressonnois and Charles Samson published their translation in 1886.
2. Bernhardt won acclaim in the title role of Jean Racine's *Phèdre* in 1874.

ELLEN TERRY

[On Ophelia] (1908)†

Ophelia only *pervades* the scenes in which she is concerned until the mad scene. This was a tremendous thing for me, who am not capable of *sustained* effort, but can perhaps manage a *cumulative* effort better than most actresses. I have been told that Ophelia has "nothing to do" at first. I found so much to do! Little bits of business which, slight in themselves, contributed to a definite result, and kept me always in the picture.

Like all Ophelias before (and after) me, I went to the madhouse to study wits astray. I was disheartened at first. There was no beauty, no nature, no pity in most of the lunatics. Strange as it may sound, they were too *theatrical* to teach me anything. Then, just as I was going away, I noticed a young girl gazing at the wall. I went between her and the wall to see her face. It was quite vacant, but the body expressed that she was waiting, waiting. Suddenly she threw up her hands and sped across the room like a swallow. I never forgot it. She was very thin, very pathetic, very young, and the movement was as poignant as it was beautiful.

I saw another woman laugh with a face that had no gleam of mirth anywhere—a face of pathetic and resigned grief.

My experiences convinced me that the actor must imagine first and observe afterwards. It is no good observing life and bringing the result to the stage without selection, without a definite idea. The idea must come first, the realism afterwards.

The Pathetic Women (1932)‡

"But soft! The fair Ophelia! Sweet rose of May!" The whole tragedy of *her* life is that she is afraid; I think I am right in saying she is Shakespeare's only timid heroine. She is scared of Hamlet when trouble changes him from the "point-devise" lover—"the glass of fashion and the mould of form"—into a strange moody creature, careless of his appearance, bitter in his speech, scornful of society. She is scared of her father, and dare not disobey him, even when he tells her to play the spy on Hamlet. She is scared of life itself when

---

† Ellen Terry, *The Story of My Life: Recollections and Reflexions* (London: Hutchinson & Co., 1908), 154–55. Ellen Terry (1847–1928) played Ophelia to Henry Irving's Hamlet in 1878, giving intensity and poignancy to the shattered love affair and exhibiting a disturbing madness, marked by sudden changes of mood.

‡ *Four Lectures on Shakespeare*, ed. Christopher St. John (1932 rpt. New York: Benjamin Blom, 1969), 165–67.

things go wrong. Her brain, her soul and her body are all pathetically weak. It is not surprising that she should think Hamlet mad,
for all he says in the scene in which she returns his presents is completely beyond her. If this scene is rightly acted, we feel a great
compassion for the poor girl, whom Hamlet at once loves and hates.
I think it ought to be suggested from the first that there is something queer about her, something which explains her wits going
astray later on. Her father's murder is assigned as the reason, but it
seems more likely that this shock developed an incipient insanity.
Ophelia is really mad, not merely metaphorically mad—with grief.

The mad were harshly treated in Shakespeare's day. Ophelia
escapes the dark house and the whip, but she is avoided by everyone.
The poor demented creature wanders about by the river, in and out
of the palace rooms, without a soul to look after her. Her father is
dead, her brother is away, the King and Queen shrink from seeing or
speaking with her. "I will not speak with her," Queen Gertrude says
impatiently. "What would she have?" [4.5.1, 3]

Ophelia makes them feel particularly uncomfortable for reasons
implied by Shakespeare in this speech by a gentleman at the court,
a very valuable speech to the actress, who can learn from it how the
famous "mad" scene ought to be played:

> She is importunate, indeed distract. . . .
> She speaks much of her father, says she hears
> There's tricks i' the world; and hems, and beats her heart;
> Spurns enviously at straws; speaks things in doubt,
> That carry but half sense: her speech is nothing,
> Yet the unshaped use of it doth move
> The hearers to collection; they aim at it,
> And botch the words up fit to their own thoughts;
> Which, as her winks, and nods, and gestures yield them,
> Indeed would make one think there might be thought,
> Though nothing sure, yet much unhappily. [4.5.1–2, 4–13]

When Laertes returns he hardly recognises his sister, "the fair
Ophelia," "the rose of May," in this poor derelict. "Had thou thy wits,
and didst persuade revenge," he cries, "it could not move thus" [164–
65]. And I think there is no "sane" scene in Shakespeare which moves
us as much as this "mad" one, this beautiful painful scene in which
Ophelia prattles and sings, making one think, as the observant courtier says, "there might be thought, though nothing sure" [12–13].[1]

"Come, my coach! Good-night, ladies! Good-night, sweet ladies;
good-night, good-night" [71–72].

---

1. When Ellen Terry delivered this lecture she usually left her reading-desk at this point,
and acted the scene. She judged it impossible to read it. She ended the lecture with
Ophelia's last words, which are printed above [*Christopher St. John's note*.]

JOHN GIELGUD

John Gielgud's *Hamlet* (1937)[†]

Scene 18

A CORRIDOR. HAMLET AND OSRIC; THE CHALLENGE
[ACT V, SCENE I]

Martin-Harvey, who played Osric at the Lyceum, says that Irving seemed to be surrounded by an aura of death in this scene. It is a very difficult passage to play, especially when the audience is flagging, and the actor out of breath from the rant in the graveyard which immediately preceded it. The necessary cuts always make one feel as if something had been left out, but even played in full there is an abrupt transition of mood and action. Again the necessary front scene demanded for the striking of the churchyard and the setting of the final scene cramps the actors for space and bores the audience, who begin to cough and look at their watches. The description of the pirate ship and the changing of the letters comes too late for the audience to be interested in it and the actors always feel, however the scene is cut, that it is difficult to settle the house so that it will be attentive for the last stretch of the play.

A good Osric does much to remedy this, and I have been very lucky in those who played the part with me—Alex Guinness in London and Morgan Farley in New York. Mr. Granville-Barker has an interesting theory about Hamlet's attitude in this last part of the play, and I think there is much to be said for his suggestion that he should be keen, ruthless, his mind made up. But with this must be weighed the half affectionate, half philosophical mood of the scene with the gravedigger, of his words about Yorick, and his touching farewell to Horatio. These moments win such obvious sympathy from the audience that no doubt this is apt to encourage the actor at the end of a long part to play for pathos and sentiment more than he should.

The fatalistic vein in which he speaks "It is no matter . . . A man's life's no more than to say 'One!' . . . If it be not to come, it will be now"—these are simple moments which, when spoken sincerely, will move almost any audience. But the general attitude of the character all through these last three scenes is extremely diffi-

---

† *John Gielgud's* Hamlet: *A Record of Performance*, by Rosamond Gilder (New York: Oxford UP, 1937), 68–71; reprinted by permission of Methuen. Equipped with acute intelligence and a voice capable of registering nuance and subtlety, Gielgud (1904–2000) played the title role in six productions (1930–45) and directed the play several times, notably in 1964 with Richard Burton. Gielgud's Hamlet was a romantic prince of patrician refinement and grace but also one who at times displayed bitterness and brutality.

cult to reconcile with the violent and often more showy passages in the earlier scenes and the actor has to take the line which he feels is most justified by his reading of the text and his whole conception of the character.

Scene 19

The final scene is apt to be a little ridiculous unless everybody concerned is very careful. Irving made his one really ill-judged cut in this play here, and left out Fortinbras altogether. The rest of his acting version is well arranged and compares favourably with his other Shakespearian texts, which were maltreated and bowdlerized to a shameless degree. Recent productions have made the fight tremendously pictorial and built the whole scene around it, especially in the productions in which Raymond Massey and Laurence Olivier played. As I am not a good swordsman I have never myself attempted more than is absolutely necessary. Frankly, also, I haven't the energy for it at the end of such a long and exhausting part. But the better the fight is done, of course, the better for the scene, and if the stage can be arranged for different levels to be used for the duelling the effect is proportionately greater.

I have always fought with rapier and dagger as the text seems to demand. Moissi, to my amazement, after an elaborate but quite anachronistic eighteenth-century fight with foils (in a Gothic production) took the poisoned sword by the blade with both hands, and stabbed the King in the back! The guards, in diagonally striped cloaks, then closed in in three groups covering the bodies of the King and Queen and Laertes, making a background for Hamlet himself to die against. This was too much of a stunt and I prefer my own arrangement of the scene, in which the Queen and Laertes died on big thrones, one on each side of the stage close to the footlights, and the King in a big cloak and crown was pursued up to a centre platform where he fell in a swirl of red folds. There were still steps below for Hamlet and Horatio to play their final scene, and Fortinbras and his army in grey cloaks and banners came from above over a kind of battlement and dipped their flags at the final curtain.

Forbes-Robertson died sitting on the throne with the King's crown set on his lap, and was then borne off on locked shields. Leslie Howard also, I believe, was carried off in a great procession to end the play. The poisoning of the Queen is difficult to manage and Mr. Granville-Barker has a fine idea that she should really play her death scene on the ground like the pictures of the death of Queen Elizabeth, suffering and moaning in her ladies' arms, and not die until Hamlet says "Wretched queen, adieu!" 1 had never noticed what he so brilliantly points out—that the King, being a professional poisoner, was unable to resist using a device a second time, as so many great criminals have done. It is indeed ironic for Hamlet to realize at this moment that his mother has died just as his father did, and undoubtedly the King should have poison in a ring and the audience should see him pour it into the cup. In Tyrone Guthrie's production the scene was produced for violent melodrama, and the Queen fell from a six-foot platform into the arms of the attendants.

The supers in the scene are an added problem, for one cannot think of actions which appear violent enough to express their horror at these tragic happenings without distracting from the main characters and the dialogue and action of the scene that follows. In London I had soldiers holding the people back, but in New York the courtiers left the stage altogether just before the King was killed. There is reason, however, to keep them on the scene in order that they should be in contrast to the corpses and also so that Hamlet may have someone to whom to address his "You that look pale and tremble at this chance." I should like, another time, to use the old councillors and ladies-in-waiting of whom I spoke in the play scene, for it would give point to Hamlet's lines if he could indicate this group of important people in the kingdom as those to whom Horatio would afterwards justify all that Hamlet has done.

Mr. McClintic invented for me the device of standing until the very end. I have never seen this done by anyone in the part and rebelled against trying it at first. It proved an admirable departure from tradition, for there are three recumbent figures on the stage already, and Hamlet in Horatio's arms is always faintly reminiscent of "Kiss me, Hardy" at the death of Nelson.[1] The standing figure holds the audience's attention just as they are on the verge of reaching for their hats, and "The rest is silence," spoken standing, appears to gain greater simplicity and significance if the actor can still command the audience with his full height.

A Note on *Hamlet* (1963)[†]

The part demands declamation, macabre humour, passionate violence, philosophical reflection. There are scenes of love and tenderness, outbursts of bitterness and despair. It is a temptation for the

---

1. Admiral Horatio Nelson, England's greatest naval hero, is said to have spoken these words to Captain Thomas Hardy before dying from a battle wound in 1805 [*Editor's note.*]

† John Gielgud, *Stage Directions* (London: Heinemann, 1963), 57–59. Reprinted by permission of Pearson UK.

actor to develop the possibilities of each scene for its individual histrionic effect, instead of presenting a complete basic character in which the part may progress in a simple convincing line. Hamlet must seem to experience before the audience everything that happens to him in the course of the play, and the actor must find in himself his own sincerest personal reactions to every episode— grief at his father's death, disillusionment with his mother and Ophelia, horror and anguish with the Ghost, and so on. The scenes themselves are so strikingly dramatic that they may betray the actor into sheer effectiveness (in a theatrical sense), more easily attained than the truth that will reveal the man himself. It was only as I grew older and more experienced that I became aware of these pitfalls (after I had worked with two or three different talented directors, and when, in two different productions, I directed the play myself as well as acting in it), though I tried continually to find a way to simplify, to use the verse and prose to express the variety of emotions conveyed so wonderfully in the text, and to balance the neurotic youthful side of the part by adding to it maturer qualities of strength, manliness and wit.

Hamlet is the many-sided, many-talented Elizabethan man— prince, son, courtier, swordsman, philosopher, lover, friend. In the Renaissance world a gifted, vital man crammed into fifty years all the variety of experience that may be spread over eighty years of life today. In the exquisite character of Hamlet, there is a richness of expression, a delicate perceptivity, a general curiosity; he has distinctive grace and breeding, which never degenerates into snobbery or decadence. The other principal characters, Claudius, Polonius, Laertes, Osric, Rosencrantz and Guildenstern, the foolish Ophelia, the sensual Gertrude—are shifting, worldly creatures drawn in deliberate contrast to the finer natures in the play—the forthright, sensitive Hamlet, the agonized, wronged Ghost, the steadfast, devoted Horatio, and the simple honest men, the First Player and the Gravedigger. These last three characters are the only men in the play with whom Hamlet can talk with the ease and directness which he so longs for in the world of disillusion which surrounds him.

Fortinbras, his *alter ego*, whom he never meets, only pervades the tragedy by hearsay, until, after once passing across the stage halfway through the action, he enters magnificently in the last scene to speak the valedictory lines on a rising note of hope.

It is sometimes lucky for an actor to tackle a great role for the first time before he is fully aware of its difficulties. I acted Macbeth (and King Lear too) before I was thirty, and, even with these dark, mature, heroic figures, I was more successful, I think, in giving a broad sketch of the characters when I attempted them with an almost naïve approach, than in subsequent productions in which I had had time to realize the enormously difficult intellectual and technical problems involved. With Hamlet it was the same, though of course long practice and experiment gave my acting in that part more assurance and skill as the years went by. On the other hand I became in the end somewhat confused in some of my decisions on readings, business, and so on, through being too ready to listen to the opinions of critics, directors and members of the audience, some of whose suggestions were of course invaluable, but whose inconsistencies tended to confuse my imagination so that I feared to lose the essential basis of my original conception.

In spite of all its complicated problems of psychology, I believe Hamlet is what we actors call a "straight" part. The man who essays it must obviously be equipped with certain essential qualities—grace of person and princely bearing, youth, energy, humour and sensitivity. He must have a pleasing voice of great range, and a meticulous ear for verse and prose. He must be neither slow nor ponderous. He must have wit and gentleness, but also power, edge, and a sense of the macabre. He must fascinate by his quick changes of mood. The soliloquies and cadenzas must be spoken in a special way to distinguish them from the conversational scenes, but without losing either humanity, rhythm, pace, or urgency. Hamlet must impress us with his loneliness and agonies of soul without seeming portentous or self-pitying. He must thrill us when he sees the Ghost, drives Claudius from the Gonzago play, stabs Polonius, reveals himself at the graveside, and throws himself upon Laertes. In no other part that I have played have I found it so difficult to know whether I became Hamlet or Hamlet became me, for the association of an actor with such a character is an extraordinarily subtle transformation, an almost indefinable mixture of imagination and impersonation.

LAURENCE OLIVIER

[On Hamlet's Character] (1982)[†]

* * * For my generation, determined upon realism, the burning question was, of course: What makes him what he is? Two books had recently appeared: Dover Wilson's *What Happens in Hamlet*,

---

[†] Laurence Olivier, *Confessions of an Actor: An Autobiography* (New York: Simon and Schuster, 1982), 102. The melancholy prince of Laurence Olivier (1907–1989), memorialized in the 1948 film, was a "man who could not make up his mind" and who suffered from the Oedipus Complex, a subconscious desire for his mother; but he showed, nevertheless, moments of wit, eloquence, and athleticism. Reprinted by permission of Weidenfeld and Nicolson, an imprint of the Orion Publishing Group, London.

and a work on the Oedipus complex by Ernest Jones. Three of us—Tony Guthrie, Peggy Ashcroft and I—went to see Professor Jones.

He had made an exhaustive study of Hamlet from his own professional point of view and was wonderfully enlightening. I have never ceased to think about Hamlet at odd moments, and ever since that meeting I have believed that Hamlet was a prime sufferer from the Oedipus complex—quite unconsciously, of course, as the professor was anxious to stress. He offered an impressive array of symptoms: spectacular mood-swings, cruel treatment of his love, and above all a hopeless inability to pursue the course required of him. The Oedipus complex, therefore, can claim responsibility for a formidable share of all that is wrong with him. There is great pathos in his determined efforts to bring himself to the required boiling point, and in the excuses he finds to shed this responsibility.

Apart from Hamlet's involuntary pusillanimity, there is another important factor in the character-drawing—his weakness for dramatics. This would be reasonable if the dramatics spurred him to action, but unfortunately they help to delay it. It is as if his shows of temperament not only exhaust him but give him relief from his absorption in his purpose—like an actor who, having spent his all in rehearsal, feels it almost redundant to go through with the performance.

[On the 1948 Film] (1986)[†]

I'd played Hamlet twice in 1937 in London and at Elsinore, and once you've played Hamlet, the play's thoughts and actions are part of you forever, and so are your thoughts about the play. As I've said before, Hamlet is spectatorproof. He fascinates every member of the audience, who recognizes—always—something of himself or herself in the dramatic ebb and flow of Hamlet's moods, his inhibiting self-realizations and doubts, his pitiful failure to control events. But I wasn't inhibited in my realization that everyone has his own idea of Hamlet; no, far from it, I was exhilarated.

As Shakespeare's interpreter, I would of course have to be true to his idea of tragedy and make up my mind about the vicious mole in Hamlet's nature. I remembered seeing a Warner Brothers seafaring picture in which Gary Cooper asks an intellectual and sensitive belowdecks crewman (Alan Ladd, I think) what book he's reading. "*Hamlet*," the sailor answers. "A story about a guy who couldn't

† *On Acting* (New York: Simon and Schuster, 1986), 284–93, reprinted with the permission of Simon & Schuster Inc. Copyright © 1986 by Wheelshare Ltd.

make up his mind"—which showed that not every Hollywood script-writer was ignorant of Shakespeare or lacking in respect for him.

My earliest and deepest resolutions were to find a cinematic interpretation of the play. Emboldened (and slightly chastened) by the popular success of *Henry V*, I didn't initially want to play the part of Hamlet myself. Not because I didn't think I was suited (my stage Hamlet and my stage Romeo—Hamlet's younger brother—had been passionate and successful), but because I didn't want the audience to think, "Oh, that's just a repeat of Laurence Olivier's *Henry V*, only this time he's dressed up to look like Hamlet." That's one of the reasons I gave myself blond hair when I did decide to take the part, for I wished to get well away from the glamorous dark-haired medieval king, from my usual image; it was also to make me conspicuous in middle and long shots—not because of any actor-manager conceit, but because Hamlet is always central to the story. The story is seen through his eyes and, when he's not present, through his imagination—his paranoia. This subjective element, paradoxically, I think, has encouraged many subjective interpreta-tions over the centuries in many different media: theater, opera, mime, ballet and Emlyn Williams's very much abridged version for touring before the troops. Much of the verse has been cut out, and even though traditions are handed down, John Gielgud's 1930s Hamlet was quite different from Richard Burbage's original. I thought it quite legitimate to make my own subjective contribution, to make a filmic interpretation to add to the universal conscious-ness of Hamlet.

If my blond hair was archetypal of the Dane, so much the better; Claudius and Gertrude were dressed as the king and queen of uni-versal playing cards, Hamlet in the timeless doublet and hose of a romantic young prince. The core of Hamlet is his loneliness and desolation after the death of his father, and his feeling of alienation from the new court. In my mind's eye I saw the camera seeing most things through Hamlet's eyes, wandering, or running, through the empty corridors, piercing the vast shadows of Elsinore's great rooms of state for some joy or the sight of some familiar object; but in vain: as lonely as a cloud, with no color, no silver lining. I was having a flaming row with the Technicolor people at the time—another reason, perhaps, for thinking in black-and-white—but I would have overcome my sulks if I'd really wanted Technicolor. I liked its sub-dued shades—grays, sepias and black. But I was terrified by its tan-gerine and apricot faces, which were not the faces I wished to haunt my melancholy Hamlet.

Black-and-white had another big, big advantage. I could use deep-focus photography. Deep focus is simply this: the character in the foreground (usually Hamlet) is in focus, so are the characters in the middle ground, and *so* are the characters in the far ground. I say "simply this": technically it was very difficult—but Desmond Dickinson, my lighting cameraman, was a genius.

People said I was far too interested in moving the camera, and in *Hamlet* I was accused of being overly self-conscious about film directing. But I wanted to exercise myself with the camera. Maybe I overdid it. But it pays off sometimes. For instance, at the end of the very first soliloquy when the camera simply goes all the way across an interesting courtyard, goes up, shows a very interesting bedroom, which you know wasn't shown you for nothing. That works nicely.

With deep focus I could beset Hamlet with faces around him which were, to him, too, too solid; I could create distances between characters, creating an effect of alienation, or of yearning for past pleasure as when Hamlet sees Ophelia, in her innocent Victorian dress, an eternity away down the long corridor (150 feet away, actually), sitting on a solid wooden chair—in focus—with love clearly in her eyes. While the camera was showing much of Hamlet's melancholy and the decadence and desolation of Claudius's court, I was able to use the empty spaces for exciting physical action, showing Hamlet's athleticism which is in the play's text—and in my repertoire as an actor, or at least, it was.

That climax really was tremendous. That fifteen-foot dive, with an open sword, onto Claudius! I first saw the finished version of the film in Australia, and I heard the ladies in the audience go "Wow!" And then, of course, the film ends with the dead Hamlet's sad, drumbeat journey up the dark flights of steps and battlements of Elsinore towards his father, the blackness lit by firelight (and if I may say so, by William Walton's music, which is where my first images of the film began).

Nothing pretty or artificial about the stone of Elsinore; gray, black, sometimes crumbling, sometimes oppressive, sometimes cavernous. At the ends and beginnings of sequences I dissolved the solid flesh of the deep-focus characters away from and into scenes, so that they looked like ghosts. At the beginning of a long walk towards Hamlet, Ophelia looked like a specter; and it seemed the most natural thing in the world to have Hamlet's soliloquies as words in his head, with his "To be or not to be" uttered to the sound of a roaring sea, like the sounds which fill the ears of troubled spirits. I once said the film was "An Essay in *Hamlet*," but that's not quite right. A bit demeaning to the creative impulse which Shakespeare inspired in me and my team; a bit insulting to the resourcefulness of the medium. Why not "An Interpretation of *Hamlet*"? Or just "A Film of *Hamlet*"?

Of course, I had to be ruthless in the cutting. Half of *Henry V* had had to go; so did half of *Hamlet*. *Hamlet* is the best-known play in the world. Everyone's got his favorite quotation. I approached the job with terror, and the utmost respect—not terror of the purists, but fear that my concept, and its execution, would be unfaithful to Shakespeare or to the medium; it must be utterly respectful to the spirit of Shakespeare and to the audience's consciousness of Hamlet. I kept bringing the concept sharp into my head so that I knew every second of the length of the film, without a loose moment.

Eileen Herlie, who played Gertrude as a sensual young-middle-aged woman, and I reveled in the closet scene, which, confident of the camera, we played as big as in Drury Lane. All the actors were confident; each gave a top-class Shakespearean performance: Jean Simmons as Ophelia, young and sensitive, and Peter Cushing as Osric, one of the best screen actors. Little makeup was worn, and the deep focus showed their confidence—and their sincerity. I used only actors who could speak the verse, either from experience or from their natural talent—like Stanley Holloway, who was the gravedigger. It would be foolish to do a Shakespeare film with actors who'd never been in any of his plays before: he presents his own volumes of technique to learn. I rehearsed them before each shot, with a stand-in for me, telling them what I had in mind, telling them the length of each cut, but otherwise giving them their freedom. Restraining them occasionally, perhaps, but never inhibiting them, and never letting the camera inhibit them. It's not a director's job to teach actors how to act. It's his job to make the most of the talent they already have: to make actors feel relaxed and happy in their work. Of course we missed—those of us who'd known them on the stage—some of the favorite characters, like Rosencrantz and Guildenstern, who enriched the four-and-a-half hour pattern of the play which I was changing to the tighter pattern of a two-and-a-half hour film.

If the shooting has been successful, editing a film is the pinnacle of a director's joy; if not, he must make it so, with no regrets about what exists or does not exist on film, because it's only his joy which will transform the lengths of film and sound track into the realization of his imagination. No human mind is big enough to forestall all problems, strong enough to quell the insistence of a last-minute inspiration, but problems in the editing room are usually part of the joy because that's where the medium of film really comes into its own, solving all the difficulties within itself. I was lucky in my editor, Reginald Beck, a consummate technician and a brilliant friend, who saw the point of the camera's changing directions in ways hitherto unknown and against the rules, of a character's being shot from the left instead of from the right. He realized the drama through Hamlet's eyes and noticed his odd moments of nervous agitation. I was lucky in my composer, my friend William Walton, who absorbed Hamlet's every mood—and mine. We coordinated his music and my sound effects: the sound of cannon shots on Hamlet's last journey on the battlements, Hamlet's heartbeat as he sees the ghost of his father for the first time (an effect I borrowed from Jean-Louis Barrault, for which Arthur Rank paid him £500—which was nothing compared with the royalties he didn't pay to Shakespeare).

RICHARD BURTON

Introduction to *Hamlet* (1954)[†]

It has been estimated that some ten thousand books, articles and theses have been written on *Hamlet*, which indicates that it is by far the most controversial play in the canon. It would also suggest that there can be very little left to add. Certainly an actor would prefer to simplify, rather than further complicate the issue, if only for the reason that there is a very definite limit to the number of these subtleties, suggested by generations of learned critics, which an actor can embody in one performance.

Why this controversy? Perhaps chiefly because each reader who discovers the play for the first time, and for the first time wonders at the strange, almost unworldly, and yet most human Prince of Denmark, will hold in his mind yet another—if only very slightly different—picture of him from all others held before.

Charles Lamb felt that there was a little of us all in Hamlet. Here is a character in whose sufferings we can all of us feel the throb of our own; in whose gentleness, or rage, fear, horror, in whose very love of life, or bewilderment in its difficulties, we can often hear an echo that is sadly or gladly personal.

But does that of necessity give rise to controversy on such a scale? The plot of the play, baldly considered, is simple enough. It is with the convolutions that result in the final hecatomb that the writers on *Hamlet* concern themselves; but there are many plots as complicated in contemporary dramatic writing, many plays with a more fearsome list of dead at the final curtain. It is, in the final analysis, the weird light that follows the young Prince through the windings of the story that so fascinates the commentators. For the character of Hamlet is unique in all literature—a portrait of such depth and breadth, of such tender subtlety, as filling the minds of watcher or

† Richard Burton, Introduction, *The Tragedy of Hamlet, Prince of Denmark* (London: Folio Society, 1954), 3–5. Richard Burton (1925–1984) first played Hamlet at the Old Vic (1953) and then starred in John Gielgud's production in New York (1964, available on DVD). Burton is a mesmerizing, powerful, unpredictable Hamlet, capable of sharp wit, profound reflection, and, as he argues here against Laurence Olivier, decisive action. Reprinted by permission of the Folio Society.

Richard Burton's mercurial Hamlet in grief, 1964

reader, can create in each a different picture. The mirror that is
here held up to nature flashes fires of infinite colour and intensity.

The questions to be asked are almost limitless; their answers
multitudinous, and none of them satisfactory to everyone. It is certainly not within the scope of this Introduction to attempt to answer
them, and certainly an actor faced with the part is wisest to look for
his own answers not in the critical Tower of Babel that looms over
the play, but in the text of the play itself.

John Barrymore, one of the memorable Hamlets of the century,
said: "Not only does every actor play Hamlet provided he live long
enough, but every member of the audience plays it, each in his own
unyielding fashion . . . you can play it standing, sitting, lying down
or, if you insist, kneeling. You can have a hangover. You can be cold
sober. You can be hungry, overfed, or have just fought with your wife.
It makes no difference as regards your stance or your mood. There
are within the precincts of this great rôle a thousand Hamlets, any
one of which will keep in step with your whim of the evening."

Sir John Gielgud, probably the greatest Hamlet of the contemporary theatre, gave us a Hamlet poetical—sensitive—illogical. Here
was the beautiful, effortless, tenor voice, soaring from the early
depths of misery, through the antic hysteria of a torn mind, to the
exquisite resolution of death—faced and accepted. Here Hamlet
shrank from immediacy with a mind too fine to cut through the

tangle of his fate with a bloody sword; a mind driven to near-lunacy by his mother's carnality, and pathetically finding horror even in the simplicities of Ophelia.

This was a definitive performance, but, in an indefinable part, not exclusive. It is still possible for an actor broad of face, wide of shoulder, thick of thigh and robust of voice—in brief, too solid for such a sensitive interpretation as Gielgud's, to advance his own definition, survive the onslaught of the adverse, and attempt some of the many facets of so versatile a character.

I strongly recommend that readers of *Hamlet* should, for their own enjoyment, also read some at least of the writers about the play—bearing in mind that some of the flashes of the mirror may only be will-o'-the-wisps.

A modern reflection upon *Hamlet* is that it is the tragedy of a man who could not make up his mind. To chase a possible will-o'-the-wisp, to risk death by drowning in its pursuit, let us postulate that there is "within the precincts" a Hamlet who not only could make up his mind, but who knew very well what he was about.

Hamlet vows vengeance in the presence of the Ghost. On only one occasion in the play does Hamlet find the King unattended, and, therefore, vulnerable. He comes upon him praying, alone [3.3]. Now might he do it, and now he'll do it—"that would be scanned; a villain kills my father, and for that, I, his sole son, do this same villain send to heaven." His withdrawal from action is strongly reasoned, according to the doctrine of an eye for an eye. He must not, in killing the King, be kind, take him in prayer and "season'd for his passage." He must wait until the King is again vulnerable, but in "some act that has no relish of salvation in 't," and pay home the debt of his father, who was killed in the full flush of his unrepented life.

The next time that Hamlet thinks Claudius may be within the shadow of his sword is in the Closet Scene [3.4]. A cry from an eavesdropper behind the arras draws his blade in deadly thrust, and his cry of hope, "is it the King?" It cannot be laid at the door of Hamlet's vacillation that the over-zealous Polonius should be the first fortuitous victim.

From then on Hamlet is defending his own life; his companions on the enforced voyage to England, who are to hand him over to death, are sent to their own death by him, as the result of his immediate decision. Their death is fortuitous, but results from the mounting tide of evil that stems from the first sinning of the King, not from a by-blow of Hamlet's indecision. He kills them to return to Denmark alive. Once back, he is faced with the culminating horror of evil in the Laertes plot, so that he is forced to final action. The King is killed, and with him his instrument, Laertes, and in the welter of evil Hamlet himself has to die.

There is a brief to be upheld on such a line, that is to say, there is a possible Prince of Decision who can hold the interest. The play may not be one of weakness, but a portrait of strength in its finest most certain form. Horror is pulled upon our heads perhaps by the initial horror of murder, gathering way and reflected in Hamlet's mind, not in the weakness of that mind.

The epitaph for the writer of a thousand pages or a thousand words on *Hamlet* is forever the same: the reflection from one facet of the jewel took the eye, but let no-one think that there is only one colour in the diamond.

Here is the play. Read it. The greatness is here in the bald, printed line.

KENNETH BRANAGH

Introduction to *Hamlet* (1996)[†]

As I write this, I am one month away from completing a project which has consumed me, to varying degrees, for the last twenty years.

I first encountered *Hamlet* when Richard Chamberlain, T.V.'s Doctor Kildare, played the title role on British television. I was eleven years old and from a background (Irish, Protestant, working-class) which had given me little preparation for watching Shakespeare. I was sufficiently distracted on that Sunday evening to leave my overdue homework uncompleted. I felt very uneasy when the Ghost of Hamlet's father appeared. There were no great special effects to heighten the audience's fear, but the atmosphere of the scene was unsettling. I was dragged away from the screen shortly afterwards to a tardy bedtime. It continued to affect me as I tried, unsuccessfully, to sleep. I wasn't sure that I had liked what I saw (the play I mean, not the performances) but it certainly stayed with me. Enough for me to resort to Shakespeare as an excuse when I was carpeted the following morning for my poor homework.

Over the following few years, *Hamlet* took on different shapes. One was a picture of Laurence Olivier on the cover of an old L.P. record, lying (unused) in a corner of the English Department Stock

† Kenneth Branagh, Introduction, *Hamlet* (New York: Norton, 1996), xi–xv. Branagh's 1996 four-hour film version of *Hamlet* features Hollywood stars—Julie Christie, Charlton Heston, Jack Lemmon, Billy Crystal, Kate Winslet, Robin Williams—and accomplished Shakespearean actors—Derek Jacobi, Judi Dench, Brian Blessed, Simon Russell Beale—in gorgeous and evocative settings. In the title role, Branagh (b. 1960) is athletic, aggressive, and imaginative. Copyright © 1996 by Kenneth Branagh. Reprinted by permission of Kenneth Branagh and W. W. Norton.

Kenneth Branagh as Hamlet, "To be or not to be," film, 1996

Room. Later still, the record itself was played in class, the master's sepulchral reading of "To Be Or Not To Be" set against Walton's eerie score. I knew nothing of "fardels" or "bodkins," but I knew that here was "something." By the age of fifteen, though, Shakespeare had still taken no special hold of my imagination. I was interested in soccer and girls. Shakespeare was for swots.

Surprisingly, however, what did grab my attention at this time was a television serialization of Robert Graves's *I, Claudius*. I was particularly impressed by the actor playing the title role. His name was Derek Jacobi, and I noticed, with some excitement, a small ad in the entertainment section of our local newspaper announcing that Derek Jacobi "of T.V's *I, Claudius* fame" was to appear in *Hamlet* at the New Theatre, Oxford.

I rang to book my ticket. A new adventure for me. My theatre-going had been limited to a couple of organized school trips prior to this. But I wanted to see this man in the flesh. I still hadn't read the play, so for all I knew, I might be treated to some of the stuttering which had impressed me so much in his television performance. I travelled to Oxford, some half an hour away by train, my first real independent outing as an adolescent. The pavement outside the theatre was thronged with ticket holders, and I discovered it was the very first performance of this production by the Prospect Theatre Company. Excitement was in the air, and from my first glimpse of the poster, with a haunted Jacobi staring into some bleak beyond, I was aglow with anticipation.

Much later I read a remark by the distinguished critic Kenneth Tynan, who said "the difference between a good play and a great play is that after the experience of a great play we understand a little more about why we are alive." My theatre-going experience at that point gave me little scope for comparison but I was convinced as I left the theatre that evening that I had experienced—not just watched, but truly experienced—something unique. The story was gripping, and I wanted at every moment to know "what happened next." Much of the language I did not understand and yet the actors' commitment to each line convinced me that I knew what they were feeling. As Ophelia lost her reason, I was moved to tears. I was passionate in my longing for Claudius to receive his come-uppance, and the sword fight at the end was as thrilling as any football match.

But as I travelled home that summer evening twenty years ago my overwhelming feeling was of having connected with an extraordinary energy. In the play itself and chiefly in the character of Hamlet I experienced the insistent hum of life itself. He was passionate, humorous, cruel, intelligent, courageous and cowardly, but unmistakably and gloriously brimming over with life. In the production and in Jacobi's performance I had been taken on an emotional rollercoaster. It made me reflect on my relationships with my parents, the prospects of my adolescent love affair. It set my heart and my head racing. I felt I had encountered a genuine force of nature, and on that journey home and for sometime afterwards, its memory made me glad to be alive. But then I was fifteen.

Nevertheless, the damage was done. I began to read the play, to read more of Shakespeare. I resolved to become an actor. Tempting though it is to re-write one's personal history with the benefit of hindsight, I believe much of what has followed in my life was affected by that experience.

My training at the Royal Academy of Dramatic Art was the next point at which I could pursue this passionate interest. At twenty, having "collected" as an audience member the performances of a dozen other Hamlets (including the films by Olivier and Kozintsev), I gave my first performance of the role. Regarding its success, I would borrow Richard Briers' self-assessment of his own RADA Prince—"I may not have been the best Hamlet but I was the quickest." But the experience taught me much about the practical demands of the role: massive physical exertion culminating in a complicated fight that an exhausted actor at the end of the play would happily do without. I felt the thrill of playing the role, but at the end of the run I knew little more about the Prince of Denmark than I had five years earlier.

There was a stronger sense of this four years later in 1984, when I played Laertes in a production for the Royal Shakespeare Company. It was invaluable to watch the central character (played by Roger Rees) from a different vantage point. I was able to observe much more clearly what is said about him by others, and worry less about the Prince's own words. Here too was a chance to view the whole play, but from within. I was made aware of the double family tragedy. All of the Polonius clan and all of the royal family—dead, at the finale. And in Fortinbras's accession to the throne there is the sense of a national tragedy—the end of an era. The weight of sadness is felt across the whole play, not confined to one man.

Derek Jacobi stepped back into my "Hamlet" life once more, when in 1988 he directed me in the role for The Renaissance Theatre Company. As a director of the company I had originally asked him to produce *Richard II* with another actor, but he suggested *Hamlet* and asked me to play the title role. My actor's vanity got the better of me and I said yes.

Even so, I was unready. I produced a hectic Hamlet, high on energy but low on subtlety and crucially lacking depth. I was aware that something Jacobi himself had brought effortlessly and effectively to the role was life experience. He had the confidence as an actor to do less. A longer exposure to the "whips and scorns of time" in his own life gave him an easy weight which underlined the depths of Hamlet's thinking and gave a necessary counterpoint to the frenzied and frantic element of Hamlet's personality.

The chief lesson of the production was that I should do it again and that the time must be right. It had to be when I still fulfilled the age requirements for the Prince but when I had the courage to bring a slightly older and more complex self to the role. When I had the confidence to let the acting energy take care of itself and, as Hamlet, live more completely in the moment. As the years went by, I was never less than fascinated by other actors' Hamlets. The play still held its attraction for me, but it remained artistically as unfinished business.

On radio in 1992 I had my first taste of the full text, and a splendid opportunity to explore the play's language with a focus and significance that was uniquely offered by the medium, in which the spoken word dominates. With the full text, the gravitational weight of the play seemed to increase. While arguments will always rage about exactly what constitutes a "full text" I had no doubt that this version offered rich opportunities for the actors, particularly in the supporting roles. I felt I understood much more about Polonius with the inclusion of the often cut scene with his "agent" Reynaldo. The complexity of Claudius's manipulations in the full version of the scene where he plots with Laertes, helped to flesh out a richer portrait than the conventional stage villain. And there were, to my taste, fascinating excursions on the state of the Elizabethan theatre, and jaundiced summations of the legal profession and of court life. On top of the domestic tragedy which engulfs a royal family the play seemed an all-embracing survey of life. It was harsh, vigorous and contemporary in feel.

I resolved that were I to attempt the role again, it should be using this full text.

The opportunity arose when Adrian Noble invited me to play the title role in a new Royal Shakespeare Company production which opened in 1992. He concurred with me that we should use what some critics have referred to as the "eternity" version. Now, at thirty-three, the part seemed at last to be "playing me." There were no surprises in the obstacle course of great set pieces, and I felt as if I had been in training for this attempt. The performance matured as it had not before, and continued to surprise me, not least by the way in which the full text offered a much more comfortable playing experience for the actor. It was more imaginatively paced. One could take advantage of the "breaths" that Shakespeare had given the actor. Paradoxically it was much less physically exhausting to play, and the cumulative weight of the longer evening made for an immensely powerful finale.

By this time I had had two experiences of filming Shakespeare and my film-maker's instincts made me long—even as I explored it within a fine production like Adrian's—to take the play into the cinema in its fullest form. I longed to allow audiences to join Fortinbras on the plain in Norway, to be transported, as Hamlet is in his mind's eye, back to Troy and see Priam and Hecuba. I felt that all my experience with the play and with Shakespeare was leading me in one direction.

My attempts to finance a film version had been in motion since the opening of *Henry V*, but the perpetual reluctance of film companies to finance Shakespeare had frustrated each attempt.

In 1995 Castle Rock Entertainment finally agreed to follow this dream, by financing a full-length version which would perhaps be followed by an abridged version at a more traditional length. The pages that follow, record the attempt.

The screenplay is what one might call the "verbal storyboard." An inflexion of a subjective view of the play which has developed over the years. Its intention was to be both personal, with enormous attention paid to the intimate relations between the characters, and at the same time epic, with a sense of the country at large and of a dynasty in decay.

The style is a development of my other Shakespeare film work. Among its principles are a commitment to international casting; a speaking style that is as realistic as a proper adherence to the structure of the language will allow; a period setting that attempts to set the story in a historical context that is resonant for a modern audience but allows a heightened language to sit comfortably. Above all, we have asked for a full emotional commitment to the characters, springing from belief that they can be understood in direct, accessible relation to modern life.

As I mentioned before, at the time of writing, the film is yet to be completed. The sound and music mix are in their final stages. So I for one am unsure of the results. I've brought as much intelligence as I can to its execution but in the end mine is not an intellectual approach, but an intuitive one. For better or worse, I am still connected to the feeling that had overwhelmed me all those years ago, when first I saw the play live. For audiences familiar or unfamiliar with the story, that's what I'd like to pass on.

That I should have pursued the play's mysteries so assiduously over twenty years continues to puzzle me. But, it's what I do, and this is what I've done. As the great soccer manager Bill Shankly once said, describing the importance of football, "It's not a matter of life and death. It's much more important than that." Certainly for me, an ongoing relationship to this kind of poetry and this kind of mind is a necessary part of an attempt to be civilized. I am profoundly grateful for the opportunity to explore it.

The hold it has over me will not lessen its grip. Michael Maloney, who plays Laertes in the film, told me recently of an impending production in which he will play the Prince. I found myself as excited as ever to discuss interpretation, casting, language—everything. For I believe I've come happily to realize that of course I cannot explain *Hamlet*, or even perhaps my own interpretation of *Hamlet*.

This film is simply the passionate expression of a dream. A dream that has preoccupied me for so many years. I cannot really explain that either. The reasons are in the film. The reasons are the film.

Goethe said, "A genuine work of art, no less than a work of nature, will always remain infinite to our reason: it can be contemplated and felt, it affects us, but it cannot be fully comprehended, even less than it is possible to express its essence and its merits in words."

After twenty years, I'm happy to say, I think I know what he means.

MICHAEL PENNINGTON

Hamlet: A User's Guide (1996)[†]

> It really boils down to symptoms. Pregnant replies, mystic allu-
> sions, mistaken identities, arguing his father is his mother, that
> sort of thing; intimations of suicide, forgoing of exercise, loss of
> mirth, hints of claustrophobia not to say delusions of imprison-
> ment; invocations of camels, chameleons, capons, whales, wea-
> sels, hawks, handsaws—riddles, quibbles and evasions; amnesia,
> paranoia, myopia; daydreaming, hallucinations; stabbing his elders,
> abusing his parents, insulting his lover, and appearing hatless in
> public—knock-kneed, droop-stockinged and sighing like a love-sick
> schoolboy, which at his age is coming on a bit strong . . .
> —Tom Stoppard, *Rosencrantz and Guildenstern Are Dead*

In the English theatre at least, a director who decided to do *Hamlet*
and then started looking around for a Hamlet would be an oddity.
There are a lot of good actors about, and you might embark on a
Merchant of Venice, an *As You Like It* or a *Henry V* with the confidence that someone would turn up out of the great British repertory company to play the leads—but not a *Hamlet*, or a *Lear*, or an
Antony and Cleopatra. These are the "specials": the motive is the
actor who's ready, the actress at whom the blood quickens. As Max
Beerbohm said, Hamlet is a hoop through which every eminent (let's
update him: every dangerous, marketable "hot") performer must
sooner or later jump—if he wants to. And since this is an unforgiv-
ing contest, he has to strike exceptional fire or not do it at all—a
middling Prince is no good to anyone. The interesting player is thus
taken to the part like a match to the touchpaper: you retreat and
wait for the bang.

Hamlet is perhaps the cleverest hero ever written, the subject of
the first European tragedy worthy of the name for two thousand
years: a form of genius, as Orson Welles observed, akin to Mercutio
and Richard II (I would add Berowne and perhaps Richard III), and

† Michael Pennington, *Hamlet: A User's Guide* (New York: Limelight Editions, 1996),
155–57, 78–81. Michael Pennington (b. 1943) has played a number of roles in *Hamlet*:
Fortinbras (1965), Laertes (1969), Hamlet (1980–81), the Ghost, and Claudius
(1994). His Hamlet is intellectually powerful, a natural thinker who views his own
violent passions with self-critical wonder and sardonic self-mockery. Reprinted by permission of Nick Hern Books.

a type that Shakespeare despaired of writing thereafter, having perceived that the heroes of tragedies must be sublime idiots (Lear, Othello). Among actors, the role is supposedly the object of much professional rivalry; among those who have played it, it is the source, surprisingly often, of regret, and occasionally of real self-definition. It's also said that nobody can quite fail in it, because Hamlet becomes the man (or woman) who plays it. By this reckoning, Shakespeare's character could be almost anything, and it certainly has been a garment pulled in all manner of directions. Such infinite variety does make it difficult to define the man in the usual terms: but of course there are some practical rules. Any lack of vitality in the actor translates into a sluggish Hamlet. A lack of generosity makes his Hamlet mean: only a true breadth of spirit, embracing fatalism and aspiration at the same time, will do. Most cruelly, any lack of "personality" in the player makes for a dull Prince.

But for all his resonance beyond it, Hamlet is a character in a play, confined by the play, bound by the same rules therefore as Osric; and to serve it, he must be certain measurable things. There are mileposts all the way through that the new candidate is checked off against: "O what a noble mind is here o'erthrown / The courtier's, soldier's, scholar's eye, tongue, sword" grieves Ophelia, and the audience checks back—is it so? The Players arrive and Hamlet is carried away with excitement and pleasure: can you believe he is brainy enough to remember certain of their speeches by heart? He certainly knows what acting is about and what it is for: does he personify those standards himself? Claudius says: "How dangerous is it that this man goes loose": so is his personality a real threat to the King, and are they "mighty opposites"? As well as the capacity for threat, has he a talent for lethargy ("I have of late, but wherefore I know not, lost all my mirth"), and plain silliness ("that's two of his weapons; but well")? Is he enough of a clown for Polonius, Rosencrantz and Guildenstern, and at the same time a sort of romantic lead? Is he ruthless enough to switch the packets on shipboard, sending Rosencrantz and Guildenstern to their deaths when all he strictly needed to do was save himself? Is he a good fencer, able to run Laertes close, even though he has lately "forgone all manner of exercise"? Does he have the vision to crystallise "To be or not to be," the childish cruelty to say to his mother "at your age The heyday in the blood is tame," the recklessness to make a joke in front of his father's Ghost? Sufficiently wise to say "The readiness is all," and existential enough to declare that Polonius is "Not where he eats but where he is eaten"? And what of his own estimate of himself, making allowance for his pervasive irony (he has to have that too): "I am very proud, revengeful, ambitious, with more offences at my beck than I have thoughts to put them in, imagination to give them shape, or time to act them in." And in the end, when he lies dead, does he meet the final tests (the critics are very hot on these): Horatio's "Goodnight, sweet prince And flights of angels sing thee to thy rest," and Fortinbras's "He was likely, had he been put on, To have proved most royal." Was he, will they, and would he have?

To deal with such a mass, what is the state of the actor's equipment? Is the voice strong enough to do perhaps eight performances a week? Does his stage personality have both a smack of the classical ("My father's spirit in arms? All is not well") and the provocatively modern ("In heaven, send thither to see; if your messenger find him not there, seek him in the other place yourself")? Is he mercurial enough to keep an audience interested for four hours or so? Is he a wise enough performer to know that he is not a one-man band, and that if the play is to work, he must balance himself against Claudius, Ophelia and Gertrude, with all of whom he has relationships, albeit in decay? Is he sexually attractive, since the making of honest love between him and the audience is vital to the play—though the sexuality of the part is not so much a matter of lineament as of emotional candour and Hamlet's skill, at the last moment, in mythologising himself:

> And in this harsh world draw thy breath in pain
> To tell my story

—with its overtone of a unique solitude, uniquely borne.
If the answer to more than half these questions is yes, play on.

*   *   *

[On 3.1 and "To be or not to be"]

The King now tells the Queen something she already knows: that he and Polonius mean to spy on Hamlet's meeting with Ophelia. Why he sends her away and she acquiesces isn't clear: perhaps this is man's work, and he doesn't want her humanising their efforts to flush her son out. The actress has to decide what attitude to take to this exclusion as she turns to Ophelia, hoping that her "good beauties" and "virtues" will be curative. Ophelia accepts the compliment, modestly or otherwise: "Madam, I wish it may."

Polonius sets Ophelia up with a book; after all, Hamlet was reading when he met him the previous day, so this is obviously a good means of dissimulation. She is also burdened by the "remembrances" she is going to return to Hamlet. Polonius then, improbably, laments the hypocrisy of it all (the things you have to do in politics . . .): "'Tis too much prov'd, that with devotion's visage / And pious action we do sugar o'er / The devil himself." Ophelia is hardly diabolical;

the real reason for the speech is to cue Claudius to do an even more surprising thing—he turns to the audience and announces his guilt, not specifically of the murder but of a "deed" amounting to "a heavy burden." It is hard to know why Shakespeare has done this. It would seem dramatically very much better to extend the tense open question of Claudius's crime, and with it the reliability of the Ghost, until the Prayer Scene after the Play, when he could thrillingly confess for the first time. At this earlier point he is not under pressure, least of all from the sententious Polonius: he is confident and unthreatened. The speech is therefore very difficult for the actor to motivate: in 1994 I was all for cutting it, feeling that the psychology was not worthy of Shakespeare, and that Sophocles would have made a better fist of the storytelling. In the end I'm glad we didn't. Something about Hamlet fills Claudius with a worry he can't name, and out of it comes this self-hating aside: compared to Hamlet's baffling integrity, he is no better in his own eyes than a harlot with a painted face. Beneath his every line ticks his nagging knowledge of himself: at any moment, touched by the right word, his politic skin might blister. Now that we know he is to face a very big test, it is best that we also learn of this precariousness in him.

Productions of Hamlet sometimes place To Be Or Not To Be and the Nunnery Scene with Ophelia not here but at the point of Hamlet's entrance in the previous scene, transposing the "Fishmonger" sequence from that point to this. The thin authority is the First, "Bad" Quarto, which is so unreliable throughout that there seems no particular reason to trust it on this point when the two later texts are consistent. The real reason for the change is a kind of reader's bewilderment: after his experiences on the battlements should we not next see Hamlet debating the great question of life and death and rejecting the ties of sexual love, rather than fooling around with Polonius, Rosencrantz and Guildenstern and the Players? But which is more typical of this writer? I know where my money is—Shakespeare is the first absurdist playwright, who later has Hamlet chatting with a clown who is digging a grave for his lover, who he doesn't even know is dead: who once held up the action after the apparent death of Juliet for fifty quibbling lines between Peter and a group of musicians who suddenly had no gig to play: and who goes on in *Antony and Cleopatra* to bring in a funny asp-seller to help with the Queen's suicide. He rarely does anything on the nose; and the theatrical surprise of To Be Or Not To Be following on from The Play's The Thing—Hamlet disconcerted by a mortal *coup de foudre* ["bolt of thunder"] at his moment of greatest purpose—is typically bold.

The speech that provokes this experimentation is very famous. If you mention the author to anyone who's heard his name only distantly, they will probably say or think "To Be Or Not to Be"; no doubt somebody is doing it somewhere at this moment.[1] It has become an identification tag, together with Yorick's skull, in cartoon, headline and soundbite, a sort of universal shorthand. In *Hamlet* it is not so much a narrative necessity as a haunting refrain, ostensibly leading from and to nothing; no wonder the memory of the compiler of the First Quarto played him false in placing it. Actors approaching the speech worry about it—how to get on for it, how to take the audience by surprise, how not to forget the lines because everyone knows them—and then realise it is far from the most important part of the job.[2]

According to Albert Camus, suicide is the only philosophical question of any interest; and Hamlet's eye-to-eye encounter with it, expressed with all his intellectual lucidity, is perhaps the nearest drama can come to pure philosophy. Like many great insights, it is essentially banal, a trite (or profound) phrasing of a profound (or trite) question. It is odd that the qualities we are most moved by in Hamlet—courage, wit, human optimism—are almost completely lacking in his most famous utterance: like the reflection on Yorick's skull, it is utterly negative apart from the grace of its phrasing. Perhaps that is the shocking point. The Christian inhibition against self-slaughter which Hamlet recognised in his first soliloquy has gone now, replaced by fear, and his typical strengths have deserted him: he proposes that it might be better to end your life than to endure it, but for the cowardly fact that the dreams after death would be bad, and the unknown is terrifying. Helpless to resolve this problem, we sit, courage drained, resolution "sicklied o'er with the pale cast of thought," unable to do anything at all.

How is this negation made tolerable, even definitive? Invited to empathise with the despair behind the lines, we might find its determinacy tainted by a young man's self-pity—it seems to reach out of the play and negate everything, including the activity of sitting watching *Hamlet*. But there is a particular technique at work, withdrawing the speaker from the speech. There is no personal pronoun at all in its thirty-five lines, so it is in a sense drained of Hamlet himself: although the cap fits, it also stands free of him as pure human

---

1. *Essere o non essere; questo e il dilemma. Byt' ili nye byt'; vot fchyom vapros. Iru to imasen; shitsumon-wa desu.* There must be a T-shirt. Most people can get a few lines on, though: "Whether 'tis nobler in the mind to suffer / The slings and arrows of outrageous fortune / Or to take arms against a sea of troubles / And by opposing end them" tends to lodge itself in the memory with a false meaning—"nobler-in-the-mind to suffer," rather than "nobler in-the-mind-to-suffer." In fact, "in the mind" is counterpointed with "to take arms": the alternative doesn't mean anything much.
2. Perhaps in retaliation for my comments about his first entrance, Roger Rees tells me that he remembers me once coming on for this speech at a run, as if diving into a cold pool: my feet arrived first, then my trunk and finally my head. He had never seen such a union of reluctance and eagerness.

analysis. In the earlier admission of despair, O That This Too Too Solid Flesh Would Melt, self-regard was kept at bay by humour, as when Hamlet compared himself to Hercules: To Be Or Not To Be is bleaker, drained of wit, energy and even personality, replacing them with a remorselessly clear vision, expressed in limpid, easy, but formal rhythms. The form is everything—it is Bach, not Stravinsky—the emotions are suppressed and the utterance perfect of its kind.

JUDE LAW

Interview (2009)[†]

JEFF LUNDEN   Law's *Hamlet* opened in London's West End to great excitement and acclaim last spring and has now made the trip across the pond to West 44th Street. Shakespeare's famous character may be haunted by his father's ghost, the murdered king, but Jude Law says he wasn't haunted by the 400-year tradition of great actors who've played the role, from Richard Burbage, the original, to Richard Burton.

JUDE LAW   I think what's key about this part and what we discovered very quickly is that there is no definitive Hamlet. Hamlet shifts in the skin that he is holding at the time. He has the capability, and the play has the capability, to morph with the times. And I found it almost immediately to be that he had to come from inside me. So the idea of carrying this mantle sort of disappeared immediately.

JEFF LUNDEN   Not that Law avoided outside research. He says he spent a year reading everything he could about the play, its history and its various interpretations, before he began rehearsals. Then he and director Michael Grandage spent time alone working on the part.

JUDE LAW   We started a week before everyone else, and we started on the soliloquies, and there are no stupid questions, he always says. Everyone's allowed to be an idiot and say, what the hell does that word mean? Or what am I saying here? And do we all get this? And so you start by pulling it apart, line for line, word for word.

† Jude Law, Interview with Jeff Lunden, Morning Edition, National Public Radio, Oct. 6, 2009. Jude Law (b. 1972) appeared as a precise, variable, and intelligent Hamlet in Michael Grandage's spare and modernist 2009 production. © National Public Radio, Inc. NPR® news report titled "Jude Law, Tackling Hamlet from the Inside Out" by NPR's Jeff Lunden was originally broadcast on NPR's *Morning Edition*® and additional interview extras were posted on NPR.org on October 6, 2009, and are used with the permission of NPR. Any unauthorized duplication is strictly prohibited.

JEFF LUNDEN   Michael Grandage's direction is all about clarity. The set is spare, and the director says he wanted to present a timeless modern production of *Hamlet*—contemporary dress, yes—BlackBerrys, no—so audiences could relate more directly to the characters and the situations.

MICHAEL GRANDAGE   We also knew, because Jude Law was playing Hamlet, that we would hopefully be engaging with a lot of young people, and I didn't want their first experience in the theater, let alone their first experience with Shakespeare, to be something that alienated them in any way. I wanted it to be as fresh and as modern as it could be. And so that they—first of all, I hope they will come back.

JEFF LUNDEN   Keeping Hamlet fresh is part of Jude Law's approach. Geraldine James, who plays Hamlet's mother, Gertrude, says she's constantly surprised by the range Law displays from night to night.

GERALDINE JAMES   I never know what Jude is going to do and it's often different and always amazing. Sometimes it's very, very, very emotional. Sometimes it's less emotional. Sometimes it gets more angry. Sometimes it's more frightening.

JEFF LUNDEN   Jude Law says quicksilver changes are all part of the role—Hamlet can go from high to low, from tragedy to comedy, in the space of a few lines. And even as he faces the turmoil of a father murdered, a mother marrying the murderer, and eventually committing murder himself, Hamlet is always the smartest guy in the room.

JUDE LAW   The wit and the intellect that doesn't rely on falsehood or anger or anything other than a sharp, fast mind and an equally matched tongue.

JEFF LUNDEN   Law says it's his job to bring all the aspects of this tragic role to life for the audience. He's always mindful of how this prince, destined to be king, has been violently thwarted.

JUDE LAW   Every night I want to try and fulfill the possibility that he would've been most royal, had he been put on. He actually had the possibility of being a great king and a great man. So that you see him being beaten down by the world. To me, one of the elements of the tragedy is that you see a positive human become sort of hardened and tarnished to being a murderer. And it's simply through him trying to cope with the world and surviving the world.

[Interview Extra: Hamlet as Fool—and Truth-Teller]

JUDE LAW   Hamlet's not allowed to be the king, he's not allowed to be the powerhouse, so he's the next most honest person in court, which is the fool. Because if he were the prince, he would have to tow the line of the king. Instead, he wants to be honest. And, in fact, he's never mad in his dialogue. In fact, all that he says is often very truthful; he hides it though in incredible language and by inverting people's language, and that's very much the use of the fool.

[Interview Extra: The Character's Journey from Turmoil to Peace]

JUDE LAW   To me, and it's amazing it's not a more famous speech, to me the piece he says to Horatio about the providence in the fall of the sparrow that leads through to "the readiness is all" and "Since no man knows aught of what he leaves, what is't to leave betimes. Let be," I mean to me is the most incredibly rounded and sense of fatalism and yet also of spiritual enlightenment combined that I think has ever been written. What's interesting is everyone talks about "To be or not to be," or "God, what a rogue and peasant slave am I"—I mean all the stuff when he's in turmoil. That's right at the end when he's sort of worked it out, which is, "You know what, it's better to just be present and be ready for anything, and if that's death, then I'm ready for death too." That was the first incredible sense of journey that I learned about this guy that I wasn't expecting, a real sense of peace.

CONTEXTS

The Bible[†]

† *The Geneva Bible: A Facsimile of the 1560 Edition*, introduction by Lloyd E. Berry (Madison: U of Wisconsin P, 1969). Shakespeare used this Protestant translation of the Old and New Testaments, perhaps in a later edition.

Genesis 4:1–12[1]

Afterward the man knew Eve his wife, which conceived and bare Cain, and said, "I have obtained a man by the Lord." And again she brought forth his brother Abel, and Abel was a keeper of sheep, and Cain was a tiller of the ground. And in process of time it came to pass that Cain brought an oblation unto the Lord of the fruit of the ground. And Abel also himself brought of the first fruits of his sheep, and of the fat of them, and the Lord had respect unto Abel and to his offering, but unto Cain and to his offering he had no regard. Wherefore Cain was exceeding wroth,[2] and his countenance fell down. Then the Lord said unto Cain, "Why art thou wroth? And why is thy countenance cast down? If thou do well, shalt thou not be accepted? And if thou dost not well, sin lieth at the door; also unto thee his desire shall be subject, and thou shalt rule over him."[3] Then Cain spake to Abel his brother. And when they were in the field, Cain rose up against Abel his brother and slew him. Then the Lord said unto Cain, "Where is Abel thy brother?" Who answered, "I cannot tell. Am I my brother's keeper?" Again he said, "What hast thou done? The voice of thy brother's blood crieth unto me from the ground. Now therefore thou art cursed from the earth, which hath opened her mouth to receive thy brother's blood from thine hand. When thou shalt till the ground, it shall not henceforth yield unto thee her strength; a vagabond and a renegade shalt thou be in the earth."

Judges 11:30–40[4]

And Jephtah[5] vowed a vow unto the Lord, and said, "If thou shalt deliver the children of Ammon into mine hands, then that thing that cometh out of the doors of mine house to meet me, when I come home in peace from the children of Ammon, shall be the Lord's, and I will offer it for a burnt offering. And so Jephtah went unto the children of Ammon to fight against them, and the Lord delivered them into his hands. And he smote them from Aroer even till thou come to Minnith, twenty cities, and so forth to Abel of the

1. See the allusions in *Hamlet* 1.2.105, 3.3.37–38, and 5.1.68–69.
2. Angry.
3. Cain here has the rights of the firstborn son over Abel.
4. See the allusion in *Hamlet* 2.2.330–39.
5. A military chief of ancient Israel, warring against the Ammonites.

vineyards, with an exceeding great slaughter. Thus the children of Ammon were humbled before the children of Israel.

Now when Jephtah came to Mizpeh unto his house, behold, his daughter came out to meet him with timbrels and dances, which was his only child; he had none other son nor daughter. And when he saw her, he rent his clothes and said, "Alas, my daughter, thou hast brought me low, and art of them that trouble me for I have opened my mouth unto the Lord, and cannot go back." And she said unto him, "My father, if thou hast opened thy mouth unto the Lord, do with me as thou hast promised, seeing that the Lord hath avenged thee of thine enemies, the children of Ammon." Also she said unto her father, "Do thus much for me: suffer me two months, that I may go to the mountains and bewail my virginity, I and my fellows." And he said, "Go," and he sent her away two months. So she went with her companions, and lamented her virginity upon the mountains. And after the end of two months, she turned again unto her father, who did with her according to his vow which he had vowed, and she had known no man. And it was a custom in Israel: the daughters of Israel went year by year to lament the daughter of Jephtah the Gileadite four days in a year.

Romans 12:17–21[6]

Recompense to no man evil for evil. Procure things honest in the sight of all men. If it be possible, as much as in you is, have peace with all men. Dearly beloved, avenge not yourselves, but give place unto wrath, for it is written, "Vengeance is mine,[7] I will repay," saith the Lord. Therefore, if thine enemy hunger, feed him; if he thirst, give him drink; for in so doing thou shalt heap coals of fire on his head. Be not overcome of evil, but overcome evil with goodness.

---

6. The passage articulates the Christian duty to forgive and to forbear revenge.
7. See Deuteronomy 32:35 and Hebrews 10:30.

Greek Tragedy

AESCHYLUS

The Libation-Bearers (458 BCE)[†]

ORESTES Of a surety the mighty oracle of Loxias[1] will not aban-
don me, charging me to brave this peril to the end, and, with
loud utterance, proclaiming afflictions chilling my warm heart's
blood, if I avenge not my father on the guilty; bidding me, infuri-
ated by the loss of my possessions, slay them in requital, even as
they slew. And with my own life, he declared, I should else pay
the debt revealed by many grievous sufferings. For he spake
revealing to mankind the wrath of malignant powers from underneath the earth, and telling of plagues: leprous ulcers that mount
with fierce fangs on the flesh, eating away its primal nature; and
how, upon this disease, a white down should spread forth.[2] And
of other assaults of the Avenging Spirits[3] he spake, destined to be
brought to pass from a father's blood; for the darkling bolt of the
infernal powers, who are stirred by slain victims of kindred race
calling for vengeance, and both madness and groundless terrors
out of the night torment and harass the man, who seeth clearly,
though he moveth his eyebrows in the dark;[4] so that, his body
marred by the brazen scourge, he be even chased in exile from
his country. For an offender such as this 'tis not allowed—so the

---

[†] Aeschylus, *The Libation-Bearers*, trans. Herbert Weir Smyth (London: W. Heinemann,
1922), lines 269–305. At the urging of his sister Electra, Orestes avenges the murder of
his father, Agamemnon, by slaying his own mother, Clytemnestra, and her lover, Aegisthus. This story, as often told in classical Greek tragedy, has many parallels to that of
Hamlet, though there is no evidence of any direct influence as source (see Gilbert
Murray, below).
  The Libation-Bearers is the second play of the *Oresteia* trilogy, which depicts crime,
guilt, and pollution (*miasma*) working its way through several generations. In this passage Orestes recalls the oracle of Apollo and rouses himself to vengeance. Orestes goes
on to fulfill his own will and that of the gods, who threaten punishment if he fails to
revenge his father; but, paradoxically, in so doing he commits a crime that must be punished by the Erinyes, winged women goddesses whose heads are entwined with snakes.
1. Phoebus Apollo, who ordered the revenge.
2. The skin disease is a physical manifestation of the spiritual pollution.
3. The Erinyes.
4. I.e., lies awake restless.

god declared—to have part either in the festal bowl or in the
genial draught; his father's wrath, albeit unseen, bars him from
the altar; no one receives him or lodges with him; and at last,
unhonored of all, unfriended, he perishes, shrivelled pitifully by
a death that wastes him utterly away.

In oracles such as these must I not put my trust? Nay, even if I
trust them not, the deed must still be done. For many impulses
conspire to one conclusion: besides the god's behest, my keen
grief for my father, and withal the pinch of poverty—that my
countrymen, the most renowned of mankind, who overthrew
Troy with gallant spirit, should not thus be at beck and call of a
brace of women;[5] for woman he is at heart; or, if he is not, he shall
soon put it to the test.

SOPHOCLES

Electra (c. 400 BCE)[†]

ELECTRA   But grant—for I will take thine own plea—grant that
the motive of his deed was to benefit his brother[1]—was that a
reason for his dying by thy hand? Under what law? See that, in
making such a law for men, thou make not trouble and remorse
for thyself; for, if we are to take blood for blood, thou wouldst be
the first to die, didst thou meet with thy desert.[2]

But look if thy pretext is not false. For tell me, if thou wilt,
wherefore thou art now doing the most shameless deeds of all—
dwelling as wife with that blood-guilty one, who first helped thee
to slay my sire, and bearing children to him, while thou hast cast
out the earlier-born, the stainless offspring of a stainless marriage? How can I praise these things? Or wilt thou say that this,
too, is thy vengeance for thy daughter? Nay, a shameful plea, if so
thou plead; 'tis not well to wed an enemy for a daughter's sake.

But indeed I may not even counsel thee—who shriekest that I
revile my mother; and truly I think that to me thou art less a
mother than a mistress; so wretched is the life I live, ever beset

---

5. Clyemnestra and Aegisthus (said in contempt).
† Sophocles, *The Plays and Fragments*, trans. Sir Richard C. Jebb, vol. 6, *The Electra*
  (Cambridge: Cambridge UP, 1894), lines 577–609, 1218–29. In the first passage Electra reproaches her mother for the murder of Agamemnon and for her affair with Aegisthus (cf. *Hamlet*, 3.4); in the second, Orestes, presumed dead, returns and reveals
  himself to his sister (cf. *Hamlet*, 5.1 and 5.2).
1. The deed was Agamemnon's sacrifice of his daughter, Iphigeneia, so that the Greek
  fleet could sail to Troy and retrieve Helen, wife of Agamemnon's brother, Menelaus.
2. J. H. Kells comments: "In these lines we have the crux of the whole ethical situation of
  the play: if retributive killing is wrong (*dike* in that sense), then Electra's and Orestes'
  killing of their mother is going to be just as wrong as was Clytaemnestra's killing of
  Agamemnon" (*Electra*, ed. J. H. Kells, Cambridge, 1973, 128).

with miseries by thee and thy partner. And that other, who scarce escaped thy hand, the hapless Orestes, is wearing out his ill-starred days in exile. Often hast thou charged me with rearing him to punish thy crime; and I would have done so, if I could, thou mayest be sure. For that matter denounce me to all as disloyal, if thou wilt, or petulant, or impudent; for if I am accomplished in such ways, methinks I am no unworthy child of thine.

* * *

ELECTRA And where is that unhappy one's tomb?

ORESTES There is none; the living have no tomb.

ELECTRA What sayest thou, boy?

ORESTES   Nothing that is not true.

ELECTRA The man is alive?

ORESTES   If there be life in me.

ELECTRA What? Art thou he?

ORESTES   Look at this signet,[3]
Once our father's, and judge if I speak truth.

ELECTRA O blissful day!

ORESTES   Blissful, in very deed!

ELECTRA Is this thy voice?

ORESTES   Let no other voice reply.

ELECTRA Do I hold thee in my arms?

ORESTES   As mayest thou hold
me always!

ELECTRA Ah, dear friends and fellow-citizens,
Behold Orestes here, who was feigned dead,
And now by that feigning hath come safely home!

EURIPIDES

Electra (c. 418 BCE)[†]

ORESTES What shall we do? Our mother—murder her?

ELECTRA How? Hath ruth seized thee, seeing thy mother's form?

ORESTES Woe!
How can I slay her—her that nursed, that bare me?

ELECTRA Even as she thy father slew and mine.

ORESTES O Phoebus, folly exceeding was thine hest—

ELECTRA Nay, where Apollo erreth, who is wise?

3. Ring.
† *Euripides: with an English Translation*, trans. Arthur S. Way, vol. 2 (London: Heinemann, 1916), lines 967–987. Like Hamlet, Orestes agonizes over and doubts the supernatural command to avenge his father.

ORESTES   Who against nature bad'st me slay my mother!
ELECTRA   How art thou harmed, avenging thine own sire?
ORESTES   Arraigned for a mother's murder—pure ere this.
ELECTRA   Yet impious, if thou succour not thy sire.
ORESTES   Her blood-price to my mother must I pay.[1]
ELECTRA   And *Him*![2]—if thou forbear to avenge a father.
ORESTES   Ha!—spake a fiend[3] in likeness of the God?
ELECTRA   Throned on the holy tripod!—I trow[4] not.
ORESTES   I dare not trust this oracle's utter faith!
ELECTRA   Wilt thou turn craven—be no more a man?
ORESTES   How? Must I lay the selfsame snare for her?
ELECTRA   Ay! That which trapped and slew the adulterer!
ORESTES   I will go in. A horror I essay!
    Yes, will achieve! If 'tis Heaven's will, so be it.
    O bitter strife, which I must needs hold sweet!

EURIPIDES

Orestes (408 BCE)[†]

ORESTES   Give me mine horn-tipped bow, even Loxias' gift,
    Wherewith Apollo bade drive back the fiends,
    If with their frenzy of madness they should fright me.
    A Goddess shall be smitten of mortal hand,
    Except she vanish from before mine eyes.
    Do ye not hear? Not see the feathered shafts
    At point to leap from my far-smiting bow?
    Ha! Ha!
    Why tarry ye? Soar to the welkin's height
    On wings! There rail on Phoebus' oracles!
    Ah!
    Why do I rave, hard-panting from my lungs?[1]
    Whither have I leapt, whither, from my couch?
    For after storm once more a calm I see.
    Sister, why weep'st thou, muffling o'er thine head?
    Ashamed am I to make thee share my woes,

1. I.e., her avenging furies will punish me.
2. I.e., Agamemnon's blood-price to him.
3. Avenging spirit (*alastor*).
4. Think.
† *Euripides: with an English Translation*, trans. Arthur S. Way, vol. 2 (London: Heine-mann, 1916), lines 268–306, 546–604. In the first passage, the Erinyes torment Orestes after the murder and he responds to his sister Electra; in the second, Orestes confronts Tyndareus, Clytemnestra's father. In both passages the revenger, like Hamlet in his soliloquies, wrestles with the moral paradoxes of revenge.
1. Compare Hamlet's return to sanity and self-reproach, "Why, what an ass am I" (2.2.471 ff.).

To afflict a maiden with my malady.
For mine affliction's sake break not, dear heart.
Thou didst consent thereto, yet spilt of me
My mother's blood was. Loxias I blame,
Who to a deed accursèd thrust me on,
And cheered me still with words, but not with deeds.[2]
I trow, my father, had I face to face
Questioned him if I must my mother slay,
Had[3] earnestly besought me by this beard
Never to thrust sword through my mother's heart,
Since he should not win so to light again,[4]
And I (woe's me!) should drain this cup of ills!
Even now unveil thee, sister well-beloved;
From tears refrain, how miserable soe'er
We be; and, when thou seëst me despair,
Mine horror and the fainting of mine heart
Assuage and comfort; and, when thou shalt moan,
Must I be nigh thee, chiding lovingly;
For friendship's glory is such helpfulness.
Now, sorrow-stricken, pass within the house;
Lay thee down; give thy sleepless eyelids sleep;
Put to thy lips food, and thy body bathe.
For if thou fail me, or of tireless watch
Fall sick, I am lost; in thee alone have I
Mine help, of others, as thou seest forlorn.

* * *

ORESTES   I know me guilt-stained with a mother's death,
    Yet pure herein, that I avenged my sire.
    What ought I to have done? Let plea face plea:
    My sire begat, thy child but gave me birth—
    The field that from the sower received the seed;
    Without the father, might no offspring be.[5]
    I reasoned then—better defend my source
    Of life, than her that did but foster me.
    Thy daughter—I take shame to call her mother—
    In lawless and in wanton dalliance
    Sought to a lover; mine own shame I speak
    In telling hers, yet will I utter it:
    Aegisthus was that secret paramour.

2. Blaming Apollo (Loxias), Orestes rejects divine justification for the deed; at the end of the play, however, Apollo rescues Orestes and sends him to Athens for trial and formal acquittal.
3. Would have.
4. Since he would not, by the slaying, regain his life.
5. Orestes' self-defense in these lines reflects contemporary ideas about the primacy of the father in procreation.

I slew him and my mother on one altar—
Sinning, yet taking vengeance for my sire.
Hear how, in that for which thou threatenest doom
Of stoning, I to all of Greece rendered service:
If wives to this bold recklessness shall come,
To slay their husbands, and find refuge then
With sons, entrapping pity with bared breasts,
Then shall they count in naught to slay their lords,
On whatso plea may chance. By deeds of horror—
As thy large utterance is—I abolished Law:
No, but in lawful hate I slew my mother,
Who, when her lord was warring far from home,
Chief of our armies, for all Hellas' sake,
Betrayed him, kept his couch not undefiled.
When her sin found her out, she punished not
Herself, but lest her lord should punish her,
Wreaked on my father chastisement, and slew.
By Heaven!—ill time, I grant, to call on Heaven,
Defending murder—had I justified
Her deeds by silence, what had the dead done?
Had not his hate's Erinyes haunted me?
Or on the mother's side fight Goddesses,
And none on his who suffered deeper wrong?
Thou, ancient, in begetting a vile daughter,
Didst ruin me; for, through her recklessness
Unfathered, I became a matricide.
Mark this—Odysseus' wife Telemachus
Slew not; she took no spouse while lived her lord,
But pure her couch abideth in her halls.
Mark this—Apollo at earth's navel-throne
Gives most true revelation unto men,
Whom we obey in whatsoe'er he saith.
Obeying him, my mother did I slay.
Account ye *him* unholy: yea, slay him!
He sinned, not I. What ought I to have done?
Or hath the god no power to absolve the guilt
I lay on him? Whither should one flee then.
If he which bade me shall not save me from death?
Nay, say not thou that this was not well done,
Albeit untowardly for me, the doer.
Happy the life of men whose marriages
Are blest; but they for whom they ill betide,
At home, abroad, are they unfortunate.

SENECA

Agamemnon (first century)[†]

I.I

[GHOST OF] THYESTES   Nay, better were it not to haunt the
  loathsome Limbo lakes,
Where as the Stygian porter doth advance with lusty crakes,
His triple gorge be hung with mane, shag, hairy, rusty, black,
Where Ixion's carcass linkèd fast, the whirling wheel doth
  rack
And rolleth still upon himself; where as full oft in vain   5
Much toil is lost (the tott'ring stone down tumbling back
  again),
Where growing guts the greedy gripe do gnaw with raven-
  ing bits.
Where parchèd up with burning thirst amid the waves he sits,
And gapes to catch the fleeting flood with hungry chaps
  beguiled,
That pays his painful punishment, whose feast the gods
  defiled.   10
Yet that old man, so steeped in years at length by tract of
  time,

---

† *Seneca His Tenne Tragedies, Translated into Englysh*, ed. Thomas Newton (London,
  1581), sigs. T7r–v, X7v, D8r–v. Invoked by Polonius (2.2.327–28), Lucius Annaeus
  Seneca (4? BCE–65 CE) wrote plays that became models of tragic action and language
  for Elizabethan tragedy, including *Hamlet*. The two plays here rework aspects of the
  Agamemnon and Orestes myths.
    In *Agamemnon*, translated by John Studley, the ghost of Thyestes appears to
  wreak vengeance on Atreus's house, specifically on Agamemnon, son of Atreus, who
  now returns from the Trojan War, only to be murdered by his wife Clytemnestra and
  her lover Aegisthus. Compare the ghost of Elder Hamlet (1.5).
 1. THYESTES: son of Pelops, bitter enemy of his brother Atreus, who served Thyestes in
    a banquet the flesh of Thyestes's own sons; Limbo lakes: rivers of hell
 2. Stygian porter: Charon, who ferried the souls of the dead across the rivers Styx and
    Acheron in Hades; crakes: crows
 3. His triple gorge: his three necks (a reference to Cerberus, the three-headed dog that
    guarded the underworld, in the original Latin); shag: matted, rough
 4. Ixion: father of the Centaurs, bound to a fiery wheel in the underworld; linkèd fast:
    tied tight
 5. still: always
 6. (This line describes the punishment of Sisyphus, condemned eternally to roll a stone up a hill only to have it roll down again.)
 7. gripe: vulture; bits: bites. Tityus suffers this punishment, vultures eternally eating
    his liver.
 8. he: Tantalus, for whom food and drink lay always just out of reach
 9. chaps: jaws
10. feast . . . defiled: (Tantalus killed his son Pelops and served him to the gods in a
    banquet.)
11. steeped: (for "stept"); tract: passing

How great a part belongs to me and portion of his crime!
Account we all the grisly ghosts, whom guilty found of ill,
The Gnosian judge in Pluto's pits doth toss in torments still.
Thyestes, I, in dreary deeds will far surmount the rest,   15
Yet to my brother yield I, though I gorged my bloody breast
And stuffèd have my pampered paunch even with my chil-
     dren three
That crammèd lie within my ribs and have their tomb in me;
The bowels of my swallowed babes devoured up I have.
Nor fickle Fortune me alone the father doth deprave,   20
But enterprising greater guilt than that is put in ure,
To file my daughter's bawdy bed, my lust she doth allure.
To speak these words I do not spare, I wrought the heinous
     deed,
That therefore I through all my stock might parent still
     proceed.
My daughter, driven by force of fates and destinies divine,   25
Doth breed young bones and lades her womb with sinful
     seed of mine.
Lo, nature changèd upside down and out of order turned,
This mingle-mangle hath she made (O fact to be forlorned!),
A father and a grandsire, lo, confusedly I am,
My daughter's husband both become, and father to the same.   30
Those babes that should my nephews be, when Nature
     rightly runs,
She, being tumbled, doth confound and mingle with my sons.
The crystal clearness of the day and Phoebus' beams so
     bright,
Are mixèd with the foggy clouds and darkness dim of night.
When wickedness had wearied us, too late truce taken was,   35
Even when our detestable deeds were done and brought to
     pass.

---

12. **portion:** share. Tantalus's crime, the horrific banquet of his son, is enacted in the
   next generation, with his grandson Thyestes as the victim.
13. **Account we:** let us consider
14. **Gnosian judge:** Minos from Crete (Gnosos), one of the judges in the underworld;
   Pluto: god of the underworld
15. **dreary:** bloody, cruel
17. **paunch:** stomach
20. **deprave:** corrupt
21. **enterprising:** undertaking; **ure:** use
22. **file:** defile; **daughter:** Pelopia, whose union with her father produced Aegisthus; **she:**
   i.e., Fortune
24. **parent:** as a parent
26. **lades:** loads
28. **fact . . . forlorned:** crime . . . turned away from
31. **nephews:** grandsons
32. **being tumbled:** having had intercourse
33. **Phoebus:** Apollo, the sun god

But valiant Agamemnon, he, grand captain of the host,
Who bare the sway among the kings, and rulèd all the roast,
Whose flaunting flag and banner brave, displayed in royal
   sort,
A thousand sail of sousing ships did guard to Phrygian port,   40
And with their swelling, shuttling sails the surging seas did
   hide,
That beateth on the banks of Troy, and floweth by her side.
When Phoebus' cart the zodiac ten times had overrun,
And waste the battered walls do lie of Troy destroyed and
   won,
Returned he is to yield his throat unto his trait'ress wife,   45
That shall with force of bloody blade bereave him of his life.
The glitt'ring sword, the hewing ax, and wounded weapons
   moe.
With blood for blood new set abroach shall make the floors
   to flow;
With sturdy stroke and bois'trous blow of pithy poleax given,
His beaten brains are pashed abroad, his crackèd skull is   50
   riven.

5.4

CLYTEMNESTRA O thou, thy mother's enemy, ungracious,
   saucy face,
After what sort dost thou, a maid, appear in public place?
ELECTRA I have with my virginity the bow'rs of bawds
   forsook.
CLYTEMNESTRA   What man is he that ever thee to be a virgin
   took?
ELECTRA What, your own daughter?
CLYTEMNESTRA   With thy mother more   5
   modest should thou be.
ELECTRA Do you at length begin to preach such godliness to
   me?

---

38. **rulèd . . . roast:** had full authority
39. **sort:** manner
40. **sousing:** swooping; **guard:** escort; **Phrygian:** Trojan
41. **shuttling:** (for "shatling")
43. **zodiac . . . overrun:** had made its annual journey through the heavens ten times
48. **set abroach:** shed
50. **pashed abroad:** smashed and scattered; **riven:** split
5.4. Electra, daughter of Agamemnon, confronts her mother, Clytemnestra, after the
    murder of Agamemnon. Compare Hamlet and Gertrude (3.4).
  2. **After what sort:** for what end
  3. **bow'rs of bawds:** bedrooms of pimps and prostitutes (a mocking reference to her
    home, now ruled by Clytemnestra and her lover Aegisthus)

CLYTEMNESTRA A manly stomach stout thou hast with swell-
ing, haughty heart;
  Subdued with sorrow, learn thou shall to play a woman's
part.
ELECTRA A sword and buckler very well a woman doth
beseem,
  Except I dote.
CLYTEMNESTRA Thyself dost thou hailfellow with us esteem? 10
ELECTRA What Agamemnon new is this whom thou hast got
of late?
CLYTEMNESTRA Hereafter shall I tame and teach thy girlish
tongue to prate,
  And make thee know how to a queen thy taunting to forbear.
ELECTRA The whilst, thou widow, answer me directly to this
gear:
  Thy husband is bereavèd quite of breath, his life is done. 15

Thyestes (first century)

2.1

ATREUS O dastard, cow'rd, O wretch, and—which the great-
est yet of all
  To tyrants' check I count that may in weighty things befall—
  O unrevenged! After guilts so great and brother's guile,
  And truth trod down, doth thou provoke with vain com-
plaints the while
  Thy wrath? Already now to rage all Argos town throughout 5
  In armor ought of thine, and all the double seas about
  Thy fleet to ride. Now all the fields with fervent flames of
thine
  And towns to flash, it well beseemed, and everywhere to
shine

9. **buckler:** shield; **beseem:** suit
10. **dote:** am out of my wits; **hailfellow:** equal
14. **gear:** matter
2.1. In *Thyestes*, translated by Jasper Heywood, Atreus reproaches himself for delaying his revenge; compare Hamlet's soliloquy, 2.2.471ff. Atreus also speaks with a restraining confidante, as Hamlet does with Horatio, especially in 5.2.
1. **dastard:** fearful one
2. **check:** rebuke
3. **brother's guile:** (Thyestes seduced Atreus's wife, Aërope, and stole the golden fleece that safeguarded his brother's rule in Mycenae.)
5–7. **now . . . ride:** now you ought to rage throughout all the towns of Argos in your armor, and ride your fleet through the double seas
8. **flash:** burn; **beseemed:** suited

The bright drawn sword. All under foot of horse let every
    side
Of Argos land resound, and let the woods not serve to hide   10
Our foes, nor yet in haughty top of hills and mountains
    high
The buildèd towers. The people all let them to battle cry,
And clear forsake Mycenas town. Who so his hateful head
Hides and defends, with slaughter dire let blood of him be
    shed.
This princely Pelops palace proud and bow'rs of high renown,   15
On me so on my brother to let them be beaten down,
Go to. Do that which never shall no after age allow,
Nor none it whished. Some mischief great there must be
    ventured now,
Both fierce and bloody, such as would my brother rather long
To have been his. Thou never dost enough revenge the wrong   20
Except thou pass. And fiercer fact what may be done so dire
That his exceeds? Doth ever he lay down his hateful ire?
Doth ever he the modest mean in time of wealth regard,
Or quiet in adversity? I know his nature hard,
Untractable, that broke may be but never will it bend.   25
For which, ere he prepare himself or force to fight intend,
Set first on him, lest while I rest he should on me arise.
He will destroy or be destroyed; in midst the mischief lies,
Prepared to him that takes it first.

SERVANT   Doth fame of people
    naught
Adverse thee fear?

ATREUS   The greatest good of kingdom may be   30
    thought
That still the people are constrained their princes' deeds as
    well
To praise, as them to suffer all.

SERVANT   Whom fear doth so compel
To praise, the same his foes to be doth fear enforce again;
But who indeed the glory seeks of favor true t'obtain,

---

    10. **woods:** (for "woundes")
16–17. **On . . . to:** Let it fall down on me so long as it falls on my brother too.
    18. **whished:** is silent about
    21. **Except thou pass:** unless you surpass it. (In the sentence ending with this
        phrase Heywood renders the popular Senecan maxim, *Scelera non ulcisceris, nisi
        vincis,* "Crimes you don't avenge, unless you outdo them"); **fact:** crime
    25. **untractable:** uncontrollable, stubborn
28–29. **in . . . first:** between us lies the crime placed for the one who takes it first
29–30. **fame . . . fear:** the adverse reaction of the people frighten you at all
    30. **kingdom:** royal rule

He rather would with hearts of each be praised than   35
   tongues of all.
ATREUS   The truer praise full oft hath happed to meaner men
   to fall,
   The false but unto mighty man; what nill they, let them
   will.
SERVANT   Let first the king will honest things and none the
   same dare nill.
ATREUS   Where leeful are to him that rules but honest things
   alone,
   There reigns the king by others' leave.
SERVANT   And where the shame   40
   is none,
   Nor care of right, faith, piety, nor holiness none stayeth,
   That kingdom swerves.
ATREUS   Such holiness, such piety and faith,
   Are private goods. Let kings run on in that that likes their
   will.
SERVANT   The brother's hurt a mischief count, though he be
   ne'er so ill.
ATREUS   It is but right to do to him that wrong to brother   45
   were.
   What heinous hurt hath his offense let pass to prove? Or
   where
   Refrained the guilt? My spouse he stole away for lechery,
   And reign by stealth; the ancient note and sign of empery
   By fraud he got; my house by fraud to vex he never ceased.

35. **hearts:** (for "hates")
37. **nill . . . will:** they don't want, let them choose
38. **nill:** choose otherwise
39. **leeful:** permissible
41. **none stayeth:** restrains not
43. **that that . . . will:** whatever pleases them
44. **The . . . ill:** consider it wrong to harm a brother, even if he is wicked
48. **note . . . empery:** token and guarantor of rule (i.e., the golden fleece)

SAXO GRAMMATICUS

Historica Danica (1180–1208)†

[After defeating Koller, King of Norway in battle, Horwendil (Elder Hamlet) wins Gerutha in marriage.]¹

Such great good fortune stung Feng [Claudius] with jealousy, so that he resolved treacherously to waylay his brother, thus showing that goodness is not safe even from those of a man's own house. And behold, when a chance came to murder him, his bloody hand sated the deadly passion of his soul.² Then he took the wife of the brother he had butchered, capping unnatural murder with incest.³ For whoso yields to one iniquity, speedily falls an easier victim to the next, the first being an incentive to the second. Also the man veiled the monstrosity of his deed with such hardihood of cunning that he made up a mock pretense of goodwill to excuse his crime, and glossed over fratricide with a show of righteousness. Gerutha, said he, though so gentle that she would do no man the slightest hurt, had been visited with her husband's extremest hate; and it was all to save her that he had slain his brother; for he thought it shameful that a lady so meek and unrancorous should suffer the heavy disdain of her husband. Nor did his smooth words fail in their intent; for at courts, where fools are sometimes favored and backbiters preferred, a lie lacks not credit. Nor did Feng keep from shameful embraces the hands that had slain a brother, pursuing with equal guilt both of his wicked and impious deeds.

---

† *The First Nine Books of the Danish History of Saxo Grammaticus*, trans. Oliver Elton (London: D. Nutt, 1894), 106–17, 130. Shakespeare is unlikely to have known Saxo's work directly, but the *Historia Danica* is the ultimate source for many adaptations of the Hamlet story, including that of François de Belleforest, *Histoires Tragiques* (1576). Belleforest's expanded and moralized version of the story may have influenced Shakespeare directly or indirectly through a dramatic adaptation; several years after Shakespeare's play it appeared in anonymous English translation as *The Hystorie of Hamblet* (1608), from which modernized passages appear below (excerpted from *Narrative and Dramatic Sources of Shakespeare*, ed. Geoffrey Bullough, vol. 7, London: Routledge & Kegan Paul, 1978, 81–124).

1. Belleforest tells the story "to the end that traitors may know, although the punishment of their trespasses committed be stayed for awhile, yet that they may assure themselves that, without all doubt, they shall never escape the puissant and revenging hand of God" (83–84). In his account, Horvendil [Saxo's Horwendil] is "the most renowned pirate that in those days scoured the seas and havens of the north parts" (86).

2. In Belleforest, the murder happens in public: "But Fengon, having secretly assembled certain men, and perceiving himself strong enough to execute his enterprise, Horvendil his brother being at a banquet with his friends, suddenly set upon him, where he slew him as traitorously as cunningly he purged himself of so detestable a murder to his subjects" (87).

3. Belleforest makes explicit the adultery of the wife (here named Geruth): "This princess, who at the first for her rare virtues and courtesies was honored of all men and beloved of her husband, as soon as she once gave ear to the tyrant Fengon [Feng, or Claudius], forgot both the rank she held among the greatest names and the duty of an honest wife on her behalf" (89).

Amleth beheld all this, but feared lest too shrewd a behaviour might make his uncle suspect him. So he chose to feign dulness, and pretend an utter lack of wits. This cunning course not only concealed his intelligence but ensured his safety. Every day he remained in his mother's house utterly listless and unclean, flinging himself on the ground and bespattering his person with foul and filthy dirt. His discoloured face and visage smutched with slime denoted foolish and grotesque madness. All he said was of a piece with these follies; all he did savored of utter lethargy. In a word, you would not have thought him a man at all, but some absurd abortion due to a mad fit of destiny. He used at times to sit over the fire, and, raking up the embers with his hands, to fashion wooden crooks, and harden them in the fire, shaping at their tips certain barbs, to make them hold more tightly to their fastenings. When asked what he was about, he said that he was preparing sharp javelins to avenge his father. This answer was not a little scoffed at, all men deriding his idle and ridiculous pursuit; but the thing helped his purpose afterwards.[4]

Now it was his craft in this matter that first awakened in the deeper observers a suspicion of his cunning. For his skill in a trifling art betokened the hidden talent of the craftsman; nor could they believe the spirit dull where the hand had acquired so cunning a workmanship. Lastly, he always watched with the most punctual care over his pile of stakes that he had pointed in the fire. Some people, therefore, declared that his mind was quick enough, and fancied that he only played the simpleton in order to hide his understanding, and veiled some deep purpose under a cunning feint. His wiliness (said these) would be most readily detected, if a fair woman were put in his way in some secluded place, who would provoke his mind to the temptations of love, all men's natural temper being too blindly amorous to be artfully dissembled, and this passion being also too impetuous to be checked by cunning. Therefore, if his lethargy were feigned, he would seize the opportunity, and yield straightway to violent delights. So men were commissioned to draw the young man in his rides into a remote part of the forest, and there assail him with a temptation of this nature. Among these chanced to be a foster brother of Amleth, who had not ceased to have regard to their common nurture and who esteemed his present orders less than the memory of their past fellowship. He attended Amleth among his appointed train, being anxious not to entrap, but to warn him; and was persuaded that he would suffer the worst if he showed the

---

4. Belleforest compares Hamblet's pretended dullness to that of Lucius Junius Brutus "dissembling a great alteration in his mind" to plot against the tyrant Tarquin, and to that of David "that counterfeited the mad man among the petty kings of Palestina" (90).

slightest glimpse of sound reason, and above all if he did the act of love openly. This was also plain enough to Amleth himself. For when he was bidden mount his horse, he deliberately set himself in such a fashion that he turned his back to the neck and faced about, fronting the tail, which he proceeded to encompass with the reins, just as if on that side he would check the horse in its furious pace. By this cunning thought he eluded the trick, and overcame the treachery of his uncle. The reinless steed galloping on, with rider directing its tail, was ludicrous enough to behold.

Amleth went on, and a wolf crossed his path amid the thicket. When his companions told him that a young colt had met him, he retorted, that in Feng's stud there were too few of that kind fighting. This was a gentle but witty fashion of invoking a curse upon his uncle's riches. When they averred that he had given a cunning answer, he answered that he had spoken deliberately for he was loath to be thought prone to lying about any matter, and wished to be held a stranger to falsehood. And accordingly he mingled craft and candor in such wise that, though his words did lack truth, yet there was nothing to betoken the truth and betray how far his keenness went.

Again, as he passed along the beach, his companions found the rudder of a ship which had been wrecked, and said they had discovered a huge knife. "This" said he, "was the right thing to carve such a huge ham," by which he really meant the sea, to whose infinitude, he thought, this enormous rudder matched. Also, as they passed the sandhills and bade him look at the meal, meaning the sand, he replied that it had been ground small by the hoary tempests of the ocean. His companions praising his answer, he said that he had spoken it wittingly.

Then they purposely left him, that he might pluck up more courage to practise wantonness. The woman whom his uncle had dispatched met him in a dark spot, as though she had crossed him by chance; and he took her and would have ravished her, had not his foster brother, by a secret device, given him an inkling of the trap. For this man, while pondering the fittest way to play privily the prompter's part and forestall the young man's hazardous lewdness, found a straw on the ground and fastened it underneath the tail of a gadfly that was flying past; which he then drove towards the particular quarter where he knew Amleth to be: an act which served the unwary prince exceedingly well. The token was interpreted as shrewdly as it had been sent. For Amleth saw the gadfly, espied with curiosity the straw which it wore embedded in its tail, and perceived that it was a secret warning to beware of treachery. Alarmed, scenting a trap, and fain to possess his desire in greater safety, he caught up the woman in his arms and dragged her off to a distant and impenetrable fen. Moreover, when they had lain together, he conjured her

earnestly to disclose the matter to none, and the promise of silence
was accorded as heartily as it was asked. For both of them had
been under the same fostering in their childhood and this early
rearing in common had brought Amleth and the girl into great
intimacy.[5]

So, when he had returned home, they all jeeringly asked him
whether he had given way to love, and he avowed that he had ravished the maid. When he was next asked where he did it, and what
had been his pillow, he said that he had rested upon the hoof of a
beast of burden, upon a cockscomb, and also upon a ceiling. For,
when he was starting into temptation, he had gathered fragments of
all these things in order to avoid lying. And though his jest did not
take aught of the truth out of the story, the answer was greeted with
shouts of merriment from the bystanders. The maiden, too, when
questioned on the matter, declared that he had done no such thing;
and her denial was the more readily credited when it was found that
the escort had not witnessed the deed. Then he who had marked the
gadfly in order to give a hint, wishing to show Amleth that to his
trick he owed his salvation, observed that latterly he had been singly
devoted to Amleth. The young man's reply was apt. Not to seem forgetful of his informant's service, he said that he had seen a certain
thing bearing a straw flit by suddenly, wearing a stalk of chaff fixed
on its hinder parts. The cleverness of this speech, which made the
rest split with laughter, rejoiced the heart of Amleth's friend.

Thus all were worsted, and none could open the secret lock of
the young man's wisdom. But a friend of Feng, gifted more with
assurance than judgment, declared that the unfathomable cunning
of such a mind could not be detected by any vulgar plot, for the
man's obstinacy was so great that it ought not to be assailed with
any mild measures; there were many sides to his wiliness, and it
ought not to be entrapped by any one method. Accordingly, said he,
his own profounder acuteness had hit on a more delicate way,
which was well fitted to be put in practice, and would effectually
discover what they desired to know. Feng was purposely to absent
himself, pretending affairs of great import. Amleth should be clos-
eted alone with his mother in her chamber; but a man should first
be commissioned to place himself in a concealed part of the room
and listen heedfully to what they talked about. For if the son had
any wits at all he would not hesitate to speak out in the hearing of

5. Belleforest changes the double warning of the foster brother to the warning of a faithful
   gentleman, omits the backward horseriding, the straw and the gadfly, and the dragging
   of the girl to a secret place. The lady here is more active: "by her he was likewise
   informed of the treason, as being one that from her infancy loved and favored him." She
   does not want "to leave his company without enjoying the pleasure of his body, whom
   she loved more than herself" (92). It is not clear that ever they make love, but Hamblet
   avoids the trap.

his mother, or fear to trust himself to the fidelity of her who bore him. The speaker, loath to seem readier to devise than to carry out the plot, zealously proffered himself as the agent of the eavesdropping. Feng rejoiced at the scheme and departed on pretense of a long journey. Now he who had given this counsel repaired privily to the room where Amleth was shut up with his mother, and lay down skulking in the straw.

But Amleth had his antidote for the treachery. Afraid of being overheard by some eavesdropper, he at first resorted to his usual imbecile ways, and crowed like a noisy cock, beating his arms together to mimic the flapping of wings. Then he mounted the straw and began to swing his body and jump again and again, wishing to try if aught lurked there in hiding. Feeling a lump beneath his feet, he drove his sword into the spot, and impaled him who lay hid.[6] Then he dragged him from his concealment and slew him. Then, cutting his body into morsels, he seethed it in boiling water, and flung it through the mouth of an open sewer for the swine to eat, bestrewing the stinking mire with his hapless limbs.

Having in this wise eluded the snare, he went back to the room. Then his mother set up a great wailing and began to lament her son's folly to his face; but he said: "Most infamous of women! Dost thou seek with such lying lamentations to hide thy most heavy guilt? Wantoning like a harlot, thou hast entered a wicked and abominable state of wedlock, embracing with incestuous bosom thy husband's slayer, and wheedling with filthy lures of blandishment him who had slain the father of thy son. This, forsooth, is the way that the mares couple with the vanquishers of their mates; for brute beasts are naturally incited to pair indiscriminately; and it would seem that thou, like them, hast clean forgot thy first husband. As for me, not idly do I wear the mask of folly; for I doubt not that he who destroyed his brother will riot as ruthlessly in the blood of his kindred. Therefore it is better to choose the garb of dulness than that of sense, and to borrow some protection from a show of utter frenzy. Yet the passion to avenge my father still burns in my heart; but I am watching the chances, I await the fitting hour. There is a place for all things; against so merciless and dark [a] spirit must be used the deeper devices of the mind. And thou, who hadst been better employed in lamenting thine own disgrace, know it is superfluity to bewail my witlessness; thou shouldst weep for the blemish in thine own mind, not for that in another's. On the rest see thou keep silence." With such reproaches he rent the heart of his mother

---

6. Here Belleforest's anonymous translator appears to have been influenced by Shakespeare's play: he changes the quilt to an "arras," has Hamblet cry "A rat, a rat," and stabs the counselor through the wall hangings (94).

and redeemed her to walk in the ways of virtue, teaching her to set the fires of the past above the seductions of the present.[7]

When Feng returned, nowhere could he find the man who had suggested the treacherous espial; he searched for him long and carefully, but none said they had seen him anywhere. Amleth, among others, was asked in jest if he had come on any trace of him, and replied that the man had gone to the sewer, but had fallen through its bottom and been stifled by the floods of filth, and that he had then been devoured by the swine that came up all about that place. This speech was flouted by those who heard; for it seemed senseless, though really it expressly avowed the truth.

Feng now suspected that his stepson was certainly full of guile, and desired to make way with him, but durst not do the deed for fear of the displeasure, not only of Amleth's grandsire Rorik, but also of his own wife. So he thought that the King of Britain should be employed to slay him, so that another could do the deed, and he be able to feign innocence. Thus, desirous to hide his cruelty, he chose rather to besmirch his friend than to bring disgrace on his own head. Amleth, on departing, gave secret orders to his mother to hang the hall with woven knots [tapestry], and to perform pretended obsequies for him a year thence, promising that he would then return. Two retainers of Feng then accompanied him, bearing a letter graven on wood—a kind of writing material frequent in old times; this letter enjoined the king of the Britons to put to death the youth who was sent over to him.

While they were reposing, Amleth searched their coffers, found the letter, and read the instructions therein. Whereupon he erased all the writing on the surface, substituted fresh characters, and so, changing the purport of the instructions, shifted his own doom upon his companions. Nor was he satisfied with removing from himself the sentence of death and passing the peril on to others, but added an entreaty that the king of Britain would grant his daughter in marriage to a youth of great judgment whom he was sending to him. Under this was falsely marked the signature of Feng.

Now when they had reached Britain, the envoys went to the king, and proffered him the letter which they supposed was an implement of destruction to another, but which really betokened death to themselves. The king dissembled the truth, and entreated them hospitably and kindly. Then Amleth scouted all the splendour of the royal banquet like vulgar viands, and abstaining very strangely,

---

7. Belleforest's Geruth here denies knowledge of the murder, admits wrong in marrying Claudius the "cruel tyrant and murderer," and says that she hopes to see Hamblet revenge his father and wear the crown of Denmark (98–99). (Q1 develops this hope by having Hamlet request, and the Queen promise, assistance in the revenge; see Appendix 1, passage 5, p. 143.)

rejected that plenteous feast, refraining from the drink even as from the banquet. All marveled that a youth and a foreigner should disdain the carefully-cooked dainties of the royal board and the luxurious banquet provided, as if it were some peasant's relish. So, when the revel broke up, and the king was dismissing his friends to rest, he had a man sent into the sleeping-room to listen secretly, in order that he might hear the midnight conversation of his guests.

[Amleth's companions ask him why he abstained from the feast and he answers that the bread was flecked with blood, there was iron in the liquor, and the meat smelled of human carcasses. He also says the king has the eyes of a slave and the queen acts like a bondmaid. Upon investigation the king discovers hidden truths in these cryptic sayings.]

Then the king adored the wisdom of Amleth as though it were inspired,[8] and gave him his daughter to wife, accepting his bare word as though it were a witness from the skies. Moreover, in order to fulfill the bidding of his friend, he hanged Amleth's companions on the morrow. Amleth, feigning offense, treated this piece of kindness as a grievance, and received from the king, as compensation, some gold, which he afterwards melted in the fire, and secretly caused to be poured into some hollowed sticks.

When he had passed a whole year with the king he obtained leave to make a journey, and returned to his own land, carrying away of all his princely wealth and state only the sticks which held the gold. On reaching Jutland, he exchanged his present attire for his ancient demeanour, which he had adopted for righteous ends, purposely assuming an aspect of absurdity. Covered with filth, he entered the banquet-room where his own obsequies were being held, and struck all men utterly aghast, rumour having falsely noised abroad his death. At last terror melted into mirth, and the guests jeered and taunted one another, that he whose last rites they were celebrating as though he were dead, should appear in the flesh.

When he was asked concerning his comrades, he pointed to the sticks he was carrying, and said, "Here is both the one and the other." This he observed with equal truth and pleasantry; for his speech, though most thought it idle, yet departed not from the truth; for it pointed at the weregild [price to be paid in compensation] of the slain as though it were themselves. Thereon, wishing to

---

8. Belleforest elaborates on the sources of this inspiration, observing "that in those days, the north parts of the world, living as then under Satan's laws, were full of enchanters, so that there was not any young gentleman whatsoever that knew not something therein sufficient to serve his turn. . . . And so Hamblet, while his father lived, had been instructed in that devilish art, whereby the wicked spirit abuseth mankind and advertiseth him (as he can) of things past." Belleforest then offers an alternative explanation, ascribing the power of divination perhaps to Hamblet's "over great melancholy" (104).

bring the company into a gayer mood, he joined the cupbearers, and diligently did the office of plying the drink.

Then, to prevent his loose dress hampering his walk, he girdled his sword upon his side, and purposely drawing it several times, pricked his fingers with its point. The bystanders accordingly had both sword and scabbard riveted across with an iron nail. Then, to smooth the way more safely to his plot, he went to the lords and plied them heavily with draught upon draught, and drenched them all so deep in wine, that their feet were made feeble with drunkenness, and they turned to rest within the palace, making their bed where they had revelled. Then he saw they were in a fit state for his plots, and thought that here was a chance offered to do his purpose. So he took out of his bosom the stakes he had long ago prepared, and went into the building, where the ground lay covered with the bodies of the nobles wheezing off their sleep and their debauch. Then, cutting away its supports, he brought down the hanging his mother had knitted, which covered the inner as well as the outer walls of the hall. This he flung upon the snorers, and then applying the crooked stakes, he knotted and bound them up in such insoluble intricacy, that not one of the men beneath, however hard he might struggle, could contrive to rise.

After this he set fire to the palace. The flames spread, scattering the conflagration far and wide. It enveloped the whole dwelling, destroyed the palace, and burnt them all while they were either buried in deep sleep or vainly striving to arise. Then he went to the chamber of Feng, who had before this been conducted by his train into his pavilion; plucked up a sword that chanced to be hanging to the bed, and planted his own in its place. Then, awakening his uncle, he told him that his nobles were perishing in the flames, and that Amleth was here, armed with his crooks [stakes] to help him, and thirsting to exact the vengeance, now long overdue, for his father's murder. Feng, on hearing this, leapt from his couch, but was cut down while, deprived of his own sword, he strove in vain to draw the strange one.

O valiant Amleth, and worthy of immortal fame, who being shrewdly armed with a feint of folly, covered a wisdom too high for human wit under a marvellous disguise of silliness! And not only found in his subtlety means to protect his own safety, but also by its guidance found opportunity to avenge his father. By this skilful defense of himself, and strenuous revenge for his parent, he has left it doubtful whether we are to think more of his wit or his bravery.[9]

9. Belleforest meditates on the justice of revenge: "If vengeance ever seemed to have any show of justice, it is then, when piety and affection constraineth us to remember our fathers unjustly murdered, as the things whereby we are dispensed withal, and which seek the means not to leave treason and murder unpunished" (110). He further adduces

[Amleth justifies his actions in an oration to the people and is crowned King of Jutland. Amleth then sails to England and his wife with a shield that depicts the events of his life, whereupon the King of England persuades him to sail to Scotland as part of a plot to avenge the death of Feng. In Scotland, however, Hamlet weds the fierce Hermutrude; he then journeys back to England, discovers the plot against him, slays the King, and returns to Jutland with two wives. Wiglek, the King of Denmark kills Amleth, then weds Hermutrude, who had promised not to survive her husband.]

Thus all vows of women are loosed by change of fortune and melted by the shifting of time; the faith of their soul rests on a slippery foothold, and is weakened by casual chances; glib in promises, and as sluggish in performance, all manner of lustful promptings enslave it, and it bounds away with panting and precipitate desire, forgetful of old things, in the ever hot pursuit after something fresh. So ended Amleth. Had fortune been as kind to him as nature, he would have equalled the gods in glory, and surpassed the labors of Hercules by his deeds of prowess. A plain in Jutland is to be found, famous for his name and burial place.

DANTE ALIGHIERI

Inferno (c. 1315)[†]

Canto 13: The Forest of Suicides

Then stretched I forth my hand a little forward,
And plucked a branchlet off from a great thorn,
And the trunk cried, "Why dost thou mangle me?"
After it had become embrowned with blood,
It recommenced its cry: "Why dost thou rend me?
Hast thou no spirit of pity whatsoever?
Men once we were, and now are changed to trees;
Indeed, thy hand should be more pitiful,
Even if the souls of serpents we had been."

---

the example of King David charging his son and successor Solomon to punish former enemies: "where the prince or country is interested, the desire of revenge cannot by any means (how small soever) bear the title of condemnation, but is rather commendable and worthy of praise" (111).

† Dante Alighieri, *The Divine Comedy*, trans. Henry Wadsworth Longfellow (Boston: Houghton, Mifflin and Co., 1865, rpt. 1895). In the *Inferno*, the first part of Dante's *Divine Comedy*, the pilgrim journeys through the nine circles of hell and meets Pier della Vigna in the Forest of Suicides (Canto 13). In the Ninth Circle (Canto 34), the pilgrim comes finally to Lucifer, three-faced, sunken in ice, chewing the three archtraitors—Judas Iscariot, who betrayed Christ, and Brutus and Cassius, who assassinated Julius Caesar in 44 BC. In these selections Dante represents the Christian traditions that prohibit suicide and regicide, traditions crucial to *Hamlet*.

As out of a green brand that is on fire
At one of the ends, and from the other drips
And hisses with the wind that is escaping,
So from that splinter issued forth together
Both words and blood; whereat I let the tip
Fall, and stood like a man who is afraid.
"Had he been able sooner to believe,"
My Sage[1] made answer, "O thou wounded soul,
What only in my verses he has seen,
Not upon thee had he stretched forth his hand;
Whereas the thing incredible has caused me
To put him to an act which grieveth me.
But tell him who thou wast, so that by way
Of some amends thy fame he may refresh
Up in the world, to which he can return."
And the trunk said: "So thy sweet words allure me,
I cannot silent be; and you be vexed not,
That I a little to discourse am tempted.
I am the one[2] who both keys had in keeping
Of Frederick's heart, and turned them to and fro
So softly in unlocking and in locking,
That from his secrets most men I withheld;
Fidelity I bore the glorious office
So great, I lost thereby my sleep and pulses.
The courtesan[3] who never from the dwelling
Of Caesar turned aside her strumpet eyes,
Death universal and the vice of courts,
Inflamed against me all the other minds,
And they, inflamed, did so inflame Augustus,
That my glad honors turned to dismal mournings.
My spirit, in disdainful exultation,
Thinking by dying to escape disdain,
Made me unjust against myself, the just.
I, by the roots unwonted of this wood,
Do swear to you that never broke I faith
Unto my lord, who was so worthy of honor;
And to the world if one of you return,
Let him my memory comfort, which is lying
Still prostrate from the blow that envy dealt it."
Waited awhile, and then: "Since he is silent,"

---

1. Virgil, Latin poet and the pilgrim's guide, who portrayed Harpies and a man (Poly-
   dorus) turned into a tree in *Aeneid* 3.
2. Pier della Vigna (c. 1190–1249), Sicilian poet who served Frederick II faithfully, only
   to be accused of treachery, then imprisoned and blinded. He committed suicide.
3. I.e., Envy.

The Poet said to me, "lose not the time,
But speak, and question him, if more may please thee."
Whence I to him: "Do thou again inquire
Concerning what thou think'st will satisfy me;
For I cannot, such pity is in my heart."
Therefore he recommenced: "So may the man
Do for thee freely what thy speech implores,
Spirit incarcerate, again be pleased
To tell us in what way the soul is bound
Within these knots; and tell us, if thou canst,
If any from such members e'er is freed."
Then blew the trunk amain, and afterward
The wind was into such a voice converted:
"With brevity shall be replied to you.
When the exasperated soul abandons
The body whence it rent itself away,
Minos[4] consigns it to the seventh abyss.
It falls into the forest, and no part
Is chosen for it; but where Fortune hurls it,
There like a grain of spelt it germinates.
It springs a sapling, and a forest tree;
The Harpies,[5] feeding then upon its leaves,
Do pain create, and for the pain an outlet.
Like others for our spoils shall we return;
But not that any one may them revest,[6]
For 'tis not just to have what one casts off.
Here we shall drag them, and along the dismal
Forest our bodies shall suspended be,
Each to the thorn of his molested shade." (13.31–108)

Canto 34: Satan and the Traitors

The Emperor of the kingdom dolorous
From his mid-breast forth issued from the ice;
And better with a giant I compare
Than do the giants with those arms of his;
Consider now how great must be that whole,
Which unto such a part conforms itself.
Were he as fair once, as he now is foul,
And lifted up his brow against his Maker,
Well may proceed from him all tribulation.
Oh, what a marvel it appeared to me,

4. One of the three judges in hell.
5. Winged monsters with women's faces.
6. Put back on their bodies (at the Last Judgment).

When I beheld three faces on his head!
The one in front, and that vermilion was;
Two were the others, that were joined with this
Above the middle part of either shoulder,
And they were joined together at the crest;
And the right-hand one seemed twixt white and yellow;[7]
The left was such to look upon as those
Who come from where the Nile falls valley-ward.
Underneath each came forth two mighty wings,
Such as befitting were so great a bird;
Sails of the sea I never saw so large.
No feathers had they, but as of a bat
Their fashion was, and he was waving them,
So that three winds proceeded forth therefrom.
Thereby Cocytus[8] wholly was congealed.
With six eyes did he weep, and down three chins
Trickled the tear-drops and the bloody drivel.
At every mouth he with his teeth was crunching
A sinner, in the manner of a brake,[9]
So that he three of them tormented thus.
To him in front the biting was as naught
Unto the clawing, for sometimes the spine
Utterly stripped of all the skin remained.
"That soul up there which has the greatest pain,"
The Master said, "is Judas Iscariot;
With head inside, he plies his legs without.
Of the two others, who head downward are,
The one who hangs from the black jowl is Brutus;
See how he writhes himself, and speaks no word.
And the other, who so stalwart seems, is Cassius."

(34.28–67)

---

7. Satan's three faces grotesquely parody the Trinity; red suggests anger; yellow, coward-ice; and black, ignorance.
8. One of the five rivers in hell.
9. Grinder.

Henry Fuseli, *Hamlet and the Ghost*, 1789

THOMAS MORE

The Supplication of Souls (1529)[†]

In most piteous wise[1] continually calleth and crieth upon your devout charity and most tender pity for help, comfort, and relief, your late acquaintance, kindred, spouses, companions, playfellows, and friends, and now your humble and unacquainted and half-forgotten suppliants, poor prisoners of God, the silly[2] souls in purgatory, here abiding and enduring the grievous pains and hot cleansing fire that fretteth and burneth out the rusty and filthy

---

[†] Thomas More, *The Supplication of Souls* (London, 1529), sigs. Ai[v]–Aii, Giv[v]–Hii. Lord Chancellor of England, martyr, and Catholic saint, Thomas More (1478–1535) wrote this defense of purgatory to answer Simon Fish's *A Supplication for the Beggars* (1529), a wide-ranging proto-Protestant attack on Catholic doctrines of penance, indulgence, and purgatory. The Ghost in *Hamlet* reflects the Catholic view of purgatory as an extant place of temporary punishment wherein fire cleanses the soul of sin (1.5.9–13, 74–79). (I have silently modernized spelling, punctuation, and some forms—*helped* for *holpen, sprung* for *sprongen, lose* for *leese, example* for *ensample, be* for *been,* and *eyes* for *eyen.*)

1. Manner.
2. Helpless.

220   THOMAS MORE

spots of our sin, till the mercy of almighty God, the rather[3] by your good and charitable means vouchsafe[4] to deliver us hence.

From whence if ye marvel why we more now molest and trouble you with our writing than ever we were wont before, it may like you to wit[5] and understand that hitherto, though we have been with many folk much forgotten of[6] negligence, yet hath always good folk remembered us, and we have been recommended unto God and eased, helped, and relieved both by the private prayers of good, virtuous people, and specially by the daily masses and other ghostly suffrages[7] of priests, religious, and folk of Holy Church. But now sith[8] that of late there are sprung up certain seditious persons, which not only travail and labor to destroy them by whom we be much helped, but also to sow and set forth such a pestilent opinion against ourself as once received and believed among the people, must needs take from us the relief and comfort that ever should come to us by the charitable alms, prayer, and good works of the world, ye may take it for no wonder, though we silly souls that have long lien and cried so far from you that we seldom brake your sleep, do now in this, our great fear of our utter loss forever of your loving remembrance and relief, not yet importunately bereave you of your rest with crying at your ears at unseasonable time when ye would, as we do never, repose yourself and take ease, but only procure to be presented unto you this poor book, this humble supplication of ours, which it may please you parcel meal[9] at your leisure to look over for all silly souls' sake that it may be as an wholesome treacle[1] at your heart against the deadly poison of their pestilent persuasion that would bring you in that error to ween[2] there were no purgatory.

Of all which cruel persons so procuring not the minishment[3] of your mercy toward us but the utter spoil and robbery of our whole help and comfort that should come from you, the very worst and thereby the most deadly deviser of our pains and heaviness (God forgive him!) is that dispiteous[4] and despiteful person which of late under pretext of pity made and put forth among you a book that he named *The Supplication for the Beggars*, a book indeed nothing less intending than the pity that it pretendeth, nothing minding the weal[5]

3. Especially.
4. Manage.
5. Know.
6. Because of.
7. Intercessory prayers.
8. Since.
9. Piecemeal.
1. Antidote.
2. Think.
3. Lessening.
4. Pitiless.
5. Welfare.

of any man, but as we shall hereafter show you, much harm and mischief to all men, and among other great sorrow, discomfort, and heaviness unto us, your even Christian and nigh kin, your late neighbors and pleasant companions upon earth and now poor prisoners here.

* * *

And if yet they deny Saint Peter [his reference to purgatory in Acts 2:24], we shall then allege them Saint Paul, whom they be best content to hear of because that of the difficulty of his writing they catch sometime some matter of contention for the defense of their false exposition. This blessed apostle in his first Epistle to the Corinthians, the third chapter [v. 11], speaking of our Savior Christ, the very foundation and the only foundation of all our faith and salvation, saith: "If any man build upon this foundation gold, silver, precious stones, wood, hay, or straw, every man's work shall be made open, for the day of our Lord shall declare it, for in the fire it shall be showed, and the fire shall prove what manner of thing every man's work is. If any man's work that he hath builded thereon do abide, he shall have a reward. If any man's work burn, he shall suffer harm but he shall be safe but yet as by fire" [1 Corinthians 3:12–15]. In these words the apostle showeth that likewise as some men, abiding upon Christ and his very lively faith, build up thereupon such good works as are so good and so pure that they be like fine gold, fine silver, or such fine precious stones as when they be cast in the fire, it can find no filth to fetch out of them, and therefore they remain in the fire safe and unminished.[6] So are there some on the other side, which, though they do not as many other do with mortal sins and lack of good works wound their faith unto the death and fall from Christ, the foundation that they must build upon, yet do they, abiding upon that foundation, build up thereupon many such simple and frail and corruptible works as can never enter heaven. And such be venial[7] sins as idle words, vain and wanton mirth, and such other things like, which be but like wood, hay, or straw. Which works when the soul after his departing out of the world bringeth hither into purgatory, he cannot so get through it as doth the soul whose works were wrought clean or fully purged by penance ere he died. For that soul in the fire can feel no harm, like as fine gold can in the fire nothing lose of his weight. But this soul that bringeth with him such frail works either wrought by themself or inserted peradventure[8] and mixed amidst of some good

6. Undiminished.
7. Lesser (as opposed to "mortal").
8. By chance.

and virtuous work, as for example, some lack peradventure sufficient attention and heed taken by some sudden wavering of the
mind in time of prayer, or some surreption[9] and creeping in of vain-
glory and liking of their own praise in their alms given or other
good deed done, not forthwith resisted and cast out but kept and
fed upon too long, and yet neither so long, peradventure, nor so
great as our Lord will for that thought deprive him the merit and
reward of his work.

Lo, in such cases, as the apostle saith, the day of our Lord, which
is to the whole world the day of the general judgment and to every
man particular the day of his own judgment after his death, shall
show his work, what manner thing it is, the fire shall prove and
declare. For here in purgatory, like as the fire can in the clean souls
take none hold but they shall be therein without any manner pain or
grief, so shall it in the souls that are uncleansed and have their works
imperfect, unclean, and spotted, hastily catch hold and keep them
fast, and burn them with incessant pain till the filthiness of their sin
be clean purged and gone. And that shall be in some sooner, in some
later, as their sins or the spots remaining thereof be more easy or
more hard to get out. And that is the thing that Paul signifieth by the
wood, hay, and straw, of which the one is a light flame soon ended,
the other smoldreth much longer, and the third is hottest and endur-
est longest. But yet hath it an end and so shall have at length all the
pains of them that shall be purged here. But whatsoever soul mis-
shape[1] to die in deadly sin and impenitent, sith he is thereby fallen
off forever from our Savior Christ that was his foundation, and hath
builded up wretched works upon your ghostly enemy the devil,
wherewith he hath so thoroughly poisoned himself that he can never
be purged, the fire shall therefore lie burning upon him forever and
his pain never lessed, nor his filthy spots never the more minished.

And forasmuch as ye never can conceive a very right imagination
of these things which ye never felt, nor it is not possible to find you
any example in the world very like unto the pains that silly souls feel
when they be departed thence, we shall therefore put you in remembrance of one kind of pain, which, though it be nothing like for the
quantity of the matter, yet may it somewhat be resembled by reason
of the fashion and manner. If there were embarked many people at
once to be by ship conveyed a long journey by sea of such as never
came thereon before, and should hap[2] all the way to have the seas
rise high and sore wrought, and sometime soon upon a storm to lie
long after, wallowing at an anchor, there should ye find diverse fash-

9. Stealing.
1. Has the misfortune.
2. Chance.

ions of folk. Some, peradventure, but of them very few, so clean from all evil humors and so well attempered[3] of themself, that they shall be all that long voyage by sea as lusty and as jocund as if they were on land. But far the most part shall ye see sore sick, and yet in many sundry manner, some more, some less, some longer time diseased, and some much sooner amended. And divers that a while had went[4] they should have died for pain yet after one vomit or twain so clean rid of their grief that they never felt displeasure of it after. And this happeth after[5] as the body is more or less disposed in itself thereto. But then shall ye sometime see there some other whose body is so incurably corrupted that they shall walter and tolter[6] and wring their hands and gnash the teeth and their eye water, their head ache, their body fret, their stomach wamble,[7] and all their body shiver for pain, and yet shall never vomit at all; or if they vomit, yet shall they vomit still and never find ease thereof. Lo, thus fareth it as a small thing may be resembled to a great by the souls deceased and departed the world: that such as be clean and unspotted can in the fire feel no disease at all, and on the other side, such as come thence so deadly poisoned with sin that their spots be indelible and their filthiness unpurgable, lie fretting and frying in the fire forever. And only such as neither be fully cleansed nor yet sore defiled but that the fire may fret out the spots of their sin, of this sort only be we that here lie in purgatory. Which these cruel heretics would make you believe that we feel none harm at all, whereof the blessed apostle, as we have showed you, writeth unto the Corinthians the contrary.

3. Balanced.
4. After a while.
5. Occurs accordingly.
6. Stumble and flounder.
7. Feel nauseated.

THOMAS KYD

The Spanish Tragedy (1592)[†]

I.I

Enter the GHOST OF ANDREA *and with him,* REVENGE.

GHOST   When this eternal substance of my soul
   Did live imprisoned in my wanton flesh,
   Each in their function serving other's need,
   I was a courtier in the Spanish court.
   My name was Don Andrea, my descent,   5
   Though not ignoble, yet inferior far
   To gracious fortunes of my tender youth.
   For there in prime and pride of all my years,
   By duteous service and deserving love,
   In secret I possessed a worthy dame,   10
   Which hight sweet Bel-imperia by name.
   But in the harvest of my summer joys,
   Death's winter nipped the blossoms of my bliss,
   Forcing divorce betwixt my love and me.
   For in the late conflict with Portingale   15
   My valor drew me into danger's mouth,
   Till life to death made passage through my wounds.
   When I was slain, my soul descended straight
   To pass the flowing stream of Acheron.
   But churlish Charon, only boatman there,   20
   Said that, my rites of burial not performed,
   I might not sit amongst his passengers.
   Ere Sol had slept three nights in Thetis' lap,
   And slaked his smoking chariot in her flood,

[†] Thomas Kyd, *The Spanish Tragedy* (London, 1592), sigs. A2–A3, G3v–G4, H1r–v, L2r–v. This play established the conventions of revenge drama for the Elizabethan stage and for *Hamlet*. It features a supernaturally motivated action and a protagonist who struggles in soliloquy, uses a play-within-the-play, and finally achieves a bloody revenge at the cost of his own sanity and life.

1.1. **Andrea**: Spanish courtier, killed in battle by Don Balthasar, a Portugese prince. (Compare this ghost to that in *Hamlet*.)

8. **prime**: springtime

11. **Which hight**: who was called

15. **Portingale**: Portugal

19. **Acheron**: one of the rivers of Hades. The following description of the underworld derives from Virgil's *Aeneid* 6.

23. **Ere . . . lap**: i.e., before three days had passed. Sol is the sun, envisioned in the next line as a burning chariot, which appears to rest in the ocean, i.e., the lap of Thetis, a sea-goddess.

By Don Horatio, our Knight Marshal's son,   25
My funerals and obsequies were done.
Then was the ferryman of hell content
To pass me over to the slimy strand,
That leads to fell Avernus' ugly waves.
There, pleasing Cerberus with honeyed speech,   30
I passed the perils of the foremost porch.
Not far from hence amidst ten thousand souls
Sat Minos, Aeacus, and Rhadamanth,
To whom no sooner 'gan I make approach,
To crave a passport for my wand'ring ghost,   35
But Minos, in graven leaves of lottery,
Drew forth the manner of my life and death.
"This knight," quoth he, "both lived and died in love,
And for his love tried fortune of the wars,
And by war's fortune lost both love and life."   40
"Why then," said Aeacus, "convey him hence,
To walk with lovers in our fields of love,
And spend the course of everlasting time
Under green myrtle trees and cypress shades."
"No, no," said Rhadamanth, "it were not well   45
With loving souls to place a martialist;
He died in war and must to martial fields,
Where wounded Hector lives in lasting pain,
And Achilles' Myrmidons do scour the plain."
Then Minos, mildest censor of the three,   50
Made this device to end the difference:
"Send him," quoth he, "to our infernal king,
To doom him as best seems his majesty."
To this effect my passport straight was drawn.
In keeping on my way to Pluto's court,   55
Through dreadful shades of ever-glooming night,
I saw more sights than thousand tongues can tell,
Or pens can write, or mortal hearts can think.

25. **Knight Marshal:** law officer in the king's household
29. **fell:** cruel; **Avernus:** the lake that marks the entrance to the inner regions of the underworld.
30. **Cerberus:** three-headed dog that guards the underworld
33. **Minos, Aeacus, and Rhadamanth:** judges of the underworld
36. **graven . . . lottery:** inscribed leaves describing Andrea's life on earth
46. **martialist:** soldier
48. **Hector:** Trojan leader
49. **Achilles' Myrmidons:** troops of Achilles, great Greek warrior
51. **device:** plan
52. **infernal king:** i.e., Pluto, god of the underworld
53. **doom:** judge; **seems:** suits

Three ways there were: that on the right-hand side
Was ready way unto the foresaid fields   60
Where lovers live and bloody martialists,
But either sort contained within his bounds.
The left-hand path, declining fearfully,
Was ready downfall to the deepest hell,
Where bloody furies shakes their whips of steel,   65
And poor Ixion turns an endless wheel,
Where usurers are choked with melting gold,
And wantons are embraced with ugly snakes,
And murderers groan with never-killing wounds,
And perjured wights scalded in boiling lead,   70
And all foul sins with torments overwhelmed.
Twixt these two ways I trod the middle path,
Which brought me to the fair Elysian green,
In midst whereof there stands a stately tower,
The walls of brass, the gates of adamant.   75
Here finding Pluto with his Proserpine,
I showed my passport, humbled on my knee,
Whereat fair Proserpine began to smile,
And begged that only she might give my doom.
Pluto was pleased and sealed it with a kiss.   80
Forthwith, Revenge, she rounded thee in th'ear,
And bade thee lead me through the gates of horn,
Where dreams have passage in the silent night.
No sooner had she spoke but we were here.
I wot not how, in twinkling of an eye.   85
REVENGE   Then know, Andrea, that thou art arrived
Where thou shalt see the author of thy death,
Don Balthazar, the prince of Portingale,
Deprived of life by Bel-imperia.
Here sit we down to see the mystery,   90
And serve for Chorus in this tragedy.

---

62. either sort: each kind; **his:** its
64. downfall: descent
66. Ixion: (The first human to shed kindred blood, Ixion was bound to an endlessly spin-
ning wheel.)
70. wights: persons
75. adamant: diamond
76. Proserpine: queen of the underworld, wife of Pluto
79. doom: sentence
81. rounded: whispered
82. gates of horn: i.e., the gates through which true dreams pass (*Aeneid* 6.893–6). (The
text reads "Hor" here for "horn.")
85. wot: know

3.12

Enter HIERONIMO, *with a poniard in one hand and a rope in the other.*

HIERONIMO   Now, sir, perhaps I come and see the King;
The King sees me, and fain would hear my suit.
Why, is not this a strange and seld-seen thing,
That standers-by with toys should strike me mute?
Go to, I see their shifts, and say no more.   5
Hieronimo, 'tis time for thee to trudge.
Down by the dale that flows with purple gore,
Standeth a fiery tower; there sits a judge
Upon a seat of steel and molten brass,
And twixt his teeth he holds a fire-brand   10
That leads unto the lake where hell doth stand.
Away, Hieronimo, to him be gone!
He'll do thee justice for Horatio's death.
Turn down this path, thou shalt be with him straight.
Or this, and then thou needst not take thy breath.   15
This way or that way? Soft and fair, not so.
For if I hang or kill myself, let's know
Who will revenge Horatio's murder then?
No, no, fie, no! Pardon me, I'll none of that.

He flings away the dagger and halter.

This way I'll take, and this way comes the King.   20

He takes them up again.

And here I'll have a fling at him, that's flat.
And, Balthazar, I'll be with thee to bring,
And thee, Lorenzo! Here's the King—nay, stay;
And here, ay, here, there goes the hare away.

3.12. **poniard**: dagger. Compare this and the following speech with Hamlet's soliloquies.
  1. **sir**: i.e., himself or an imaginary auditor
  2. **fain**: gladly
  3. **seld**: seldom
  4. **toys**: trifles
  5. **shifts**: tricks
  6. **trudge**: move on
7–10 **Down . . . stand**: (Hieronimo evokes the underworld described by Andrea's ghost in the previous passage.)
  7. **purple gore**: blood
  11. **lake**: i.e., Avernus
  14. **Turn . . . path**: i.e., commit suicide by stabbing
  15. **this**: i.e., suicide by hanging
  16. **Soft and fair**: easy now
  18. **Horatio**: Hieronimo's son, stabbed and hung up in an arbor
  21. **flat**: certain
  22. **Balthazar**: one of Horatio's murderers; **be . . . bring**: get even with you
  23. **Lorenzo**: another of Horatio's murderers
  24. **there . . . away**: i.e., the quarry escapes

3.13

Enter HIERONIMO, *with a book in his hand.*

[HIERONIMO]   *Vindicta mihi!*

Ay, heaven will be revenged of every ill,
Nor will they suffer murder unrepaid.
Then stay, Hieronimo, attend their will,
For mortal men may not appoint their time.   5
Per scelus semper tutum est sceleribus iter.
Strike, and strike home, where wrong is offered thee,
For evils unto ills conductors be,
And death's the worst of resolution.
For he that thinks with patience to contend   10
To quiet life, his life shall easily end.
Fata si miseros juvant, habes salutem;
Fata si vitam negant, habes sepulchrum.
"If destiny thy miseries do ease,
Then hast thou health, and happy shalt thou be;   15
If destiny deny thee life, Hieronimo,
Yet shalt thou be assured of a tomb."
If neither, yet let this thy comfort be:
Heaven covereth him that hath no burial.
And to conclude, I will revenge his death!   20
But how? Not as the vulgar wits of men,
With open, but inevitable ills,
As by a secret yet a certain mean,
Which under kindship will be cloakèd best.
Wise men will take their opportunity,   25
Closely and safely, fitting things to time.
But in extremes advantage hath no time,
And therefore all times fit not for revenge.
Thus therefore will I rest me in unrest,
Dissembling quiet in unquietness,   30

3.13. *book*: probably Seneca, who supplies some of the quotations below
   1. *Vindicta mihi*: Latin: "Vengeance is mine" (Romans 12:19).
   3. *suffer murder unrepaid*: allow murder to go unpunished
   6. *Per . . . iter*: "The safe way for crimes is always through crimes"—an adaptation of Seneca, *Agamemnon* 115.
   9. *of*: that can result from
   10. *contend*: strive
12–13. *Fata . . . sepulchrum*: (Hieronimo offers a translation of these lines from Seneca's *Troades* [510–12] in the following four lines.)
22–32. *With . . . mean*: by open means, but by those that produce inevitable results—that is, secret, certain schemes
   24. *kindship*: kindness
   26. *Closely*: secretly
27–28. *But . . . revenge*: but in desperate situations, the passing of time brings no clear advantage, though not all times are equally suitable

Not seeming that I know their villainies,
That my simplicity may make them think
That ignorantly I will let all slip.
For ignorance, I wot, and well they know.
Remedium malorum iners est.   35
Nor aught avails it me to menace them
Who, as a wintry storm upon a plain,
Will bear me down with their nobility.
No, no, Hieronimo, thou must enjoin
Thine eyes to observation, and thy tongue   40
To milder speeches than thy spirit affords,
Thy heart to patience, and thy hands to rest,
Thy cap to courtesy, and thy knee to bow,
Till to revenge thou know, when, where, and how.

4.5

Enter GHOST *and* REVENGE.

GHOST   Ay, now my hopes have end in their effects,
When blood and sorrow finish my desires:
Horatio murdered in his father's bower,
Vile Serberine by Pedringano slain,
False Pedringano hanged by quaint device,   5
Fair Isabella by herself misdone,
Prince Balthazar by Bel-imperia stabbed,
The Duke of Castile and his wicked son
Both done to death by old Hieronimo,
My Bel-imperia fallen, as Dido fell,   10
And good Hieronimo slain by himself.
Ay, these were spectacles to please my soul!
Now will I beg at lovely Proserpine
That by the virtue of her princely doom
I may consort my friends in pleasing sort,   15
And on my foes work just and sharp revenge.
I'll lead my friend Horatio through those fields,

---

34. **wot**: know
35. *Remedium* . . . *est*: Latin: "is an idle remedy for ills" (Seneca, *Oedipus* 515)
36. **aught**: anything
39. **enjoin**: urge
4.5. The play ends as it began, with the ghost of Andrea and Revenge, who now sum-
      marize the action and assign afterlife punishments and rewards. Contrast the end
      of *Hamlet*.
  5. **quaint device**: crafty plot
  6. **misdone**: killed
10. **Dido**: Carthaginian queen who committed suicide (*Aeneid* 4)
15. **consort**: accompany

Where never-dying wars are still inured;
I'll lead fair Isabella to that train
Where pity weeps but never feeleth pain;   20
I'll lead my Bel-imperia to those joys
That vestal virgins and fair queens possess;
I'll lead Hieronimo where Orpheus plays,
Adding sweet pleasure to eternal days.
But say, Revenge, for thou must help, or none,   25
Against the rest how shall my hate be shown?
REVENGE   This hand shall hale them down to deepest hell,
Where none but furies, bugs, and tortures dwell.
GHOST   Then, sweet Revenge, do this at my request:
Let me be judge, and doom them to unrest.   30
Let loose poor Tityus from the vultures' gripe,
And let Don Cyprian supply his room;
Place Don Lorenzo on Ixion's wheel,
And let the lover's endless pains surcease
(Juno forgets old wrath, and grants him ease);   35
Hang Balthazar about Chimaera's neck,
And let him there bewail his bloody love,
Repining at our joys that are above;
Let Serberine go roll the fatal stone,
And take from Sisyphus his endless moan;   40
False Pedringano, for his treachery,
Let him be dragged through boiling Acheron,
And there live, dying still in endless flames,
Blaspheming gods and all their holy names.
REVENGE   Then haste we down to meet thy friends and foes,   45
To place thy friends in ease, the rest in woes;
For here though death hath end their misery,
I'll there begin their endless tragedy.

Exeunt.

18. **inured:** practiced
19. **train:** way of life
23. **Orpheus:** mythic poet and musician
27. **hale:** drag
28. **bugs:** bugbears, i.e., frightful things
31. **Tityus:** Titan whose liver was continually eaten by vultures
34. **lover:** Ixion had tried to seduce Juno, queen of the gods
36. **Chimaera:** mythical monster—part lion, part snake, part goat
40. **Sisyphus:** king who endlessly rolled a stone up a hill only to watch it endlessly roll down
42. **Acheron:** river of fire in Hades

CRITICISM

JOHN DRYDEN

Preface to *Troilus and Cressida* (1679)†

If Shakespeare be allowed, as I think he must, to have made his
characters distinct, it will easily be inferred that he understood the
nature of the passions because it has been proved already that confused passions make undistinguishable characters. Yet I cannot
deny that he has his failings; but they are not so much in the passions themselves, as in his manner of expression: he often obscures
his meaning by his words, and sometimes makes it unintelligible. I
will not say of so great a poet that he distinguished not the blown
puffy stile from true sublimity, but I may venture to maintain that
the fury of his fancy often transported him beyond the bounds of
judgment, either in coining of new words and phrases, or racking
words which were in use into the violence of a catachresis.[1] 'Tis not
that I would explode[2] the use of metaphors from passions—for
Longinus[3] thinks 'em necessary to raise it—but to use 'em at every
word, to say nothing without a metaphor, a simile, an image, or
description, is I doubt[4] to smell a little too strongly of the buskin.[5] I
must be forced to give an example of expressing passion figuratively, but that I may do it with respect to Shakespeare, it shall not
be taken from anything of his. 'Tis an exclamation against Fortune
quoted in his *Hamlet* but written by some other poet:[6]

> Out, out, thou strumpet fortune; all you gods,
> In general synod, take away her power,
> Break all the spokes and sallies from her wheel,
> And bowl the round nave down the hill of heav'n
> As low as to the fiends. [2.2.417–21]

And immediately after, speaking of Hecuba, when Priam was killed
before her eyes:

> The mobled queen ran up and down,
> Threat'ning the flame with bisson rheum: a clout about
>   that head,

---

† John Dryden, Preface, *Troilus and Cressida* (London, 1679), sigs. b2–b3. Poet, dramatist, and arbiter of neoclassical taste, John Dryden (1631–1700) praised Shakespeare for
  his "comprehensive soul" but censured him for perceived faults in plotting and style.
1. Misuse.
2. Exclude.
3. First-century Greek author of the literary treatise "On the Sublime"
4. Fear.
5. Put on tragic airs excessively. A "buskin" was the high boot worn by ancient tragic
   actors in Athens.
6. Most today believe that Shakespeare wrote these lines in imitation of contemporary
   tragic style.

Where late the diadem stood; and for a robe
About her lank and all o'er-teemed loins,
A blanket in th'alarm of fear caught up.
Who this had seen, with tongue in venom steeped,
'Gainst Fortune's state would treason have pronounced.
But if the gods themselves did see her then,
When she saw Pyrrhus make malicious sport
In mincing with his sword her husband's limbs,
The instant burst of clamor that she made
(Unless things mortal [move] them not at all)
Would have made milch the burning eyes of heav'n,
And passion in the gods. [2.2.430–43]

What a pudder[7] is here kept in raising the expression of trifling thoughts! Would not a man have thought that the poet had been bound prentice to a wheelwright for his first rant? And had followed a ragman for the clout and blanket in the second? Fortune is painted on a wheel and therefore the writer in a rage will have poetical justice done upon every member of that engine.[8] After this execution, he bowls the nave downhill from heaven to the fiends (an unreasonable long mark a man would think). 'Tis well there are no solid orbs to stop it in the way or no element of fire to consume it, but when it came to the earth it must be monstrous heavy to break ground as low as to the center. His making milch the burning eyes of heaven was a pretty tolerable flight too; and I think no man ever drew milk out of eyes before him; yet to make wonder even greater, these eyes were burning. Such a sight indeed were enough to have raised passion in the gods, but to excuse the effects of it he tells you perhaps they did not see it.

Wise men would be glad to find a little sense couched under all those pompous words for bombast is commonly the delight of that audience which loves poetry but understands it not, and as commonly has been the practice of those writers who, not being able to infuse a natural passion into the mind, have made it their business to ply[9] the ears and to stun their judges by the noise. But Shakespeare does not often thus.

7. Stir.
8. Contrivance.
9. Address.

NICHOLAS ROWE

Some Account of the Life, &c. of
Mr. William Shakespeare (1709)†

Hamlet is founded on much the same tale with the *Electra* of Sopho-cles. In each of 'em a young prince is engaged to revenge the death of his father; their mothers are equally guilty, are both concerned in the murder of their husbands, and are afterwards married to the murderers. There is in the first part of the Greek tragedy something very moving in the grief of Electra; but, as Mr. D'Acier[1] has observed, there is something very unnatural and shocking in the manners he has given that princess and Orestes in the latter part. Orestes imbrues his hands in the blood of his own mother; and that barba-rous action is performed, though not immediately upon the stage, yet so near that the audience hear Clytemnestra crying out to Aegis-thus for help and to her son for mercy; while Electra, her daughter and a princess—both of them characters that ought to have appeared with more decency—stands upon the stage and encourages her brother in the parricide. What horror does this not raise! Clytemnes-tra was a wicked woman and had deserved to die; nay, in the truth of the story, she was killed by her own son. But to represent an action of this kind on the stage is certainly an offence against those rules of manners proper to the persons that ought to be observed there.

On the contrary, let us only look a little on the conduct of Shake-speare. Hamlet is represented with the same piety towards his father, and resolution to revenge his death, as Orestes; he has the same abhorrence for his mother's guilt, which, to provoke him the more, is heightened by incest. But 'tis with wonderful art and just-ness of judgment that the poet restrains him from doing violence to his mother. To prevent anything of that kind, he makes his father's ghost forbid that part of his vengeance:

> But howsoever thou pursuest this act,
> Taint not thy mind; nor let thy soul contrive
> Against thy mother ought; leave her to heav'n,
> And to those thorns that in her bosom lodge,
> To prick and sting her. [1.5.84–88]

This is to distinguish rightly between horror and terror. The latter is a proper passion of tragedy, but the former ought always to be

---

† Nicholas Rowe, ed., *The Works of Mr. William Shakespeare*, 6 vols. (London, 1709), 1:xxxi–xxxiii. Nicholas Rowe (1674–1718), the first critical editor of Shakespeare, here compares Sophocles's *Electra* to *Hamlet*.
1. André Dacier (1651–1722), French classical scholar and translator.

carefully avoided. And certainly no dramatic writer ever succeeded better in raising terror in the minds of an audience than Shakespeare has done. The whole tragedy of *Macbeth*, but more especially the scene where the King is murdered (in the Second Act), as well as this play, is a noble proof of that manly spirit with which he writ; and both show how powerful he was in giving the strongest motions to our souls that they are capable of.

I cannot leave *Hamlet* without taking notice of the advantage with which we have seen this masterpiece of Shakespeare distinguish itself upon the stage by Mr. Betterton's fine performance of that part.[2] A man who, though he had no other good qualities, as he has a great many, must have made his way into the esteem of all men of letters by this only excellency. No man is better acquainted with Shakespeare's manner of expression, and indeed he has studied him so well and is so much a master of him that whatever part of his he performs, he does it as if it had been written on purpose for him, and that the author had exactly conceived it as he plays it.

VOLTAIRE

Preface to *Sémiramis* (1748)[†]

The Roman philosophers had no faith in ghosts in the time of the emperors, and yet young Pompey raises one in the *Pharsalia*. The English have certainly no more belief in spirits than the Romans had, and yet they see every day with pleasure, in the tragedy of *Hamlet*, the ghost of a king, who appears nearly the same as the apparition of Ninus did at Paris.[1] I am at the same time far from justifying the tragedy of *Hamlet* in every respect; it is a gross and barbarous piece, and would never be borne by the lowest of the rabble in France or Italy. Hamlet runs mad in the second act, and his mistress in the third; the prince kills the father of his mistress and fancies he is killing a rat; and the heroine of the play throws herself into the river. They dig her grave on the stage, and the gravediggers, holding the dead men's skulls in their hands, talk nonsense worthy of them. Hamlet answers their abominable stuff by some

2. Thomas Betterton (1635–1710), leading actor of the English Restoration, played the role of Hamlet from 1661 to 1709. Surviving accounts praise his expression of terror upon seeing the ghost, and his passion in the closet scene, wherein he knocked over a chair.
† *The Works of Voltaire: A Contemporary Version with Notes*, trans. William F. Fleming, et al., 42 vols. (Paris: Du Mont, 1901), 37:136–38. François-Marie Arouet or Voltaire (1694–1778), dramatist, philosopher, and man of letters, praised Shakespeare's genius but sharply criticized perceived violations of dramatic decorum, especially the mingling of comedy and tragedy.
1. The ghost of the murdered King Ninus appears in Voltaire's own play *Sémiramis*.

whimsies not less disgusting; during this time one of the actors makes the conquest of Poland. Hamlet, his mother, and father-in-law, drink together on the stage: they sing at table, quarrel, beat and kill one another: one would think the whole piece was the product of the imagination of a drunken savage. And yet, among all these gross irregularities which make the English theatre even at this day so absurd and barbarous, we find in *Hamlet*, which is still more strange and unaccountable, some sublime strokes worthy of the greatest genius. It seems as if nature took pleasure to unite in the head of Shakespeare all that we can imagine great and forcible, together with all that the grossest dullness could produce of everything that is most low and detestable.

It must be acknowledged that among the beauties that shine forth in the midst of all these horrid extravagancies, the ghost of Hamlet's father is one of the most striking. It has always a strong effect on the English—I mean, on those who are the best judges and are most hurt by the irregularity of their old theatre. This ghost inspires more terror, even in the reading, than the apparition of Darius in the *Persians* of Aeschylus. And why does it? Because Darius in Aeschylus only appears to foretell the misfortunes of his family whereas in Shakespeare the ghost of Hamlet appears to demand vengeance and to reveal secret crimes. It is neither useless nor brought in by force but serves to convince mankind that there is an invisible power, the master of nature. All men have a sense of justice imprinted on their hearts and naturally wish that heaven would interest itself in the cause of innocence; in every age, therefore, and in every nation, they will behold with pleasure the Supreme Being engaged in the punishment of crimes which could not come within the reach of human laws. This is a consolation to the weak and a restraint on the insolence and obstinacy of the powerful.

Du Théâtre Anglais (1761)[†]

The good lord chamberlain [Polonius] was an old fool, and is represented as such, as has already been seen; his daughter Ophelia, who, no doubt, resembled him in this respect, becomes raving mad when she is informed of her father's death: she runs upon the stage with flowers and straw upon her head, sings ballads, and then goes and drowns herself. Thus there are three mad people in the play, the chamberlain, and Hamlet, without reckoning the other buffoons who play their parts.

* * *

[After rehearsing in detail the plot of *Hamlet*] Here there are two important questions to be solved. The first is, How could so many wonderful things be generated in one head alone? For it must be acknowledged that all the plays of the divine Shakespeare are in the very same taste. The second is, How have audiences been able to work themselves up to see these pieces with transport, and how can they still be attended to in an age which has produced the *Cato* of Addison?[2]

The astonishment occasioned by the first wonder will cease entirely when it is known that Shakespeare has taken the subjects of all his tragedies from history or romances; and that he has done nothing more than turn into dialogues the romances of Claudius, Gertrude and Hamlet, written entirely by Saxo, the grammarian, to whom the whole glory of the performance is due.

The second question, that is, as to the pleasure taken in seeing these tragedies, is somewhat more difficult to be accounted for; but this seems to be the reason of it, according to the profound reflections of certain philosophers:

Chairmen, sailors, hackney-coachmen, apprentice boys, butchers, and clerks are passionately fond of fights; give them cock-fights, bull-fights, or prize-fights, buryings, duels, executions, witchcraft and ghosts, and they crowd to the theatre; many a nobleman is as curious as the populace. The citizens of London found in the tragedies of Shakespeare everything that can please the curious. Those at court were obliged to conform to the current taste. How could they avoid admiring what the most rational of the citizens admired? There was nothing better to be seen during a hundred and fifty years; admiration gathered strength, and was converted into idolatry. A few strokes of genius, a few happy lines replete with nature and force, which spectators got by heart whether they would or no, procured indulgence for the rest; and soon the whole piece succeeded by means of a few detached beauties.

2. Joseph Addison's *Cato* (1712) is a premier example of neoclassical tragedy—observant of the unities, decorous in style, and didactic in purpose. Admired in its day and forgotten in ours, it extolled the republican virtue of Cato, a Roman enemy of Caesar.

SAMUEL JOHNSON

Notes on *Hamlet* (1765)[†]

This speech [3.3.73ff., Hamlet's refusal to kill the King at prayer], in which Hamlet, represented as a virtuous character, is not content with taking blood for blood, but contrives damnation for the man that he would punish, is too horrible to be read or to be uttered.

* * *

If the dramas of Shakespeare were to be characterised, each by the particular excellence which distinguishes it from the rest, we must allow to the tragedy of *Hamlet* the praise of variety. The incidents are so numerous that the argument of the play would make a long tale. The scenes are interchangeably diversified with merriment and solemnity; with merriment that includes judicious and instructive observations, and solemnity not strained by poetical violence above the natural sentiments of man. New characters appear from time to time in continual succession, exhibiting various forms of life and particular modes of conversation. The pretended madness of Hamlet causes much mirth, the mournful distraction of Ophelia fills the heart with tenderness, and every personage produces the effect intended, from the apparition that in the first act chills the blood with horror, to the fop in the last that exposes affectation to just contempt.

The conduct is perhaps not wholly secure against objections. The action is indeed for the most part in continual progression, but there are some scenes which neither forward nor retard it. Of the feigned madness of Hamlet there appears no adequate cause, for he does nothing which he might not have done with the reputation of sanity. He plays the madman most when he treats Ophelia with so much rudeness, which seems to be useless and wanton cruelty.

Hamlet is, through the whole play, rather an instrument than an agent. After he has by the stratagem of the play convicted the King, he makes no attempt to punish him, and his death is at last effected by an incident which Hamlet has no part in producing.

The catastrophe is not very happily produced; the exchange of weapons is rather an expedient of necessity than a stroke of art. A

† Samuel Johnson, ed. *The Plays of William Shakespeare*, 8 vols. (London, 1765), 8:236, 311. Great essayist, poet, critic, and editor, Samuel Johnson (1709–1784) held neoclassical principles about the importance of probability, unity in plot and character, and moral representation. Admiring the variety of *Hamlet*, he also objected to elements of its design and conclusion.

David Tennant (Hamlet) and Patrick Stewart (Claudius) in
the Prayer Scene, 2008. © Tristram Kenton.

scheme might easily have been formed to kill Hamlet with the dagger, and Laertes with the bowl.

The poet is accused of having shown little regard to poetical justice, and may be charged with equal neglect of poetical probability.
The apparition left the regions of the dead to little purpose; the
revenge which he demands is not obtained but by the death of him
that was required to take it; and the gratification which would arise
from the destruction of an usurper and a murderer is abated by the
untimely death of Ophelia, the young, the beautiful, the harmless,
and the pious.

GEORGE STEEVENS

Letter to David Garrick (1771)[†]

I expect great pleasure from the perusal of your altered *Hamlet*. It is a circumstance in favour of the poet which I have long been wishing for. Dr. Johnson allots to this tragedy the praise of variety; but in my humble opinion, that variety is often impertinent, and always languishing on the stage. In spite of all he has said on the subject, I shall never be thoroughly reconciled to tragi-comedy, for if the farce of theatrical deceptions is but short-lived at best, their slightest success ought not to be interrupted. This play of Shakespeare, in particular, resembles a looking-glass exposed for sale, which reflects alternately the funeral and the puppet-show, the venerable beggar soliciting charity, and the blackguard rascal picking a pocket.

I am sure when you personate the Danish Prince, you wish your task concluded with the third act, after which the genius of Shakespeare retires, or only plays bo-peep through the rest of the piece. I confess I am talking a kind of poetical blasphemy; but I am become less afraid of you, since you have avowed your present design.

I think you need not fear that the better half of your audience, (as Othello says) *should yawn at alteration*. No performer whatever would be able to recite all that Shakespeare has put into the mouth of his prince with equal energy. You are therefore furnished with a plea for declaring that performers must either check their powers, or shorten the drama where it grows to an unreasonable length. Every man in his senses must think you had done right in making the latter your choice; for you will then be enabled to do justice to all you retain, and to retain no more than deserves that justice. I cannot answer for our good friends in the gallery. You had better throw what remains of the piece into a farce, to appear immediately afterwards. No foreigner who should happen to be present at the exhibition would ever believe it was formed out of the loppings and excrescences of the tragedy itself. You may entitle it, *The Grave-Diggers; with the pleasant Humours of Osrick, the Danish Macaroni*.[1]

† George Steevens, in *The Private Correspondence of David Garrick*, ed. James Boaden, 2 vols. (London: H. Colburn and R. Bentley, 1831–32), 1:451–54; ed., *The Plays of William Shakespeare. Volume the Tenth* (London, 1785), 520–22. A cantankerous, scholarly editor of Shakespeare, Steevens (1736–1800) wrote David Garrick (1771–1779), the greatest Shakespearean actor of the eighteenth century, to commend his adaptation of *Hamlet* (1772) and its radically abridged ending (see "Afterlives," p. 363). Steevens also attacked Hamlet as immoral and the play as poorly designed.
1. Dandy, fop.

As you intend to stab the usurper I beg, for your own sake, you will take care that this circumstance is not on his part awkwardly represented. Those who die on the stage either in single combat or by suicide generally meet with applause; but Henry the Sixth standing still to receive the dagger of Richard too often excites merriment. Poor Gibson was sure to convulse the audience with laughter whenever he fell in that character, and yet it is no more than justice to his memory to observe that all who knew him were sincerely sorry when he died a natural death. A stab given to an unarmed or a defenceless man has seldom a very happy effect. An Englishman loves a spirited, but abhors a phlegmatic exit.

Excuse this liberty I have taken with you in your profession; but the idea struck me immediately on reading your intended change in the catastrophe of *Hamlet*, which I am very impatient to see.

I think myself much obliged to you, both for a letter which is highly flattering to my vanity, and for the entertainment I expect from your promised communication. That I may not appear totally ungrateful I will cease to trespass on your patience any longer, and once more assure you that I am, with great truth, your much obliged,

G. STEEVENS

[On Hamlet's Character] (1785)

Let us review for a moment the behaviour of Hamlet, on the strength of which Horatio sounds this eulogy, and recommends him to the patronage of the angels [5.2.333–34].

Hamlet, at the command of his father's ghost, undertakes with seeming alacrity to revenge his murder; and declares he will banish all other thoughts from his mind. He makes, however, but one effort to keep his word, and that is when he mistakes Polonius for the king. On another occasion, he defers his purpose till he can find an opportunity of taking his uncle when he is least prepared for death that he may insure damnation to his soul. Though he assassinated Polonius by accident, yet he deliberately procures the execution of his schoolfellows, Rosencrantz and Guildenstern, who appear to have been unacquainted with the treacherous purposes of the mandate which they were employed to carry. Their death (as he declares in a subsequent conversation with Horatio) gives him no concern, for they obtruded themselves into the service, and he thought he had a right to destroy them. He is not less accountable for the distraction and death of Ophelia. He comes to interrupt the funeral designed in honour of this lady, at which both the king and queen were present; and by such an outrage to decency renders it still more necessary for the usurper to lay a second stratagem for his life, though the first had proved abortive. He comes to insult the brother of the dead, and to boast of an affection for his sister, which before he had denied to her face; and yet at this very time must be considered as desirous of supporting the character of a madman, so that the openness of his confession is not to be imputed to him as a virtue. He apologizes to Horatio afterwards for the absurdity of this behaviour, to which, he says, he was provoked by that nobleness of fraternal grief, which, indeed, he ought rather to have applauded than condemned. Dr. Johnson has observed that to bring about a reconciliation with Laertes, he has availed himself of a dishonest fallacy;[2] and to conclude, it is obvious to the most careless spectator or reader, that he kills the king at last to revenge himself, and not his father.

Hamlet cannot be said to have pursued his ends by very warrantable means; and if the poet, when he sacrificed him at last, meant to have enforced such a moral, it is not the worst that can be deduced from the play, for as Maximus in Beaumont and Fletcher's *Valentinian* says: "Although his justice were as white as truth, / His way was crooked to it; that condemns him" [5.3.15–16].

The late Dr. Akenside[3] once observed to me that the conduct of Hamlet was every way unnatural and indefensible, unless he were to be regarded as a young man whose intellects were in some degree impaired by his own misfortunes; by the death of his father, the loss of expected sovereignty, and a sense of shame resulting from the hasty and incestuous marriage of his mother.

I have dwelt the longer on this subject, because Hamlet seems to have been hitherto regarded as a hero not undeserving the pity of the audience, and because no writer on Shakespeare has taken the pains to point out the immoral tendency of his character.

JOHANN WOLFGANG VON GOETHE

Wilhelm Meister's Apprenticeship (1795)[†]

[Wilhelm:] "Conceive a prince such as I have painted him, and that his father suddenly dies. Ambition and the love of rule are not the passions that inspire him. As a king's son he would have been

---

2. I.e., the excuse that he is mad (5.2.198–99). Johnson said, "I wish Hamlet had made some other defence; it is unsuitable to the character of a good or a brave man, to shelter himself in falsehood" (*Plays*, 1785, 10:513).
3. Mark Akenside (1721–1770), English poet and physician.
† Johann Wolfgang von Goethe, *Wilhelm Meister's Apprenticeship* (1795), trans. Thomas Carlyle (Edinburgh: Oliver & Boyd, 1824), 2:72–75. Wilhelm discusses *Hamlet* with Serlo (the theater manager) and his sister Aurelia, and articulates the classic reading of Hamlet as a delicate and noble soul, unfit for the charge of revenge.

contented; but now he is first constrained to consider the difference which separates a sovereign from a subject. The crown was not hereditary yet a longer possession of it by his father would have strengthened the pretensions of an only son, and secured his hopes of the succession. In place of this, he now beholds himself excluded by his uncle, in spite of specious promises, most probably for ever. He is now poor in goods and favor, and a stranger in the scene which from youth he had looked upon as his inheritance. His temper here assumes its first mournful tinge. He feels that now he is not more, that he is less, than a private nobleman; he offers himself as the servant of every one; he is not courteous and condescending, he is needy and degraded.

"His past condition he remembers as a vanished dream. It is in vain that his uncle strives to cheer him, to present his situation in another point of view. The feeling of his nothingness will not forsake him.

"The second stroke that came upon him wounded deeper, bowed still more. It was the marriage of his mother. The faithful tender son had yet a mother, when his father passed away. He hoped, in the company of his surviving noble-minded parent, to reverence the heroic form of the departed. But his mother too he loses, and it is something worse than death that robs him of her. The trustful image, which a good child loves to form of its parents, is gone. With the dead there is no help, on the living no hold. She also is a woman; and her name is Frailty, like that of all her sex.

"Now only does he feel completely bent and orphaned; and no happiness of life can repay what he has lost. Not reflective or sorrowful by nature, reflection and sorrow have become for him a heavy obligation. It is thus that we see him first enter on the scene. I do not think that I have mixed aught foreign with the play, or overcharged a single feature of it."

Serlo looked at his sister and said, "Did I give thee a false picture of our friend? He begins well; he still has many things to tell us, many to persuade us of." Wilhelm asseverated loudly, that he meant not to persuade but to convince: he begged for another moment's patience.

"Figure to yourselves this youth," cried he, "this son of princes; conceive him vividly, bring his state before your eyes, and then observe him when he learns that his father's spirit walks; stand by him in the terrors of the night when the venerable ghost appears before him. A horrid shudder passes over him; he speaks to the mysterious form; he sees it beckon him; he follows it and hears. The fearful accusation of his uncle rings in his ears, the summons to revenge, and the piercing, oft-repeated prayer, 'Remember me!'

"And when the ghost has vanished, who is it that stands before us? A young hero panting for vengeance? A prince by birth, rejoicing to be called to punish the usurper of his crown? No! Trouble and astonishment take hold of the solitary young man: he grows bitter against smiling villains, swears that he will not forget the spirit, and concludes with the expressive ejaculation—

> The time is out of joint: O! cursed spite,
> That ever I was born to set it right! [1.5.195–96]

"In these words, I imagine, will be found the key to Hamlet's whole procedure. To me it is clear that Shakespeare meant, in the present case, to represent the effects of a great action laid upon a soul unfit for the performance of it. In this view the whole piece seems to me to be composed. There is an oak-tree planted in a costly jar, which should have borne only pleasant flowers in its bosom; the roots expand, the jar is shivered.

"A lovely, pure, noble and most moral nature, without the strength of nerve which forms a hero, sinks beneath a burden which it cannot bear and must not cast away. All duties are holy for him: the present is too hard. Impossibilities have been required of him—not in themselves impossibilities, but such for him. He winds, and turns, and torments himself; he advances and recoils; is ever put in mind, ever puts himself in mind; at last does all but lose his purpose from his thoughts; yet still without recovering his peace of mind."

SAMUEL TAYLOR COLERIDGE

Lecture on *Hamlet*, January 2, 1812[†]

We will now pass to *Hamlet*, in order to obviate some of the general prejudices against the author, in reference to the character of the hero. Much has been objected to, which ought to have been praised, and many beauties of the highest kind have been neglected, because they are somewhat hidden.

The first question we should ask ourselves is—What did Shakespeare mean when he drew the character of Hamlet? He never wrote any thing without design, and what was his design when he sat

---

[†] Samuel Taylor Coleridge, *Seven Lectures on Shakespeare and Milton*, ed. J. Payne Collier (London: Chapman and Hall, 1856), 141–49. Poet, philosopher, intellectual, Samuel Taylor Coleridge (1772–1834) mesmerized audiences with his lectures on literature, especially Shakespeare. Defending the character of Hamlet against the attacks of George Steevens, Samuel Johnson, and others, Coleridge presents the prince as brilliant and sensitive but fatally weak and irresolute.

down to produce this tragedy? My belief is, that he always regarded his story, before he began to write, much in the same light as a painter regards his canvas, before he begins to paint—as a mere vehicle for his thoughts—as the ground upon which he was to work. What then was the point to which Shakespeare directed himself in *Hamlet*? He intended to portray a person, in whose view the external world, and all its incidents and objects, were comparatively dim, and of no interest in themselves, and which began to interest only, when they were reflected in the mirror of his mind. Hamlet beheld external things in the same way that a man of vivid imagination, who shuts his eyes, sees what has previously made an impression on his organs.

The poet places him in the most stimulating circumstances that a human being can be placed in. He is the heir apparent of a throne; his father dies suspiciously; his mother excludes her son from his throne by marrying his uncle. This is not enough; but the Ghost of the murdered father is introduced, to assure the son that he was put to death by his own brother. What is the effect upon the son?—instant action and pursuit of revenge? No, endless reasoning and hesitating—constant urging and solicitation of the mind to act, and as constant an escape from action; ceaseless reproaches of himself for sloth and negligence, while the whole energy of his resolution evaporates in these reproaches. This, too, not from cowardice, for he is drawn as one of the bravest of his time—not from want of forethought or slowness of apprehension, for he sees through the very souls of those who surround him, but merely from that aversion to action, which prevails among such as have a world in themselves.

How admirable, too, is the judgment of the poet! Hamlet's own disordered fancy has not conjured up the spirit of his father, it has been seen by others: he is prepared by them to witness its reappearance, and when he does see it, Hamlet is not brought forward as having long brooded on the subject. The moment before the Ghost enters, Hamlet speaks of other matters: he mentions the coldness of the night, and observes that he has not heard the clock strike, adding, in reference to the custom of drinking, that it is "More honour'd in the breach than the observance" [1.4.16]. Owing to the tranquil state of his mind, he indulges in some moral reflections. Afterwards, the Ghost suddenly enters.

> HORATIO Look, my lord! it comes.
> HAMLET Angels and ministers of grace defend us! [38–39]

The same thing occurs in *Macbeth*: in the dagger-scene, the moment before the hero sees it, he has his mind applied to some indifferent matters; "Go, tell thy mistress," etc. [2.1.31ff.]. Thus, in both cases, the preternatural appearance has all the effect of abruptness, and the reader is totally divested of the notion that the figure is a vision of a highly wrought imagination.

Here Shakespeare adapts himself so admirably to the situation—in other words, so puts himself into it—that, though poetry, his language is the very language of nature. No terms, associated with such feelings, can occur to us so proper as those which he has employed, especially on the highest, the most august, and the most awful subjects that can interest a human being in this sentient world. That this is no mere fancy, I can undertake to establish from hundreds, I might say thousands, of passages. No character he has drawn, in the whole list of his plays, could so well and fitly express himself, as in the language Shakespeare has put into his mouth.

There is no indecision about Hamlet, as far as his own sense of duty is concerned; he knows well what he ought to do, and over and over again he makes up his mind to do it. The moment the players, and the two spies set upon him, have withdrawn, of whom he takes leave with a line so expressive of his contempt, "Ay so; good bye you.—Now I am alone" [2.2.470], he breaks out into a delirium of rage against himself for neglecting to perform the solemn duty he had undertaken, and contrasts the factitious and artificial display of feeling by the player with his own apparent indifference:

> What's Hecuba to him, or he to Hecuba,
> That he should weep for her? [480–81]

Yet the player did weep for her, and was in an agony of grief at her sufferings, while Hamlet is unable to rouse himself to action, in order that he may perform the command of his father, who had come from the grave to incite him to revenge:—

> This is most brave!
> That I, the son of a dear father murder'd,
> Prompted to my revenge by heaven and hell,
> Must, like a whore, unpack my heart with words,
> And fall a cursing like a very drab,
> A scullion. [503–11]

It is the same feeling, the same conviction of what is his duty, that makes Hamlet exclaim in a subsequent part of the tragedy:

> How all occasions do inform against me,
> And spur my dull revenge! What is a man.
> If his chief good, and market of his time.
> Be but to sleep and feed? A beast, no more. . . .
>   I do not know
> Why yet I live to say—"this thing's to do,"
> Sith I have cause and will and strength and means
> To do't. [4.4.33–36, 44–47]

Yet with all this strong conviction of duty, and with all this resolution arising out of strong conviction, nothing is done. This admirable and consistent character, deeply acquainted with his own feelings, painting them with such wonderful power and accuracy, and firmly persuaded that a moment ought not to be lost in executing the solemn charge committed to him, still yields to the same retiring from reality, which is the result of having, what we express by the terms, a world within himself.

Such a mind as Hamlet's is near akin to madness. Dryden has somewhere said, "Great wit to madness nearly is allied" [*Absalom and Achitophel*, 1.163], and he was right; for he means by "wit" that greatness of genius, which led Hamlet to a perfect knowledge of his own character, which, with all strength of motive, was so weak as to be unable to carry into act his own most obvious duty.

With all this he has a sense of imperfectness, which becomes apparent when he is moralising on the skull in the churchyard. Something is wanting to his completeness—something is deficient which remains to be supplied, and he is therefore described as attached to Ophelia. His madness is assumed, when he finds that witnesses have been placed behind the arras to listen to what passes, and when the heroine has been thrown in his way as a decoy.

Another objection has been taken by Dr. Johnson, and Shakespeare has been taxed very severely. I refer to the scene where Hamlet enters and finds his uncle praying, and refuses to take his life, excepting when he is in the height of his iniquity. To assail him at such a moment of confession and repentance, Hamlet declares, "Why, this is hire and salary, not revenge" [3.3.79]. He therefore forbears, and postpones his uncle's death, until he can catch him in some act "That has no relish of salvation in't" [92].

This conduct, and this sentiment, Dr. Johnson has pronounced to be so atrocious and horrible, as to be unfit to be put into the mouth of a human being.[1] The fact, however, is that Dr. Johnson did not understand the character of Hamlet, and censured accordingly: the determination to allow the guilty King to escape at such a moment is only part of the indecision and irresoluteness of the hero. Hamlet seizes hold of a pretext for not acting, when he might have acted so instantly and effectually: therefore, he again defers the revenge he was bound to seek, and declares his determination to accomplish it at some time,

> When he is drunk, asleep, or in his rage,
> Or in th'incestuous pleasures of his bed. [89–90]

1. See p. 239 of this Norton Critical Edition.

This, allow me to impress upon you most emphatically, was merely the excuse Hamlet made to himself for not taking advantage of this particular and favourable moment for doing justice upon his guilty uncle, at the urgent instance of the spirit of his father.

Dr. Johnson farther states, that in the voyage to England, Shakespeare merely follows the novel as he found it, as if the poet had no other reason for adhering to his original; but Shakespeare never followed a novel, because he found such and such an incident in it, but because he saw that the story, as he read it, contributed to enforce, or to explain some great truth inherent in human nature. He never could lack invention to alter or improve a popular narrative; but he did not wantonly vary from it, when he knew that, as it was related, it would so well apply to his own great purpose. He saw at once how consistent it was with the character of Hamlet, that after still resolving, and still deferring, still determining to execute, and still postponing execution, he should finally, in the infirmity of his disposition, give himself up to his destiny, and hopelessly place himself in the power, and at the mercy of his enemies.

Even after the scene with Osrick, we see Hamlet still indulging in reflection, and hardly thinking of the task he has just undertaken: he is all dispatch and resolution, as far as words and present intentions are concerned, but all hesitation and irresolution, when called upon to carry his words and intentions into effect; so that resolving to do everything, he does nothing. He is full of purpose, but void of that quality of mind which accomplishes purpose.

Anything finer than this conception, and working out of a great character, is merely impossible. Shakespeare wished to impress upon us the truth, that action is the chief end of existence—that no faculties of intellect, however brilliant, can be considered valuable, or indeed otherwise than as misfortunes, if they withdraw us from, or render us repugnant to action, and lead us to think and think of doing, until the time has elapsed when we can do anything effectually. In enforcing this moral truth, Shakespeare has shown the fullness and force of his powers: all that is amiable and excellent in nature is combined in Hamlet, with the exception of one quality. He is a man living in meditation, called upon to act by every motive human and divine, but the great object of his life is defeated by continually resolving to do, yet doing nothing but resolve.

JOHN QUINCY ADAMS

Letter to James H. Hackett, February 7, 1839[†]

Hamlet is the personification of *Man*, in the prime of life, with a mind cultivated by the learning acquirable at an university, combining *intelligence* and *sensibility*, in their highest degrees, within a step of the highest station attainable upon earth, crushed to extinction by the pressure of calamities inflicted not by nature but against nature, not by physical but by moral evil. Hamlet is the heart and soul of man in all their perfection and all their frailty, in agonizing conflict with human crime also in its highest preeminence of guilt. Hamlet is all heart and all soul. His ruling passions are filial affections, youthful love, manly ambition. His commanding principles are filial duty, generous friendship, love disappointed and subdued, ambition and life sacrificed to avenge his father.

* * *

The reasoning faculty of Hamlet is at once sportive, sorrowful, indignant, and melancholy. His reflections always take the tinge of the passion under which he is labouring but his conduct is always governed by the *impulse* of the moment. Hence his madness, as you have remarked, is sometimes feigned and sometimes real. His feigned madness, Polonius, without seeing through it, perceives has *method* in it. His real madness is *towering passion*, transient, momentary, the *furor brevis* which was the ancient definition of anger. It overwhelms at once the brightest genius, the soundest reason, and the kindliest heart that ever was exhibited in combination upon the stage. It is *Man* in the ideal perfection of his intellectual and moral nature, struggling with calamity beyond his power to bear, inflicted by the crime of his fellow man, struggling with agonizing energies against it, sinking under it, to extinction. What can be more terrific?[1] What can be more piteous?

† John Quincy Adams, Letter to James H. Hackett, Folger MS. Y.c.10(3). Writing to the American Shakespearean actor Hackett (1800–1871), Adams (1767–1848), the sixth president of the United States (1824–28), follows Goethe in seeing Hamlet as a sensitive, intellectual, and moral man overwhelmed by evils he cannot overcome. (See also Abraham Lincoln's letter to Hackett on p. 252.)
1. Terrifying.

EDGAR ALLAN POE

Review of William Hazlitt, August 16, 1845†

In all commentating upon Shakespeare, there has been a radical error, never yet mentioned. It is the error of attempting to expound his characters, to account for their actions, to reconcile his inconsistencies, not as if they were the coinage of a human brain, but as if they had been actual existences upon the earth. We talk of Hamlet the man, instead of Hamlet the *dramatis persona*—of Hamlet that God, in place of Hamlet that Shakespeare, created. If Hamlet had really lived, and if the tragedy were an accurate record of his deeds, from this record (with some trouble) we might, it is true, reconcile his inconsistencies and settle to our satisfaction his true character. But the task becomes the purest absurdity when we deal only with a phantom. It is not (then) the inconsistencies of the acting man which we have as a subject of discussion—(although we proceed as if it were, and thus *inevitably* err)—but the whims and vacillations, the conflicting energies and indolences of the poet. It seems to us little less than a miracle that this obvious point should have been overlooked.

While on this topic we may as well offer an ill-considered opinion of our own as to the *intention of the poet* in the delineation of the Dane. It must have been well know to Shakespeare that a leading feature in certain more intense classes of intoxication (from whatever cause) is an almost irresistible impulse to counterfeit a farther degree of excitement than actually exists. Analogy would lead any thoughtful person to suspect the same impulse in madness—where beyond doubt it is manifest. This Shakespeare *felt*, not thought. He felt it through his marvelous power of *identification* with humanity at large—the ultimate source of his magical influence upon mankind. He wrote of Hamlet as if Hamlet he were; and having, in the first instance, imagined his hero excited to partial insanity by the disclosures of the ghost—he (the poet) *felt* that it was natural he should be impelled to exaggerate the insanity.

---

† Edgar Allan Poe, review of William Hazlitt, *The Characters of Shakespeare's Plays* (1817), *Broadway Journal*, August 16, 1845, 89. American poet, short-story writer, and editor, Poe (1809–1849) here objects to the prevailing Romantic tendency to treat fictional characters as real people and explores Shakespeare's representation of insanity in *Hamlet*.

ABRAHAM LINCOLN

Letter to James H. Hackett, August 17, 1863[†]

For one of my age, I have seen very little of the drama. The first presentation of Falstaff, I ever saw, was yours here, last winter or spring.
Perhaps the best compliment I can pay is to say, as I truly can, I am
very anxious to see it again. Some of Shakespeare's plays I have
never read; while others I have gone over perhaps as frequently
as any unprofessional reader. Among the latter are *Lear, Richard
Third, Henry Eighth, Hamlet* and especially *Macbeth*. I think nothing
equals *Macbeth*. It is wonderful. Unlike you gentlemen of the profession, I think the soliloquy in *Hamlet* commencing "Oh my offense is
rank" surpasses that commencing, "To be or not to be." But pardon
this small attempt at criticism.

LEO TOLSTOY

Shakespeare and the Drama (1908)[‡]

My disagreement with the established opinion about Shakespeare
is not the result of an accidental frame of mind nor of a light-
minded attitude towards the matter, but is the outcome of many
years' repeated and insistent endeavours to harmonize my own views
of Shakespeare with those established amongst all civilized men of
the Christian world.

I remember the astonishment I felt when I first read Shakespeare.
I expected to receive a powerful aesthetic pleasure, but having read,
one after the other, works regarded as his best—*King Lear, Romeo
and Juliet, Hamlet*, and *Macbeth*—not only did I feel no delight but
I felt an irresistible repulsion and tedium, and doubted as to whether

[†] Transcribed and annotated by the Lincoln Studies Center, Knox College, Galesburg,
Illinois. Available at Abraham Lincoln Papers at the Library of Congress, Manuscript
Division (Washington, D.C.: American Memory Project, [2000–02]), http://memory.
loc.gov/ammem/alhtml/alhome.html, accessed 11/2/2008. Hackett, a prominent American actor, had recently sent Lincoln (1809–1865) a copy of his book on Shakespeare
(1863). The sixteenth president of the United States (1861–65) here voices his admiration for *Macbeth* and for Claudius's "O my offense is rank" speech, the soliloquy of a
ruler haunted by a guilty conscience.
[‡] Leo Tolstoy, "Shakespeare and the Drama," trans. V. Tchertkoff, et al., in *Tolstoy on
Shakespeare* (London: The Free Age Press, 1906), 7–9, 48–50, 78–79. Though he found
occasional beauties in Shakespeare, Leo Tolstoy (1828–1910) thought *Hamlet* full of
irrelevancies and the prince a hopelessly inconsistent character. The great Russian
novelist, moreover, declared all of Shakespeare's work to be overrated, tedious, and
trivial, wholly lacking in religious seriousness and largely responsible for a general
decline in dramatic art.

I was senseless in feeling works regarded as the summit of perfection by the whole of the civilized world to be trivial and positively bad, or whether the significance which this civilized world attributes to the works of Shakespeare was itself senseless. My consternation was increased by the fact that I always keenly felt the beauties of poetry in every form; then why should artistic works recognized by the whole world as those of a genius—the works of Shakespeare— not only fail to please me, but be disagreeable to me? For a long time I could not believe in myself, and during fifty years, in order to test myself, I several times recommenced reading Shakespeare in every possible form, in Russian and in English and in German and in Schlegel's translation, as I was advised. Several times I read the dramas and the comedies and historical plays, and I invariably underwent the same feelings: repulsion, weariness and bewilderment. At the present time, before writing this preface, being desirous once more to test myself, I have as an old man of seventy-five, again read the whole of Shakespeare, including the historical plays, the Henry's, *Troilus and Cressida*, *The Tempest*, *Cymbeline*, etc., and I have felt with even greater force, the same feelings—this time, however, not of bewilderment, but of firm, indubitable conviction that the unquestionable glory of a great genius which Shakespeare enjoys, and which compels writers of our time to imitate him and readers and spectators to discover in him nonexistent merits—thereby distorting their aesthetic and ethical understanding—is a great evil, as is every untruth.

* * *

On this subject [Hamlet] he writes his own drama, introducing quite inappropriately (as indeed he always does) into the mouth of the principal person, all such thoughts of his own as appeared to him worthy of attention. Putting into the mouth of his hero these thoughts: about life (the gravedigger), about death ("To be or not to be")—the same which are expressed in his sixty-sixth sonnet— about the theater, about women. He is utterly unconcerned as to the circumstances under which these words are said, and it naturally turns out that the person expressing all these thoughts is a mere phonograph of Shakespeare, without character, whose actions and words do not agree.

In the old legend, Hamlet's personality is quite comprehensible: he is indignant at his uncle's and his mother's deeds, and wishes to revenge himself upon them, but is afraid his uncle may kill him as he had killed his father. Therefore he simulates insanity, desiring to bide his time and observe all that goes on in the palace. Meanwhile his uncle and mother, being afraid of him, wish to test whether he is feigning or is really mad, and send to him a girl whom he loves.

He persists, then sees his mother in private, kills a courtier who is eavesdropping, and convicts his mother of her sin. Afterwards he is sent to England, but intercepts letters, and returning from England, takes revenge of his enemies, burning them all.

All this is comprehensible and flows from Hamlet's character and position. But Shakespeare putting into Hamlet's mouth speeches which he himself wishes to express, and making him commit actions which are necessary to the author in order to produce scenic effects, destroys all that constitutes the character of Hamlet and of the legend. During the whole of the drama, Hamlet is doing not what he would really desire, but what is necessary for the author's plan. One moment he is awestruck at his father's ghost, another moment he begins to chaff it, calling it "old mole"; one moment he loves Ophelia, another moment he teases her and so forth. There is no possibility of finding any explanation whatever of Hamlet's actions or words, and therefore no possibility of attributing any character to him.

*   *   *

If there were not that exaggerated praise of Shakespeare's dramas, recognised as the most perfect model of the drama, the men of the eighteenth and nineteenth centuries would have had to understand that the drama, to have a right to exist and to be a serious thing, must serve, as it always has served and cannot but do—the development of the religious consciousness. And having understood this, they would have searched for a new form of drama corresponding to their religious understanding.

But when it was decided that the height of perfection was Shakespeare's drama, and that we ought to write as he did, not only without any religious, but even without any moral intention, then all writers of dramas began in imitation of him, to compose such empty pieces as are those of Goethe, Schiller, Hugo, and, in Russia, of Pushkin, or the chronicles of Ostrovski, Alexis Tolstoy, and an innumerable quantity of other more or less celebrated dramatic productions which fill all the theaters and are prepared wholesale by anyone who happens to have the idea or desire to write a play. It is only thanks to such a low, trivial understanding of the significance of the drama, that there appears amongst us that infinite quantity of dramatic works describing men's actions, positions, characters and frames of mind, not only void of any spiritual substance, but often of any human sense.

Let not the reader think that I exclude from this estimate of contemporary drama the theatrical pieces I have myself incidentally written. I recognize them, as well as all the rest, as not having that religious character which must form the foundation of the drama of the future.

The drama then, the most important branch of art, has in our time become the trivial and immoral amusement of a trivial and immoral crowd. The worst of it is, moreover, that to dramatic art—fallen as low as it is possible to fall—is still attributed an elevated significance no longer appropriate to it. Dramatists, actors, theatrical managers, the press—this last publishing in the most serious tone reports of theaters and operas—and the rest, are all perfectly certain that they are doing something very worthy and important.

GILBERT MURRAY

Hamlet and Orestes (1914)[†]

Now to our comparison.

1. The general situation. In all the versions, both Northern and Greek, the hero is the son of a king who has been murdered and succeeded on the throne by a younger kinsman—a cousin, Aegisthus, in the Greek; a younger brother, Feng or Claudius, in the Northern. The dead king's wife has married his murderer. The hero, driven by supernatural commands, undertakes and carries through the duty of vengeance.

In Shakespeare the hero dies as his vengeance is accomplished; but this seems to be an innovation. In Saxo, *Ambales*, and the Greek he duly succeeds to the kingdom. In Saxo there is no mention of a ghost; the duty of vengeance is perhaps accepted as natural. In *Ambales*, however, there are angels; in the English, a ghost; in the Greek, dreams and visions of the dead father, and an oracle.

2. In all versions of the story there is some shyness about the mother-murder. In Saxo the mother is not slain; in Shakespeare she is slain by accident, not deliberately murdered; in *Ambales* she is warned and leaves the burning Hall just in time. In one of the variants the mother refuses to leave the Hall and is burnt with her husband.[1] In the Greek versions she is deliberately slain, but the

---

† Gilbert Murray, *Hamlet and Orestes: A Study in Traditional Types*, *The Annual Shakespeare Lecture* (London: Humphrey Milford, 1914), 6–16. Celebrated classicist and translator of Greek drama, Murray (1866–1957) adopted a mythical and anthropological approach to literature. Here he explores the remarkable parallels between two revengers, Orestes and Hamlet, as they appear in various legends, stories, and representations. Murray examines Orestes in Greek tragedy—Aeschylus's *Choephori* and *Eumenides*, Sophocles' *Electra*, and Euripides' *Electra*, *Orestes*, *Iphigenia in Tauris*, and *Andromache*—and Hamlet in the Hamlet plays, Saxo's *Historia*, and the Icelandic *Ambales Saga*.

1. Halfdan is killed by his brother Frodi, who also takes his wife. Halfdan's sons Helgi and Hroar eventually burn Frodi at a feast. See Prof Elton's appendix to his translation of Saxo, edited by York Powell.

horror of the deed unseats the hero's reason. We shall consider this mother more at length later on.

3. In all the versions the hero is in some way under the shadow of madness. This is immensely important, indeed essential, in his whole dramatic character. It is present in all the versions, but is somewhat different in each.

In *Hamlet* the madness is assumed, but I trust I am safe in saying that there is something in the hero's character which at least makes one wonder if it is entirely assumed. I think the same may be said of Amloði and Ambales.

In the Greek the complete madness only comes as a result of the mother-murder; yet here too there is that in the hero's character which makes it easy for him to go mad. In the *Choephori*, where we see him before the deed, he is not normal. His language is strange and broken amid its amazing eloquence; he is a haunted man. In other plays, after the deed, he is seldom actually raving. But, like Hamlet, in his mother's chamber he sees visions which others cannot: "You see them not: 'tis only I that see" (*Cho.* 1061, cf. *Or.* 255–79); he indulges freely in soliloquies (*I. T.* 77–94, *El.* 367–90; cf. *I. T.* 940–78; *Cho.* 268–305 and last scene); especially, like Hamlet, he is subject to paralysing doubts and hesitations, alternating with hot fits. For instance, once in the *Iphigenia* he suddenly wishes to fly and give up his whole enterprise and has to be checked by Pylades (*I. T.* 93–103):

> O God, where hast thou brought me? what new snare
> Is this?—I slew my mother, I avenged
> My father at thy bidding. I have ranged
> A homeless world, hunted by shapes of pain. . . .
> . . . We still have time to fly for home,
> Back to the galley quick, ere worse things come.
> PYLADES   To fly we dare not, brother: 'tis a thing
> Not of our custom.

Again, in the *Electra* he suspects that the God who commands him to take vengeance may be an evil spirit in disguise: "How if some fiend of Hell / Hid in God's likeness spake that oracle?" (*El.* 979; cf. *Hamlet*, [2.2.519–20]) "The spirit that I have seen / May be the devil."

At the moment before the actual crisis he is seized with horror and tries to hold back. In the *Choephori* this is given in a line or two: "Pylades, what am I do? Let me spare my mother!"—or "Shall I spare," if we put a query at the end of the line (*Cho.* 899). In the *Electra* it is a whole scene, where he actually for the moment forgets what it is that he has to do; he only remembers that it has something to do with his mother.

The scene is so characteristic that I must quote several lines of it. Aegisthus has just been slain: Clytemnestra is seen approaching (*Electra*, 962–87).

ORESTES   What would we with our mother? . . . Didst thou say
    Kill her?
ELECTRA   What? Is it pity? , . . Dost thou fear
    To see thy mother's shape?
ORESTES   Twas she that bare
    My body into life. She gave me suck.
    How can I strike her?
ELECTRA   Strike her as she struck
    Our father!
ORESTES   (*to himself, brooding*)
                Phoebus, God, was all thy mind
    Turned unto darkness?
ELECTRA   If thy God be blind,
    Shalt thou have light?
ORESTES (*as before*)   Thou, Thou, didst bid me kill
    My mother: which is sin.
ELECTRA   How brings it ill
    To thee, to raise our father from the dust?
ORESTES   I was a clean man once. . . . Shall I be thrust
    From men's sight, blotted with her blood?

Again he vows, too late, after the mother-murder, that his Father's Ghost, if it had known all, would never have urged him to such a deed; it would rather "have knelt down / And hung his wreath of prayers about my beard, / To leave him unavenged" (*Or.* 288–93). In *Hamlet* this belief is made a fact; the Ghost specially charges him not to kill Gertrude: "Taint not thy mind, nor let thy soul contrive / Against thy Mother aught" [1.5.85–86; cf. also the tone in 3.4].

Is it too much to say that, in all these strangely characteristic speeches of Orestes, every line might have been spoken by Hamlet, and hardly a line by any other tragic character except those directly influenced by Orestes or Hamlet?

Now what do we find in the sagas? Both in Saxo and in *Ambales* the madness is assumed, entirely or mainly, but in its quality also it is utterly different. Hamlet in both sagas is not a highly wrought and sensitive man with his mind shaken by a terrible experience, he is simply a Fool, a gross Jester, covered with dirt and ashes, grinning and mowing and eating like a hog, spared by the murderer simply because he is too witless to be dangerous. The name "Amloði" itself means a fool. This side is emphasized most in *Ambales*, but it is clear enough in Saxo also and explains why he has combined his hero with the Fool Brutus. Hamlet is a Fool, though his folly is partly assumed and hides superhuman cunning.

4. The Fool. It is very remarkable that Shakespeare, who did such wonders in his idealized and half-mystic treatment of the real Fool, should also have made his greatest tragic hero out of a Fool transfigured. Let us spend a few moments on noticing the remains of the old Fool characteristics that subsist in the transfigured hero of the tragedies. For one thing, as has often been remarked, Hamlet's actual language is at times exactly that of the regular Shakespearian Fool: e.g. with Polonius in II.2; just before the play in III.2, and after. But apart from that, there are other significant elements.

(a) The Fool's Disguise. Amloði and Brutus and Shakespeare's Hamlet feign madness; Orestes does not. Yet the element of disguise is very strong in Orestes. He is always disguising his feelings: he does so in the *Choephori*, Sophocles' *Electra*, Euripides' *Electra* and *Iphigenia in Tauris*. In two passages further, *Andromache* 980 and *I. T.* 956, he narrates how, in other circumstances, he had to disguise them: "I suffered in silence and made pretence not to see." "I suffered, Oh, I suffered; but as things drove me I endured." This is like Shakespeare's Hamlet. It is also very like the saga Hamlet, who laughs in pretended idiocy to see his brother hanged.

Again, it is a marked feature of Orestes to be present in disguise, especially when he is supposed to be dead, and then at some crisis to reveal himself with startling effect. He is apt to be greeted by such words as "Undreamed of phantom!" or "Who is this risen from the dead?" (*Or.* 879, 385, 478f.; *I. T.* 1361, cf. 1321; *Andr.* 884). He is present disguised and unknown in the *Choephori*, Sophocles' *Electra*, Euripides' *Electra* and *Iphigenia in Tauris*; he is in nearly every case supposed to be dead. In the *Choephori* and Sophocles' *Electra* he brings the funeral urn that is supposed to contain his own ashes; in the *Iphigenia* he interrupts his own funeral rites.

No other character in Greek Tragedy behaves in this extraordinary way. But Saxo's Amloði does. When Amloði goes to England he is supposed to be dead, and his funeral feast is in progress, when he walks in, "striking all men utterly aghast" (Saxo, 95).

In *Hamlet* there is surely a remnant of this motive, considerably softened. In Act V. 2, the Gravedigger scene, Hamlet has been present in disguise while the gravedigger and the public thought he was in England, and the King and his confidants must have believed him dead, as they do in Saxo. Then comes the Funeral—not his own but Ophelia's; he stays hidden for a time, and then springs out revealing himself: "This is I, Hamlet the Dane!" [5.1.235–36]. The words seem like an echo of that cry that is so common in the Greek tragedies: "'Tis I, Orestes, Agamemnon's son!" (*Andr.* 884; *I. T.* 1361; cf. *Cho.* 212ff.; *El.* 220; also the recognition scenes). And one is reminded, too, of the quotation from the pre-Shakespearian *Hamlet* in Dekker's *Satiromastix* of 1602: "My name's Hamlet! Revenge!"

I suspect that these melodramatic appearances were perhaps more prominent in the tradition before Shakespeare.

(b) The Disorder of the Fool. This disguise motive has led us away from the Fool, though it is closely connected with him. Another curious element of the Fool that lingers on is his dirtiness and disorder in dress. Saxo says that Amloði "remained always in his mother's house, utterly listless and unclean, flinging himself on the ground and bespattering his person with foul dirt" (Saxo, 88). Ambales was worse; enough to say that he slept in his mother's room and "ashes and filth reeked off him" (*Ambales*, pp. 73–75, 77). We remember Ophelia's description of Hamlet's coming to her chamber

> his doublet all unbraced;
> No hat upon his head; his stockings fouled,
> Ungartered and down-gyvèd to the ankle,
> Pale as his shirt . . . [2.1.76–79]

Similarly Orestes, at the beginning of the play that bears his name, is found with his sister, ghastly pale, with foam on his mouth, gouts of rheum in his eyes, his long hair matted with dirt and "made wild with long unwashenness." "Poor curls, poor filthy face," his sister says to him (*Or.* 219–26). In the *Electra* too, he is taken for a brigand (*El.* 219), which suggests some lack of neatness in dress; in the *I. T.* we hear of his foaming at the mouth and rolling on the ground (307 f.). In both plays, it is true, Orestes carries with him an air of princely birth, but so, no doubt, did Hamlet, whatever state his stockings were in.

(c) The Fool's Rudeness of Speech. Besides being dirty and talking in riddles the Fool was abusive and gross in his language. This is the case to some degree in Saxo, though no doubt the monk has softened Amloði's words. It is much emphasized in Ambales. That hero's language is habitually outrageous, especially to women. This outrageousness of speech has clearly descended to Hamlet, in whom it seems to be definitely intended as a morbid trait. He is obsessed by revolting images. He does "like a whore unpack his heart in words / And fall a-cursing like a very drab" [2.2.506–07] and he rages at himself because of it.

(d) The Fool on Women. Now the general style of Greek tragedy will not admit any gross language. So Orestes has lost this trait. But a trace of it perhaps remains. Both Orestes and Hamlet are given to expressing violently cynical opinions about women (*Or.* 246–51, 566–72, 935–42). The *Orestes* bristles with parallels to the ravings of Hamlet's "Get-thee-to-a-Nunnery" scene (III. 1). The hero is haunted by his "most pernicious woman." All women want to murder their husbands; it is only a question of time. Then they will fly in tears to their children, show their breasts and cry for

sympathy. We may, perhaps, couple with these passages the famous
speech (*Or.* 552 ff. based on Apollo's ruling in the *Eumenides*), where
he denies any blood relationship with his mother; and the horrible
mad line where he says he could never weary of killing evil women
(*Or.* 1590).

Both heroes also tend—if I may use such an expression—to bully
any woman they are left alone with. Amloði in Saxo mishandles his
foster-sister—though the passage is obscure—and utters violent
reproaches to the Queen. (The scene is taken over by Shakespeare.)
Ambales is habitually misbehaving in this way. Hamlet bullies
Ophelia cruelly and "speaks daggers" to the Queen. He never meets
any other woman. Orestes is very surly to Iphigenia (*I. T.* 482 ff.);
draws his sword on Electra in one play, and takes her for a devil
in another (*El.* 220 ff.; *Or.* 264); holds his dagger at the throat of
Hermione till she faints (*Or.* 1575 ff.); denounces, threatens, and kills
Clytemnestra, and tries to kill Helen. There are not many tragic
heroes with such an extreme anti-feminist record.

The above, I think, are all of them elements that go deep down
into the character of the hero as a stage figure. I will now add some
slighter and more external coincidences.

1. In both traditions the hero has been away from home when the
main drama begins, Orestes in Phocis, Hamlet in Wittenberg, This
point, as we shall see later, has some significance.

2. The hero in both traditions—and in both rather strangely—
goes on a ship, is captured by enemies who want to kill him, but
escapes. And as Hamlet has a sort of double escape, first from the
King's treacherous letter, and next from the pirates, so Orestes in
the *Iphigenia* escapes once from the Taurians who catch him on the
shore, and again from the pursuers in the ship. Ambales has similar
adventures at sea; and the original Amloði seems to have had nauti-
cal connexions, since the sea was his meal-bin, and the ship's rudder
his knife.[2]

3. Much more curious, and indeed extraordinary, is the following point, which occurs in Saxo, *Ambales*, and the Greek, but not in
Shakespeare. We have seen that the hero is always a good deal connected with the dead and graves and ghosts and funerals. Now in
the sagas he on one occasion wins a great battle after a preliminary
defeat by a somewhat ghastly stratagem. He picks up his dead—or
his dead and wounded—and ties them upright to stakes and rocks,
so that when his pursuers renew their attack they find themselves
affronted by an army of dead men standing upright, and fly in dismay. Now in *Electra*, 680, Orestes prays to his Father: "Girt with

2. See also a pamphlet *Grotta Söngr and the Orkney and Shetland Quern* by A. W. Johnston, 1912.

thine own dead armies wake, Oh wake," or, quite literally, "Come bringing every dead man as a fellow-fighter." One would almost think here that there was some direct influence—of course with a misunderstanding. But the parallel may be a mere chance.

4. I would not lay much stress on the coincidence about the serpent. Clytemnestra dreams that she gives birth to a Serpent, which bites her breast. Orestes, hearing of it, accepts the omen: he will be the serpent. And at the last moment Clytemnestra so recognizes him: "Oh, God; / This is the serpent that I bore and suckled." We are reminded of the Ghost's words: "The serpent that did sting thy Father's life / Now wears his crown" [1.5.39–40]. However, Shakespeare abounds in serpents, and I have found no trace of this serpent motive in the sagas (*Cho.* 527–50, 928; *Or.* 479).

5. Nor yet would I make anything of the point that both Hamlet and Orestes on one occasion have the enemy in their power and put off killing him in order to provide a worse death afterwards. This is important in *Hamlet*, "Now might I do it pat, now he is praying [3.3.73]," but only occurs as a slight incident in Sophocles' *Electra*, 1491 ff., and may be due merely to the Greek rule of having no violent deaths on the stage. Nor is there much significance in the fact that in both traditions the hero has a scene in which he hears the details of his father's death and bursts into uncontrollable grief (*Cho.* 430 ff.; *El.* 290; *Hamlet*, 1.5 [92 ff.], "Oh, all you host of heaven," &c). Such a scene is in both cases almost unavoidable.

Let us now follow this Father for a little while. He was, perhaps naturally, a great warrior. He "slew Troy's thousands"; he "smote the sledded Polacks on the ice." It is a particular reproach that the son of such a man should be so slow-tempered, "peaking like John-a-dreams" and so chary of shedding blood (*El.* 245, 336 ff., 275 ff., 186 ff.). The old king was also generally idealized and made magnificent. He had some manly faults, yet "He was a man, taking him all in all". . . . He was "a king of kings" (*El.* 1066 ff.). A special contrast is drawn between him and his successor (*El.* 320 ff., 917, 1080):

> It was so easy to be true. A King
> Was thine, not feebler, not in any thing
> Below Aegisthus; one whom Hellas chose
> Above all kings.

One might continue: "Look on this picture and on this [3.4.54]."

We may also notice that the successor, besides the vices which are necessary, or at least desirable, in his position, is in both cases accused of drunkenness (*Hamlet*, I. 4; *El.* 326), which seems irrelevant and unusual.

Lastly, and more important, one of the greatest horrors about the Father's death in both traditions is that he died without the due religious observances. In the Greek tragedies, this lack of religious burial is almost the central horror of the whole story. Wherever it is mentioned it comes as something intolerable, maddening; it breaks Orestes down. A good instance is the scene in the *Choephori*, where Orestes and Electra are kneeling at their father's grave, awakening the dead and working their own passion to the murder point.

> ELECTRA   Ah, pitiless one, my mother, mine enemy! With an enemy's burial didst thou bury him: thy King without his people, without dying rites; thine husband without a tear!
> ORESTES   All, all, in dishonour thou tellest it, woe is me! And for that dishonouring she shall pay her punishment: by the will of the Gods, by the will of my hands: Oh, let me but slay, and then perish!

He is now ripe for the hearing of the last horror: "LEADER OF THE CHORUS *His body was mangled to lay his ghost!* There, learn it all . . ." and the scene becomes hysterical (*Cho.* 435 ff.; cf. Soph. *El.* 443 ff.; Eur., *El.*, 289, 323 ff.).

The atmosphere is quite different in the English. But the lack of dying rites remains and retains a strange dreadfulness: "Cut off even in the blossom of my sin, / Unhouselled, disappointed, unannealed" [1.5.76–77].

To turn to the other characters: in both the dramatic traditions the hero has a faithful friend and confidant, who also arrives from Phocis-Wittenberg, and advises him about his revenge. This friend, when the hero is threatened with death, wishes to die too (*Or.* 1069 ff.; *I.T.* 675 ff.), but is prevented by the hero and told to "absent him from felicity awhile." This motive is worked out more at length in the Greek than in the English.

Also the friendship between Orestes and Pylades is more intense than between Hamlet and Horatio; naturally, since devoted friendship plays always a greater part in antiquity. But Hamlet's words are strong:

> Give me the man
> That is not passion's slave, and I will wear him
> In my heart's core, yea, in my heart of hearts;
> As I do thee. [3.2.64–66]

I find no Pylades-Horatio in the sagas; though there is a brother to Hamlet, sometimes older and sometimes a twin, and in some of the variants, such as the stories of Helgi and Hroar, there are pairs of avengers, one of whom is mad or behaves like a madman.

Next comes a curious point. At first sight it seems as if all the Electra motive were lacking in the modern play, all the Ophelia-Polonius
motive in the ancient. Yet I am not sure.

In all the ancient plays Orestes is closely connected with a strange
couple, a young woman and a very old man. They are his sister Electra and her only true friend, an old and trusted servant of the dead
King, who saved Orestes' life in childhood. This old man habitually
addresses Electra as "my daughter"—not merely as "Child," παῖς, but
really "daughter," θυγάτηρ (El. 493, 563). She in return carefully
avoids calling him "Father"; that is to her a sacred name, and she will
never use it lightly, at least in Euripides. But in Sophocles she says
emphatically: "Hail, Father. For it is as if in thee I saw my Father!"
(Soph. El. 1361).

In the Elizabethan play this couple—if we may so beg the
question—has been transformed. The sister is now the mistress,
Ophelia; the old servant of the King—for so we must surely describe
Polonius or Corambis—remains, but has become Ophelia's real
father. And their relations to the hero are quite different.

The change is made more intelligible when we look at the sagas.
There the young woman is not a sister but a foster-sister; like Electra she helps Amloði, like Ophelia she is his mistress. The old servant of the King is not her father—so far like the Greek; but there
the likeness stops. He spies on Amloði in his mother's chamber and
is killed for his pains, as in the English.

We may notice, further, that in all the Electra plays alike a peculiar effect is got from Orestes' first sight of his sister, either walking
in a band of mourners or alone in mourning garb (Cho, 16; Soph. El.
80; El. 107 ff.). He takes her for a slave, and cries, "Can that be the
unhappy Electra?" A similar but stronger effect is reached in Hamlet,
V. 1, when Hamlet, seeing an unknown funeral procession approach,
gradually discovers whose it is and cries in horror; "What, the fair
Ophelia?" [220].

Lastly, there is something peculiar, at any rate in the Northern Tradition [. . .] about the hero's mother. Essentially it is this; she has
married the murderer of her first husband and is in part implicated
in the murder, and yet the tradition instinctively keeps her sympathetic. In our Hamlet she is startled to hear that her first husband
was murdered, yet one does not feel clear that she is perfectly honest with herself. She did not know Claudius had poisoned him, but
probably that was because she obstinately refused to put together
things which she did know and which pointed towards that conclusion. At any rate, though she does not betray Hamlet, she sticks to
Claudius and shares his doom. In the First Quarto she is more definitely innocent of the murder; when she learns of it she changes

sides, protects Hamlet and acts in confidence with Horatio. In Saxo her attitude is as ambiguous as in the later *Hamlet*; she is friendly to Hamlet and does not betray him, yet does not turn against Feng either.

A wife who loves her husband and bears him children, and then is wedded to his slayer and equally loves him, and does it all in a natural and unemotional manner: somewhat unusual.

And one's surprise is a little increased to find that in Saxo Amloði's wife, Hermutrude, does the same as his mother has done. On Amloði's death she marries his slayer, Wiglek. Again, there is an Irish king, historical to a great degree, who has got deeply entangled with the Hamlet story. His name is Anlaf Curan. Now his wife, Gormflaith, carried this practice so far that the chronicler comments on it. After Anlaf's defeat at Tara she marries his conqueror Malachy, and on Malachy's defeat marries Malachy's conqueror Brian. We will consider later the Greek parallels to this enigmatic lady. For the present we must admit that she is very unlike the Clytemnestra of Greek tragedy, whose motives are studied in every detail, who boldly hates her husband and murders him. There are traces in Homer of a far less passionate Clytemnestra.

ERNEST JONES

A Psycho-analytic Study of *Hamlet* (1922)[†]

The complete expression of the "repressed" wish is not only that the father should die but that the son should then espouse the mother. This was openly expressed by Diderot in speaking of boys: "If we were left to ourselves and if our bodily strength only came up to that of our phantasy we would wring our fathers' necks and sleep with our mothers." The attitude of son to parents is so transpicuously illustrated in the Oedipus legend,[1] as developed for instance in Sophocles' tragedy, that the group of mental processes in question is generally known under the name of the "Oedipus-complex."

† Jones, *A Psycho-analytic Study of* Hamlet (London: The International Psycho-analytic P, 1922), 50–59. Following Sigmund Freud, Ernest Jones (1879–1958) wrote a classical psychoanalysis of Hamlet as an illustration of the Oedipus complex, the unconscious desire to possess the parent of the child's same sex. According to this reading, Claudius has acted out Hamlet's repressed desires and thereby caused Hamlet's turmoil, cruelty to Ophelia, and delay in revenge. See Olivier, "The Actors Gallery," p. 168.
1. See Freud, *Die Traumdeutung*, 1900, S. 181. Valuable expositions, of the mythological aspects of the subject are given by Abraham, *Traum und Mythus*, 1909, and Rank, *Der Mythus von der Geburt des Helden*, 1909. Rank has also worked through in great detail the various ways in which the same theme is made use of in literature: *Das Inzest-Motiv in Dichtung und Sage*, 1912, especially Kap. VIII which contains an excellent analysis of the Oedipus legend.

Laurence Olivier (Hamlet) and Eileen Herlie (Gertrude) in Oedipal embrace, film, 1948

We are now in a position to expand and complete the suggestions offered above in connection with the Hamlet problem.[2] The story thus interpreted would run somewhat as follows.

As a child Hamlet had experienced the warmest affection for his mother, and this, as is always so, had contained elements of a disguised erotic quality. The presence of two traits in the Queen's character go to corroborate this assumption, namely her markedly sensual nature and her passionate fondness for her son. The former is indicated in too many places in the play to need specific reference, and is generally recognised. The latter is also manifest; Claudius says, for instance "The Queen his mother lives almost by his looks" [4.7.12–13]. Nevertheless Hamlet seems to have with more or less success weaned himself from her and to have fallen in love with Ophelia. The precise nature of his original feeling for Ophelia is a little obscure. We may assume that at least in part it was composed of a normal love for a prospective bride, though the extravagance of the language used (the passionate need for absolute certainty, etc.)

2. Here, as throughout this essay, I closely follow Freud's interpretation given in the footnote previously referred to. He there points out the inadequacy of the earlier explanations, deals with Hamlet's feelings toward his mother, father, and uncle, and mentions two other matters that will presently be discussed, the significance of Hamlet's reaction against Ophelia and of the probability that the play was written immediately after the death of Shakespeare's own father.

suggests a somewhat morbid frame of mind. There are indications
that even here the influence of the old attraction for the mother is
still exerting itself.

Although some writers, following Goethe,[3] see in Ophelia many
traits of resemblance to the Queen, surely more striking are the
traits contrasting with those of the Queen. Whatever truth there
may be in the many German conceptions of Ophelia as a sensual
wanton[4]—misconceptions that have been confuted by Loening[5]
and others—still the very fact that it needed what Goethe happily
called the "innocence of insanity" to reveal the presence of any
such libidinous thoughts demonstrates in itself the modesty and
chasteness of her habitual demeanour. Her naive piety, her obedi-
ent resignation and her unreflecting simplicity sharply contrast
with the Queen's character, and seem to indicate that Hamlet by
a characteristic reaction towards the opposite extreme had unknow-
ingly been impelled to choose a woman who should least remind
him of his mother. A case might even be made out for the view
that part of his courtship originated not so much in direct attraction for Ophelia as in an unconscious desire to play her off against
his mother, just as a disappointed and piqued lover so often has
resort to the arms of a more willing rival. It would be hard otherwise to understand the readiness with which he later throws himself into this part. When, for instance, in the play scene he replies
to his mother's request to sit by her with the words "No, good
mother, here's metal more attractive" [3.2.101–02] and proceeds to
lie at Ophelia's feet, we seem to have a direct indication of this
attitude; and his coarse familiarity and bandying of ambiguous
jests with the woman he has recently so ruthlessly jilted are hardly
intelligible unless we bear in mind that they were carried out
under the heedful gaze of the Queen. It is as though his unconscious were trying to convey to her the following thought: "You
give yourself to other men whom you prefer to me. Let me assure
you that I can dispense with your favours and even prefer those of
a woman whom I no longer love." His extraordinary outburst of
bawdiness on this occasion, so unexpected in a man of obviously
fine feeling, points unequivocally to the sexual nature of the underlying turmoil.

3. Goethe, *Wilhelm Meister*, IV, 14. "Her whole being hovers in ripe, sweet voluptuous-
   ness." "Her fancy is moved, her quiet modesty breathes loving desire, and should the
   gentle Goddess Opportunity shake the tree the fruit would at once fall."
4. For instance, Storffrich, *Psychologische Aufschlüsse über Shakespeares Hamlet*, 1859,
   S. 131; Dietrich, Hamlet, *Der Konstabel der Vorsehung, Shakespeare-Studie*, 1883,
   S. 129; Tieck, *Dramatargische Blätter*, II, S. 85, etc.
5. Loening, *Die Hamlet-Tragödie Shakespeares*, 1893, Cap. XIII. "'Charakter' und Liebe
   Ophelias."

Now comes the father's death and the mother's second marriage. The association of the idea of sexuality with his mother, buried since infancy, can no longer be concealed from his consciousness. As Bradley[6] well says: "Her son was forced to see in her action not only an astounding shallowness of feeling, but an eruption of coarse sensuality, 'rank and gross,' speeding post-haste to its horrible delight." Feelings which once, in the infancy of long ago, were pleasurable desires can now, because of his repressions, only fill him with repulsion. The long "repressed" desire to take his father's place in his mother's affection is stimulated to unconscious activity by the sight of someone usurping this place exactly as he himself had once longed to do. More, this someone was a member of the same family, so that the actual usurpation further resembled the imaginary one in being incestuous. Without his being in the least aware of it these ancient desires are ringing in his mind, are once more struggling to find conscious expression, and need such an expenditure of energy again to "repress" them that he is reduced to the deplorable mental state he himself so vividly depicts.

There follows the Ghost's announcement that the father's death was a willed one, was due to murder. Hamlet, having at the moment his mind filled with natural indignation at the news, answers normally enough with the cry:

> Haste me to know 't, that I, with wings as swift
> As meditation or the thoughts of love,
> May sweep to my revenge. [1.5.29–31]

The momentous words follow revealing who was the guilty person, namely a relative who had committed the deed at the bidding of lust.[7] Hamlet's second guilty wish had thus also been realised by his uncle, namely to procure the fulfilment of the first—the possession of the mother—by a personal deed, in fact by murder of the father. The two recent events, the father's death and the mother's second marriage, seemed to the world to have no inner causal relation to each other, but they represented ideas which in Hamlet's unconscious fantasy had for many years been closely associated. These ideas now in a moment forced their way to conscious recognition in spite of all "repressing forces," and found immediate expression in his almost reflex cry: "O my prophetic soul! My uncle?" The frightful truth his unconscious had already intuitively divined his consciousness had now to assimilate, as best it could. For the rest of the interview Hamlet is stunned by the effect of the internal conflict

---

6. Bradley, [*Shakespearean Tragedy*, 2nd ed., 1905,] p. 118.
7. It is not maintained that this was by any means Claudius' whole motive, but it was evidently a powerful one and the one that most impressed Hamlet.

thus re-awakened, which from now on never ceases, and into the essential nature of which he never penetrates.

One of the first manifestations of the awakening of the old conflict in Hamlet's mind is his reaction against Ophelia. This is doubly conditioned, by the two opposing attitudes in his own mind. In the first place, there is a complex reaction in regard to his mother. As was explained above, the being forced to connect the thought of his mother with sensuality leads to an intense sexual revulsion, one that is only temporarily broken down by the coarse outburst discussed above. Combined with this is a fierce jealousy, unconscious because of its forbidden origin, at the sight of her giving herself to another man, a man whom he had no reason whatever either to love or to respect. Consciously this is allowed to express itself, for instance after the prayer scene, only in the form of extreme resentment and bitter reproaches against her. His resentment against women is still further inflamed by the hypocritical prudishness with which Ophelia follows her father and brother in seeing evil in his natural affection, an attitude which poisons his love in exactly the same way that the love of his childhood, like that of all children, must have been poisoned. He can forgive a woman neither her rejection of his sexual advances nor, still less, her alliance with another man. Most intolerable of all to him, as Bradley well remarks, is the sight of sensuality in a quarter from which he had trained himself ever since infancy rigorously to exclude it. The total reaction culminates in the bitter misogyny of his outburst against Ophelia, who is devastated at having to bear a reaction so wholly out of proportion to her own offence and has no idea that in reviling her Hamlet is really expressing his bitter resentment against his mother.[8] "I have heard of your paintings too, well enough; God has given you one face, and you make yourselves another; you jig, you amble, and you lisp, and nickname God's creatures, and make your wantonness your ignorance. Go to, I'll no more on't; it hath made me mad." [3.1.137–40] On only one occasion does he for a moment escape from the sordid implication with which his love has been impregnated and achieve a healthier attitude toward Ophelia, namely at the open grave when in remorse he breaks out at Laertes for presuming to pretend that his feeling for her could ever equal that of her lover.

---

8. His similar tone and advice to the two women show plainly how closely they are identified in his mind. Cp. "Get thee to a nunnery: why wouldst thou be a breeder of sinners" [3.1.122–23] with "Refrain tonight; And that shall lend a kind of easiness To the next abstinence" [3.4.168–70]. The identification is further demonstrated in the course of the play by Hamlet's killing the men who stand between him and these women (Claudius and Polonius).

The intensity of Hamlet's repulsion against woman in general, and Ophelia in particular, is a measure of the powerful "repression" to which his sexual feelings are being subjected. The outlet for those feelings in the direction of his mother has always been firmly dammed, and now that the narrower channel in Ophelia's direction has also been closed the increase in the original direction consequent on the awakening of early memories tasks all his energy to maintain the "repression." His pent up feelings find a partial vent in other directions. The petulant irascibility and explosive outbursts called forth by his vexation at the hands of Guildenstern and Rosencrantz, and especially of Polonius, are evidently to be interpreted in this way, as also is in part the burning nature of his reproaches to his mother. Indeed towards the end of his interview with his mother the thought of her misconduct expresses itself in that almost physical disgust which is so characteristic a manifestation of intensely "repressed" sexual feeling.

> Let the bloat king tempt you again to bed;
> Pinch wanton on your cheek; call you his mouse;
> And let him, for a pair of reechy kisses,
> Or paddling in your neck with his damn'd fingers,
> Make you to ravel all this matter out . . . [3.4.185–89]

Hamlet's attitude towards Polonius is highly instructive. Here the absence of family tie and of other similar influences enables him to indulge to a relatively unrestrained extent his hostility towards the prating and sententious dotard. The analogy he effects between Polonius and Jephthah[9] is in this connection especially pointed. It is here that we see his fundamental attitude towards moralising elders who use their power to thwart the happiness of the young, and not in the over-drawn and melodramatic portrait in which he delineates his father: "A combination and a form indeed, where every god did seem to set his seal to give the world assurance of a man." [3.4.61–63]

It will be seen from the foregoing that Hamlet's attitude towards his uncle-father is far more complex than is generally supposed. He of course detests him, but it is the jealous detestation of one evildoer towards his successful fellow. Much as he hates him, he can never denounce him with the ardent indignation that boils straight from his blood when he reproaches his mother, for the more vigorously he denounces his uncle the more powerfully does he stimulate to activity his own unconscious and "repressed" complexes. He is therefore in a dilemma between on the one hand allowing his natural

9. What Shakespeare thought of Jephthah's behaviour towards his daughter may be gathered from a reference in *Henry VI, Part III*, Act V, Sc. 1. See also on this subject Wordsworth, *On Shakespeare's Knowledge and Use of the Bible*, 1864, p. 67.

detestation of his uncle to have free play, a consummation which would stir still further his own horrible wishes, and on the other hand ignoring the imperative call for the vengeance that his obvious duty demands. His own evil prevents him from completely denouncing his uncle's, and in continuing to "repress" the former he must strive to ignore, to condone, and if possible even to forget the latter; *his moral fate is bound up with his uncle's for good or ill.* In reality his uncle incorporates the deepest and most buried part of his own personality, so that he cannot kill him without also killing himself. This solution, one closely akin to what Freud[1] has shown to be the motive of suicide in melancholia, is actually the one that Hamlet finally adopts. The course of alternate action and inaction that he embarks on, and the provocations he gives to his suspicious uncle, can lead to no other end than to his own ruin and, incidentally, to that of his uncle. Only when he has made the final sacrifice and brought himself to the door of death is he free to fulfil his duty, to avenge his father, and to slay his other self—his uncle.

There is a second reason why the call of duty to kill his step-father cannot be obeyed, and that is because it links itself with the unconscious call of his nature to kill his mother's husband, whether this is the first or the second; the absolute "repression" of the former impulse involves the inner prohibition of the latter also. It is no chance that Hamlet says of himself that he is prompted to his revenge "by heaven and hell."

In this discussion of the motives that move or restrain Hamlet we have purposely depreciated the subsidiary ones, which also play a part, so as to bring out in greater relief the deeper and effective ones that are of preponderating importance. These, as we have seen, spring from sources of which he is quite unaware, and we might summarise the internal conflict of which he is the victim as consisting in a struggle of the "repressed" mental processes to become conscious. The call of duty, which automatically arouses to activity these unconscious processes, conflicts with the necessity of "repressing" them still more strongly; for the more urgent is the need for external action the greater is the effort demanded of the "repressing" forces. Action is paralysed at its very inception, and there is thus produced the picture of apparently causeless inhibition which is so inexplicable both to Hamlet[2] and to readers of the play. This

---

1. Freud, "Trauer und Melancholie," *Vierte Sammlung kleiner Schriften*, 1918, Kap. XX.
2. The situation is perfectly depicted by Hamlet in his cry: "I do not know / Why yet I live to say 'This thing's to do,'/ Sith I have cause, and will, and strength, and means, / To do't" [4.4.44–47]. With greater insight he could have replaced the word "will" by "pious wish," which as Loening (op. cit., S. 246) points out, it obviously means. Curiously enough, Rolfe (Introduction to Werder, *The Heart of Hamlet's Mystery*, trans. E. Wilder, 1907, p. 23) quotes this very passage in support of Werder's hypothesis that Hamlet was inhibited by the thought of the external difficulties of the situation, which shows the straits the supporters of this untenable hypothesis are driven to.

paralysis arises, however, not from physical or moral cowardice, but from that intellectual cowardice, that reluctance to dare the exploration of his inner soul, which Hamlet shares with the rest of the human race. "Thus conscience does make cowards of us all."

HARRY LEVIN

[Irony in *Hamlet*] (1959)†

Our third trope, *ironia*, is more than a figure of speech or even of thought; it may be a point of view, a view of life, and—as such—a resolvent for contrarieties. Its most clear-cut form, designated in Puttenham's *Arte of English Poesie* as "the drye mock," is a statement which means the contrary of what it purports to say. Caesar was ambitious; Brutus was honorable; yet Antony contrives, by his mocking inflection, to carry the opposite impression in both regards. Dubious statements could be reversed by simply adding the Elizabethan interjection *quotha*. Hamlet makes the controversion explicit, when his mother asks him, "What shall I do?" [3.4.183]. He has just told her, directly, "go not to my uncle's bed." Now he elaborates, "Not this, by no means, that I bid you do." In other words, what follows is to be taken ironically: "Let the bloat King tempt you again to bed . . ." And Hamlet dwells, with ambivalent detail, on the endearments he would have her avoid. Given the hypocrisy of the court, where one may not say what one means, honesty must either hold its tongue or express itself through indirection. When Polonius begs to take his leave, Hamlet's tone of politeness thinly disguises his eagerness to confer the favor begged: "You cannot, sir, take from me anything that I will more willingly part withal—" Whereupon his dry mock deepens into a thrice-uttered heartcry: "except my life, except my life, except my life" [2.2.211–12]. To the initial queries of Claudius and Gertrude, his hedging answers are verbal ironies. Gertrude's naïve reaction to the Play-Queen—"The lady doth protest too much, methinks"—unconsciously lays bare her own standards of conduct. Hamlet's double-edged comment, "O, but she'll keep her word," is ostensibly another bit of polite conversation [3.2.217–18]. Actually, he is distorting the play-within-the-play in order to drive home an invidious contrast. The Play-Queen

† Harry Levin, *The Question of Hamlet*, paper (New York: Oxford University Press, 1959), 80–92, 103–106. After exploring *interrogation* and *doubt*, Harry Levin (1912–1994), a founder of comparative literature studies, here explores *irony* in the language, action, and characters of *Hamlet*. Reprinted by permission of Oxford University Press.

will have no chance to keep her word; the Queen of Denmark had a chance and failed.

As for the King, his usual mode is merely hypocritical; but, under the goading of Hamlet, he too waxes ironic. When he announces the excursion to England, and Hamlet assents with "Good," Claudius says, "So is it, if thou knew'st our purposes" [4.3.47–48]. He is having his grim little joke, and assuming Hamlet is unaware that what might be good for Claudius would not be good for himself. But the joke is on Claudius; for he does not know that Hamlet knows his purposes, that he himself is rather a step behind than a step ahead of his opponent. Hamlet's retort is enigmatic, if not ironic, with its cryptic allusion to the Ghost: "I see a cherub that sees them." The irony now lies not in the statement but in the situation, which will turn out to be the contrary of what Claudius designs. Hamlet has already ventured a prediction, in his farewell to his mother. There, in hinting at the treachery of Rosencrantz and Guildenstern, whom he will trust as would "adders fang'd," he has defined the process of dramatic irony:

> For 'tis the sport to have the engineer
> Hoist with his own petar . . . [3.4.206, 209–10]

It is always exciting when craft meets equal craftiness in a battle of wits. But there is peculiar satisfaction in watching, when vaunted cleverness overreaches itself. The comic formula of the cheater cheated, *Wily Beguiled*, is transmuted into the imagery of siege and explosion, as Hamlet conspires with himself to blow his enemies at the moon. The actual conspiracy, when it happens, will be literary rather than military; it will consist of forging a royal mandate, so that Rosencrantz and Guildenstern will be executed in Hamlet's place; and this will be retrospectively disclosed by Hamlet to Horatio, with rhetorical flourishes parodying the style of Claudius. Thus the episode has been somewhat glossed over, particularly the incidental deaths of the schoolfellows; but it has been a conspicuous feature of the primitive legend; and its elements, widely diffused in folklore, persist through the *motif* of a lucky youth with an ill-fated letter. Hamlet's prototype is the unsuspecting hero, sent on a journey, bearing his own death-warrant; jolted into some realization of the hazards confronting him, he finally turns adversity into advantage.

Another element in the archaic tale has proved susceptible of endless refinement. This was the spectacle of a cunning hero forced to wear a mask of stupidity, which originally lent Hamlet his oafish name. In dissembling, in counterfeiting madness, in playing his antic part, he exemplifies the humanistic tradition of the wise fool. In his wayward fashion, he pursues the wisdom of Socrates, which characteristically masqueraded as ignorance. Hamlet's behavior has been

characterized by a student of Shakespeare's wit and humor, John
Weiss, as "a sustained gesture of irony." It is that gesture which
enables the questioner to reject seeming for being, which helps the
doubter to distinguish between appearance and reality. In the dual
role of an ironist, Hamlet can remain his tragic self while presenting a quasi-comic front. The dissembler of Aristophanic comedy, the
eiron, had shrewdly exposed the impostor or *alazon*. Neo-classicists
like Voltaire were historically warranted in associating the ironic
with the comic and deeming it inappropriate for tragedy. The concept was broadly extended by Bishop Thirwall's essay "On the Irony
of Sophocles." If the Greek tragedians had been ironists, it was not
because they mocked at their fellow men, but because they concerned themselves with the mockery of fate. Oedipus is the engineer of his own downfall; and his blinding is a requital for taunting
the blind Tiresias, as well as an expiation of his trespasses. Human
agency seems to confound itself through the workings of some cosmic design. So it seems to the Play-King:

> Our wills and fates do so contrary run
> That our devices still are overthrown . . . [3.2.198–99]

That overthrow is made ironic by the perception of counter-devices,
by the aptness with which fates are matched against wills. The outcome must belie the expectation, the disappointment must become
concrete, through some logical connection or personal association.
This correspondence between device and counter-device takes its
most obvious form in the equivocal oracle. The riddling prophecies
that cajole and betray Macbeth are the merest plays upon words,
which are carried out by charades on the part of Birnam Wood and
Macduff. In *King Lear* the irony is classical when the gods are said
to have justly taken Cornwall's life for Gloucester's sight; it is more
problematic when Gloucester accuses them of treating mortals as
wanton boys treat flies. Poetic justice, which prevails in *Macbeth*,
miscarries in *King Lear*, where the ways of providence are as unfathomable as in *Hamlet*.

With *Hamlet*, as we have seen, we are involved in two sets of complementary problems. One set is speculative: why? wherefore? who is
the ghost? and what is the ultimate mystery that it prefigures? The
other is practical: what shall we do? how should Hamlet bear himself
amid these unexampled difficulties? and how should he accomplish
his unsought vocation, revenge? Shakespearean tragedy is deeply
concerned with the individual as he faces opportunity, responsibility,
and moral choice. It is equally preoccupied with the pattern of events,
and whether this is determined by casual accident, fatal necessity, or
divine intervention. Given the motive, one must await one's cue. The
interplay between these preoccupations is the source of innumerable

ironies, both conscious and unconscious, some of them attached
to the hero's viewpoint, others detached in a reminiscent overview.
"Hamlet has no plan, but *Hamlet* has," as Goethe observed, with a
fellow-dramatist's understanding. The play has a plot; and, so, in
another sense, has the Prince; but he cannot foresee the fulfilment
of his intentions; he can only test them against hugger-mugger conditions. Yet, as producer of "The Murder of Gonzago," he can take
charge of a miniature drama which exerts an effect on the drama at
large; he can play god and look down on his creation, in the self-
conscious mood of romantic irony. Whereas in *Hamlet* itself, he is no
more than a leading actor, whose body will be placed "on a stage"—on
a funeral bier which may likewise be viewed as a theatrical platform—
among the other corpses at the end. It will then become Horatio's
function to play the commentator, and to report upon the ironic
upshot of the whole story: "purposes mistook / Fall'n on th'inventors'
heads" [5.2.358–59].

Hamlet points the analogy himself when he addresses the surviving onlookers as "audience to this act" [308]. The verb "to act" is
synonymous with "to do," in the patient explanation of the Gravedigger, but also with the ambiguous "to perform." "The name of
action" has further branches for Hamlet; it often takes on this theatrical inflection, as when he declares that the customs of mourning are "actions that a man might play" [1.2.84]. Conversely, he is
pleading for sincerity, when he tells the Players: "Suit the action to
the word, the word to the action" [3.2.16–17]. The noun "act" conveys a sexual innuendo, when it is bandied back and forth between
Hamlet and Gertrude in the Closet Scene. Some of these ambigui-
ties might be clarified in the light of God's law, if not of man's; for
above us "the action lies / In his true nature," as Claudius confesses
to himself [3.3.61–62]. Here below, deeds may be obfuscated by
words, as they have been in his own case; or else they may be
retarded by thoughts, as they are in Hamlet's.

> I do not know
> Why yet I live to say "This thing's to do,"
> Sith I have cause, and will, and strength, and means
> To do't. [4.4.44–47]

Again and again he reproaches himself in this tone; but self-reproach
is a sign of conscientiousness rather than cowardice. The Ghost
reappears, at an awkward moment, to whet Hamlet's "almost blunted
purpose"; but ghosts, after all, are notorious for nagging, especially
on the Elizabethan stage [3.4.112]. It takes no less than five of them
to rouse Chapman's Senecal hero to *The Revenge of Bussy D'Ambois*;
and yet his bravery is widely and loudly attested. Because we are
privileged to overhear Hamlet's moments of self-questioning, or to

glimpse his incertitude before psychic phenomena, we should not make the mistake of considering him a weak or passive figure. That his native disposition is active and resolute, though it has been temporarily sicklied over with the pale cast of melancholy—such an impression is fully confirmed by objective testimony from the other characters. "*Hamlet* is not a drama of weakness," its Russian translator, Boris Pasternak, has clairvoyantly noted, "but of duty and self-denial."

The critical sentimentalization of Hamlet's personality has leaned heavily on the expression, *Gedankenschauspiel*, wrenched from its context in A. W. Schlegel's lectures and mistranslated as "tragedy of thought." This has encouraged the obscurantist conclusion that thought is Hamlet's tragedy; Hamlet is the man who thinks too much, ineffectual because he is intellectual; his nemesis is a failure of nerve, a nervous prostration. Schlegel wanted merely to underline the well-taken point that *Hamlet* was, above all, a drama of ideas, a dramatization of man's intellectual curiosity. By the canons of the humanists, the highest virtue was knowledge put into action. But how to know what to do? That was the question; there was the rub. Hamlet's plight is magnified by the tension between the stream of his highly skeptical consciousness and the undercurrents of murky superstition and swirling paganism. Hence he stands as the very archetype of character at odds with destiny, of the incompatibility between will and fate. He is a virtual prisoner, figuratively straining at gyves and fetters, yet capable of breaking away from "the mutines in the bilboes" [5.2.6]. When he complains, "I lack advancement," Rosencrantz assumes that he is anxious for promotion; more likely, he is impatient to get on with his revenge [3.2.317]. "The time is out of joint," he sighs, as romantics and sentimentalists have sighed after him. But, though he curses the circumstance of his birth, he accepts his mission: "O cursed spite / That ever I was born to set it right" [1.5.195–96]. A similar tag, concluding the next act, marks his advance toward a plan: "The play's the thing / Wherein I'll catch the conscience of the King" [2.2.525–26]. Hamlet's progress through the acts is marked by a sequence of such broken couplets, which seem to evoke an answering rhythm in the diction of Claudius: "O come away! / My soul is full of discord and dismay!" [4.1.44–45]. While Claudius seems to falter, Hamlet's threats become firmer, until he terminates his last soliloquy with a decision which moves from thought to action: "from this time forth / My thoughts be bloody or nothing worth!" [4.4.67–68].

Hamlet begins with a scholar's request to resume his studies at the university. He ends by being given a soldier's funeral. He is drawn into a psychological conflict: "Sir, in my heart there was a kind of fighting . . ." [5.2.4]. This *agon* gradually leads to physical

struggles, accompanied by vivid metaphors of reconnoitering spies
and deploying battalions. His first maneuver is a strategic retreat,
pursued by his antagonist's followers, who do not succeed in flushing him out. Then, as occasion will have it, he presses the Players
into his service, and succeeds in outmaneuvering Claudius. Our
attention shifts to the King with his first aside, which reveals to us
that he has a conscience to be caught: "O heavy burthen!" [3.1.55].
Without this confession, we should not be certain of his guilt, and
the play-within-the-play would lack its dimension of irony. What
interests us, along with Hamlet and Horatio, is not the melodrama
on the court stage but the psychodrama in Claudius' mind. "This
play is the image of a murther done in Vienna"—not at Elsinore
[3.2.223–24]. The name of the duke's wife is Baptista, not Gertrude. No one would remember the late King, anyway; like the
hobbyhorse, he is forgotten. Any resemblances to real people or
local situations are—or are they?—purely coincidental. "The players cannot keep counsel," says Hamlet, acting as prologue to the
prologue, "they'll tell all" [129–30]. They will lodge the accusation
that he has kept to himself, and we shall see if Claudius can keep
counsel. Though their rhymes are stiff and didactic, they echo
Hamlet's obsessions. One of his bitterest ironies was to attribute the
haste of Gertrude's remarriage to palace economy, since it permit-
ted the leftovers from the wake to be served at the wedding. "Thrift,
thrift, Horatio!" [1.2.180]. This becomes a matter of principle in the
Play-Queen's protestations: "The instances that second marriage
move / Are base respects of thrift, but not of love" [3.2.169–70].

To the Players Hamlet has expressed his distaste for "inexplicable
dumb shows" [3.2.11]. The pantomime that precedes and anticipates
"The Murder of Gonzago" is all too explicable; since we are not to see
the whole of the play, it shows us what we shall miss. Yet Hamlet's
presentation of something like his father's murder has been too
emphatically straightforward for some of Shakespeare's critics, notably Dover Wilson, who has argued that the King must somehow have
missed the dumb show in order to be able to sit through the ensuing
production as long as he does. Mr. Wilson's hyper-ingenious interpretation seems to rest on the simple-minded postulate that, if Claudius
witnessed the miming of his misdeed, he would react at once with
reflexive alacrity. But, though he is guilty, Claudius is a hardened
character, skilled at hiding his feelings and nearly able to brazen out
Hamlet's test. Therein, to be precise, the scene derives its dramatic
suspense: a murderer is being put through the third degree, and we
are waiting and watching for signs of the psychological impact. These
are not altogether wanting; as long as the actors are silent, so is
Claudius; but when deeds are articulated by words, he voices his
uneasiness with the suspicion that the play may contain offensive

material; and it is under the cumulative ordeal that he breaks down, calls for lights, and stops the performance. The crucial business is the poisoning, together with the incantation of the poisoner, Lucia- nus. Now Lucianus is not Gonzago's brother; as Hamlet takes pains to point out, he is "nephew to the King" [229]. It follows, by implica- tion, that what we have witnessed was not so much a re-enactment of King Hamlet's death as it was a preview of young Hamlet's revenge. The conscience of Claudius is trapped by fear for his life, as well as by remorse for his offence.

If the cap fits, Hamlet has taunted Claudius, put it on. "Let the gall'd jade winch; our withers are unwrung" [227–28]. At the top of his bent, amid the abrupt confusion that closes the Play Scene, he versifies that sentiment: "Why, let the stricken deer go weep, / The hart ungalled play . . ." The huntsman has hit his mark, and the beast has been caught napping. "For some must watch, while some must sleep . . . [254–57]. The symbolic torches, hastily sum- moned, have cast their flickering light into dark corners. It is an exorcism, not of the honest ghost, but of the courtly dishonesty that obscures more sinister creatures, now "frighted with false fire" [F 3.2.257]. The comedy of masks is over, at all events; Hamlet has unmasked Claudius, revealing the inward villain behind the exte- rior smile. For the first time, Hamlet is sure of his object and free to act. His failure to do so, in the Prayer Scene, is a baffling mixture of coincidence and compunction, where fate tempts and will is puz- zled. Here, it may seem in retrospect, Hamlet found the right moment and took the wrong turn. But would it have been better to plunge his rapier into the back of that proud man upon his knees at the *prie-dieu*? Claudius would live to say, "No place indeed should mur- ther sanctuarize" [4.7.126]. Ironically, he would not realize that his own life had been spared through this momentary impulse of piety. Still more ironically, as he realizes, he has only been going through pious motions. He has desperately tried to pray, but he is too unre- generate a hypocrite: "Words without thoughts never to heaven go" [3.3.98]. Meanwhile, his soliloquy has been crossed, so to speak, by Hamlet's; and Hamlet has decided to put up his sword, on the erro- neous assumption that Claudius is purging his soul. Since Claudius does not succeed in repenting, Hamlet is retroactively deprived of his single reason for delay.

These cross-purposes were summed up in the word "purgation," when Rosencrantz and Guildenstern announced the King's indispo- sition after the play [3.2.285–86]. That purge has two double mean- ings, one physical and the other spiritual: blood-letting in a medical and in a homicidal sense, and purification through penance or through purgatory. Having brought to a stalemate the only scene in which he is alone with his archenemy, Hamlet plunges on to his mother's closet, where he makes the mistake of not hesitating. Slashing through the arras, he kills whoever is lurking there, presumably the King. It turns out to be Polonius, master of indirections, whose machination has reaped its reward by springing a final trap on himself. Consequently, Hamlet must withdraw for an interval, which is concentrated upon the two victims of the underplot: Laertes, forced to become his father's revenger; Ophelia, driven to madness and to death by water. Whether or not to accept the verdict of suicide is a doubtful question which we may leave to the Gravediggers. It is significant that Polonius, in rendering his mistaken diagnosis of Hamlet, blundered into a correct prognosis for his daughter. Hamlet's malady, he averred, was "the very ecstasy of love," to be feared because its violence "foredoes itself" [2.1.100–01]. The verb is prognostic; for Hamlet, as an unknown and unknowing spectator, will notice that the funeral rites are "maimed" because the corpse "did with desp'rate hand / Foredo its own life" [5.1.198–99]. It is he who entertains the idea of self-slaughter; but it is the defenseless Ophelia whom the sea of troubles overwhelms. It is she who pronounces him insane, his noble mind overthrown, "Like sweet bells jangled, out of tune and harsh" [3.1.157]. But it is she who truly loses her mind, and drowns while singing "snatches of old tunes" [4.7.176].

Imagery functions as a guide to Shakespeare's irony. Reason, like the music of the spheres, is a harmonious ideal; mental breakdown, transposed into sound, should be discordant; yet Ophelia, with her off-key ballads, turns "affliction" into "prettiness," discord into harmony [4.5.181–82]. Gertrude, lyrically recounting Ophelia's "muddy death," emphasizes her "melodious lay" [4.7.181–82]. Gertrude's elegy also draws on that floral symbolism which Ophelia poignantly invoked on her round of farewells, and which has wreathed her in a special fragrance from her first scene to her burial. Laertes, warning her that Hamlet's affection may be "sweet" but "not lasting," has compared it to "A violet in the youth of primy nature" [1.3.7–8]. To his forbidding "No more," she responds with a gentle tremor: "No more but so?" Whereupon he repeats his rigid denial: "Think it no more." In the Graveyard Scene, the same language and meter re-echo when Laertes asks, "Must there no more be done?" And the Priest replies with the sepulchral refrain, "No more be done" [5.1.213]. Whereupon Laertes cries, "Lay her i' th' earth; / And from her fair and unpolluted flesh / May violets spring! [216–18]. Like the adverb "nevermore," so indelibly associated with the death of a beautiful young woman by Edgar Allan Poe, the hopeless phrase "no more" runs through the play. It figures meaningfully in Hamlet's soliloquies: "To die—to sleep— / No more . . ." "A beast, no more [3.1.61–2; 4.4.36]." It is repeated three times by the Queen in her effort to stave off Hamlet's reprimand [3.4.89, 95, 102]. Gertrude, again, takes up the theme of flowers in strewing Ophelia's grave—not with "dust to dust" but with "Sweets to the sweet!" [5.1.221]. The harsh priest believes that Ophelia should have stones instead of her "virgin crants" or maiden garland; she should have been buried in unhallowed ground, without any ceremony whatever. She has been most distressed by the unceremonious interment accorded to her ceremonious father. She has even modified one of her songs to make it clear that flowers were omitted; since that day, the violets have all withered [4.5.39, 177–78]. In lamenting Hamlet's distraction, she evoked another flower, a Tudor emblem, "Th' expectancy and rose of the fair state" [3.1.151]. When her brother first beholds her in her distraught condition, he exclaims, "O rose of May!" [4.5.157].

                              *   *   *

Self-mastery may alternatively demand an exertion of will or a submission to fate. Circumstances are beyond our control, much more often than not; our best endeavor is to control ourselves, if we can. "Lord, we know what we are," Ophelia moans prophetically, "but we know not what we may be" [4.5.43]. Hamlet, the scholar-prince, dies suddenly like a soldier-king on a battlefield, eulogized by the belligerent Fortinbras, and borne off the stage to a higher stage for a military funeral. This is the most striking of many contrasts, when we are invited to measure him beside his contemporary, Don Quixote, who retires in defeat to his study and to a lucid and peaceful deathbed. Until that belated hour of self-recognition, he has never doubted that he was born to set things right. Nor could he be accused of lacking a plan; whenever it miscarried, as it has invariably done, he has offered some sort of contingent excuse. But his rout and retirement have thoroughly demonstrated the impracticality of his project for combining the two professions of arms and letters. Thought, instead of guiding retarded action, has overleaped itself. The irony of Cervantes is based on the rhetorical device of *antiphrasis*—or, more concretely, on the mock-heroic disparity between the style and the subject. What happens to the hero is a joke to everyone except himself. What happens in *Hamlet* is a secret discernible to the hero alone. He knows what the others do not; the others know what Don Quixote does not. Hamlet, as *eiron*, exposes the high and mighty pretensions of the *alazon*, Claudius; and when the pretender falls, the whole superstructure of courtly appearances collapses with him. But Shakespeare, as the master ironist, is not content to undermine superficial ideals; his profounder concern is with the recognition of underlying realities.

Circumstantial irony, at its simplest, may be exemplified by Lucian's Charon, who laughs because he has seen a falling tile kill a man who has just accepted an invitation to dinner. The situation

became more comprehensive, but scarcely more complex, when the
Lisbon earthquake erupted to shatter Voltaire's optimistic faith in
a rational cosmos, where everything was teleologically ordained for
human convenience and comfort. Such encounters with sheer con-
tingency may be as inevitable as they are unpredictable; and tragedy
is at least a forewarning against them, a warning lest our blessings
be turned into curses. Moreover, it is an attempt to indicate limits
which we may overstep at our peril, to locate the point where our
wills converge with our fates, to discern the odds that confront and
confound our best-laid plans. Vengeance is its most habitual theme
because the revenger is called upon to take into his own hands what
might better be left to providence, however we define it; and if the
revenge gets out of hand and goes amiss, as it is almost bound to do,
if the mistaken purposes fall upon their inventors' heads, then that
reversal is an ironic commentary upon the ways of human destiny.
Since we cannot altogether arrange our lives, we are constantly seeking some principle of arrangement in the universe, whether it be the
finger of deity or the determination of chance. Thwarted, we may
blame fickle fortune with Seneca, or malicious fate with Thomas
Hardy, or original sin with Kierkegaard. Otherwise, our quest for
retribution, with Dante, must be continued in another world. Lesser
dramatists are easily tempted to intervene in the little worlds they
have created, making sure that the good have their rewards when the
evil have their punishments; but insofar as they improve upon life,
they weaken their dramaturgy With Shakespeare the dramatic resolution conveys us, beyond the man-made sphere of poetic justice,
toward the ever-receding horizons of cosmic irony.

   This is peculiarly the case with Hamlet, for the same reasons
that it excites such intensive empathy from actors and readers, critics and writers alike. There may be other Shakespearean characters who are just as memorable, and other plots which are no less
impressive; but nowhere else has the outlook of the individual in a
dilemma been so profoundly realized; and a dilemma, by definition,
is an all but unresolvable choice between evils. Rather than with
calculation or casuistry, it should be met with the virtue of readiness; sooner or later it will have to be grasped by one or the other of
its horns, These, in their broadest terms, have been—for Hamlet,
as we interpret him—the problem of what to believe and the problem
of how to act. Hamlet is unwittingly compelled to act as if life were
a duel, with unbated swords and against a series of furtive assail-
ants. He is unwillingly led to believe that death comes as a cup, filled
with poisonous wine and containing a flawless pearl. His doom is
generalized in Fulke Greville's chorus: "Oh, wearisome condition of
humanity, / Born under one law, to another bound." Irony cannot
solve the incalculable contradictions between the personal life and

the nature of things. Yet it can teach us to live with them; and that is no mean achievement; for Hamlet's knowledge was not idle reflection, according to Nietzsche. It was an insight which hindered action by stripping the veil of illusion from the terrible truth, the terror or the absurdity of existence. This would be intolerable, were it not for the transformations of art, which asserts man's conquest over his fears, and which thereby allays his vexation of spirit. Thus Hamlet's limited victory commences with the play-within-the-play, a working-model of the play itself, which repeats the lesson in mastery on a larger scale within our minds. From its very commencement, after the stroke of midnight, we are brought face to face with the supernatural. Volleys of gunfire augment and accelerate the sound effects until, at the conclusion of the dead-march, "*a peal of ordnance*" signalizes a battle lost and won.

ELAINE SHOWALTER

Representing Ophelia: Women, Madness, and the Responsibilities of Feminist Criticism (1985)†

"As a sort of a come-on, I announced that I would speak today about that piece of bait named Ophelia, and I'll be as good as my word." These are the words which begin the psychoanalytic seminar on *Hamlet* presented in Paris in 1959 by Jacques Lacan. But despite his promising come-on, Lacan was *not* as good as his word. He goes on for some 41 pages to speak about Hamlet, and when he does mention Ophelia, she is merely what Lacan calls "the object Ophelia"—that is, the object of Hamlet's male desire. The etymology of Ophelia, Lacan asserts, is "O-phallus," and her role in the drama can only be to function as the exteriorized figuration of what Lacan predictably and, in view of his own early work with psychotic women, disappointingly suggests is the phallus as transcendental signifier.[1] To play such a part obviously makes Ophelia "essential,"

---

† Elaine Showalter, "Representing Ophelia: Women, Madness, and the Responsibilities of Feminist Criticism," in *Shakespeare and the Question of Theory*, ed. Patricia Parker and Geoffrey Hartman (London: Methuen, 1985), 77–94. In this seminal essay, Showalter examines theatrical, critical, and artistic representations of Ophelia in their specific cultural and historical contexts.Reprinted by permission of Methuen.

1. Jacques Lacan, "Desire and the interpretation of desire in *Hamlet*," in *Literature and Psychoanalysis: The Question of Reading, Otherwise*, ed. Shoshana Felman (Baltimore, 1982), 11, 20, 23. Lacan is also wrong about the etymology of Ophelia, which probably derives from the Greek for "help" or "succour." Charlotte M. Yonge suggested a derivation from "ophis," "serpent." See her *History of Christian Names* (1884, republished Chicago, 1966), 346–47. I am indebted to Walter Jackson Bate for this reference.

John Everett Millais, *Ophelia*, 1852. Reprinted by permission of Art Resource.

as Lacan admits; but only because, in his words, "she is linked forever, for centuries, to the figure of Hamlet."

The bait-and-switch game that Lacan plays with Ophelia is a cynical but not unusual instance of her deployment in psychiatric and critical texts. For most critics of Shakespeare, Ophelia has been an insignificant minor character in the play, touching in her weakness and madness but chiefly interesting, of course, in what she tells us about Hamlet. And while female readers of Shakespeare have often attempted to champion Ophelia, even feminist critics have done so with a certain embarrassment. As Annette Kolodny ruefully admits: "it is after all, an imposition of high order to ask the viewer to attend to Ophelia's sufferings in a scene where, before, he's always so comfortably kept his eye fixed on Hamlet."[2]

Yet when feminist criticism allows Ophelia to upstage Hamlet, it also brings to the foreground the issues in an ongoing theoretical debate about the cultural links between femininity, female sexuality, insanity, and representation. Though she is neglected in criticism, Ophelia is probably the most frequently illustrated and cited of

2. Annette Kolodny, "Dancing through the minefield: some observations on the theory, practice, and politics of feminist literary criticism" (*Feminist Studies*, 6 [1980]), 7.

Shakespeare's heroines. Her visibility as a subject in literature, popular culture, and painting, from Redon who paints her drowning, to
Bob Dylan, who places her on Desolation Row, to Cannon Mills,
which has named a flowery sheet pattern after her, is in inverse relation to her invisibility in Shakespearean critical texts. Why has she
been such a potent and obsessive figure in our cultural mythology?
Insofar as Hamlet names Ophelia as "woman" and "frailty," substituting an ideological view of femininity for a personal one, is she
indeed representative of Woman, and does her madness stand for the
oppression of women in society as well as in tragedy? Furthermore,
since Laertes calls Ophelia a "document in madness," does she represent the textual archetype of woman *as* madness or madness *as*
woman? And finally, how should feminist criticism represent Ophelia in its own discourse? What is our responsibility towards her as
character and as woman?

Feminist critics have offered a variety of responses to these questions. Some have maintained that we should represent Ophelia as
a lawyer represents a client, that we should become her Horatia, in
this harsh world reporting her and her cause aright to the unsatisfied. Carol Neely, for example, describes advocacy—speaking for
Ophelia—as our proper role: "As a feminist critic," she writes, "I
must 'tell' Ophelia's story."[3] But what can we mean by Ophelia's
story? The story of her life? The story of her betrayal at the hands of
her father, brother, lover, court, society? The story of her rejection
and marginalization by male critics of Shakespeare? Shakespeare
gives us very little information from which to imagine a past for
Ophelia. She appears in only five of the play's twenty scenes; the
pre-play course of her love story with Hamlet is known only by a
few ambiguous flashbacks. Her tragedy is subordinated in the play;
unlike Hamlet, she does not struggle with moral choices or alternatives. Thus another feminist critic, Lee Edwards, concludes that it
is impossible to reconstruct Ophelia's biography from the text: "We
can imagine Hamlet's story without Ophelia, but Ophelia literally
has no story without Hamlet."[4]

If we turn from American to French feminist theory, Ophelia
might confirm the impossibility of representing the feminine in
patriarchal discourse as other than madness, incoherence, fluidity,
or silence. In French theoretical criticism, the feminine or "Woman"
is that which escapes representation in patriarchal language and
symbolism; it remains on the side of negativity, absence, and lack.
In comparison to Hamlet, Ophelia is certainly a creature of lack.

3. Carol Neely, "Feminist modes of Shakespearean criticism" (*Women's Studies*, 9 [1981]),
   11.
4. Lee Edwards, "The labors of Psyche" (*Critical Inquiry*, 6 [1979]), 36.

"I think nothing, my lord," she tells him in the Mousetrap scene, and he cruelly twists her words:

> HAMLET That's a fair thought, to lie between maid's legs.
> OPHELIA What is, my lord?
> HAMLET Nothing. [3.2.109–11]

In Elizabethan slang, "nothing" was a term for the female genitalia, as in *Much Ado About Nothing.* To Hamlet, then, "nothing" is what lies between maids' legs, for, in the male visual system of representation and desire, women's sexual organs, in the words of the French psychoanalyst Luce Irigaray, "represent the horror of having nothing to see."[5] When Ophelia is mad, Gertrude says that "Her speech is nothing," mere "unshaped use." Ophelia's speech thus represents the horror of having nothing to say in the public terms defined by the court. Deprived of thought, sexuality, language, Ophelia's story becomes the Story of O—the zero, the empty circle or mystery of feminine difference, the cipher of female sexuality to be deciphered by feminist interpretation.[6]

A third approach would be to read Ophelia's story as the female subtext of the tragedy, the repressed story of Hamlet. In this reading, Ophelia represents the strong emotions that the Elizabethans as well as the Freudians thought womanish and unmanly. When Laertes weeps for his dead sister he says of his tears that "When these are gone, / The woman will be out" —that is to say, that the feminine and shameful part of his nature will be purged. According to David Leverenz, in an important essay called "The Woman in *Hamlet*," Hamlet's disgust at the feminine passivity in himself is translated into violent revulsion against women, and into his brutal behavior towards Ophelia. Ophelia's suicide, Leverenz argues, then becomes "a microcosm of the male world's banishment of the female, because 'woman' represents everything denied by reasonable men."[7]

It is perhaps because Hamlet's emotional vulnerability can so readily be conceptualized as feminine that this is the only heroic male role in Shakespeare which has been regularly acted by women, in a tradition from Sarah Bernhardt to, most recently, Diane Venora, in a production directed by Joseph Papp. Leopold Bloom speculates

5. Luce Irigaray: see *New French Feminisms*, ed. Elaine Marks and Isabelle de Courtivron (New York, 1982), 101. The quotation above from III.ii is taken from the Arden Shakespeare, *Hamlet*, ed. Harold Jenkins (London and New York, 1982), 295. All quotations from *Hamlet* are from this text. [References to this Norton Critical Edition are substituted in brackets.]
6. On images of negation and feminine enclosure, see David Wilbern, "Shakespeare's 'nothing,'" in *Representing Shakespeare: New Psychoanalytic Essays*, ed. Murray M. Schwartz and Coppélia Kahn (Baltimore, 1981).
7. David Leverenz, "The woman in Hamlet: an interpersonal view" (*Signs*, 4 [1978]), 303.

on this tradition in *Ulysses*, musing on the Hamlet of the actress Mrs Bandman Palmer: "Male impersonator. Perhaps he was a woman? Why Ophelia committed suicide?"[8]

While all of these approaches have much to recommend them, each also presents critical problems. To liberate Ophelia from the text, or to make her its tragic center, is to re-appropriate her for our own ends; to dissolve her into a female symbolism of absence is to endorse our own marginality; to make her Hamlet's anima is to reduce her to a metaphor of male experience. I would like to propose instead that Ophelia does have a story of her own that feminist criticism can tell; it is neither her life story, nor her love story, but rather the *history* of her representation. This essay tries to bring together some of the categories of French feminist thought about the "feminine" with the empirical energies of American historical and critical research: to yoke French theory and Yankee knowhow.

Tracing the iconography of Ophelia in English and French painting, photography, psychiatry, and literature, as well as in theatrical production, I will be showing first of all the representational bonds between female insanity and female sexuality. Secondly, I want to demonstrate the two-way transaction between psychiatric theory and cultural representation. As one medical historian has observed, we could provide a manual of female insanity by chronicling the illustrations of Ophelia; this is so because the illustrations of Ophelia have played a major role in the theoretical construction of female insanity.[9] Finally, I want to suggest that the feminist revision of Ophelia comes as much from the actress's freedom as from the critic's interpretation.[1] When Shakespeare's heroines began to be played by women instead of boys, the presence of the female body and female voice, quite apart from details of interpretation, created new meanings and subversive tensions in these roles, and perhaps most importantly with Ophelia. Looking at Ophelia's history on and off the stage, I will point out the contest between male and female representations of Ophelia, cycles of critical repression and feminist reclamation of which contemporary feminist criticism is only the most recent phase. By beginning with these data from cultural history, instead of moving from the grid of literary theory, I hope to conclude with a fuller sense of the responsibilities of feminist criticism, as well as a new perspective on Ophelia.

8. James Joyce, *Ulysses* (New York, 1961), 76.
9. Sander L. Gilman, *Seeing the Insane* (New York, 1981), 126.
1. See Michael Goldman, *The Actor's Freedom: Toward a Theory of Drama* (New York, 1975), for a stimulating discussion of the interpretative interaction between actor and audience.

"Of all the characters in *Hamlet*," Bridget Lyons has pointed out,
"Ophelia is most persistently presented in terms of symbolic
meanings."[2] Her behavior, her appearance, her gestures, her costume, her props, are freighted with emblematic significance, and for
many generations of Shakespearean critics her part in the play has
seemed to be primarily iconographic. Ophelia's symbolic meanings,
moreover, are specifically feminine. Whereas for Hamlet madness is
metaphysical, linked with culture, for Ophelia it is a product of the
female body and female nature, perhaps that nature's purest form.
On the Elizabethan stage, the conventions of female insanity were
sharply defined. Ophelia dresses in white, decks herself with "fan-
tastical garlands" of wild flowers, and enters, according to the
stage directions of the "Bad" Quarto, "distracted" playing on a lute
with her "hair down singing." Her speeches are marked by extravagant metaphors, lyrical free associations, and "explosive sexual
imagery."[3] She sings wistful and bawdy ballads, and ends her life
by drowning.

All of these conventions carry specific messages about femininity
and sexuality. Ophelia's virginal and vacant white is contrasted with
Hamlet's scholar's garb, his "suits of solemn black." Her flowers suggest the discordant double images of female sexuality as both innocent blossoming and whorish contamination; she is the "green girl"
of pastoral, the virginal "Rose of May" and the sexually explicit madwoman who, in giving away her wild flowers and herbs, is symboli-
cally deflowering herself. The "weedy trophies" and phallic "long
purples" which she wears to her death intimate an improper and discordant sexuality that Gertrude's lovely elegy cannot quite obscure.[4]
In Elizabethan and Jacobean drama, the stage direction that a
woman enters with dishevelled hair indicates that she might either
be mad or the victim of a rape; the disordered hair, her offense
against decorum, suggests sensuality in each case.[5] The mad Ophelia's bawdy songs and verbal license, while they give her access to "an
entirely different range of experience" from what she is allowed as
the dutiful daughter, seem to be her one sanctioned form of self-
assertion as a woman, quickly followed, as if in retribution, by her
death.[6]

2. Bridget Lyons, "The iconography of Ophelia" (*English Literary History*, 44 [1977]), 61.
3. See Maurice and Hanna Charney, "The language of Shakespeare's madwomen" (*Signs*,
   3 [1977]), 451, 457; and Carroll Camden, "On Ophelia's madness" (*Shakespeare Quarterly* [1964]), 254.
4. See Margery Garber, *Coming of Age in Shakespeare* (London, 1981), 155–57; and
   Lyons, op. cit., 65, 70–72.
5. On dishevelled hair as a signifier of madness or rape, see Charney and Charney,
   op. cit., 452–53, 457; and Allan Dessen, *Elizabethan Stage Conventions and Modern
   Interpreters* (Cambridge, 1984), 36–38. Thanks to Allan Dessen for letting me see
   advance proofs of his book.
6. Charney and Charney, op. cit., 456.

Drowning too was associated with the feminine, with female fluidity as opposed to masculine aridity. In his discussion of the "Ophelia complex," the phenomenologist Gaston Bachelard traces the symbolic connections between women, water, and death. Drowning, he suggests, becomes the truly feminine death in the dramas of literature and life, one which is a beautiful immersion and submersion in the female element. Water is the profound and organic symbol of the liquid woman whose eyes are so easily drowned in tears, as her body is the repository of blood, amniotic fluid, and milk. A man contemplating this feminine suicide understands it by reaching for what is feminine in himself, like Laertes, by a temporary surrender to his own fluidity—that is, his tears; and he becomes a man again in becoming once more dry—when his tears are stopped.[7]

Clinically speaking, Ophelia's behavior and appearance are characteristic of the malady the Elizabethans would have diagnosed as female love-melancholy, or erotomania. From about 1580, melancholy had become a fashionable disease among young men, especially in London, and Hamlet himself is a prototype of the melancholy hero. Yet the epidemic of melancholy associated with intellectual and imaginative genius "curiously bypassed women." Women's melancholy was seen instead as biological, and emotional in origins.[8]

On the stage, Ophelia's madness was presented as the predictable outcome of erotomania. From 1660, when women first appeared on the public stage, to the beginnings of the eighteenth century, the most celebrated of the actresses who played Ophelia were those whom rumor credited with disappointments in love. The greatest triumph was reserved for Susan Mountfort, a former actress at Lincoln's Inn Fields who had gone mad after her lover's betrayal. One night in 1720 she escaped from her keeper, rushed to the theater, and just as the Ophelia of the evening was to enter for her mad scene, "sprang forward in her place . . . with wild eyes and wavering motion."[9] As a contemporary reported, "she was in truth Ophelia herself, to the amazement of the performers as well as of the audience—nature having made this last effort, her vital powers failed her and she died soon after."[1] These theatrical legends reinforced the belief of the age that female madness was a part of female nature, less to be

---

7. Gaston Bachelard, *L'Eau et les rêves* (Paris, 1942), 109–25. See also Brigitte Peucker, "Dröste-Hulshof's Ophelia and the recovery of voice" (*The Journal of English and Germanic Philology* [1983]), 374–91.
8. Vieda Skultans, *English Madness: Ideas on Insanity 1580–1890* (London, 1977), 79–81. On historical cases of love-melancholy, see Michael MacDonald, *Mystical Bedlam* (Cambridge, 1981).
9. C. E. L. Wingate, *Shakespeare's Heroines on the Stage* (New York, 1895), 283–84, 288–89.
1. Charles Hiatt, *Ellen Terry and Her Impersonations* (London, 1898), 11.

imitated by an actress than demonstrated by a deranged woman in a performance of her emotions.

The subversive or violent possibilities of the mad scene were nearly eliminated, however, on the eighteenth-century stage. Late Augustan stereotypes of female love-melancholy were sentimentalized versions which minimized the force of female sexuality, and made female insanity a pretty stimulant to male sensibility. Actresses such as Mrs Lessingham in 1772, and Mary Bolton in 1811, played Ophelia in this decorous style, relying on the familiar images of the white dress, loose hair, and wild flowers to convey polite feminine distraction, highly suitable for pictorial reproduction, and appropriate for Samuel Johnson's description of Ophelia as young, beautiful, harmless, and pious. Even Mrs Siddons in 1785 played the mad scene with stately and classical dignity. For much of the period, in fact, Augustan objections to the levity and indecency of Ophelia's language behavior led to censorship of the part. Her lines were frequently cut, and the role was often assigned to a singer instead of an actress, making the mode of representation musical rather than visual or verbal.

But whereas the Augustan response to madness was a denial, the romantic response was an embrace.[2] The figure of the madwoman permeates romantic literature, from the gothic novelists to Wordsworth and Scott in such texts as "The Thorn" and *The Heart of Midlothian*, where she stands for sexual victimization, bereavement, and thrilling emotional extremity. Romantic artists such as Thomas Barker and George Shepheard painted pathetically abandoned Crazy Kates and Crazy Anns, while Henry Fuseli's "Mad Kate" is almost demonically possessed, an orphan of the romantic storm. In the Shakespearean theater, Ophelia's romantic revival began in France rather than England. When Charles Kemble made his Paris debut as Hamlet with an English troupe in 1827, his Ophelia was a young Irish ingénue named Harriet Smithson. Smithson used "her extensive command of mime to depict in precise gesture the state of Ophelia's confused mind."[3] In the mad scene, she entered in a long black veil, suggesting the standard imagery of female sexual mystery in the gothic novel, with scattered bedlamish wisps of straw in her hair. Spreading the veil on the ground as she sang, she spread flowers upon it in the shape of a cross, as if to make her father's grave, and mimed a burial, a piece of stage business which remained in vogue for the rest of the century.

2. Max Byrd, *Visits to Bedlam: Madness and Literature in the Eighteenth Century* (Columbia, 1974), xiv.
3. Peter Raby, *Fair Ophelia: A Life of Harriet Smithson Berlioz* (Cambridge, 1982), 63.

The French audiences were stunned. Dumas recalled that "it was the first time I saw in the theatre real passions, giving life to men and women of flesh and blood."[4] The twenty-three-year-old Hector Berlioz, who was in the audience on the first night, fell madly in love, and eventually married Harriet Smithson despite his family's frantic opposition. Her image as the mad Ophelia was represented in popular lithographs and exhibited in bookshop and printshop windows. Her costume was imitated by the fashionable, and a coiffure "à la folle," consisting of a "black veil with wisps of straw tastefully interwoven" in the hair, was widely copied by the Parisian beau monde, always on the lookout for something new.[5]

Although Smithson never acted Ophelia on the English stage, her intensely visual performance quickly influenced English productions as well; and indeed the romantic Ophelia—a young girl passionately and visibly driven to picturesque madness—became the dominant international acting style for the next 150 years, from Helena Modjeska in Poland in 1871, to the eighteen-year-old Jean Simmons in the Laurence Olivier film of 1948.

Whereas the romantic Hamlet, in Coleridge's famous dictum, thinks too much, has an "overbalance of the contemplative faculty" and an overactive intellect, the romantic Ophelia is a girl who feels too much, who drowns in feeling. The romantic critics seem to have felt that the less said about Ophelia the better; the point was to look at her. Hazlitt, for one, is speechless before her, calling her "a character almost too exquisitely touching to be dwelt upon."[6] While the Augustans represent Ophelia as music, the romantics transform her into an *objet d'art*, as if to take literally Claudius's lament, "poor Ophelia / Divided from herself and her fair judgment, / Without the which we are pictures."

Smithson's performance is best recaptured in a series of pictures done by Delacroix from 1830 to 1850, which show a strong romantic interest in the relation of female sexuality and insanity.[7] The most innovative and influential of Delacroix's lithographs is *La Mort d'Ophélie* of 1843, the first of three studies. Its sensual languor, with Ophelia half-suspended in the stream as her dress slips from her body, anticipated the fascination with the erotic trance of the hysteric as it would be studied by Jean-Martin Charcot and his students, including Janet and Freud. Delacroix's interest in the drowning Ophelia is also reproduced to the point of obsession in later nineteenth-century painting. The English Pre-Raphaelites painted her again and again, choosing the drowning which is only

4. Ibid., 68.
5. Ibid., 72, 75.
6. Quoted in Camden, op. cit., 247.
7. Raby, op. cit., 182.

described in the play, and where no actress's image had preceded
them or interfered with their imaginative supremacy.

In the Royal Academy show of 1852, Arthur Hughes's entry
shows a tiny waif-like creature—a sort of Tinker Bell Ophelia—in a
filmy white gown perched on a tree trunk by the stream. The over-
all effect is softened, sexless, and hazy, although the straw in her
hair resembles a crown of thorns. Hughes's juxtaposition of childlike femininity and Christian martyrdom was overpowered, however, by John Everett Millais's great painting of Ophelia in the same
show. While Millais's Ophelia is sensuous siren as well as victim,
the artist rather than the subject dominates the scene. The division
of space between Ophelia and the natural details Millais had so
painstakingly pursued reduces her to one more visual object; and
the painting has such a hard surface, strangely flattened perspective, and brilliant light that it seems cruelly indifferent to the
woman's death.

These Pre-Raphaelite images were part of a new and intricate traffic
between images of women and madness in late nineteenth-century
literature, psychiatry, drama, and art. First of all, superintendents
of Victorian lunatic asylums were also enthusiasts of Shakespeare,
who turned to his dramas for models of mental aberration that
could be applied to their clinical practice. The case study of Ophelia was one that seemed particularly useful as an account of hysteria or mental breakdown in adolescence, a period of sexual
instability which the Victorians regarded as risky for women's mental health. As Dr John Charles Bucknill, president of the Medico-
Psychological Association, remarked in 1859, "Ophelia is the very
type of a class of cases by no means uncommon. Every mental physician of moderately extensive experience must have seen many
Ophelias. It is a copy from nature, after the fashion of the Pre-
Raphaelite school."[8] Dr John Conolly, the celebrated superin-
tendent of the Hanwell Asylum, and founder of the committee to
make Stratford a national trust, concurred. In his Study of Hamlet
in 1863 he noted that even casual visitors to mental institutions
could recognize an Ophelia in the wards: "the same young years,
the same faded beauty, the same fantastic dress and interrupted
song."[9] Medical textbooks illustrated their discussions of female
patients with sketches of Ophelia-like maidens.

8. J. C. Bucknill, The Psychology of Shakespeare (London, 1859, reprinted New York,
1970), 110. For more extensive discussions of Victorian psychiatry and Ophelia figures,
see Elaine Showalter, The Female Malady: Women, Madness, and English Culture,
1830–1980 (New York, 1985).
9. John Conolly, Study of Hamlet (London, 1863), 177.

But Conolly also pointed out that the graceful Ophelias who dominated the Victorian stage were quite unlike the women who had become the majority of the inmate population in Victorian public asylums. "It seems to be supposed," he protested, "that it is an easy task to play the part of a crazy girl, and that it is chiefly composed of singing and prettiness. The habitual courtesy, the partial rudeness of mental disorder, are things to be witnessed. . . . An actress, ambitious of something beyond cold imitation, might find the contemplation of such cases a not unprofitable study."[1]

Yet when Ellen Terry took up Conolly's challenge, and went to an asylum to observe real madwomen, she found them "too theatrical" to teach her anything.[2] This was because the iconography of the romantic Ophelia had begun to infiltrate reality, to define a style for mad young women seeking to express and communicate their distress. And where the women themselves did not willingly throw themselves into Ophelia-like postures, asylum superintendents, armed with the new technology of photography, imposed the costume, gesture, props, and expression of Ophelia upon them. In England, the camera was introduced to asylum work in the 1850s by Dr Hugh Welch Diamond, who photographed his female patients at the Surrey Asylum and at Bethlem. Diamond was heavily influenced by literary and visual models in his posing of the female subjects. His pictures of madwomen, posed in prayer, or decked with Ophelia-like garlands, were copied for Victorian consumption as touched-up lithographs in professional journals.[3]

Reality, psychiatry, and representational convention were even more confused in the photographic records of hysteria produced in the 1870s by Jean-Martin Charcot. Charcot was the first clinician to install a fully-equipped photographic atelier in his Paris hospital, La Salpêtrière, to record the performances of his hysterical stars. Charcot's clinic became, as he said, a "living theatre" of female pathology; his women patients were coached in their performances for the camera, and, under hypnosis, were sometimes instructed to play heroines from Shakespeare. Among them, a fifteen-year-old girl named Augustine was featured in the published volumes called *Iconographies* in every posture of *la grande hystérie*. With her white hospital gown and flowing locks, Augustine frequently resembles the reproductions of Ophelia as icon and actress which had been in wide circulation.[4]

1. Ibid., 177–78, 180.
2. Ellen Terry, *The Story of My Life* (London, 1908), 154.
3. Diamond's photographs are reproduced in Sander L. Gilman, *The Face of Madness: Hugh W. Diamond and the Origin of Psychiatric Photography* (New York, 1976).
4. See Georges Didi-Huberman, *L'Invention de l'hystérie* (Paris, 1982), and Stephen Heath, *The Sexual Fix* (London, 1983), 36.

But if the Victorian madwoman looks mutely out from men's pictures, and acts a part men had staged and directed, she is very differently represented in the feminist revision of Ophelia initiated by
newly powerful and respectable Victorian actresses, and by women
critics of Shakespeare. In their efforts to defend Ophelia, they invent
a story for her drawn from their own experiences, grievances, and
desires.

Probably the most famous of the Victorian feminist revisions of the
Ophelia story was Mary Cowden Clarke's *The Girlhood of Shakespeare's Heroines*, published in 1851. Unlike other Victorian moralizing and didactic studies of the female characters of Shakespeare's
plays, Clarke's was specifically addressed to the wrongs of women,
and especially to the sexual double standard. In a chapter on Ophelia called "The rose of Elsinore," Clarke tells how the child Ophelia was left behind in the care of a peasant couple when Polonius
was called to the court at Paris, and raised in a cottage with a foster-
sister and brother, Jutha and Ulf. Jutha is seduced and betrayed by
a deceitful knight, and Ophelia discovers the bodies of Jutha and her
still-born child, lying "white, rigid, and still" in the deserted parlor
of the cottage in the middle of the night. Ulf, a "hairy loutish boy,"
likes to torture flies, to eat songbirds, and to rip the petals off roses,
and he is also very eager to give little Ophelia what he calls a bear-
hug. Both repelled and masochistically attracted by Ulf, Ophelia is
repeatedly cornered by him as she grows up; once she escapes the
hug by hitting him with a branch of wild roses; another time, he
sneaks into her bedroom "in his brutish pertinacity to obtain the
hug he had promised himself," but just as he bends over her trembling body, Ophelia is saved by the reappearance of her real
mother.

A few years later, back at the court, she discovers the hanged
body of another friend, who has killed herself after being "victim-
ized and deserted by the same evil seducer." Not surprisingly,
Ophelia breaks down with brain fever—a staple mental illness of
Victorian fiction—and has prophetic hallucinations of a brook
beneath willow trees where something bad will happen to her. The
warnings of Polonius and Laertes have little to add to this history of
female sexual trauma.[5]

On the Victorian stage, it was Ellen Terry, daring and unconventional in her own life, who led the way in acting Ophelia in feminist
terms as a consistent psychological study in sexual intimidation, a

5. Mary Cowden Clarke, *The Girlhood of Shakespeare's Heroines* (London, 1852). See also
George C. Gross, "Mary Cowden Clarke, The Girlhood of Shakespeare's Heroines, and
the sex education of Victorian women" (*Victorian Studies*, 16 [1972]), 37–58, and Nina
Auerbach, *Woman and the Demon* (Cambridge, Mass., 1983), 210–15.

girl terrified of her father, of her lover, and of life itself. Terry's debut
as Ophelia in Henry Irving's production in 1878 was a landmark.
According to one reviewer, her Ophelia was "the terrible spectacle
of a normal girl becoming hopelessly imbecile as the result of overwhelming mental agony. Hers was an insanity without wrath or
rage, without exaltation or paroxysms."[6] Her "poetic and intellectual
performance" also inspired other actresses to rebel against the conventions of invisibility and negation associated with the part.

Terry was the first to challenge the tradition of Ophelia's dressing
in emblematic white. For the French poets, such as Rimbaud, Hugo,
Musset, Mallarmé and Laforgue, whiteness was part of Ophelia's
essential feminine symbolism; they call her "blanche Ophélia" and
compare her to a lily, a cloud, or snow. Yet whiteness also made her
a transparency, an absence that took on the colors of Hamlet's
moods, and that, for the symbolists like Mallarmé, made her a blank
page to be written over or on by the male imagination. Although
Irving was able to prevent Terry from wearing black in the mad
scene, exclaiming "My God, Madam, there must be only one black
figure in this play, and that's Hamlet!" (Irving, of course, was playing Hamlet), nonetheless actresses such as Gertrude Eliot, Helen
Maude, Nora de Silva, and in Russia Vera Komisarjevskaya, gradually won the right to intensify Ophelia's presence by clothing her in
Hamlet's black.[7]

By the turn of the century, there was both a male and a female
discourse on Ophelia. A. C. Bradley spoke for the Victorian male
tradition when he noted in *Shakespearean Tragedy* (1906) that "a
large number of readers feel a kind of personal irritation against
Ophelia; they seem unable to forgive her for not having been a heroine."[8] The feminist counterview was represented by actresses in
such works as Helena Faucit's study of Shakespeare's female characters, and *The True Ophelia*, written by an anonymous actress in
1914, which protested against the "insipid little creature" of criticism,
and advocated a strong and intelligent woman destroyed by the
heartlessness of men.[9] In women's paintings of the fin de siècle as
well, Ophelia is depicted as an inspiring, even sanctified emblem of
righteousness.[1]

6. Hiatt, op. cit., 114. See also Wingate, op. cit., 304–05.
7. Terry, op. cit., 155–56.
8. Andrew C. Bradley, *Shakespearean Tragedy* (London, 1906), 160.
9. Helena Faucit Martin, *On Some of Shakespeare's Female Characters* (Edinburgh and
   London, 1891), 4, 18; and *The True Ophelia* (New York, 1914), 15.
1. Among these paintings are the Ophelias of Henrietta Rae and Mrs F. Littler. Sarah
   Bernhardt sculpted a bas relief of Ophelia for the Women's Pavilion at the Chicago
   World's Fair in 1893.

While the widely read and influential essays of Mary Cowden Clarke are now mocked as the epitome of naive criticism, these Victorian studies of the girlhood of Shakespeare's heroines are of course alive and well as psychoanalytic criticism, which has imagined its own prehistories of oedipal conflict and neurotic fixation; and I say this not to mock psychoanalytic criticism, but to suggest that Clarke's musings on Ophelia are a pre-Freudian speculation on the traumatic sources of a female sexual identity. The Freudian interpretation of *Hamlet* concentrated on the hero, but also had much to do with the re-sexualization of Ophelia. As early as 1900, Freud had traced Hamlet's irresolution to an Oedipus complex, and Ernest Jones, his leading British disciple, developed this view, influencing the performances of John Gielgud and Alec Guinness in the 1930s. In his final version of the study, *Hamlet and Oedipus*, published in 1949, Jones argued that "Ophelia should be unmistakably sensual, as she seldom is on stage. She may be 'innocent' and docile, but she is very aware of her body."[2]

In the theater and in criticism, this Freudian edict has produced such extreme readings as that Shakespeare intends us to see Ophelia as a loose woman, and that she has been sleeping with Hamlet. Rebecca West has argued that Ophelia was not "a correct and timid virgin of exquisite sensibilities," a view she attributes to the popularity of the Millais painting; but rather "a disreputable young woman."[3] In his delightful autobiography, Laurence Olivier, who made a special pilgrimage to Ernest Jones when he was preparing his Hamlet in the 1930s, recalls that one of his predecessors as actor manager had said in response to the earnest question, "Did Hamlet sleep with Ophelia?"—"In my company, always."[4]

The most extreme Freudian interpretation reads Hamlet as two parallel male and female psychodramas, the counterpointed stories of the incestuous attachments of Hamlet and Ophelia. As Theodor Lidz presents this view, while Hamlet is neurotically attached to his mother, Ophelia has an unresolved oedipal attachment to her father. She has fantasies of a lover who will abduct her from or even kill her father, and when this actually happens, her reason is destroyed by guilt as well as by lingering incestuous feelings. According to Lidz, Ophelia breaks down because she fails in the female developmental task of shifting her sexual attachment from her father "to a man who can bring her fulfillment as a woman."[5] We see the effects of this Freudian Ophelia on stage productions since the 1950s, where direc-

2. Ernest Jones, *Hamlet and Oedipus* (New York, 1949), 139.
3. Rebecca West, *The Court and the Castle* (New Haven, 1958), 18.
4. Laurence Olivier, *Confessions of an Actor* (Harmondsworth, 1982), 102, 152.
5. Theodor Lidz, *Hamlet's Enemy: Madness and Myth in Hamlet* (New York, 1975), 88, 113.

tors have hinted at an incestuous link between Ophelia and her father, or more recently, because this staging conflicts with the usual ironic treatment of Polonius, between Ophelia and Laertes. Trevor Nunn's production with Helen Mirren in 1970, for example, made Ophelia and Laertes flirtatious doubles, almost twins in their matching fur-trimmed doublets, playing duets on the lute with Polonius looking on, like Peter, Paul, and Mary. In other productions of the same period, Marianne Faithfull was a haggard Ophelia equally attracted to Hamlet and Laertes, and, in one of the few performances directed by a woman, Yvonne Nicholson sat on Laertes' lap in the advice scene, and played the part with "rough sexual bravado."[6]

Since the 1960s, the Freudian representation of Ophelia has been supplemented by an antipsychiatry that represents Ophelia's madness in more contemporary terms. In contrast to the psychoanalytic representation of Ophelia's sexual unconscious that connected her essential femininity to Freud's essays on female sexuality and hysteria, her madness is now seen in medical and biochemical terms, as schizophrenia. This is so in part because the schizophrenic woman has become the cultural icon of dualistic femininity in the mid-twentieth century as the erotomaniac was in the seventeenth and the hysteric in the nineteenth. It might also be traced to the work of R. D. Laing on female schizophrenia in the 1960s. Laing argued that schizophrenia was an intelligible response to the experience of invalidation within the family network, especially to the conflicting emotional messages and mystifying double binds experienced by daughters. Ophelia, he noted in *The Divided Self*, is an empty space. "In her madness there is no one there. . . . There is no integral selfhood expressed through her actions or utterances. Incomprehensible statements are said by nothing. She has already died. There is now only a vacuum where there was once a person."[7]

Despite his sympathy for Ophelia, Laing's readings silence her, equate her with "nothing," more completely than any since the Augustans; and they have been translated into performances which only make Ophelia a graphic study of mental pathology. The sickest Ophelias on the contemporary stage have been those in the productions of the pathologist-director Jonathan Miller. In 1974 at the Greenwich Theatre his Ophelia sucked her thumb; by 1981, at the Warehouse in London, she was played by an actress much taller and heavier than the Hamlet (perhaps punningly cast as the young actor Anton Lesser). She began the play with a set of nervous tics

6. Richard David, *Shakespeare in the Theatre* (Cambridge, 1978), 75. This was the production directed by Buzz Goodbody, a brilliant young feminist radical who killed herself that year. See Colin Chambers, *Other Spaces: New Theatre and the RSC* (London, 1980), especially 63–67.
7. R. D. Laing, *The Divided Self* (Harmondsworth, 1965), 195n.

and tuggings of hair which by the mad scene had become a full set of schizophrenic routines—head banging, twitching, wincing, grimacing, and drooling.[8]

But since the 1970s too we have had a feminist discourse which has offered a new perspective on Ophelia's madness as protest and rebellion. For many feminist theorists, the madwoman is a heroine, a powerful figure who rebels against the family and the social order; and the hysteric who refuses to speak the language of the patriarchal order, who speaks otherwise, is a sister.[9] In terms of effect on the theater, the most radical application of these ideas was probably realized in Melissa Murray's agitprop play *Ophelia*, written in 1979 for the English women's theater group "Hormone Imbalance." In this blank verse retelling of the *Hamlet* story, Ophelia becomes a lesbian and runs off with a woman servant to join a guerrilla commune.[1]

While I've always regretted that I missed this production, I can't proclaim that this defiant ideological gesture, however effective politically or theatrically, is all that feminist criticism desires, or all to which it should aspire. When feminist criticism chooses to deal with representation, rather than with women's writing, it must aim for a maximum interdisciplinary contextualism, in which the complexity of attitudes towards the feminine can be analyzed in their fullest cultural and historical frame. The alternation of strong and weak Ophelias on the stage, virginal and seductive Ophelias in art, inadequate or oppressed Ophelias in criticism, tells us how these representations have overflowed the text, and how they have reflected the ideological character of their times, erupting as debates between dominant and feminist views in periods of gender crisis and redefinition. The representation of Ophelia changes independently of theories of the meaning of the play or the Prince, for it depends on attitudes towards women and madness. The decorous and pious Ophelia of the Augustan age and the postmodern schizophrenic heroine who might have stepped from the pages of Laing can be derived from the same figure; they are both contradictory and complementary images of female sexuality in which madness seems to act as the "switching-point, the concept which allows the co-existence of both sides of the representation."[2] There is no "true" Ophelia for whom feminist criticism must unambiguously

---

8. David, op. cit., 82–83; thanks to Marianne DeKoven, Rutgers University, for the description of the 1981 Warehouse production.
9. See, for example, Hélène Cixous and Catherine Clément, *La Jeune Née* (Paris, 1975).
1. For an account of this production, see Micheline Wandor, *Understudies: Theatre and Sexual Politics* (London, 1981), 47.
2. I am indebted for this formulation to a critique of my earlier draft of this paper by Carl Friedman, at the Wesleyan Center for the Humanities, April 1984.

Julia Stiles (Ophelia) rages at Diane Venora (Gertrude) in the
Guggenheim Museum, Almereyda's film, 2000

speak, but perhaps only a Cubist Ophelia of multiple perspectives,
more than the sum of all her parts.

But in exposing the ideology of representation, feminist critics
have also the responsibility to acknowledge and to examine the
boundaries of our own ideological positions as products of our gender and our time. A degree of humility in an age of critical hubris
can be our greatest strength, for it is by occupying this position of
historical self-consciousness in both feminism and criticism that
we maintain our credibility in representing Ophelia, and that, unlike
Lacan, when we promise to speak about her, we make good our
word.

STEPHEN GREENBLATT

Hamlet in Purgatory (2001)†

Dark Hints

"When the ghost has vanished," says Goethe's Wilhelm Meister, in what is probably the most influential of all readings of *Hamlet*, "what do we see standing before us? A young hero thirsting for revenge? A prince by birth, happy to be charged with unseating the usurper of his throne? Not at all!" The tragedy is more inward: "A fine, pure, noble and highly moral person, but devoid of that emotional strength that characterizes a hero, goes to pieces beneath a burden that it can neither support nor cast off."[1] Generations of critics have agreed, responding in effect to the startling Shakespearean shift from vengeance to remembrance. But what motivated this unprecedented shift? Where did it come from? How did it connect successfully with a popular London audience in 1601? And why, more specifically, is the injunction to remember spoken by a ghost? The overwhelming emphasis on the psychological dimension, crowned by psychoanalytical readings of the play in the twentieth century, has the odd effect of eliminating the Ghost as ghost, turning it into the prince's traumatic memory or, alternatively, into a conventional piece of dispensable stage machinery. ("When the ghost has vanished," Goethe's account tellingly begins.) But if we do not let the Ghost vanish altogether, we can perhaps begin to answer these questions, by recognizing that the psychological in Shakespeare's tragedy is constructed almost entirely out of the theological, and specifically out of the issue of remembrance that, as we have seen, lay at the heart of the crucial early-sixteenth-century debate about Purgatory.

More's souls are in a panic that they will be forgotten, erased by "slothful oblivion." They are heartsick that they will fade from the minds of the living, that their wives will remarry, that their children will mention them only, if at all, "so coldly and with so dull affection that it lies but in the lips, and comes not near the heart" (*The Supplication of Souls, Complete Works*, Yale edn., 7:149). They are harrowed above all by the fear that their sufferings will cease even to be credited, that their prison house will be dismissed as a "fantastic fable," and that their very existence, in its horrible, prolonged pain,

---

† Princeton: Princeton UP, 2001, 229–40. A contemporary critic and founder of New Historicism, Greenblatt here examines the theological contexts of the play, specifically the matter of Purgatory. © 2001 Princeton University Press. Reprinted by permission of Princeton University Press.
 1. Johann Wolfgang von Goethe, *Wilhelm Meister's Apprenticeship*, trans. Eric Blackall (Princeton: Princeton UP, 1989), p. 146.

will be doubted. It is this fear that seems to shape Shakespeare's depiction of the Ghost and of Hamlet's response.

The Ghost makes clear to Hamlet that he is in what Thomas White's early-seventeenth-century text called "the middle state of souls,"[2] not damned for eternity but forced to suffer torments in a "prison-house" designed to purge him of the crimes he had committed in his life:

> I am thy father's spirit,
> Doomed for a certain term to walk the night,
> And for the day confined to fast in fires
> Till the foul crimes done in my days of nature
> Are burnt and purged away. [1.5.9–13]

"For a certain term"—the bland phrase, which looks at first as though it serves only to fill out the syllables of a line of blank verse, is in fact significant, since it helps to set up the theological claim of the word "purged."[3] In a mid-eleventh-century report on moans that had been heard to rise out of the crater of Stromboli, Jotsuald explained that the souls of sinners were being tortured there *ad tempus statutum*, for a certain term.[4] "In purgatory my soul hath been / a thousand years in woe and teen," the "Imperator Salvatus" says in the Chester mystery play *The Last Judgment* (ca. 1475):

> As hard pains, I dare well say,
> in purgatory are night and day
> as are in hell, save by one way—
> that one shall have an end.[5]

In church teachings, the excruciating pains of Purgatory and of Hell were, as we have seen, identical; the only difference was that the former were only for a certain term.

That one difference, of course, was crucial, but the Catholic Church laid a heavy emphasis upon the horrors of purgatorial tor-

---

2. Thomas White, *The Middle State of Souls from the hour of death to the day of judgment* (London, 1659).
3. "Claim" rather than "meaning" because the Ghost may only be lying, luring Hamlet into a belief that Purgatory actually exists and then luring him further toward damnation by inducing him to commit an act of vengeance.
4. See Le Goff, *The Birth of Purgatory*, p. 227.
5. *The Last Judgment* in *The Chester Mystery Cycle* (1475), ed. R. M. Lumiansky and David Mills, Early English Text Society, s.s., 3 (London: Oxford UP, 1974), p. 441. See, similarly, *A lyttel boke . . . of Purgatorye* (London, [1534?]):

> Betwene the payne of hell / certaynly
> And betwene the payne / of Purgatorye
> Is no dyfference / but certes that one
> Shall haue an ende / and that other none.

(Quoted in Germain Marc'hadour, "Popular Devotions Concerning Purgatory," in the Yale Edition of *The Supplication of Souls*, in *The Complete Works of St. Thomas More*, ed. Frank Manley, Germain Marc'hadour, Richard Marius, and Clarence Miller [New Haven: Yale UP, 1990], Appendix E, 7:447.)

ments, so that the faithful would be as anxious as possible to reduce the term they would have to endure. The intensity of the anguish is brilliantly represented in the greatest of English morality plays, *Everyman* (ca. 1495), where God sends his agent Death to demand of the hero "a sure reckoning / Without delay or any tarrying."[6] Everyman frantically begs for time, for his "book of reckoning" is not ready, but Death will grant him only the briefest of respites. Still, the interval is enough for the penitent to begin to scourge himself: "Take this, body, for the sin of the flesh!" (613). The grotesque spectacle of a dying man scourging himself makes sense only in the context of a desperate, last-minute attempt to alter the "reckoning" by substituting penitential pain in this life for the far more terrible pain that lies ahead. "Now of penance I will wade the water clear," declares Everyman, intensifying his blows, "To save me from purgatory, that sharp fire" (618–19).

Everyman has thus narrowly escaped one of the worst medieval nightmares, a sudden death.[7] This nightmare, of course, is the fate that befalls Hamlet's father: the horror is not only the fact of his murder, at the hands of his treacherous brother, but also the precise circumstances of that murder, in his sleep, comfortable and secure. Contemplating killing Claudius at prayer, Hamlet remembers that Claudius took his father "grossly, full of bread, / With all his crimes broad blown, as flush as May" [3.3.80–81]. Hamlet continues with lines that are perfectly orthodox, from a theological point of view, but extremely strange in the wake of what he has witnessed and heard:

> And how his audit stands, who knows save heaven?
> But in our circumstance and course of thought
> 'Tis heavy with him. [82–84]

The phrase "circumstance and course of thought" is a hendiadys, or nearly so: it means something like circumstantial or indirect course of thought. But Hamlet has precisely had a more direct testimony, which he has professed, only a minute before, to credit absolutely: "I'll take the Ghost's word for a thousand pound" [3.2.268–69]. That is, his father's ghost has told him quite explicitly how his audit

6. *Everyman*, in *Medieval Drama*, ed. David Bevington (Boston: Houghton Mifflin, 1975), lines 70–71.
7. Cf. Paget, *The Revelation to the Monk of Evesham Abbey*, p. 141: "I saw numberless people there, who had died suddenly, and who were being punished almost beyond measure." William of Auvergne (regent and master of theology at Paris from 1222 to 1228 and bishop of Paris from 1228 until his death in 1249) argued that Purgatory is a continuation of earthly penance. It is necessary because "those who die suddenly or without warning, for example, 'by the sword, suffocation, or excess of suffering,' those whom death takes unawares before they have had time to complete their penance, must have a place where they may do so" (Le Goff, *The Birth of Purgatory*, p. 242).

stands, but once again Hamlet has "forgotten," as he earlier forgot
that a traveler has in fact returned from the bourns of the death's
undiscovered country.

Having just glanced indirectly at the question of where his father
resides in the afterlife, and having avoided directly naming Purgatory, Hamlet goes on to ask himself, with regard to murdering his
uncle, "[A]m I then revenged / To take him in the purging of his
soul, / When he is fit and seasoned for his passage?" [3.3.84–86]
The word "purging" is striking here, since it links prayer in this
world (and the preparation or seasoning of a soul for the "passage"
to the other world) to the purgation that may or may not follow.
Similarly, a few minutes earlier, in response to Guildenstern's saying
that the king is "distempered" (a word that recurs in *Hamlet*) with
"choler," Hamlet jokes, "Your wisdom should show itself more richer
to signify this to his doctor, for for me to put him to his purgation
would perhaps plunge him into far more choler" [3.2.284–86]. Here
purgation has a meaning in humoral medicine, but the joke is a deep
one, since for Hamlet to put the king to his purgation would mean
to kill him, and that would, in Hamlet's account, plunge him into
choler, that is, into the rage of infernal punishment and torture.

These strange, angry jests seem like a series of anxious, displaced
reflections on the middle state in which the Ghost is condemned to
suffer as a result of being taken "full of bread." Old Hamlet's condition is a grievous one—the term of his sufferings or their intensity
vastly increased—because of the way he was dispatched, unprepared for death:

> Cut off even in the blossoms of my sin,
> Unhouseled, dis-appointed, unaneled,
> No reck'ning made, but sent to my account
> With all my imperfections on my head.
> O horrible, O horrible, most horrible! [1.5.76–80]

That he can speak of "imperfections" presumably means that his sins
were not mortal; after all, he will eventually burn and purge away his
crimes. But his inability to make a proper reckoning and his failure
to receive the Catholic last rites weigh heavily against him.[8]

---

8. On the importance of deathbed houseling, for example, see a sermon by John Mirk. A
   Christian man, dying, sends for the priest to "come to hym wyth Godys body." He
   receives the sacrament steadfastly believing that it is the real body of Christ, "And so
   wyth his perfite beleue he armeth hym, and maketh hym strong and myghty forto
   aghenstond the fendes that wol assayle hym, when he passeth oute from the body, in
   al wyse that thai con, forto assay, ghef thei mow bryng hym oute of the beleue. Then
   schal the sacrament that he receyvet make hym so myghty, that he schal overcome
   hem and sett noght by hem" (quoted in C. W. Dugmore, *The Mass and the English
   Reformers* [London: Macmillan, 1958], p. 68). The specificity of the Catholic nature
   of these last rites is open to debate, since some version of each of them was compatible
   with Protestantism.

When he first encounters the apparition, Hamlet envisages only two possibilities for the Ghost's origin:

> Be thou a spirit of health or goblin damned,
> Bring with thee airs from heaven or blasts from hell,
> Be thy intents wicked or charitable,
> Thou com'st in such a questionable shape
> That I will speak to thee. [1.4.40–44]

Nothing Hamlet says in the wake of his fateful exchange with his father's spirit explicitly acknowledges a third possibility, a middle state between Heaven and Hell, a place within the earth where souls are purged. But "there are more things in heaven and earth, Horatio," he tells his Wittenberg friend, as the Ghost moves restlessly beneath the stage, "Than are dreamt of in your philosophy" [1.5.174–75]. And a moment later, hearing the Ghost's voice once again, he addresses it directly in words that would have been utterly familiar to a Catholic and deeply suspect to a Protestant: "Rest, rest, perturbèd spirit" [1.5.189].[9]

There is, moreover, something suspect (or at least strange), as scholars have long noted, about the precise terms of Hamlet's response to Horatio's remark, "There's no offense, my lord":

> Yes, by Saint Patrick, but there is, Horatio,
> And much offence, too. Touching this vision here,
> It is an honest ghost, that let me tell you. [1.5.141–44]

The assertion that the Ghost is "honest" seems to mark Hamlet's acceptance of its claim that it has come from a place of purgation, and that acceptance may in turn be marked by the invocation—unique in Shakespeare's works—of Saint Patrick, the patron saint of Purgatory. By the eighteenth century Warburton thought the invoca-

---

9. Hamlet's "Rest, rest, perturbèd spirit" may be compared to the mad Ophelia's prayer for her murdered father: "God 'a' mercy on his soul. / And of all Christian souls, I pray God" ([4.5.189–90]. What would these prayers have sounded like to Elizabethan ears? "Prayer for the dead was such a deeply engrained practice in mid-Tudor England that it took several decades of preaching and discipline to draw it to a close. Some people believed that the soul still lingered in the vicinity of the body during the first thirty days after burial, a liminal situation requiring great ritual caution. During the Elizabethan period, especially in the early part of the reign, some testators continued to provide for this 'triginal' period by ordering a black cover for their coffin or grave during this month's mind, or arranging for another service, dole, and funeral feast when it came to an end. Though repudiated by the Reformation, the traditional month-mind and year-mind had a customary half-life in many parts of England as far apart as Lancashire and Essex. Provisions for obits and month-minds and prayers for all Christian souls were not uncommon in wills of the 1550s, 1560s, and 1570s, though heirs and executors were increasingly hard-pressed to carry them out." David Cressy, *Birth, Marriage, and Death: Ritual, Religion and the Life-Cycle in Tudor and Stuart England* (New York: Oxford UP, 1997), p. 398. Cressy writes, however, that the disciplinary process, though prolonged, was basically completed by the second half of Elizabeth's reign, so Hamlet in 1601 would seem to hark back to a world lost.

tion of Patrick must have been made "at random,"[1] but a specific association with Purgatory would have probably seemed obvious to a late-sixteenth-century audience. "I come not from Trophonius care [*sic*], for then I should be loathed," declares a character in John Grange's *The Golden Aphroditis* (1577), "[n]or from S. Patrick's purgatory."[2] [These allusions] make clear the strong association between Saint Patrick and Purgatory, along with the association, to which we will return, between Purgatory and fiction.

To the Saint Patrick allusion in Hamlet, whose association with Purgatory was remarked as early as the 1860s by the learned German philologist Benno Tschischwitz, we can add another, a few lines further on, that has not, to my knowledge, been noted. When Hamlet adjures his friends to take an oath that they will not reveal what they have seen, the Ghost, from under the stage, cries "Swear." When they shift ground to a new position, the Ghost once again cries out beneath them, and Hamlet asks, "*Hic et ubique?*" [1.5.164]. The Latin tag here has never been adequately explained.[3] The words obviously refer to restless movement, a certain placelessness, comparable in Othello to Roderigo's description of Othello as "an extravagant and wheeling stranger / Of here and everywhere" (1.1.137–38). The use of Latin—besides suggesting that Hamlet is, like his friend Horatio, something of a scholar—may also convey a theological resonance, one evidently in Shakespeare's mind at the time that he wrote *Hamlet*. In *Twelfth Night*, a play of the same year, Sebastian, baffled by the appearance of his double, declares that there cannot be "that deity in my nature / Of here and everywhere" (5.1.220–21). The words refer in jest to the divine power to violate the laws of physics, a power that became an issue in the Reformation in a dispute over the Lutheran doctrine of Christ's Ubiquity. If this resonance is present in Hamlet, as it well may be, the prince's jest is deepened by a disquieting association of his father's ghost with the omnipresence of God.

But I believe that there is a further theological resonance to these words, specifically relevant to Purgatory. Traditional Catholic ritual in England included a prayer to be recited for the dead who

---

1. Quoted in Furness, *Variorum, Hamlet*, 1:111.
2. John Grange, *The Golden Aphroditis* (London, 1577; reprint, New York: Scholars' Facsimiles and Reprints, 1939), fol. Cv.
3. See, however, the speculation in Fr. Christopher Devlin, *Hamlet's Divinity, and Other Essays* (London: Rupert Hart-Davis, 1963), pp. 31–32: "One may find another [reference to the Roman Breviary] in Hamlet's first reaction to the Ghost, 'Angels and ministers of grace defend us' [1.4.39]. For the prayer in the Office of St. Michael, 'May we be defended on earth by the ministers in heaven' is accompanied by an antiphon which invokes the Angelic protection HIC ET UBIQUE [1.5.164]. An ironic echoing of the Liturgy may be sufficient explanation of Hamlet's odd irruption in Latinity, 'Hic et ubique!', when the Ghost moans beneath him."

had been laid to rest in the churchyard. God's mercy and forgiveness of sin are begged on behalf of all of those souls here and everywhere (*hic et ubique*) who rest in Christ.[4] The point is not only that
such pleas for the dead make use of the key phrase *hic et ubique* but
also that they are specifically connected to a belief in Purgatory. In
The Catholic Doctrine of the Church of England (1607), the Protestant Thomas Rogers, ridiculing this connection, quotes the papal
indulgence from the Sarum *Horae Beatissimae Virginis Mariae*: "Pope
John the Twelfth hath granted to all persons, which, going through
the churchyard, do say the prayer following, so many years of pardons as there have been bodies buried since it was a churchyard."[5]
The prayer begins "Avete, omnes animae fideles, quarum corpora hic
et ubique requiescunt in pulvere" ("Hail all faithful souls, whose
bodies here and everywhere do rest in the dust"). In the context of
the Ghost's claim that he is being purged, and in the context, too, of
Hamlet's invocation of Saint Patrick, the words *hic et ubique*,
addressed to the spirit who seems to be moving beneath the earth,
seem to be an acknowledgment of the place where his father's spirit
is imprisoned.

There is a famous problem with all of these heavy hints that the
Ghost is in or has come from Purgatory: by 1563, almost forty years
before Shakespeare's *Hamlet* was written, the Church of England
had explicitly rejected the Roman Catholic conception of Purgatory
and the practices that had been developed around it. The twenty-
second of the Thirty-Nine Articles declares that "[t]he Romish
doctrine concerning Purgatory, Pardons, Worshipping, and Adoration, as well of Images as of Reliques, and also invocation of Saints,
is a fond thing, vainly invented, and grounded upon no warranty of
Scripture, but rather repugnant to the word of God."[6] This fact
alone would not necessarily have invalidated allusions to Purgatory: there were many people who clung to the old beliefs, despite
the official position, and Elizabethan audiences were in any case
perfectly capable of imaginatively entering into alien belief systems.[7] Hence the spectators could watch the Lupercalia in *Julius*

4. "*Pro quiescentibus in cimiterio. Oratio:* Deus, in cujus miseratione animae fidelium
requiescunt; animabus famulorum famularumque tuarum omnium, hic et ubique in
Christo quiescentium, da propitius veniam peccatorum, ut a cunctis reatibus absoluti,
tecum sine fine laetentur. Per Dominum," in *Missale Ad Usum Insignis et Praeclarae
Ecclesiae Sarum* [*Missale Sarum*], ed. Francis Dickinson (Oxford: J. Parker, 1861–
1883), p. 878. The phrase *hic et ubique* is repeated in the *Secreta* and *Postcommunio* as
well.
5. Thomas Rogers, *The Catholic Doctrine of the Church of England* (Cambridge: UP for
the Parker Society, 1882), p. 221.
6. Edgar C. S. Gibson, *The Thirty-Nine Articles of the Church of England*, 2 vols. (London: Methuen & Co., 1897), 2:537.
7. In *The Fate of the Dead: A Study in Folk Eschatology in the West Country after the
Reformation* (Ipswich: Rowan and Littlefield, 1979), Theo Brown argues that in repu-
diating the "Romish doctrine" of Purgatory, the English church had not meant to

Caesar or Lear's solemn invocation of Hecate, and Shakespeare's plays frequently (and not unsympathetically) represent the monks and friars from the outlawed Catholic orders. But the theater, like the press, was censored, and, though the censors were often slipshod in some respects, they were acutely sensitive to controversial political and doctrinal questions. It was, as we saw in the last chapter, possible in the Elizabethan theater to represent the afterlife in many different ways, and it was possible (indeed, perfectly orthodox) for Shakespeare to absorb some of the imagery of Purgatory into the representation of ordinary life. But it would have been highly risky to represent in a favorable light any specifically Roman Catholic doctrines or practices, just as it would have been virtually impossible to praise the pope.

A playwright could ridicule Purgatory, as Marlowe does in *Doctor Faustus*: when the invisible Faustus snatches food and drink away from the pope, the baffled archbishop of Rheims speculates that it may "be some ghost crept out of purgatory and now is come unto your holiness for his pardon."[8] So, too, in a pamphlet written about 1590, *Tarlton's News Out of Purgatory*, the anonymous author pretends that he left the theater, in order to avoid the huge crowd, walked in the nearby fields, and, falling asleep under a tree, was astonished to be approached by the ghost of the popular Elizabethan clown, Richard Tarlton. "Ghost thou art none," he told Tarlton, "but a very devil, for the souls of them which are departed, if the sacred principles of theology be true, never return into the world again till the general resurrection." But Tarlton saucily replied that he resided not in Heaven or Hell but in "a third place that all our great grandmothers have talked of." "What, sir," the clown continued, "are we wiser than all our forefathers? and they not only feared that place in life, but found it after their death: or else was there much land and annual pensions given in vain to morrow-mass priests for dirges, trentals, and such like decretals of devotion."[9] As this and many similar moments in Tudor and Stuart texts bear witness, belief in Purgatory could be represented as a sly jest, a confidence trick, a mistake, or what Knevet, in a poem quoted in chapter 2, calls "a fable or a story, / A place of fancy." But it could not be represented as a

abolish Purgatory altogether but only the abuses of the doctrine, abuses associated with Rome. The wholesale assault on suffrages for the dead makes this argument implausible, but, as we have seen, early reformers like Tyndale kept open the imaginative possibility that there might be an unspecifiable process of purgation. It is this imaginative possibility, rather than any practice, that the careful Anglican language seems to preserve—and that Shakespeare, as I have been arguing, realized he could exploit.
8. *Doctor Faustus* (B-text), 3.2.79–81, in Christopher Marlowe, *Doctor Faustus and Other Plays*, ed. David Bevington and Eric Rasmussen (Oxford: Clarendon P, 1995).
9. Quoted in Bullough, *Narrative and Dramatic Sources*, 7:170–71.

frightening reality. *Hamlet* comes closer to doing so than any other play of this period. But Shakespeare, with his remarkable gift for knowing exactly how far he could go without getting into serious trouble, still only uses a network of allusions: "for a certain term," "burned and purged away," "Yes, by Saint Patrick," "*hic et ubique.*"

Moreover, even were these allusions less cautiously equivocal, there remains a second famous problem: souls in Purgatory were saved. The fact that old Hamlet died suddenly and hence without time for last rites—"unhouseled, dis-appointed, unaneled"—left him with a heavy burden of earthly sins that had painfully to be burned away after death, but he could not possibly commit new sins. The trouble is that Purgatory, along with theological language of communion (houseling), deathbed confession (appointment), and anointing (aneling), while compatible with a Christian (and, specifically, a Catholic) call for remembrance, is utterly incompatible with a Senecan call for vengeance.[1] Such a call for vengeance—and Hamlet understands that it is premeditated murder, not due process, that is demanded of him—could come only from the place in the afterlife where Seneca's ghosts reside: Hell.

Uncertainty and Interrogation

It would be quite possible for an audience not to notice this problem at all—after all, this is a play, not a theological tract, and there are many comparable contradictions that are simply ignored throughout Shakespeare and Elizabethan drama—were it not for the fact that Hamlet notices it and broods about it. Even before the Ghost has uttered a syllable, Hamlet anticipates the problem and articulates the key question that the *discretio spirituum* was meant to address.

> Angels and ministers of grace defend us!
> Be thou a spirit of health or goblin damned,
> Bring with thee airs from heaven or blasts from hell,
> Be thy intents wicked or charitable,
> Thou com'st in such a questionable shape
> That I will speak to thee. [1.4.39–44]

The initial injunction functions like the prophylactic prayers that precede Jean Gobi's encounter with the ghost, and the paired options that follow make clear that Hamlet goes into the encounter fully understanding the dangerous ambiguity that characterized all

1. The issue has been the subject of extensive scholarly discussion. Arguing for the Catholic position, I. J. Semper has suggested that, under certain circumstances, vengeance could be called for, but there is no evidence that Hamlet's circumstances in any way match those that might possibly justify the assassination of Claudius. See I. J. Semper, *Hamlet without Tears* (Dubuque, Iowa: Loras College P, 1946). For the dominant counterview, see Prosser, *Hamlet and Revenge*.

spectral returns. But there is an odd sense in which Hamlet leaps over the questions that were traditionally asked of "questionable" apparitions. This is precisely not the beginning of a clerical interrogation: in the almost unbearable intensity of the moment, he acknowledges the ambiguity only to brush it aside as irrelevant. "I'll call thee Hamlet," he declares impetuously, before the Ghost has named himself, "King, father, royal Dane" [1.4.44–45].

The desperate impatience that Hamlet expresses is to know why the Ghost has returned, not whence it has returned. Indeed, he addresses the apparition not as a spirit at all but as a "dead corpse" that has burst out from its tomb:

> Let me not burst in ignorance, but tell
> Why thy canonized bones, hearsed in death,
> Have burst their cerements, why the sepulchre
> Wherein we saw thee quietly enurned
> Hath oped his ponderous and marble jaws
> To cast thee up again. [1.4.46–51]

This is not an image of Jonah miraculously cast up from the belly of the fish; rather, it is as if Hamlet pictures his father vomited forth, like something undigested, from one of those horrible mouths that artists painted to represent Hell or Purgatory. Hamlet had been deeply mourning his father, seeking him, as his mother said, in the dust. But this vision of his father out of the grave, weirdly intact and clad in armor, is hideous. Instead of "cerements" (that is, grave clothes), the First Quarto reading is "ceremonies." The alternative calls attention to something in any case insistently present in the lines: a sense of shattered ritual, a violation of what it means for a corpse to be "canonized," "hearsed," quietly laid to rest in its sepulchre. The violation, Hamlet thinks, must have a meaning, and, horribly shaken "with thoughts beyond the reaches of our souls" [1.4.56], he is willing to risk his life to find out what the meaning is.

It is only when he has discovered this meaning, when he has received the Ghost's charge to revenge and to remember, that Hamlet returns to the question of the Ghost's status.

> The spirit that I have seen
> May be the devil, and the devil hath power
> T'assume a pleasing shape; yea, and perhaps,
> Out of my weakness and my melancholy—
> As he is very potent with such spirits—
> Abuses me to damn me. [2.2.519–24][2]

---

2. In the Second Quarto, the spirit that Hamlet has seen may be "a deale [*devil*]." The singular has the effect of individualizing this particular apparition—that is, individual devils, in the service of Satan, could impersonate individuals or inhabit pagan statues.

The test he devises to establish the veracity of the Ghost's accusation—"The play's the thing / Wherein I'll catch the conscience of the King" [2.2.525–26]—seems to satisfy Hamlet, but it notoriously leaves the question of the Ghost's origin unanswered.

My intention here is not to rehearse a long series of debates by Eleanor Prosser, Christopher Devlin, Miriam Joseph, Peter Milward, Roy Battenhouse, and others whose intricate arguments, for me at least, are not completely evacuated by the fact that they are almost certainly doomed to inconclusiveness.[3] In the ingenious attempt to determine whether the apparition is "Catholic" or "Protestant," whether it is a spirit of health or a goblin damned, whether it comes from Purgatory or from Hell—as if these were questions that could be decisively answered if only we were somehow clever enough—the many players in the long-standing critical game have usefully called attention to the bewildering array of hints that the play generates.[4] Perhaps most striking is simply how much evidence on all sides there is in the play, and not only from those scenes in which the status of the Ghost is being directly discussed. Hence, for example, Ophelia tells her father that the distracted Hamlet appeared to her in her chamber

> with a look so piteous in purport
> As if he had been loosed out of hell
> To speak of horrors. . . . [2.1.80–82]

Spirits loosed out of hell do not normally have "piteous" looks; it is as if Ophelia had begun by thinking about purgatorial suffering and then shifted in midstream to a figure from a pagan or Christian Hell.

The issue is not, I think, simply random inconsistency. There is, rather, a pervasive pattern, a deliberate forcing together of radically incompatible accounts of almost everything that matters in *Hamlet*. Is Hamlet mad or only feigning madness? Does he delay in the pursuit of revenge or only berate himself for delaying? Is Gertrude

---

3. For a sampling, see Dover Wilson, *What Happens in "Hamlet"*; Roy Battenhouse, "The Ghost in *Hamlet*. A Catholic 'Linchpin'?" *Studies in Philology* 68 (1951): 161–92; John Vyvyan, *The Shakespearean Ethic* (London: Chatto & Windus, 1959); Miriam Joseph, "Discerning the Ghost in *Hamlet*," *PMLA* 76 (1961): 302; Christopher Devlin, *Hamlet's Divinity* (Carbondale: Southern Illinois UP, 1963); Miriam Joseph, "*Hamlet*, a Christian Tragedy," *Studies in Philology* 59 (1962): 119–40; Prosser, *Hamlet and Revenge*; Robert F. Fleissner, "Subjectivity as an Occupational Hazard of 'Hamlet Ghost' Critics," *Hamlet Studies* (New Delhi) 1 (1979): 23–33; Walter N. King, *Hamlet's Search for Meaning* (Athens: U of Georgia P, 1982), pp. 22–40; Roland Mushat Frye, *The Renaissance "Hamlet": Issues and Responses in 1600* (Princeton: Princeton UP, 1984), pp. 11–24.

4. Robert West, among others, has trenchantly argued that "Shakespeare knowingly mixed the evidence and did it for the sake of dramatic impact" (Robert H. West, *Shakespeare and the Outer Mystery* [Lexington: U of Kentucky P, 1968], p. 63). West notes that quite a few critics have preceded him in this perception.

innocent or was she complicit in the murder of her husband? Is the strange account of the old king's murder accurate or distorted? Does the Ghost come from Purgatory or from Hell?—for many generations now audiences and readers have risen to the challenge and found that each of the questions may be powerfully and convincingly answered on both sides. What is at stake is more than a multiplicity of answers. The opposing positions challenge each other, clashing and sending shock waves through the play. In terms of the particular issues with which this book has been concerned, a young man from Wittenberg, with a distinctly Protestant temperament, is haunted by a distinctly Catholic ghost.

KENNETH S. ROTHWELL

An Annotated and Chronological Screenography (2002)†

This chronological compilation includes major Shakespearean adaptations and a few derivatives such as Chabrol's *Ophelia* (1962) but omits most educational documentaries and bypasses the countless *Hamlet* references in feature films such as Katharine Hepburn's recitation of the "To be or not to be" soliloquy in *Morning Glory* (1933) or Danny DeVito's teaching army recruits about the play in *Renaissance Man* (1994).

So-called *Hamlet* films and videos and DVDs come in many guises, ranging from full-scale adaptations like Kenneth Branagh's 1996 *Hamlet* down to passing references to the play (as in Steve Martin's 1991 *L.A. Story*), to documentaries such as *The Great Hamlets* (1985). Luke McKernan, British Film Institute archivist, has informally counted nearly 250 titles bearing on *Hamlet*, but even that unpublished listing is incomplete. Commentaries on and credits for most screened *Hamlet*s can be found in Bernice W. Kliman's *Hamlet: Film, Television, and Audio Performance*, which is abbreviated here as "Kliman, *Film*," and Kenneth S. Rothwell and Annabelle Henkin Melzer's *Shakespeare on Screen*, which is cited here as *SoS*. Of critical importance also is Luke McKernan and Olwen Terris's *Walking Shadows: Shakespeare in the National Film and Television Archive*. For silent film versions of *Hamlet*, which for the most part are

† Rothwell, "An Annotated and Chronological Screenography: Major *Hamlet* Adaptations and Selected Derivatives," from *Approaches to Teaching Shakespeare's* Hamlet, ed. Bernice W. Kliman (New York: Modern Language Association, 2001), 14–27. Reprinted by permission of the Modern Language Association.

omitted here, there is no substitute for Robert H. Ball's 1968 *Shakespeare on Silent Film* (cited here as "Ball"), which lists twenty-six entries for *Hamlet*, though many are of questionable status, sometimes having only borrowed the title for other scenarios. Updated commentary is also in my *History of Shakespeare on Screen* (1999). In addition, references at the close of each entry suggest other readings. Abbreviations in the screenography follow MLA and British Film Institute guidelines:

bw=black and white

col=color

mins=duration, though run times vary depending on the condition of the print and the speed of projection. Allow for some leeway especially for older films.

sd=sound

st=silent

tv=television or nonterrestrially transmitted video

Hamlet. Dir. Clément Maurice. Perf. Sarah Bernhardt (Hamlet), Pierre Magnier (Laertes). Phono-Cinéma-Théâtre. St/bw, with supplementary Edison sound cylinders. France, 1900. 3 mins.

The inaugural example of *Hamlet* in moving images and the second ever Shakespeare "movie," this fragment showing the great Bernhardt in the duel scene followed closely on the heels of the first Shakespeare movie, the Sir Herbert Beerbohm Tree *King John*, produced in 1899 by British Mutoscope and Bioscope. References: *SoS*, entry 74; Ball 23–28; Taranow 129 (see also Taranow's 13 frame enlargements, 231–34).

Hamlet. Dir. E. Hay Plumb and Cecil Hepworth. Perf. Sir Johnston Forbes-Robertson (Hamlet), Gertrude Elliott (Ophelia). Hepworth Manufacturing Company. St/bw. UK, 1913. 59 mins.

The first feature-length adaptation of *Hamlet*, which even though employing the Drury Lane London cast moves beyond theatricality into a cinematic grammar, as shown, for example, in the Méliès-like special effects of the ghost scene and the ambitious outdoor sets constructed on location at Dorset's Lulworth Cove. Sixty-one-year-old Forbes-Robertson had made a career of playing Hamlet on stage. Clips from the film appear in a 1984 documentary narrated by Trevor Nunn, *The Great Hamlets* (see below). References: *SoS*, entry 82; Kliman, *Film* 247–74; Ball 186–92; Rothwell, *History* 21–25.

Hamlet, the Drama of Vengeance. Dir. Svend Gade and Heinz Schall. Perf. Asta Nielsen (Hamlet), Mathilde Brandt (Gertrude). Art-Film. St/bw. Germany, 1920. 117 mins.

If it were not for the awkward fact that the movie considerably departs from the *Hamlet* text by turning the prince into a cross-dressed woman and by raiding the Saxo Grammaticus legend for numerous plot elements, this gender-bending movie would have to be unequivocally declared the best of the silent *Hamlet*s. Even so, postmodernist theory licenses indulgence for a film with a great actress, a protofeminist agenda, and the indubitable cinematic virtues of the Weimar expressionist school. Since Bernhardt's foray, the casting of women as Hamlet has gained considerable cachet, though Asta Nielsen departs from the Bernhardt formula somewhat by playing the prince not so much as a cross-dressed woman [but] as a woman disguised as a man, actually more in the British "breeches" tradition than in the French *travesti*. References: *SoS*, entry 86; Ball 272–78: McKernan and Terris 47–48; Guntner 90–102; Rothwell, *History* 3. Thompson.

Hamlet: Test Shots. Dir. Robert Jones. Perf. John Barrymore (Hamlet). Irving Pichel, Reginald Denny, Donald Crisp. RKO Studios. Sd/col. USA, 1933. 10 mins.

Test shots of the fabulous John Barrymore as Hamlet for a film that never materialized include the "O what a rogue and peasant slave" soliloquy and the ghost scene in act 1. They suggest how he appeared in his sublime performances on the Broadway and London stages during the 1920s at the peak of a brilliant career. An interesting sidebar for any student of the play, when it can be located. References: *SoS*, entry 89; Kliman, *Film* 316.

To Be or Not to Be. Dir. Ernst Lubitsch. Perf. Jack Benny, Carole Lombard, Robert Stack. United Artists, Sd/bw. USA, 1942. 99 mins.

This backstage pic, directed by Ernst Lubitsch, one of Hollywood's Weimar exiles, is a clever derivative of *Hamlet* that has stood the test of time and remains useful for stirring up the interest of lethargic students in Shakespeare's play. Ask them, for example, how the scenario of Lubitsch's movie logically fits the play. References: *SoS*, entry 93; Willson, *"To Be."*

Strange Illusion. Dir. Edgar G. Ulmer. Perf. James Lydon (Paul Cartwright and Hamlet), Warren William (Brett Curtis and Claudius), and Mary McLeod (Lydia and Ophelia). A PRC Picture. Sd/bw. USA, 1945. 80 mins.

A modernized *Hamlet*, like Kurosawa's *The Bad Sleep Well* (qv), *Strange Illusion* is the film noir work of a German exile, Edgar G. Ulmer, who struggled on Hollywood's Poverty Row making B horror movies until, in the 1950s, he was magically declared by the French critics to be an auteur. Some students with a keen eye for film may enjoy comparing it to *Hamlet*. Reference: *SoS*, entry 94.

Hamlet. Dir. George More O'Ferrall. Perf. John Byron (Hamlet), Sebastian Shaw (Claudius). BBC. Tv/bw. UK, 1947. 180 mins, transmitted in two parts.

Now of course unavailable, because before Kinescope there was
no handy technology for recording these early transmissions, this
ambitious *Hamlet* with a cast of seventy filling forty-eight roles was
broadcast live from the BBC's Alexandra Palace studio (actually a
derelict ex-resort) to the handful of Londoners then owning television sets. It has special interest also for, anecdotally anyway, having
influenced the deep-focus camera work in the subsequent Olivier
Hamlet. Reference: *SoS*, entry 97.

Hamlet. Dir. Laurence Olivier. Perf. Olivier (Hamlet), Jean Simmons (Ophelia), Eileen Herlie (Gertrude). Two Cities Films. Sd/bw.
UK, 1948. 152 mins.

So famous a movie as this one hardly needs additional commentary here, though worth mentioning again is the consistent and
beautiful camera work that tirelessly escorts the spectator through
the vast rooms of Elsinore and, almost literally, even into the inner-
most recesses of Hamlet's being. References: Davies 40–64; Jorgens 207–17; Kliman, *Film* 23–36.

Hamlet. Dir. George Schaefer. Perf. Maurice Evans (Hamlet),
Sarah Churchill (Ophelia). Hallmark Greeting Cards. Tv/bw. USA,
1953. 98 mins.

In the early days of television, sponsors like Hallmark Greeting
Cards actively sought to bring culture to the lobotomized masses,
though the perpetual quavering of Maurice Evans, famous for his
World War II "GI *Hamlet*," left millions with the impression that
Shakespeare was more unpalatable than palatable. References:
SoS, entry 101; Griffin; Kliman, *Film* 117–29.

Hamlet. Dir. Kishore Sahu. Perf. Mala Sinha, Venus Bannerjee.
Hindustan Chitra. Sd/bw, in Urdu. India, 1953. 80 mins (?).

Listed here simply as a reminder that nonanglophone Shakespeare
movies, including *Hamlet*, are a worldwide reality. From all accounts,
Olivier's *Hamlet* heavily influenced this film, which opened with
much fanfare in Bombay but received merciless reviews from local
critics. References: *SoS*, entry 104; Rothwell, *History* 169.

Hamlet. Dir. Ralph Nelson (CBS) and Michael Benthall (Old Vic).
Perf. John Neville (Hamlet), Barbara Jefford (Ophelia), Frederic
March (Host). DuPont Show of the Month and CBS. Tv/bw. USA,
1959. 90 mins.

An abbreviated version of an Old Vic production, imported for
the DuPont Show of the Month on television at a time when corporate sponsors had not yet reserved most of their advertising budgets
for professional athletics. In Regency costumes, the production
features a thin, rather neurasthenic John Neville as the prince and
a compelling Barbara Jefford as Ophelia. It manages some brilliant

camera work in the chaos and confusion capping the play-within-the-play scene. References: *SoS*, entry 107; Kliman, *Film* 130–38.

The Bad Sleep Well. Dir. Akira Kurosawa. Perf. Toshiro Mifune (Nishi and Hamlet), Kyoko Kagawa (Kieko and Ophelia). Toho Films. Sd /bw, Japanese with subtitles. Japan, 1960. 135 mins.

A nonanglophone *Hamlet* derivative that recontextualizes the play into contemporary Japan. Despite the gap between the cinematic and Shakespearean text, Kurosawa's epistemological anxieties strike a chord reminiscent of Shakespeare's own obsession with the interplay between illusion and reality. References: *SoS*, entry 107; Perret; Rothwell, "Akira Kurosawa."

Hamlet: Prinz von Danemark. Dir. Franz Wirth. Perf. Maximilian Schell (Hamlet), Hans Caninenberg (Claudius), Dunja Mobar (Ophelia). Bavaria Attelier. Tv/bw, dubbed-in English. West Germany, 1960. 127 mins.

It was originally filmed for Austrian television, then later brought to America by Edward Dmytryk and screened theatrically with dubbed-in English. Schell makes a precise, Teutonic Hamlet whose perturbed spirit lends power even to the minimalist set. References: *SoS*, entry 110; Kliman, *Film* 139–53; Coursen, "A German *Hamlet*"; Wilds.

Ophelia. Dir. Claude Chabrol. Perf. André Jocelyn (Yvan and Hamlet), Juliette Maniel (Lucie and Ophelia). Boreal Pictures. Sd/bw, English subtitles. France, 1962. 150 mins.

A derivative from *Hamlet*, not an adaptation, but so incredibly resourceful and compelling in its exploration of the interplay between what seems and what is that it effectively mirrors the quandaries of Hamlet himself. Like other serious derivatives, it offers a sounding board for discovering fresh possibilities of interpretation. References: *SoS*, entry 111; Kliman, "Chabrol's *Ophelia*"; Newman.

Hamlet at Elsinore. Dir. Philip Saville. Perf. Christopher Plummer (Hamlet), Michael Caine (Horatio), Robert Shaw (Claudius), Donald Sutherland (Fortinbras), Lindsay Kemp (Player Queen). BBC and Danmarks Radio. Bw/tv. UK and Denmark, 1963. 170 mins.

At the time a critic rhapsodized over Plummer's portrayal as the embodiment of Goethe's romantic idea of the prince of Denmark as "a gentle spirit broken by a burden too heavy for him to bear," which tells part of the story. What needs to be added is mention of Plummer's wit and resourcefulness in capturing the full flavor of Hamlet's intricate personality, though the use of the castle at Elsinore as location actually does not embellish the production much at all. This memorable performance with a remarkable cast rivals the nearly contemporaneous Burton *Hamlet* and should not be allowed to go gently into the night. References: *SoS*, entry 118; Kliman, *Film* 154–66; Coursen, *Watching Shakespeare* 62–63.

Gamlet. Dir. Grigori Kozintsev. Perf. Innokenti Smoktunovsky (Hamlet), Anastasia Vertinskaya (Ophelia), Elza Radzin-Szolkonis (Gertrude). LenFilm. Sd/bw, English subtitles. USSR, 1964. 148 mins.

Grigori Kozintsev thought that the secret of filmic success lay in the ability "to point a cine camera," a creed that he practiced as successfully as he advocated. Searing, explosive images fill the screen as the late Innokenti Smoktunovsky unforgettably places Hamlet's story into a Russian context against harsh images of stone, water, and iron. Ophelia straitjacketed in an iron farthingale becomes the ultimate icon for female subjugation, while Boris Pasternak's translation and Dmitri Shostakovich's score lend even more interest. Legal tangles have unhappily prevented this wonderful film from being recorded on videocassette, though it is available on 16mm film from Corinth Films, 34 Gansevoort Street, New York City, NY 10014. For rates, phone 800 221-4720. References: *SoS*, entry 116; Jorgens 218–34; Kliman, *Film* 87–11:3. [The film is now available on DVD.]

Hamlet. Dir. John Gielgud. Perf. Richard Burton (Hamlet), Hume Cronyn (Polonius), Alfred Drake (Claudius), Eileen Herlie (Gertrude), Linda Marsh (Ophelia). Electronovision Theatrofilm. Sd/bw. USA, 1964. 199 mins.

Acted in "rehearsal clothes" (whatever that means, as some actors wear sweaters and others coats and ties) at New York's Lunt-Fontanne Theatre, this stage production was later, by a now obsolete technology called electronovision, simultaneously released on film throughout the hinterlands nationwide to give provincial folk a taste of Shakespeare live on Broadway. Burton's raw power as a virile Hamlet prevents the endeavor from teetering over into disaster. Long out of circulation, it recently reemerged in the UK on PAL, then in the USA on NSTC VHS formats, and in 2000 on a shiny new DVD. References: *SoS*, entry 117; McKernan and Terris 55–56; Sterne.

Enter Hamlet. Dir. Fred Mogubgub. Perf. Maurice Evans (Narrator). Janus New Cinema. Sd/animation. USA, 1965 or 1967 (?). 10 mins.

An animation of the "To be or not to be" soliloquy with Maurice Evans as the offscreen narrator that is distinguished for an intricate fugue of visual and verbal puns paralleling Shakespeare's words. Reference: Kliman, "Enter Hamlet."

Shakespeare Wallah. Dir. James Ivory. Prod. Ismail Merchant. Screenplay Ruth Prawer Jhabvala and James Ivory. Perf. Shashi Kapoor (Sanji), Felicity Kendal (Lizzie Buckingham), Madhur Jaffrey (Manjulla), Geoffrey Kendal (Mr. Buckingham), Laura Liddell (Mrs. Buckingham). Sd/col. India, 1965. 115 mins.

An early Merchant-Ivory production about a British acting troupe touring India, based on the lives of the Kendal family, featuring an East-West love story as well as scenes from Shakespeare plays, including *Hamlet*. No one should miss this wonderful brew of heartache and humor, which measures the height and depth of the human spirit against the exquisitely refined interplay between British and Indian culture. Reference: Wayne (takes a position at variance with the above comments).

Hamlet. Dir. Tony Richardson. Perf. Nicol Williamson (Hamlet), Judy Parfitt (Gertrude), Anthony Hopkins (Claudius), Marianne Faithfull (Ophelia). A Woodfall Production. Sd/col. UK, 1969. 117 mins.

Nicol Williamson's Hamlet is closer to a seismic upheaval than to the neo-Victorian representation of the prince as a sensitive young fellow. He doesn't just act, he gyrates and wheels and spins and spits out his anger against stuffy bourgeois values so energetically, one fears he will self-destruct. His stage performances as Hamlet in London and in North America had already made him famous for tantrums, which linger on in this hastily made movie shot in the claustrophobic cellars of London's Roundhouse Theatre. The decision to film almost entirely in close and mid shot deprives the actors of legs, but authentic feeling emerges anyway in the elegant portraiture of the tight shots. An excellent film for showing students how *Hamlet* resists stereotypes, it was probably also produced as a small-screen experience with residual television rights in mind. References: *SoS*, entry 123; Kliman, *Film* 167–79; Manvell 127–30; Mullin.

Hamlet. Dir. Peter Wood. Perf. Richard Chamberlain (Hamlet), Michael Redgrave (Polonius), John Gielgud (Ghost). Hallmark Hall of Fame and NBC. Tv/col. UK, 1970. 115 mins.

A drastically cut made-for-television version in Regency period costumes, filmed on location at Raby Castle. This was an early example of the Masterpiece Theatre syndrome, by which highbrow American tastes, largely ignored by commercial networks, were catered to by British television. Jay Halio saw Chamberlain's Hamlet as a rather high-minded young man whose worldview was underwritten by a notable use of Christian iconography. Kliman thought the visual codes splendid but Chamberlain too "bland" for the mercurial role. References: *SoS*, entry 126; Halio; Kliman, *Film* 180–87.

Hamlet. Dir. David Giles and Robert Chetwyn. Perf. Ian McKellen (Hamlet), John Woodvine (Claudius), Tim Pigott-Smith (Laertes), Susan Fleetwood (Ophelia). BBC-2 and Prospect Theatre. Tv/col. UK, 1972; USA (CBS), 1982. 115 mins.

In this London stage play adapted to television, a youthful Ian McKellen was allowed an opportunity to show his considerable talents in a production later televised in the United States. Despite McKellen's impressive performance, a limited budget undercut him with sparse sets and a propensity to cramp him with excessive close and mid shots. References: *SoS*, entry 129; Kliman, *Film* 188–94.

Hamlet. Dir. Celestino Coronado. Perf. Anthony Meyer and David Meyer (Hamlet and Hamlet's Father), Helen Mirren (Gertrude and Ophelia), Vladek Sheybal (First Player and Player Queen and Lucianus). Cabochon Films and Royal College of Art. Tv/col. UK, 1976. 67 mins.

Coronado's two transgressive Shakespeare movies (this and *Midsummer Night's Dream*, 1984) eagerly ferret out the subtext's darkest, most hidden secrets (usually sexual) and are therefore not recommended for beginning students. This *Hamlet*, however, is caviar for the cognoscenti who can tolerate a split vision of Hamlet (played by the Meyer brothers) that dissects the psyche of a human being torn by conflicting attachments to father, mother, and girlfriend. Shot on video in one week by enthusiastic young people and later transferred to 16mm film, this is not a movie for persons unacquainted with the play. References: *SoS*, entry 132; Holderness 63–74; McKernan and Terris 58–59; Rothwell, *History* 202–03.

Dogg's Troupe Hamlet. Dir. Ed Berman. Perf. Jane Gambia, Katina Noble, John Perry. Inter-Action and Hornsey Coll. of Art. Sd/col/16mm. UK, 1977. 15 mins.

Tom Stoppard's fifteen-minute version of *Hamlet* performed on the steps of the National Theatre. See also his 1995 version below. Reference: Terris 4.

Hamlet. Dir. Rodney Bennett. Prod. Cedric Messina. Perf. Derek Jacobi (Hamlet), Claire Bloom (Gertrude), Patrick Stewart (Claudius), Lalla Ward (Ophelia). BBC and Time-Life's The Shakespeare Plays. Tv/col. UK, 1980. 210 mins.

One of the productions in the Shakespeare Series made by the BBC with United States financing that was partially designed to please "purist" American classroom teachers but neglected to use any American actors. The result is a splendid reading of *Hamlet* by distinguished actors like Derek Jacobi and Patrick Stewart (Captain Jean-Luc Picard of *Star Trek* fame), but not much in the way of visual excitement. When it is assigned for library study, students tend to read the text as they screen the video, which suggests that they'd be better off with a plain audio rather than an audiovisual experience. This is not to say that there aren't grand moments, especially the play-within-a-play when Jacobi as the prince and

Stewart as the corrupt king come to their moment of truth. References: *SoS*, entry 140; *Shakespeare Plays*; Coursen, *"Hamlet"*; Kliman, *Film* 195–201; Rothwell, *"Hamlet"*; Taylor.

Hamlet Act. Dir. Robert Nelson and Joseph Chang. Perf. Dick Blau (Hamlet), Bob Whitney (Polonius). Univ. of Wisconsin Film Dept. Sd/col (?). USA, 1982. 21 mins.

An avant-garde postmodernist exploration of the epistemological puzzles in *Hamlet*, built around the metadrama of Hamlet's advice to the players. As the scene is enacted through the use of an on-site video camera, the play becomes nested in other plays, until Hamlet begins to become the spectator for his own play. This is an interesting essay but probably more bewildering than enlightening for the novice student. References: *SoS*, entry 144; Birringer; Kliman, *Film* 317.

The Great Hamlets, Parts 1 and 2. Dir. Derek Bailey. Perf. Trevor Nunn (interviewer) and interviewees playing themselves and Hamlet: Laurence Olivier, John Gielgud, Richard Burton, Maximilian Schell, Jean Louis Barrault, Vittorio Gassman, Mandy Patinkin, Innokenti Smoktunovsky, Nicol Williamson, and Ben Kingsley. Tv/col. Thames. UK, 1982. Part 1, 53 mins; part 2, 56 mins.

In this most absorbing educational documentary, the RSC director Trevor Nunn interrogates famous twentieth-century Shakespearean actors about their interpretations of *Hamlet*. They comment not only on their own performances but on their colleagues' as well, Laurence Olivier's contrasting his Hamlet with John Gielgud's being a case in point. Backing up the talking but passionate heads are clips from all their films, which highlight differences among the mercurial Burton, diffident Kingsley, meditative Olivier, decisive Schell, and forth. There is even a clip or two from the Sir Johnston Forbes-Robertson 1913 silent *Hamlet*, which adds a detritus of historic richness. It's full of interesting tidbits, such as the revelation from Olivier that his *Hamlet* was in black and white because he was having fights with Technicolor, Inc., about the color of the *Henry V* prints, and that Olivier got his much-contested summary sentence about the work being about "a man who could not make up his mind" from a Gary Cooper film (probably *Souls at Sea*, 1937). References: Mahon, *"Hamlet"*; Writing Company Catalogue (1999) 30.

Playing Shakespeare. An eleven-part program originally aired on UK Channel 4 Television, now available from Films for the Humanities (qv). Written and dir. John Barton. Perf. RSC actors, including Ben Kingsley, Ian McKellen, Michael Pennington, Judi Dench, and others. Tv/col. UK, 1984. c. 50 mins. each.

A skillfully directed series by John Barton that really aims more at acting students than at typical undergraduates, but it does have three or four absorbing segments from *Hamlet*, particularly in programs 1, 3, and 6. More directly concerned with *Hamlet* is *The Great Hamlets*, above. References: *SoS*, entries 723–34; Huffman.

To Be or Not to Be. Dir. Alan Johnson. Perf. Mel Brooks (Frederick Bronski), Anne Bancroft (Anna Bronski), Tim Matheson (Lieutenant Andre Sobinski), Charles Durning (Colonel Erhardt), Christopher Lloyd (Captain Schultz), José Ferrer (Professor Siletski). Sd/col. USA, 1983. 108 mins.

A remake of the 1942 Jack Benny version, which lacks the sparkle of its predecessor, though so gifted a comic as Mel Brooks should never be underestimated. References: *SoS*, entry 147; Willson, "*To Be or Not to Be* Once More."

Den tragiska historien om Hamlet, prinz av Danmark. Dir. Ragnar Lyth. Perf. Stellan Skarsgaard (Hamlet), Mona Malm (Gertrude), Frej Lindquist (Claudius), Pernilla Wallgren (Ophelia). SVT 1. Tv/col. English subtitles. Sweden, 1984. 160 mins.

Ragnar Lyth never flags in his feverish quest for originality from the opening sequence, which shows an Elsinore steeped in domesticity, to the macabre burial of poor Ophelia in a cheap wooden coffin, to the prince's wild revenge, when a demonic Skarsgaard turns the duel scene with Laertes into a grotesque but lethal farce. Here is a Hamlet who progresses from an unkempt hippie into a vicious skinhead and who benefits from the imaginative settings, which turn a nineteenth-century Nobel explosives factory into a bizarre ambiance for dire events presided over by a caged crow. A daring and intelligent translation of Shakespeare's words into images. References: *SoS*, entry 148; Kliman, *Film* 202–24; Rothwell, *History* 173–76.

Hamlet. Dir. Roland Kenyon and Rod MacDonald. Perf. Tricia Hitchcock (Ophelia), Melanie Revill (Gertrude), Richard Spaul (Claudius), entire cast (Hamlet). Cambridge Experimental Theatre. Tv/col. UK, 1987. 96 mins.

Like the Coronado *Hamlet* unapologetically experimental, this offbeat production turns the entire cast into Hamlet, with masked actors speaking separately, simultaneously, and contrapuntally. It thereby underscores how Hamlet substantially reflects or mirrors the play's other characters. We are all Hamlet, in a sense. Not for beginners, this highly choreographed production with overtones of rock video will provide the basis for spirited discussion by people who know the play. References: *SoS*, entry 154; Crowl, "Fragments"; Maher, "Stage into Film"; Spaul, Ritchie, and Wheale. In 1987, the videocassette was available for $195.00 from Audio-Visual Unit, Cambridgeshire College of Arts and Technology, East Road, Cambridge CB1 1PT.

Hamlet Goes Business. Dir. Aki Kaurismaki. Perf. Pirkka-Pekka
Petelins (Hamlet), Kati Outinen (Ophelia), Elina Salo (Gertrude),
Esko Salminen (Klaus), Kari Väänänen (Polonius), Hannu Valtonen
(Simo), Mari Rantasila (Helena). Finnkino and Villealfa. Sd/bw.
Finland, 1989. 86 mins.

Another postmodernist take on *Hamlet*, along the lines of the
Cambridge Experimental Theatre production described above, only
this one is possibly more a destruction than a deconstruction of the
text. In a film noir mode, its modern-day characters closely follow
the *Hamlet* story line, which has been reshaped to echo an old Warner Bros. thriller. Screened at the seventeenth Norwegian Film
Festival, it kept the audience "wide awake." Reference: Kell.

Hamlet. Dir. Kevin Kline and Kirk Browning. Perf. Kline (Hamlet),
Peter James (Horatio), Dana Ivey (Gertrude), Diane Venora (Ophelia). New York Shakespeare Festival and WNET. Great Performances. Tv/col. USA, 1990. 150 mins.

Kevin Kline accomplishes the double feat of simultaneously directing and acting in this Hamlet, which was originally produced for the
New York Shakespeare Festival and subsequently transmitted on
public television. His special niche was to explore the potential madness of Hamlet, so that he was constantly walking a fine line between
jocularity and a lunatic behavior spiced with razor-edged wit. Besides
Kline's obvious talents, I found Peter James's Horatio one of the best
ever, in the way James makes this static character kinetic. References: Maher, "American *Hamlet*" and "Kevin Kline"; Pall.

Hamlet. Dir. Franco Zeffirelli. Perf. Mel Gibson (Hamlet), Glenn
Close (Gertrude), Alan Bates (Claudius), Helena Bonham Carter
(Ophelia), Paul Scofield (Ghost), John McEnery (Osric). Carolco.
Sd/col. USA, 1990. 134 mins.

Although technically credited to the United States, this Shakespeare movie—with an Italian director, Australian star, British supporting players, and an American like Glenn Close sprinkled in here
and there—obviously reflects the internationalization of the cinema
industry that has long abandoned the "classical Hollywood cinema"
of the 1930s and 1940s. Nowadays the stars do not inhabit storybook
homes in Beverly Hills like Pickfair but jet in from everywhere. True
to his belief in popularizing art for the masses, Franco Zeffirelli
brilliantly chose the unlikely Mel Gibson, macho survivor of shoot
'em, slash 'em, blow 'em up action movies, for his prince of Denmark. And why not? Hamlet is a one-man exercise in cultural diver-
sity who can be tweaked into virtually any kind of behavior, but
Gibson confounded his critics by playing the role with sensitivity
and imagination—almost too much so, one critic argued, finding
the production "dour." So powerful is the aura projected by Glenn
Close that Hamlet's paternal obsession gets overshadowed by his

passion for the maternal. The scenarists further redirected the script into cinematic idiom, dropping Fortinbras (who is often sacrificed both on stage and screen to the exigencies of time) and adding a highly inventive opening scene of King Hamlet's burial. Gone also are the vivid colors of Zeffirelli's Italian films, to be replaced by a kind of blue-gray haze, but the supporting cast, the location settings in crumbling British castles like Dover, and the movie's surging energy reassert the timeless appeal of Shakespeare's great tragedy. References: Quinn; Romney 48–49; Impastato; Skovmand; Rothwell, *History* 137–42.

L.A. Story. Dir. Mick Jackson. Prod. Mario Kassar and Steve Martin. Screenplay by Martin. Perf. Martin (Harris K. Telemacher), Victoria Tennant (Sara McDowel), and Rick Moranis (Gravedigger, uncredited). Rastar Productions. Sd/col. USA, 1991. 95 mins.

Steve Martin's witty spoof on the gravedigger scene from *Hamlet* becomes a memento mori from late medievalism displaced into a mawkish Hollywood cemetery. Moments like this prove once again the essentialist nature of Shakespeare's obsession with human mortality. References: Buhler, "Antic Dispositions"; Floyd.

Rosencrantz and Guildenstern Are Dead. Dir. and screenplay by Tom Stoppard. Perf. Gary Oldman (Rosencrantz), Tim Roth (Guildenstern), Richard Dreyfuss (Player). Brandenberg Intl. Cinecom Entertainment. Sd/col. USA, 1991. 118 mins.

In the tradition of Luigi Pirandello's *Six Characters in Search of an Author*, Stoppard turns two minor characters from Hamlet loose to blunder into a web of intrigue and inevitable doom. Their fate underscores the fallout from Hamlet's strange behavior, though what happens to them is absurd but not funny. References: Aspden; Wheeler.

Shakespeare: The Animated Tales: Hamlet. Screenplay Leon Garfield. Dir. Natalia Orlova. Designers Peter Kotov, Natasha Demidova. Soyusmultifilm et al. Sd/col. Moscow and Cardiff, 1992. 30 mins.

Generations of literature teachers have railed against the subversion of academic standards when indolent students swap the printed text for a comic book. If it were done, though, "'twere well / It were done [well]," as it is in this ingenious animation. Reference: Osborne.

Last Action Hero. Dir. John McTiernan. Prod. McTiernan et al. Written by Zak Penn. Perf. Arnold Schwarzenegger (Jack Slater and Himself), Charles Dance (Benedict), Tom Noonan (Ripper and Himself), Robert Prosky (Nick), Austin O'Brien (Danny Madigan), Joan Plowright (Teacher), Apollo Dukakis (Polonius). SA/col. USA, 1993. 130 mins.

A metadramatic treatment of *Hamlet* that offers yet another insight into the play from a fresh perspective. The distinction between illusion and reality blurs as a little boy watches his modern hero take on some of the coloration of the prince of Denmark—with allusions to Olivier's *Hamlet*. Reference: Mallin.

The Lion King. Dir. Roger Allers and Rob Minkoff. Perf. (voices only) James Earl Jones, Nathan Lane, Whoopi Goldberg. Walt Disney Productions. Sd/col. USA, 1994. 88 mins.

The obvious parallels to *Hamlet* in this elaborate animation provided quite a stir when it was released several years ago, some parents even worrying about its being too traumatic for children. Since then it has been staged by Julie Taymor, the director of the 1999 film *Titus*, with Anthony Hopkins as the emperor Titus. References: Klass; Myers.

The Fifteen-Minute Hamlet. Dir. Todd Louiso. Prod. Gina Belafonte et al. Based on play by Tom Stoppard. Perf. Austin Pendleton (Hamlet), Ernest Perry Jr. (Claudius and Polonius), Angie Phillips (Gertrude), Todd Louiso (Ophelia). Cin-cine 19. Sd/col. USA, 1995. 22 mins.

In this Tom Stoppard spoof, the main gag has Shakespeare throwing away sheets of his work so that *Hamlet* can be squeezed into a fifteen-minute and then a two-minute film. Transmitted recently on cable television. Reference: www.imdb.com/title?0125746.

In the Bleak Midwinter (USA: *A Midwinter's Tale*). Dir. Kenneth Branagh. Screenplay Branagh. Prod. David Barron et al. Perf. Michael Maloney (Joe Harper and Hamlet), Richard Briers (Henry Wakefield and Claudius and Ghost, and Player King), Hetta Charnley (Molly), Joan Collins (Margaretta D'Arcy), Nicholas Farrell (Tom Newman and Laertes and Fortinbras), Mark Hadfield (Vernon Spatch and Polonius and Marcellus and First Gravedigger), Julia Sawalha (Nina and Ophelia). Rank and Midwinter Films. Sd/bw. UK, 1995. 98 mins.

A group of down-at-the-heels actors assemble in an abandoned church to rehearse and produce *Hamlet*, a play that to them is not just larger than life but life itself. In its Chekhovian nostalgia for a lost past, Branagh's low budget movie reminds me of *Shakespeare Wallah*, in which there are also tears for things in the midst of not just bleak midwinter but a redemptive life force. Reference: Jays.

Hamlet. Dir. Kenneth Branagh. Perf. Branagh (Hamlet), Derek Jacobi (Claudius), Julie Christie (Gertrude), Brian Blessed (Ghost and Old Hamlet), Michael Maloney (Laertes), Nicholas Farrell (Horatio), Kate Winslet (Ophelia), Charlton Heston (Player King), Rosemary Harris (Player Queen), Rufus Sewall (Fortinbras), Billy

Crystal (First Gravedigger), Gerard Depardieu (Reynaldo), Robin
Williams (Osric), Jack Lemmon (Marcellus), John Gielgud (Priam),
Judi Dench (Hecuba). Castle Rock Entertainment. Sd/col. UK,
1996. 242 mins.

Kenneth Branagh achieved the unachievable in managing to produce, direct, and star in an uncut, four-hour *Hamlet* with a cast of
big-name stars filmed on wintry location at Blenheim Palace and
indoors on a Shepperton set opulent enough for Sigmund Romberg's
Student Prince. Branagh's prince emerges as an activist, aggressive
young man, who ends the picture by literally swinging on a rope like
a circus acrobat, though the energy, supported by a swooping, swirling, almost dizzying camera, tends to erase the prince's more
thoughtful side. Branagh's supporting cast of famous actors is a daring exercise in code switching, a device that some critics stigmatized
as "stunt casting" but that others praised as a clever scheme to
ensnare the audience's attention. Who ever paid any attention to
Marcellus until Jack Lemmon played the role? Taken all in all, this
is a dazzling film of *Hamlet* that will delight students even when some
of their teachers are hunting for ways to find fault with it. References:
Branagh; Pendleton; Mahon, "Editor's View"; Felperin; Bidder,
"Double Takes"; Crowl, *"Hamlet"* (1997); Rothwell, *History* 253–58.

Shakespeare in Love. Dir. John Madden. Written by Marc Norman and Tom Stoppard. Perf. Joseph Fiennes (Will Shakespeare),
Gwyneth Paltrow (Viola de Lesseps), Judi Dench (Queen Elizabeth), Ben Affleck (Ned Alleyn), Colin Firth (Lord Wessex),
Geoffrey Rush (Philip Henslowe), Rupert Everett (Christopher
Marlowe), Imelda Staunton (Nurse). Miramax Films. Sd/col. UK,
1998. 122 mins.

Nothing much to do with *Hamlet*, everything with *Romeo and
Juliet*, but listed here simply because it's the most popular Shakespeare movie of recent times, one that is guaranteed to stir the
interest of even the grumpiest student. Historically accurate? Of
course not, but then neither were Shakespeare's history plays. Reference: Rothwell, *"Elizabeth."*

Hamlet. Dir. Michael Almereyda. Perf. Ethan Hawke (Hamlet),
Kyle MacLachlan (Claudius), Sam Shepard (Ghost), Diane Venora
(Gertrude), Bill Murray (Polonius), Casey Affleck (Fortinbras),
Julia Stiles (Ophelia). Miramax. Sd/col. USA, 2000. 111 mins.

This bold modernization set in New York City with much of the
text intact intrigued a sophisticated preview audience at the April
2000 Montreal convention of the Shakespeare Association of America. It's full of witty surprises, including Hamlet's discovery while
airborne on a jet en route to England of a laptop with Claudius's
message on the hard drive ordering the executions of Rosencrantz

and Guildenstern. As Hamlet, Ethan Hawke manages to be contemporary cool and yet passionate; as Claudius, jut-jawed star Kyle MacLachlan radiates corporate power; as Gertrude, Diane Venora is both wary and ravishing; as Ophelia, Julia Stiles goes wonderfully mad in the Guggenheim Museum; as the Ghost, a chilling, frozen-faced Sam Shepard almost steals the show; and as Polonius, Bill Murray seems properly bewildered. Undergraduates will probably love it. References: The Internet Movie Database (www.imdb.com); Crowl, "Hamlet" (2000).

Where Do I Buy or Lease These Films? To the question of how to obtain these films there is no simple answer, because ownership and availability are as unstable as the soil on a California hillside. The best strategy is to get on the telephone and begin calling or to get on the Internet and begin surfing. For that reason there has been no attempt, with a few exceptions, to give definitive information about dealers and distributors of specific films. Silent movies are, when not entirely lost, generally unavailable except in such archives as the NFTVA at the British Film Institute in London; the Folger Library and Library of Congress Motion Picture Division in Washington, DC; and the Museum of Modern Art in New York City. But at times *Hamlet* segments appear in anthology collections such as *The Great Hamlets* (see above). Prolix video distributor lists are available in such easily accessible annual paperback publications as *VideoHounds Golden Movie Retriever* (New York: Gale Research, 1998). It may, however, be worth trying the following retailers that have shown a special commitment to Shakespeare on video.

Poor Yorick CD and Video Emporium, 89a Downie Street, Stratford, Ontario, Canada N5A 1W8. Phone 519 272-1999; fax 519 272-0979; yorick@bardcentral.com. Web site: www.bardcentral.com/category.html.

The Writing Company, 10200 Jefferson Blvd., PO Box 802, Culver City, CA 90232-0802. Phone 800 421-4246; fax 800 944-5432; access@writingco.com. Web site: writingco.com.

Facets Multimedia Incorporated, 1517 West Fullerton Avenue, Chicago, IL 60614. Phone 800 331-6192; fax 773 929-5437; sales@facets.org. Web site: www.facets.org.

Films for the Humanities, PO Box 2035, Princeton, NJ 08513, Phone 800 257-5126.

The Web site of the Internet Movie Database, www.imdb.com/Credits?/, can also be extremely useful.

Note: The author is grateful to Neal-Schuman Publishers for permission to use here updated and revised material from his (with

Annabelle Henkin Melzer) *Shakespeare on Screen: An International Filmography and Videography.*

Works Cited

Aspden, Peter. Rev. of *Rosencrantz and Guildenstern Are Dead.* Dir. Tom Stoppard. *Sight and Sound* ns 1.2 (1991): 58.

Ball, Robert H. *Shakespeare on Silent Film: A Strange Eventful History.* London: Allen, 1968.

Barton, John. *Playing Shakespeare.* London: Methuen, 1984.

Birringer, Johannes H. "Rehearsing the Mousetrap: Robert Nelson's *Hamlet Act.*" *Shakespeare on Film Newsletter* 9.1 (1984): 1+.

Boose, Lynda E., and Richard Burt, eds. *Shakespeare, the Movie: Popularizing the Plays on Film, TV, and Video.* London: Routledge, 1997.

Branagh, Kenneth. Hamlet: *Screenplay and Introduction.* New York: Norton, 1996.

Buhler, Stephen M. "Antic Dispositions: Shakespeare and Steve Martin's *L. A. Story.*" *Shakespeare Yearbook* 8 (1997): 212–29.

———. "Double Takes: Branagh Gets to *Hamlet.*" *Post Script. Essays in Film and the Humanities* 17.1 (1997): 43–52.

———. "Text, Eyes, and Videotape: Screening Shakespeare Script." *Shakespeare Quarterly* 46 (1995): 236–44.

Bulman, J. C., and H. R. Coursen. *Shakespeare on Television: An Anthology of Essays and Reviews.* Hanover: U P of New England, 1988.

Burnett, Mark Thornton. "The 'Very Cunning of the Scene': Kenneth Branagh's *Hamlet.*" *Literature/Film Quarterly* 25.2 (1997): 78–82.

Coursen, Herbert R. "A German *Hamlet.*" *Shakespeare on Film Newsletter* 11.1 (1986): 4.

———. "*Hamlet.*" *Shakespeare on Film Newsletter* 5.2 (1981): 5+.

———. *Watching Shakespeare on Television.* London: Assoc. UP, 1993.

Crowl, Samuel. "Fragments." *Shakespeare on Film Newsletter* 13.1 (1988): 7.

———. "*Hamlet.*" *Shakespeare Bulletin* 15.1 (1997): 34–35.

———. "*Hamlet.*" *Shakespeare Bulletin* 18.4 (2000): 39–40.

Davies, Anthony. *Filming Shakespeare's Plays: The Adaptations of Laurence Olivier, Orson Welles, Peter Brook, and Akira Kurosawa.* Cambridge: Cambridge UP, 1988.

Donaldson, Peter S. "Ghostly Texts and Virtual Performances: Old Hamlet in New Media." Multimedia presentation. Meeting of the Shakespeare Assn. of Amer. Atlanta. 2 Apr. 1993.

———. *Shakespearean Films / Shakespearean Directors.* Boston: Unwin, 1990.

Felperin, Leslie. *"Hamlet."* Rev. of *Hamlet.* Dir. Kenneth Branagh. *Sight and Sound* 7.2 (1997): 46–47.

Floyd, Nigel. Rev. of *L.A. Story.* Dir. Mick Jackson. *Sight and Sound* ns. 1.1 (1991): 53.

Griffin, Alice. "Shakespeare through the Camera's Eye." *Shakespeare Quarterly* 4 (1953): 33–34.

Guntner, Lawrence. "Expressionist Shakespeare: The Gade/Nielsen *Hamlet* (1920) and the History of Shakespeare on Film." *Post Script: Essays in Film and the Humanities* 17.2 (1998): 90–102.

Halio, Jay. "Three Filmed *Hamlets.*" *Literature/Film Quarterly* 1.4 (1973): 317–18.

Holderness, Graham. "Shakespeare Rewound." *Shakespeare Survey* 45 (1993): 63–74.

Huffman, Clifford. "The RSC *Playing Shakespeare* Tapes in a College Classroom." *Shakespeare on Film Newsletter* 14.2 (1990): 3.

Impastato, David. "Zeffirelli's *Hamlet* and the Baroque." *Shakespeare on Film Newsletter* 16.2 (1992): 1+.

———. "Zeffirelli's *Hamlet*: Sunlight Makes Meaning." *Shakespeare on Film Newsletter* 16.2 (1991): 1+.

Jackson, Russell. "Film Diary." *Branagh* 175–208.

Jays, David. Rev. of *In the Bleak Midwinter.* Dir. Kenneth Branagh. *Sight and Sound* ns 5.12 (1995): 47.

Jorgens, Jack J. *Shakespeare on Film.* Bloomington: Indiana UP, 1977.

Kell. Rev. of *Hamlet Goes Business.* Dir. Aki Kaurismäki. *Variety* 30 Aug. 1989.

Klass, Perri. "A 'Bambi' for the 90's via Shakespeare." Rev. of *The Lion King.* Dir. Roger Allers and Rob Minkoff. *New York Times* 19 June 1994, sec. 2: 1+.

Klein, Holger, and Dimiter Daphinoff, eds. *Hamlet on Screen. Shakespeare Yearbook* 8. Lewiston: Mellon, 1997.

Kliman, Bernice W. "Chabrol's *Ophelia.*" *Shakespeare on Film Newsletter* 3.1 (1978): 1+.

———. "'Enter Hamlet': A Demythologizing Approach to *Hamlet.*" *Shakespeare on Film Newsletter* 15.1 (1990): 2+.

———. *Hamlet: Film, Television, and Audio Performance.* London: Assoc. UP, 1988.

Maher, Mary Z. "Kevin Kline: 'In Action How like an Angel.'" *Modern Hamlets and Their Soliloquies.* Iowa City: Iowa UP, 1992. 175–200.

———. "Kevin Kline's American *Hamlet*: Stage to Screen." *Shakespeare on Film Newsletter* 15.2 (1991): 12.

———. "Stage into Film Doesn't Go." *Shakespeare on Film Newsletter* 13.1 (1988): 7.

Mahon, John W. "Editor's View." Rev. of Branagh's *Hamlet*. *Shakespeare Newsletter* 46.3 (1996): 66+.

———. "*Hamlet* on Video." *Shakespeare Newsletter* 46.4 (1996): 80+.

Mallin, Eric S. "You Kilt My Foddah'; or, Arnold, Prince of Denmark." *Shakespeare Quarterly* 50 (1999): 127–51.

Manvell, Roger. *Shakespeare and the Film*. 1971. New York: A. Barnes, 1979.

McKellen, Ian, and Richard Loncraine. *William Shakespeare's Richard III: A Screenplay*. New York: Overlook, 1996.

McKernan, Luke, and Olwen Terris. *Walking Shadows: Shakespeare in the National Film and Television Archive*. London: British Film Inst., 1994.

McMurtry, Jo. *Shakespeare Films in the Classroom: A Descriptive Guide*. Hamden: Archon, 1994.

Mullin, Michael. "Tony Richardson's *Hamlet*: Script and Screen." *Literature/Film Quarterly* 4.2 (1976): 123–33.

Myers, Caren. Rev. of *The Lion King*. Dir. Roger Allers and Rob Minkoff. *Sight and Sound* ns. 4.10 (1994): 47–48.

Newman, Karen. "Chabrol's *Ophelia*." *Shakespeare on Film Newsletter* 6.2 (1982): 1+.

Norman, Marc, and Tom Stoppard. *Shakespeare in Love*. Filmscript. London: Faber, 1999.

Osborne, Laurie. "Poetry in Motion: Animating Shakespeare." Boose and Burt 103–20.

Pall, Ellen. "Kevin Kline Discovers There's a Rub in TV." *New York Times* 28 Oct. 1990: H35.

Pendleton, Thomas. "And the Thoughts of the Other Editor." Rev. of Branagh's *Hamlet*. *Shakespeare Newsletter* 46.3 (1996): 60.

Perret, Marion D. "Kurosawa's *Hamlet*." Samurai in Business Dress." *Shakespeare on Film Newsletter* 46.3 (1996): 6.

Quinn, Edward. "Zeffirelli's *Hamlet*." *Shakespeare on Film Newsletter* 15.2 (1991): 1+.

Romney, Jonathan. "*Hamlet*." *Sight and Sound* ns. 1.1 (1991): 48–49.

Rothwell, Kenneth S. "Akira Kurosawa and the Shakespearean Vision: *The Bad Sleep Well* as a 'Mirror up to Nature.'" *Shakespeare Worldwide: Translation and Adaptation*. Vol. 14–15. Ed. Yoshiko Kawachi. Tokyo: Yushodo, 1995. 168–85.

———. "*Elizabeth and Shakespeare in Love*." Rev. of *Shakespeare in Love*. Dir. John Madden. *Cineaste* 34.2–3 (1999): 78–80.

———. "*Hamlet* and the Five Plays of [BBC] Season Three." *Shakespeare Quarterly* 32 (1981): 396.

———. *A History of Shakespeare on Screen: A Century of Film and Television*. Cambridge: Cambridge UP, 1999.

Rothwell, Kenneth S., and Annabelle Henkin Melzer. *Shakespeare on Screen: An International Filmography and Videography*. London: Neal, 1990.

The Shakespeare Plays: Hamlet. London: BBC; New York: Mayflower, 1980.

Simmons, James R., Jr. "In the Rank Sweat of an Enseamed Bed: Sexual Aberration and the Paradigmatic Screen *Hamlets*." *Literature/Film Quarterly* 25.2 (1997): 111–18.

Skovmand, Michael, "Mel's Melodramatic Melancholy: Zeffirelli's *Hamlet*." *Screen Shakespeare*. Ed. Skovmand. Aarhus: Aarhus UP, 1994. 113–31.

Spaul, Richard, Charlie Ritchie, and Nigel Wheale. Hamlet: *A Guide*. Cambridge: Cambridgeshire Coll. of Arts and Technology, 1988.

Sterne, Richard L. *John Gielgud Directs Richard Burton in* Hamlet: *A Journal of Rehearsals*. New York: Random, 1967.

Taranow, Gerda. *The Bernhardt* Hamlet: *Culture and Context*. New York: Lang, 1996.

Taylor, Neil. "The Films of *Hamlet*." *Shakespeare and the Moving Image: The Plays on Film and Television*. Ed. Anthony Davies and Stanley Wells. Cambridge: Cambridge UP, 1994. 180–95.

Terris, Olwen. *Shakespeare: A List of Audio-visual Materials Available in the UK*. 2nd ed. London: British Universities Film and Video Council, 1987.

Thompson, Ann. "Asta Nielsen and the Mystery of *Hamlet*." Boose and Burt 215–24.

Wayne, Valerie. "*Shakespeare Wallah* and Colonial Specularity." Boose and Burt 95–102.

Wheeler, Elizabeth. "Light It Up and Move It Around: *Rosencrantz and Guildenstern Are Dead*." *Shakespeare on Film Newsletter* 16.1 (1991): 5.

Wilds, Lillian. "On Film: Maximilian Schell's Most Royal Hamlet." *Literature/Film Quarterly* 4.2 (1976): 134–40.

Willson, Robert F., Jr. "Lubitsch's *To Be or Not to Be*." *Shakespeare on Film Newsletter* 1.1 (1976): 2+.

———. "*To Be or Not to Be* Once More." *Shakespeare on Film Newsletter* 8.2 (1984): 1+.

TONY HOWARD

Women as Hamlet (2007)†

> How can woman put herself into the text—into the world and into history?

> —Helène Cixous, "The Laugh of the Medusa," 1975[1]

The first Hamlet on film was a woman, Sarah Bernhardt (1900). Probably the first Hamlet on radio was a woman, Eve Donne (1923). The "observed of all observers," the "glass of fashion and the mould of form," the "hoop through which every actor must jump" according to Max Beerbohm, Hamlet is also the role that has since the late eighteenth century most inspired tragic actresses to challenge expectations and cross gender lines. Several of the most brilliant performances of the part in our time have been by women, and the issue of Hamlet's "femininity" has fascinated artists in all media. Crossing boundaries, contesting convention, disrupting or reflecting the dominant sexual politics, this regendering of Hamlet has involved repeated investigations into the nature of subjectivity, articulacy, and action—investigations with radically different consequences depending on the cultural situation. It has been an extraordinary history, but until recently, with the re-evaluation of such unconventional actresses as Charlotte Charke, Charlotte Cushman, Asta Nielsen and Eva Le Gallienne, it was largely ignored. Why, at certain points, was it thought appropriate for women to play this role, and why were many other artists, male and female, fascinated by them? To establish some parameters we begin with a German actress, a French painter, and an amateur American critic who each in different ways and for different reasons explored what has been seen as the femininity of Hamlet.

Performance: Hamlet 2000

> Hamlet raises all the questions that human beings ask throughout their lives . . . Today, in a world in which science and politics want to make us believe that all questions can be answered,

---

† Tony Howard, *Women as Hamlet: Performance and Interpretation in Theatre, Film and Fiction* (Cambridge: Cambridge UP, 2007), 1–11. A contemporary critic, Tony Howard tells selected stories of the many women who have played the role of Hamlet; here he recreates Angela Winkler's acclaimed performance in Berlin 2000, which revealed Hamlet's multiplicity and capacity for love at "the end of history." Reprinted by permission of Cambridge University Press.
1. Helène Cixous, "The Laugh of the Medusa." See Kelly Oliver, *French Feminism Reader* (Lanham: Rowman and Littlefield, 2000), p. 257.

Sarah Bernhardt, the first female Hamlet, 1880–85

> our instincts tell us that this is all wrong . . . What will this
> "Hamlet 2000" be like? What will be his questions to the
> world, on the eve of the new millennium?[2]

Angela Winkler, one of Germany's leading actresses, played Hamlet
at the Hanover Schauspielhaus as part of the millennial Expo 2000.
Best known internationally for her role in the film *The Lost Honour
of Katherina Blum* (1975) as an innocent bystander embroiled in
state terror, she won Germany's Best Actress award as Hamlet. The
director was Peter Zadek. *Hamlet 2000* was tied into the politics of
Germany and Europe after the Wall; few performances have carried
such symbolic weight. It was a Berlin Schaubühne production but it
was co-financed by Expo 2000 and the Avignon Festival, rehearsed
in Strasbourg, premiered in Vienna in 1999, and climaxed its Berlin
run that December, the week the world's leaders assembled in the
reunified city to mark the rebuilding of the Reichstag.[3] In response
to the end of a brutal century, Angela Winkler made Hamlet an
embodiment of bruised hope. If Hamlet always shows "the very age
and body of the time his true form and feature" (and many saw the
advice to the Players as the key to her contained realism), after such
an age of violence must not the "form and feature" of consciousness
itself, which Hamlet has for so long represented, be refigured? Zadek
said he sensed "instinctively" that at that moment a woman must
ask "the questions," and the androgyny of Winkler's Hamlet had col-
lective resonance.

Angela Winkler was fifty-five, the same age as Bernhardt when
she played Hamlet a century earlier. "I didn't set out to play a man,"
Winkler said, "I don't find that interesting."[4] Rather, she saw theatre as "a different way of living"—"It's very important for me that
the work corresponds to a precise moment in my life." She had four
children and rationed herself ("I couldn't act all the time. I had to
have pauses, to be with my family") and in the 1990s she chose to
collaborate with particular directors on major projects. "Why did
Zadek want a woman to play Hamlet?" she was asked: "Why did he
choose me? I don't know. I never ask directors to explain." She had
had no driving interest in *Hamlet* ("I'd only seen the play once, in
1977, 1 hadn't read it, and I've never played Shakespeare") but its
difficulty attracted her ("If it's not a struggle, I don't accept") and

2. 1999 Vienna Festival publicity.
3. Premiere: Volkstheater, Vienna, 21 May.
4. *Le Monde* 12 May 1999. The following account is based on performance notes made
   in Hamburg. Journalists consulted: Barbara Villiger Heilig, *Neue Zürcher Zeitung*
   (25 May); Gerhard Stadelmaier, *Frankfurter Allgemeine Zeitung* (25 May); Roland
   Koberg, *Berliner Zeitung* (26 May); Reinhold Reiterer, *Berliner Morgenpost* (26 May);
   Lothar Sträter, *Nürnburger Zeitung* (27 May); Gerhard Jörder, *Die Zeit* (27 May); Urs
   Jenny, *Der Spiegel* (31 May); Stefan Steinberg, *World Socialist Website* (30 September
   1999).

there were private echoes. Late in World War II Winkler's father was shot and assumed dead on the Russian Front; when she was six like a ghost he returned to Germany. As we shall see, any effective performance of Hamlet, by man or woman, resonates with auto-biography. Angela Winkler made Hamlet emotionally raw and unprotected, consumed by an insatiable hunger for truth, observing history with amazement.

Somewhere near "the end of history" on an empty windswept stage, a modern soldier wrapped in leather and furs kept watch (NATO's bombing of Belgrade began during rehearsals). In an age of grand architectural statements like the new Reichstag, Elsinore was a metal box, a giant version of the portakabins® seen on build-ing sites everywhere. Its blank impermanence made European crit-ics think of migrant workers, refugees, and the construction of false realities: "What symbolizes postmodern randomness better?"[5] As nervous guards clicked their rifles, the container opened, and to murmurs of ecclesiastical music from a distant time of belief, the Ghost emerged rattling bells and beads and toting a ring-binder ledger of sins. It ignored the soldiers and locked itself back in: there was no dialogue between numb present and grotesque past. Then a business-suited new Court emerged from the box for a photocall; Claudius' white uniform unified elements from East and West Ger-many. Otto Sadler made him a canny working-class politician who easily solved the Norway problem and smiled, complacent as Clin-ton, Blair and Schröder in the post-ideological age. Women's con-dition however had not altered—Ophelia was a timid doll and Gertrude a scarlet woman forever in red. Elizabeth Plessen's trans-lation interlaced Schlegel's Romantic rhetoric with everyday idioms and the acting veered between the conversational and caricature. Dressed in 1940s fashions, Ophelia and her fighter-pilot brother were what Claudius and Gertrude might once have been: time slipped; people coexisted with their own past; *Hamlet* was haunted by memories from Germany's postwar reconstruction and from Angela Winkler's life.

Hamlet arrived late, in black tunic and hose, disrupting every-thing and taking all the culture's contradictions and suppressed anxieties into his/her self. Winkler pushed through to the front, slammed down a kitchen chair and sat taut and sullen, unable to stay still, shaking her long dark hair, fingers drumming. Everyone tried to ignore her till she laughed out loud to hear of Laertes' escape. Gertrude came over from the party but Hamlet could hardly speak: "I know not seems . . ." The production made nothing of Winkler's gender, nor did she "play a man": rather, as Michael Billington

5. Steinberg, *World Socialist Website*.

observed, "she absorbs Hamlet's emotions into her own personality" and crucially, like Sarah Bernhardt, she played a child. Hamlet became pre-gendered—"the problem child," Roland Koberg said, "at a dinner party, whose behaviour is disturbed . . . And all simultaneously stare, perplexed, and shy away because they cannot deal with it." Claudius delivered a pep-talk. In *Hamlet*—and this was one reason why the role beckoned many actresses—there is no division between history and the private sphere.

Winkler was one of many actresses who played Hamlet in the 1990s. In Stockholm (1996) and Cincinnati (1997), the character was made female (Princess Hamlet) while in other cases (e.g. London, 1992) there was a thorough male impersonation. The experience varied from country to country. For example specific languages are more or less gendered so there were no personal pronouns to define Leea Klemola's Finnish punk Hamlet (1995) as either "he" or "she": Hamlet was "*han*." Cultural contexts varied, sometimes unpredictably. In Giles Block's 1995 Japanese production (Shochiku Theatre, Tokyo) Hamlet was Rei Asami, from the all-female Takorasaka company who were reversing the centuries-old *onnagata* tradition of all-male casting. Takorasaka implicitly critiqued a society that had clung to conventions of gender representation from a distant age; yet a group of actresses had staged *Hamlet* in Japan as early as 1907 and the kabuki-trained actress Yaeko Mizutani played Hamlet successfully in 1933 and 1935. Block's 1995 production was less revolutionary than it sounded and, he said, "As soon as rehearsals started everyone forgot about the sex of the person, she was like any other performer, playing Hamlet."[6] All cross-cast *Hamlet*s involve decisions regarding the nature of gender—biologically or culturally determined? learned, improvised or imposed?—and may universalise the character or focus on *difference*. But what most female Hamlets have in common is that they are catalysts—inassimilable figures alien to the norms around them. The paradoxes and dissident intensities of Hamlet's beliefs and language become sharper through the figure of an actress/prince whose very presence exposes artifice—the theatrical conventions we might otherwise not question, the political banalities masking Elsinore's lies, and the structures of power and gender that normally trap women in *Hamlet* in the roles of Mother, Virgin and Whore. The female Hamlet is a walking, speaking alienation effect. Angela Winkler confronted the fact that Hamlet embodies contradiction.

In public Winkler was scarcely audible, but alone with the audience tempestuous energy burst through. She punched the air ("Her-

---

6. Giles Block "In Conversation" on Shakespeare's Globe website 1999 discussing his all-male *Antony and Cleopatra*, 1999. For earlier Japanese performances see Takashi Sasayama, J. R. Mulryne and Margaret Shewring, *Shakespeare on the Japanese Stage* (Cambridge: Cambridge UP, 1998).

cules!"), hit her shoe thinking of Gertrude's new ones, jumped into
the audience to explain incest ("My father's brother!"), but retreated
to the lonely stage and blew her nose on her sleeve. Horatio delighted
her with magic tricks but she confided in the spectators, almost
naively: "It is not nor it cannot come to good." Winkler made the
famous pronouncements seem simple, even trite ("Frailty thy name is
woman," "To be or not to be, that is the question") but new and
astonishing to Hamlet, who was so intrigued by the "vicious mole of
nature" that s/he nearly missed the Ghost. Winkler showed that each
individual encounters life and death as if for the first time, and the
fact that women cannot normally speak this text in public intensified
the effect: she gave Hamlet a compulsive need for knowledge, and
articulation. Reviewers spoke of *The Little Prince* and *Peter Pan*. As
Koberg noted, everyone suppressed their past except Winkler's Hamlet, who "believes in the past, corresponds with it . . . Hamlet has the
longest memory and the shortest life."

We shall see that when gender is put in question, so is genre. Farce
and tragedy overlapped: Winkler pulled a gun on Marcellus and
Horatio to comic effect; seeing the Ghost on its knees in shame—
"strange, tattered, half-shaman half fool" (Kolberg)—Hamlet gave
it a chair, but it fell off. "My uncle?" expressed amazement. Winkler
was volatile: "Oh but there is, Horatio!" was a mature explosion of
rage, but then she banged on the stage ("Swear!") like a six-year-old
whose father had returned from the dead, and told Horatio in all
simplicity that there are lots of things in heaven and earth. At the
2000 Edinburgh Festival some British reviewers complained that
Zadek was identifying femininity with immaturity, but this ignored
Winkler's force and intellect. There was a profound visible disparity
between her *performance*—variously a disturbed adolescent, a college rebel, and Pippi Longstocking—and her *physical self*. There
were superficial similarities, for example, to Rebecca Hall's Hamlet
(Soho Theatre Company 1997) in a production aimed at London
teenagers that addressed questions of alienation and self-harm
among adolescent girls (Hall yelled the soliloquies as if confiding in
her pals at a disco) but Winkler's Hamlet was multi-dimensional: lost
child and experienced woman, past and present overlaid. In action
she created a restless, ebullient figure of "childlike radiance," yet
photographs showed her mature features and haunted eyes. She created a post-Brechtian collage of clashing but truthful emotional
moments: "Not male, not female, not boyish, . . . simply a person,
who happens to be an actress," said *Le Pais*, and *Le Monde* added: "A
child, neither girl nor boy."[7] But to be a child in this smug Denmark
was to be the one person observing life as an outsider—that is,
truthfully—"cold reality seen through the eyes of a child." Winkler

7. 11 and 12 May 1999.

made *Hamlet* about individuation, the forging of a consciousness over three hours and a lifetime.

Her encounter with Polonius was uniquely pointed. He was played by Ulrich Wildgrüber, who had been Zadek's Hamlet in 1977 in an iconoclastic but outrageously pre-feminist production where Gertrude was half-naked with painted breasts, Ophelia was a sex-toy, and women played Claudius' parasites (Polonius, Rosencrantz, Guildenstern). Now Wildgrüber's fat, scant of breath, myopic and flustered Polonius was the male Hamlet tradition gone rotten—"a large pompous duck flapping his wings inconsequentially, darting his beady eyes left and right to emphasise his regurgitation of chewed-over nostrums and commonplaces.[8] He gabbled and interrupted himself, frustrated by his inability to find the *mot juste*, distracted by his own false gestures. He shrieked when crossed. Written into the man's body was "disastrous uncertainty" (Koberg), the loss of the postwar generation's promise. (Wildgrüber died during the run.) Twenty years on, Hamlet was in Claudius' pay, but Winkler and Katherina Blum had not lapsed—"the face is unaffected, betrays no age"[9]—and the radical spirit—greasy-haired and dishevelled, laughing at third-hand "words, words, words"—was younger than ever.

So Angela Winkler's Hamlet negotiated her identity in relation to gross middle-aged men: Rosencrantz and Guildenstern were faded chorus boys dancing to "Singing in the Rain" and the Players were bored, camp exhibitionists whose show featured onstage sex and a murderer who spewed on his audience. Their Voice Beautiful star ruined the Hecuba speech, but Hamlet's heartfelt version crystallised a young person's first discovery that art might transfigure pain. In "O what a rogue and peasant slave am I" Winkler used her rich natural voice for the first time. The actor acts out true "dreams," she stressed, and raking the fully-lit auditorium with her eyes, "addressing flaming words clearly and directly to the public,"[1] she challenged them to consider their relationship to this play: what was Hecuba to *them*? Then she was back in infancy, scuffing the floor and confiding what she'd heard about Theatre—that it touches the guilty. . . . She ran out. It was the first of two intervals, and before each break Hamlet confronted the audience of this expensive "festival production." Faced with Elsinore's bland meritocracy, German critics admitted "these are people like you and I, petty plotters, inconspicuous and interchangeable."[2] When Winkler rushed back, she was murmuring "To be or not to be." She spoke the soliloquies directly but drifted

8. Steinberg.
9. *Le Pais*, 11 May 1999.
1. Barbara Villiger Heilig.
2. Lothar Sträter.

into introspection; her unprotected face was "an open book."[3] With
the last lines (". . . lose the name of action"), Hamlet understood the
appalling complexity of existence for the first time and lapsed into
shocked isolation.

For the psychologist Nancy Chodorow, the "masculine sense of
self" is separate, the "feminine sense of self remains connected to
others in the world."[4] Hamlet's struggle for individuation occupied
both grounds. Noticing Ophelia, Winkler smiled at their comic
disparateness—Ophelia was a prim 1950s *debutante* clutching a
handbag, Hamlet now resembled a drowned rat—but identified a
potential ally. In all productions where an actress plays Hamlet, the
clashes with Ophelia and Gertrude gain importance; even if there
has been a suspension of disbelief, it now becomes impossible to
ignore the leading artist's gender. The Nunnery and Closet scenes
comment on choice and female identity in a patriarchal world. All
Hamlets are surrounded by models of masculinity, from the Ghost
to Fortinbras, Laertes, Horatio and even Claudius, but this Hamlet's
psyche incorporated fragments of Ophelia and Gertrude too. Annet
Renneberg's Ophelia, trapped in a time-warp of domestic confor-
mity, shocked by Hamlet's slovenly disrespect, returned the gifts
robotically and horrified Hamlet, who had never before experienced
rejection, only false grins. Winkler ripped the letters to pieces and
hurled the scraps in Ophelia's face; all Hamlet's pain erupted—
"*Dummkopf!*"—and was misdirected at her: Hamlet emptied Ophelia's handbag on the floor and drew a knife on her in a scene of
great physical violence, but at the end the young people's shared
tragedy was shocking. Both actresses crawled on the floor as Ophelia spoke her soliloquy, "Blasted with ecstasy," and Hamlet scrab-
bled wretchedly for the letters. Not only did the politicians ignore
Ophelia's pain, they actually planned Hamlet's removal with Winkler
at their feet: a child was not worth lying to, nor a woman. Hamlet
was totally alienated, even from the Self ("Now I am alone!"), but as
she gathered the last letters Winkler spoke "Speak the speech . . ."
half to herself: "Suit the action to the word . . . obey the modesty of
nature." Can art offer answers? The decadent play-within-the-play
was a travesty of Shakespeare, but alongside it Angela Winkler's
reanimated *travesti*, the tradition of female-to-male cross-dressing,
presenting it as an exploration of identity, not the jaded replication
of roles.

The Prayer scene focused the production's dialectic onto Winkler's Hamlet and Sadler's King. Hamlet writhed as she imagined

3. Barbara Villiger Heilig.
4. Nancy Chodorow, *The Reproduction of Mothering: Psychoanalysis and the Sociology of
   Gender* (Berkley: U of California P, 1978), p. 169.

Claudius' torment, he mocked his own glib prayers; it was disturbing to register Hamlet's naivety against his cynical intimacy with
corruption. A total pragmatist, he used whatever means a situation
required—kindness, diplomacy, religious mantras, murder—while
Gertrude inhabited a fantasy world. Eve Mattes was Zadek's Queen
in 1977; two decades later she showed her still clinging to the sensual illusion that luxury meant fulfilment. Frustrated, unable to
articulate anything but adoration for the dead and hatred for the
living, Hamlet beat and dragged her across the floor; but when
the Ghost entered, Gertrude put on 1940s dance music and swayed
to it, and the dead man joined her, escaping into nostalgia too.
Mother and child sat close in exhausted silence, and Winkler
became gentler. What followed was unexpected. Claudius invaded
the bedroom, Hamlet hid under the bed, the pain of psychological
separation unresolved; but s/he re-emerged to confront the King,
and grew up. Claudius sank on the mattress, convinced life was a
sty where only violence worked ("No-one is monstrous. Everyone is
wretched. They are all fatalists" [Le Monde]) but Angela Winkler
stepped in front of the stage curtain in a beret and leather jacket,
an image of the Baader-Meinhof era. Costumes had subtly taken
Winkler from her 1940s childhood to the 70s and her own identification with the cinema of conscience. "What is a man / If his
chief good and market of his time / Be but to sleep and feed?": sur-
veying the audience on their little patch of EU ground, Hamlet
transcended the immediate moment for the first time, and committed to action.

    William Hazlitt wrote, "It is we who are Hamlet." Women who
take the role pose recurrent questions. Is Hamlet a "universal"
figure whose dilemmas everyone shares, male or female? Is Hamlet
a "feminine" character whose words invite a woman's voice? What
is the relationship between Shakespeare's all-male theatre and the
conventions that have succeeded it? How may the sexual and state
politics of an English Renaissance play relate to the time and place
of its re-enactment? Hamlet 2000 for example was typical of its
period in its inventive treatment of Ophelia and the fact that in
madness—here signified by the loss of one glove, shocking in this
coded world—she became a second Hamlet. Winkler shaped the
production even in her absence: she unleashed energy. Ophelia's
hair went awry, she played off the kitchen chair like Winkler, stalked
Gertrude, and when Claudius shook her she shook him back. But
unlike Hamlet she empathised with Gertrude, wept for her, stared
inside the older woman's handbag and saw nightmares there. Laertes
blamed his sister for his shame, hitting her viciously till she let out
frightening birdlike cries. She ripped her flowers and scattered them
as Hamlet had the letters. Then Gertrude described Ophelia's death

to the audience, beginning her own awkward journey in Winkler's footsteps, from female Sign to female Subject.[5]

The graveyard scene laid social corruption bare. Hamlet and Horatio stood on the roof of the steel container while down below gravedigger-clowns in masked fumigation suits waded through mountains of rubbish and found human remains. Some read this as a scene of ecological disaster, a mass exhumation after ethnic cleansing, or the excavation of Germany's secrets.[6] Winkler covered her mouth against the stench and descended, forcing Horatio—the increasingly terrified Intellectual—to follow the woman's lead. The rest tried to deny reality, so perversely this became the only spectacular scene: the container opened, revealing a shrine and the royal party in Victorian mourning. Ophelia's coffin was metal; she was toxic. The clowns robbed graves and men played tug-of-war with her corpse. Laertes and Hamlet collapsed, victims who had forgotten their real enemies.

Winkler's Prince always retained something of the child— Rosencrantz and Guildenstern had to die because they broke the rules—but the play's final movement began with a farcical *anagnorisis*: when Osric entered he was Polonius in a long blond wig, one last degenerate recycling of "Hamlet 1977." The "fall of a sparrow" speech was calm and happy; Hamlet could see through masks now, yet was not tainted. Winkler embraced Laertes. To quote Heilig, she made Hamlet "addicted to life," a feeling intelligence who "hangs on to life by every fibre of the senses . . . The world has disappointed Hamlet beyond measure, more than the heart can bear" but "the heart remains the most reliable, the only interlocutor."[7] In a tatty jumper, Winkler fought the duel like a talented novice with infectious humour. *Hamlet* is theatre's greatest meditation on death, and Zadek's production opposed four perspectives. Gertrude drank the poison as an instinctive act of rebellion. Laertes died bitterly. Claudius, the absolute materialist, studied a tiny fatal scratch on his forearm, chuckling at its absurdity. Only Hamlet, though regretful, accepted death. Winkler arranged herself carefully on her kitchen chair, there was a comic interruption when Osric announced Fortinbras, and suddenly mid-sentence Hamlet was dead. Whatever answers to "The Questions" s/he had learnt, they were not for spectators: "the rest is silence." To drums, Fortinbras entered in a greatcoat and helmet. It was Ophelia. But Ophelia turned hectoring tyrant—Zadek short-circuited any feminist reading or sense of collectivity. The humanity of Angela Winkler's Hamlet was unique.

5. Sue-Ellen Case, *Feminism and Theatre* (London and New York: Methuen, 1988), pp. 112–17.
6. *Le Pais*, 11 May 1999.
7. Barbara Villiger Heilig.

Reviewers across Europe were lyrical in their attempt to define Winkler's achievement. Gerhard Stadelmaier argued that the twentieth century's Hamlets had stood for partial visions—the intellectual, the Oedipal, the existential—but "now this century is almost ended" so on this emptied millennial stage Winkler's Prince "for the first time bears the memories of not just one sector, but of the whole world." Hamlet's androgyny meant amplitude, and for Michael Billington "What Winkler brings out—in a way that no man I have ever seen quite has—is Hamlet's enormous capacity for love, a capacity that is constantly baffled and frustrated."[8] Stadelmaier honoured her "beautiful seriousness": "Hamlet's death is a miracle, a smile in sleep . . . [Winkler] burns out like a holy candle—the child's dream was to create beauty and reason in a mad and ugly world . . . The attempt failed . . . It was nevertheless a wonderful children's game."[9] Roland Koberg praised Winkler for reinventing the heroic: "One wants to live in the country from which Angela Winkler comes."

In one sense that country has been densely populated. Amongst many others Hamlet has been played by Judith Anderson, Sarah Bernhardt, Charlotte Cushman, Alla Demidova, Nuria Espert, Olwen Fouere, Fatma Girik, Clare Howard, Elizabeth Inchbald, Mme. Judith, Bertha Kalisch, Eva Le Gallienne, Siobahn McKenna, Asta Nielsen, Nance O'Neil, Giacinta Pezzana, Anna Maria Quinn, Julianna Ramaker, Sarah Siddons, Frances de la Tour, Diane Venora, Angela Winkler, Margarita Xirgu, Clara Ziegler."[1] Over the past century and a half, Hamlet has been played by women in Britain, the USA, Australia, Eire, Russia, France, Italy, Japan, Germany, Spain, Sweden, Denmark, Poland, Finland, Mexico and elsewhere. The list could be expanded to include the names of at least two hundred professional actresses but would still be incomplete, and out of date within months. Some, like Bernhardt, essayed it because Hamlet is Everest, the part male actors traditionally *must* play, and these women declined to be excluded. Some had specific professional, personal or political agendas while others, like Winkler, were cast by male directors. Many appeared in low-status fringe or provincial theatres, others on the most distinguished stages in the world; some caused little stir because theatrical cross-dressing was at that time commonplace, others were denounced. In the 1950s the English theatre historians Mander and Mitcheson categorised female Hamlets alongside children and trained dogs, but in Germany, Turkey and Canada women played Hamlet in full-

8. *Guardian*, 23 August 2000.
9. Gerhard Stadelmaier.
1. Gerda Taranow, *The Bernhardt Hamlet* (New York: Lang, 1996), p. 123.

length films; many movies told of fictional actresses who long for the role; and the female Hamlet surfaced in novels and plays. What might playing Hamlet have meant to an actress and her public in Regency Dublin, Victorian London, Berlin in the 1920s, or Manhattan at the height of the Women's Movement? It was sometimes an act of transgression and it always involved empowerment of a kind.

MARGRETA DE GRAZIA

Empires of World History (2007)†

Within two years of its publication, *Hamlet* was cited in the report of a recent, almost concurrent, event in world history: the fall of Boris Godunov, the Tsar of Russia. In 1605, the anonymous author of *Sir Thomas Smithes Voiage and Entertainment in Rushia* likened the demise of Russia's regime in 1605 to the tragedy of *Hamlet*. At the time of writing, Boris Godunov, who had obtained the throne in 1598 after allegedly poisoning the rightful heir, died suddenly, and the empire passed to his own son Theodor. Within a month's time, a young man claiming to be the rightful heir appeared from obscurity to avenge Godunov's usurpation by slaying his relations and supporters. To the anonymous English reporter, the episode possessed all the makings of an Aristotelian tragedy.

> [H]is fathers Empire and Government [was] but as the *Poeti-call Furie in a Stage-action*, compleat yet with horrid and wofull Tragedies: a first, but no second to any Hamlet; and that now *Revenge*, just *Revenge* was comming with his Sworde drawne against, his royall Mother, and dearest Sister, to fill up those Murdering Sceanes, the *Embryon* whereof was long since Modeld, yea digested (but unlawfully and too-too vive-ly) by his dead selfe-murdering Father: such and so many being their feares and terrours.[1]

Springing from the "Embryon" of Godunov's treachery and driven toward its fatal dénouement by peripatetic revenge, the downfall of the Godunovs comprised a "compleat" action. The collapse of an imperial regime appeared as dramatic as tragedy itself, "a first, but

---

† Margreta de Grazia, *"Hamlet" without Hamlet* (Cambridge: Cambridge UP, 2007), 45–46, 63–73, 79–80. A contemporary critic, de Grazia turns critical attention to the imperial politics and histories inscribed in the play. Reprinted by permission of Cambridge University Press.
1. Anon., *Sir Thomas Smithes Voiage and Entertainment in Rushia. With the tragicall ends of two Emperors, and one Empresse, within one Moneth during his being there* (London, 1605), sig. K.

no second to any Hamlet."² Like the "Stage-action" of *Hamlet*, the
contemporary event featured usurpation, a dispossessed prince,
revenge, self-slaughter, and dynastic collapse. Horatio's sensational-
ized synopsis at the conclusion of *Hamlet* applies as well to the Russian upheaval as the Danish: "So shall you hear / Of carnal, bloody,
and unnatural acts" [5.2.354–55].³ The resemblance between events
in the world historical arena and on the professional stage suggests the close association between tragedy and history. As Aristo-
tle's redactors had maintained, tragedy commonly looked to history
for its materials. And as this traveler's account indicates, history
turned to tragedy to give form to tumultuous political upheaval.

That this allusion to the demise of Godunov has received scant
critical attention is not surprising, for it highlights a feature of
Hamlet rarely noted in modern discussions: its preoccupation with
the stuff of history—the fall of states, kingdoms, and empires. The
play begins with the threat of invasion and ends with foreign occupation. Its action blocks out the major event punctuating one of the
earliest schema for organizing world history: the fall of empire.
From the days of the early church, exegetes schematized history
into a series of four monarchies, kingdoms, or empires, each one
rising from the ashes of its predecessor until all would be subsumed
by a final fifth. Although the theory had pagan precedents, Christian exegetes found a basis for the schema in the prophet Daniel's
interpretation of King Nebuchadnezzar's dream.⁴ A statue with a
head of gold, shoulders of silver, stomach of brass, and legs of iron
and clay is smashed by a falling stone which then expands into a
mountain so vast as to cover the face of the earth (Dan. 2:36–45).
Daniel interprets the dream as a prophecy: the statue's head stands
for Nebuchadnezzar's Babylon, the other three body parts represent the three great kingdoms yet to come, and their smashing by
the stone foretells the eventual subsuming of them all by the final
and eternal heavenly kingdom.⁵ By the start of the fifth century,
Jerome in his commentary on Daniel was able to identify the statue's four parts with the four great monarchies which had emerged
since the time of Abraham: Babylon, Media-Persia, Greece, and

2. Ibid., sig. M2.
3. Harold Jenkins, ed., *Hamlet*, Arden ed. (London and New York: Methuen, 1982),
   5.2.385–86 [340–41]. Unless otherwise indicated, all subsequent quotations from the
   play follow this edition and appear parenthetically in the text. [References to this Norton Critical Edition are substituted in brackets.]
4. For pagan precedents, Eastern as well as Western, to the schema as established by
   Jerome and Orosius, see Joseph Ward Swain, "The Theory of the Four Monarchies:
   Opposition History under the Roman Empire," *Classical Philology* 35:1 (1940), 1–21.
5. This dream was borne out by a later vision of four great beasts rising from the sea to be
   destroyed by a greater beast; see G. W. Trompf, *The Idea of Historical Recurrence in
   Western Thought: From Antiquity to the Reformation* (Berkeley, CA: U of California P,
   1979), 186, 222–29, 282, 343–45.

Rome, as illustrated in the series of magnificent engravings by
Marten de Vos (1600). Prevalent throughout the middle ages, the
schema survived in England well into the seventeenth century, as
is testified by the emergence after the execution of Charles I of
the Fifth Monarchy Men, a radical millenarian sect determined to
bring Daniel's prophecy to fulfillment by preparing the way for the
everlasting fifth kingdom.[6]

✻   ✻   ✻

Because *Hamlet* has been read as timeless tragedy, the specificity
of its historical setting has been overlooked.[7] As the references to
England indicate, however, Shakespeare set the play sometime after
Denmark's invasion of England in 1017, the beginning of the Third
Rule, just after the Danish King Canute's defeat of the English, dra-
matized in the anonymous *Edmund Ironside* (c. 1632). Conquered by
Denmark, Britain retained its tributary status until conquered again
in 1066 by the Normans. Indeed the Norman invasion occurred so
fast upon the Danish, that some chroniclers consolidated the two,
considering them "a double blow as it were in the necke one after
another within a few yeares," "a two-fold conquest of the land."[8] The
proximity of the two invasions might shed light on the gratuitous
introduction of the mysterious Norman horseman.

> KING   Two month since
>   Here was a gentleman of Normandy . . .
> LAERTES   A Norman was't?
> KING   A Norman.
> LAERTES   Upon my life, Lamord [*Lamound* F].
> KING   The very same.
> LAERTES   I know him well. He is the brooch indeed
>   And gem of all the nation. [4.7.80–81, 89–93]

The "gentleman of Normandy," by Claudius' report, is the equestrian
marvel who piqued Hamlet's envy by lavishly praising Laertes' skill at
fencing. His praise "[d]id Hamlet so envenom with his envy / That he
could nothing do but wish and beg / Your sudden coming o'er to play
with you" [4.7.102–04]. But why must Laertes' praises be sung by a

---

6. For Luther's use of Daniel's Four Monarchies scheme, see Robin Bruce Barnes, *Prophecy and Gnosis: Apocalypticism in the Wake of the Lutheran Reformation* (Stanford:
   Stanford UP, 1988), 39–41. For Milton's use of it, see Andrew Barnaby, "Another Rome
   in the West?': Milton and the Imperial Republic, 1654–1670," *Milton Studies* 30 (1993),
   67–84. For the Fifth Monarchists' self-legitimization in Daniel 2, see James Holstun,
   A Rational Millennium: Puritan Utopias of Seventeenth-Century England and America
   (New York and Oxford: Oxford U P, 1987), 149–50.
7. In his generic reconfiguration of Shakespeare's canon, Leonard Tennenhouse groups
   Hamlet with the chronicle histories because of their shared "strategies of representation," in *Power on Display: The Politics of Shakespeare's Forms* (New York and London:
   Methuen, 1986), 72.
8. Stow, *Annales*, 4r.

Norman? The Folio's name for the Norman, *Lamound*, has led some
editors to take the horseman as a "personal allusion" to a cavalier in
Castiglione's *The Courtier*, Pietro Monte or, in Hoby's translation,
Peter Mount. But why cast the Italian cavalier as a Norman? Another
strain of commentary finds allegorical significance in Q2's rendition
of his name. Harry Levin has identified *Lamord* as the apocalyptic
rider from Revelation (6:2), "a vision of Death on a pale horse," and
Margaret Ferguson also argues for his association with death, a subtle "*memento mori* admonition" intended for the reader."[9] But, again,
why should this mysterious figure originate in Normandy? Here it
may be helpful to distinguish Normandy from modern France, the
location of Paris, the city to which Laertes is keen to return, the
fashion capital where the best in rank are "rich, not gaudy" [1.3.70] in
their dress, where even rapiers and poiniards are stylishly attired
[5.2.128–30]. The Normandy of *Lamord/Lamound* belongs to an earlier time frame, after the region was conquered by the eponymous
Norsemen in the tenth century and before they charged across the
Channel to conquer England in the eleventh. It was their skill on
horseback that gave them the advantage over the English at the Battle of Hastings, as is commemorated by the Bayeux tapestry. As
Claudius remembers of the Normans, "they can well on horseback"
[4.7.83]. The horseman's association with the invading Normans by
no means rules out Revelation as his provenance. Norman and apocalyptic horsemen are both conquerors. The deathly resonance of
Lamord is appropriate to both. So, too, are the two senses of mound
in *Lamound*: a burial tumulus and the globe-like orb mounted with a
cross, often featured in imperial portraits.

Extraneous to the plot, Claudius' fifty-line disquisition on the
Norman makes for a clean theatrical cut. Even Laertes seems puz-
zled by its purpose: "What out of this, my lord?" [4.7.105]. Claudius's response suggests that it is intended to warm Laertes up to duel
with Hamlet, but surely the incensed Laertes needs no fueling. The
ambiguous horseman, belonging to both England's eleventh century past and its unprescribed eschatological future, is an anachro-
nous composite. He serves the same admonitory and premonitory
function as the Ghost, who simultaneously references the historical past of ancient Rome's "sheeted dead" [1.1.117] as well as the
looming future of the rising dead. Both specters presage fatality to
the state and its prince.

In an attempt to identify topical allusions, scholarly attention has
focused on England's relation to Denmark around 1600. Scholars

9. Harry Levin, *The Question of Hamlet* (New York: Oxford UP, 1959), 95; and Margaret
    W. Ferguson, "Hamlet: Letters and Spirits," in *Shakespeare and the Question of Theory*,
    ed. Patricia Parker and Geoffrey Hartman (New York and London: Methuen, 1985),
    303.

have determined that the Baltic Sea was then infested by pirates, that a Danish embassy arrived in Edinburgh to demand the return of the isles of Orkney and Scotland, that negotiations were underway for the marriage of James VI to Anne of Denmark. Yet England is pulled into the play through a much earlier relation to Denmark. A period of English history was named after it: the fifty-year period just before the Norman Conquest known as the Rule of the Danes. The long tradition that has seen *Hamlet* as the inaugural work of the modern period has been blind to the historical moment in which the play situates itself. But it has also ignored the play's own preoccupation with the process of history, the alternations of state that punctuate world history, as one kingdom gives way to another in what might be called a premodern imperial schema that assumes the eventual fall of all kingdoms and their final subsumption by the apocalyptic kingdom-to-come.

Set within the fifty-year period in which Britain fell first to the Danes and then to the Normans, the play alludes to the most famous imperial falls of ancient history. The speech Hamlet "chiefly loved" derives from Virgil's great imperial epic. Extracted from Aeneas' extended account of the Trojan War, it was widely translated and imitated during Shakespeare's time in both school exercises and poetic set-pieces. The speech climaxes when Pyrrhus, after wending his way through burning Troy, comes upon his royal victim and slays him as the towers of Troy come crashing down. King and kingdom go down together, the felling of Priam and fall of Troy. The fall marks the extinction of a great race, as Thomas Heywood concludes in his great poem, "Thus is King *Priam* and Queene *Hecubs* race, / Extinct in dust," and the beginning of a new, as Aeneas flees Troy to found what by Virgil's time was imperial Rome.[1] The context in which Aeneas narrates the fall of Troy is also important: he recounts it to Dido, the Queen of an emergent empire, on his voyage to found a new empire. As he surveys the newly erected edifices of Carthage, he thinks back on the destruction of his native kingdom and looks ahead to the long task of founding a new one. At the time of Aeneas' recounting, Troy was the kingdom of the past, Carthage of the present, and Rome of the future. By the time Virgil wrote his great epic, however, Carthage had been reduced to salty ashes by Rome's infamous Carthaginian peace. Carthage had followed the course of Troy; and, in due time, Rome would cede to the same fate. Even at the height of its power, historically minded Romans knew what the future held in store. In an account in Appian's *History of Rome* which Shakespeare may have known, at the very moment of Rome's victory

---

1. Heywood, *Troia*, 15.93, 406.

over Carthage, Scipio Africanus at once remembered the fall of Troy, foresaw the fall of Rome, and wept:

> After being wrapped in thought for long, and realizing that all cities, nations, and empires, just like men, must meet their doom, that this was what the once fortunate city of Troy suffered, as did the might of the Assyrians, the Medes, the Persians, and the very recent and brilliant empire of Macedonia, he uttered, whether voluntarily or otherwise, the words of the poet: "The day shall come when sacred Troy shall perish; as also Priam, with the people over whom spear-bearing Priam rules."[2]

When asked by his tutor what he meant by quoting from the *Iliad* (6.448–90), Scipio allowed that he feared the same fate would befall Rome.[3] Recollection and prolepsis produce the same narrative of the "precurse of fear'd events" [1.1.123]. As Carthage fell, so, too, had past kingdoms and so, too, would future ones. In his *History of the World*, Raleigh observed the same pattern in commenting on Carthage's decline: "So this glorious citie, ranne the same fortune, which many other great ones have done, both before and since." As in the history of the Four Monarchies, the long series of imperial falls would finally culminate in the end of the world portended by every fall: "The ruine of the goodliest pieces of the world foreshews the dissolution of the whole world."[4]

The great example of imperial collapse is featured in the "excellent play" [2.2.364] from which the Player recites. Within the speech Hamlet "chiefly loved" [370], Aeneas' tale to Dido, lies the passage he "especially" loved of "Priam's slaughter" [372]. The relevance of the speech is generally seen through Hamlet's eyes: he seeks inspiration from the bloodthirsty avenger Pyrrhus. But the importance of the speech extends beyond Hamlet's personal situation. The death of Priam was the foundational moment of England's own history. Like Virgil's Rome, Britain traced its origins back to "Priam's slaughter" or the fall of Troy. From Caxton's *Chronicles of England* (1480) to Holinshed's *Chronicles* (1586), the event was routinely present at the threshold of British chronicle history. Gyles Godet's pictorial account of British kings opens with a woodcut of the burning of Troy.[5] The Historical Preface to *The Mirror for Magistrates*

2. Appian, *Punica*, cited by Trompf, *Recurrence*, 79. For Shakespeare's knowledge of Appian, see Ernest Schanzer, ed., *Shakespeare's Appian: A Selection from the Tudor Translation of "Appian's Civil Wars"* (Liverpool: Liverpool UP, 1956), xix–xxviii.
3. Appian, *Appian's Roman History*, trans. Horace White (London: William Heinemann, and New York: Macmillan, 1912), xix, 637-8.
4. Raleigh, *History*, 1.2.314.
5. Gyles Godet's *A briefe Abstract of the Genealogy of All the Kinges of England* (1560) opens with Priam's fall, and situates it within salvational history between the Creation and the Incarnation, tracing Priam's descent back beyond the Flood to Japthet, founder of Europe, and son of Noah. For "Shakespeare and the Troy legend," see Heather

takes the same starting point, "When Troy was sackt, and brent, and could not stand."[6] As Jeffrey Knapp has shown, the story of Britain's founding as narrated by Geoffrey of Monmouth both extended and patterned itself after Virgil's great epic.[7] After the fall of Troy, Aeneas fled to found Rome; from there his great-grandson Brut was also thrown into exile (for the accidental killing of his father) and into multiple adventures while sailing around the Mediterranean before arriving, as prophesied, to the land over which he and his descendants would rule. *Nomen est omen*: embedded in the name given that isle was its link to that history: "Brute did first inhabit this land, and called it then after his owne name, Britaine."[8] A punning reference to Britain's founder has been heard in Hamlet's quip to Polonius when he boasts of having played Caesar at the university, "It was a brute part" [3.2.98].[9]

But the play is more interested in the brutal part played by the Roman Brutus. Polonius recalls having played the part of Caesar in a university production, "I did enact Julius Caesar" [3.2.96]. The scene he remembers represented the very "fear'd events" [1.1.123] portended by the prodigies in the "high and palmy state of Rome" [1.1.115]. "I was killed i'th'Capitol" [3.2.96–97], says the man who played Caesar. As Stephen Orgel has noted, the reference to Caesar's assassination in the Capitol refers to Shakespeare's own *Julius Caesar*, written shortly before *Hamlet*, for in Plutarch it occurs elsewhere, in Pompey's Theatre.[1] Named according to Pliny after the *caput* or head, the Capitol better suited Caesar's offending ambition to be alone at the top, in the position his name posthumously came to signify. As Polonius emphasizes, though all the conspirators set upon Caesar, the fatal stab was dealt by Brutus, the man he valued as a son, as his final words in Plutarch record, "*Et tu, mi fili, Brute*." "It was a brute part of him to kill so capital a calf' [3.2.98], quips Hamlet, who will end up playing that brutish part himself when he stabs the former impersonator of Caesar behind the arras, mistaking him for the King ("Is it the king?") [3.4.26]. His victim, however, turns out to be not the head of state but only a "capital" calf. The drop from Caesar to calf is one from ruler to slave, both types of movable property or cattle/chattel, deriving from the Latin for the chief source of wealth, *capitale* or property. In a repertory theatre that ran the two plays in close proximity, the link between

James, *Shakespeare's Troy: Drama, Politics, and the Translation of Empire* (Cambridge and New York: Cambridge U P, 1997), 7–41.
6. Lily B. Campbell, ed., *The Mirror for Magistrates* (New York: Barnes and Noble, 1960).
7. Jeffrey Knapp, *An Empire Nowhere: England, America, and Literature from* Utopia *to* The Tempest (Berkeley: U of California P, 1992), 42–48.
8. Holinshed, *Chronicles*, 1:202.
9. See Jenkins, ed., *Hamlet*, 294, n. 104.
1. Stephen Orgel, *Authentic Shakespeare*, 241–43.

Hamlet and Brutus would have been more apparent still if, as has been suggested, Richard Burbage (the English counterpart to the Roman Roscius [2.2.319], played the parts of both Brutus and Hamlet and John Heminge of both Caesar and Polonius.[2] As Cassius and Brutus had predicted in Shakespeare's dramatization of Caesar's assassination, the deed would be reenacted, time after time, in other states and other tongues, on stage and off.

The play relates Hamlet to another Brute or Brutus, Lucius Junius Brutus, the ancestor of Marcus Brutus. Whether he came to know the story of Hamlet from the fifth volume of the French *Histories Tragiques* or from a manuscript version of the English translation, *The Hystorie of Hamblet*, Shakespeare would have found that the model for Hamlet's feigned idiocy was Lucius Junius Brutus. In the English translation, Hamlet is said to have known how to counterfeit madness because he "had been at the schoole" of this Brutus. It was from him that he learned how to bide his time by playing the fool: "running through the streets like a man distraught," begriming himself, speaking nonsense, "all his actions and jestures" proper only to a man deprived of his wits, "fitte for nothing but to make sport."[3] Hamlet adopts an ancient model, as is intimated by the unusual adjective he uses to describe his "disposition": "antic" shared both spelling and pronunciation with "antique."[4] One of the printed marginal notations of *The Hystorie of Hamblet* instructs the reader where to look for a fuller account of Brutus' "counterfeiting the foole" or "antic": "Read Titus Livius."[5] In the recently translated *The Romane Historie* (1600), Livy explained that this Brutus counterfeited "a noddie and a verie innocent" in order to conceal his conspiracy against the tyrannous king Tarquin, enduring the indignity of being called *Brutus*, "a name appropriate to unreasonable creatures." His disguise enabled him to "abide the full time and appear in due season."[6] At the end of Shakespeare's *The Rape of Lucrece*, at the moment when Tarquin's crime is disclosed, Brutus casts off his "folly's show" and "shallow habit" and sparks an insurrection against Tarquin, ending in his "everlasting banishment."[7] In Livy, the very

2. For the likelihood that Burbage played both Hamlet and Brutus and John Heminge both Caesar and Polonius, see E. A. J. Honigmann, "The Date of *Hamlet*," *Shakespeare Survey* 9 (1956), 27–29.

3. *The Hystorie of Hamblet* (1608), in Bullough, ed., *Sources of Shakespeare*, VII:90.

4. Hamlet assumes an "Anticke" (Q1 Dv, Q2 D4v, F 258) disposition; Priam wields his "antike" (Q1 E4v) or "antike" (Q2 F 3v, F 263) sword; and Horatio is more an "antike" (Q1 I 3v), "anticke"(Q2 O), or "Antike" (F 281) Roman than Dane.

5. See Bullough, ed., *Sources of Shakespeare*, VII:90 and n. 4. The note also recommends reading Dionysius of Halicarnassus who relates how Junius feigned stupidity after Tarquin had killed his father and brother and confiscated the ancient family's inheritance, in *Roman Antiquities*, trans. Ernest Cary, 7 vols. (London: William Heinemann, and Cambridge, MA: Harvard U P, 1937), II, IV:68–69.

6. From *The Romane Historie* by Titus Livius, trans. Philemon Holland (1600), in Bullough, ed., *Sources of Shakespeare*, VII:80.

7. Shakespeare, *The Rape of Lucrece*, 1810, 1814, 1815.

historian the reader of the English narrative is instructed to read, this event put an end not only to the Tarquinian line of kings, but to monarchy itself, thereby clearing the way for the rise of the Roman republic.[8] In his republican commentary on Livy, Machiavelli also describes Lucius Junius Brutus' dilatory folly and hails him as founder of the Roman republic and father of Roman liberty.[9]

Junius Brutus figured as consequentially at the beginning of republican Rome as his descendant did at its end. As the elder Brutus inaugurated the Republic so the younger Brutus attempted to preserve it by eliminating the man who aspired to the sovereignty that became synonymous with his name. The two Brutuses were often paired, one at either end of the 500-year duration of the Republic. Plutarch connects them in the opening sentence of his Life of the younger Brutus, "Marcus Brutus came of that Junius Brutus."[1] Lucan in his *Pharsalia* has the ghost of Junius Brutus anticipating the success of his descendant and namesake in the assassination of the absolutist Caesar.[2] Depending on their constitutional position, commentators either credited or blamed the Brutuses for felling kings. In the early 1600s, both Samuel Daniel and William Fulbecke wrote Roman histories condemning "the two Bruti," centuries apart, as haters of monarchy; for Fulbecke, the assassination was an act of "regicide," for once he had assumed sovereign power, Caesar was a *de facto* monarch.[3] Shakespeare stresses their kinship in *Julius Caesar* by having Cassius remind Brutus of his ancestor's hatred of kingship ("There was a Brutus once . . .") and Brutus takes that reminder to heart in reflecting on his predecessor, "My ancestor did from the streets of Rome / The Tarquin drive when he was called a king."[4]

Hamlet could be said to play the part of both Brutuses. He adopts the "antic disposition" of the former and the "brute part" of the latter. Might he also have shared their politics? As many scholars have pointed out, the circle forming around the Earl of Essex had a particular interest in Livy's *History of Rome*.[5] One member of this circle paired two Shakespearean works as the particular favorites of the learned. In a note to his edition of Chaucer's *Works* (1598), Gabriel Harvey maintained that *The Rape of Lucrece* and Hamlet

8. See also the comparison of Prince Hal's vanities to "the outside of the Roman Brutus / Covering discretion with a coat of folly," in *Henry V*, 2.4.37–38.

9. Niccolò Machiavelli, *Discourses upon Livy*, trans. Harvey C. Mansfield and Nathan Tarcov (Chicago: U of Chicago P, 1996), 216–18.

1. Plutarch, "The Life of Marcus Brutus," in *The Lives of the Noble Grecians and Romanes*, trans. Thomas North (1579; New York: AMS Press, 1967), 182.

2. David Norbrook, *Writing the English Republic: Poetry, Rhetoric and Politics, 1627–1660* (Cambridge: Cambridge UP, 1999), 451.

3. Woolf, *Idea*, 180.

4. *Julius Caesar*, 2.1.160 and 53–54.

5. On the study of Roman history, particularly Tacitus, for the instability of its constitutional forms, see R. Malcolm Smuts, *Culture and Power in Early Stuart England, 1585–1685* (New York: St. Martin's Press, 1999), 39, 70–72.

both "haue it in them, to please the wiser sort."[6] Could "the wiser sort" have been those who like Harvey pored over Livy, readers who heeded the marginal instruction in the *The Hystorie of Hamblet*— "Read Livy"—and were sympathetic with the political leanings of the republican historian?[7] In the same note, Harvey cites one of the most celebrated readers of Livy, the Earl of Essex, whose fatal uprising against the monarch in February 1601 has often been identified with the civic disturbance or "late innovation" [2.2.290] Rosencrantz associates with the Players' flight from the city.[8]

Although bent on one in particular, Hamlet seems to take pleasure in the death of sovereigns in general. His favorite speech, as we have seen, describes the slaughter of a king. In both silent and spoken versions, the performance he sponsors requires that a king be poisoned. He stabs the man he thinks is king ("Is it the King?") [3.4.26]; he considers, "too curiously" [5.1.185], the reduction of kings to dust, as well as their passage through "the guts of a beggar" [4.3.30]. All these regicides—represented, mistaken, reflected upon—resemble rehearsals for the final debacle when he first stabs and then poisons the King of Denmark, to the frantic cry of "Treason! treason!" [5.2.297].

The play, too, targets monarchs with unusual frequency, in word and deed. It features a long graphic description of a king's poisoning, as well as an extended exposition on the dire consequences attending the end of kings or "cess [cease F] of majesty" [3.3.15]. Sentries strike with their partisans at the "majestical" figure [1.1.147] they have just identified with the King: "Looks a not like the King?" [1.1.45] and "Is it not like the King?" [60]. Backed by a "riotous head" [4.5.101], Laertes, "arm'd" as the Folio stage directions specify, breaks through the King's bodyguard—"Where is my Switzers?" [97]; "The doors are broke"—and draws on the King, "O thou vile king" [116]. The messenger describes the violence of this outbreak as unprecedented, "as the world were now but to begin" [103]. In this respect, it qualifies as an "innovation" [2.2.290], the term used to describe the civil disturbance that forced the "inhibition" [289] or ban on playing in the city. After so many assaults on

6. Jenkins transcribes Harvey's manuscript note in his edition of *Hamlet*, Appendix, 573–74. For evidence of Harvey's reading of Livy with the "wiser sort," including members and associates of the Sidney circle, see Lisa Jardine and Anthony Grafton, "'Studied for Action': How Gabriel Harvey Read his Livy," *Past and Present* 129 (November 1990), 30–78, esp. 54–55.

7. For Hamlet's republican leanings as derived from Tacitus' *History* and *Annals* and especially Livy's *History of Rome*, see Andrew Hadfield's discussion of *Hamlet* as "a distinctly republican play," in *Shakespeare and Republicanism* (Cambridge: Cambridge UP, 2005), 189. I am grateful to the author for sharing Chapter 6, "The Radical *Hamlet*" with me before publication.

8. On "innovation" as a synonym for "rebellion" or "insurrection" as well as the identification of the "late innovation" with the recent Essex rebellion, see Jenkins, ed., *Hamlet*, 4, 471–72.

the King's person and office, represented or enacted, the play leaves Denmark with no king on the throne, at least no Danish king.

In Q1, the Norwegian conqueror, upon spotting the heap of royal bodies strewn on the palace floor, cries out, "O imperious death!" (I4r). The carnage bears witness to both the death of an empire and the imperial sway of Death. The death of "so many princes at a shot" [5.2.340] leaves the empire without a ruling family. As with Priam's slaughter and Caesar's assassination, the "cess of majesty" takes the state with it. As the English Ambassador is moved to observe in Q1, "O most most unlooked for time! unhappy country" (I4r). Denmark has fallen, without a fight, into the hands of Denmark's inveterate enemy. Horatio knows full well what this means, "I am more an antique Roman than a Dane" [5.2.315]. Editors stop short of a full gloss here, identifying his "antique" Romaness with a preference for suicide over dishonorable life without explaining that the source of dishonor derives from submission. Cato the younger and Brutus and even Portia chose death by their own hands in order to avoid the indignity of subjection. The import of these lines has been missed because tragedy has been defined to play down, if not rule out, historical events like a regime's downfall or foreign occupation. Also ignored are the multiple references to the pattern of imperial succession set in the ancient world by the four kingdoms and extended or translated into the present by the modern imperial ambitions of Europe and the East whose expiration was expected to coincide with the apocalyptic ushering in of a new heaven and new earth.

The same prodigies which presaged the fall of empire, in ancient "palmy Rome" and modern "pursy" Denmark, were also expected to herald the eschaton.[9] Horatio's description of the eclipse foreshadowing Caesar's death has precedents in both Plutarch and Lucan. Yet neither Roman would have recognized the phrase used to indicate the degree of darkness—"the moist star . . . Was sick almost to doomsday with eclipse" [1.1.120–22]—for it echoes the biblical prophecy in Isaiah that "the moon shall not cause her light to shine" (13:10) as well as Christ's predictions of his own Second Coming in both Mark (13:24) and Matthew (24:29).[1] So too, the evacuated graves—"the graves stood tenantless" [117]—that preceded Caesar's fall also prefigure the rising of the dead at Judgment Day. [In] the graveyard scene, the remains of imperial Alexander and Caesar are contemplated in the shadow of Doomsday. The grave-digger makes "houses" to last until Doomsday while the great imperial houses (of Alexander, Caesar, and King Hamlet) terminate in dust.

9. For the grave-digger in *Hamlet* and the Diggers, see Annabel Patterson, *Shakespeare and the Popular Voice* (Oxford: Blackwell, 1989), 101, 179, n. 22.
1. Jenkins provides the reference to Matthew (Jenkins, ed., *Hamlet*, 174, n. 123); John Parker in conversation provided parallels from Isaiah and Mark.

These overlaps recall the celebrated point in time when imperial history and salvational history converged. During the *pax Romana*, the seven-year duration when the Roman Empire was at peace, Christ was born. Prophecies of the auspicious concurrence were retrospectively identified in both classical and biblical texts, in Virgil's fourth eclogue and Isaiah's prophecy in 2:4. The "time of peace" invoked to comfort the watch after the eerie disturbance of the Ghost is Christmas, "that season / Wherein our Saviour's birth is celebrated" when "this bird of dawning singeth all night long" [1.1.162–64]; "So hallow'd and so gracious is that time" [168]. Christmas marks the beginning of the salvational history which ends with the Second Coming or Doomsday. Eusebius and other Church historians believed that the two histories were coterminous: when the Roman Empire expired, so too would the world come to an end. Yet the world did not end when Rome fell in 476.[2] Nor did the history of empire. The Danielic process began all over again. Through the mechanism of *translatio imperii*, imperial power was transferred first to the Eastern Roman Empire at Byzantium (the "new Rome"), then to the Franks with the crowning of Charlemagne as Holy Roman Emperor in 800, and then through the Habsburgs to the Vienna of Charles V in 1555; its destination after Charles' abdication was a major European concern.[3]

Hamlet goes out of his way to specify that *The Murder of Gonzago* "is the image of a murder done in Vienna" [3.2.223–24]. It has been conjectured that Vienna may be a compositor's misreading of Urbino in an alphabet in which V and U were interchangeable. Indeed Urbino would be a more plausible location for a play which was purportedly "written in very choice Italian" [246–7] and which scholars have identified with a crime documented in 1538: the poisoning of the Duke of Urbino through the ear by a Gonzago.[4] And yet in the context of the play's concern with ancient and modern empires, the appearance of Vienna is not implausible, especially when backed by a punning allusion to Charles V's empire. When asked the whereabouts of the slain Polonius, Hamlet says he is "At supper" [4.3.17],

2. For Eusebius, the two events converged "not by mere human accident" but "of God's arrangement," as proven by the prophecies they fulfill; Augustine, however, passes over this coincidence with a mere sentence, eager to dissociate the eternal City of God from recently sacked Rome, Christian History from Roman History. See Theodor Ernst Mommsen, "St. Augustine and the Christian Ideal of Progress: The Background of *The City of God*" in *Medieval and Renaissance Studies*, ed. Eugene F. Rice, Jr. (Ithaca, NY: Cornell UP, 1966), esp. 282; 296.
3. On this providentially driven transfer of imperial power, see Ernst Robert Curtius, *European Literature and the Latin Middle Ages*, trans. Willard R. Trask (New York: Pantheon, 1953), 28–30. On its destination after Charles V's abdication, and England's prospects, see Frances A. Yates, *Astraea: The Imperial Theme in the Sixteenth Century* (London and Boston: Routledge and Kegan Paul, 1975), 20–28, 51–59.
4. See "The Murder of Francesco Maria I, Duke of Urbino," in Bullough, ed., *Sources of Shakespeare*, 172–73.

or more accurately he *is* supper: "A certain convocation of politic worms are e'en at him. Your worm is your only emperor for diet" [4.3.19–21]. A transposition of Hamlet's response allows for a more specific reference: to the convocation or Diet at Worms presided over by the emperor Charles V. At this momentous assembly in 1521, Luther was condemned by the Holy Roman Emperor for refusing to recant. It was this standoff at Worms between Vienna's Holy Roman Emperor and Wittenberg's protesting monk that split Christendom in two.[5] Foxe's detailed account of the Diet at Worms illustrated "how, and by what means this reformation of the church first began, and how it proceeded, increasing by little and little unto this perfection which now we see, and more I trust shall see."[6]

Another German city is woven into the play's imperial backdrop. Wittenberg was considered the "German Rome," the Protestant alternative to the great papal city. Hamlet, Horatio, Rosencrantz, and Guildenstern have all studied at Wittenberg, the university which had "growen famous, by reason of the controversies and disputations of religion, there handled by Martin Luther, and his adherents: the Doctors thereof at this day the greatest propugnators of the confession of Ausburge, and retaine in use the meere Lutherane religion."[7] Luther held an appointment at the University of Wittenberg, and famously posted his incendiary 95 theses on the Castle Church door. It was at Wittenberg, according to Foxe, that Luther repudiated the material presence of Christ in the Eucharist. "The mass [was] laid down first at Wittenberg," and on the advice of the learned, it was determined there that "the use of the mass [was] to be abrogated through [Duke Frederic's] dominion."[8] The context of supping on a corpse sharpens the reference since it was Luther's position on the substance of the Last Supper's bread and wine that posed the greatest threat to the established Church. From the vantage of the Protestant historiographers like Foxe, the Reformation witnessed the same convergence of the imperial and salvational as the Incarnation. For Samuel Daniel, too, it marked the beginning of the final fifth period before Doomsday which by reforming "religio" would complete the political and cultural "alternation" ushered in by the Norman Conquest.

There is no denying that the play produces a sense of contemporaneity: the university at Wittenberg (founded in 1502) is foregrounded, various types of cutting-edge weaponry (rapiers, petards, ordnances, Swiss mercenaries) are in view, recent or concurrent

5. Foxe, *Actes and Monuments*, IV:260.
6. "The Acts and Doings of Martin Luther Before the Emperor, at the City of Worms," ibid., IV:281–92, 252.
7. Samuel Lewkenor, *A Discourse . . . of forraine cities* (London, 1600), 15–16.
8. Foxe, *Actes and Monuments*, IV:293.

theatrical practices (jigs, chopines, boy acting companies) are mentioned, and topical events are referenced, like the theatrical flare-up
between the rival boy and adult companies in 1600 and, more con-
jecturally, Essex's political "innovation" or insurrection in 1601.
And yet through scattered allusions, tropes, and puns, the play also
references events of world historical magnitude, all bearing on
England's own remote and recent history, from the ancient Fall of
Troy from which Britain claimed its own origins to the modern
breakup of Christendom at Worms and Wittenberg from which it
marked its spiritual Reformation. While the play is set in Denmark,
England is drawn into the picture by the time period shared by
the two nations, the Danish Rule preceding the great epochal divide
of the Norman Conquest from which regnal succession traced its
beginnings. Rather than a continuous time line running through
this play we have a temporal jumble. A heavy Roman presence is
created by the high number of Latinate names circulating in the
play. Some are borne by characters (Lucianus, Cornelius, Reynaldo,
Barnado, Francisco), including one belonging to an Augustan poet
(Horatio) and another to a Roman emperor of the same dynasty as
Augustus (Claudius) and still another of a man who was Augustus'
son-in-law and prospective heir (Marcellus); additional Latin names
are mentioned, referring to Roman figures, both historical (Seneca,
Plautus, Roscius, Nero) and legendary (Hercules, Juno, Mars, Mercury); there is also, of course, the long set-piece recited by the Player
of the Fall of Troy derived from Virgil's great Augustan imperial
epic. Salvational history also spans the play: at the start the Incarnation is invoked to dispel the fear of the risen dead, and Doomsday
looms over the remains of the dead at the end. History of empire,
ancient history, history of the Four Rules, salvational history all
impinge upon the play's contemporaneity, saturating it with the
past, in preparation for another imperial fall.

* * *

Horatio was right in inferring that the Ghost's visitation portended
"some strange eruption to the state." As it turns out, the "strange
eruption" is not caused by *strangers*, the Norwegian foreigners who
threatened attack from the border. The "eruption" arises from
elsewhere—from "th'imposthume of much wealth and peace." Denmark's history comes full circle: the era which began thirty years
ago in territorial and dynastic expansion ends in collapse, as the
result not of outward conquest but of inner degeneracy. It is this
epochal structure that has been lost to the tradition of Hamlet
criticism. When the play loses its historical context, the Ghost performs no "precursive" or proleptic function. It sets the revenge plot
into motion. Nor does the threat of attack signify, except as a cover

or decoy for the "real danger" that exists to Hamlet's psyche; it is there that penetration and contamination are feared.[9] The play's multiple allusions to the large sweep of imperial history remain inert. The sluggishness of the state and its princes goes unremarked. Or rather, it is remarked only in respect to Prince Hamlet, and interpreted in terms of some form of psychological difficulty.

As we have seen, the play situates the fall of the Danish empire in a context of imperial rises and falls that includes Priam's Troy, Alexander's Greece, Dido's Carthage, Caesar's Rome, and the notional Duke of Urbino's Vienna. It also signals the two great modern threats to Christendom: the standoff between Luther and Charles V that split Christendom in two and the hovering threat of the Turks who in the sixteenth century had made their way to the very gates of Vienna, the seat of the Holy Roman Emperor. And England is included in this imperial panorama, obliquely, by turning back the clock five centuries to the time when it was itself a subjugated colony between the Danish and Norman Rules. England is not in the dominant role of a nascent imperial kingdom, as we might expect, but in the submissive colonial one of paying taxes and obeying foreign commands.

In the context of this imperial vicissitude, two notorious variants from Q1, both consistently rejected by editors, seem less far-fetched. In Q2 and F, Hamlet announces that the Mousetrap play represents "a murder done in Vienna" [3.2.224]; in Q1, however, the murder is done in "*guyana*."[1] The imagined seat of the Inca Empire slips into the place of the capital of the Holy Roman Empire. In F, Hamlet derides players who in their excessive histrionics resemble no human species: neither "Christian, Pagan, or Norman" [Q2 nor man]. In Q1, humanity is divided into a more comprehensive triad of Christian, pre-Christian, and non-Christian: "Christian, Pagan, / Nor Turke" (F2r). The "Turke," the prospective conqueror of Europe, slips into the place of the Norman, the last conqueror of Britain, as if one outlandish conquering stranger were as good as another. It is as if moveable type were conforming to the same principle of imperial interchangeability as history itself.

9. See, for example, Janet Adelman, *Suffocating Mothers: Fantasies of Maternal Origin in Shakespeare's Plays* (New York: Routledge, 1992), 28–29.
1. Patricia Parker takes issue with the editorial bias against Q1's "guyana" in "Murder in Guyana," *Shakespeare Studies* 28 (2000), 169.

AFTERLIVES

Der Bestrafte Brudermord *or* Fratricide Punished (seventeenth century)†

[3.11]

[*Enter*] PHANTASMO, OPHELIA.

PHANTASMO Wherever I go or stay, that darned girl, that Ophelia, runs after me out of every corner. I can get no peace along of her. She keeps saying that I am her lover, and it is not true. If I could only hide myself somewhere where she could not find me! Now the plague is loose again! There she comes again!

OPHELIA Where can my sweetheart be? The rogue won't stay with me, but had rather run away. —But see, there he is! Listen, my love: I have been at the priest's, and he will join us this very day. I have made all ready for the wedding, and bought chickens, hares, meat, butter, and cheese. There is nothing else wanting but the musicians to play us to bed.

PHANTASMO I can only say yes. Come then, let us go to bed together.

OPHELIA No, no, my puppet, we must first go to church together, and then we'll eat and drink, and then we'll dance. Ah, how merry we shall be!

PHANTASMO Ay, it will be right merry—three eating out of one dish.

OPHELIA What sayest thou? If thou wilt not have me, I'll not have thee! [*She strikes him.*] Look there! There is my love beckoning to me! See there, what fine clothes he has on! See, he is enticing me to him! He throws me a rose and a lily. He wants to take me in his arms. He beckons me. I am coming, I am coming. [*Exit.*]

PHANTASMO Near to, she's not wise, but farther off, she's downright mad. I wish she were hanged, and then the carrion could not run after me so. [*Exit.*]

† Anonymous, *Der Bestrafte Brudermord*, trans. Horace Howard Furness, *Hamlet*, 2 vols. (Philadelphia: J. B. Lippincott, 1877), 2: 135–37. This German prose play represents a touring version of *Hamlet* that appears to derive from the quartos but that differs from them significantly, including a prologue with Hecate and the Furies, German topical references, an Ophelia who is crudely comic in her madness, and many new actions. In these scenes Ophelia pursues Phantasmo, a courtier, and Hamlet comically outwits those appointed to kill him.

Ethan Hawke as a modern Hamlet, contemplating action, Almereyda's film, 2000

[4.1]

[*Enter*] HAMLET, *Two* BANDITS.

HAMLET This is a pleasant spot, here on this island. Let us stay here a while and dine. There's a pleasant wood, and there a cool stream of water. So fetch me the best from the ship; here we'll make right merry.

BANDIT 1 Gracious sir, this is no time for eating, for from this island you will never depart; for here is the spot which is chosen for your churchyard.

HAMLET What sayest thou, thou scoundrel, thou slave? Knowest thou who I am? Wouldst thou jest so with a royal prince? However, for this time, I forgive you.

BANDIT 2 No, it is no jest, but downright earnest. Just prepare yourself for death.

HAMLET Why so? What injury have I ever done you? For my part, I can think of none. Therefore, speak out: why do you entertain such bad thoughts?

BANDIT 1 It is our orders from the King; as soon as we get Your Highness on this island, we are to kill you.

HAMLET Dear friends, spare my life! Say that you have done your work, and so long as I live I will never return to the King. Think well what good you gain by having your hands covered with the blood of an innocent prince! Will you stain your consciences with my sins? Alas, that most unfortunately I am unarmed! If I only had something in my hands! [*He snatches at a dagger.*]

BANDIT 2 I say, comrade, take care of thy weapon!

BANDIT 1   I'll take care. Now, Prince, get ready. We haven't much
time.

HAMLET   Since it cannot be otherwise and I must die at your
hands at the bidding of the tyrannical king, I will submit without
resistance, although I'm innocent. And you, bribed to the deed
through poverty, I willingly forgive. My blood, however, must be
answered for by the murderer of his brother and of my father at
the great Day of Judgement.

BANDIT 1   What has that Day to do with us? We must do this day
what we were told.

BANDIT 2   That's true, brother. Hurry up, there's no help for it! Let
us fire, I on one side and thou on the other.

HAMLET   Hear me, one word more. Since the very worst of male-
factors is not denied a time for repentance, I, an innocent prince,
beg you to let me raise to my Maker a fervent prayer. After that, I
am ready to die. But I will give you a signal: I will turn my hands
toward heaven, and the moment I stretch out my arms, fire! Aim
both pistols at my sides, and when I say "Shoot," give me as
much as I need, and be sure and hit me so that I shall not be long
in torture.

BANDIT 2   Well, we can easily grant him this favor. Therefore, go
ahead.

HAMLET   [Spreads out his hands.] Shoot! [He throws himself forward
on his face between the two, who shoot each other.] O just Heaven!
Thanks be to thee for this angelic idea! I will praise forever the
guardian angel who through my own idea has saved my life. But
these villains—as was their work, so is their pay. The dogs are
still stirring; they have shot each other. But out of revenge I'll
give them a death-blow to make sure, else one of the rogues
might escape. [He stabs them with their own swords.] I'll search
them and see whether they have by chance any warrant of arrest
about them. This one has nothing. Here on this murderer I find a
letter; I will read it. This letter is written to an arch-murderer in
England; should this attempt fail, they had only to hand me over to
him, and he would soon enough blow out the light of my life! But
the gods stand by the righteous. Now will I return to my "father,"
to his horror. But I will not trust any longer to water; who knows
but what the ship's captain is a villain too. I will go to the first
town and take the post. The sailors I will order back to Denmark.
These rascals I will throw into the water.   [Exit.]

360

HENRY FIELDING

[Partridge and the Ghost] (1749)†

As soon as the play, which was *Hamlet, Prince of Denmark*, began, Partridge was all attention; nor did he break silence till the entrance of the ghost, upon which he asked Jones, "What man that was in the strange dress; something," said he, "like what I have seen in a picture. Sure it is not armor, is it?" Jones answered, "That is the ghost." To which Partridge replied with a smile, "Persuade me to that, sir, if you can. Though I can't say I ever actually saw a ghost in my life, yet I am certain I should know one, if I saw him, better than that comes to. No, no, sir, ghosts don't appear in such dresses as that, neither." In this mistake, which caused much laughter in the neighborhood of Partridge, he was suffered to continue till the scene between the ghost and Hamlet, when Partridge gave that credit to Mr. Garrick, which he had denied to Jones, and fell into so violent a trembling that his knees knocked against each other. Jones asked him what was the matter, and whether he was afraid of the warrior upon the stage. "O la, sir," said he, "I perceive now it is what you told me. I am not afraid of anything for I know it is but a play. And if it was really a ghost, it could do one no harm at such a distance and in so much company; and yet, if I was frightened, I am not the only person." "Why, who," cries Jones, "dost thou take to be such a coward here besides thyself?" "Nay, you may call me coward if you will, but if that little man there upon the stage is not frightened, I never saw any man frightened in my life."

"Ay, ay, go along with you![1] Ay, to be sure! Who's fool then? Will you? Lud have mercy upon such foolhardiness! Whatever happens, it is good enough for you. Follow you? I'd follow the devil as soon. Nay, perhaps it is the devil for they say he can put on what likeness he pleases. Oh, here he is again! No farther! No, you have gone far enough already; farther than I'd have gone for all the king's dominions." Jones offered to speak, but Partridge cried "Hush, hush! Dear sir, don't you hear him?" And during the whole speech of the ghost he sat with his eyes fixed partly on the ghost and partly on Hamlet, and with his mouth open, the same passions which succeeded each other in Hamlet, succeeding likewise in him.

When the scene was over Jones said, "Why, Partridge, you exceed my expectations. You enjoy the play more than I conceived possible."

---

† *The History of Tom Jones, a Foundling* (London, 1749), 162–68. The great novelist Henry Fielding (1707–1754) praises David Garrick's famous performance in the ghost scene by having his naïve playgoer, Mr. Partridge, decry it comically.
1. Partridge here and below speaks directly to the ghost, who has commanded Hamlet to follow him, and to Hamlet, who obeys the ghost.

"Nay, sir," answered Partridge, "if you are not afraid of the devil, I can't help it; but to be sure, it is natural to be surprised at such things, though I know there is nothing in them: not that it was the ghost that surprised me neither, for I should have known that to have been only a man in a strange dress; but when I saw the little man so frightened himself, it was that which took hold of me." "And dost thou imagine then, Partridge," cries Jones, "that he was really frightened?" "Nay, sir," said Partridge, "did not you yourself observe afterwards, when he found it was his own father's spirit, and how he was murdered in the garden, how his fear forsook him by degrees and he was struck dumb with sorrow, as it were, just as I should have been, had it been my own case? But hush. O la, what noise is that? There he is again. Well, to be certain, though I know there is nothing at all in it, I am glad I am not down yonder, where those men are." Then turning his eyes again upon Hamlet, "Ay, you may draw your sword; what signifies a sword against the power of the devil?"

During the second act, Partridge made very few remarks. He greatly admired the fineness of the dresses; nor could he help observing upon the king's countenance. "Well," said he, "how people may be deceived by faces! *Nulla fides fronti* ["there is no trust in appearances"] is, I find, a true saying. Who would think, by looking in the king's face, that he had ever committed a murder?" He then inquired after the ghost but Jones, who intended he should be surprised, gave him no other satisfaction than "that he might possibly see him again soon, and in a flash of fire."

Partridge sat in fearful expectation of this; and now, when the ghost made his next appearance, Partridge cried out, "There, sir, now, what say you now? Is he frightened now or no? As much frightened as you think me and, to be sure, nobody can help some fears. I would not be in so bad a condition as what's-his-name, squire Hamlet, is there, for all the world. Bless me! What's become of the spirit? As I am a living soul, I thought I saw him sink into the earth." "Indeed, you saw right," answered Jones. "Well, well," cries Partridge, "I know it is only a play, and besides, if there was anything in all this, Madam Miller would not laugh so. For as to you, sir, you would not be afraid, I believe, if the devil was here in person. There, there. Ay, no wonder you are in such a passion. Shake the vile, wicked wretch to pieces! If she was my own mother, I would serve her so. To be sure all duty to a mother is forfeited by such wicked doings. Ay, go about your business, I hate the sight of you."

Our critic was now pretty silent till the play which Hamlet introduces before the king. This he did not at first understand till Jones explained it to him, but he no sooner entered into the spirit of it than he began to bless himself that he had never committed murder. Then turning to Mrs. Miller, he asked her, "If she did not imagine the king looked as if he was touched; though he is," said he, "a good actor, and doth all he can to hide it. Well, I would not have so much to answer for as that wicked man there hath, to sit upon a much higher chair than he sits upon. No wonder he run away; for your sake I'll never trust an innocent face again!"

The grave-digging scene next engaged the attention of Partridge, who expressed much surprise at the number of skulls thrown upon the stage. To which Jones answered, "That it was one of the most famous burial-places about town." "No wonder then," cries Partridge, "that the place is haunted. But I never saw in my life a worse grave-digger. I had a sexton, when I was clerk, that should have dug three graves while he is digging one. The fellow handles a spade as if it was the first time he had ever had one in his hand. Ay, ay, you may sing. You had rather sing than work, I believe." Upon Hamlet's taking up the skull, he cried out, "Well, it is strange to see how fearless some men are! I never could bring myself to touch anything belonging to a dead man, on any account. He seemed frightened enough too at the ghost, I thought, *Nemo omnibus horis sapit*" ["no one is wise at all hours"].

Little more worth remembering occurred during the play, at the end of which Jones asked him, "Which of the players he had liked best?" To this he answered with some appearance of indignation at the question, "The king, without doubt." "Indeed, Mr. Partridge," says Mrs. Miller, "you are not of the same opinion with the town for they are all agreed that Hamlet is acted by the best player who ever was on the stage." "He the best player!" cries Partridge, with a contemptuous sneer, "why, I could act as well as he myself. I am sure if I had seen a ghost, I should have looked in the very same manner and done just as he did. And then, to be sure, in that scene, as you called it, between him and his mother, where you told me he acted so fine, why, Lord help me, any man, that is, any good man, that had had such a mother would have done exactly the same. I know you are only joking with me but indeed, madam, though I was never at a play in London, yet I have seen acting before in the country and the king for my money, he speaks all his words distinctly, half as loud again as the other. Anybody may see he is an actor."

While Mrs. Miller was thus engaged in conversation with Partridge, a lady came up to Mr. Jones, whom he immediately knew to be Mrs. Fitzpatrick. She said, she had seen him from the other part of the gallery and had taken that opportunity of speaking to him as she had something to say which might be of great service to himself. She then acquainted him with her lodgings, and made him an appointment the next day in the morning, which, upon recollection, she presently changed to the afternoon, at which time Jones promised to attend her.

Thus ended the adventure at the playhouse, where Partridge had afforded great mirth not only to Jones and Mrs. Miller, but to all who sat within hearing, who were more attentive to what he said than to anything that passed on the stage.

He durst not go to bed all that night for fear of the ghost and for many nights after sweated two or three hours before he went to sleep, with the same apprehensions, and waked several times in great horrors, crying out, "Lord have mercy upon us! There it is!"

DAVID GARRICK

[The Ending of *Hamlet*] (1772)[†]

4.5

OPHELIA There's fennel for you and columbines; there's rue for you, and here's some for me. We may call it herb of grace o' Sundays. Oh, you may wear your rue with a difference. There's a daisy. I would give you some violets but they all withered when my father died. They say he made a good end. [*Sings*]

"For bonny sweet Robin is all my joy."

LAERTES Thought and affliction, passion, hell itself
She turns to favour and to prettiness!
OPHELIA [*Singing*]

"And will he not come again?
And will he not come again?
No, no, he's dead.
Go to thy death bed,
He never will come again.

"His beard as white as snow,
All flaxen was his pole.
He is gone, he is gone,

---

† David Garrick, adapter, *Hamlet* (London, 1747), 73–75 [Promptbook 16, with alterations in Garrick's hand]. Garrick (1717–1779), the greatest Shakespearean actor of the eighteenth century, radically abbreviated the ending of the play: he cut 4.6 (Horatio with Hamlet's letter), 4.7 (Claudius and Laertes with Hamlet's letter, their plot, the report of Ophelia's death), and much of 5.1 (the gravediggers, the funeral, the conversation of Hamlet and Horatio on Claudius's plot, the deaths of Rosencrantz and Guildenstern, Osric and the wager, the duel, the poisoned rapier, the poisoned drink, Gertrude's death, Laertes's death, and Fortinbras's return and resumption of rule). This selection begins in 4.5 after Ophelia enters. On Garrick's *Hamlet* see Illustration (p. 364), Steevens in "Criticism" (p. 241), and Dickens in "Afterlives" (p. 372).

364

David Garrick's terrified Hamlet, recoiling from the Ghost, 1754

And we cast away moan,
And peace be with his soul, and with all lovers' souls." [*Exit.*]

LAERTES   Oh, treble woe
Fall ten times double on that cursèd head
Whose wicked deed deprived thee of
Thy most ingenious sense! Let me but see him, heav'n!
'Twould warm the very sickness of my heart,
That I should live and tell him to his teeth,
"Thus didst thou!"

Enter HAMLET.

HAMLET   What is he, whose griefs
  Bear such an emphasis? Whose phrase of sorrow
  Conjures the wand'ring stars and makes them stand
  Like wonder-wounded hearers? This is I,
  Hamlet the Dane!
LAERTES [*Drawing his sword*]   Then my revenge is come!
HAMLET   I prithee take thy fingers from thy sword,
  For though I am not splenitive and rash,
  Yet have I in me something dangerous,
  Which let thy wisdom fear.
KING   Keep them asunder!
HAMLET   Why, I'll fight with him upon this theme
  Until my eyelids will no longer wag.
QUEEN   O my son! What theme?
HAMLET   I loved Ophelia. Forty thousand brothers
  Could not with all their quantity of love
  Make up my sum. What wilt thou do for her?
KING   Oh, he is mad, Laertes.
HAMLET   Show me what thou wilt do.
  Wilt weep? Wilt fight? Wilt fast? Wilt tear thyself?
  Wilt drink up eisel? Eat a crocodile?
  I'll do't, and more. Nay, an you'll mouth it, sir,
  I'll rant as well as thou—
QUEEN   O Hamlet, Hamlet!
  [*To* LAERTES] For love of heaven forbear him!
KING   We will not bear this insult to our presence.
  Hamlet, I did command you hence to England.
  Affection hitherto has curbed my pow'r,
  But you have trampled on allegiance,
  And now shall feel my wrath. —Guards!
HAMLET   First feel mine! [*He stabs the* KING.]
  Here thou incestuous, murd'rous, damnèd Dane!
  There's for thy treachery, lust, and usurpation!
KING   Oh, yet defend me, friends, I am but hurt— [*He falls and dies.*]
QUEEN   O, mercy, heaven! Save me from my son— [*She runs out.*]
LAERTES   What treason, ho! Thus then do I revenge
  My father, sister, and my king—

    [HAMLET *runs upon* LAERTES's *sword and falls.*]

HORATIO   And I my prince, and friend— [*He draws.*]
HAMLET   Hold, good Horatio. 'Tis the hand of heav'n,
  Administers by him this precious balm
  For all my wounds. Where is the wretched queen?

    Enter MESSENGER.

MESSENGER   Struck with the horror of the scene, she fled,
But ere she reached her chamber door, she fell,
Entranced and motionless, unable to sustain the load
Of agony and sorrow.
HAMLET   O my Horatio, watch the wretched queen.
When from this trance she wakes, oh, may she breathe
An hour of penitence ere madness ends her.
Exchange forgiveness with me brave Laertes,
Thy sister's, father's death, come not on me,
Nor mine on thee.
LAERTES   Heav'n make us free of 'em.
HAMLET   Oh, I die Horatio. But one thing more:
Oh, take this hand from me, unite your virtues

    [*He joins* HORATIO's *hand to* LAERTES's *hand.*]

To calm this troubled land. I can no more,
Nor have I more to ask but mercy, heav'n.   [*He dies.*]
HORATIO   Now cracks a noble heart. Good night, sweet prince,
And flights of angels sing thee to thy rest.
—Take up the body. Such a sight as this
Becomes the field but here shows much amiss.

Hamlet Travesties[†]

JOHN POOLE

Hamlet Travestie (1817)

[3.4]

[POLONIUS *hides behind the arras;* HAMLET *enters to the* QUEEN.]

HAMLET   Well, mother, what's the matter with you now?
QUEEN   Your father, sir, has made a pretty row. (*a*)
HAMLET   Mother, you've put my father in a passion.
QUEEN   Zounds, sir, don't answer in this idle fashion.
HAMLET   None of your blarney, it won't do tonight.
QUEEN   Have you forgot me, puppy?
HAMLET   No, not quite:
   You are the Queen—wife to your husband's brother;
   And (though I blush to own you), you're my mother.
QUEEN   Behave yourself; be decent, sir, I beg.
HAMLET   Sit down—and dam'me if you stir a peg[1]
   Till I have let you see your very soul—
QUEEN   what! Wouldst thou kill me? Help, ho! Watch!
POLONIUS (*behind*)   Patrol!
HAMLET   A rat—a rat!—by Jove, that's just the thing—
   He's dead as sure as two-pence.

> (HAMLET *draws, and stabs* POLONIUS *behind the arras, then
> returns, sliding down the stage.*)
>   Is't the king?

---

† The nineteenth century was the great age of Shakespeare "travesties," comic rewrit-
ings that treated the high moments in low style. The first selection from John Poole,
Hamlet Travestie (London, 1817), 34–36, 62, also ridicules the learned commentators
of the preceding century, Samuel Johnson and George Steevens (see "Criticism"). The
second selection is attributed to Francis Talfourd, *Hamlet Travestie* (Oxford, 1849),
38–39; the third, to George Edward Rice, *An Old Play in a New Garb: Hamlet, Prince
of Denmark* (Boston: Ticknor, Reed, and Fields, 1853), 28–29.
1. Move at all.

QUEEN   O Hamlet, you have done a deed felonius;
  You've killed our poor lord chamberlain, Polonius!
HAMLET   They who throw stones should mind their windows,
    mother.
  Who killed a king and married with his brother?
QUEEN   If I know what you mean, the devil burn me.
HAMLET (*Lifts up the arras; sees* POLONIUS)
  Thou'st paid for listening to what don't concern thee.
(*To* QUEEN) Leave wringing of your hands: before we part,
  I'll take the liberty to wring your heart.
          (*Brings chairs; they sit.*)
QUEEN   What have I done that you dare make me so free,
  As thus to blow me up, and bully me?
HAMLET   Oh, such an act—it scarcely can be named—
  So bad—I wonder you're not more ashamed.
  Jump o'er a broomstick (*b*) but don't make a farce on
  The marriage ceremonies of the parson.
QUEEN   What act d'you mean?—You hoax—there's nothing
  in it.
HAMLET   I'll let you know my meaning in a minute.

            Song (Hamlet)
         (Tune: "Drops of Brandy")
    Come sit you down here, ma'am, a little,
    And I'll show you two counterfeit faces;
       They're done from the life to a tittle—
    Come, none of your fine airs and graces.
    Look on this first: the likeness you well know,
       Like a ploughman, so plump and so chubby;
         A good-looking, fine, strapping fellow—
         Now, madam, this was once your hubby.
              Ri tol, &c.
       You'll now please to look upon this:
    I'd have married a monkey as soon—
       An old, ugly, undersized quiz[2]—
    Zounds, the fellow looks like a baboon.
       How could you take this—and forgo
    The one I now hold in my hand, mother?
    You can't say 'twas for love; for you now know
       That you're almost as old as my grandmother.
              Ri tol, &c.

              *   *   *

2. Odd person.

(a) *Row—*

A breeze; a kick-up.

JOHNSON.

I find this word used, in the same sense, in an old ballad (which, no doubt, was within our author's knowledge), called *Molle in ye Wadde*, bl. let.[3] 1564:

> "Molle in ye Wadde and I fell outte
> And what doe you thinke it was aboutte,
> She wanted monnie—I had nonne,
> And that's ye way y^e *row* begun." [began]

STEEVENS.

(b) *Jump o'er a broomstick*

We might, with more propriety, read *mop-stick*; but, as I do not approve of alterations unsupported by authority, or of emendations captious and arbitrary, I leave the text as I found it.

JOHNSON.

Broomstick is certainly right. The allusion is to an ancient custom, noticed in *Quiz 'em's Chronicles*, printed by Stephen Typpe, at the sign of the Catte and the Fiddelle, London, 1598, bl. let.[3] and entered into the books of the Stationers' company, November, 1598. " ___ And ye bryde and ye brydegroome, not Handyely fyndeing a Parson, and being in grievous hayst to bee wed; they did take a *Broome-stycke*, and they did jumpe from one syde of ye *Broome-stycke* over ye other syde thereof; and having so done, they did thinke them lawfulle Man and Wyffe."

STEEVENS.

FRANCIS TALFOURD

Hamlet Travestie (1849)

[3.1.57 ff.]

> *Enter* HAMLET (*advances thoughtfully to the front, and produces a bottle, labeled "Old Tom."*)

HAMLET   To drink, or not to drink! That is the question.
Whether 'tis better to let cares infest one,
And put up with misfortunes, such as are

---

3. Black letter (a type of print).

A wicious[4] mother and a poisoned Pa,
Or, with this pocket pistol to my brain,
Plunge in blue ruin the blue devil's train!
To drink—to feel with each successive "Go"
Some pang depart, till hope alone doth glow,
As in Pandora's reticule[5]—the plan
Looks a good opening for a nice young man!
So easy too—to drink, to sleep, to dream—
There's more in that though than at first doth seem;
For I have heard the restless toper[6] knows
(When he has shuffled off his bed the clothes)
Nocturnal horrors! *Spirits*, floored by day,
Rise up in vengeance and assert their sway:
Some grin like gargoyles; like nightmares infest
His sleep and chaff him; some upon his breast
Dance endless polkas; some fan fever's flame,
Vex him with thirst, and of his thirst make game;
Bring Schweppes'[7] iced waters to his dreaming gaze,
Just to his mouth the claret cup they raise,
And while, like Tantalus,[8] he may not sip,
Cool lumps of Wenham[9] bob against his lip!
—I will *not* drink! No bottle imp shall make
Of me a sponge and then a tipsy-cake.[1]
Yet I've a deed to do and need to prime,
Like a mild lover at the "popping" time,[2]
Like cockney fox-hunter of lily heart,
Who needs the jumping-powder[3] ere he start,
Like the dread toothache's victim, ere he try
The artist who can draw on ivory,[4]
Like waking men who find that over night
They've lost quite a sum 'tis not convenient quite
To pay, or those by whose bed-side doth stand,
The punctual second,[5] pistol-case in hand!
Like—soft, she comes; I must feign mad a while,
If the cook flirt, the goose is sure to spoil.

4. Vicious.
5. Handbag. The mythical Pandora opened a bag and let all troubles out into the world; only hope remained.
6. Drinker.
7. A beverage company.
8. Mythical figure whose punishment in Hades was to have food and drink always just beyond his reach.
9. Pudding.
1. Cake saturated with wine or spirits.
2. Time for making love.
3. Stimulant taken to embolden riders.
4. I.e., the dentist.
5. Backup (in a duel).

GEORGE EDWARD RICE

An Old Play in a New Garb (1853)

[3.1.57 ff.]

HAMLET To be or not to be (that is the question)
Relieved of an attack of indigestion!
The fact is, I am sadly out of tune,
And if some change don't take place very soon,
I am determined (*takes out a revolver*) something rash to do,
And rid myself of this existence. (*Looks into the muzzle.*)
    Whew!
It don't look pleasant. (*Puts it up.*) I think not, just yet,
A little longer I'll contrive to fret.
It isn't manly, though 'tis very easy
To shoot yourself if everything don't please ye.
But when all earthly troubles thus you've ended,
And gone elsewhere—is the matter mended?
We can't be certain, and that very doubt
Keeps very many young men from putting out
The lamp of life, for who, think you, would bear
The insolence of duns,[6] the rich man's stare,
The pangs of tooth-ache, and the mail's delay
That always happens when one's love's away,
And he's a little anxious, the distress
Of finding the last shirt quite buttonless,
A stupid servant, or a sulky wife,
And all the other miseries of life,
When such annoyances he might get rid of
      (*Takes out the revolver again.*)
If he'd pull this and blow his stupid head off.
But, as I said before, it is the dread
Of what comes after death that saves his head!

6. Demands for payment.

CHARLES DICKENS

[Mr. Wopsle's *Hamlet*] (1861)[†]

On our arrival in Denmark, we found the king and queen of that
country elevated in two arm-chairs on a kitchen-table, holding
a Court. The whole of the Danish nobility were in attendance;
consisting of a noble boy in the wash-leather boots of a gigantic
ancestor, a venerable Peer with a dirty face who seemed to have
risen from the people late in life, and the Danish chivalry with a
comb in its hair and a pair of white silk legs, and presenting on the
whole a feminine appearance. My gifted townsman stood gloomily
apart, with folded arms, and I could have wished that his curls and
forehead had been more probable.

Several curious little circumstances transpired as the action proceeded. The late king of the country not only appeared to have
been troubled with a cough at the time of his decease, but to have
taken it with him to the tomb, and to have brought it back. The
royal phantom also carried a ghostly manuscript round its truncheon, to which it had the appearance of occasionally referring and
that, too, with an air of anxiety and a tendency to lose the place of
reference which were suggestive of a state of mortality. It was this,
I conceive, which led to the Shade's being advised by the gallery to
"turn over!"—a recommendation which it took extremely ill. It was
likewise to be noted of this majestic spirit that whereas it always
appeared with an air of having been out a long time and walked an
immense distance, it perceptibly came from a closely contiguous
wall. This occasioned its terrors to be received derisively. The
Queen of Denmark, a very buxom lady, though no doubt historically brazen, was considered by the public to have too much brass
about her; her chin being attached to her diadem by a broad band
of that metal (as if she had a gorgeous toothache), her waist being
encircled by another, and each of her arms by another, so that she
was openly mentioned as "the kettledrum." The noble boy in the
ancestral boots, was inconsistent; representing himself, as it were
in one breath, as an able seaman, a strolling actor, a gravedigger, a
clergyman, and a person of the utmost importance at a Court
fencing-match, on the authority of whose practised eye and nice
discrimination the finest strokes were judged. This gradually led to
a want of toleration for him, and even—on his being detected in
holy orders, and declining to perform the funeral service—to the

---

[†] *Great Expectations* (London: Chapman and Hall, 1861), 198–203. The main character,
Pip, watches an actor, Mr. Wopsle, play Hamlet pretentiously to a heckling audience.

general indignation taking the form of nuts. Lastly, Ophelia was a
prey to such slow musical madness, that when, in course of time,
she had taken off her white muslin scarf, folded it up, and buried it,
a sulky man who had been long cooling his impatient nose against
an iron bar in the front row of the gallery, growled, "Now the baby's
put to bed, let's have supper!" Which, to say the least of it, was out
of keeping.

Upon my unfortunate townsman all these incidents accumulated
with playful effect. Whenever that undecided Prince had to ask a
question or state a doubt, the public helped him out with it. As for
example, on the question whether 'twas nobler in the mind to suffer,
some roared yes, and some no, and some inclining to both opinions
said "toss up for it"; and quite a Debating Society arose. When he
asked what should such fellows as he do crawling between earth and
heaven, he was encouraged with loud cries of "Hear, hear!" When he
appeared with his stocking disordered (its disorder expressed, according to usage, by one very neat fold in the top, which I suppose to be
always got up with a flat iron), a conversation took place in the gallery respecting the paleness of his leg, and whether it was occasioned
by the turn the ghost had given him. On his taking the recorders—
very like a little black flute that had just been played in the orchestra
and handed out at the door—he was called upon unanimously for
"Rule, Britannia." When he recommended the player not to saw the
air thus, the sulky man said, "And don't *you* do it, neither; you're
a deal worse than *him!*" And I grieve to add that peals of laughter
greeted Mr. Wopsle on every one of these occasions.

But his greatest trials were in the churchyard: which had the
appearance of a primeval forest, with a kind of small ecclesiastical
wash-house on one side, and a turnpike gate on the other. Mr.
Wopsle in a comprehensive black cloak, being descried entering at
the turnpike, the gravedigger was admonished in a friendly way,
"Look out! Here's the undertaker a-coming, to see how you're a getting on with your work!" I believe it is well known in a constitutional country that Mr. Wopsle could not possibly have returned
the skull, after moralizing over it, without dusting his fingers on a
white napkin taken from his breast; but even that innocent and
indispensable action did not pass without the comment "Wai-ter!"
The arrival of the body for interment (in an empty black box with
the lid tumbling open) was the signal for a general joy which was
much enhanced by the discovery, among the bearers, of an individual obnoxious to identification. The joy attended Mr. Wopsle
through his struggle with Laertes on the brink of the orchestra
and the grave, and slackened no more until he had tumbled the
king off the kitchen-table, and had died by inches from the ankles
upward.

We had made some pale efforts in the beginning to applaud Mr. Wopsle; but they were too hopeless to be persisted in. Therefore we had sat, feeling keenly for him, but laughing, nevertheless, from ear to ear. I laughed in spite of myself all the time, the whole thing was so droll; and yet I had a latent impression that there was something decidedly fine in Mr. Wopsle's elocution—not for old associations' sake, I am afraid, but because it was very slow, very dreary, very up-hill and down-hill, and very unlike any way in which any man in any natural circumstances of life or death ever expressed himself about anything.

MARK TWAIN

[Huck Finn on *Hamlet*] (1885)[†]

The duke told him, and then says:

"I'll answer by doing the Highland fling or the sailor's hornpipe;[1] and you—well, let me see—oh, I've got it—you can do Hamlet's soliloquy."

"Hamlet's which?"

"Hamlet's soliloquy, you know; the most celebrated thing in Shakespeare. Ah, it's sublime, sublime! Always fetches the house. I haven't got it in the book—I've only got one volume—but I reckon I can piece it out from memory. I'll just walk up and down a minute, and see if I can call it back from recollection's vaults."

So he went to marching up and down, thinking, and frowning horrible every now and then; then he would hoist up his eyebrows; next he would squeeze his hand on his forehead and stagger back and kind of moan; next he would sigh, and next he'd let on to drop a tear. It was beautiful to see him. By-and-by he got it. He told us to give attention. Then he strikes a most noble attitude, with one leg shoved forwards, and his arms stretched away up, and his head tilted back, looking up at the sky; and then he begins to rip and rave and grit his teeth; and after that, all through his speech, he howled, and spread around, and swelled up his chest, and just knocked the spots out of any acting ever *I* see before. This is the speech—I learned it, easy enough, while he was learning it to the king:

[†] *Adventures of Huckleberry Finn.* New York: Harper and Brothers, 1895 rpt. 1901), 181–83. Here a con man, claiming to be the Duke of Bridgewater, tries to teach a soliloquy from *Hamlet* to another con man, who claims to be the Dauphin, or heir apparent to the throne of France. The narrator, Huck himself, is impressed with the speech, though it consists of disjointed fragments from *Hamlet*, *Macbeth*, and *Richard III*.

1. Types of dances.

To be, or not to be; that is the bare bodkin
That makes calamity of so long life;
For who would fardels bear, till Birnam Wood do come to
    Dunsinane,
But that the fear of something after death
Murders the innocent sleep,
Great nature's second course,
And makes us rather sling the arrows of outrageous fortune
Than fly to others that we know not of.
There's the respect must give us pause:
Wake Duncan with thy knocking! I would thou couldst;
For who would bear the whips and scorns of time,
The oppressor's wrong, the proud man's contumely,
The law's delay, and the quietus which his pangs might take,
In the dead waste and middle of the night, when churchyards
    yawn
In customary suits of solemn black,
But that the undiscovered country from whose bourne no
    traveler returns,
Breathes forth contagion on the world,
And thus the native hue of resolution, like the poor cat i' the
    adage,
Is sicklied o'er with care,
And all the clouds that lowered o'er our housetops,
With this regard their currents turn awry,
And lose the name of action.
'Tis a consummation devoutly to be wished.
But soft you, the fair Ophelia:
Ope not thy ponderous and marble jaws,
But get thee to a nunnery—go!

    Well, the old man he liked that speech, and he mighty soon got it so he could do it first-rate. It seemed like he was just born for it; and when he had his hand in and was excited, it was perfectly lovely the way he would rip and tear and rair up[2] behind when he was getting it off.

2. Stand up straight.

BORIS PASTERNAK

Hamlet (1946)†

The buzz subsides. I have come on stage.
Leaning in an open door
I try to detect from the echo
What the future has in store.

A thousand opera-glasses level
The dark, point-blank, at me.
Abba, Father, if it be possible
Let this cup pass from me.

I love your preordained design
And am ready to play this role.
But the play being acted is not mine.
For this once let me go.

But the order of the acts is planned,
The end of the road already revealed.
Alone among the Pharisees I stand.
Life is not a stroll across a field.

TOM STOPPARD

Rosencrantz and Guildenstern Are Dead (1967)‡

[ROSENCRANTZ *and* GUILDENSTERN *discover the* PLAYERS
hiding in three large barrels.]

GUILDENSTERN And you?
PLAYER In disfavour. Our play offended the King.
GUILDENSTERN Yes.
PLAYER Well, he's a second husband himself. Tactless, really.

---

† *Selected Poems*, trans. Jon Stallworthy and Peter France (New York: Norton, 1983), 125.
Pasternak (1890–1960), Russian poet, novelist, and translator of *Hamlet*, has the Prince
echo Christ here, praying to his Father that the cup of suffering be passed from him if
possible, but finally accepting God's will. Reprinted by permission of Penguin UK.
‡ From Tom Stoppard, *Rosencrantz and Guildenstern Are Dead* (New York: Grove Press,
1994), 115–18. Stoppard's absurdist tragicomedy reimagines *Hamlet* from the viewpoint of Rosencrantz and Guildenstern, who ponder their fate as extras trapped in
someone else's play. Aboard ship to England in this scene, they do not know that Hamlet has secretly discovered the letter ordering his death and replaced it with one ordering their deaths. Copyright © 1967 by Tom Stoppard. Used by permission of Grove/
Atlantic Inc and Faber & Faber Ltd.

ROSENCRANTZ   It was quite a good play nevertheless.

PLAYER   We never really got going—it was getting quite interesting when they stopped it. (*Looks up at Hamlet.*) That's the way to travel. . . .

GUILDENSTERN   What were you doing in there?

PLAYER   Hiding. (*Indicating costumes.*) We had to run for it just as we were.

ROSENCRANTZ   Stowaways.

PLAYER   Naturally—we didn't get paid, owing to circumstances ever so slightly beyond our control, and all the money we had we lost betting on certainties. Life is a gamble, at terrible odds—if it was a bet you wouldn't take it. Did you know that any number doubled is even?

ROSENCRANTZ   Is it?

PLAYER   We learn something every day, to our cost. But we troupers just go on and on. Do you know what happens to old actors?

ROSENCRANTZ   What?

PLAYER   Nothing. They're still acting. Surprised, then?

GUILDENSTERN   What?

PLAYER   Surprised to see us?

GUILDENSTERN   I knew it wasn't the end.

PLAYER   With practically everyone on his feet. What do you make of it, so far?

GUILDENSTERN   We haven't got much to go on.

PLAYER   You speak to him?

ROSENCRANTZ   It's possible.

GUILDENSTERN   But it wouldn't make any difference.

ROSENCRANTZ   But it's possible.

GUILDENSTERN   Pointless.

ROSENCRANTZ   It's allowed.

GUILDENSTERN   Allowed, yes. We are not restricted. No boundaries have been defined, no inhibitions imposed. We have, for the while, secured, or blundered into, our release, for the while. Spontaneity and whim are the order of the day. Other wheels are turning but they are not our concern. We can breathe. We can relax. We can do what we like and say what we like to whomever we like, without restriction.

ROSENCRANTZ   Within limits, of course.

GUILDENSTERN   Certainly within limits.

HAMLET *comes down to footlights and regards the audience. The others watch but don't speak.* HAMLET *clears his throat noisily and spits into the audience. A split second later he claps his hand to his eye and wipes himself. He goes back upstage.*

ROSENCRANTZ   A compulsion towards philosophical introspection is his chief characteristic, if I may put it like that. It does not mean he is mad. It does not mean he isn't. Very often, it does not mean anything at all. Which may or may not be a kind of madness.

GUILDENSTERN   It really boils down to symptoms. Pregnant replies, mystic allusions, mistaken identities, arguing his father is his mother, that sort of thing; intimations of suicide, forgoing of exercise, loss of mirth, hints of claustrophobia not to say delusions of imprisonment; invocations of camels, chameleons, capons, whales, weasels, hawks, handsaws—riddles, quibbles and evasions; amnesia, paranoia, myopia; day-dreaming, hallucinations; stabbing his elders, abusing his parents, insulting his lover, and appearing hatless in public—knock-kneed, droop-stockinged and sighing like a love-sick schoolboy, which at his age is coming on a bit strong.

ROSENCRANTZ   And talking to himself.

GUILDENSTERN   And talking to himself.

     ROSENCRANTZ *and* GUILDENSTERN *move apart together.*

Well, where has that got us?

ROSENCRANTZ   He's the Player.

GUILDENSTERN   His play offended the King—

ROSENCRANTZ   —offended the King—

GUILDENSTERN   —who orders his arrest—

ROSENCRANTZ   —orders his arrest—

GUILDENSTERN   —so he escapes to England—

ROSENCRANTZ   On the boat to which he meets—

GUILDENSTERN   Guildenstern and Rosencrantz taking Hamlet—

ROSENCRANTZ   —who also offended the King—

GUILDENSTERN   —and killed Polonius—

ROSENCRANTZ   —offended the King in a variety of ways—

GUILDENSTERN   —to England. (*Pause.*) That seems to be it.

     ROSENCRANTZ *jumps up.*

ROSENCRANTZ   Incidents! All we get is incidents! Dear God, is it too much to expect a little sustained action?!

    And on the word, the PIRATES *attack. That is to say:*
    Noise and shouts and rushing about. "Pirates!"
Everyone visible goes frantic. HAMLET *draws his sword and rushes downstage.* GUILDENSTERN, ROSENCRANTZ, *and* PLAYER *draw swords and rush upstage. Collision.* HAMLET *turns back up. They turn back down. Collision. By which time there is general panic right upstage. All four charge upstage with* ROSENCRANTZ, GUILDENSTERN, *and* PLAYER *shouting:*

At last!
To arms!

Pirates!
Up there!
Down there!
To my sword's length!
Action!

*All four reach the top, see something they don't like, waver,
run for their lives downstage:* HAMLET, *in the lead, leaps
into the left barrel.* PLAYER *leaps into the right barrel.*
ROSENCRANTZ *and* GUILDENSTERN *leap into the middle
barrel. All closing the lids after them. The lights dim to
nothing while the sound of fighting continues. The sound
fades to nothing. The lights come up. The middle barrel
(Rosencrantz's and Guildenstern's) is missing. The lid of
the right-hand barrel is raised cautiously. The heads of*
ROSENCRANTZ *and* GUILDENSTERN *appear.*

*The lid of the other barrel (Hamlet's) is raised. The head
of the* PLAYER *appears.*

All catch sight of each other and slam down lids.

Pause.

HEINER MÜLLER

Hamletmachine (1977)[†]

[HAMLET *is alone on stage with a suit of armor that has an axe
stuck in the helmet, a refrigerator, and three television screens.
He takes off his make-up and costume.*]

HAMLET   Television The daily nausea Nausea
   Of prefabricated babble Of decreed cheerfulness
   How do you spell GEMÜTLICHKEIT[1]
   Give us this day our daily murder
   Since thine is nothingness Nausea
   Of the lies which are believed
   By the liars and nobody else
   Nausea
   Of the lies which are believed Nausea

[†]   Heiner Müller, Hamletmachine *and Other Texts for the Stage,* trans. Carl Weber (New
   York: Performing Arts Journal Publications, 1984), 56–58. © Copyright 1984 by PAJ
   Publications. Reprinted by permission of PAJ Publications and Suhrkamp Verlag.
   Heiner Müller (1929–1995), an important German playwright, adapts *Hamlet* into a
   series of disturbing poetic fragments. This selection meditates on the problem of terrorism,
   the corruption of government, and the failure of human revolution.
1.   German idiom: coziness, pleasantness.

By their struggle for positions votes bank accounts
Nausea A chariot armed with scythes sparkling with punchlines
I walk through streets stores Faces
Scarred by the consumers battle Poverty
Without dignity Poverty without the dignity
Of the knife the knuckleduster the clenched fist
The humiliated bodies of women
Hope of generations
Stifled in blood cowardice stupidity
Laughter from the dead bellies
Hail Coca Cola
A kingdom
For a murderer
I WAS MACBETH
THE KING HAD OFFERED HIS THIRD MISTRESS TO ME
I KNEW EVERY MOLE ON HER HIPS
RASKOLNIKOV[2] CLOSE TO THE
HEART UNDER THE ONLY COAT THE AX FOR THE
ONLY
SKULL OF THE PAWNBROKER
In the solitude of airports
I breathe again I am
A privileged person My nausea
Is a privilege
Protected by torture
Barbed wire Prisons

    [He takes out a] Photograph of the author

I don't want to eat drink breathe love a woman a man a child an
    animal anymore.
I don't want to die anymore. I don't want to kill anymore.

    Tearing of the author's photograph.

I force open my sealed flesh. I want to dwell in my veins, in
the marrow of my bones, in the maze of my skull. I retreat into
my entrails. I take my seat in my shit, in my blood. Somewhere
bodies are torn apart so I can dwell in my shit. Somewhere bodies are opened so I can be alone with my blood. My thoughts are
lesions in my brain. My brain is a scar. I want to be a machine.
Arms for grabbing Legs to walk on, no pain no thoughts.

    *TV screens go black. Blood oozes from the refrigerator. Three
    naked women [enter]:* MARX, LENIN, MAO. *They speak simul-
    taneously, each one in his own language, the text:*

---

2. The protagonist of Dostoevsky's *Crime and Punishment* (1866) who murders a pawnbroker with an ax.

THE MAIN POINT IS TO OVERTHROW ALL EXISTING
   CONDITIONS . . .

The actor of HAMLET *puts on make-up and costume.*

HAMLET THE DANE PRINCE AND MAGGOT'S FODDER
STUMBLING FROM HOLE TO HOLE TOWARDS THE
   FINAL
HOLE LISTLESS IN HIS BACK THE GHOST THAT ONCE
MADE HIM GREEN LIKE OPHELIA'S FLESH IN CHILDBED
AND SHORTLY ERE THE THIRD COCK'S CROW A CLOWN
WILL TEAR THE FOOL'S CAP OFF THE PHILOSOPHER
A BLOATED BLOODHOUND'LL CRAWL INTO THE ARMOR

He steps into the armor, splits with the ax the heads of MARX,
LENIN, MAO. *Snow. Ice Age.*

JAWAD AL-ASSADI

Forget Hamlet (1994)†

HAMLET *and* OPHELIA

OPHELIA   Hamlet—Laertes is in danger!
HAMLET   (*Calmly and coldly*)   Why is Laertes in danger?
OPHELIA   Don't you know why?
HAMLET   Where is he now?
OPHELIA   In heaven, building a kingdom of pain.
HAMLET   Are you ill? Exhausted? You should see a doctor!
OPHELIA   Could I please have back the rest of the letters I gave to
you?
HAMLET   Never! I've perfumed them and hidden them away in my
treasure chest.
OPHELIA   Hamlet! Give them back to me! I want to tear up the
words that I inscribed once upon a time with such impassioned
feelings.
HAMLET   Didn't you write them to me?
OPHELIA   They were for you.

---

† Jawad al-Assadi, an Iraqi exile and leading theatrical figure in the Arab world, wrote
Forget Hamlet in Arabic for performance in Cairo, 1994 (trans. Margaret Litvin). In
al-Assadi's adaptation everyone knows about the crime and Claudius, a tyrant like Saddam Hussein, eventually orders the weak Hamlet and the rebellious, blind Laertes
killed; a strong Ophelia proclaims the truth. In the first selection al-Assadi rewrites the
Nunnery scene (3.1); in the second, the gravediggers, a constant presence in the tyrannical regime, supply a mocking epilogue. Reprinted by permission of Jawad al-Assadi
and Margaret Litvin.

HAMLET   So they're my property.

OPHELIA   Everything in me has been extinguished now. My feelings have dried up, and my tears too. I did love you once. But now, no more.

HAMLET   Don't be in such a hurry. Soon your fire will die down and you'll return to your old promises.

OPHELIA   You've disappointed me. Oh God, who planted this tune in your head? You're just sick, just a dumb kid. That's how I see you now.

HAMLET   I guess that means our bed will be less thunderous.

OPHELIA   Are you trying to kill me with this lethargy? Even your lips that used to be smoldering hot are cold now. And some kind of stupor has descended over your whole being.

HAMLET   Next Saturday is the wedding day. That's how your father has arranged everything having to do with me, and with you.

OPHELIA   Get yourself to a monastery; that would be more merciful. There you can focus your body and your mind on the pressing theological questions. There you can have more peace and quiet to ask and re-ask your question, "to be or not to be."

HAMLET   I love you, even if the world has stumbled and fallen on its knees.

OPHELIA   Search for the cause of your father's death! Search for his killer! That will bring back your manliness!

HAMLET   (*conjugates*) He died, we will die, he will die. A long train of dead people. This is the poem of non-being. No fear. We die with a knife in the back or a kiss on the lips. Or with a long sleep. We open the door to the quietude that our soul desires. Death is a sleep. Sleep is a sleep in death. What's the difference? I love you.

OPHELIA   Who do you think you are? You're presumptuous! What a catastrophe for Denmark. You were her prince and her pride—now you've become her little lamb. Go away, Hamlet! Get out of my sight!

Exit HAMLET.

Enter HORATIO.

HORATIO   Ophelia, don't get frustrated and don't be afraid. We're up against an unholy grinder. A letter from Laertes just arrived. I'll read it to you, but please be strong, and keep a grip on yourself.

OPHELIA   Oh Horatio! Everything has collapsed on us at once. Hamlet's defeat, Laertes' madness. Denmark has become one big prison, Horatio. A basin of rot! Or else how could Claudius the ignorant appoint himself king over us, and take possession of us? Then he mocks our heritage, laughs at our deaths. He's turning the country into a general graveyard.

HORATIO   (*Opens the letter and reads*) "My dear Ophelia!

I hope to see you. That is the only dream I have left. I want to hear your laughter—oh God, what could be sweeter than your laughter.

Here I am constantly at a party with my friends in a sanatorium big enough for our screams and curses.

I still remember Claudius, the new king.

That stately rat, he put on the crown in the blink of an eye and started acting as though all of Denmark were in his shirt pocket.

The guillotine is active—impossible news. The death of sense and the freedom of appearance. A winged buffalo is sitting on all of us, crushing us one by one without paying attention to any of us. Even Hamlet with his keen mind and his motives collapsed before the blows of Claudius his uncle.

I love you, my sister, although my body has wasted away like the mummies—the really old ones!

Love, your brother, Laertes."

EPILOGUE

GRAVEDIGGERS

DIGGER 1   Look at this skull! Used to belong to the best violinist in Denmark.

DIGGER 2 (*Chuckles*)   I wonder where are the hands he used to play with.

DIGGER 1   The worms ate them.

DIGGER 2   The same worms that will eat Hamlet the prince of Denmark.

DIGGER 1   Isn't this Hamlet's skull?

DIGGER 2   Where is the sparkle of his eyes? Look at his wide brow! And at his tongue! That's the tongue of the prince of Denmark.

Comes across a book.

DIGGER 1   What a priceless book.

DIGGER 2   Read me a little of it.

DIGGER 1   Listen! (*Laughs*)

DIGGER 2   Read, you fool.

DIGGER 1   Listen! Listen! (*Laughs harder*)

DIGGER 2   (*Takes the book from him and reads*)

O, what a rogue and peasant slave am I!
Is it not monstrous that this player here,
But in a fiction, in a dream of passion,
Could force his soul so to his own conceit
That from her working all his visage wann'd,
Tears in his eyes, distraction in's aspect,

A broken voice, and his whole function suiting
With forms to his conceit? and all for nothing!
Yet I,
A dull and muddy-mettled rascal, peak,
Like John-a-dreams, unpregnant of my cause,
And can say nothing.
Am I a coward? Who,
Prompted to my revenge by heaven and hell,
Must, like a whore, unpack my heart with words,
And fall a-cursing, like a very drab,
A scullion! (*Long silence*)

DIGGER 1   Hamlet died a horrible death.

DIGGER 2   His problem was his tongue. He kept philosophizing.
Look, here's his tongue!

DIGGER 1   Leave his tongue between the leaves of his book, and
toss it up to heaven.

The GRAVEDIGGER *indeed tosses the book up to the sky, and the
pages fly high in the air.*

JOHN UPDIKE

Gertrude and Claudius (2000)†

I

[The wedding night of Gerutha and Horwendil]

They passed through a bare anteroom, where a lone guard slept.
Horwendil cuffed him awake as they passed. A fire had been kept
blazing in their bed-chamber for hours, so the space was stiflingly
hot. Readily Gerutha shed her heavy hooded cloak lined with
miniver,[1] her sleeveless surcoat of gold cloth diapered in a pattern of
crosses and florets, her blue tunic with wide flowing sleeves and a
band of jewelled embroidery at the throat, under that a white cotte[2]
with longer, tighter sleeves, and, lastly, the thin camise worn next to
the skin, sweated with much dancing. A thick silent woman with

† New York: A. A. Knopf, 2000, 24–25, 79–81, 208–10. Updike (1932–2009) writes a
prequel to *Hamlet* in three parts, the first adopting the names of the characters as
given in Saxo Grammaticus's medieval account, the second, as in Belleforest's early
modern adaptation, and the third, as in Shakespeare's play. He portrays Gertrude
(Gerutha, Geruthe) as sensitive, intelligent, and sensual, trapped in a marriage to the
oafish King Hamlet (Horwendil, Horvendile), and attracted to his sensitive brother
Claudius (Fengon); the parents worry about Hamblet [Hamlet], but Claudius thinks
that he has gotten away with the murder and usurpation. Copyright © 2000 by John
Updike. Used by permission of Alfred A. Knopf, a division of Random House.
1. Fur, usually ermine.
2. Matted wool garment.

Glenn Close's sensual, remorseful Gertrude in Mel Gibson's film, 1990

trembling hands undid the laces and cord belt and wrist ties, leaving it to her, in Horwendil's company alone, to shed the camise. This she did, stepping from the cast-off cloth as from a cleansing pool.

By the snapping firelight her nakedness felt like a film of thin metal, an ultimate angelic costume. From throat to ankles her skin had never seen the sun. Gerutha was as white as an onion, as smooth as a root fresh-pulled from the earth. She was intact. This beautiful intactness, her life's treasure, she roused herself—betranced before the leaping fire, the tips of her falling hair reflecting its hearthbound fury—to bestow, as decreed by man and God, upon her husband. She was aroused. She turned to show Horwendil her pure front, vulnerable as his had been when he had bared it, for a famous dangerous moment, to the possibility of Koll's thrust.

He was asleep. Her husband, in a coarse-knit boxy nightcap, had collapsed from excessive festivity, and from the three-hours' bath in winter air followed by this sauna of a bedchamber. One long strong arm lay relaxed upon the blanket as if severed up to the shoulder, where a naked ball of muscle gleamed beneath an epaulette of golden fur. A strand of saliva from his slumped lips glittered like a tiny arrow.

My poor dear hero, she thought, *carrying that great soft frame through life with but his wits and a leather shield to keep it from being hacked to death.* Gerutha discovered in this moment a woman's secret: there is a pleasure in feeling love that answers, as with the heat of two opposing fireplaces, to that of being loved.

II

[Concern about Hamblet at University]

The King was irate. "But what can the boy still be studying at Wittenberg?" Horvendile asked. "He is twenty-nine! I am all of sixty, with aches and pains and spells of irresistible lethargy. It is high time Hamblet came home and studied kingship."

Geruthe kept brushing out her thick hair, which in the half-light of this gloomy winter morning emanated a coruscating halo of static phosphorescence as she brushed. Some sparks were blue, and others yellow and remarkably long as they leaped from where with her brush of stiffest boar bristle she sharply pulled taut an extended coppery strand. The more she brushed, the more filaments stood up all over her head. "I think he finds us unsubtle," she said. "We drink too much. We eat crudely, with hunting knives. We are barbarians compared with his professors down there."

"Unsubtle! What does he think life is—a theatrical performance to be minced through by boys in women's clothes?"

"He doesn't talk to me about what he thinks," she said, "or indeed about anything. But I understand from what Corambis [Polonius] has let drop of what Laertes tells *him*, there's a ferment going on in cultivated circles to the south, various bits of ancient knowledge the Crusaders brought back, the Arabs and the Byzantine monks have been transcribing them for centuries but nobody read them, something about a new way of looking at the world *scientifically*, whatever that is, letting nature tell us about itself in little details, one after another, as if women and children and millers and farmers haven't been doing that all along. Instead of taking everything on faith from the priests and the Bible, I mean. Instead of arguing from first principles, you deduce your principles from a host of observed particulars. I'm sorry, I'm not making a great deal of sense; it's still too early in the morning, my dearest."

"You confirm my worst suspicions. My son is down there on the Elbe learning how to *doubt*—learning mockery and blasphemy when I'm trying to instill piety and order into a scheming, rebellious conglomeration of Danes."

"What else did Corambis say?" Geruthe mused, as colorful electricity played about her head. "Something about man being the measure of things, which makes a kind of sense, really, since men and women are right here all around us while God, though we can all feel He's here somewhere, is a lot harder to observe. Still, you can't help wondering if people are ready to be the measure of things. We can hardly measure ourselves. We are the only animal that makes *mistakes*."

"We must get Hamblet back, or the regional *thing* will choose another when I—if I were to—As I say, I have these uncanny spells of fatigue."

"Normal aging, merely, darling. I too need a nap more than formerly. You'll live another twenty years at least," his wife told the King, whipping an especially impressive blue spark from her long hair, as if the thought were not entirely soothing to her. "You Jutes are tough as nails. Look at your brother. Five wounds in a Turkish ambush, and still he moves like a panther, with a bear's thick head of hair." It soothed her to mention Fengon, lately returned from his lifetime of knightly exile, and suddenly very attentive to those who lived in Elsinore. His scalp and beard, becomingly sprinkled with gray, flourished, whereas Horvendile's curly pale locks, once so spectacularly Nordic, had thinned touchingly above his brow and at the back of his skull. His skull showed its mineral hardness, its marmoreal gloss.

"Yes," he said loudly, stalking about and summing up: "My rogue of a brother returned and hanging as close about the castle as if he smells his future here, and Hamblet, who should be in residence cutting a successor's stalwart figure, impressive and engaging yet not too much so, off instead in Wittenberg wasting his days in fruitless logic-chopping and his nights in whorish follies that might not disgrace a nineteen-year-old but sit sluggishly on a man ten years older."

III

*[Gertrude and Claudius at the beginning
of Shakespeare's play, 1.2]*

The royal couple took their two thrones, whose coat of gilt had not prevented rot from nibbling at the ancient sticks of linden and ash, including it was said bits of the True Cross and of the primal tree Yggdrasil. Claudius spoke his lines so all could hear. The speech went well, he thought. The regrets and compliments were distributed with a calm grace, the general collusion in his actions tersely made clear, and the situation with Fortinbras and the King's response ringingly outlined. Laertes, having done his duty in attending the King's coronation, asked for leave to go back to Paris, and this of course was granted, with compliments to Polonius that only the self-important old courtier would not recognize to be distancingly excessive.

Then, when Hamlet rebuffed with some muttered puns the King's fatherly inquiry after his health, Gertrude surprised Claudius by speaking up at his side, entreating her son to stop looking for his father in the dust. "All that lives must die," she gently told him, "passing through nature to eternity." Not the least of the King's reasons

for loving her was that female realism which levelly saw through the
agitations and hallucinations of men.

And when the boy—boy! thirty years old!—wordily implied, with
the whole court listening, that only he was truly grieving King
Hamlet, Claudius took it upon himself to continue her instruction
in the obvious: men die, each father in turn has lost a father, it is
unmanly and impious to persist in unavailing woe. "Think of us as
of a father," he commanded, reminding him, "You are the most
immediate to our throne." He elaborated on this theme of his love,
and as he spoke, one iambic cadence smoothly succeeding another,
Claudius was distracted by a clatter of birds—starlings, he guessed,
shriller-voiced than rooks—at the blue clerestory windows above.
The birds, scenting spring here at the height of winter, were stirred
up and flocking to the sun-warmed roof of crumbling slates.

Some persons in attendance glanced up, the drama before them
having perhaps stretched long. The day was revolving overhead,
dropping rhomboids of sun upon the multi-colored finery and the
hall's broad oak planks, worn and scarred. In olden days bored
knights would clatter their horses up the stone stair and joust
beneath the beams, where captured pennants faded and frayed.

Claudius finished with Hamlet by bluntly stating—where others
had been pussyfooting for years—that he did not want Hamlet to
return to Wittenberg: "It is most retrograde to our desire." He rel-
ished the imperious ring of this, but softened it by beseeching his
stiff nephew to bend, to stay here, in Elsinore, "here in the cheer
and comfort of our eye, our chiefest courtier, cousin, and our son."

Gertrude played her part, adding, "Let not thy mother lose her
prayers, Hamlet: I pray thee, stay with us; go not to Wittenberg."

Trapped by their twin professions of love, the Prince from beneath
his clouded brow studied the two glowing middle-aged faces hung
like lanterns before him—hateful luminaries fat with satisfaction and
health and continued appetite. He tersely conceded, to shunt away
the glare of their conjoined pleas, "I shall in all my best obey you."

"Why," Claudius exclaimed, startled by the abrupt concession,
"'tis a loving and a fair reply." They had him. He was theirs. The
King's imagination swayed forward to the sessions of guidance and
lively parry he would enjoy with his surrogate son, his only match
for cleverness in the castle, and to the credit such a family relation
would win him in the heart of the boy's newly fond mother.

The era of Claudius had dawned; it would shine in Denmark's
annals. He might, with moderation of his carousals, last another
decade on the throne. Hamlet would be the perfect age of forty
when the crown descended. He and Ophelia would have the royal
heirs lined up like ducklings. Gertrude would gently fade, his
saintly gray widow, into the people's remembrance. In his jubilation
at these presages the King, standing to make his exit, announced

boomingly that this gentle and unforced accord of Hamlet sat so smiling to his heart that, at every health he would drink today, the great cannons would tell the clouds. And his queen stood up beside him, all beaming in her rosy goodness, her face alight with pride at his performance. He took her yielding hand in his, his hard sceptre in the other. He had gotten away with it. All would be well.

JASPER FFORDE
Something Rotten[†]

It was a bright and clear morning in mid-July two weeks later that I found myself on the corner of Broome Manor Lane in Swindon, on the opposite side of the road to my mother's house with a toddler in a stroller, two dodos, the Prince of Denmark, an apprehensive heart and hair cut way too short. The Council of Genres hadn't taken the news of my resignation very well. In fact, they'd refused to accept it at all and given me instead unlimited leave, in the somewhat deluded hope that I might return if actualizing my husband "didn't work out." They also suggested I might like to deal with escaped fictionaut Yorrick Kaine, someone with whom I had crossed swords twice in the past.

Hamlet had been a late addition to my plans. Increasingly concerned over reports that he was being misrepresented as something of a "ditherer" in the Outland [the real world], he had requested leave to see for himself. This was unusual in that fictional characters are rarely troubled by public perception, but Hamlet would worry about having nothing to worry about if he had nothing to worry about, and since he was the indisputable star of the Shakespeare canon and had lost the Most Troubled Romantic Lead to Heathcliff once again at this year's BookWorld awards, the Council of Genres thought they should do something to appease him. Besides, Jurisfiction had been trying to persuade him to police Elizabethan drama since Sir John Falstaff had retired on grounds of "good health," and a trip to the Outland, it was thought, might persuade him.

"'Tis very strange!" he murmured, staring at the sun, trees, houses and traffic in turn. "It would take a rhapsody of wild and whirling words to do justice of all that I witness!"

[†] *Something Rotten* (New York: Penguin, 2004), 20–22. Jasper Fforde has written a fantasy series about a policing agency inside books, Jurisfiction, which has Prose Resource Operatives who maintain the continuity of narratives, holding authors and readers to the guidelines of the Council of Genres. One operative, Thursday Next, the narrator and female hero, enters into fictions to restore order but finds that fictional characters have wills of their own and often enter into her world, as Hamlet does here. Copyright © 2004 by Jasper Fforde. Used by permission of the author and Viking Penguin, a division of Penguin Group (USA) Inc.

"You're going to have to speak English out here."

"All this," explained Hamlet, waving his hands at the fairly innocuous Swindon street, "would take millions of words to describe correctly!"

"You're right. It would. That's the magic of the book imagino-transference technology," I told him. "A few dozen words conjure up an entire picture. But in all honesty the reader does most of the work."

"The reader? What's it got to do with him?"

"Well, each interpretation of an event, setting or character is unique to each of those who read it because they clothe the author's description with the memory of their own experiences. Every character they read is actually a complex amalgam of people that they've met, read or seen before—far more real than it can ever be just from the text on the page. Because every reader's experiences are different, each book is unique for each reader."

"So," replied the Dane, thinking hard, "what you're saying is that the more complex and apparently contradictory the character, the greater the possible interpretations?"

"Yes. In fact, I'd argue that every time a book is read by the same person it is different again—because the reader's experiences have changed, or he is in a different frame of mind."

"Well, that explains why no one can figure me out. After four hundred years nobody's quite decided what, *exactly*, my inner motivations are." He paused for a moment and sighed mournfully. "Including me. You'd have thought I was religious, wouldn't you, with all that not wanting to kill Uncle Claudius when at prayer and suchlike?"

"Of course."

"I thought so, too. So why do I use the atheistic line: *there is nothing either good or bad, but thinking makes it so*? What's that all about?"

"You mean you don't know?"

"Listen, I'm as confused as anyone."

I stared at Hamlet and he shrugged. I had been hoping to get some answers out of him regarding the inconsistencies within his play, but now I wasn't so sure.

"Perhaps," I said thoughtfully, "that's why we like it. To each our own Hamlet."

"Well," snorted the Dane unhappily, "it's a mystery to me. Do you think therapy would help?"

"I'm not sure. Listen, we're almost home. Remember: to anyone but family you're—who are you?"

"Cousin Eddie."

"Good. Come on."

Resources

ONLINE

The Complete Works of William Shakespeare   Transcriptions of the plays.
http://shakespeare.mit.edu/works.html

Internet Shakespeare Editions
http://internetshakespeare.uviv.ca/

DEEP: Database of Early English Playbooks   A user-friendly database that enables research in the publishing, printing, and marketing of every play-book produced in England, Scotland, and Ireland up to 1660.
http://deep.sas.upenn.edu/

Early English Books Online   An indispensable digital library of over 100,000 English books from 1475 to 1700.
http://eebo.chadwyck.com/home/

Early English Books Online Text Creation Partnership   A searchable full-text database of many early English books.
http://quod.lib.umich.edu/e/eebo/

Eighteenth Century Collections Online   A searchable full-text database of over 136,000 works.
www.gale.cengage.com/DigitalCollections/products/ecco/index.htm

English Short Title Catalogue   A listing of over 460,000 items published between 1473 and 1800, mainly but not exclusively in English.
http://estc.bl.uk/

Folger Shakespeare Library   Links to many scholarly and popular Shakespeare sites and an impressive Digital Image Collection.
www.folger.edu

Geneva Bible (1560/1599)   Transcriptions of the Bible translation Shakespeare is likely to have used.
www.genevabible.org

Google Books   A digital archive of many scholarly monographs and reference books (see also the Online Books Page, Project Gutenberg, and the Universal Digital Library).
http://books.google.com

Hamlet Online   A site with links to general Shakespeare topics and Hamlet texts, humor, movies, and spinoffs.
www.tk421.net/hamlet/hamlet.html

Hamlet on the Ramparts   Texts (including adaptations and promptbooks), images, and film clips related to Hamlet's first encounters with the ghost (1.4, 1.5).
http://shea.mit.edu/ramparts/

Hamlet Works   An exhaustive compilation of textual and literary criticism on virtually every line of *Hamlet*, with full bibliographies, reference links, and

essays on global productions, including Kaori Ashizu on Japan and Roger Paulin on Germany.
www.hamletworks.org

JSTOR   An archive of scholarly articles and reviews (see also Project Muse).
www.jstor.org

LEME: Lexicons of Early Modern English   A database of dictionaries and lexicons from 1480 to 1702.
http://leme.library.utoronto.ca/

Literature Online   A database of many works of English and American Literature, as well as many literature journals.
http://lion.chadwyck.com

Modern Language Association International Bibliography   Citations of scholarly books and articles from 1926 to the present.
www.mla.org/bibliography

Open Source Shakespeare   Site that enables text, word, and character searches in Shakespeare's works (see also The Works of the Bard).
www.opensourceshakespeare.com/concordance

Oxford Dictionary of National Biography   Authoritative, illustrated biographies of people important to British history.
www.oxforddnb.com

Oxford English Dictionary   The authoritative historical dictionary.
www.oed.com

Rare Book Room   Digital images of Shakespeare quartos and the First Folio, including some from copies in Scotland.
www.rarebookroom.org

Royal Shakespeare Company   A resource on theatrical productions. Click on the Education link for a complete Internet guide to Shakespeare.
www.rsc.org.uk

Royal Shakespeare Company Archive: "Plays in Focus"   Galleries of pictures and exhibitions from RSC productions.
www.rsc.org.uk:8080/picturesandexhibitions/jsp/index.jsp or tingurl.com/yf2smxv

Schoenberg Center for Electronic Text & Image   A digital collection of rare Shakespeare materials, including the Furness Collection.
http://sceti.library.upenn.edu/

Shakespeare: An International Database of Shakespeare on Film, Television and Radio   An international database from 1899 to the present.
www.bufvc.ac.uk/shakespeare/

Shakespeare in Europe   A collection of resources including many adaptations.
http://pages.unibas.ch/shine

The Shakespeare Quartos Archive   Cover-to-cover digital images and transcriptions of early quartos, including thirty-two copies of pre-1642 editions of Hamlet.
www.quartos.org

Treasures in Full: Shakespeare in Quarto   The British Library's collection of Shakespeare quartos in digital images with links to other digitalized quartos under "Partners."
www.bl.uk/treasures/shakespeare/homepage.html

University of Virginia Shakespeare Resources   Transcriptions of early quartos and the Folio, as well as playhouse promptbooks, modern editions, and criticism.
http://etext.virginia.edu/shakespeare/

World Shakespeare Bibliography   Annotated citations for books, articles, reviews, and productions related to Shakespeare from 1960 to the present. www.worldshakesbib.org

PRINT

• indicates works included or excerpted in this Norton Critical Edition.

• Adams, John Quincy. Letter to James H. Hackett. February 7, 1839. Folger MS. Y.c.10(3).
• Aeschylus. *The Libation-Bearers*. Trans. Herbert Weir Smyth. London: W. Heinemann, 1922.
• al-Assadi, Jawad. *Forget Hamlet*. Trans. Margaret Litvin. Manuscript.
  al-Shetawi, Mahmoud F. "*Hamlet* in Arabic." *Hamlet Studies* 22 (2000): 77–109.
  Allen, Michael J. B. and Kenneth Muir, eds. *Shakespeare's Plays in Quarto*. Berkeley: U of California P, 1981.
  Barrymore, John. *Confessions of an Actor*. Indianapolis: The Bobbs-Merrill Company, 1926.
  ———. Interview with Beauvais Fox. *New York Tribune*, 14 Jan. 1923.
  Battenhouse, Roy. "The Ghost in *Hamlet*: A Catholic 'Linchpin'?" *Studies in Philology* 48 (1951): 161–92.
• Bernhardt, Sarah. *The Art of the Theatre*, trans. H. J. Stenning. London: Geoffrey Bles, 1924.
  Bertram, Paul, and Bernice W. Kliman, eds. *The Three-Text* Hamlet: *Parallel Texts of the First and Second Quartos and First Folio*. 1991, 2nd ed., New York: AMS Press, 2003, with an introduction by Eric Rasmussen.
  Bevington, David, ed. *Hamlet*. New York: Bantam, 1988.
• *Bible. The Geneva Bible: A Facsimile of the 1560 Edition*, Introduction by Lloyd E. Berry. Madison: U of Wisconsin P, 1969.
  Blayney, Peter W. M. *The First Folio of Shakespeare*. Washington, DC: Folger Library Publications, 1991.
• Booth, Edwin. Letter to William Winter. Folger MS. Y.c.215 (412b).
• ———. *Shakespeare's Tragedy of Hamlet, as Presented by Edwin Booth*, ed. William Winter. New York: Francis Hart and Co., 1878, with notes in Booth's hand.
  Bowers, Fredson. "Hamlet as Minister and Scourge." *PMLA* 70 (1955): 740–49.
  Bowers, Fredson. "Hamlet's 'Sullied' or 'Solid' Flesh: A Bibliographical Case-History." *Shakespeare Survey* 9 (1956): 44–48.
  Bradley, A. C. *Shakespearean Tragedy: Lectures on* Hamlet, Othello, King Lear, Macbeth. 1904, 4th ed., Basingstoke: Palgrave Macmillan, 2007, with an introduction by Robert Shaughnessy.
• Branagh, Kenneth. Introduction, *Hamlet*. New York: Norton, 1996.
  Brower, Reuben Arthur. *Hero & Saint: Shakespeare and the Graeco-Roman Heroic Tradition*. New York: Oxford UP, 1971.
• Bullough, Geoffrey, ed. *Narrative and Dramatic Sources of Shakespeare*. 8 vols. London: Routledge & Kegan Paul, 1957–75.
• Burton, Richard. Introduction, *The Tragedy of Hamlet, Prince of Denmark*. London: Folio Society, 1954.
  Clayton, Thomas, ed. *The Hamlet First Published (Q1, 1603): Origins, Form, Intertextualities*. Newark: U of Delaware P, 1992.
• Coleridge, Samuel Taylor. *Seven Lectures on Shakespeare and Milton*, ed. J. Payne Collier. London: Chapman and Hall, 1856.
• Dante Alighieri. *The Divine Comedy*, trans. Henry Wadsworth Longfellow. Boston: Houghton, Mifflin and Co., 1865, rpt., 1895.
  Davison, Peter Hobley. *Hamlet. Text and Performance*. London: Macmillan, 1983.

Dawson, Anthony B. *Hamlet (Shakespeare in Performance)*. Manchester: Manchester UP, 1995.
• De Grazia, Margreta. Hamlet *without* Hamlet. Cambridge: Cambridge UP, 2007.
Dent, R. W. *Shakespeare's Proverbial Language: An Index*. Berkeley: U of California P, 1981.
• *Der Bestrafte Brudermord*, trans. Horace Howard Furness. *Hamlet. A New Variorum Edition of Shakespeare*. 2 vols. Philadelphia: J. B. Lippincott, 1877. Vol. 2.
Dessen, Alan C., and Leslie Thomson. *A Dictionary of Stage Directions in English Drama, 1580–1642*. Cambridge: Cambridge UP, 1999.
Dessen, Alan C. "Hamlet's Poisoned Sword: A Study in Dramatic Imagery." *Shakespeare Studies* 5 (1970): 53–69.
• Dickens, Charles. *Great Expectations*. London: Chapman and Hall, 1861.
• Dryden, John. *Troilus and Cressida*. London, 1679.
Duffy, Kevin Thomas, et al. *The Elsinore Appeal: People vs. Hamlet*. New York: St. Martin's Press, 1996.
Dusinberre, Juliet. *Shakespeare and the Nature of Women*. 1975, 2nd ed., New York: St. Martin's Press, 1996.
Edwards, Philip, ed. *Hamlet, Prince of Denmark*. 1985, updated, Cambridge: Cambridge UP, 2003.
Erne, Lukas. *Shakespeare as Literary Dramatist*. Cambridge: Cambridge UP, 2003.
• Euripides. *Euripides with an English Translation*, trans. Arthur S. Way. Vol. 2. London: William Heinemann, 1916. (*Electra* and *Orestes*)
Farley-Hills, David, et al., eds. *Critical Responses to Hamlet, 1600–1900*. 4 vols. in 5. New York: AMS Press, 1996–2006.
• Fforde, Jasper. *Something Rotten*. New York: Penguin, 2004.
• Fielding, Henry. *The History of Tom Jones, a Foundling*. London, 1749.
Foakes, R. A. *Hamlet versus Lear: Cultural Politics and Shakespeare's Art*. Cambridge: Cambridge UP, 1993.
Frye, Roland Mushat. *The Renaissance Hamlet: Issues and Responses in 1600*. Princeton: Princeton UP, 1984.
• Garrick, David, adapter. *Hamlet*. London, 1747. Folger Shakespeare Library, Promptbook 16, with alterations in Garrick's hand.
Gibínska, Marta and Jerzy Limon, eds. *Hamlet East-West*. Gdánsk: Theatrum Gedanese Foundation, 1998.
• Gielgud, John. *Stage Directions*. London: Heinemann, 1963.
• Gilder, Rosamond. *John Gielgud's* Hamlet: *A Record of Performance*. New York: Oxford UP, 1937.
• Goethe, Johann Wolfgang von. *Wilhelm Meisters Apprenticeship* (1795), trans. Thomas Carlyle. 3 vols. Edinburgh: Oliver & Boyd, 1824. Vol. 2.
• Greenblatt, Stephen. *Hamlet in Purgatory*. Princeton: Princeton UP, 2001.
Gurr, Andrew. *The Shakespearean Stage, 1574–1642*. 1970, 4th ed., Cambridge: Cambridge UP, 2009.
Hapgood, Robert, ed. *Hamlet, Prince of Denmark* (*Shakespeare in Production* Series). Cambridge: Cambridge UP, 1999.
Hattaway, Michael, Boika Sokolova, and Derek Roper, eds. *Shakespeare in the New Europe*. Sheffield: Sheffield Academic Press, 1994.
Hibbard, G. R., ed. *Hamlet*. New York: Oxford UP, 1987.
Hinman, Charlton, ed. *The Norton Facsimile: The First Folio of Shakespeare*. 2nd ed. New York: Norton, 1996, with an introduction by Peter W. M. Blayney.
Holderness, Graham. "'Silence Bleeds': Hamlet across Borders: The Shakespearean Adaptations of Sulayman Al-Bassam." *European Journal of English Studies* 12 (2008): 59–77.
• Howard, Tony. *Women as Hamlet: Performance and Interpretation in Theatre, Film and Fiction*. Cambridge: Cambridge UP, 2007.

Hunter, Joseph. *New Illustrations of the Life, Studies, and Writings of Shake-speare*. London: J. B. Nichols and Son, 1845.

Irace, Kathleen O., ed. *The First Quarto of Hamlet*. New York: Cambridge UP, 1998.

• Irving, Henry and Frank A. Marshall, eds. *The Works of William Shakespeare*. 8 vols. London: Blackie, 1888–90. Vol. 8.

Jenkins, Harold, ed. *Hamlet*. London: Methuen, 1982.

• Johnson, Samuel, ed. *The Plays of William Shakespeare*. 8 vols. London, 1765. Vol. 8.

• Jones, Ernest. *Essays in Applied Psycho-analysis*. London: The International Psycho-analytic P, 1923.

Kastan, David Scott. "'His semblable is his mirror': *Hamlet* and the Imitation of Revenge." *Shakespeare Studies* 19 (1987): 111–24.

Kennedy, Dennis, ed. *Foreign Shakespeare: Contemporary Performance*. Cambridge: Cambridge UP, 1993.

Kilroy, Gerard. "Requiem for a Prince: Rites of Memory in *Hamlet*." *Theatre and Religion: Lancastrian Shakespeare*, Richard Dutton, Alison Findlay and Richard Wilson, eds. Manchester: Manchester UP, 2003, 143–60.

King, T. J. *Casting Shakespeare's Plays: London Actors and Their Roles, 1590–1642*. Cambridge: Cambridge UP, 1992.

Kliman, Bernice W. *Hamlet: Film, Television, and Audio Performance*. London: Associated U Presses, 1988.

• Kyd, Thomas. *The Spanish Tragedy*. London, 1592.

• Law, Jude. Interview with Jeff Lunden. Morning Edition, National Public Radio, 6 Oct. 2009.

Lennox, Charlotte. *Shakespear Illustrated*. 2 vols. London: A. Millar, 1753–54.

• Levin, Harry. *The Question of Hamlet*. New York: Oxford UP, 1959.

Litvin, Margaret. "Vanishing Intertexts in the Arab *Hamlet* Tradition." *Critical Survey* 19 (2007): 74–94.

Mack, Maynard. "The World of *Hamlet*." *The Yale Review* 41 (1952): 502–23.

Madariaga, Salvador de. *On Hamlet*. 1948, 2nd ed., London: Cass, 1964.

McGee, Arthur. *The Elizabethan Hamlet*. New Haven: Yale UP, 1987.

Mercer, Peter. *Hamlet and the Acting of Revenge*. Iowa City: U of Iowa P, 1987.

• More, Thomas. *The Supplication of Souls*. London, 1529.

• Müller, Heiner. Hamletmachine *and Other Texts for the Stage*, trans. Carl Weber. New York: Performing Arts Journal Publications, 1984.

• Murray, Gilbert. *Hamlet and Orestes: A Study in Traditional Types. The Annual Shakespeare Lecture*. London: Published for the British Academy by Humphrey Milford, 1914.

• Olivier, Laurence. *Confessions of an Actor: An Autobiography*. New York: Simon and Schuster, 1982.

• ———. *On Acting*. New York: Simon and Schuster, 1986.

• Pasternak, Boris. *Selected Poems*, trans. Jon Stallworthy and Peter France. New York: Norton, 1983.

• Pennington, Michael. *Hamlet: A User's Guide*. New York: Limelight Editions, 1996.

• Poe, Edgar Allan. Review of William Hazlitt, *The Characters of Shakespeare's Plays* (1817). *Broadway Journal*, August 16, 1845, 89.

• Poole, John. *Hamlet Travestie*. London, 1817.

Pope, Alexander, ed. *The Works of Shakespear*. 6 vols. London: Jacob Tonson, 1723. Vol. 6.

Prosser, Eleanor. Hamlet *and Revenge*. 1967, 2nd ed., Stanford: Stanford UP, 1971.

Quince, Rohan W. "*Hamlet* on the South African Stage." *Hamlet Studies* 10 (1988): 144–51.

———. *Shakespeare in South Africa: Stage Productions during the Apartheid Era*. New York: Peter Lang, 2000.

• Rice, George Edward. *An Old Play in a New Garb: (Hamlet, Prince of Denmark) in Three Acts*. Boston: Ticknor, Reed, and Fields, 1853.

Rosenberg, Marvin. *The Masks of Hamlet*. Newark: U of Delaware P, 1992.

• Rothwell, Kenneth S. "An Annotated and Chronological Screenography: Major *Hamlet* Adaptations and Selected Derivatives," in *Approaches to Teaching Shakespeare's* Hamlet, ed. Bernice W. Kliman. New York: Modern Language Association, 2001. Pp. 14–27.

Rowe, Eleanor. *Hamlet: A Window on Russia*. New York: New York UP, 1976.

• Rowe, Nicholas, ed. *The Works of Mr. William Shakespeare*. 6 vols. London: Jacob Tonson, 1709. Vols. 1, 5.

• Saxo Grammaticus. *The First Nine Books of the Danish History of Saxo Grammaticus*, trans. Oliver Elton. London: D. Nutt, 1894.

Schick, Josef, ed. *Corpus Hamleticum:Hamlet in Sage und Dichtung, Kunst und Musik*. 4 vols. Berlin: E. Felber, 1912–38.

Schlegel, August Wilhelm von. *A Course of Lectures on Dramatic Art and Literature*. 1808, trans. John Black, London: H. G. Bohn, 1846.

Schleiner, Louise. "Latinized Greek Drama in Shakespeare's Writing of *Hamlet*." *Shakespeare Quarterly* 41 (1990): 29–48.

Scofield, Martin. *The Ghosts of Hamlet: The Play and Modern Writers*. Cambridge: Cambridge UP, 1980.

• Seneca, Lucius Annaeus. *Seneca His Tenne Tragedies, Translated into Englysh*, ed. Thomas Newton. London, 1581.

Shaheen, Naseeb. *Biblical References in Shakespeare's Plays*. Newark: U of Delaware P, 1999.

Shapiro, James S. *A Year in the Life of William Shakespeare: 1599*. New York: HarperCollins, 2005.

Shaw, George Bernard. Review of Forbes-Robertson production. *The Saturday Review*, October 2, 1897, 364–65. Available online at tingurl.com/yzy5cb9.

• Showalter, Elaine. "Representing Ophelia: Women, Madness, and the Responsibilities of Feminist Criticism," in *Shakespeare and the Question of Theory*, ed. Patricia Parker and Geoffrey Hartman. London: Methuen, 1985, 77–94.

Snyder, Susan. *The Comic Matrix of Shakespeare's Tragedies*: Romeo and Juliet, Hamlet, Othello, *and* King Lear. Princeton: Princeton UP, 1979.

• Sophocles. *The Plays and Fragments*, trans. Sir Richard C. Jebb. Vol. 6, *The Electra*. Cambridge: Cambridge UP, 1894.

• Steevens, George. Letter to David Garrick, in *The Private Correspondence of David Garrick*, ed. James Boaden. 2 vols. London: H. Colburn and R. Bentley, 1831–32. Vol. 1.

• ———, et al., eds. *The Plays of William Shakespeare*. 3rd ed. 10 vols. London, 1785. Vol. 10.

Stern, Tiffany. *Documents of Performance in Early Modern England*. Cambridge: Cambridge UP, 2009.

———. *Making Shakespeare: From Stage to Page*. New York: Routledge, 2004.

Sterne, Richard L. *John Gielgud directs Richard Burton in* Hamlet: *A Journal of Rehearsals*. New York: Random House, 1967.

Stone, George Winchester, Jr. "Garrick's long lost alteration of *Hamlet*." *PMLA* 49 (1934): 890–921.

• Stoppard, Tom. *Rosencrantz and Guildenstern Are Dead*. 1967, rpt., New York: Grove Press, 1994.

Stříbrný, Zdeněk. *Shakespeare and Eastern Europe*. Oxford: Oxford UP, 2000.

Taylor, Gary. "*Hamlet* in Africa, 1607," in *Travel Knowledge: European "Discoveries" in the Early Modern Period*, eds. Ivo Kamps and Jyotsna G. Singh. New York: Palgrave, 2001, 223–48.

• Talfourd, Francis. *Hamlet Travestie*. Oxford, 1849.

• Terry, Ellen. *Four Lectures on Shakespeare*, ed. Christopher St. John. 1932, rpt., New York: Benjamin Blom, 1969.

• ———. *The Story of My Life: Recollections and Reflexions*. London: Hutchinson & Co., 1908.

Theobald, Lewis. *Shakespeare Restored*. London: R. Francklin, J. Woodman and D. Lyon, and C. Davis, 1726.

Thompson, Ann, and Neil Taylor, eds. *Hamlet. The New Arden Shakespeare*. London: Arden Shakespeare, 2006. (Q2 is in one volume; Q1 and F, in another.)

• Tolstoy, Leo. "Shakespeare and the Drama," trans. V. Tchertkoff, et al., in *Tolstoy on Shakespeare*. London: Free Age Press, 1906.

• Twain, Mark. *Adventures of Huckleberry Finn*. 1885, rpt., New York: Harper and Bros., 1901.

• Updike, John. *Gertrude and Claudius*. New York: Knopf, 2000.

Vickers, Brian, ed. *Shakespeare: The Critical Heritage*. 6 vols. London: Routledge & K. Paul, 1974–81.

Vining, Edward Payson. *The Mystery of* Hamlet: *An Attempt to Solve an Old Problem*. Philadelphia: Lippincott, 1881.

• Voltaire. *The Works of Voltaire: A Contemporary Version*, trans. William F. Fleming, et al. 42 vols. Paris: Du Mont, 1901. Vols. 37, 39.

Wells, Stanley, and Gary Taylor, gen. eds. *William Shakespeare: The Complete Works*. Oxford: Clarendon, 1986.

———. *William Shakespeare: A Textual Companion*. 1987, rpt. with corrections, New York: Norton, 1997.

Werstine, Paul. "The Textual Mystery of *Hamlet*." *Shakespeare Quarterly* 39 (1988): 1–26.

Williams, Simon. *Shakespeare on the German Stage*. Cambridge: Cambridge UP, 1990.

Wilson, John Dover. "Hamlet's Solid Flesh." *Times Literary Supplement*, May 16, 1918: 233.

———. *The Manuscript of Shakespeare's* Hamlet *and the Problems of Its Transmission*. 2 vols. Cambridge: Cambridge UP, 1934.

Wright, George T. "Hendiadys and *Hamlet*." *PMLA* 96 (1981): 168–93.

Young, Alan R. *Hamlet and the Visual Arts, 1709–1900*. Newark: U of Delaware P, 2002.